THE
'OLYMPIC' CLASS
SHIPS

OLYMPIC TITANIC BRITANNIC

THE
'OLYMPIC' CLASS
SHIPS

OLYMPIC   TITANIC   BRITANNIC

MARK CHIRNSIDE

The
History
Press

The inventions of man proved mightier than the brute force of the inanimate elements. The unsinkable ship builded [sic] by all the resources of centuries of science withstood the shock, messages carried by the harnessed waves of the air brought speedy help, and every life, it seems, was saved, and the ship herself proceeded unaided to port.

Daily Mirror, 16 April 1912

DEDICATION

To my wonderful parents, Ghislaine and David, without whose constant and valued support and encouragement this book would never have been written.

Back cover: A striking image of HMHS *Britannic*, taken by Nurse H.K. Moore in 1916. (Imperial War Museum, HU 090768)

First published 2004
Reprinted 2005, 2006
This edition 2011
Reprinted 2011

The History Press
The Mill, Brimscombe Port
Stroud, Gloucestershire, GL5 2QG
www.thehistorypress.co.uk

© Mark Chirnside, 2004

British Library Cataloguing in Publication Data.
A catalogue record for this book is available from the British Library.

ISBN 978 0 7524 5895 3

Typesetting and origination by The History Press
Printed in Great Britain

CONTENTS

INTRODUCTION

The story of the 'Olympic' class ships is one of 'triumph and tragedy', as one history of *Titanic* aptly describes it. At a time of continued advancement in technology and naval architecture, the White Star Line's plan to build two ships, followed by a third, that would be almost 50 per cent larger than the largest ships then in existence was an ambitious one.

By the time *Olympic* arrived in New York on her maiden voyage in the summer of 1911, the company's confidence appeared to have been well rewarded. She had performed well and was highly regarded by those passengers who had chosen her. She was soon setting records for the highest number of first-class passengers who had ever embarked on one ship. It is unlikely that anyone foresaw at the time the fact that she would be the only one of the three sister ships ever to complete a single commercial voyage; the only one ever to reach New York.

Olympic's career spanned a quarter of a century and she carried hundreds of thousands of commercial passengers, establishing a reputation for reliability and regularity. Her record of government service during the war was extraordinary, as the most successful troopship. Her career demonstrated the potential of her sisters. A potential that was never fulfilled.

This is the story of her success and her sisters' failure.

Mark Chirnside
August 2004

AUTHOR'S INTRODUCTION TO THE SECOND EDITION

Since the first words of this book were written, twelve years have passed. There have been many new discoveries and developments as the history of the 'Olympic' class ships continues to evolve. My own research and interest in the subject has continued. The defeatist perception that little new could be learned has been shown to be entirely false: an entirely predictable development. The centenary of *Olympic*'s maiden voyage is a good point to look back, improving the existing book and bringing the story up to date with a new edition.

It was an immense privilege to become a published author and I remain extremely proud of my accomplishment with my first book, particularly at such a young age. Given the commercial realities of publishing and the inevitable constraints, long after the wave of interest in *Titanic* had subsided at the end of the 1990s, it provided a reasonably comprehensive look at the lives of three ships whose histories can only be understood in their proper context. Like many new authors I struggled occasionally to find my own voice, but I was delighted with the enthusiastic reception that the book received. A great deal of information was published that was either little-known or never before published in book form: for instance, naval architect Leonard Peskett's professional assessment of *Olympic* when he sailed in August 1911. (Much of my *Olympic* research was expanded upon in *RMS Olympic: Titanic's Sister*, whose publication was brought forward to less than a month after this book's original publication.) However much hard work went into researching the subject, the hard fact remains that I have now spent more time researching *after* the book was published than before. That gives a different perspective in some important respects, but on the other hand I am pleased that much of the original work stood the test of time. On the whole, I believe it was more right than wrong, and was a positive contribution, but there is always room for improvement, without discarding the original product entirely.

The new edition offers an opportunity to do just that, retaining the original book's strengths and addressing weaknesses. The text incorporates new information and discoveries that were not available a decade ago, some improvements based upon readers' suggestions and feedback, and changes due to ongoing research which revealed errors in some of the secondary sources used. There have been editorial changes in order to improve the flow of the text, aimed at improving the reader's enjoyment.

As well as changes to the existing text, additions to the later chapters help to bring the story up to date, with new material about the wrecks of *Britannic* and *Titanic*, while the original appendices have been improved (or removed) and eight new ones added.

An expanded index helps to make the book a better reference tool, while advantage has been taken of the additional pages to add an entirely new colour section with a number of rare and previously unpublished images; another thirty-two pages have been added to the original book's 352 pages.

Perhaps it is inevitable that some valuable new nuggets of information only come to light after a book has been published. There are undoubtedly many researchers who can sympathise with the feeling of frustration when they unearth an interesting new anecdote or story, only for it to be too late to add to their completed project. It has been a pleasure to remedy that with the new edition, while some material that is already adequately covered elsewhere has been removed. There are always limitations in trying to tell such an extensive story in a single volume. Not only is the sheer volume of information too much to put into print, but in deciding what to include, different readers will be interested in different aspects of the ships' lives: whether it be structural and technical details of their design; the design progression from ship-to-ship and changes over *Olympic*'s lengthy career; the people who sailed on them, from passengers to crew, stoker to commander; the sinking of *Titanic* and *Britannic*; the broader development and decline of the White Star Line and contemporary ships; and modern-day explorations of the shipwrecks. One person's fascination is another's tedium.

Undoubtedly, there will be new discoveries and further developments in the years ahead. Hopefully, in the meantime this revised and expanded volume will go a small way towards implementing a better understanding of *Olympic*, *Titanic* and *Britannic*'s history.

Mark Chirnside,
May 2011

EXPLANATORY NOTE

There are a number of reasons behind the changes that have been made for this new edition. When a subject such as *Titanic* has been covered in so many books, articles and documentaries, the danger is that the gems of accurate information are buried in an avalanche of popular misconceptions which are repeated time and again, even though the factual basis behind them is questionable. The subject appears to be better known than it is. Even serious researchers who have been researching a subject for a long time can make errors; nobody is perfect, nor should they claim to be. Meanwhile, the popularity of the subject can attract those more interested in profit rather than a worthwhile contribution to historical accuracy.

Just as it was important to place *Titanic* in context as one of three sister ships, it was necessary to place the 'Olympic' class liners in context with the White Star Line fleet, other companies' competing liners, as well as those ships that preceded them. However, it is important not to lose focus. The original book described the fate of *Olympic*'s running mates in the Cunard White Star fleet following the merger of the two companies, even to the point of following *Aquitania* to her scrapping in 1950. It related a popular anecdote about a piano which allegedly fell through one of the decks in the late 1940s, but following my ongoing research (which resulted in *RMS Aquitania: The 'Ship Beautiful'*), it seems to be one of those stories which is repeated even though there seems to be no contemporary, reliable evidence that it occurred. As a result, this is one of a number of statements that have been removed.

While it is inevitable that the narrative of such a broad subject will involve published works and secondary sources, the original book certainly had plenty of original research and helped to dispel a number of myths. I have sought to retain that quality in this edition. A number of published sources repeat the view that the company's planned *Germanic/ Homeric* was intended as a replacement for *Titanic*. However, as researchers such as Mark Baber have discovered, IMM's own annual report for 1913 clearly stated she was intended for the Liverpool to New York service. Her tonnage and intended speed indicate that she was an enlarged and slightly faster version of ships such as *Adriatic*, employing the new combination machinery to drive her three propellers. Another source, a statement Harold Sanderson made in June 1914, offers the final confirmation that she was not being built as a new running mate for *Olympic*. (Further information about this ship and rumours of *Titanic*'s replacement can be found in one of the new appendices.)

Plenty of secondary sources repeat the traditional timeline that was established by Lord Mersey's report in 1912 in regard to when each of *Titanic*'s lifeboats left the ship, yet parts of the sequence can be shown to be incorrect and some of the departure times are questionable. Perhaps that is unsurprising in regard to the short amount of time available when the report was compiled, but modern researchers have the luxury of both additional time and additional survivor accounts for their analysis. Although the original book was a step forward in some respects, for instance in challenging the order in which lifeboats 16, 14 and 12 left the ship from my own research, there were still errors in regard to other lifeboats, such as number 10. I have therefore cited the work of other, more knowledgeable researchers who have done so much study in this area and produced a comprehensive and valuable study of the lifeboats and the order in which they were lowered. (See Bill Wormstedt, Tad Fitch and George Behe's article, 'The Lifeboat Launching Sequence' in *Titanic Commutator*, *Titanic* Historical Society, 2001. A revised and expanded version was made available online in 2009 and 2010 with contributions from researchers Sam Halpern and J. Kent Layton.)

Even if errors can be introduced through secondary sources, there are sometimes problems even with original material. A prime example is the duration of the voyage as reported on *Olympic*'s maiden voyage souvenir log cards, which was in error. This mistake, which went unnoticed for ninety-five years, will undoubtedly persist in other sources as it is repeated and cited again. Even a researcher who does not cite a published work, instead relying on the original log card in isolation, would be prone to repeating the mistake. (See the article co-authored by myself and Sam Halpern, '*Olympic* and *Titanic*: Maiden Voyage Mysteries' in *Voyage*, *Titanic* International Society, 2007.) That error led to other problems: Ismay's figures for *Olympic*'s average coal consumption each day were slightly wrong, as he had based them on an overall time and average speed for the voyage that were not correct. In turn, that meant that it was necessary to re-examine my research into *Titanic*'s coal consumption, although my original conclusions have not changed.

The original book did set to rest a number of myths. Many published works state that *Olympic* and *Titanic* displaced (or weighed) 66,000 tons. In fact, it is an error that can be dated back to at least 1910. When all the evidence is considered, there is no doubt that the true figure was 14,000 tons less. (See my article, 'The 66,000 ton Myth', in *White Star Journal*, Irish *Titanic* Historical Society, 2007, setting out the available evidence.) Other books and articles document the moments on *Titanic*'s bridge during and after the fatal collision. While it is often taken as a fact that First Officer Murdoch had ordered the engines reversed prior to the collision, the statement relies solely on Fourth Officer Boxhall's recollection. The accounts from those in the engine room make clear that the engines were ordered to 'stop'. However, Mersey's report summarising the events on the bridge stated as a fact that the engines were reversed and that statement appears in many modern sources as well. There is an argument to be made as to whether Boxhall was right or wrong, but at the very least his statement should not be taken as fact if the other testimonies do not support it. The first edition mentioned some of these issues and further clarification has been added. Another debate is whether the engines could have been reversed in time even if the order had been given. These points call into question modern criticism of Murdoch's actions in allegedly reversing the engines. It is very easy and very dangerous to make judgements or criticisms based on knowledge in hindsight. Murdoch would not have been on *Olympic*'s maiden and early voyages and then *Titanic*'s maiden voyage if he had not been a highly qualified and competent officer. Nor did he live to explain his actions or defend himself.

There have been quite a few further changes regarding *Britannic* and her name, following the discovery of additional material. This material has been added and a number of recent articles on the subject referenced. The discovery of an entry in a Harland & Wolff engineering notebook, which specified *Titanic*'s propellers and stated that the centre propeller had three blades, is another interesting point. At present, it seems to be the only source that directly specified the number of blades for this propeller and, with all photographs claiming to be *Titanic* actually those of *Olympic*, it raises a question about an aspect of *Titanic* that might not have been considered otherwise. Whether other documentation might appear contradicting it, perhaps the only definitive answer lies with the wreck itself. Unfortunately, this area is buried beneath the mudline. (See: 'The Mystery of *Titanic*'s Central Propeller', in *Voyage*, *Titanic* International Society, 2008.)

Simple spelling mistakes can also occur. John Thearle, who served on board *Olympic* when she entered service and remained until he retired as *Olympic*'s chief engineer at the end of 1929, appears early in the story. His name was incorrectly recorded as 'Therle' in 1911 and in this original book, however it was subsequently corrected from other documentation (and in *RMS Olympic: Titanic's Sister*). His grandson, Nick Thearle, confirmed the correct spelling. Captain Alexander Elvin Sherwin Hambelton, one of *Olympic*'s commanders, is variously recorded as 'Hambeldon', 'Hambledon' and 'Hambleton'. His service record seems to confirm the correct spelling.

Hopefully, these comments have given some insight into a few of the many changes – large and small – that have been made and the reasons behind them. As well as the articles referenced in this note there are others that have been cited in the text for the interested reader to pursue. These comments highlight the difficulty in chronicling such a broad subject, but also the importance of scepticism and the need to rely on primary source material. Past experience shows all too clearly that many other errors will remain. Responsibility for those errors is mine alone.

1

THE OCEANIC STEAM
NAVIGATION COMPANY

I n 1869 the Oceanic Steam Navigation Company (otherwise known as the White Star Line) was formed with a capital of £400,000[1] in £1,000 shares. This was primarily the result of a meeting between Gustav Schwabe and T.H. Ismay,[2] at which Schwabe had promised Ismay financial backing if Ismay's newly purchased shipping company ordered its ships from Harland & Wolff.[3] (Gustav Schwabe's nephew, Gustav Wolff, was a junior partner in Harland & Wolff.[4]) Orders for six ships were placed with Harland & Wolff later that year[5]; the sister-ships *Oceanic, Atlantic, Baltic, Republic, Celtic* and *Adriatic*.[6] These vessels were around 4,000grt, were built of iron, and had single propellers.[7]

Designed to carry 1,166 passengers, 166 in 'saloon' and the remainder in steerage, the pioneering forerunner *Oceanic* cost £120,000; her accommodation was 'superb' and she was capable of a competitive 14 knots.[8] But although she was fast, the ship consumed only 58 tons of coal per day, compared to her rival Cunard's 110-ton equivalent.[9] She had initial engine troubles and a lack of passengers, but soon proved popular.[10] Her accommodation was arresting:

> …the partners planned totally novel passenger accommodation. The saloon ran the breadth of the ship…a built-in smoking room was provided instead of a canvas deck-house…cabins were doubled in size and fitted with large portholes and electric bells.

Cunard did not launch a worthy competitor for ten years.[11]

'The interior decorations are on a most magnificent scale,' it was said. 'The lounges and fixed seats are upholstered in crimson velvet; the [wall] panels are damasked with white and pink and the pilasters, brackets and cornices are of teak, picked out with gold. The bed hangings of the staterooms and sleeping berths…and the apartments are in all respects elegant and complete.'[12]

Oceanic was one of the first ships where the first-class accommodation and dining saloon were situated amidships, rather than near the stern as on earlier vessels; her length-to-beam ratio was ten-to-one rather than the then usual eight-to-one; instead of many deckhouses there was a single superstructure, 'which provided generous deck space'.[13] Her dining saloon was a large, plush area, 'where coal-burning fireplaces with marble mantels gave the illusion of a grand country house, passengers for the first time sat down to dinner in separate armchairs, albeit ones bolted to the floor, rather than the long padded benches of yore.'[14] Yet more new features included steam heating in every cabin and lighting which came from adjustable oil lamps rather than candles.[15]

The ship overall looked 'more like an Imperial yacht' than a conventional passenger vessel.[16] '*Oceanic* established the White Star Line as the arbiter of comfort on the North Atlantic.' [17]

The company was dealt a severe below when *Atlantic* ran aground off Nova Scotia in April 1873. Although a number of passengers and crew survived, there was a severe loss of life and hundreds of people died. Accusations that the steamer was short of coal were strongly disputed by the company, but they did nothing for its reputation. Nevertheless, the disaster did not break the firm.

The first *Britannic*, and the *Germanic*, built in 1874–75, were capable of over 16 knots and reduced a crossing to 7½ days. These were very successful ships of 5,004grt. Essentially the same as her sister, *Britannic*'s registry records her length as 455ft between perpendiculars, with a beam a little over 45ft. Compound engines, as were usual at the time, drove her twin propellers. Interestingly, *Britannic*'s propeller shaft was initially adjustable so that it could be lowered for more thrust in deeper water, although the shaft snapped several times and was soon removed, to be replaced by a conventional one.[19] Harland & Wolff were not yet building engines at their yard, so the Lambeth firm of Maudslay, Sons & Field produced the twin-cylinder engines, which produced 760 nominal horse power (nhp). As with the previous ships, their superstructure was a single deckhouse, but their masts numbered four and the two ships featured barque rigging. They became White Star's premier liners for the time.

In 1889 White Star had commissioned two Blue Riband-winning sister-ships, the 10,000-gross ton, twin-screw, 20-knot ships *Teutonic* and *Majestic*, which were very smart looking ships, of an impressive 582ft length.[20] *Teutonic*'s port propeller was 5ft further forward than her starboard propeller, with the port propeller running at eighty-two revolutions per minute and the starboard counterpart running at seventy-nine revolutions, in order to counter torque.[21] The company was doing well, building ships that bettered the competition on all of its different services.

As the company grew, J. Bruce Ismay and his younger brother James were admitted to White Star in 1891 and when Thomas Henry Ismay retired the following year, the brothers effectively gained control of the company.[22] However, Thomas Ismay maintained an interest in the line.

There was fierce rivalry during this decade between the German shipping companies and their British counterparts.[23] Despite this, the White Star Line continued to prosper. White Star introduced in 1899 to its express service a liner regarded as the pinnacle of nineteenth-century shipbuilding, the *Oceanic* (II).[24] Billed 'the ship of the century' she was the 'world's largest' by a good margin and her launching was attended by a huge crowd.[25] The new liner measured 17,200grt and had engines capable of developing 28,000hp, which drove twin propellers.[26] *Oceanic* had extensive, comfortable and luxurious first-class accommodation which included a large, plush smoking room; a lounge; a library, one of the finest afloat; a reading and writing room; and a lavish dining saloon that was capped by a large dome. Her second- and third-class accommodation was also of a very good standard. *Oceanic* could carry 410 first-class, 300 second-class, and 1,000 third-class passengers.[27]

She proved popular with the travelling public and developed a sound reputation for reliability. Her powerful engines ensured that she had plenty of reserve power to make up for delays, although even she could not defy the hostile Atlantic ocean at its worst. As one newspaper put it: 'She is designed to insure absolute regularity of service without regard

The White Star Line advertised 'low rates' on their Liverpool to New York service in the 1870s. Second-class accommodation was very limited in comparison with future steamships. (Author's collection)

to the elements… It is believed that the White Star Line has, in truth, built a vessel which will combine the luxury of the express steamer and the capacity of the slower leviathans, with a speed approaching that attained by the every day greyhound of the period, but without attempting to outdo the best that has been accomplished in speed. Yet no one would be surprised if the *Oceanic* should come in [to New York] on Tuesday next, instead of Wednesday, when she should be due under the company's schedule.' Eighteen months after her debut, J. Bruce Ismay told a reporter in New York that, 'The line was so well pleased with the success of the *Oceanic* that it would not build boats any faster than that vessel.'

In fact, the company's focus was switching towards larger vessels whose large carrying capacity, combined with economy of operation, would deliver increasing profits. When *Celtic* entered service in 1901, she was the largest vessel in the world and had the capacity to carry more than 2,000 third-class passengers in addition to her extensive first- and second-class accommodation. Despite her great size, at almost 21,000 gross tons, her speed designated her as an intermediate liner, since she was able to maintain a dependable 16 knots. However, she proved popular on the company's secondary service to New York from Liverpool. Her first-class fittings were not as grand as *Oceanic*'s, nor as vulgar as some of the German liners of the period, but her public rooms were handsomely finished and spacious. Her success with passengers combined with a very large cargo capacity, while her coal consumption was extremely low at around 260 tons each day. *Oceanic* consumed closer to 400 tons: around 50 per cent higher to give her an advantage in speed of a mere three or four knots.

Unsurprisingly, *Celtic* proved a model for future ships. Her nearly identical sister, *Cedric*, entered service in 1903, and she was followed – in turn – by *Baltic* the following year. Each ship grew increasingly popular, even to the point of surpassing *Oceanic*'s own popularity with first-class passengers. During her first year of service it was claimed that *Cedric* 'carried more first cabin passengers trip for trip than any other liner sailing from New York'. She certainly bettered all the other ships in the White Star fleet, relegating *Oceanic* to second place. *Adriatic*, laid down within months of *Baltic*, did not enter service until 1907, since her construction had been suspended for a period as *Baltic*'s progress continued apace. Each ship was larger than her predecessor, so that *Adriatic*'s size reached 24,541 gross tons. Collectively, they were known as the 'Big Four' and earned substantial profits for the company over the following decades.

Even as the 'Big Four' progressed from the design stage to physical reality, the White Star Line itself saw considerable changes. After buying controlling interests in a host of steamship companies, through his firm J.P. Morgan & Co., the American banker J.P. Morgan set his sights on the line. In January 1902, Ismay had been reported as saying: 'Money can't buy the White Star Line. It's not for sale.' Although the Ismay family wanted to resist initially, Morgan's generous offer – at over ten times the line's profits based on its bumper results in 1900 – was agreeable to the company's shareholders, who approved it on 18 May 1902. Control of the company was fairly complex. The White Star Line itself, the trading name used by the Oceanic Steam Navigation Company, was registered in Britain with J. Bruce Ismay as chairman and managing director; Lord Pirrie, of Harland & Wolff, and Harold Sanderson as directors. However, from 1902 nearly all the company's shares were held by the International Navigation Company, registered in Liverpool.★ Its directors were J. Bruce Ismay as chairman, supported by Harold Sanderson, Charles Torrey and Henry Concanon. The International Navigation Company also held 'practically the whole of the issued share capital of the British and North Atlantic Steam Navigation Company, and the Mississippi and Dominion Steamship Company (the Dominion Line)'; as well as almost 'the whole of the issued share capital' of the Dominion and Leyland Lines. In turn, the shares in the International Navigation Company were held by the International Mercantile Marine Company (IMM), which was itself an American company based in New Jersey.

★ The exceptions were eight shares held by Messrs E.C. Grenfell, Vivian H. Smith, W.S.M. Burns, James Gray, J. Bruce Ismay, Harold Sanderson, A. Kerr, and Lord Pirrie.

From 1904, Ismay – at Morgan's request – headed IMM, helping to whip the unwieldy combine into shape. By 1911, the company's ninth annual report was stating: 'The number of vessels now in the various services is 120, representing a gross tonnage of 1,067,425 tons, to which will be added, when the six steamers now building are completed, 113,700 tons gross, making in all a total tonnage of your own and subsidiary companies of 1,181,125 tons...' The White Star Line's own profits rose strongly during the period. Despite the poor years experienced by the shipping industry in 1908 and 1909, profits exceeded a seven-figure sum for the first time in 1910.

One German company, Albert Ballin's Hamburg-Amerika Line (HAPAG), followed White Star's lead and abandoned any thought of speed records. In 1905, their new *Amerika* won praise from many quarters for her luxurious interiors and comfortable accommodation. Laid down by Harland & Wolff on the same slip that *Baltic* vacated when she was launched in November 1903, she was designed on very similar lines, but her first-class accommodation was far more extravagant. Faced with stiff competition from foreign companies and worries in Britain about Morgan's intentions, Cunard sought to take advantage of the situation, obtaining a low-interest loan from the British government to construct two fast liners, *Lusitania* and *Mauretania*. Not only would they be the largest in the world when they entered service in 1907, but they would enhance British pride as the world's fastest. Once they had settled into their routine, it became clear that their speed was ten knots greater than the 'Big Four'. The White Star Line could not pause for breath. *Adriatic* had seen remarkable improvements compared to her sister ships, particularly in her first- and second-class accommodation. She was the first ship fitted with a plunge bath (a tiny swimming pool), not to mention a Turkish and electric bath establishment, while a gymnasium was available as well. Although she was also designed for comfort rather than speed, her engines were more powerful than her sisters' and gave her additional reserve power, since she would start her career sailing from Southampton after White Star moved their express service there in 1907. *Celtic*, *Cedric* and *Baltic* continued to operate a secondary service from Liverpool, maintaining the company's traditional connection with the port.

Although it is popularly believed that plans for the *'Olympic'* class liners were discussed first between J. Bruce Ismay and Lord Pirrie at a London dinner party in the summer of 1907, in fact the order for the first two ships can be traced back to at least 30 April 1907.[26] It seems probable that ideas had been floated over several years as competition intensified on the Atlantic, although it is quite plausible that the dinner party conversation took place as they became more definite. They saw the merits of larger liners, incorporating many improvements based upon the 'Big Four' and other ships. While they would be slightly faster than *Oceanic*, in order to maintain a credible service, no attempt would be made to build record breakers. The first two ships would replace the ageing *Teutonic* and *Majestic*, while the order for a third would follow afterwards.

2
HARLAND & WOLFF

P erhaps it was fitting that Harland & Wolff's 400th ship was such an important one as *Olympic*. The White Star Line's relationship with the shipbuilding firm was close and it endured throughout the company's existence. When the first *Oceanic* was completed, she was not built to a contract or set price. Instead, the arrangement with Harland & Wolff was to the effect that they would construct the ship to a high quality with sound materials and then add 4 or 5 per cent to the overall bill. While they were not limited to a set price, there was clearly a recognition that the shipbuilder would not overindulge with lavish or unnecessary expenditure: nevertheless, the arrangement ensured that they would make money from the construction of each White Star liner. The 'cost plus' arrangement continued for decades and was satisfactory to both parties. It helped that Harland & Wolff and their customer were closely linked, with Lord Pirrie one of the White Star Line's directors. Had that *not* been the case, Cunard's Lord Inverclyde drew attention to potential problems: 'The difficulty in building without a [fixed price] contract is where the shipbuilder is not also interested as a ship owner, as Harland & Wolff are. They are very apt to mount up the cost, regardless of what it will come to, not only because the higher the cost the better their percentage, but also because they can spend what they choose in getting the results aimed at.'

Edward Harland, senior partner in Harland & Wolff, noted that the shipbuilder had not manufactured the engines for *Oceanic*. At that time, they had to be subcontracted and were made by Forester & Co. at Liverpool to Harland & Wolff's own design: 'So satisfactorily did they work in the *Oceanic* and *Atlantic* that we are at present [May 1873] building larger vessels for the same owners on identically the same plan,' Harland explained. 'They were built for the New York trade expressly.' William Taylor, principal surveyor to the Board of Trade, described *Oceanic*'s younger sister *Atlantic* as a sound ship: 'She showed no symptom of weakness… She was a very long ship; but a fine shaped one…I examined the rivets of the *Atlantic*…; they were firm and staunch.' Certainly, the White Star Line were pleased with their early performances, notwithstanding *Atlantic*'s devastating loss. The young William James Pirrie was already working for Harland & Wolff as an apprentice in 1862 and he was admitted to the partnership in 1874,[1] at a time when even larger and better ships were being built for the White Star Line. *Britannic* and *Germanic* proved successful, but few at the time could have foreseen that *Germanic* would survive life under various owners for an astonishing three-quarters of a century.

Economy of operation was not only achieved by the propelling machinery. A ship's hull form could have a considerable impact on her efficiency. Edward Harland's concept

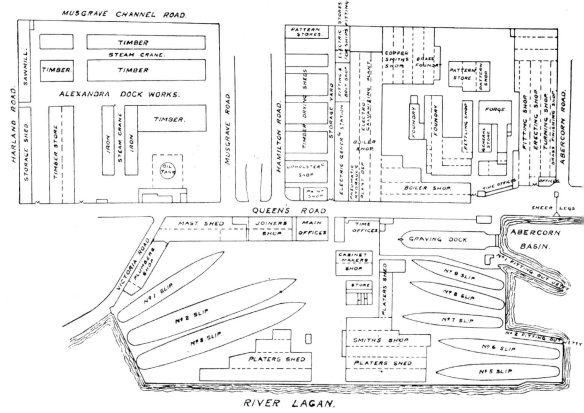

Fig. 3.—Plan of the Queen's Island Works.

Harland & Wolff's works at Queen's Island, as they were at the time of *Olympic* and *Titanic*'s construction. (*The Shipbuilder*, 1911/Ioannis Georgiou collection)

for longer ('coffin') ships had been applied with two ships for John Bibby & Sons, and they and the White Star Line benefited: 'Of the greater carrying power and accommodation, both for cargo and passengers, that would be gained by constructing the new vessels of increased length, without any increase in the beam…the hull of the ship was converted into a box girder of immensely increased strength.'[2] The concept proved itself in service. He described *Oceanic* and *Atlantic*, stating: 'Even at half boiler power against a gale of wind they would make from five to six knots.' In the early days, ships such as White Star's first *Adriatic* logged 375 miles in a single day at a speed of almost 16 knots, under the command of Captain Digby Murray, White Star's commodore from March 1871 until February 1873. Throughout the late nineteenth century, Harland & Wolff developed a number of other innovations and continued to develop larger and finer steamers.

The completion of *Oceanic* in 1899 and the 'Big Four' over the following years enhanced the shipbuilder's reputation. By September 1908, the White Star Line's fleet had expanded to include twenty-three steamships with a total combined tonnage of 311,403 gross tons, or an average size of 13,539 gross tons. All of them were twin screw steamers

Giant and Floating Cranes, Loading and Transporting Plants, Shipbuilding Slips.

OLYMPIC

Deutsche Maschinenfabrik A.G.,

Duisburg   Germany

An interesting illustration of *Olympic* and a floating crane lifting one of the boilers into the ship through the first funnel casing. The crane was ordered in 1908 and built by the Benrather *Maschinenfabrik*, Düsseldorf. Following a merger with another firm, Bechem & Keetmann, they became Duisburger *Maschinenfabrik*; and another merger in 1910 formed the larger *Deutsche Maschinenfabrik Aktien Gesellschaft* (DEMAG). It weighed over 200 tons and was capable of lifting heavy machinery more than 150ft. (*Shipbuilding & Shipping Record*, 1914/Author's collection)

and Harland & Wolff had constructed every single one, since the White Star Line only ever ordered new tonnage from them. (The sole exception was *Cretic*, which had been built by R. & W. Hawthorn, Leslie & Co. at Newcastle. Even then, she was only an exception because she had originally been ordered by the Leyland Line. She was subsequently transferred within IMM to the White Star fleet.)

Following Edward Harland's death in 1896 and the retirement of Gustav Wolff in 1906, Pirrie became the company's chairman.[3] The company's Belfast works underwent a significant programme of expansion and improvement, including two enormous slipways large enough to hold *Olympic* and *Titanic*, which replaced three smaller slipways:

> First of all a bed sufficiently strong to take their enormous weight had to be constructed. For this purpose the ground was heavily piled, and then a concrete floor reaching in places four feet six inches thick was laid on, and around the piles in such a manner that the latter take the load... The gantry... was designed by [Harland & Wolff] and constructed by Messrs Sir William Arrol & Co. Ltd, the electric cranes being supplied by Messrs Stothert & Pitt. The space covered is more than 850ft long by 270ft broad, while the height is 150ft. No fewer than twenty-three crane hooks are fitted... these cranes support the hydraulic riveting machines, by which the bulk of the work [is] done.

Pirrie's shipyard was ready to produce the largest ships that the world had seen.

3

THE COMPETITION:

LUSITANIA, MAURETANIA & AQUITANIA

Cunard's magnificent trio were to prove key in the inspiration for the White Star Line's fabulous new express steamships. Their histories often inter-twined with the *Olympic*-class liners, and it appears entirely justifiable to devote a chapter to detail their design and entry into transatlantic service.

Lusitania and *Mauretania* were laid-down at the Clydebank shipyard of John Brown & Co. and Swan, Hunter & Wigham Richardson Ltd., respectively, in 1904. Principal specifications were and would be:[1]

	Lusitania	Mauretania
Length	785ft	790ft
Breath	88ft	88ft
Moulded depth	60ft 4in	60ft 6in
Draught	Over 30ft	Over 30ft
Gross tonnage	31,550 tons	31,938 tons
Displacement (fully-loaded)	44,060 tons	44,640 tons
Engines	Four turbines	Four turbines
Horsepower	Over 68,000	Over 68,000
Service speed	24½ knots	24½ knots

In order to finance the new vessels Cunard had secured a low-interest twenty-year loan for the sum of £2.6 million. The company had had to give a guarantee that they would remain a British concern for the next twenty years and that the new ships would be available for service in the event of war. Additionally, the new ves-sels were to be built to Admiralty specification. This meant, briefly, that there would be increased watertight subdivision, including longitudinal watertight bulkheads, and special deck mounts for guns.

Lusitania was launched first in 1906 and her sister soon followed on the same day as White Star's *Adriatic*. However, it is interesting to note that at launching, the White Star ship was actually slightly heavier, although she was shorter and thinner. Both Cunard ships entered service in 1907, *Lusitania* in September and her sister in November.[2] Soon both were exchanging the Blue Riband for the fastest crossing. Two high-pressure and two low-pressure turbines were run by twenty-three main boilers and two single-ended auxiliary boilers.[3] The speed was slowly pushed-up from under 24 knots to over 26 knots. *Mauretania* had in fact actually achieved a top speed of 27¾ knots during her

Cunard's *Lusitania*, seen at Liverpool several years after she entered service. (Author's collection)

speed trials on the 'measured mile'.[4] By 1929, she would complete her best-ever crossing at an average of only a little less than this.

Cunard advised that their new vessels were the 'fastest, finest and largest quadruple-screw express steamships in the world'.

Although built for speed, the ships did not stint on luxury and could carry many passengers. *Mauretania*, for example, when she entered service could accommodate 563 first-class 'saloon' passengers, 464 second-class ('cabin') passengers and 1,138 third-class passengers, with a crew numbering 812:[5] a total of 2,977 people.

Saloon accommodation included a lounge and music room; writing room and library; smoke room and veranda café. In addition, there was a children's nursery. There were also several parlour suites with en-suite bathrooms and regal suites on the higher decks; cold and hot water supplies were available to first-class staterooms on decks A and B and some of the finest rooms had telephone connections with the exchange. The staterooms varied between Adam, Sheraton and Chippendale styles.[6]

Undoubtedly the dining saloons were the ships' showpieces. They also marked the greatest contrast between the two vessels. Designer James Millar had worked on the *Lusitania* and Harold Peto on the newer vessel. While both saloons were two decks high and capped by a dome, *Lusitania*'s was full of white plaster and gold leaf – 'cool elegance,' as one writer once said – *Mauretania*'s was lavish in the use of rich mahogany, giving a more substantial feel.[7] But one detail showed the ships up: the chairs were swivel chairs, not adjustable and bolted to the floor. In addition, there were no private alcoves.[8]

One other notable failing was the lack of a swimming pool on either vessel and no Turkish baths,[9] which were facilities of the best of White Star's 'Big Four'. Nevertheless, at the time of entering service both ships claimed to be the most luxurious in the world. It may have been said that the vessels had failed to excel the luxury of the White Star ships, but certainly in terms of top speeds they left the competition crawling. 18 knots was about the maximum speed attained by the 'Big Four', the German ships were somewhat faster, but both Cunarders could reach over 27 knots.

However, when these two vessels were surpassed in size and luxury by the White Star ships that followed, luring away passengers, not to mention further German competition, Cunard decided that a third vessel to join them would be slower and more luxurious.[10]

After much discussion, in December 1910 the contract for *Aquitania* was signed with John Brown & Co., builders of the *Lusitania*;[11] she was to be 45,647grt with a speed of 23 knots and so was slightly smaller than *Olympic*'s 1913 tonnage of 46,358grt.

Principally, *Aquitania*'s statistics were:

Length	901ft 6in
Breadth	97ft[12]
Moulded depth	64ft 6in
Draught	34ft
Gross tonnage	45,647
Displacement (fully loaded)	49,430
Engines	Four turbines
Horsepower	Over 56,000
Service speed	23 knots

Launched in April 1913, *Aquitania* entered service a little over a year later. She was able to carry 618 first-class passengers, 614 second-class passengers, plus a staggering 1,998 third-class passengers; a total of 4,202 people including crew. Primarily, her large capacity was due to all of the machinery being below the waterline, which was a deliberate feature so that the ship could carry enough passengers to make up for the lack of a mail subsidy.[13] Her maiden voyage total of 1,055 passengers in all classes, roughly one-third of her maximum capacity, proved disappointing – even though nobody had cancelled because of the tragic *Empress of Ireland* sinking in Canada – but in other respects the voyage was perfect; the ship averaged over 23 knots and it was noted how little vibration there was.[14]

First-class accommodation was certainly very luxurious and the ship soon earned the nickname 'Ship Beautiful'. In fact, *Aquitania* was the first ever Cunarder to have a swimming pool, her first-class accommodation comprising a gymnasium, Elizabethan grill, main restaurant, smoke room, long gallery, two writing salons, two 'garden lounges', Palladian lounge and drawing room.[15] She had eight special B-deck suites – comprising a sitting room, baths, hall and bedrooms (three with small verandas) – named after painters such as Holbein, Gainsborough, Rembrandt and Romney, the suites being decorated in each painter's style.[16] *Aquitania* proved popular and many consider her to be one of the finest liners ever built.

Cunard's nascent quadruple-screw three-ship express service was finally established by *Aquitania*'s maiden voyage in mid-1914, but soon war intervened and the service was shattered.

4
BIRTH OF THE *OLYMPICS*

From the White Star Line's main offices a party of distinguished guests arrived at the Harland & Wolff shipyard on 29 July 1908.[1] They had come to view the builder's concepts for the new vessels, bearing the legend,

> 400 Plan – July 29th 1908 (Proposed General Arrangement)
> 'SS no. 400
> '850 x 92 x 64½
> Design 'D'[2]

They certainly liked what they saw, as the 'letter of agreement' for construction to proceed was signed two days later. Along the promenade deck, a first-class reading and writing room, lounge, smoke room and two veranda cafés ensured that passengers had plenty of choice where to spend their day; the first-class dining saloon occupied a single deck, with a central dome extending its height a further two; a reception room next to the saloon was a new innovation; and the establishment of a gymnasium, swimming pool and Turkish and electric bath was an expansion of features seen on *Adriatic*. In first class, a high proportion of single-berth staterooms were a great stride forward at a time when it was still commonplace to share with a stranger. Although some open berths were retained, the vast majority of third-class passengers were berthed in enclosed rooms. Building upon the initial concept, changes and improvements were made. The removal of the dome above the first-class dining saloon allowed the space to be used for first-class staterooms; the two first-class elevators became three and the second-class elevator, a new feature for that class, was retained; the second-class smoke room, originally situated beneath its first-class counterpart, was moved elsewhere and replaced with a new innovation for a British ship, an *á la carte* restaurant where a variety of dishes could be ordered outside of the normal sittings in the dining saloon. The original straight first-class staircases, which appeared rather plain, were transformed so that they curved in a magnificent sweep from deck to deck. The gymnasium was moved to the boat deck.

The original concept showed 600 first-, 716 second- and 1,788 third-class passengers so that, including crew, each ship would accommodate around 4,000 people. As it was refined, passenger capacities changed markedly: first class was expanded further, while second class was reduced slightly, and third class saw a dramatic reduction. The model moved away from that of the 'Big Four' and their enormous third-class capacities, to earlier express liners such as *Teutonic* and *Majestic*, which could carry around 1,000 third-class passengers. For their size, the new liners carried fewer passengers than might have been expected. *Olympic*'s net tonnage (commercially useful space, excluding, for example, the engine and boiler rooms which were included in the gross tonnage figure) was three times greater than that of *Oceanic*, the White Star Line's most recent express liner. Her passenger capacity, on the other hand, increased by a little over 40 per cent: the biggest increase coming in luxurious first- and second-class accommodation. *Mauretania* carried a similar number of passengers to *Olympic*, even though her net tonnage was smaller than each of the 'Big Four'.

Following the necessary preparation work after the White Star Line had agreed that construction could proceed, Harland & Wolff's yard and engine works had been busy. By 16 December 1908, *Olympic*'s keel had been laid – 'Yard Number 400'; on 31 March 1909 *Titanic*'s followed – 'Yard Number 401'.

Lord Pirrie 'practically designed' the new liners, in terms of specifying the length, beam, depths and modelling. But the details, decorations and general vessels' equipment were the responsibility of Alexander Montgomery Carlisle, chairman of the shipyard managing directors and general yard manager (who was to retire in mid-1910); Thomas Andrews was the managing director of the Drafting Department (to succeed Carlisle); while J. Bruce Ismay and the White Star Line directors had the final say.

Olympic and *Titanic* were to have an overall length of 882ft 9in and an extreme breadth of 92ft 6in, so that their gross tonnages were projected at 45,000grt each. When they were at their designed load in service, drawing 34ft 7in of water, their displacement (or weight) would be 52,310 tons each. Together, they represented a substantial record in size as they were built side by side at the same shipyard at the same time.

It seems doubtful that anyone was unduly worried at the time about the arrangements that were being made for their lifeboat provision. Government regulations had long been outdated. In the 1850s, 'nearly the whole of the passenger traffic was carried on by wooden sailing ships of about 1,200 to 1,500 tons' and lifeboat provision was based upon their registered tonnage, 'which in those days of sailing ships gave a very good idea of the vessel's size and of her capabilities for stowing boats…' Cunard's *Pavonia* could carry 1,141 passengers and 155 crew, but she was only required by law to have lifeboat accommodation for 17 per cent of the maximum number of people on board, and Cunard provided it for 29 per cent. The law did not require any passenger ship greater than 1,500 tons to carry more than seven lifeboats, even though construction of ships such as *Teutonic* and *Majestic* demonstrated the advent of ships six times the size by the late 1880s. One official, Sir Digby Murray, had been impressed by the White Star Line's own *Britannic*, which had entered service in 1875 and suffered flooding on more than one occasion:

> The *Britannic* especially has been saved twice by her [watertight] bulkheads; once with two compartments full; this last time with one compartment full. And I need not tell you that there is very great risk to life even in smooth weather the moment you have to lower your boats… I think you can make ships perfectly safe by subdivision of them; I think the *Britannic* has amply proved that.

The Merchant Shipping Act (1854) and Passenger Act (1855) remained in force more than thirty years after they had been passed, but a proposed improvement in 1875 had never gone into effect. Murray freely admitted that 'the old rules on this subject are entirely obsolete, and we are perfectly well aware at the Board of Trade that they are obsolete.' He made his comments as the rules were being reviewed in 1887, but expert opinion continued to focus on keeping a damaged ship afloat rather than having to evacuate her passengers and crew in relatively small boats on the open sea. Sound watertight subdivision was 'most important for saving life at sea, and a thing upon which the full efficiency of lifesaving appliances largely depends.' By 1894, ships of over 10,000grt were required to carry sixteen lifeboats under davits 'with a minimum capacity of 5,500 cubic feet'. Cunard supplied *Lusitania* and *Mauretania* with this number when they entered service in 1907, as they met the legal requirements. Their naval architect explained:

> When the question of boat capacity of such ships as the *Mauretania* and *Lusitania* was brought forward, the special [watertight] subdivision of those particular vessels was taken into account, and it was considered that owing to the extraordinary precautions which had been taken, the total capacity of boats necessary to be carried would be fully met by the existing Rules.

Olympic and *Titanic* had grown to thirty times the size of their forerunners of the 1850s yet, even as the legal requirements were occasionally updated, the broad consensus had seen little challenge. No longer could a ship's tonnage be a reliable guide as to the required lifeboat capacity, insofar as it had ever been. The German liner *President Lincoln* complied to American, British and German laws and could carry over 4,100 people, even more than the much larger *Olympic* and *Titanic*, but her lifeboat capacity fell short of that by 2,643 persons.

The great new liners would be fitted with the new double-acting Welin davits; each set of davits able to 'handle four lifeboats'. Due to the increasing size of liners, a revision of the rules was being discussed. If the regulations did end up being changed then it would be more convenient to be able to add the extra lifeboats without the extra davits that would cause a clutter on the boat deck. An additional advantage was that there would be no extra expense. Alexander Carlisle later recalled:

> When working out the designs of the *Olympic* and *Titanic* I put my ideas (for a davit set that could handle more than one lifeboat) before the davit constructors, and got them to design for me [special] davits; these would allow me to place, if necessary, four lifeboats on each pair of davits, which would have meant a total of over forty lifeboats. Those davits were fitted in both ships, but the Board of Trade [regulations] did not require anything over sixteen lifeboats.

Sixteen sets of the double-acting davits were to be fitted on both of the first two ships. Each set of davits could handle up to four lifeboats, a total of sixty-four; if three boats were fitted, a total of forty-eight; if two boats were fitted, a total of thirty-two; or if only one lifeboat was fitted, a total of sixteen boats. Alexander Carlisle thought personally that the ships should have at least forty-eight lifeboats each, and when seeing the Merchant Shipping Advisory Committee later on 19 and 26 May 1911, he stated his concern about the lack of lifeboats generally on larger liners, despite signing a report that would have the effect of *reducing* lifeboat accommodation on such large vessels.

Nevertheless, although a total of only twenty lifeboats would be fitted to the two liners after Carlisle's June 1910 retirement, the other lifesaving appliances were very complete. Fourteen wooden lifeboats of the 'standard type' were built, 30ft long by 9ft 1in breadth and 4ft in depth. These had a cubic capacity of 655.2 cubic feet and were constructed to carry sixty-five people each, although in terms of weight they could carry quite a lot more. Two wooden 'emergency' cutters were to be fitted either side of the navigating bridge, and kept permanently swung out in readiness for cases such as somebody falling overboard. Both cutters were not identical: both were 25ft 2in long and 3ft in depth, but the breadths were 7ft 1in and 7ft 2in; these had a cubic feet capacity of 322.1 and 326.6 and were constructed to hold forty people. Four Englehardt 'collapsible' boats were 27ft 5in in length, 8ft in breadth and 3ft in depth; the cubic feet capacities were 376.6 and these boats could carry forty-seven people. All of these different types of boats were constructed in basically the same way: the keels were elm; stems and sternposts oak; clinker-built of yellow pine and double-fastened with copper nails clinched over rooves. Timbers were spaced 9in apart and the seats were pitch pine with galvanised iron double-knees securing them; the buoyancy tanks were copper and weighed 18oz, and their capacities exceeded British Board of Trade regulations.

All lifeboats under davits were fitted with 'Murray's Patented Release Gear'; both ends of the lifeboats could be simultaneously released from the falls and the gear was fastened to suit the new advanced davits. Lifelines were fitted along the gunwales on the lifeboats to aid anyone falling overboard. The blocks for the ropes (falls) used to lower the lifeboats were treble for the lifeboats, and double for the cutters; these were made of elm with lignum vitae roller sheaves, were bound inside with iron, and had swivel eyes. Manilla was the material used for the falls, which were long enough to lower the lifeboats to the waterline with a light draught and enough to pull the boats back up and reach the electrically driven winches on the deck. Hinged wooden chocks on the deck supported the boats in groups of three at the forward lifeboat ends and four at the after boat ends. There were two 'groups' of lifeboats on the boat deck, four sets of davits with four standard wooden boats aft, then an open space of nearly 200ft and four sets of davits with three wooden boats and an emergency cutter on the first davit set. The cutters were, as previously mentioned, to be always swung out, and the collapsibles were next to them on the deck. One collapsible was at the inboard side of each 'cutter' and the others were stowed one either side of the first funnel on the roof of the officers' quarters.

Forty-eight lifebuoys were supplied of the pattern approved by the Board of Trade for each vessel and there were 3,560 lifebelts distributed throughout the sleeping accommodation and these contained cork and were white in colour. Rockets and various other signals of every conceivable type were also to be kept aboard.

The enormous hulls showed a remarkable similarity with earlier vessels. Although they did not quite match the old length-to-breadth ratio of ten to one, their measurements were fairly close. The gracious lines would not become apparent until time had passed, but even in the early stages of construction the ships' keels and double bottom structures were an indication of their great length. Harland & Wolff followed tried and tested methods of construction: in many ways, they represented an enlarged and improved version of earlier structural designs for ships such as *Oceanic* and *Adriatic*. Lessons were learned from the White Star liner *Laurentic*, whose triple-screw configuration was a much smaller version of *Olympic* and *Titanic*'s; while *Adriatic* undoubtedly provided valuable insights, since the company drew upon her design. At an early stage of the design process, it was being proposed that the two new liners would be dry docked on a single line of blocks beneath the centre of the ship, which required 'special consideration' in regard to strengthening the hull and ensuring that the sides of the ship would not drop in that situation when they were unsupported. Similarly, the hull plating was doubled along the ship's length at strategic points to ensure longitudinal (lengthways) strength. Edward Wilding explained that Harland & Wolff's previous experience indicated that 'riveting was the weak point in big ships' and, therefore, 'we adopted, to an unusual extent, hydraulic riveting wherever possible, to insure the rivets being thoroughly well closed. This was of course a slow and expensive affair, but it was done.'

To use a human analogy, each ship's keel could be likened to her 'spine', which was surrounded by the strong cellular double bottom structure; the hull frames which extended from the double bottom to the top of the structural hull could be seen as the 'ribcage' and then the hull (or shell) plating as the 'skin' of the ship, keeping the structure watertight. The plating of the bridge deck (B-deck) formed the top of the structural hull and was met at the ship's side with the thicker (doubled) hull plating that ran along the side of uppermost decks and was referred to as the sheer strake. Essentially, the hull could be visualised as an enormous hollow girder, while the decks were supported by a complex combination of beams, girders, stanchions and pillars. The superstructure sat *supra*, above, the structural hull itself. It consisted of the deckhouses on the bridge, promenade and boat decks, constructed to withstand the North Atlantic's most hostile storms.

The Design 'D' plan that the White Star Line had approved at the end of July 1908 already envisaged a combination arrangement of propelling machinery. Earlier White Star liners, including the 'Big Four', were twin screw ships with two reciprocating engines, each one driving one of the ship's propellers. It was a tried and tested arrangement and had proved satisfactory. However, Cunard's *Lusitania* and *Mauretania* had demonstrated the benefits of turbine engines for high speed ships. Harland & Wolff's designers had come up with a compromise arrangement. The new ships would be powered by two enormous reciprocating engines, driving the port and starboard propellers, while a low-pressure steam turbine would drive a centre propeller. The turbine would be able to take advantage of the low-pressure steam exhausted from the reciprocating engines. While the reciprocating engines could not make any further use of it, the turbine could use this low-pressure steam, and it provided a substantial boost to the power generated by the propelling machinery. Another considerable advantage was that it contributed to the ships' overall fuel economy. The two Cunarders could consume over 1,000 tons of coal every twenty-four hours if they were driven at high speed, but the White Star ships were expected to consume several hundred tons of coal less than that.

The theory was undoubtedly sound, but it would have been a considerable leap forward to take. *Olympic* and *Titanic* would require more than twice as much power as the older *Oceanic*, which had the most powerful propelling machinery of any White Star liner to date. Fortunately, the opportunity arose for a small practical experiment before the decision was finalised. On 30 April 1907 two new ships had been ordered that became *Laurentic* and *Megantic*, for use on the Canadian service. Just like the larger ships, they were essentially identical twins. The significant difference lay in their propelling machinery: *Laurentic*'s design employed two reciprocating engines exhausting steam into a low-pressure turbine; *Megantic*'s used the traditional two reciprocating engines alone. *Laurentic* was not launched until 9 September 1908 and she was delivered on 15 April 1909. Her performance appears to have been immediately satisfactory and was reflected in the orders given to the engine works at the shipyard. On 26 February 1909, the shipyard and engine works had been ordered to proceed with the boilers for *Olympic* and *Titanic* and five days after *Laurentic* had been delivered the order was also given to proceed with the remainder of the propelling machinery, their reciprocating and turbine engines. Over a longer period, *Laurentic*'s performance was shown to be better than that of her sister and she was more economical to operate, which would have reassured Harland & Wolff and the White Star Line's management as construction proceeded on the machinery for their great new express liners.

Enough power would be available to maintain a service speed of 21 knots with plenty of additional power in reserve to cope with the inevitable delays that could be encountered on the hostile North Atlantic.

With their large cylinders and stroke length, not to mention all of the other massive parts, the main reciprocating engines were very impressive; the crankshafts and thrust shafts were 27in diameter, the line shaft being 26¼in and the tail shaft 28½in. These two engines drove the wing propellers that were 23ft 6in diameter and three-bladed, having a steel cast boss and bronze blades and weighing 38 tons.

Another impressive piece of machinery was the turbine which, as mentioned before, was mounted on the ships' centreline and drove the centre propeller of 22 tons. This propeller was 16ft 6in diameter and had four blades, unlike the wing propellers, this was all bronze. Of course, this propeller was much smaller, driven by the more powerful engine; but it had more blades and revolved much faster than the wing propellers did. The turbine itself was built in the usual way of steel forgings, was 12ft in diameter, had blades varying in length from 18-25½in, and its rotor was 13ft 8in long. It was made at the Belfast works; the rotor's total weight was 130 tons and the whole turbine weighed 420 tons. It was out of action when the ships were reversing because the two main engines were thought sufficient to be able to manoeuvre the ships in harbour.

Harland & Wolff opted for a tried and tested design in the ships' watertight subdivision, and it was thought to be very complete, although the watertight bulkheads amidships that divided the boiler rooms only went as high as E-deck's underside. It was not thought necessary to take the bulkheads up to D-deck's underside or higher because the ships could float with four compartments flooded. The worst imagined collision would flood two compartments, which would not in any way effect the ships' safety; each compartment was on average 50ft long and 92ft wide, and four could be flooded and the ships would still float – such a great engineering achievement.

While *Olympic* and *Titanic* were in the early stages of construction, the White Star Line suffered an unfortunate blow when one of their ships was lost at sea. *Republic* was rammed by the liner *Florida*. She suffered severe and fatal flooding. Ultimately, however, she remained afloat for around one-and-a-half days, enabling passengers and crew to be rescued when other ships came to her assistance, and her lifeboats were employed in a lengthy service ferrying people from one ship to another. It would have been far worse if she had foundered quickly. Although the ship's wireless apparatus was able to summon assistance, it did not arrive instantly. If she had gone down before help arrived, her lifeboat provision would not have been adequate to prevent significant loss of life.

Republic's passengers and crew were, in fact, remarkably lucky. Her loss in January 1909 did nothing to challenge the prevailing wisdom of the safety of life at sea, and that of modern liners. To the contrary, it seems to have reinforced it. Meanwhile, *Olympic* and *Titanic* grew.

Olympic's sleek lines were reminiscent of *Oceanic*'s a decade earlier. Her light painted hull contrasted her profile with the overhead gantry. (Georgiou/Chirnside/Klistorner/Layton Collection)

From the river, the two enormous ships could easily be seen dominating the skyline. Many craft going down the river slowed to get a good look at the ships. Such a sight had never been seen by the world before.

White Star's 1911 seventy-eight-page-long advertising brochure proudly described to the fascinated public – or at least the technically minded segment of the public – the details of the new liners' stern frame and boss arms, rudder, stem, steering gear, anchor gear, navigating appliances, cargo cranes, manoeuvring gear and electric lighting plant. Here are some extracts:

> The stern frame of such a vessel is of special interest. The Darlington Forge Co. made it, and some idea of its size may be formed by the fact that the total weight of the casting was about 190 tons, the stern frame being seventy tons, the side propeller brackets 73¼ tons and the forward boss arms 45 tons. The centre propeller, (driven by the turbine), works in the usual stern frame aperture, while the wing propellers are supported in brackets. The Chief dimensions of the stern castings are as follows:

Stern frame:
Height	67ft½in
Length of keel post	37ft 4in
Section of gudgeon post	21 by 13in

After brackets:
Centre of shafts	38ft 10¼in
Diameter of bosses	5ft 2¼in
Forward brackets:	
Centres of shafts	38ft 5in
Diameter of bosses	6ft 2in

The stern frame is of Siemens-Martin mild cast steel, of hollow or dish section, in two pieces, with large scarphs, one on the forward post and one on the after post, connected with best Lowmoor iron rivets two inches in diameter, with a total weight of rivets being over a ton. The care exercised in fitting these to ensure a strong connection is suggested by the fact that they were all turned and fitted and specially closed with rams. There are in all fifty-nine rivets in the forward and fifty-three rivets in the after scarphs. In the stern frame there is, of course, the boss for the shaft driven by the turbine, the lower portion of this part of the stern frame having a large palm cast on its extreme forward end, to give a solid connection to the after boss arms and main structure of the vessel.

Tried and tested equipment was supplied for handling the ship's anchors:

The centre anchor involved an addition to the usual design of windlass gear, which in these, as in other large liners, is by Messrs Napier Brothers Limited, Glasgow, and has proved by the test of time to be very reliable. In addition to working the windlass, one of the two engines fitted drives through worm gear a large drum at the forward end and opposite the central aperture on the stem. This drum is grooved to take the wire rope of the centre fifteen-ton central anchor, adopted instead of the more usual cable. Clutch-engaging and brake gear has been fitted, and every detail embodied to ensure the satisfactory working of the cables under all conditions.

A strongly built crane is fitted at the centre line of the forecastle deck for handling the fifteen-ton anchor, which is placed in a well in the deck immediately abaft the stem.

The capstan gear, operated by steam engines, is also Messrs Napier Brothers Limited, Glasgow, and includes on the forecastle two capstans worked by the windlass engines, two with independent engines, and on a lower level one for handling mooring ropes. Aft there are five capstans, with four steam engines, one of which actuates two capstans.

The vessels' navigating equipment was detailed, yielding data which have become well known to technically minded enthusiasts of the *Olympic* class:

The navigating appliances are most complete. In addition to the two compasses on the captain's bridge and one on the docking bridge aft, there is a standard compass on an isolated brasswork platform in the centre of the ship, at a height of twelve feet above all ironwork and seventy-eight feet above the waterline. Adjacent to the bridge there are two electrically driven sounding machines, arranged with spars to enable soundings to be taken when the ship is going at a good speed. All observations can thus be taken under the direct control of the Officer in command. The telegraphs are by Messrs J.W. Ray & Co., of Liverpool, and communicate with engine room, capstan and other stations. As already indicated, there is also telemotor gear for the steering of the ship. The vessels are fitted with complete installation for receiving submarine signals.

Another array of technical details flowed forth in the description of the vessels' cargo hatches, winches, and electric cranes.

There are three cargo hatches forward and aft. Two of the forward hatches are served by steam winches, the gins being fixed to cargo spans, while the third hatch – that nearest the passengers' quarters – is served by two Stothert and Pitt electric cranes, designed to lift 50cwt. They have a radius of 27ft, a height from the deck to the centre of the pulley of 29ft and a total lift of 100ft. The hoisting motors fitted are of 40bhp and the slewing motors 5bhp.

All the hatches in the after part of the ship are served by electric cranes of the same make; two of these are on the promenade deck, there being two small hatches to the hold below, so as to form a minimum of interference with the promenading space. The cranes here are of 30cwt capacity, the radius being 21ft. The height between deck and pulley is 20ft, while the total lift is 80ft. In this case the hoisting motors are of 30bhp, and the slewing motors of 3bhp. For the remaining two hatches aft there are four electric cranes of 50cwt capacity, corresponding exactly with those already referred to, except as regards the radius, which is, in the case of the two cranes, 28ft, and those of the other two, 29ft. The height to the centre of the pulley is, however, slightly less than the forward cranes, being 27ft and 26ft respectively.

The lifting speed at full load is 160ft per minute in the case of the 50cwt cranes, and two hundred feet in the case of the 30cwt cranes, and increases automatically at lighter loads, whilst the slewing speed in all cases is 500ft per minute.

In addition to the electric cranes, there are four three-ton electric cargo winches at the hatches, operating through gins on the cargo spans; also four fifteen cwt electric boat and baggage winches.

An impressive summary of the ships' electricity generating equipment concluded:

A complete system of electric lighting is, of course, provided, and electricity is also largely employed for heating, as well as for motive power, including no fewer than seventy-five motor-driven 'Sirocco' fans from 55in to 20in diameter, for ventilating all the passenger and crew spaces, as well as the engine and boiler rooms. All fan motors are provided with automatic and hand speed regulation.

While construction continued on the new liners, however, problems of a serious nature were worrying the White Star Line's management: the lack of dry-docking facilities at Southampton, the berthing facilities at New York and also the depth of the River Test at Southampton.

Southampton's port facilities were under a program of continuous expansion. The London & South Western Railway, known as the LSWR, had loaned £250,000 to aid the construction of the 1890 Empress Dock berths at Southampton.[3] Five years later, Southampton's fifth dry dock, the 745ft Prince of Wales Graving Dock, was opened. During January 1900, the LSWR awarded the contract for a sixth dry-dock to J. Aird. Extensive excavations were seen and the 875 x 90 x 33ft dock, known as the Trafalgar Dock, was opened in 1905.[4] With the White Star Line's forthcoming *Olympic* class of liners planned for the express service from Southampton, it became obvious that yet another dry-dock and berths were required. LSWR found that it would be best to extend the existing Trafalgar Dock. Accordingly, in October 1910, Topham Jones & Railton began excavation to enlarge the dock to 897ft long and to increase its depth and width. This was completed in the spring of 1913.[5] In the meantime, as part of Harland & Wolff's ongoing development, the new dry dock was nearing completion and it would be ready to receive *Olympic* in April 1911.★

LSWR awarded the £492,231 contract for the new wet dock berthing in October 1907 to Topham Jones & Railton. This came to be known as the 'White Star Dock', but the facility was renamed in 1922 as the 'Ocean Dock'.[6] To cover sixteen acres, the new dock was planned to consist of 3,806ft of quay over a 400ft width with a depth of about 40ft at low tide and 53ft at high tide.[7] Berths were numbered 43, 44, 46 and 47; these were flanked by four large cargo and passenger sheds, with lavatories and waiting rooms, one storey in height, but with passenger gantries that had a height of a good two storeys.[8] Corrugated metal sides of the sheds were painted green, the LSWR house colour; but, in time 'this faded to a dull, somewhat-bluish green'.[9]

Southampton's Harbour Board controlled the inadequately deep River Test, which White Star made efforts to deepen, but little progress was made until 1910.[10] On 6 January 1910, General Manager Harold Sanderson, Assistant Local Manager Philip Curry, Marine Superintendent Ben Steel, Captain Haddock of *Oceanic* and Pilot George Bowyer formed an official deputation to the Harbour Board. However, this initially failed, but the LSWR eventually granted a loan of the necessary funds to complete the dredging.[11]

At New York, an IMM special appeal in Washington succeeded in obtaining permission for the pier to be lengthened and deepened.[12]

On 20 September 1910 the ordering of new chinaware by the White Star line for use on the new ships commenced.[13] Other supplies were also being organised. *Olympic's* hull had been fully plated since 15 April 1910 and *Titanic's* hull plating was completed by 19 October 1910.

Holding the shell plating to the 'skeleton' frames were millions of rivets, driven home by squads of four men at the rate of two hundred per day per squad.[14] Siemens-Martin steel had been used on the vessels *Teutonic* and *Majestic*, and, after twenty years' service, the hulls of both were in remarkable condition for their age. It had also been decided that this was the best steel that could be used for the new vessels of the *Olympic* class.[15]

Olympic's launch was set for late 1910.

★ Described at the time as the largest dry dock in the world, it was not named at the time that *Olympic* was completed. On 20 May 1915, it was finally named the Thompson Graving Dock by the Lord Lieutenant of Ireland, in the presence of Robert Thompson, chairman of the Belfast Harbour Commissioners.

Thursday 20 October 1910 dawned 'fairly bright', but with quite a strong North wind, which fortunately ceased before the launch. From then on, 'conditions could not have been more fortunate. The sun shone with a warmth and power reminiscent of spring; indeed there was a vernal breath in the atmosphere such as often characterises Indian summer on the other side of the "pond" above the forty-ninth parallel,' the *Belfast News-Letter* recorded. It was the scheduled day for the *Olympic*'s launching.

'Transcending in interest every other event last year in the world of shipbuilding and marine engineering, the launch of the Royal Mail Triple-screw White Star liner *Olympic* from the stocks of the Queen's Island shipbuilding establishment of Messrs Harland & Wolff, Limited, on October 20th, attracted not only the attention of those associated with shipbuilding and the subsidiary industries, but also of that much wider section of the general public who watch closely the international struggle for supremacy on the Atlantic,' *The Shipbuilder* would later write.

From an early hour, trams going to Queen's Island were crowded. 'The scene at the yard was one of great interest and anticipation.' Stands had been constructed for the department heads, their friends, guests, pressmen, the builders and White Star Line representatives. As was his usual custom, Lord Pirrie was at the yard early, sporting his nautical yachting cap. Meanwhile, the Queen's Road was busy, overflowing with automobiles, carts and pedestrians. Even before 10 a.m., 'admiring crowds were gazing with awe at the leviathan which reared her gigantic hull far above their heads.' Numerous dignitaries would be in attendance: Miss Asquith, the Prime Minister's daughter; Captain Hunter, ADC; Captain Warner, ADC; Lord and Lady Aberdeen; the Lord Mayor and Lady Mayoress of Belfast, Miss Carlisle, and the Lord Mayor's Private Secretary Mr F.W. Moneypenny, MVO; the High Sheriff; the Lord Chief Baron and Miss Palles; Lord Powerscourt; Lord and Lady Dartrey; Lady Cole; Lady Mary Lawson; Earl Annesley; Lord Trimblestown… Some had boarded a special train from Dublin, reaching the Great Northern Railway terminal in Great Victorian Street at 10.05 a.m., to journey to the shipyard with the Lord Mayor's carriages… Lord Pirrie then gave them a tour of the shipyard, before they were seated in the stand draped in white and crimson cloth.

White Star had chartered the steamer *Duke of Cumberland* of Fleetwood, Lancashire, to bring to the launching over one hundred pressmen from England, America and the continent, not to mention the numerous executives, among them: Messrs Joseph Bruce Ismay; Harold Sanderson; E.C. Grenfell; J.W. Scott; P.E. Curry; E.L. Fletcher; A.B. Canty; J.R. Dagnall; P.A. Griffiths; T.H. Allan; H.A. Pickthall; M. Fothergill; T.C. Swain; A. Kerr; Bruce Scott; C. Baldwin; R.J.A. Shelley; C. Buchanan; A. Hillen; W.J. Willet-Bruce; Major Maitland Kersey, DSO; Captain P.D. Murray; Captain C.F.D. Beresford, and Captain R.P. Graham.

When the time reached 10.50 a.m., two rockets were fired to signal the imminent launching. Another rocket followed just before 11 a.m. Then, from the white and crimson draped stand, Lord Pirrie called the launching command to Managing Director Charles Payne: 'Now!'

Hundreds of workmen had previously knocked away the shores and wedges, leaving the hydraulic triggers and launching rams, but now that these were released, *Olympic* began to move. The vast crowds cheered, as did the shipyard workers at her stern and forecastle deck. Whoops, whistles and shouts erupted as she entered her natural element: 'There she goes!'

Shipyard workers aboard had been prepared to lower her anchors if any emergency had occurred, but there was no need. Sixty-two seconds after she began to move, *Olympic* was fully waterborne, having reached 12½ knots, and now the six heavy anchors – three

Olympic in the water, with the paraphernalia of launching still attached to her bow. (Georgiou/ Chirnside/Klistorner/ Layton Collection)

on each side of the ship – connected by 8in-thick wire hawsers came into successful effect; it took another forty-five seconds for her to be brought to a halt, in slightly more than her nearly 900ft-length.

'Her towering sides showing virgin white behind the sombre interlacery of the massive gantry present a bulk which beggars description,' an observer recorded. 'Her sharp bow, beautiful lines, and clean run from stem to stern suggest speed, her tremendous weight, rigidity, and strength indicate stability, and like the *Oceanic* eleven years ago she may proudly claim the title of "Queen of the Seas."'

'There is something awe-inspiring in the proportions of the *Olympic*. She bulks largely in one's imagination, and suggests marvellous developments in future transmarine operations. Moderate terms and comparison between this gigantic creation of shipbuilder's genius and her predecessors fail of their purpose when applied to such a ship, and the mind is almost staggered by her wonderful size, her general dimensions internally, and the luxury and completeness of her appointments. She is the apotheosis of skill as applied to the dominion of the ocean, and really dominates and triumphs over all previous achievements...'

After tugs had trained to pull the vessel to her outfitting wharf, *Olympic* suffered her first accident. While being towed, the wind that had earlier decreased returned and a gale caught *Olympic*'s towering 24,600-ton hull. As a result, she came into the side of the buttress, merely denting slightly some of her hull plates and scraping her paintwork even though it had been quite a heavy blow. The denting was so slight, Edward Wilding – Thomas Andrews' Deputy – would later say, that there had been no reason to doubt the hull's integrity. It would later be suggested that this warned of the potential difficulties of navigating such a large vessel, but nobody thought so at the time.

Now that the launch was over, Lord Pirrie entertained the numerous guests at a special luncheon at Queen's Island. It was not until 2.15 p.m. that they left for Dublin aboard a special train from the Great Victoria Street terminal.

Numerous others – special correspondents, artists and photographers – were treated to a repast at Belfast's lavish Grand Central Hotel, hosted by Messrs Ismay, Imrie & Company,

Shortly after launching, *Olympic* had been brought to a halt. The chimney for the graving dock's pump house can be seen above the ship's stern. (Georgiou/Chirnside/Klistorner/Layton Collection)

White Star's owners. Among the speeches was that of the well-known nautical commentator Mr Frank T. Bullen; the launch had been a 'world-thrilling event', he said, without hyperbole, conducted in an unpretentious manner that was 'particularly British'. There was much applause. He proposed a toast to 'the Builders and Owners of the *Olympic*'.

Mr R.J. Shelley, representing the line, extended thanks to all involved in making the day such a success and honoured Bullen's toast.

Mr Saxon J. Payne, of Harland & Wolff, thanked warmly those who had had the foresight to build and propose such a ship. Harland & Wolff 'were prepared at any time to turn out another vessel like the *Olympic*'. Those present were cordially thanked for their reception of the toast. 'Hear, hear!' many cried, applauding.

Mr J. Barker said he had seen over two hundred vessels launched at the shipyard and 'thought nothing of them'. But when he saw *Olympic*'s launching, he was quite moved. It had been a pleasure to serve under people who believed in 'deeds, not words'. The pressure on the two hydraulic triggers just before the ship had been released had been 435 tons, while over 22 tons of tallow had been used to grease the ways (about £1,000-worth). All engines, boilers and machinery would be put in at the yard, but although the ship's departure date could not be announced officially, it might be at any time between May and July 1911. As his speech finished, he was greeted with applause.

That evening the cross-Channel visitors 'were entertained to dinner previous to leaving for England and Scotland'.

Harland & Wolff now concentrated on completing *Olympic*'s interiors as quickly as possible, while work continued on the new large graving dock that would service the largest liners in the world:

> The work in connection with this necessary adjunct to modern and successful ship-building enterprise is now in its final stages, and it is expected that the dock will be ready for the admission of vessels in December or January at the very latest, but the formal opening will not take place until the spring or summer.

The next seven months saw the hull's completion and the installation of the elaborate fittings required for the cavernous interiors, the detailing of which was taken from the builder's 'Specification Book', an immense document of over 300 pages.

Meanwhile, advertisement for the new vessels included a builder's model, completed during 1910, which represented *Olympic* and *Titanic*. Built to a 1:48 scale, it was 22ft long and weighed in excess of half a ton. Housed in a large glass case that stood on a grand total of eight legs, the model was lit up from inside and a large electric sign on top of the case housing proclaimed 'White Star Line R.M.S. *Olympic* & *Titanic*. Largest Ships in the World'. The model, however, became in many ways inaccurate when the *Titanic's* layout was altered.

The prestigious nautical magazine *The Shipbuilder* – often described as 'the bible of shipping' – devoted an entire issue to the latest wonders of the shipping world in mid-1911, describing the liners in great detail.

During construction and now while outfitting, Board of Trade inspectors visited *Olympic* 2,000 times, checking that the workmanship was of a good standard and that all of the ship met their strict requirements.

Partitions were installed then the individual cabin bulkheads and finally the fine, ornate wood panelling was fitted. Carpet installers fitted the thousands of square feet of carpeting. Slowly, the white hull was painted a colour of black; at the load line and below the hull was painted a deep shade of red, and a gold band joined the hull and the gleaming-white-painted superstructure. All four funnels were a colour of buff-yellow, and were capped by a band of black so that the emissions of soot would not show.

As the liner neared completion, numerous companies advertised that their products were either being installed or would be used aboard… The Regulator Patent Furnace Bridge Co. Ltd's regulator patent furnace bridge; Dorman & Smith's electric switch gear, with 'thumb type fuses, throughout'; Bullivant & Co. Ltd's 9½in 'circular galvanised special extra flexible steel wire mooring rope'; Henry Wilson & Co. Ltd's impressive cooking apparatus; Wailes, Dove & Co.'s Bitumastic covering (holding 'the world's record as an anti-corrosive') throughout the whole of the tank tops in the boiler rooms and passages; Perry & Co.'s royal appointed light fittings from Bond Street (their fitting 'number 20610' was fitted in the first-class entrances, the 'fifty light dome light fitting, number 20570' for the forward grand staircase dome, lamps of 'number 20590' for use in the Turkish bath's cooling room…); and the Newalls Insulation Company Ltd's magnesia coverings for steam pipes and boilers… their nonpareil cork for cold storage insulation…[16] Probably the most famous advertisement belonged to the Vinolia Company Ltd's Vinolia Otto toilet soap: 'it is not only in size, but in the luxury of her appointments that the *Titanic* takes first place among the big steamers of the world,' the company proclaimed, by the provision of Vinolia Otto toilet soap, as 'offering a higher standard of toilet luxury and comfort at sea'. Numerous companies advised their products were 'supplied to the great new liners, SS *Olympic* and SS *Titanic*'.

As *Olympic's* completion drew nearer, items arrived at the shipyard for installation. At the foot of the forward first-class grand staircase was a twenty-one-light candelabra, which arrived – as with most of the other light fittings – from Perry & Co.[17]

Assigned signal letters were given to the ship, among them her three-letter wireless code: 'MKC'. 1 April 1911 saw dry-docking of *Olympic* and her massive propellers being fitted, plus a final coat of paint being applied.[18]

Olympic's basin trials took place on 2 May 1911. Her engines were run to be sure of their abilities and before leaving for her sea trials she was opened to the public at a cost of five shillings each[19] (the proceeds going to the Belfast hospitals). *Olympic's* performance was superb. Although designed to produce 15,000hp at 75rpm, at 78rpm her port engine developed nearly 19,000hp; 81rpm was later achieved briefly on the maiden voyage.[20]

Testing of one of *Olympic*'s wooden standard lifeboats took place on 9 May 1911 to check that the boats could hold their full designed complement and that the lowering gear was in order and working properly. Many half-hundredweights were placed in the lifeboat, corresponding to a weight of sixty-five people; the lifeboat was then raised and lowered six times without any signs of strain on the boat or the davits and lowering gear.

Olympic's two-day sea trials commenced on 29 May 1911. 3,000 tons of best Welsh coal filled the bunkers and a crew of two hundred and fifty boarded the ship.[21]

At high water on the morning of 28 May 1911, the task of swinging the liner had been completed, the Mersey tugs *Wallasey*, *Alexandra*, *Hornby* and *Herculaneum*, as well as Harland & Wolff's tug *Hercules*, completing the operation without a hitch.[22]

Olympic – accompanied by the new tenders *Nomadic* and *Traffic* – was guided by the five tugs down the Victoria Channel and into Belfast Lough on the morning of 29 May 1911.[23]

Compasses were adjusted. This could not be done in the shipyard because of the large quantities of iron and steel surrounding the vessel.

Steam was fed into the reciprocating engines for the second time, but for the first time at sea. Turning abilities were tested. With both main reciprocating engines running at full speed ahead, a port turn was ordered; in another test the starboard engine was put at 'full astern' to assist. The helm was put hard over and both main engines were at 'full ahead' and a complete circle was turned at high speed. Other manoeuvres were completed, although history's account of *Olympic*'s trials is not complete.

During *Olympic*'s trials she did not run the 'measured mile', and no attempt was made to push the ship as fast as possible. It was not the custom of the White Star Line. But, her designed speed had been exceeded by at least three-quarters of a knot.

Olympic's wireless equipment was tested and tuned by her two operators, and messages were sent to the White Star Line's Liverpool offices describing the success of the trials.[24]

All passenger clearance and seaworthiness certificates were signed, valid for one year, and the liner was handed over on 31 May 1911, the owners accepting the builder's product.

With the tender *Magnetic* at her side and another tender pulling away, *Olympic* is shown here on her one-day stop at Liverpool at the end of May 1911. (J.&C. McCutcheon collection)

Titanic's launching had been scheduled for the same day and so the double event drew an enormous crowd.

J.P. Morgan, J. Bruce Ismay and other distinguished guests, along with a number of eager reporters, travelled to Belfast for the event aboard the steamer *Duke of Argyll*, which had been specially chartered for the occasion.

The mechanical launching arrangements that had been so successful for *Olympic* seven months previously were repeated. Indeed, at her launch, *Titanic* was identical to her sister (not 3in longer), but her hull was painted black instead of white. At the time, it was reported that at launching she was actually slightly lighter than her older sister as she had not been completed to quite the same standard, but the weight was given as 24,600 tons, identical to *Olympic's*.

'Without any flourish, beyond the enthusiastic cheering of an immense concourse of people, the *Titanic*, sister-ship of the *Olympic*,' wrote the *Irish News* the following day, 'was successfully launched from the Queen's Island yesterday morning, and Belfast enjoyed for one day the world's record of having over 90,000 tons of shipping in her port.'[25]

The luncheon at the Grand Central Hotel concluded with a telegram to Lord and Lady Pirrie, wishing them a happy birthday and offering many heartfelt congratulations of the *Olympic's* successful trials and *Titanic's* launch.[26]

At 4.30 p.m. on 31 May 1911 *Olympic* left Belfast for a one-day stop at Liverpool, where she was opened for public inspection, before leaving for Southampton on the evening of 1 June 1911 for preparations for her maiden voyage.[27] Half a crown was the charge of visiting the liner (12½ pence in today's money).[28]

Meanwhile, her sister had been towed to the outfitting basin by straining tugs. Lessons learned from the *Olympic's* outfitting would be applied to the new vessel.

Soon, the army of workers would begin to install the luxurious fittings in the extensive passenger areas required for the ship to enter service. They would eventually occupy nearly 22,000 tons of space, compared to the nearly 21,000 tons of her elder sister. The larger third sister's passenger areas would later total an even larger 24,500 tons.

It was well known that the new liner would be 'the *Olympic* perfected' and that in several aspects her accommodations would be more luxurious. Her outfitting would take ten months, three months more than required for *Olympic*. Finally, shortly after 9 a.m. on Saturday 3 February 1912, the tugs *Hercules*, *Jackal* and *Musgrave* were able to tow *Titanic* from the outfitting wharf to the entrance of the dry-dock. High tide allowed a perfectly comfortable dry-docking, supervised continually by Lord Pirrie and a few members of the public. Propellers would be fitted and a final coat of paint in the White Star Line colours applied to the new vessel before she left the dry dock exactly two weeks later on 17 February 1912.

Only eight days before she commenced her maiden voyage, *Titanic* went through her day-long trials in the Irish Sea, beginning just off Carrickfergus when her five escorting tugs cast off.[29] Twenty main boilers were alight for her trials,[30] but this did not stop her touching 21 knots when she passed Copeland Island during her running trials just after 2 p.m.[31] Around lunch time, while running at over 20 knots, the helm was put hard over and she steamed a circle of a 3,850ft diameter with some 2,100ft of forward movement.[32] Perhaps the most important test was the 'crash stop' in mariner's vernacular. Running at 20 knots, 'full ahead', the engine telegraphs were thrust to 'full astern' and – with a severe shuddering as the engines pounded in reverse – *Titanic* stopped in 850 yards, having taken three minutes fifteen seconds to come to a complete halt.[33] It was an impressive performance, much credit being due to the reciprocating engines, which could reverse much more quickly than turbines. As with her sister, she did not attempt the 'measured mile', but she had impressively reached her designed speed, albeit briefly, with only 75% of the furnaces operating.

But for the meantime, all focus was on the huge *Olympic* as her maiden voyage drew nearer.

CATERING DEPARTMENT OF THE "OLYMPIC."

THIS department looms very largely in the success of the modern passenger liner and the owners of the *Olympic*, evidently recognising this fact, have spared neither pains nor expense to carry the arrangements to a successful issue. Space is absolutely unlimited. Light, drainage and ventilation have all been carefully considered, and above all the apparatus itself is of the most modern type.

The first-class kitchen is fitted with two immense ranges, probably the largest ever made, each fitted with " bain maries " and hot closets on port and starboard sides. Large patent roasters for meat and game, silver grills, steam ovens, brass stockpots, triturators, electric slicing and mincing machines are all most conveniently placed for working. The absence of funnels is a very noticeable feature. They have all been led under the decks, thus minimising radiation of heat in the kitchen itself.

There are two large bakeries for the making of bread. These are fitted with electric dough-making machines, dough dividers, Vienna water-tube ovens, hot-air pastry ovens, provers, etc. In addition there is a special apartment with apparatus for the practice of the confectioner's art, which also includes electric cake making, whisking, freezing machines and hot plates. There are also rooms for the preparation of vegetables, fitted with "Cornhill" potato peeling machines. The restaurant has a special kitchen entirely devoted to it, and this kitchen, though not so large, is just as completely fitted as that already described for the first and second-class passengers.

The third-class passengers have not been overlooked in any respect, their culinary arrangements being absolutely perfect, and including large ranges, steam stockpots, steam ovens, clean steam producers, potato peeling machines and everything likely to assist in preparing food under the most hygienic conditions. The pantries and serving rooms have been arranged with a view to obtaining a rapid service, and are in close proximity to the dining saloons. The installation includes hot presses, hot closets, entrée presses, silver coffee apparatus, automatic egg boilers, " bain maries," milk scalders, and a hundred and one other items that we cannot pretend to technically describe. However, taken on the whole we consider it would be impossible to find anything more complete, either ashore or afloat.

Not only are the first and second-class passengers well provided with pantries and serving rooms, but the third-class passengers are equally well catered for, so that the chance of obtaining a cold dinner on board the *Olympic* is somewhat remote.

The owners evidently hold very strong views on the necessity of absolute perfection in the preparation and serving of food, and much credit is due to Messrs. Henry Wilson & Co., Ltd., of Cornhill Works, Liverpool, who are responsible for the complete outfit of the department.

A number of articles were devoted to *Olympic* in the maritime and technical journals of the day. This one provides an interesting description of her 'catering department'. (*The Marine Engineer and Naval Architect*, 1911/ Georgiou/ Chirnside/Klistorner/Layton Collection)

5
RMS OLYMPIC

'The finest ship in my estimation that has ever been built or ever will be'
– Sir Bertram Hayes, Captain.

During the early hours of 3 June 1911 the Royal Mail Steamship *Olympic* arrived in Southampton to begin preparations for her maiden voyage. As the new dock was not quite finished, the ship entered bow first for ease.[1] She had passed the Lizard, Cornwall, at 2.45 p.m. on 2 June 1911 and arrived for docking at 3 a.m., the operation being completed by 4 a.m. Her run from Liverpool had been successful, 'and her officers were well-pleased with the manner in which she performed the passage.' When she had arrived on the early morning high tide, five tugs had met her, the docking being completed safely with no trouble despite the liner's enormous size. 'Her hull was a thing of wonder and awe, and the visitors who thronged to the dock from the early hours of the morning were greatly impressed with the biggest ship the world has ever known,' recorded the local press. There were many reports of her luxury, amazing size and 'practical unsinkability'. The *Southern Daily Echo* described her as 'an unparalleled achievement', reporting that '*Titanic* will be ready at the end of the year.' It also said 'the third giant has yet to be built' and mentioned the sum of £4.5 million as the cost of all three vessels.

In the well-chosen words of John Maxtone-Graham, *Olympic* was 'in the same breathtaking instance, the last of the lean, yacht-like racers and the first "floating palace".'[2] He wrote that 'she was an entirely new breed, the first sumptuous superliner'.[3]

'If she did not look such a "greyhound" as the Cunarders she had an unrivalled magnificence,' wrote J.H. Isherwood in the February 1956 *Sea Breezes* magazine. 'She was undoubtedly a really magnificent ship, high-sided, with a nice sweeping sheer and her masts and funnels beautifully proportioned.'[4] Her interiors were no less worthy of such praise.

When veteran pilot George Bowyer first saw her, he recalled: 'We could hardly believe our eyes there was such a ship!'[5]

All considered it fitting that Britain should own the largest liner in the world, to complement its splendid merchant fleet and the Royal Navy, which was also the largest in the world at the time.

At 11 a.m., Colonel E. Bance, VD, DL, Mayor of Southampton, visited the new ship, accompanied by Alderman C.J. Sharp, Deputy-Mayor, Alderman E.R. Knsor and Mr R.R. Lindthorne, the Town Clerk. They were received by the captain on board and after an inspection of the ship, when the visitors 'were charmed and delighted with all they saw', luncheon was served to a vast assembly to the sound of the fine orchestra in the splendid first-class dining saloon, including company executives and numerous local dignitaries.

A 'book card' depicts *Olympic* in 1911. Her impressive profile was noted on the reverse: 'Isn't this a beautiful boat?' (Author's collection)

White Star had issued invitations to luncheon on the ship on Thursday 8 June 1911, while it was also announced that on Saturday 10 June the new vessel would be open for public inspection, the entrance funds going to various local charities, as was the usual custom at the time. Even though the ship would be open for those days, there was still ample time for the final maiden voyage preparations, and throughout the week the press enthusiastically went over many details of the incredible liner.

As with the second ship the following year, newspapers reported the ship's provisioning as an illustration of her size. Stores included:

Fresh meat	75,000lb
Fresh fish	11,000lb
Fresh butter	6,000lb
Sausages	2,500lb
Eggs	40,000
Sugar	10,000lb
Potatoes	40 tons
Salt fish	4,000lb
Bacon and ham	7,500lb
Poultry	8,000 heads
Sweetbreads	1,000lb
Coffee	2,200lb
Tea	800lb
Jams	1,120lb
Flour	200 barrels
Apples	36,000
Oranges	36,000
Beer and stout	20,000 bottles
Wines	1,500 bottles
Spirits	850 bottles
Grapefruit	13,000
Lemons	16,000

Grapes	1,000lb
Tomatoes	3,500lb
Onions	3,500lb
Lettuce	7,000 heads

The ship's linen stores were just as extensive, as evidenced by this selection:

Miscellaneous	40,000
Table napkins	45,000
Single sheets	15,000
Fine towels	25,000
Blankets	7,500
Pantry towels	6,500

Also on board were some 58,000 items of crockery, about 44,000 pieces of cutlery and roughly 30,000 pieces of glassware, to name but a few of the many items and stores needed. There were alone 11,500 cups, 14,200 glasses and 12,000 dinner plates included in these numbers.

F.G. Bealing & Son of Southampton brought aboard the 400 plants to decorate the ship's interiors, initially placing them all in the first-class reception room before they were distributed to the first-class reading and writing room, the *à la carte* restaurant and the veranda café, but some plants remained in the reception room in fretwork containers. Small plants stood in vases, on tables or in pots in other various lounges.[6] It seems that plants were placed among the wicker furniture of the grand staircase landings, throughout odd corners, and on the second-class stair landings.

Coal for White Star vessels was brought out to the ships by R. & J.H. Rea, who were able to transfer over 4,000 tons in fifteen hours from their barges, a world record in 1911. Although the maiden voyage was to be overshadowed by a coal strike, strike breakers bunkered the new ship with the necessary capacity.[7] In fact, the White Star Line had to search as far a field as the North of England to find the necessary unofficial labour. The following year, an attempt to hire a 'scratch crew' would result in the desertion of one-quarter of the ship's complement.

To command their new flagship the White Star Line had chosen their senior captain Edward John Smith, known as 'E.J.' Born in 1850, Smith had gone to sea aged thirteen and he had been associated with the Liverpool firm Messrs Gibson & Co., who had given him command of the *Lizzie Fennell* in May 1876. He joined the White Star Line as a junior officer in 1880, aged thirty. He worked his way up as an officer on board such ships as the company's first *Celtic*, *Coptic*, *Britannic* and *Republic*. Smith had temporary command of *Republic* (April and May 1887) and *Baltic* (April and May 1888), but it was not until he joined *Cufic* as her commander in December 1888 that he permanently settled in the post. The next six years had seen him in charge of a succession of ships and he joined *Majestic* in 1895, serving for nine years, interrupted only by his command of the old *Germanic* from December 1902 to May 1903. Distinguishing himself during the Boer War, making trips to the Cape with troops and earning the Transport Medal, Captain Smith became a Commander in the Royal Naval Reserve. A trend began when he took *Baltic*, the largest vessel in the world, to New York on her maiden voyage in June 1904; he joined *Adriatic* for her maiden voyage in May 1907 and then *Olympic* four years later. By this time, Smith was reputed to be the highest paid seaman afloat, earning £1,250 ($6,250) a year. Whether that was true or not may be an interesting question, but it was also said that he gained an additional bonus of £200 ($1,000) if no ships under his command were involved in an accident during the year.[8]

Perhaps Smith was a bit of a showman. When *Baltic* came into New York on her maiden voyage, he explained: 'I tried to see how she would work coming around the tail of the Southwest Spit, and, as the channel was clear, I sent her around at full speed. She behaved admirably.' He had experienced several groundings in ships under his command. Nevertheless, the same could be said for a number of his contemporaries, and although some sources reported that he was in command of *Germanic* when she capsized and sank in New York in 1899, the claim was not true. He told the press in 1907:

> Of course there have been winter gales and storms and fog and the like in the forty years I have been on the seas. But I have never been in an accident worth speaking of...I never saw a wreck. I have never been wrecked. I have never been in a predicament that threatened to end in disaster.

Captain Smith had great faith in the safety of such great new liners, particularly the one that he had just taken command of. He had previously remarked when commanding the *Adriatic*:

> I cannot imagine any condition which would cause a ship to founder. I cannot conceive of any disaster happening to this vessel. Modern shipbuilding has gone beyond that.

Some idea of the 'wonder ship' could be gained from this comparison view of her, issued as a company postcard. (J.&C. McCutcheon collection)

He was a man of 'very high standing' and it was later said that with one exception, 'there had never been any collision in any vessel which he had commanded'. Passengers crossed on vessels just because of his presence and undoubtedly many altered their schedules to fit in with Smith's sailing times.

It was during the first year of *Olympic*'s life that he showed King Alfonso and the Queen of Spain, as well as Princess Henry of Battenberg, around the vessel. Smith obviously made an impression on the king, for the following year when he perished with *Titanic*, King Alfonso sent a special message to Smith's widow Eleanor expressing his grief.

Olympic's maiden voyage on 14 June 1911 was reasonably well booked, considering the coal strike, with passengers who wanted to sample the world's latest and largest liner. Yet the return trip would be virtually full. A crew, hand-picked from other ships of the line, mustered on sailing day, feeling immensely proud.[9]

Harland & Wolff's Managing Director Thomas Andrews – making the trip to observe *Olympic* in action – was soon given a 'magnificent walking stick' by the victualling department's staff who wanted to thank him because of his great efforts to increase the quality of all the crew accommodation.[10]

He was quite a remarkable figure, for no detail was beyond his attention and as well as having a brilliant engineering mind, Andrews also loved dealing with the aesthetics of ship construction.[11] His accomplishments at the Harland & Wolff shipyard, and especially with the *Olympic*-class ships, were certainly amazing for somebody of only thirty-seven years of age by the time of *Olympic*'s maiden trip. 'Andrews was a universally popular figure and an extraordinarily hard worker, often arriving at the shipyard by 4 a.m. in his paint-smeared bowler hat, the pockets of his jacket stuffed with plans.'[12] Reportedly, he had said of the achievement of the new vessels: 'It takes three million rivets and a lot of sweat to make a fine ship.'[13] Stewardess Violet Jessop would remember that Andrews was 'one of the finest and kindliest of men it has been my privilege to meet'.[14] Joseph Bruce Ismay and his wife were also on board, as Ismay wanted to note any possible improvements to the ship.

The liner got underway without difficulty, drawing 34ft 1in of water, and five tugs supplied by the Isle of Wight Company (the present day Red Funnel) attended her.

'On sailing day we had to go out stern first,' Pilot George Bowyer remembered, '… and then on down to the entrance to the Itchen, where at the time was the only swinging ground then dredged.'[15] It took an hour for the tugs to move the ship into the channel, her bow pointing down Southampton Water ready for the narrow channel.[16]

Enormous crowds watched the manoeuvre, the tugs *Hector* and *Hercules* leading at the stern, and at 12.45 p.m. the tugs departed. Aboard *Olympic*, a correspondent wrote:

> Perhaps the most striking thing about her departure was the practical comparison which it allowed between the size of the *Olympic* and that of what may now almost be called the last generation of liners. The Red Star ship *Kroonland* and the *New York*, of the American Line, were moored hard by. The *Kroonland* is about 15,000 tons and the *New York* over 10,000, yet from the highest deck of the *Olympic* they seemed to be dwarfed into bewildering insignificance.

Olympic was westward bound for New York via Cherbourg and Queenstown. She made the leisurely trip to the French port by 7 p.m. in fine weather, and once at Cherbourg the new tenders *Nomadic* and *Traffic*, built especially for the new class of ship, served her for the first time.

Running with the *Majestic* and *Oceanic*, the new liner's schedule was thus: leaving Southampton on Wednesday, a call at Cherbourg was made in the evening and then the run to Queenstown made overnight, while New York would normally be reached early Wednesday morning; on Saturday, the ship left New York, calling firstly at Plymouth and then Cherbourg before arriving in Southampton on Friday evening.[17]

Leaving Queenstown, there were many days for the passengers to enjoy themselves on this wonderful vessel. In order to make the new liner the most luxurious in the world, first-class accommodation included a lounge in Louis XIV style, 1½ decks high, lit by a massive electrolier in a curved recess in the centre of the ceiling. It seems worth quoting contemporary descriptions in full:

> The lounge, being a room dedicated to reading, cards, tea drinking and other social usages, is decorated in the style which was in vogue in France when Louis XIV was on the throne, when social intercourse was the finest of fine arts, and when the Salon was the arena in which the keenest intellects of the age "crossed swords" and then exchanged the most delicate conversational thrust and parry.
>
> Now, as then, the British workman is supreme in the production of finely carved "boiseries" with which the walls are covered, and in which, without interfering with the symmetry of the whole, the fancy of the carver has everywhere shown itself in ever-varying details.
>
> When talk becomes monotonous, we may here indulge in bridge and whist, or retire with our book or our letters to one of the many quiet retreats which reveal themselves to the thoughtful explorer. The chairs and sofas are so soft and cosy, however, that on them inducements to slumber may easily prevail, to the detriment of our literary efforts.

There was a 1½-deck-high smoking room panelled with the finest mahogany available inlaid with mother-of-pearl and with coloured stain-glass panels lit from behind, depicting mythological scenes. Many of the 100 carvers who had worked on the interiors had contributed to this 'masterpiece'. Etched-patterned mirrors and gilt marble-topped tables with comfortable leather chairs completed the effect:[18]

> The walls are panelled with the finest mahogany, carved in the taste of our Georgian forefathers, and relieved everywhere with inlaid work in mother-of-pearl.
>
> Here, seated around the home-like fire, we may enjoy Mr Norman Wilkinson's fine painting of the *Approach to the New World*, and meanwhile smoke and drink as wisely and well as we feel inclined.
>
> The light comes tempered and softened through the painted windows, where the voyager sees the depicted ports and beauty spots with which he is familiar or hopes to visit. As well some of the happy and glorious ships which in the past wore so beautiful an aspect, with their low prows and their soaring sterncastles.
>
> Here, too, are personifications of the Arts – Poetry, Painting, and the like – that have adorned our surroundings and ministered to our pleasures.
>
> Passing through the silently revolving doors, we emerge upon a happy little Veranda, over whose green trellis grow climbing plants, which foster the illusion that

we are still on the fair, firm earth, but one glance through the windows, with their beautifully chased bronze framing, adds to the charm. We realise that we are still on the restless sea, once so dreaded a barrier to normal intercourse. Set in this flowery arbour are numerous inviting little tables, at which we can take our coffee or absinthe in the open air, much as we do in our own summery gardens on land.

As already mentioned, revolving doors led from the smoking room into two veranda cafés, with trellised walls and green climbing plants, wicker furniture, chequered floors, and high bronze-framed windows overlooking the sea. *The Shipbuilder* commented:

> ...the verandas are completely enclosed on all sides with the exception of the openings provided in the after end for access from the promenade space...the cafés are less liable to draughts and the effects of inclement weather than is the case with he wide open-ended cafés adopted in other vessels. To maintain the impression of sitting in the open, windows of exceptional size have been provided...The style is *Treillage* of the Louis Seize period; and to create the illusion that the cafés are on shore, ivy and climbing plants are trained up the green trellis-work panels.[19]

With the smoking room used as a men's retreat, a ladies room in Jacobean style, 1½ decks in height, was also provided. There was a large bay window overlooking the sea, and an arched opening leading to an inner recess. The apartment had a thick velvety carpet:

> The pure white walls and the light and so elegant furniture show us that this is essentially a ladies' room.
> Through the great bow window, which almost fills one side of the room, we look out past the deck on which our companions in travel are taking the air, over the vast expanse of sea and sky.
> An atmosphere of refined retirement pervades the apartment; a homely fire burns in the cheerful grate; our feet move noiselessly over the thick, velvety carpet, and an arched opening leads to an inner recess – a sanctuary so peaceful that here it would seem as if any conversation above a whisper would be a sacrilege.

A fully equipped gymnasium had the latest exercise bicycles, rowing machine and mechanical camels:

> The gymnasium is...provided with all the latest appliances. It is 44ft long, by 18ft wide, is 9ft 6in high, and is lighted by eight windows of exceptional size. Here passengers can indulge in the action of horse riding, cycling, boat rowing, etc., and obtain beneficial exercise, besides endless amusement. The gymnasium appliances have been supplied by Messrs Rossel, Schwarz and Co., of Wiesbaden.[20]

There was also the first squash court ever to go to sea. 30ft in length and complete with a spectator's gallery, it was situated forward on G-deck, being two decks high.

There was a swimming pool, which was not only the largest afloat but also one of the first ever installed on an ocean liner. Immediately forward of the Turkish baths on F-deck, it was 30ft in length, 14ft in width and was no doubt superior to some on shore.

The elegant first-class reading and writing room. Its light panelling made it appear even more spacious. (Library of Congress, Prints and Photographs Division, Daniel Klistorner collection)

Another luxury was *Olympic*'s Turkish bath establishment. The cooling room of the baths was described extensively in contemporary advertising, and it seems worth quoting in detail:

> The Cooling room on the middle deck in connection with the Turkish Baths is in many respects one of the most interesting and striking rooms on the ship. The portholes are concealed by an elaborately carved Cairo curtain, through which the light fitfully reveals "something of the grandeur of the mysterious East."
>
> The walls are completely tiled, from the dado to the cornice, in large panels of blue and green, surrounded by a broad band of tiles in a bolder and deeper hue.
>
> The dado and doors and panelling are in a warm-coloured Teak, which makes a perfect setting to the gorgeous effect of the tiles and ceiling, the cornice and beams of which are gilt, and the intervening panels picked-out in dull red. From these panels are suspended bronze Arab lamps. The stanchions are cased also in teak, carved all over with an intricate Moorish pattern, and surmounted by a carved cap.
>
> Over the doors are small gilt domes, semicircular in plan, with their soffits carved in a low relief geometrical pattern.
>
> As those who partake of Turkish Baths are constrained to spend a considerable time in the Cooling Room, no pains have been spared to make it interesting and comfortable.

Around the walls are low couches, and between each an inlaid Damascus table, upon which one may place one's coffee, cigarettes, or books.

As the drinking of fresh water is one of the concomitant features of the benefits of taking the bath, there is a handsome marble drinking fountain set in a frame of tiles. There is also a teak dressing table and mirror with all its accessories, and a locker to which valuables may be committed, whilst scattered around the room are numerous canvas chairs.

First-class passengers had many places to eat: the veranda cafés, the main dining saloon or the glistening *à la carte* restaurant. The *à la carte* restaurant was the best on board:

The restaurant is of the Louis XVI period in design, and is panelled from floor to ceiling in beautifully marked French walnut of a delicate light fawn brown colour, the mouldings and ornaments being richly carved and gilded. In the centre of the large panels hang electric light brackets, cast and finely chased in brass and gilt holding candle lamps. On the right of the entrance is a counter with a marble top of *fleur de pêche*, supported by panelling and pilasters recalling the design of the wall panels…

The room is well lighted by large bay windows that are a distinctive and novel feature, and give a feeling of spaciousness. These are draped with plain fawn silk curtains with flowered borders and pelmets richly embroidered. The windows themselves are divided into squares by ornamented metal bars. Every small detail, down to the fastenings and hinges, has been carried out with regard to purity of style.

With the floor covered by a rich pile Axminster carpet, the quality of the décor and finishing was clear, while the restaurant was furnished with small tables that accommodated between two and eight people each – 'with crystal standard lamps and rose-coloured shades to illuminate each table.'

The first-class reception room and dining saloon were both in Jacobean style. The reception room's panelling was white and delicately carved, while there were handsome bronze ceiling lights, wicker furniture, lit panels and a specially woven tapestry at the foot of the 16ft-wide first-class staircase which led into the room:

…Some of the passengers will stand to gaze at the magnificent tapestry directly facing the staircase, specially woven on the looms at Aubusson, or will await their friends seated upon the capacious Chesterfields or grandfather chairs upholstered in a floral pattern of wool damask, or the comfortable can furniture distributed at intervals.

Upon a dark, richly coloured carpet, which will further emphasise the delicacy and refinement of the panelling and act as a foil to the light dresses of the ladies, this company will assemble – the apotheosis surely, of ocean-going luxury and comfort. What more appropriate setting than this dignified Jacobean room redolent of the time when the Pilgrim Fathers set forth from Plymouth on their rude bark to brave the perils of the deep!

The dining saloon was also magnificent, as the largest room afloat in 1911, with floor space totalling more than 10,000sq.ft.

One of *Olympic*'s running mates early in her career, White Star's *Oceanic* is seen here leaving New York. (Library of Congress, Prints and Photographs Division)

The immense room has been decorated in a style particularly English – that, in fact, which was evolved by the eminent architects of early Jacobean times. It differs from most of the great halls of that period, Chiefly in being painted white instead of the sombre oak that the sixteenth and seventeenth century builders would have used.

For details, the splendid decorations at Hatfield, Haddon Hall, and other contemporary great houses have been carefully studied, the coved and richly moulded ceilings being particularly characteristic of the plasterers' art of that time.

The furniture of oak is designed to harmonise with its surroundings, and at the same time to avoid the austere disregard for comfort which our forefathers evidently found no hindrance to the enjoyment of a meal.

As it was on *Olympic*'s maiden voyage, the first-class dining saloon could accommodate 532 passengers at a single sitting. Privacy had been dutifully considered in the design of the saloon, and so recessed bays were provided where 'families or friends can dine together practically alone', away from the centre of the saloon.

A typical evening menu in the wonderful saloon might have included:

Hors d'oeuvres variés
Oysters
Consomme olga, cream of barley
Salmon, mousseline sauce, cucumber

★ ★ ★

Filet mignons lili
Sauté of chicken lyonnaise
Vegetable marrow farcis
Lamb, mint sauce
Roast duckling, apple sauce
Sirloin of beef, château potatoes
Green peas, creamed carrots
Boiled rice
Parmentier & boiled new potatoes

★ ★ ★

Punch Romaine

★ ★ ★

Roast squab
Cold asparagus vinaigrette
Pâté de foie gras
Celery

★ ★ ★

Waldorf pudding
Peaches in chartreuse jelly
Chocolate and vanilla éclairs
French ice cream[21]

The crowning glory of the first-class accommodation was the 'grand staircase', which has become so well known:

> We leave the deck and pass through one of the doors that admit us to the interior of the vessel. And, as if by magic, we at once lose the feeling that we are on board a ship, and seem instead to be entering the hall of some great house on shore. Dignified and simple oak panelling covers the walls, enriched in a few places by a bit of elaborate carved work, reminiscent of the days when Grinling Gibbons collaborated with his great comtemporary, Wren.
>
> In the middle of the hall rises a gracefully curving staircase, its balustrade supported by light scrollwork of iron with occasional touches of bronze, in the form of flowers and foliage. Above all a great dome of iron and glass throws a flood of light down the stairway, and on the landing beneath it a great carved panel gives its note of richness to the otherwise plain and massive construction of the wall. The panel contains a clock, on either side of that is a female figure, the whole symbolising Honour and Glory crowning Time…

White Star enthused that the staircase would be admired, 'as being without doubt the finest piece of workmanship of its kind afloat'.

The liner's staterooms were described as 'exceptionally large and beautifully furnished'. Suite rooms on the bridge and shelter decks, B and C, were described with pride as being 'unusually large in number', decorated in varying styles and periods – from Louis Seize, Empire, Italian Renaissance, and Adams, to Georgian, Regence, Queen Anne, and Modern and New Dutch. Every single first-class stateroom was fitted with a large cot bed in either brass, oak or mahogany, while the beds in most of the suites were 4ft wide – a 'distinct feature' in 1911.

Second-class passengers had nothing to complain about, for their accommodation was very comfortable, if not luxurious. Contemporary publicity proudly described:

> The White Star Line has done much to increase the attractions of second-class accom-
> modation during recent years, having made a special feature of this in a number of their
> vessels… it will be found that this class of passenger has been generously provided for…
> Nothing has been omitted in the determination to place the new White Star leviathans
> beyond criticism as to the excellence of the accommodation both in the second and
> third classes.

Second-class passengers enjoyed a dining saloon that might not have been as impressive as its first-class counterpart, but nonetheless it was impressive. Extending the full width of the ship, it was described in 1910 as 'an exceedingly fine room'. Because it extended the width of the ship, large portholes which opened in pairs were fitted, allowing much light into the large room. Likewise, the ports aided ventilation. Oak panelling, based on a seventeenth-century design, made up the bulk of the decoration, while the mahogany furniture was no less impressive and a piano was even included in the room's features.

It was made clear that the other rooms were equally well-equipped. Second-class passengers also enjoyed a library and lounge on C-deck, above the dining saloon. Panelled in sycamore with beautifully crafted carvings, the furniture, fittings and dado were constructed of mahogany. At the forward end of the room was a large bookcase, ready to supply a range of cultured works for passengers to enjoy. Large windows along the port and starboard sides of the room supplied a plentiful amount of light, arranged in pairs and draped with curtains made of silk. On the floor of the large room, a 'handsome Wilton carpet' completed what the White Star Line described as a 'comfortable – indeed, luxurious' apartment, no doubt worthy of first-class accommodation on earlier liners, such as those of the 1890s.

Of the second-class smoke room, it was explained:

> …in this room the decoration is a variation of Louis XVI period; the panelling and
> dado are of oak relieved with carving; the furniture is of oak of special design, covered
> with plain, dark green morocco; the floor is laid with linoleum tiles of special design.

Linking the second-class decks were two staircases, both panelled in oak, the forward stairway extending through seven decks, with an elevator running from the boat deck to F-deck.

Second-class staterooms had great appeal, arranged on the tandem principle, which allowed natural light to every cabin by means of a 'corridor' – or thinner section of the inside cabins extending to the ship's exterior. Finished in enamel white, the staterooms had mahogany furniture covered with moquette, while linoleum tiles covered the floors.

Their features included fans, heaters and plush washbasin fittings, varying according to the standard of each individual stateroom.

'They are hardly inferior to first-class ordinary staterooms, except that four passengers are accommodated in one room instead of three,' *The Shipbuilder* explained.[22]

Second-class promenades were 'unusually spacious', being enclosed and open. It was an additional detail that the second-class corridors were wood-panelled and carpeted in either two-tone red or two-tone green.[23]

Third-class accommodation was equally well-designed, for the public rooms were 'large, airy compartments, suitably furnished, and in excellent positions', while staterooms were also described as such.

> The third-class dining saloon is situated amidships on the middle deck, consisting of two saloons extending from ship's side to ship's side, well lighted with sidelights, and all finished enamel white; the chairs are of special design. The position of this apartment – i.e., in the centre of the ship – illustrates the wonderful strides made in passenger accommodation in modern times. Third-class passengers today have greater comfort on the ocean than first-class passengers had before the great developments had taken place for which the White Star Line is largely responsible.

In contrast to the typical first-class menu listed, third-class meals were plain. Breakfast consisted of cereal, kippers or boiled eggs, bread, marmalade and tea or coffee; at midday there was soup, followed by a meat dish with vegetables and fruit; tea was a cooked course, of bread or buns, cooked fruit or another light dessert and tea; a late supper of cheese and biscuits or gruel and coffee was also on offer.[24]

Third-class passengers enjoyed a smoke room, situated aft on the shelter deck, panelled and framed in oak with teak furniture. Opposite the smoke room was the general room, panelled and framed in pine and finished in white enamel, also with teak furniture. Although the furnishings may not have been as plush, the third-class public rooms enjoyed fittings that were of a high standard compared to earlier liners, and probably superior to what their occupants had experienced ashore.

> Third-class promenades – to add, as it were, the finishing touch to the excellent provision made for the comfort and well being of the third-class passengers, there is a large apartment arranged under the forecastle as a third-class promenade, and fitted with tables and seats, so as to be useful in any kind of weather.

The Shipbuilder, the nautical 'bible' of shipping, covered in great detail the passenger accommodation, devoting to it nearly forty pages of its summer 1911 issue. Much was similar to the previously quoted advertising, but in general more detail was given.

'Full advantage has been taken of the great size of *Olympic* and *Titanic* to provide passenger accommodation of unrivalled extent and magnificence,' the periodical enthused. '…the arrangement has been most carefully considered from all points of view, and the excellent result defies improvement.'[25]

Of the first-class accommodation it said, 'everything has been done in regard to the furniture and fittings to make the first-class accommodation more than equal to that provided in the finest hotels on shore.'[26] Many features were new to passenger vessels, but in particular were listed the barber's shop, photographers' dark room, clothes pressing room,

Olympic's first-class smoke room in 1911, looking aft from the forward port side of the room. The painting above the fireplace is Norman Wilkinson's *Approach to the New World*, which can be seen today in Southampton's maritime museum. *Titanic*'s smoke room painting was called *Plymouth Harbour* and was recreated for the museum by the artist's son. (Library of Congress, Prints and Photographs Division, Daniel Klistorner collection)

maids' and valets' saloon, library, magnificent telephone installation and wireless equipment.[27] Many more features could have been listed.

When introducing the second-class passenger accommodation *The Shipbuilder* stated that: 'It would have been difficult a few years ago to conceive such sumptuous apartments as have been provided in the *Olympic* and *Titanic*.'

'Everything has been done to make the accommodation superior to anything previously seen afloat.'[28]

Even of the third-class accommodation, the praise was high. 'The accommodation for third-class passengers is of a very superior character,' the periodical began. 'Third-class passengers today have greater comforts provided than had first-class passengers before the great modern developments in passenger carrying, for which the White Star Line is largely responsible.'[29]

Many general details of the accommodation followed the descriptions of each class's accommodation.

Most beds, supplied by Messrs Hoskins & Sewell Ltd of Birmingham in the case of the brass beds, were the widest afloat. All brass berths used the 'Varnoid' process, a form of lacquer that was durable and of high quality. The same firm fitted 'Tapex' spring mattresses to second and first -class berths, but 'Orex' spring and chain mattresses to third-class berths.[30]

Of the vessels' kitchens – 'galleys', in nautical vernacular – *The Shipbuilder* observed, 'the culinary departments in these ships are among the most complete in the world.'[31] It listed the first/second-class galley's two huge 96ft fronted ranges and nineteen ovens, 'possibly the largest ever made'.

'There are also four silver grills, two large roasters, ranges of steam ovens, steam stockpots, hot closets, *bain-maries* (used for steaming food, especially fish), and electrically driven triturating, slicing, potato peeling, mincing, whisking and freezing machines.'[32] The potato peelers were missing from the crew's galley, J. Bruce Ismay soon noted; they were fitted as soon as possible.

The flues' design was 'a new departure', if not revolutionary: '…these are all taken below the deck, the object being to minimise the radiation of heat.'[33]

Olympic's bakery, cold storage rooms, vegetable preparing room and larder, plus pantries and storage rooms, were not lacking any gadgets or details.

'The service of plate,' explained *The Shipbuilder*, 'which comprises in all about ten thousand pieces, has been supplied by the Goldsmiths & Silversmiths Co. Ltd, of London.'[34] Novel features had been introduced: a huge duck press; 'neat portable spirit lamp with quick heating flame, for keeping warm special sauces and making Turkish coffee'; 'fruit tymbal and caviar dishes', in which the contents were cooled by an ice bath after being taken out of cold storage; 'electrically heated Rêchaud stands of the Goldsmiths Company's special type.' Attention had been lavished upon everything.[35]

'The ventilation and heating system of these vessels is more elaborate and probably more perfect than any yet attempted on-board ship,' began the publication on yet another aspect of the new vessels. It detailed the great installation, concluding: 'the mechanical system of ventilation renders superfluous the numerous cowls which encumber the decks of so many liners.'[36]

Sidelights and windows were detailed, especially the first-class dining saloon and reception room's inner windows. 'A special glass, supplied by the Maximum Light Window Glass Company, of London, has been used,' began the explanation. 'By means of the combination of lenses and prisms introduced in this glass, the light from the [double] portholes is dispersed over a greater area than would be the case if ordinary glass had been adopted.'[37]

Finally, the elevators were mentioned. 'The lift service, for which Messrs R. Waygood & Co., of London, have been responsible, is considerably in advance of that of any previous vessel,' enthused *The Shipbuilder*. 'Each elevator will raise a load of 15cwt between the Upper [C] and Promenade [A] decks, a height of 37ft 6in… The cages are about 5ft 4in by 6ft, by 7ft high, and are made of dark mahogany.'[38] The second-class lift was mechanically the same, but with plainer cage furnishing.

At the first-class pursers' office on C-deck, first-class passengers could pay 12*s* 6*d* to send a ten-word wireless message; 9*d* was charged for every additional word (for messages going to the United States) – the messages were sent to the wireless room via pneumatic tube. Messages going to Canada were charged at the rate of 7½*d* for ten words and 4*d* for each additional word; messages to the United Kingdom were 10*d* per word and ship-to-ship messages varied, but were usually around 8*d* per word. The wireless room via pneumatic tube sent incoming messages to the pursers' office; a bell boy then dispatched them to the addressee's cabin.

Deck chairs could be hired at a charge of 4*s* each for the voyage and rugs could also be hired at a 4*s* charge.

The gymnasium was open to children from 1 to 3 p.m. and open to ladies between 10 a.m. to 1 p.m.; it was open to gentlemen from 2 p.m. to 7 p.m. F-deck's squash racquet court was in the charge of a professional player. Tickets were available from the pursers' office for 2s (50 cents) per half-hour – this included the services of the professional. It was available for a maximum of one hour if other passengers were waiting to use the court.

The clothes pressing and cleaning room was in charge of an expert attendant who would 'carry out any work for this kind for ladies or gentlemen, in accordance with a fixed tariff of charges which can be had on application to the bedroom steward.'

Turkish baths, Electric bath and swimming bath were available for ladies between 10 a.m. to 1 p.m. and for gentlemen between 2 p.m. and 7 p.m.; tickets were obtainable from the pursers' office at a charge of 4s ($1). The swimming bath was open free to gentlemen from 6 a.m. to 9 a.m. and open to ladies and gentlemen during the day like the Turkish baths. However, there was a charge of 1s (25 cents) for passengers who did not book the Turkish Bath as well.

The veranda café and Palm Court served light refreshments. These were open between 8 a.m. and 11 p.m. for passengers; after dinner coffee was sometimes served in these.

B-deck's *à la carte* restaurant was open from 8 a.m. to 11 p.m. for passengers with more unusual tastes. If passengers stated that they would take all meals in here instead of the dining saloon, they were offered rebates in recognition that they would pay in the restaurant for any meals taken. Rebates were (per adult) £3 ($15) on tickets under £35 ($175) or £5 ($25) for tickets over £35 ($175);★ passengers applied to the restaurant's manager for reservation of seats.

The A-deck lounge and D-deck reception room were intended for the use of both ladies and gentlemen and afternoon tea, after-dinner coffee, etc., were served. Liqueurs, cigars and cigarettes were available for passengers to purchase. Books placed on the lounge's bookcase by *The Times* of London book club could be seen upon application to the steward in charge; a supply of recent works was placed here each voyage. D-deck's reception room was open until 11 p.m. and the lounge was open until 11.30 p.m. (both from 8 a.m.).

While the passengers relaxed, the ship's victualling department staff worked overtime, but there were compensations. 'I got a fresh thrill every time I went through *Olympic*'s beautiful staterooms,' stewardess Violet Jessop later wrote, 'the Adams room, the Regency room, the Dutch, Georgian and so on, with their exquisite woodwork and sumptuous silk furnishings. I have always maintained that never before or since have such materials of so perfect a quality been used to fit out any ship.'

Olympic's speed was increased gradually throughout the voyage and she did better than expected. After a first day's run of 428 miles, averaging 20½ knots, she logged 534 miles at 21½ knots, 542 miles at an average of nearly 22 knots, 525 miles at 21¼ knots and 548 miles at over 22 knots. She slowed a little for the remaining 317 miles and averaged 21¼ knots. The performance was all the more impressive given that five boilers remained unlit, while she had slowed for a short period one day due to the weather.

J. Bruce Ismay initially cabled Lord Pirrie: '*Olympic* is a marvel and has given unbounded satisfaction. Once again accept my warmest and most sincere congratulations.'[39]

He also sent a cable to the White Star Line's Liverpool Offices.

> Arrived at lightship 2.24 [a.m.], docked at 10 a.m. Everything worked most satisfactorily, passengers delighted. Passage 5 days 16 hours 42 minutes, average speed 21.7; [total] coal consumption given 3,540 [tons], think it liberal estimate. Delayed by fog 1½ hours. Daily runs…Single-ended boilers not lighted. Communicate this to Pirrie, Harland, Belfast.[40]

★ The rebate was only granted when 'passengers announce their intention to book without meals, and of making use of the restaurant, at the time of purchasing their ticket and no other rebate can be assured under any other circumstance,' stated a contemporary brochure.

In a letter written after the ship docked to other White Star Line officials, J. Bruce Ismay suggested that larger first-class suites could be installed on *Titanic*'s B-deck because he thought the deck space on *Olympic* excessive.

'The deck space, with the number of passengers on board going out, was certainly excessive, and I think, in another ship, we might carry out the rooms on B-deck the same as those on C-deck,' Ismay wrote.[41]

Additionally, he thought an enlarged *à la carte* restaurant could be fitted and a café parisien[42] installed on part of the second-class promenade, imitating a 'sidewalk café'. He recommended a potato peeler should be fitted in the crew galley and some cigar holders in the first-class bathrooms, plus some slightly firmer mattresses.[43]

The mattresses were a little too soft, thereby accentuating the vibration from the engines, but nevertheless it was reported: 'passengers said that there was very little vibration.' (However, in the aft passenger areas the wing propellers' thud could be felt on occasion.) *Olympic*'s smooth running at high speeds was particularly pleasing. During the early age of the express steamships – and indeed, sometime afterwards – vibration was a problem that plagued many vessels. As a few examples, Hamburg Amerika's *Deutschland* of 1900 and the swift Cunarders *Lusitania* and *Mauretania* spring to mind; *Lusitania*'s stern suffered 'a violent shuddering convulsion that rattled through

Olympic's spacious passenger decks and promenade space drew considerable praise when she entered service. In this view, looking aft along the starboard promenade on A-deck, the bay windows of the first-class lounge can be seen in the distance. (Library of Congress, Prints and Photographs Division, Daniel Klistorner collection)

her steel plates' at high speed, while her sister vibrated worst in the area of the forward superstructure. *Deutschland*'s engines caused excessive rattling noises, in addition to heavy vibration. Usually, the problem could be and would be solved – or at least reduced – with additional hull strengthening, general stiffening and propeller redesign.[44]

The first-class reception room required fifty additional cane chairs and ten tables because it had proved so popular; it was duly arranged for them to be added by Harland & Wolff.[45]

Ismay was not distracted by such minor details and sent a wireless before the maiden voyage was over.[46] Harland & Wolff were given the 'go ahead' to begin construction on a larger and finer sister ship, to complete the planned three ship express service. All indications are that *Olympic*'s pleasing performance merely confirmed the White Star Line's intentions.

After passing the Ambrose Lightship at 2.24 a.m., she was delayed at Quarantine for a while. 'The *Olympic* left Quarantine at 7.45 a.m., and was saluted on her way up the harbour by all kinds of craft, from tiny motorboats to ferryboats plying on the North River and lower bay.' As Ismay reported, it appeared to have taken her 5 days, 16 hours and 42 minutes to complete the 2,894-mile crossing, a very pleasing result, but there was an unfortunate error. The distance and time were calculated from the Daunt's Rock light vessel, which *Olympic* passed shortly after leaving Queenstown, to the Ambrose Lightship as she came up the channel into New York. From passing Daunt's Rock at 4.22 p.m. on 15 June 1911 to the arrival at the Ambrose Lightship at 2.24 a.m. on 21 June 1911, it had actually taken her 5 days, 15 hours and 2 minutes, allowing for the time differences. An error of 100 minutes had crept into the calculations. Consequently, *Olympic*'s average speed was a quarter of a knot higher than Ismay or anybody else realised, at nearly 21½ knots over the entire crossing.

'The view of the liner at Quarantine as she loomed up off Staten Island gave an impression of immense bulk to observers,' recorded the *New York Times*. 'She looked to be a genuine sea monster. Two daring passengers emerged through the cloud of galley smoke coming up from the depth and waved their hats as they walked around the rim inside the fourth funnel.'

Pilot Julius Adler and Captain Smith docked the ship by 10 a.m., having needed almost an hour, as well as the assistance of twelve straining tugs. But the operation was not without drama. 'With the exception of a playful touch given to the stern of a tugboat, drawn under the counter of the *Olympic*,' it was recorded, 'the liner was made fast without incident to the newly extended pier.'

The 'playful touch' had been a potentially disastrous incident; the tug *O.L. Hallenbeck* was at the stern, sucked into the liner's side,[47] under the counter, when the starboard propeller briefly turned to increase *Olympic*'s momentum while berthing.[48] *O.L. Hallenbeck*'s owner sued White Star for $10,000 but the case was dropped along with White Star's countersuit for 'lack of evidence'.[49]

While *Olympic* received numerous whistle salutes from vessels around her, 'the *Lusitania* did not salute the latest addition to the Atlantic fleet as she passed...It was thought that in the hurry of getting his ship underway and receiving congratulations upon his coronation honour of Commander of the Bath, Captain Charles, skipper of the *Lusitania*, overlooked the *Olympic* as she passed the Cunard pier.'

There was – very predictably – much more publicity. In the *New York Times* one cartoon depicted a well-dressed passenger asking for directions to the *Olympic*'s fictitious racecourse: 'Walk up two blocks,' a deckhand said, 'take a red car and – on second thought, take the subway…'[50]

'Captain Smith said she had done all that was expected of her, and behaved splendidly,' it was reported.

'Will she ever dock on Tuesday?' a reporter enquired.

'No,' Smith responded, 'and there will be no attempt to bring her in on Tuesday. She was built for a Wednesday ship and her run this first voyage has demonstrated that she will fulfil the expectations of the builders.' Yet *Olympic* would later manage some Tuesday arrivals.

Purser McElroy said that his daily 10.30 a.m. inspection of the ship – with Captain Smith, Dr O'Loughlin and Chief Steward Andrew Latimer – had seemed like 9 miles.

In one more recent account, 'the *Olympic* was an enormous success. Wealthy Americans flocked to her, as intended, along with her other second and third-class passengers.'[51] It was surely due in no small part to *Olympic* that the White Star Line became a millionaires' favourite, transporting during 1911 more passengers in first-class than any other steamship line in history.[52]

Passengers asked about the ship referred to her as 'a big hotel in which it was hard to imagine oneself afloat, she was so steady'.

The second steward's task of checking that the crew who were supposed to be assisting with baggage were not skiving was made all the more difficult by the warrens of passageways and rooms, and he told one man hanging around near the squash court: 'I am not going to try to round you up again as it would be impossible for me to keep track of you, but remember this: I may not see you again today, but I shall see you some day, and if you don't get to work on the baggage…'

Chief Engineer Bell completed his report of the voyage to the management on 24 June 1911. He reported that the boilers and engines 'worked very well' without trouble at all, while the boiler room telegraphs worked satisfactorily, the reciprocating engines specifically performing 'exceptionally well' and the turbine not giving 'the slightest trouble' at all. Bell suggested that slight changes be made to the electric engine pipes, although the generators had supplied plenty of power 'without approaching the maximum load' they had been designed to take; engine room telegraphs were 'remarkably easy' to use; watertight doors were fine; but boiler room telephones needed better insulation. Further comments included the steering gear being 'an exceptionally good fitting', telemotors, steam whistles and controls needing no adjustment whatsoever during the voyage, and the ventilation fans working well, although he recommended that additional fans be fitted.

Although *Olympic* had been opened to the public following her maiden arrival, 8,000 people visited her before she cast off at 3 p.m. on 28 June 1911 to begin the return voyage, watched by 10,000 people, with 2,301 passengers aboard (731 first-class, 495 second-class and 1,075 third-class passengers), compared to the 1,313 passengers she had previously carried (489 first, 263 second and 561 third class); thus for her first round trip she carried an amazing 3,614 passengers, 1,220 of them in first-class.

Among her passengers were Mrs William K. Vanderbilt and her three children; William Truesdale, president of the Lackawanna Railroad; George Baer, president of the Philadelphia & Reading Railroad; and a Hamburg-Amerika Line director, eagerly sampling the new class of liner.

'Every pier head in the vicinity was crowded,' a journalist recorded. 'The thousands cheered and waved handkerchiefs from the minute the biggest ship in the world began to move into the North River until she finally straightened out and headed down the bay. Many remained until she was lost to view.'

Aviator Tommy Sopwith added to the excitement by flying over the ship and dropping a package containing some replacement spectacles for a passenger who had recently lost his; unfortunately the package missed the ship and sank.

'I was particularly glad to accomplish the flight,' he said afterwards, unaware that he had missed the ship, 'for I had been prevented from greeting the *Olympic* on her arrival and I did not want her first trip to America to be completed without extending my congratulations to her captain. There was a special letter to him in my bundle. I only hope he got it.'

On the crossing home, eastbound, she averaged over 22¼ knots, which was later increased much further.[53] Her combined speed for the round trip was 21¾ knots, a very impressive performance all things considered. On *Olympic*'s return home, she arrived at Southampton with the expectation of being well booked on her next trip; leaving with well over seven hundred first-class passengers alone.

At Southampton, a diver routinely inspected her propeller blade routes, bosses and bolts, finding that they were still in fine condition.

Of interest – especially when considering the fate of *Olympic*'s sister – were the boat drills. Captain Smith tested some of the lifeboats regularly, but only two boats each time, once every round trip. He had to report to the company every time:

The beautiful first-class grand staircase, perhaps the most impressive interior space on board. Its smaller counterpart, situated aft, was a contrast in that it had a rather plain surround for its clock. (Library of Congress, Prints and Photographs Division, Daniel Klistorner collection)

Southampton, December 15th 1911.
General Remarks – Boat numbers 1 and 3 lowered and crews exercised at Southampton. All davits and falls in good order.

January 30th 1912.
Before leaving Southampton boats 10 and 12 lowered and crews exercised. All davits and falls in good order.

During her first year of service, *Olympic* achieved excellent crossing times as her engines were run in and the speed increased. On her second westbound crossing, she improved her time to 5 days, 13 hours and 6 minutes with an average speed of around 21¾ knots. Her runs each day were 525, 560, 534, 526 and 518 miles. The second day was particularly impressive because it was her highest to date and her average speed exceeded 22½ knots. Even though she slowed down quite markedly, to less than 21 knots for the final complete day, she arrived at the Ambrose Lightship at 10.08 p.m. on the Tuesday evening, 19 July 1911. Returning from New York, she raised her best day's run for the eastbound crossing to 540 miles. Accounting for the fact that a day on an eastbound crossing was shorter due to clock adjustments, the average speed for the day worked out at 23¼ knots, aided by the current.

Her fourth westbound crossing showed her reducing the time taken to 5 days, 7 hours and 29 minutes, arriving at the Ambrose Lightship early on Tuesday evening and docking in New York several hours later. She was helped by one of the highest average speeds she had yet recorded westbound, combined with the fact that it was her first voyage on the shorter northern track to New York.

Harold Sanderson would later state that *Olympic's* fastest eastbound crossing had taken 5 days, 14 hours and 32 minutes, but she did better than that at least once in her first year, bettering the time he quoted by more than two hours. All in all, her performance was enough to make it abundantly clear that she had ample power in reserve to maintain her designed service speed or to exceed it over an extended time period.

It did not take long for *Olympic's* performance to raise some questions as to her schedule. An increase in speed from 21 knots to 22½ knots resulted the crossing time being reduced by almost ten hours. Even though she had left Queenstown later than expected on her maiden voyage, she had arrived at the Ambrose Lightship at 2.24 a.m. on Wednesday. *Olympic* was more than capable of arriving in New York on Tuesday evening when she was on the longer southern track to New York, or even docking on Tuesday evening if she was on the shorter northern track which was in use from the middle of August to the middle of January each year. The White Star Line had a long standing policy that if a ship arrived early (or late) in the evening then passengers were welcome to stay on board overnight and take breakfast in the morning, so that they would not be inconvenienced if their ship arrived at a time they had not expected.

Philip Franklin and other American directors at IMM had strongly recommended that on *Olympic's* second westbound crossing she should dock on the Tuesday evening, aiding the turnaround and re-stocking of the ship in addition to pleasing the passengers. Ismay initially disagreed, but had said that if it was discussed with Lord Pirrie, Captain Smith and Chief Engineer Bell and the suggestion was favoured, he would not stand in the way. On 11 August 1911 Captain Smith was advised: '…it will be right for you to go full speed when on the short [northern] track, subject to your considering it prudent and in the interests of safe navigation to do so.' It applied to both westbound and eastbound

passages. Frederick Toppin enthused to J. Bruce Ismay on 18 August 1911 that the decision would 'insure her arriving here [New York] almost regularly on Tuesday afternoon',
certainly adding 'materially to her attractiveness and popularity this side'. More practically,
he noted: 'It will also enable us to more satisfactorily handle her coaling here.'[54]

Olympic's third westbound crossing was the last one for 1911 where she would be on
the longer southern track to New York. She ran 516, 543, 536, 544 and 553 miles, maintaining an average speed that varied from 21¾ to 22 knots. She completed the remaining
198 miles to New York, arriving at the Ambrose Lightship at 9.10 p.m. It was all the
more impressive given that the engines had been limited to 78rpm, leaving ample power
in reserve even during the fastest day's run, while as usual for a westbound crossing the
prevailing current had been against her. Her speed 'through the water' was therefore
greater than her speed 'over the ground'.

Her third crossing eastbound was recorded by a Cunard observer, their naval architect
Leonard Peskett who was on board as a passenger and had an eye for detail:[55] she carried a
large cargo, 7,000 tons of coal and a full load of fresh water, was drawing 35ft 5in of water,
transporting 447 first-class, 205 second-class and 914 third-class passengers, a grand total of
1,596 passengers. *Olympic* sailed from New York on 19 August 1911 at 1 p.m., passing
the Ambrose light vessel at 3.05 p.m. Her daily runs were 449, 505, 529, 519, 506 and 494
miles, with average speeds of about 22¼, 21¾, 22¾, 22¼, 21¾, 21¼ and 22 knots. She
completed the 3,086-mile crossing in 5 days, 20 hours and 12 minutes, arriving at Plymouth
at 4.17 p.m. on 26 August 1911. Throughout the passage, he poked his nose into every
corner of the ship. There was a 'superabundance' of promenade space; the cavernous first-
class reception room was extremely popular; the *à la carte* restaurant was a success, receipts
totalling £1,730, £1,400 and about £1,250 on each of the three round voyages; 'very
little fault' could be found with the main dining saloon seating, the lighting being 'very
effective' but also making parts of the saloon too warm; and the service was so quick that
'nothing better could be desired'. He noted that 2,164 passengers had used the swimming
pool since the ship had been in commission, while 448 people had used the Turkish
baths; the gymnasium was 'fairly well patronised', while the squash court was well used
continuously by a number of passengers. In meticulous detail, he wrote that there were
404 light bulbs in the first-class dining saloon, 180 in the reception room and 330 in the
smoke room. One observation was that in parts of the ship additional ventilation would
be an improvement, a detail White Star had already noted and would soon be rectified.
The *à la carte* restaurant's creation appeared to be creating a consciously superior kind of
first-class passengers, that inevitable *crème de la crème* who felt privileged to dine on even
grander food than that found in the 'ordinary' first-class saloon.

Electric lights in the lavatories were turned on when the doors closed and off when
the doors were opened, which was better than a switch and saved electricity; the baths
of the private suites were fitted with sprays and showers; while wash basins were fitted in
marble slabs. Hot and cold water was supplied to all first-class staterooms apart from those
on E-deck, the supply being 'clean and quick'.

Noting the standards of accommodation, he wrote of the first-class areas:

> ...the corridors to the best class of rooms on B and C-decks are framed up with pilasters
> and fielded panels. The framing of all other sections of the first-class cabins is made up
> of machined stiles and long plain panels.

Personally, he thought that there was a lack of drawer space in some of the cabins without the special wardrobes. Framing of the second-class cabins was similar to that he had described for the ordinary first-class staterooms. In the third-class dining saloon, the chairs were 'large, comfortable and spaced 26in apart centre to centre' which was 'rather more than is usually allowed'. The 'large covered promenade space' forward of the main third-class entrance was 'fitted with tables and seats at the sides and very popular'. Third-class rooms were 'framed up with chamfered-edged stiles' and wash basins were 'provided in the rooms intended for married people and single women, but no wash basins are provided in the rooms intended for men only.'

The greatest the ship had ever rolled was between 3 and 5 degrees, in twenty seconds, which was hardly bad and surely scarcely perceptible. Personally, he thought that although the combination of reciprocating engines and the turbine saved coal and undoubtedly performed well as did the boilers, he was not in favour of it as the main engine room required a great space which might otherwise be used as passenger accommodation.

★   ★   ★

Olympic completed four round trips to New York and on 20 September 1911 she left Southampton on her fifth trip, in fine clear weather but with moderate breezes. Her voyage did not begin auspiciously, because shortly before sailing time some of the crew belonging to the British Seamen's & Firemen's Union had refused to join the ship because there were two non-unionists working aboard, but, shortly before sailing, the problem was fortunately averted when the two men in question were withdrawn from the ship, allowing the liner to sail on time. In fact, *Olympic* was carrying 1,313 passengers from Southampton,[56] beginning her journey down Southampton Water. At 12.29 p.m. the liner reached Calshot Castle, then the Black Jack Buoy one minute later, reaching Calshot Spit at 12.34 p.m. to proceed on a course of south 65° west.

To get to sea she had to round a shoal called the Bramble, then move into Spithead and head south-east to Cherbourg from the Isle of Wight, Captain Smith's regularly-chosen route.[57]

Travelling at 17½ knots through the water, she reached the North Thorn Buoy at about 12.37 p.m., then passed Thorn Knoll Buoy three minutes later, when the port engine was put 'slow ahead' and the turbine stopped. *Olympic* slowed to 11 or 12 knots for the turn around the West Bramble Buoy at 12.42 p.m. – which was completed with the port engine stopped and reversed at 'half astern', followed by 'full speed astern'. At the same time, the helm was put hard over for a port turn, while two short two-second blasts on the whistles sounded to indicate the turn. At 12.43 p.m., the port engine was stopped and ordered 'full speed ahead', the helm straightened-up. *Olympic* then began slowly accelerating up to twenty knots; the 'reduced maximum speed' in effect for coastal waters, on a course of south 59° east.

Meanwhile, HMS *Hawke* – a twenty-year-old twin-screw first-class protected cruiser 360ft long, 60ft wide, with a mean draft of 23ft 5in and a displacement of 7,600 tons, which had just completed engine power trials and was returning to Portsmouth – was going down the narrow waters of Spithead and altered her course slightly to south 74° east in order to give the liner more room, but she was on a crossing course. As she neared the liner, *Hawke* was said to be making 15¼ knots and started to move ahead, before dropping

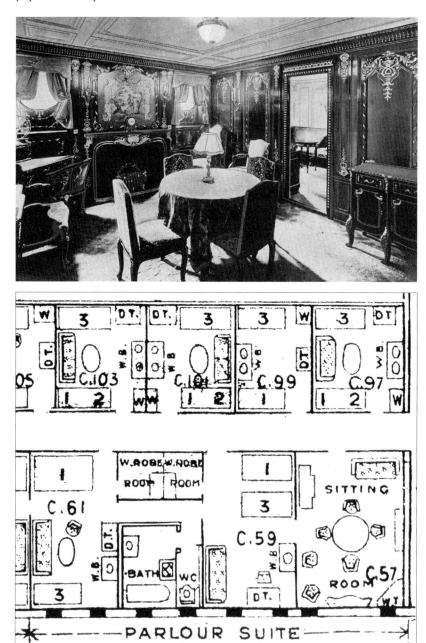

Top: The sitting room of the starboard 'parlour suite' on C-deck, decorated in Regence style, was one of the most elaborate rooms on the ship. In 1924, the Prince of Wales was reported to have said 'this is too grand for me'. (Author's collection)

Above: A plan showing the layout of the suite and its size compared with the ordinary first-class staterooms across the corridor. C57 was the Regence sitting room; C59 was a stateroom in Empire style; and C61 was a stateroom in Louis XV, the Harland & Wolff 'Bedroom A' design with oak French-style panelling. From 1913, the rooms were renumbered C53, C55 and C57, as they were on the equivalent suite aboard *Titanic*. (*The Shipbuilder*, 1911/Ioannis Georgiou collection)

back once she had nearly reached a point level with the liner's bridge as the larger vessel increased speed.

Olympic's main engines were now making about 60–65rpm, while her turbine's speed was somewhat higher.

Hawke's movements did not go unnoticed on the larger ship. When the much smaller vessel began to drop back and move towards the ship's stern, Captain Smith and Pilot George Bowyer watched from the bridge. Smith had believed there was no danger from the smaller vessel, but now it was clear that there was a dangerous situation developing.

'I don't believe he will get under our stern, Bowyer.' said Smith, thinking that the *Hawke* was attempting to pass under the stern.

'If she is going to strike sir, let me know in time so I can put the helm hard over to port.'

'Is she going to strike sir?'

'Yes, she is going to strike us in the stern!' Smith replied; 'He is starboarding and he is going to hit us.'

Aboard *Hawke*, Commander Blunt had ordered a turn to starboard to keep away from the huge *Olympic*, but *Hawke* swung up to 57° to port.

'What are you doing?' he yelled to the quartermaster. 'Port! Port, hard to port!'

Blunt was forced to reverse the port and then the starboard engine to turn the vessel as the quartermaster yelled 'helm jammed!' Then the other three men on the bridge applied

One of the innovative features of the first-class dining saloon was the provision of semi-private alcoves, away from the central portion of the large saloon. On the right, directly behind the leaded glass windows were strips of Linolite, illuminated at night to give the effect of daylight coming through the windows. During the day, the Luxfer prismatic panes, situated between the windows and the outer porthole, evenly dispersed the light so that the porthole's shape was not visible: 'Inside the window and on each side of the frame there is a strip of Linolite fitted which proves very effective at night'. (Author's collection)

The light and elegant first-class dining saloon was the largest room afloat when *Olympic* entered service. It had changed little by the time of this photograph in 1920. The fixed round swivel chairs on earlier liners such as *Lusitania* were gone. (Daniel Klistorner collection)

all their strength to the wheel, delivering a 15-degree turn to starboard before the helm failed again. However, due to forces now beyond her control, *Hawke* was unavoidably heading towards *Olympic*.

Hawke was designed to sink enemy ships by ramming them and so she was fitted with an underwater ram of thick steel filled with concrete. With the sound of 'a howitzer going off', *Hawke*'s bow pierced *Olympic*'s hull and paint was stripped from the liner. In fact, the noise of the collision was heard more than a mile away by observers ashore.

As *Olympic* quickly continued forward, her starboard propeller shaft and later the propeller were hit, jolting the starboard engine. Chief Engineer Fleming, on the top platform, felt the collision 'slightly' and was moving down to the bottom platform when the starboard engine 'pulled up'. 'Just for a moment,' he recalled, 'and [it] then cleared itself.' It must have been quite a shock, as the engine had been making over 60rpm. Fleming reached the bottom platform just after the telegraphs rang 'stop' from the bridge.

Hawke's ram fell off and the vessel briefly scraped forcefully along the ship's hull, causing much damage above and below the waterline over a roughly 40ft-length. As *Hawke* eventually cleared *Olympic* she took a massive roll to port, listing sharply and nearly capsizing before she righted herself.

Water now surged through *Olympic*'s ruptured hull, a smashing and surging assault. On the bridge the warning bell was rung to warn those below that the watertight doors were closing, then the doors were closed at Pilot Bowyer's orders and the engines were stopped. The rough log's entry simply recorded: '12.46 [p.m.] Struck on starboard quarter by His Majesty's ship.'

The watertight doors controlled the water's inrush through the holes in the hull: one 15ft high by 14ft wide and 8ft deep was mostly above the waterline, plus the other damage. Two of the largest watertight compartments had been flooded and several hundred tons of water had entered a third that had had to be pumped dry. The damage extended all the way up to D-deck and was situated approximately 87ft from the sternpost, even the starboard propeller bossing being damaged.

'Full astern' was telegraphed at 12.50 p.m., to be quickly followed by 'stop' one minute later, the ship slowly coming to a stop.

Despite this serious damage, nobody was hurt and *Olympic* steamed to Osborne Bay, in the Isle of Wight, as she could not return to Southampton owing to the tide, on her port engine. She had never been in any danger of sinking following the collision and in fact was drawing only 35ft 6in of water aft, a mere one foot more than when she was normally loaded, but her Plimsoll line was partly submerged.

Passengers disembarked by tender, among them twenty millionaires valued at a total of $500,000,000 (some £100,000,000), including Mr Waldorf Astor, MP, and His Highness Prince Jaisinh Gaekwar. 'It is stated that the number of the vessel's first-class passengers was the largest ever carried in a single ship for New York,' a reporter noted.

White Star lost no time in issuing an apology to the passengers, stating:

Olympic's second-class dining saloon was a marked advance on previous ships. She followed an innovation from *Adriatic* where the second-class dining saloon extended the entire width of the ship. (Daniel Klistorner collection)

> The service of the White Star Line offices in London, Southampton and Liverpool will
> be placed at the disposal of passengers for securing accommodation, and passage money
> will be returned forthwith to those passengers who wish to make their own arrangements.

Two special trains ran to London, one carrying 200 first-class passengers and various mails,
the other second- and third-class passengers.

Eight of the passengers who had left the ship by tug the night after the collision managed to board the boat train from Euston the following afternoon to get to Liverpool to
catch the *Adriatic*. Mr E.P. Sheldon, President of the United States Trust Company, New
York, was so anxious to get to New York that he hired a special train for a £78 first-class
fare, leaving Southampton at 12.33 p.m. He managed to board *Adriatic* with a mere few
minutes to spare, making a total of nine passengers who reached the liner.

During a later voyage aboard *Olympic*, Captain Smith was among a group discussing
the collision. 'Anyhow, the *Olympic* is unsinkable, and *Titanic* will be the same when she
is put in commission,' he remarked. He said that either vessel could be cut in halves and
each section would remain afloat. 'I venture to add,' he finished, 'that even if the engines
and boilers were to fall through their bottoms, the vessels would remain afloat.'[58]

A little before 11.00 a.m. on Thursday 21 September 1911, *Olympic* was berthed at
Southampton, having left her Osborne Bay anchorage at 8.50 a.m. with the assistance of tugs
from the Isle of Wight towing company, proceeding under her own steam with her port
engine. Six tugs had been needed for the docking, watched by numerous interested spectators. Soon, divers went down for an inspection of the damage. Cargo was discharged.

After *Olympic* docked, the crew left her by 5.00 p.m. on Friday 22 September 1911,
but were dissatisfied with the offer of three days' pay, claiming that they were entitled for
wages for the entire round trip under the Merchant Shipping Act of 1894. It all depended
on whether the liner was considered a 'wreck', for although she had not sunk, she had
been damaged sufficiently to force cancellation of the voyage. White Star did indeed
consider her a wreck and under the Act justified their decision:

> When the service of a seaman terminates before the date contemplated in the agreement by reason of a wreck or loss of the ship,…he shall be entitled to wages up to the
> time of such termination, but not for any longer period.

However, under the very same legislation, the men cited Section 162:

> If a seaman, having signed an agreement is discharged otherwise than in accordance
> with the terms thereof before the commencement of the voyage…without fault on his
> part justifying the discharge…he shall be entitled to receive…in addition to the wages
> he may have earned…due compensation for the damage caused to him by the discharge
> not exceeding one month's wages…

On 29 September 1911, the case went before Southampton County Court, but was
referred on 11 October 1911 to a March 1912 Admiralty Court when a verdict was not
reached.[59] Finally, on 1 April 1912 Mr Justice Bargrave Deane delivered judgement. 'The
Olympic, he ruled, was a wreck within the meaning of the Act. If a vessel foundered at sea
she would be a loss, not a wreck…*Olympic* was so badly damaged that she ceased to be
navigable, and the men were not entitled to more than three days' wages…'[60]

Meanwhile, *Olympic* had been temporarily repaired at Southampton and she left on 3 October 1911, taking three days to arrive back at Belfast for a full survey and permanent repair work. Among other problems, the ship's refrigerated cargo space had been 'badly damaged through the effect of the silicate cotton becoming saturated with water'; the litosilo deck covering 'for the extent of [the] deck and shell [plating] damage has been destroyed'; and there were concerns about the ship's starboard engine, as it had been in operation during the collision. Every length of the propeller shafting had to be 'removed and tested' and 'replaced, or renewed if found necessary'. One of Harland & Wolff's directors, Mr Cummings, noted on 14 October 1911: '*Titanic*'s shafting is available if necessary but if used would entail considerable delay in that ship's completion, as the engines are now being put into her.' While she was at the yard, Harland & Wolff took advantage of the situation and made improvements to the port and starboard propellers: the pitch of the blades was increased to improve their efficiency, similar to changes that would be made to *Titanic*. *Olympic* left at 4.31 p.m. on 20 November 1911 and arrived at Southampton two days later. Two months after the collision, she was ready for service.

It had not taken as long for the naval authorities to investigate the collision's cause. On 21 September 1911, the commander in chief at Portsmouth, Admiral Moore, directed two commanders to undertake a 'strict and careful enquiry into the circumstances of the case' on board *Hawke*. Only naval personnel were questioned and they concluded that 'We are of the opinion that from the evidence heard that the *Olympic* is alone to blame.' Unsurprisingly, the White Star Line had come to a different conclusion. They sued the navy who, in turn, sued them. The two cases were heard together by the Probate, Divorce and Admiralty Division with Sir Samuel Evans presiding. Messrs Laing, Stephens and Dumas appeared for the White Star Line; the attorney general, Sir Rufus Isaacs, Messrs Butler Aspinall, Bateson and Dunlop appeared for the navy when the first day's evidence began on 16 November 1911.

Captain Smith was the first witness. He spoke of his vessel's course, speed and movements. Speaking of the moments before the collision, he was asked: 'When you saw her [*Hawke*] drawing up, had you any anxiety about her at that time?'

'No, not at all,' he replied. '…She continued to overhaul until she got with her stem almost abreast of our bridge. I could see the stem through the aperture on the bridge shelter.'

Smith recalled that the two ships were 'running practically on a parallel course'. '…We [either] gathered speed, drew ahead a little, or she dropped astern.' He had never experienced the suction phenomenon in either the *Baltic*, *Adriatic* or *Olympic*; before the collision it had seemed that the *Hawke* was 'starboarding her helm' (turning to port). 'It seemed inconceivable, a manoeuvre I could not understand.'

'Did it occur to you at all, Captain Smith, that the ship had got out of control, the *Hawke* I mean?'

'No.'

'…Or that her steering gear had got out of control?'

'No, that did not occur to me.'

He thought the *Hawke* had misjudged a manoeuvre to go 'under our stern'. *Olympic*'s speed was reduced to twenty knots in such waters as the Solent, but out at sea he would have accelerated up to 22½ knots after passing the Nab Lightship.

Quartermaster Haines testified that between steadying on course at 12.43 p.m., it had taken five minutes for the collision to occur; but was flatly contradicted by the other evidence that the collision occurred at 12.46 p.m. His estimate was 'just my idea', he said.

Suspicious of his estimate, Sir Samuel Evans asked him how long he had been in the witness box. 'About ten minutes, I think.' The actual time is not recorded; but it was one of many incidents of the liner's civilian witnesses being weaker than the Royal Navy's.

Chief Engineer Robert Fleming (Chief Engineer Bell had been transferred to the *Titanic*) testified that the *Olympic's* engines developed a maximum of '59,000hp' with the main engines at a maximum of 83rpm and the turbine operating at full power. The turbine was only activated when the main engines were set at 'half ahead' and 'full ahead'; 'slow ahead', 30rpm, gave a speed of 9 knots without the turbine in operation. 60 or 65rpm was the main engines' speed at the time of the collision, he judged, which he roughly estimated at 16 knots (or over); at 12.48 p.m. (after the collision) the turbine was stopped, having been operating for twenty-five minutes at an average of 106rpm.

Senior Second Engineer John Herbert Thearle, with the line for eleven years, had been in charge of the port engine at the time of the collision and testified about the liner's speed. Much testimony was given on the subject by witnesses from the engine room. With the main engines doing 80rpm, the turbine would be working at about 175 or 180rpm, he said; the turbine did a maximum of 190rpm with the main engines at their highest speed. Thearle said that at the time of the collision he had estimated the port engine to be doing 62 or 65 rpm; after the order for 'full speed ahead' at 12.43 p.m. he had been 'gradually opening up [the stop valve] and giving her more steam to increase the speed'. His questioner suspected he was putting down the ship's speed in his testimony:

'It is very difficult to get any information,' he remarked. 'Had you your full boiler pressure?'

'Within a few pounds.'

'What pressure had you?'

'About 200lb.'

'Are you trying to reduce the speed of your engines as much as possible?'

'No.'

'...Are you trying by your evidence to cut down the speed of this ship as much as possible?'

'No.'

'With a pressure of 200lb you will not get quite so good a speed as with 215lb?'

'Quite so,' Thearle responded. He thought the difference in pressure about 4rpm.

'...I have got your log, and I see the boiler pressure is recorded there as 215lb.'

'We had been carrying 215lb, but in leaving port the pressure varies a good deal,' Thearle explained. '...At one time I would look at the pressure gauge and it would be one thing, and a few minutes later it might be another. When we stop suddenly the pressure goes up...'

'...I ask you again, are you not trying by your evidence to reduce the speed of this ship?'

'It may appear so, but I was not trying to do so.'

'...Of course, if you had 215lb pressure it would give you a better speed than what you have been describing in the bow, would it not?'

'Yes,' he responded.

In later questioning, he explained patiently that the boiler pressure was available for the engines, but only if the stop valve in the engine room was opened-up fully. The President asked him: 'I suppose that with this 215lb pressure of steam that you had you could have driven your engines slow or half speed all the time could you not?'

R.M.S. OLYMPIC
IN NEW YORK HARBOUR

A pre-war postcard demonstrates *Olympic*'s appearance coming into New York. (Author's collection)

'Yes.'

'Then it does not appear to be material,' the President announced.

Chief Engineer Fleming confirmed to the court when he was recalled that the steam pressure changed as the engines operated, while Junior Second Engineer Charles McKimm and several others were called to testify.

Giving details as to *Olympic*'s course and speed, Professor J.H. Biles produced detailed calculations for the court; at 21 knots, the resistance of the ship would be 165 tons assuming a displacement of 53,000 tons, based on an indicated horsepower at that speed of 46,000, while he had made calculations to show her speed at various times, taken from the times in the log. 'It is very difficult to arrive at any conclusion as to what the speed is at 12.43 p.m.,' he said, but if it was 12 knots then by the time of the collision three minutes later it would have been roughly 17 knots; the liner's speed would have been 18 knots if the collision had occurred four minutes later rather than the three recorded in the log. 'If you take 18 knots at the collision point, and 12 knots at 12.43 p.m., then we get a mean speed of 15 [knots],' he testified, but Biles said that it did 'not seem very probable' that the speed had been as low as 12 knots as the court had suggested. This put *Olympic*'s speed up somewhat and Biles' calculations agreed with Captain Smith's rough estimate of how long it would take for the ship to accelerate; but the evidence from the engine room was that it would take longer for the ship's speed to increase to the same extent.

Commander Blunt described that due to the sight of the *Olympic* he 'kept more to my own side of the channel. That was south 74 degrees east [magnetic]. My proper course [i.e. if *Olympic* had not been in the channel] would have been south 85 degrees east.' Speaking of the moments before the collision, as he was ordering 'full speed astern' on both engines and with the helm jammed, he described: 'screws without helm, or helm without screws, was not going to stop her.' 'In my opinion,' he said, 'undoubtedly the *Olympic* [was going faster at the time of the collision]…In my estimation her speed was anything from 19–20 knots.' *Hawke*'s engines were going astern before the collision, he asserted, as he could feel the vibration, resulting in the cruiser's speed being 'materially lessened'.

Called to give *Olympic*'s displacement figures, Thomas Andrews, Harland & Wolff's managing director, stated that the ship displaced 50,500 tons when drawing 33ft 6in of water; or 51,340 tons at 34ft (at the time of the collision the liner was drawing 33ft 9in).

Despite the question regarding whether the two vessels were on parallel or converging courses, there was also the question of which vessel had been overtaking or trying to and thus which vessel was responsible for avoiding a collision if they had been on parallel courses, but in the case of converging courses the ship to starboard had the right of way. Obviously, *Olympic* was much faster than the *Hawke*, which had reached 19½ knots when new, but because she had been accelerating after the turn it was unclear about her precise speed at any time. When she had completed the turn, *Hawke* was far faster, but *Olympic* soon accelerated. 'It was pleaded and stated in evidence at the time of the collision [that] her speed through the water was 16 knots,' it was later concluded, '…her captain said that from about 12 knots it would take her three or four minutes to attain her maximum reduced speed of 20 knots.' It was considered 'doubtful' as to whether the liner's speed had ever been as low as 11 or 12 knots at the time of the turn. Evidence supported that the collision had taken place some three or four minutes after she had straightened on her course. 'She must have reached a speed nearer 20 knots than 16 knots,' it was concluded. If this had been the case, then on a parallel course *Olympic* had then become an overtaking vessel and it was her responsibility to have avoided a collision. Yet although *Hawke*'s speed had been stated as 15¼ knots, some witnesses placed it higher, not just the White Star officers. One yachtsman's estimate was 16 knots. (Even though the *Hawke* had a dirty bottom, with her engines on 92rpm she was still able to achieve 17 knots, it had been found during her power trials earlier that morning; but if her bottom had been cleaned 18½ knots was a more likely speed.)

The point of the collision was another factor which nobody seemed to be in agreement on. The *Hawke*'s given place of collision 'is where it must be taken to have actually occurred', it was concluded. Later events would prove this was not the case, but those on *Olympic* were also in disagreement. Captain Smith said it had taken place 400 yards north by west from the place the court decided; Pilot George Bowyer estimated that the collision had occurred 500 yards away, in a direction north-north-west, while Colonel White gave his position 650 yards distant in an east-south-easterly direction. 'The place of collision will be very important, as I afterwards point out, in deciding as to the courses of the two vessels and the lines of those courses in the channel,' Evans later stated.

He ruled that *Olympic* was at fault for the collision. She had:

> … ample room and water in the channel to the northward. She came too close to the cruiser on the south side of the channel. She did not take the proper steps to keep out of the way. She might have averted the collision right up to the last if she had put her helm hard a starboard. Even when the pilot saw the *Hawke* come towards his vessel, he delayed action; and even when he took it, he ordered the helm hard a port, which was a very doubtful manoeuvre.

Although Captain Smith was responsible for the ship, *Olympic* was under pilot control at the time so he was not directly held responsible, but he saw it as a blemish on his career.

'The collision… was due solely to the faulty navigation of the pilot,' it was recorded, 'and there is not a shadow of…foundation for saying that the negligence of any of the owner's servants partly caused it. The owners of the *Olympic* therefore succeed on the defence of compulsory pilotage.'

'Suction' was the main cause of the collision, as the court heard. The 45,324grt *Olympic* was moving forward, with water being pushed out on either side of the hull and then surging back into the ship's wake, the force causing any small object near the stern to be sucked in. In this case it was the *Hawke* that had fallen victim to the force, which had been described in detail.

> Any ship's movement through the water is accompanied by a change of pressure. In the centre there is a reduced pressure, and when in shallow water that increases. If anything is put within that field they will feel reduction of pressure. When they get further aft they are partly in the reduced pressure and partly in the field of increased pressure. When a vessel overtakes another and is so placed that the bows feel the power of the reduced pressure and the stern is in the field of increased pressure, the bow will turn in and the stern move out.

White Star continued to believe that their vessel was blameless and appealed. Following a number of hearings, their appeal was dismissed in April 1913. The judges were unconvinced that *Hawke*'s ram, which had been located and recovered, had fallen off immediately after the collision, and so they did not feel that it helped pinpoint the location. They

Olympic approaches her New York pier for the first time. (Library of Congress, Prints and Photographs Division)

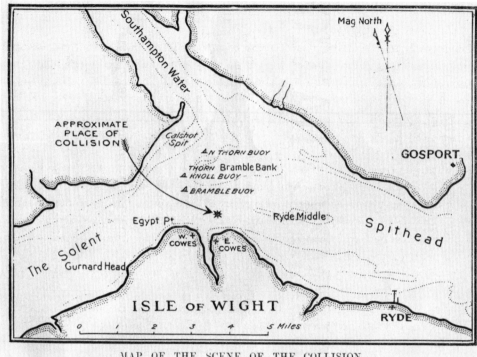

MAP OF THE SCENE OF THE COLLISION.

An interesting map of the area where the collision between *Olympic* and *Hawke* took place, published by the *Journal of Commerce* in 1911. Proceeding down Southampton Water, *Olympic* reached the North Thorn Buoy at 12.37 p.m. and the Thorn Knoll Buoy at 12.40 p.m. After passing the West Bramble Buoy at reduced speed and completing her turn to head towards Spithead, *Olympic*'s engines were ordered 'full speed ahead'. Unknown to anyone at the time, the positions of the Thorn Knoll and West Bramble Buoys – useful to navigation – were shown incorrectly on naval charts. *Hawke* was therefore sixty to seventy yards nearer to the middle of the channel than her navigators assumed, fatefully close to *Olympic*. (Author's collection)

reaffirmed Evans' findings, since White Star had not established that '*Hawke* was the over-taking vessel and bound to keep out of the way'; the vessels were crossing and therefore *Olympic* had been required to keep out of *Hawkes*'s way; and, as *Hawke* was not to blame for 'what she did or omitted to do' then it followed 'that the cause of the collision was the faulty navigation of the *Olympic*'. White Star took their case to the House of Lords, then Britain's highest court. By December 1913, it had been discovered that some of the navigating buoys' locations were incorrectly shown on the Admiralty charts in use aboard *Hawke* at the time: since they were shown sixty to seventy yards further south, then she had been further north and therefore closer to the middle of the channel than previously assumed. However, their final appeal was dismissed with costs in November 1914. One estimate indicated that the company had lost £250,000 in terms of the potential profits they had lost from cancelling several heavily booked crossings, as well as the necessary repairs.

Olympic was back in service by the end of November 1911, but the North Atlantic in winter was eventful without any further accidents. On her first westbound cross-ing after the repairs, she 'experienced very rough weather… and in spite of her great size her forward decks were swept by great waves rolling over her bows on Saturday and Sunday. Ventilators were smashed and one sea poured down the galley funnel and washed out the cooks as they were preparing breakfast,★ and another wave broke three of the steerage ports. According to the officers, some of the combers were as high as the crow's nest.' In January 1912, *Olympic* again encountered bad weather and 'in spite of her enormous size she shipped one huge sea over her bows on Sunday afternoon that tore off the cover of No.1 hatch on the foc'sle deck and lifted it bodily over the guard rails at the break of the deck and deposited it safely on the well deck below.' Captain Smith thought it one of the worst storms that he had witnessed, while the *New York Times* reported that J. Bruce Ismay, who was travelling to New York on business, had one of his stateroom's portholes smashed by the sea's ferocity. It seems more likely that it might have been left open. These frustrations were relatively minor in terms of their impact on the ship's schedule, but in February 1912 *Olympic*'s port propeller dropped a blade and she had to return to Harland & Wolff for repairs in the only dry dock capable of accommodating her. On 29 February 1912, she left Southampton for Belfast. Once again, she incurred expenses being repaired rather than earning profits for the company.

Early March 1912 saw *Olympic* and *Titanic* together for the last time at the Belfast shipyard. The local paper described *Olympic*'s visit and departure:

> The mammoth vessel was taken in tow by five tugs and proceeded slowly down the channel stern first; but after she had reached the second buoy it was decided to bring her back, and she was subsequently redocked. A statement was widely circulated in the city during the day to the effect that the *Olympic* had got out of the channel and touched the sandbank, but this is emphatically denied by Messrs Harland & Wolff Limited. A leading official informed a representative of this newspaper that after the vessel had been undocked the weather became boisterous, and as the tugs were not quite able to handle her satisfactorily in the channel owing to the strong wind, it was deemed advisable, in order to obviate any further trouble, to bring the liner back. The *Olympic* was placed in the graving dock again, because there was no other available berth to accommodate her... It is certain that the vessel did not receive the slightest damage, and she will leave for Southampton as soon as the weather moderates...
>
> Naturally, many people made their way down to the graving dock during the weekend to see the big ship, but they did not gain admission to the dock itself, as Harbour Police were on duty and only those on business were permitted to enter.
>
> The *Olympic* should leave Southampton for New York on Thursday next [14 March 1912].

On 7 March 1912, *Olympic* left for Southampton. When she arrived in New York on 20 March 1912, she brought with her 1,586 passengers and arrived with no more than 500 tons of coal, but the White Star Line had another problem to worry about in the form of the coal strike in Britain that was causing severe disruption. One internal com-

---

★ This referred to the crew's galley beneath the forecastle deck. It was equipped with a funnel which led up alongside the foremast, as well as a skylight. In August 1911, Leonard Peskett noted 'several times on the passage across the smell of cooking – and sometimes of burning fat – was perceptible at the fore end of the first-class promenade'. *Titanic*'s arrangement was improved, while *Olympic* would see changes when the opportunity arose.

pany letter noted: 'The trouble now existing may continue in a more or less acute form for some time. In any case coal will not be forthcoming under normal conditions for an indefinite period and we feel our principal [sic] consideration will be the *Olympic* & *Titanic* (cancelling the *Oceanic* as may be necessary).' As a consequence, when *Olympic* left New York three days later, she carried considerable extra coal. The company reported that she took on board no fewer than 9,210 tons: consisting of 8,160 tons stowed throughout the bunkers, the stokehold plates and the reserve bunker; an additional 1,050 tons in boiler room 3 and even crammed into the third-class dining saloon. (It hardly seems credible, but with only 270 third-class passengers for the eastbound crossing then the entire two compartments of the dining saloon would not have been required.) While they felt that they had 'sufficient coal at Southampton for the next sailing of each ship' (*Olympic* on 3 April and *Titanic* on 10 April 1912), it was 'not a safe position' and a draft cable for New York on 28 March 1912 advised: 'Owing to outlook coal position will sail *Olympic Titanic* twenty knots per hour each way *pro tem* This ensuring future sailings Advise agents please.' Fortunately, the coal strike was not as prolonged as they feared and it had been resolved by early April.

Captain Smith had completed his last crossing as *Olympic*'s commander and on her return to Southampton he left for Belfast to transfer to *Titanic*, now ready for her sea trials. Smith was now aged sixty-two, but in signing on as *Titanic*'s master he said he was fifty-nine. The transfer had been announced when *Olympic* left New York, by the *Southampton Times*:

> It has been definitely decided that Captain Smith, who has commanded the *Olympic* since she was first placed in commission, will be transferred to the new steamer *Titanic*, which is due at Southampton in the course of the next ten days…
>
> It is understood that Captain Haddock will be promoted in succession to Captain Smith. He, too, is an old and trusted servant of the White Star, having recently had charge of the *Oceanic*.

Sure enough, Haddock was on *Olympic*'s bridge when she left for New York on 3 April 1912. He must have been a proud man. She was still the largest vessel in service and the 2,043 passengers were her highest number for a westbound crossing to date. She arrived on the same day that *Titanic* was leaving Southampton, leaving New York again on 13 April 1912. It was reported that there were already 600 first-class bookings for her sister ship's scheduled departure from New York on 20 April 1912, but Haddock received a worrying message.

Olympic was barely a day out of New York when, at 10.50 p.m. on Sunday 14 April 1912, New York time, she received a wireless message that *Titanic* was signalling that she had struck an iceberg. Due to trouble with atmospheric conditions, initially it was difficult to ascertain whether it was really *Titanic* in trouble. Ten minutes later, it was clear the sister-ship was sending-out signals of distress. At 11.10 p.m., *Titanic* gave her position as 41° 46' north 50° 14' west: 'We have struck an iceberg.' Captain Haddock by this time had worked out the necessary course to reach the position, altering course towards her, while sending for the Chief Engineer 'to get up full power'. Unfortunately, *Olympic*'s distance from her stricken sister was 505 miles.

At 11.20 p.m. New York time, *Titanic* asked: 'Tell Captain get your boats ready and what is your position?'

Olympic replied: 'Commander, *Titanic*, 4.24 a.m. Greenwich Mean Time 40° 52' north 61° 18' west. Are you steering southerly to meet us? Haddock.'

It became apparent *Titanic* was in a bad condition when she signalled: '…we are putting the passengers off in small boats.' Haddock was well aware it would take time to reach her and only asked what weather she had, which fortunately was clear and calm.

Haddock signalled: 'Commander, *Titanic*, am lighting up all possible boilers as fast as can. Haddock,' at 11.50 p.m. By *Titanic*'s local time, it was 1.50 a.m. Her bow was largely submerged and she had less than an hour left. There was no chance that her sister ship would get there in time. As she rushed towards the disaster site *Olympic* was continually calling *Titanic* only to receive no reply.

By 7.45 a.m. New York time, about 9.00 a.m. ship's time, *Olympic* was still 310 miles from her sister, having covered 195 miles in 8 hours 35 minutes at fractionally under 23 knots, her low speed due to the fact that the additional boilers had needed some time to provide a good head of steam and thus additional power for the engines. However, her speed had increased considerably since she had first headed for her sister.

One passenger, Earl (surname unknown) wrote home: 'Monday morning, and a great morning it is too. The sea has quieted down some and the sun is shining today… *Titanic*, a sister-ship is in distress off the coast of Newfoundland. We have altered our course since three o'clock [sic] this morning and we are racing to her at full speed. Are making 25 knots an hour and expect to reach her about three o'clock this afternoon [sic].'

One passenger, the novelist R.H. Benson, wrote a diary of the day, stating: 'On coming down from mass this morning I heard a sentence from a lift boy that made me wonder…I asked what was the matter and was told that the *Titanic* had communicated with us that she was in a sinking condition; that we were moving full speed towards her…'

By that evening, passengers had 'been receiving various messages – e.g. that all passengers are saved…but now we have heard that only 675 are saved [sic: 712 later reported], crew and passengers, and that the passengers are chiefly women and children.'

All concerts on board were cancelled as a mark of respect and a quietness came upon the ship, *Olympic*'s passengers raising some £1,400 (nearly $7,000) to go towards a fund for the sunken liner's survivors.

'We steamed hard towards her for fourteen hours before we picked up the *Carpathia* signals and knew there was nothing more we could do,' Captain Haddock recalled. *Titanic* had sunk before any ships could reach her, the Cunard liner *Carpathia* arriving first, but only in time to rescue the survivors from the small fleet of lifeboats. In the event all the *Olympic* could do was notify New York of the disaster and assist with the transmission of survivor listings, *Carpathia*'s captain stating in response to Haddock's offer to embark survivors that it was not advisable for the survivors to see *Titanic*'s nearly identical-looking sister-ship.

Olympic arrived at Southampton Docks by 2.00 a.m. on 21 April 1912, roughly a day late, despite her fourteen-hour all-out-speed run.

'He [Haddock] was so fatigued,' the *Daily Mirror* reported on 22 April 1912, 'with his extra work during the last twenty-four hours and so upset by his distress at the terrible news of the *Titanic*, full details of which only reached him yesterday at Plymouth, that he slept through all this morning.'

As part of a public promise to provide enough lifeboats for every soul on board their ships, White Star saw collapsible boats from some of His Majesty's Transports installed on the boat deck, originally to number forty, but as the ship was by no means full and the additional boats crowded the deck, surplus boats were removed, and so twenty-four additional collapsibles

Hawke and *Olympic* after the collision. The White Star liner settled noticeably at the stern. (Author's collection)

made a total of forty-four boats, quite an adequate number. On sailing day, they were examined and found in good order, while the crew were quite able to lower them quickly.

However, believing the new boats unseaworthy, nearly 300 stokehold crew left the ship. *Olympic* moved into the Solent, while some 100 crew were hastily hired in Portsmouth and more in Liverpool and Sheffield.

Early the next morning Board of Trade Assistant Marine Surveyor Captain Maurice Harvey Clarke put the crew through their paces lowering the boats, but that time it was a lengthy process and the appearance of passengers on deck stopped the proceedings.

Union delegates were kept waiting for some time before boarding the ship for negotiations with Captain Haddock and others, including White Star's Southampton manager Philip E. Curry.

Some of the boats were lowered to the water to prove that they were safe, with pleasing results, although one of the Berthon collapsible boats was found to have water in it after two hours. A small hole in the outer skin and another below were found to be responsible, but two hours' leaking was easily disposed of within minutes.

The union delegates agreed to advise their members that the boats were safe if number 38 – the faulty one – was replaced, and in fact it was concluded that the damage had been caused during lowering. Unfortunately, the assurances had little effect.

The new crew were brough out to the ship by tug late on Thursday night, around 10.30 p.m. However, it proved only to be a temporary solution.

Those who had remained aboard were now unsatisfied with the new non-union crew, and so at around midnight there was commotion as fifty-three sailors hurried down the gangway to the tug which had brought out the new crew.

At 12.20 a.m., Friday 26 April 1912, with his ship some thirty-six hours behind schedule, Captain Haddock ordered them back, to no avail. He signalled by lamp to the cruiser HMS *Cochrane* for assistance: 'Crew deserting ship, request your assistance; Haddock, Master.'

The cruiser's ten-oar pinnace appeared at 1.15 a.m., to be made fast to the tug. Captain Goodenough was greeted by Haddock who apologised for bothering him, then after ten minutes' discussion in his cabin with Marine Superintendent Captain Benjamin Steel, the two men returned to the gangway, joined by a lieutenant and two other Navy men, to address the mutineers.

'Have you a spokesman among you?' Goodenough asked. 'What exactly is the matter?'

'We are all ready to go on board, sir, if they put on bona-fide firemen. The men say that these men who have just come on board from Portsmouth have not a dozen good

THE SOLENT COLLISION.
H MS HAWKE RETURNING TO HARBOUR
AFTER THE TERRIFIC IMPACT WITH THE OLYMPIC

Hawke's bow suffered severe damage in the collision. (Günter Bäbler collection)

men among the whole lot of them. The boats are not serviceable – the collapsible boats.' They thought it dangerous to set sail and objected to the non-union 'scab' crew. They refused to go to sea unless they had proof that the non-union men were qualified firemen and greasers.

'These men assured me that the boats were perfectly serviceable last night,' Haddock interrupted.

'Am I to take it from you men,' Goodenough slowly replied, '– that the men who are being shipped are not firemen?'

'Yes, sir.'

'I do not think it is a matter of pure seamanship,' Goodenough told them. 'You have no right to leave the ship having signed on. I have been thirty years at sea and know you cannot leave a ship you have started a voyage upon. It is my duty to tell you that what you are doing now in combining to leave the ship when she is afloat in an open stead, as she is now, is an act of open mutiny.'

Finally, he asked them: 'Are you coming back to your ship or are you not?'

'No, sir.'

Above left: Members of *Olympic*'s crew inspect the damage in the ship's side. (J.&C. McCutcheon collection)

Above right: Olympic returned to Southampton: 'Divers employed by the White Star company report that there is a large pear shaped hole in [the] shell plating below water…also the boss plating around [the] starboard [propeller] shaft is badly strained for a distance of about 12 to 14 feet; and [the] blades of [the] starboard propeller broken. It is understood that temporary repairs are to be made at Southampton, to enable the *Olympic* to be navigated to Belfast for docking, and that a further complete survey will then be made'. (Daniel Klistorner collection)

Irritated, if not furious, Goodenough asked his lieutenant to get a signaller, then decided to return to his cruiser to inform the Admiral Commanding-in-Chief at Portsmouth. As he left, the sailors laid on the deck of the tug to go to sleep, tiny compared to the enormous liner towering above them, but powerful and significant.

That Friday morning, *Olympic*'s Fifth Officer was ordered to go with the mutineers to Portsmouth, to hand them to Superintendent Moore on arrival.

Early that morning, yet more crew had been found to replace the deserters, while Captain Clarke would clear the ship for departure as soon as the replacements were found adequate. Seventy-two passengers had previously volunteered to work in the stokeholds, while the Duke of Sunderland had tried to raise a deck crew of volunteer yachtsmen, but by morning the ship was so far behind schedule that despite everyone's best efforts it was decided to cancel the voyage completely, while the passengers were compensated, and *Olympic* was berthed back at Southampton by 8.00 p.m. Many passengers hoped to catch the *Lusitania*, others boarding German liners at Le Havre and Southampton.

Fifty-three prisoners from the *Olympic* appeared in court at Portsmouth shortly after 3.00 p.m. on Friday 26 April 1912. Appearing on behalf of the White Star Line was Mr

C. Hiscock, while Mr S.H. Emanuel appeared for the crew belonging to the British Seafarers' Union and Mr G.H. King of Portsmouth appeared for the other defendants. The Merchant Shipping Act of 1894, section 225 sub-section B, stated that if any seaman was ruled guilty of wilful disobedience to a lawful command he would be liable to imprisonment for a period of not more than four weeks; and that was what the crew were charged with.

Olympic's Fifth Officer John E.J. Withers was grilled by Mr Emanuel. 'Was it because the men engaged did not know their work that the others left the ship?' he enquired.

'The only reason I have heard given was that non-union men were being employed,' Withers responded. He said that he had not heard any objections that the crew could not stoke a boiler or handle a lifeboat.

'Did you hear it said that the firemen refused to risk their lives with men in the stokehold who knew nothing about the work?'

'No.'

'Did any of them make complaints about the boats?'

'No.'

'Or that you had not proper tackle on board for lowering the "Berthon" boats?'

'No. As a matter of fact the "Berthon" boats were lowered and the tackle responded satisfactorily.'

After facing Emanuel, it was Mr King's turn.

Withers maintained that the crew had only complained about the non-union men to his knowledge.

'Do you know that 284 men left the ship at Southampton?'

'I don't know the number.'

'As a matter of fact were you not so short of a crew when you left Southampton that officers had to let go from the stern end of the ship?'

'Yes,' Withers admitted.

'And that you had to send stewards down to stoke the ship?' King persisted.

'I heard so.'

'You set out to pick up anything with a suit of clothes on?' he continued, displaying the total lack of respect that existed at the time between the various class levels of society. Mr Hiscock objected, but he was overruled by the bench who did not see any harm in the question. King continued: 'Well, I suggest that the men complained about the very badly manned ship.'

'Not personally to me,' Withers responded, admitting, 'I heard it in conversation.'

'I suggest that they complained that the boats put on board at Southampton were totally unseaworthy?'

'I don't know.'

'I will put it that three or four of the boats were totally unseaworthy?'

'They only complained about one boat that I know of.'

'I put it to you that, broadly, it was a "scratch" crew?'

'Well,' Withers smiled back, 'I don't know.'

'Is it true,' King began, irritated, 'that of the 200 men taken on board only three were able to show discharges to prove that they had ever been to sea as stokers?'

'I can't say.'

'Was it your intention,' King continued, 'to take on a lot of Frenchmen at Cherbourg?'

'This is the first that I have heard of it.'

'Do you know that Mr Curry [White Star's assistant local manager at Southampton] had given instructions to take on as many French firemen as possible at Cherbourg and complete the remainder at Queenstown?'

'I could not say.'

Magistrates allowed bail for the defendants until 11.00 a.m. the following Tuesday, 30 April 1912. The day the hearing finished, *Olympic*'s mails were forwarded to Liverpool from Southampton to sail on the arch-rival *Lusitania*.

Opening before the same bench magistrates, Second Engineer Charles William McKimm told the court that he and another officer from the *St Louis* had selected 168 firemen and greasers.

Norman Raeburn, appearing for White Star, questioned him.

'You selected them in the ordinary way?'

'Yes, by examining their hands, general appearance and pay books.' They were perfectly competent.

'Would you call firing a ship skilled labour?'

'No, sir, not skilled labour, but hard work.' The court laughed.

Many firemen didn't have signing-on books, but they were 'used to hard work' and some had been to sea before on *Adriatic*.

The Chairman, Sir Thomas Bramsdon, asked several questions.

'Is it fair to say that you were glad to get any men for the job?'

'I don't know. We could fill up with plenty of men.'

'Are we to understand that you wanted men badly?'

'Not badly.'

'Did you accept men you would not under ordinary circumstances?'

'Well, with regard–'

'Cannot you answer that? It is a simple question.'

'It is a hard one to answer.'

'It is a curious thing,' Bramsdon persisted, 'you will not answer yes or no.'

'Well, sir we should have taken them.'

They were fit for the job, but he admitted that better people could have been employed.

White Star's Southampton superintending engineer said extra men had been signed on in addition because they wanted to try and make-up some of the lost time.

(Even if the ship had been driven at over 23 knots, only one-third of the thirty-six hours or so could have been made up. Over 28 knots would have barely made-up the time, hard even for *Mauretania*.)

Purser Claude Lancaster said five-eighths of the men had been to sea before, but only seven had produced signing-on books without being asked.

Senior First Assistant Engineer William Joyce of the *St Louis*, who had helped select the crew, said that they were satisfactory.

'Would you have taken them aboard the *St Louis*?' Emanuel asked him.

'Yes.'

Captain Benjamin Steel, White Star's Southampton Marine Superintendent, stated that special wire falls had been provided for the boats. Many of the boats were twelve months old, but ten from the HMT *Soudan* were ten years old. They were sound, but no doubt looked their age.

Defending, Mr Emanuel concluded that under Section 458 of the Merchant Shipping Act, the White Star Line had a duty to ensure that their ships were seaworthy, but 'the placing of an incompetent crew on board amounted almost to rendering her as unseaworthy as if she had a hole in her hull'.

Mr King also spoke, saying that the deserters 'were anxious and willing to serve the company, but they refused to endanger their lives with the scallywags of Portsmouth and elsewhere, very many of whom were known to the bench and the police.'

After two hours' consideration, the Chairman told the court that although all of the charges against the men had been proved, it was considered 'inexpedient to send the men to prison or impose a fine'. Special circumstances dictated that they should be let off; specifically the sinking of the *Titanic* and the loss of many crew, whom some of the seamen would have known. 'The bench, however, hoped the differences would be settled, and that the men should return to work.'

If the 'mutineers' had been charged, then surely public opinion would have gone against the verdict. The president of the British Seafarer's Union advised the men that although they had achieved the (undue) cancellation of the voyage, in future they should consult the union before taking independent action.[61] *Olympic* was to remain at Southampton until her next voyage, with approved boats and crew.

Lord Mersey and his assessors came on board on 6 May 1912 to examine the lowering of a lifeboat and to look at the watertight doors. *Olympic* took part in some tests for the benefit of the inquiry, to establish how long it would take to turn two points at various speeds. With both the port side and starboard side reciprocating engines running at 74rpm ahead and the centre turbine in operation *Olympic* was making a speed of 21½ knots. The helm was ordered 'hard a starboard' and *Olympic* turned two points to starboard in 37 seconds, revealing the approximate time that it had taken the *Titanic* to turn that distance before the collision with the iceberg causing her to sink.

Olympic began her next round trip to New York on 15 May 1912. She carried 527 passengers, largely composed of third class as there were only eighty-eight first and ninety-seven second-class passengers on board. Perhaps the cancellation of her previous voyage and the loss of *Titanic* played a part, but although it was disappointing for a new ship it was similar to the number that the older *Oceanic* and *Majestic* carried that month. It was the first of five consecutive westbound crossings where she carried less than 1,000 passengers, although some of her eastbound passenger lists were better and before June was out she carried 666 first-class passengers from New York. By the start of September 1912, *Olympic* appeared to be doing much better and she brought into New York 713 first-class passengers. It was her highest number that year, slightly below the record she had made in 1911.

If her popularity began to recover as the summer of 1912 wore on, *Olympic* did not have an uneventful time. The White Star Line cannot have been pleased at her continuing run of bad luck, although if one account is to believed she avoided near-destruction a matter of weeks after *Titanic* sank. At the start of June 1912, *Olympic*'s eleventh eastbound crossing was drawing to a close and the light began to fade one evening at 10 p.m. Suddenly, the officer on watch was horrified to see broken water ahead and ordered an emergency 'full astern', sending a shudder throughout the ship as *Olympic* was brought to a halt. Owing to a navigational error, *Olympic* was far north of where she should have been and narrowly avoided going aground off Land's End. Captain Steel, White Star's marine superintendent at Southampton, was horrified when he learned of the error once *Olympic* was safely in port.

Olympic's lifeboats undergo tests, under the watchful eye of a number of interested passengers. This image helps to visualise the scenes on *Titanic*'s decks as her lifeboats were prepared. (*Illustrated London News*, 1912/ Author's collection)

He felt that it had to be reported to J. Bruce Ismay for an internal company investigation. Steel knew that 'if the information ever got out it would have done irreparable harm to the company… just imagine how the public would have reacted on hearing this immediately after the loss of the *Titanic*.' Captain Haddock, a public figure whose dismissal might have aroused suspicions, retained command and it appears that he won back the company's confidence over time. Nevertheless, the company kept a close eye on Haddock's performance.[62]

Olympic was delayed early in July 1912 when her bow grounded on a mud bank as she was leaving New York. On 8 August 1912, a blade came off her starboard propeller shortly after she had left Queenstown, delaying her arrival at New York. After completing the eastbound crossing, she left Plymouth for Belfast, where she would be dry docked and repaired. Harland & Wolff did the job and she was able to return to Southampton. She left for New York a day late and carried her large list of first-class passengers. Unfortunately, as she returned to Plymouth on the eastbound crossing she lost another propeller blade – this time from the port propeller, and the third blade to be lost that year! The vibration caused some of her second-class passengers to rush on deck, worried that a collision had occurred. Clearly, the missing blade needed to be replaced, necessitating another trip back to Belfast, but she completed one final round trip to New York at reduced speed. Her average speed was cut to less than 18 knots on the westbound crossing. Perhaps it was this delay that prompted 'a cruel rumour' that *Olympic* had foundered, resulting in numerous enquiries at the White Star Line's Southampton offices from concerned people who had relatives on board. The White Star Line eventually announced that she would be returning to Belfast a month earlier than expected, for her annual overhaul and an extensive refit.

During her refit from 10 October 1912 to 2 April 1913, *Olympic*'s hull was gutted. Several of the watertight bulkheads were extended up to B-deck and an inner watertight skin was fitted that ran the length of the boiler and engine room compartments:

The inner shell is very strongly constructed, so as to withstand heavy water pressure if necessary. The frames are of heavy channel steel, and the longitudinals, giving increased strength to the structure, extend the entire length of the double skin. The inner shell or hull, as it might be called, consists of strong steel plating. The space between the outer and inner shells has been specially subdivided, both vertically and horizontally, by retaining out to the inner shell and the introduction of intermediate watertight vertical divisions between the two shells, while the top…of the structure and upper longitudinal have been specially fitted as watertight flats, so that each side of the ship has been converted into a series of watertight compartments.

An alteration was made to the liner's pumping apparatus, with the addition of an extra line of piping, large in diameter, running through the ship, enabling all pumps to draw through it in case of emergency, so that any watertight compartment could be pumped. As an added safety feature, the apparatus could be operated from E-deck, if it was not possible otherwise.

If *Olympic* were involved in the sort of collision that had sunk her ill-fated sister, then she would be able to survive. Four of the compartments forward would be flooded, and the watertight inner skin would restrict flooding in the forward boiler rooms. The ship could now float with six watertight compartments open to the sea. It was too difficult to install longitudinal bulkheads because of the internal boiler arrangements and the naval architects at Harland & Wolff thought an inner skin better. Longitudinal watertight compartmentalisation would cause the ship to list seriously and unduly if holed (in fact this was exactly what happened to the doomed *Lusitania* three years later).

In fact, to extend the watertight bulkheads as they were extended, 'meant taking many of the boilers out of the ship and this, in turn, of course, meant landing the funnels, taking all the uptakes apart and removing all the mass of platforms, piping, etc…in order to get the boilers out and the new steelwork in…It also meant an almost complete re-arrangement of the enormous and complex piping system and a more than considerable amount of electric rewiring…apart from the actual new structural work itself.' According to one expert, the ship was now 'in all probability the safest afloat'.[63] Due to the inner skin, in boiler room 5 the central boiler, 20ft long with a diameter of 15ft 9in, was replaced with a new smaller boiler with a diameter of 13ft 6in.

Olympic's propellers underwent change during this refit. Her central turbine-driven propeller, originally with a diameter of 16ft 6in and a pitch of 14ft 6in, was changed to a propeller of 17ft in diameter and a pitch of 14ft, meaning that revolutions would increase to produce the same power; the new propeller design quite probably had three blades instead of the original four, although, if this was the case, the design was changed to the original configuration of four blades following the war. Both wing propellers were changed – from a diameter of 23ft 6in and pitch of 34ft 6in to a diameter of 22ft 9in and a pitch of 36ft. The higher pitch meant that the propeller would theoretically move the ship further for a given number of revolutions, but at the same time the engine had to work harder to achieve the same revolutions, which may be the explanation for the diameter being slightly reduced.

Ventilation systems were upgraded and improved, while heating apparatus was altered, and the engineers', officers' and crew accommodation were improved.

It had been planned to outfit the ship with sufficient lifeboats to accommodate all on board, but although it was one year after the *Titanic* disaster there was still a high

Once it had been confirmed that the voyage to New York had been abandoned, a number of *Olympic*'s passengers were able to leave the ship. (*Illustrated London News*, 1912/Author's collection)

demand for lifeboats; in fact, even the smaller liners frequently had not had enough lifeboats to accommodate all on board. The high demand meant that although Harland & Wolff had constructed the twenty additional wood lifeboats needed, they had only completed sixteen of the thirty-two required deck lifeboats (these fifty-two additional boats would supplement sixteen original lifeboats for a total complement of sixty-eight boats, it had been planned). On 11 March 1913 they informed the Board of Trade that 'to get over the difficulty temporarily' they would keep ten (April 1912) Berthon boats aboard, supplemented by six Henderson collapsible boats; in the meantime they were 'doing all possible to expedite the delivery of the remaining sixteen decked lifeboats' which would be 'placed on board at the earliest possible opportunity'.

While *Olympic* stayed at Belfast some small modifications were made to the accommodation. On promenade deck A, between the reading and writing room and the forward first-class entrance, there was a space for storage of deck chairs that was not used much. Five extra first-class cabins were installed here, also occupying part of what had been the reading and writing room, which had not proved as popular as expected; these initially did not have their own private bathrooms but there were two bathrooms and one lavatory. Other changes included two more cabins, one port and starboard, off the aft grand staircase, like the last-minute cabins that had been added to her sister. The forward third of the promenade deck was not enclosed like *Titanic*'s had been, presumably because the unbroken lifeboat fence did not allow open sea views on the boat deck and the enclosure of the deck could have caused difficulties when lowering the lifeboats, but by keeping the promenade deck open the boats could all be lowered to this level and loaded quite safely and efficiently. One further alteration on the promenade deck was the addition of extra cloakroom accommodation.

Changes to B-deck included the installation of a 'café parisien', similar to the café on the *Titanic*, in place of what was a section of second-class promenade on the starboard side aft. On the port side of the second-class promenade, the *à la carte* restaurant was extended. Two first-class cabins and a wine room to the starboard side, forward of the restaurant but aft of the aft first-class staircase, were taken-out and a small reception room for the restaurant was added. This reception room could seat around thirty-two people. The promenade space outside the first-class suites and bank of cabins forward remained – enclosing it would have reduced the promenade area available to first-class passengers because of the extra boats on the boat deck.

C-deck remained unaltered, but the first-class staterooms forward on D-deck were slightly changed. Several staterooms were converted to private bathrooms to the staterooms next door. There were a few small alterations to the second-class accommodation similar to those in first class.

Olympic's passenger capacities had changed to 735 first-class, 675 second-class and 1,030 third-class passengers; she now had a net tonnage of 22,350 tons, the highest it would ever be, while her gross tonnage increased by 1,035 tons to 46,359grt.

The White Star Line naturally wanted to state to the travelling public the great improvements made for the *Olympic*'s safety. An advertisement stated 'The new *Olympic*, "virtually two ships in one"…thus enhancing to the utmost the safety of the vessel,' and it described the modifications[64] in detail. Public confidence in the ship returned and memories of the *Titanic* disaster gradually faded.

Although there was soon fierce new competition, especially from the ever-threatening German liners, 'the next 1½ years saw her popularity mounting steadily'. By August 1914, the line's flagship had established 'a reputation second to none'.[65]

After June 1913, two months after re-entering service, *Olympic* was no longer the holder of the now clichéd title 'Largest Liner in the World', as the 52,000grt German liner *Imperator* had entered service for the Hamburg Amerika Line. However, *Olympic* was still the largest British ship and would remain so until the time of the *Queen Mary*, only briefly displaced while her second sister was in service.★

Olympic's running mates, *Oceanic* and the ageing *Majestic*, were hardly ideal partners. She enjoyed a successful year in 1913, carrying almost 32,000 passengers, which was fractionally under half the total passengers carried by all three ships. *Majestic* herself would be withdrawn from service the following year, by which time *Olympic* carried nearly two thirds of the traffic running alongside *Oceanic*. Although it is popularly believed that White Star's plans for the liner *Germanic* envisaged her as *Titanic*'s replacement, in fact she was conceived as a smaller liner for the Liverpool service, to enter service by 1916. Harold Sanderson described her as 'a larger ship than the *Adriatic*.' Her accommodation would be further improved, while she would have the same triple screw configuration as *Olympic*. She was projected at over 33,000 gross tons with a service speed of 19 knots.

Olympic settled into the schedule, but there were occasional dramas. Early in February 1914, while she was travelling from New York to Southampton, stormy seas smashed nine portholes: eight of them amidships in the first-class dining saloon and another in a potato-

---

★ Contrary to popular belief, the Cunard liner *Aquitania* – launched in April 1913 and in service by May 1914 – was not the largest British liner. In terms of tonnage, *Aquitania* was smaller with a tonnage of 45,647grt. *Aquitania* was longer at 901ft compared to *Olympic*'s 882½ft, but her tonnage was 800 tons less.

cleaning room on the deck below. Several passengers were injured by glass, either from the broken portholes or the shattered stained glass windows inside. The damage caused a storm of another sort when a team of professional gamblers took advantage of some of the first-class passengers who were betting on the day's run. If one news report could be believed, 'the high seas smashed in several portholes on Saturday when the day's run was slightly more than 500 miles. The passengers figured that 50 miles deduction would be about right on account of the storm and so the high number for Sunday's pool was 445. The gamblers bought in the low field and then managed to get passengers to lay heavy bets that the low field had no chance to win. When the *Olympic* lay to for a couple of hours to repair the damaged portholes the passengers who had made the bets became suspicious.' One of the ship's officers denied that the gamblers had any 'inside information' but 'this did not shake the belief of the losers'. Following a threat of physical violence, 'the gamblers took the hint and sneaked away to their staterooms, where they remained throughout the rest of the trip.'

The outbreak of war occurred while *Olympic* was westbound for New York. Captain Haddock halted the usual wireless reports, ordered portholes covered, stopped the showing of any lights on the promenade decks, and arranged for the use of dimmer emergency lamps rather than the usual interior lighting. The ship's speed was increased and she arrived at quarantine on Tuesday evening, where she anchored for the night before docking the next morning, 5 August 1914. Passengers thanked Haddock for bringing them safely into New York. Although a number of them thought that *Olympic* had exceeded 25 knots, he 'admitted that she had been going at full speed, which meant about 24 knots'. Artist May Wilson Preston described the arrival at the Ambrose Channel Lightship: 'The big liner, with her decks and port holes in darkness, stopped in the heaving sea, the interested passengers crowding the rail of the promenade deck, watching the bobbing light on the pilot boat bringing the pilot from the cutter to the *Olympic*.'

Olympic departed New York for Liverpool on Sunday 9 August 1914, 'suddenly, without passengers, mails or cargo'. As she moved down the river, the crew of the German liner *Vaterland* looked forlornly at her, as she was bound for home; while they would be in New York for the foreseeable future, officially awaiting orders as to what to do. *Olympic's* crew 'lined the decks and greeted them with derisive gestures'. While she departed, an officer of the *Florida* came aboard to check her papers, which 'were made out for Liverpool when Captain Haddock cleared her on Saturday at Custom House'. Indeed, that day Philip Franklin had made an announcement in which he stated that the *Olympic* was ready to sail at any hour, so it had come as little surprise when she did the following morning. She had over 6,000 tons of coal on board, and while it was planned for the ship to use the northern track, it was understood that all of the ship's twenty-nine boilers would be fired, seven of them usually being held in reserve, in order to allow an average speed of 24 knots to be achieved with the aid of the Gulf Stream. *Olympic* was escorted as far as Sable Island by the cruiser *Essex*, after which she would rely on her swift speed to maintain her safety against German submarines, before being escorted again by the *Drake* once she was near the Irish coast. Indeed, the ship was blessed with good luck and she completed the journey successfully.

The White Star Line improvised a passenger service out of Liverpool. *Olympic* arrived in New York on 29 August 1914 with no fewer than 810 first-class passengers crowded on board, the highest number she ever carried; on her return, the figure was eighty-seven first-class passengers. Passengers were naturally leaving Europe after war's outbreak and eastbound numbers were very low. Her next westbound crossing saw another large number of passengers: 776 first, 711 second and 558 third, but the White Star Line directed her away from Liverpool and Captain Haddock was told to return to Glasgow. Even this did not last. She left Glasgow for New York with 956 passengers in total, but the return crossing had very few passengers booked. *Olympic* would be withdrawn from commercial service, while other ships such as *Baltic* and *Adriatic* accommodated a reduced demand from passengers as the year drew to a close.

Dr Beaumont later described: 'We sailed from New York on 21 October 1914 with the smallest number of passengers that the *Olympic* has ever carried. There were thirty-five first cabin, eighteen second cabin and one hundred steerage,' a total of 153 passengers. After the New York departure, some passengers were shocked by the news, as Bandmaster Beames recalled: '…we heard for the first time that the north-east coast of Ireland was reported to have been mined and that certain shipping men in New York had bet as high as forty to one that the ship would not reach Greenock safely. All went well, however, until 10.00 a.m. on 27 October 1914 when we sighted Tory Island of the Irish coast…'

HMS *Audacious*, under the command of Captain C.R. Dampier, struck a mine off Tory Island during gunnery practice, one of two hundred mines laid by the converted German liner *Berlin*.[66] Captain Haddock spotted the sinking battleship and stopped the ship, giving the order for the crew to man the ship's lifeboats. 'Fourteen lifeboats were swung out on the port side first,' recalled one passenger, 'under the direction of Staff Captain Metcalff, but they were swung in again, and the boats were lowered from the starboard side. They were manned by sailors, firemen and stewards from the *Olympic* without any excitement. When the order was given the stewards all rushed for the boats and a bell boy, not [yet] fifteen years old, climbed into lifeboat number 2 and hid under a thwart, where he was not discovered until the boat had left the ship.'

Lifeboats from HM Troopship *Soudan* lie ready to be fitted to *Olympic* after the sinking of her sister. Two of the dockside cranes are lowering lifeboats on to the ship's portside boat deck. It is popularly believed that *Titanic*'s lifeboats were reused on *Olympic*. In fact, they were still at New York when *Olympic* returned to Belfast in October 1912; and her permanent additional lifeboats, installed during 1912-13, were different in size. (J.&C. McCutcheon collection)

Stewardess Violet Jessop – who seemed to be on each *Olympic* whenever something happened – watched as the boats made the perilous journey to the battleship in heavy seas, rowed back, were raised, and the crew came aboard. She noticed the crew's simple wonder as they compared *Olympic*'s luxurious appointments to their previous 'austere surroundings'.[67] Attention now turned to the sinking battleship and efforts to keep her afloat.

In 'a splendid piece of seamanship', the destroyer HMS *Fury* came right up to the liner and took a light steel hawser over to the sinking battleship, where the crew stationed on the forecastle made it secure. Efforts would be made to tow the *Audacious* into Lough Swilly, more than 20 miles distant.

Captain Haddock demonstrated perfect manoeuvring skills, beginning a slow tow at about 2.00 p.m. Alas, the heavy seas effected even the enormous *Olympic*, and when her stern rose slightly the hawser snapped owing to the battleship's weight moving in the trough of the sea.

On the next attempt, HMS *Liverpool* was asked to tow. Although *Fury* carried the line over, it fouled one of *Liverpool*'s propellers and was cut. By 4.00 p.m., with the stricken battleship deteriorating, a final attempt was made to try and take her in tow. The collier *Thornhill* was asked to try and perhaps all involved hoped that it would be 'third time lucky'. Once again, *Fury* took the line over to *Thornhill*, but it parted when it became taught.

The skies were darkening and *Audacious*' quarterdeck was awash. Captain Dampier signalled to Captain Haddock that *Olympic* had better depart for Lough Swilly. The lifeboats were left in the event that they were needed for saving the remaining crew. *Olympic* put into Lough Swilly that evening. Meanwhile, *Liverpool* was ready to take on board *Audacious*' crewmen when it should prove necessary.

For *Audacious*, the end came barely hours after the *Olympic* had left the scene. At 6.15 p.m. she was abandoned, her list reaching 30° by 6.50 p.m., and the vessel capsized at 8.45 p.m. She blew up at 9.00 p.m., in 'a tremendous explosion', before settling rapidly at the stern and disappearing under the sea. Several passengers and crew aboard *Olympic* observed the battleship's death from Lough Swilly, in spite of the distance. Passenger Hugh Griffiths recalled: 'I was standing on deck just after two bells had struck, when suddenly a bright glow shot up 3–400 feet into the sky in a direct line from the spot where we had left the *Audacious*. It lit up the whole ship's decks like day for a period of about ten seconds, and then came a low, rumbling report that was re-echoed from the shore. When the 200 men who were left on the *Audacious* were brought on board…about midnight by trawlers and destroyers they told us that the *Audacious* had been blown-up by wireless orders from the Admiralty[!].'

Olympic then returned to Lough Swilly where she anchored from 27 October 1914 to 2 November 1914, before returning to Belfast to be laid up, and her passengers were forced to remain on board for a long while so that they wouldn't be able to say anything to anybody else about the rescue, although the American millionaire Charles Schwab was given preferential treatment and allowed to disembark.[68] This predictably futile attempt to suppress the news ultimately failed, although the fact that the Admiralty mocked up the Canadian Pacific Line's *Montcalm* to resemble the lost battleship illustrates the lengths that they went to.[69]

Despite the censorship of the British media, American papers were able to gain some information, although of course little or nothing appeared at all in the British press. On 30 October 1914, the *New York Times* reported:

London, Oct. 29 – A notice posted this afternoon at Lloyd's, which caused considerable excitement, was to the affect that coast guards at Malin Head, on the North coast of Ireland, saw an unidentified vessel torn asunder and sunk by what was supposed to be contact with a mine. No further information was obtainable…

Another report in the paper, on the same page, read:

Olympic Avoids Mines
Lands Passengers In [County] Donegal To Escape Perils Farther North.
London, Oct. 29 – The steamer *Olympic*, which left New York on 21 October 1914 for Glasgow [sic], having been warned by wireless that there were German mines off Tory Island, put into Lough Swilly, on the North coast of Ireland today.
The passengers were loaded and sent by special train to Londonderry, Lough Swilly, in Country Donegal, Ireland.

By 15 November 1914 the truth was out in America.

Some days after the rescue, five boats from *Olympic* were salvaged by Tory Island inhabitants, although a sixth was driven ashore in bad weather onto the rocky cliff-bound north-eastern side of the island and subsequently smashed to pieces. James Ward, Lloyd's Tory Island agent, later wrote to the White Star Line on the behalf of the salvers, for although they had said that the case was in the hands of the Admiralty, by January 1915 nothing had been done. The Receiver of Wrecks, accompanied by the assistant naval officer, went to Tory Island and on 10 February 1915 they were able to inspect the boats.[70] Four of the boats, salved by Fisherman Ned Rogers and his crew, were valued at £39 and the fifth, salved by Denis Dougan and his crew, was estimated to be worth £9, or £48 for the five boats altogether. It would have been difficult to move the boats from the remote island, but considering the difficulty the locals had had in salvaging, salvage was taken to be one-third of their estimated value, which the fishermen accepted with reluctance, as they had expected a sum nearer to £50, based on two *Californian* lifeboats salvaged the previous summer.

Extracts from one of Ward's letters to White Star questioning the loss of the lifeboats confirm the curiosity of many people and the standard of success of the Admiralty's 'information blackout' regarding the *Audacious* disaster:

…By the way, how did the *Olympic* lose those boats? Or how did she come to lower them at all off Tory? It has been a puzzle to me and I've never seen it explained or solved since.

In the place I saw the *Olympic* pass homeward close to Tory Island about noon on 27 October [1914] – (just a day after the loss of the *Manchester Commerce* by mines off Tory Island). When the *Olympic* had gone past Tory Island and perhaps as far east as Horn Head or thereabouts she wheeled round and went off to a point in the horizon north-east from Tory Island and there "brought-up". At the same time there was a rush of warships of various descriptions – cruisers, destroyers, etc. – converging from different points towards the same spot and each ship as she arrived brought up and lay there. I could see with my telescope that all were deeply engrossed in something, but it was too distant to enable me to see what was going on or what had happened. They lay there till night, and I don't know how long thereafter. It was

An interesting, mottled view of Southampton docks around 1913. *Olympic*, on the left at berth 43, is considerably larger than the other steamers, including two American Line ships at berths 46 and 47. (Author's collection)

likely at that place that the *Olympic* lowered her lifeboats. Then there must have really been some serious occurrence there. Probably when returning to Lough Swilly from that scene the *Olympic* was towing those lifeboats astern, the tow-rope broke and the boats drifted before the wind, a day or so later, to Tory Island where they were picked up as already described.

By the way a life buoy marked in gold lettering 'HMS *Audacious*' was washed ashore here and picked up by a fisherman about those same days too.

I closely scanned the newspaper for weeks after, but never could see anything about all that commotion in which your *Olympic* played a prominent part – and also those other warships. However about a month later I saw in some London paper a quotation from an article in *The Times* criticising our Government censorship of war news in which that article hinted at some catastrophe that had occurred about 'a month ago' – a catastrophe well known then in Portsmouth and in all the Naval ports; known and published all over America; and even all over Germany but yet not allowed to appear in any of our own papers. I reckoned 'a month back' and found it practically coincided with date your *Olympic* was to the fore off Tory. I've been wondering if it was the *Audacious* was in trouble that day...[71]

★ ★ ★

On 7 May 1915 the Cunarder *Lusitania* was disastrously lost to a German torpedo off the southern Irish coast. It marked a further reduction in the possible ships available for troop transport, particularly since numerous large liners were laid up.

The Admiralty[72] wrote: 'so many ships having been taken, it is impossible to procure ships without seriously interfering with other services such as the food and munition supply; except by taking the large ships now laid up like the *Olympic* and *Aquitania*. These ships will accommodate large numbers – between 5,000 and 6,000 men each – but the risk of loss from submarine attack owing to their great size is only justifiable if the emergency warrants it being taken…'

It was, however, decided that such ships were too useful a resource to waste and on 11 May 1915 *Mauretania* and *Aquitania* became military transports at the rate of fifteen

The White Star Line advertised the 'New *Olympic*' when she returned to service in 1913. (Author's collection)

shillings per gross ton per month. On 26 June 1915 the rates were fixed at £10,000 per ship per month, but by 23 August 1915 it was revised. From then on, ten shillings was paid to Cunard per gross ton per month, amounting to £15,350 for *Mauretania* and £22,820 for *Aquitania*, quite an increase on the previous agreement, but still well below what the company was entitled to; the favourable rate had been agreed in order for Cunard to retain some of their smaller vessels.

Meanwhile, enquiries were being made regarding the *Olympic's* availability, capacity, speed and range. In many of these respects she was similar to the *Aquitania*, ideal for trooping to the Mediterranean campaigns. While *Olympic's* designed service speed of 21 knots allowed her to travel over 4,250 miles without even using her reserve coalbunker, or some 8½ days of steaming, and was more than adequate for avoiding submarines, Harold Sanderson was able to confirm that she had previously maintained 24¼ knots for twenty-four hours in the Atlantic. It was expected that *Olympic* would not have to carry more than 6,000 men (5,400 soldiers, 200 non-commissioned officers and 400 officers), which was within her capabilities, although she would have been able to carry 7,000 if necessary.

However, on 21 June 1915, Harland & Wolff informed Harold Sanderson that *Olympic* would need to be dry-docked if she were to become a transport, as she had been laid up for some time in dirty water at Belfast. It would be impossible for this to be done at Belfast until the end of the month due to the tides, but the divisional transport officer in Liverpool confirmed that the Gladstone Dock could not be used either because it was currently occupied by the *Aquitania*. If *Olympic* could be moored at the Sloyne Cunard Buoy in Liverpool, at least ten days would be needed to prepare the ship. It would be possible for the work to be done in the Belfast dry-dock if the Admiralty gave her priority, but in the event *Olympic* was not needed.

It was not to last. Towards the end of August 1915, *Aquitania* was outfitted for hospital duties, costing £63,000 including her trooping, and she became HMHS *Aquitania* on 4 September 1915. *Mauretania* followed her on 22 October 1915, at a cost of £68,000. Increasing demand for these ships from the medical authorities dictated that the still-unfinished *Britannic* was taken over for duties at the end of the year, costing £90,000. The resulting loss of troop-carrying capacity was heavy and on 2 September 1915 Harold Sanderson was advised: 'SS *Olympic* required for government service…'

He accepted the rate of ten shillings per gross ton per month, the same rate as Cunard had accepted, which amounted to a little over £23,000 per month. However, Harold Sanderson was unable to get the captain he wanted. As *Olympic* was 'quite an exceptional ship' he requested that Captain Haddock be reappointed if the Admiralty would spare him from their service at Belfast, adding: 'if this cannot be arranged, we will have to make the next best appointment.' He suggested that it would be quicker for the ship to be completed at Liverpool or Southampton as if she was completed at the shipyard it would not be possible to coal her at the same time, which the Admiralty agreed with, getting the Gladstone Dock ready. Harland & Wolff were able to provide boats and rafts for everybody on board. Although initially 'hopeful of succeeding' to re-appoint Captain Haddock, the Admiralty decided in the end that he was too important to them where he was and so Sanderson decided to appoint Captain Bertram Fox Hayes.

Captain Bertram Fox Hayes would command the *Olympic* longer than any other of the vessel's commanders. He had joined the White Star Line back in March 1889 and by 1891 Hayes was fourth officer of the *Teutonic*. Having held an Extra Master's Certificate since

1897, Hayes was a commander on the Royal Naval Reserve's 'Active list', and by June 1899 he had risen to command the first White Star Line ship with the name *Britannic*. He commanded the White Star Line's 1909 vessel *Laurentic* on the Canadian route for two years and was to later become the White Star Line's Commodore.

When Hayes first went aboard *Olympic*, in the Gladstone Dock, she was 'more or less in a condition of bewilderment'. He nearly got into trouble during his first interview with the principal naval transport officer, who was very concerned that Hayes was not in uniform, despite the fact that merchant service officers always wore civilian clothes on land. Other than that, the interview generally seemed to go well.[73]

It is interesting to record the layout of *Olympic* as a troopship, for records do survive. Her gymnasium remained in use serving its original function throughout the early stages of her trooping career, and may even have remained in use as a gymnasium until after the spring 1917 refitting. On the shelter deck, C, officers were berthed in the comfortable first-class staterooms, the senior non-commissioned officers being allocated to the starboard aide. Aft at this deck level, the second-class library had become a 'troops hospital' with one hundred beds. Just forward of the after grand staircase, the maids' and valets' dining saloon had become the 'warrant officers' mess', while the third-class smoke room and general room, aft in the poop deck, had sleeping accommodation for 200 troops in hammocks. Her famed first-class dining room and reception on D-deck became available as hammock and mess arrangements for 1,804 and 1,499 troops respectively, while the second-class dining saloon became an officers' mess. 'Upper deck E' housed numerous troops forward and aft, with NCOs amidships, while crew found accommodation on the port side, along the famous 'Park Lane'. All in all, *Olympic* could accommodate more than 6,000 troops.

In September 1915 *Olympic* left for her first trooping run, sailing under the merchant 'Red Duster' rather than the transport flag Blue Ensign, as it was considered that the naval flag was an incentive to enemy attacks. Her official designation was 'T2810', transport number 2,810. After conversion, *Olympic* sailed from Liverpool via Gibraltar and La Spezia to Mudros.[74] Once there, troops would be disembarked to fight in the Dardanelles and other Middle-Eastern campaigns. As she was a very important vessel, Hayes discovered that two guns were mounted aboard, a twelve-pounder gun forward and one 4.7in gun aft, while four Naval ratings were aboard to handle them.

Even on *Olympic*'s first voyage she was to encounter enemy action. On 1 October 1915, as she approached Mudros, survivors from the French steamer *Provincia* were sighted, their vessel having been sunk by an enemy submarine. Captain Hayes decided to stop and rescue the survivors, but he did so at considerable risk. Not only had he stopped his enormous vessel, but he had stopped in an area of the Aegean Sea where submarines were dangerously active. *Olympic* would have been an unmissable target and even if she had put on maximum speed if a submarine was spotted, it would have taken some minutes for her to speed out of danger, during which time she could easily have been hit and damaged, or even sunk. If she had been torpedoed with 6,000 people on board the loss could have been terrible, but it seems to have been another one of those occasions when she was blessed with far more luck than her sisters ever had. Upon rescuing the survivors the lifeboats were sunk and the journey resumed at full speed.

Several hours later, a submarine's periscope was spotted six points off the port bow. Hayes ordered the ship's course to be altered, while the guns fired on it and she zigzagged until the danger had passed. A number of soldiers on board mentioned sightings of a torpedo passing astern of *Olympic*, as did Hayes himself, but perhaps the perceived dangers of wartime were playing tricks on them. After sinking *Provincia*, *U33* left the scene. No mention was made of encountering *Olympic*, nor did *U33*'s log record any torpedo being fired, even though she was the only German submarine in the vicinity and every torpedo had to be accounted for.

Although Admiral de Robeck criticised Hayes' actions, French Vice-Admiral Dartige du Fournet proposed to honour him with a Gold Medal of Honour.[75] The French wrote to the Admiralty Transport Division on 21 November 1915 notifying them and requesting to know Hayes' name so that it could be engraved on the medal. The Transport Division were surprised to hear of the rescue and no doubt even more surprised when they heard of the proposed honour, noting on 27 November 1915; 'although prompted no doubt by the highest motives [this rescue action] was dangerous, as the *Olympic* had 6,000 troops on board at the time.'

As she was under naval discipline, *Olympic*'s captain being in the Royal Naval Reserve, the director of transport submitted the French Naval Attaché's letter to the Admiralty in case they desired 'to take up with the French authorities the propriety of such a presentation'. In the event, it seems the medal was awarded.

It would be the most dangerous time of the liner's existence. Strict instructions were issued along with the normal Sailing Orders for ships entering the Mediterranean, stipulating among other things for a constant wireless watch to be kept east of Cape Matapan for submarine warnings, which were addressed to all British merchant ships and would not be answered. 'High speed is the best protection against submarine attack,' captains were told, it being preferable for ships to use longer courses rather than reducing speed for arrival times. Good lookout was 'essential', while watertight doors were to be closed at all times, navigating lights were to only be used when absolutely necessary, and otherwise the ships should be thoroughly darkened. Bells were not to be sounded and no calls sounded on deck.

Olympic enjoyed more luck than her sisters ever did, particularly during the early phase of her war service in the Mediterranean. Captain Hayes remembered a plane from Bulgaria dropping bombs around the ship during her final round trip to Mudros. The day before she arrived, a submarine was sighted on 23 February 1916: *Olympic*'s guns opened fire, but *U35*'s log made clear that she had been unable to mount an attack on the four funnelled steamer; and on 28 February 1916, the day after she left Mudros, she reported sighting the same submarine.

On one occasion, Hayes recalled, arriving at Spezia to take on coal, there was no Pilot boat about, so he was forced to steam slowly toward the breakwater; it was then that there was a gun shot and an Italian destroyer rushed out signalling for *Olympic* to follow as there were mines in the area.

The routine aboard His Majesty's Transport *Olympic* is recorded in a partial diary of her second trip.[76] On 14 November 1915 at 6.00 p.m., 490 officers, 24 warrant officers, 452 non-commissioned officers and 5,126 soldiers embarked for the Mediterranean, a total of 6,092 people, who were allocated their quarters and issued rations of tea. A mere hour later, there was a lecture by the Officer Commanding Troops to all of the officers in the smoking room.

Early the following day, at 6.30 a.m., *Olympic* left Liverpool's Prince's Dock escorted by two destroyers. Physical training took up most of the day apart from meals, but at 10.00 a.m. there was a one-hour officers' parade and inspection of quarters and at 3.00 p.m. there was an emergency practice alarm when troops had to quickly fall-in at their alarm stations. Lights were out at 10.00 p.m.

Olympic and the Caledonian Steam Packet Co. paddle steamer *Duchess of Fife* on the Clyde on 3 October 1914. *Olympic* had left New York on 26 September 1914, returning to Gourock rather than Liverpool. (J.&C. McCutcheon collection)

16 November 1915 saw the escorts depart at 4.00 a.m., while the day's training and parades followed the same course, although there was a 9.00 p.m. officers' conference in the smoking room to those in charge of the various decks. Various regiments underwent cholera vaccinations.

Similar parades continued the next day as standard routine, but at 10.30 a.m. there was an alarm for the lifeboat crews to stand at boat stations.

By 20 November 1915, *Olympic* was well on her way to the Aegean and passed Malta at 8.15 p.m. During that day a Greek steamer was observed under escort by two torpedo boats and three trawlers on patrol.

On 22 November 1915 at 12.15 p.m., *Olympic* entered Mudros harbour and dropped anchor. Unfortunately, due to inefficient organisation it was not for some time that the process of disembarking and turning-around was completed, while various ratings embarked. Orders were received on 2 December 1915 for all officers and troops to be ready to disembark the next day, and four hospital cases disembarked to join the *Mauretania*. The next day, 1,220 officers and other ranks disembarked and by 5 December 1915 *Olympic* was able to return home via La Spezia, where she disembarked various regiments who had boarded at Mudros.

By early 1916, however, following the disastrous failure and abandonment of the Gallipoli campaign, the forces were locked in 'bloody stalemate', resulting in a reduction of the required trooping capacity.

The fact that so many troopers would not be needed was probably greeted with enthusiasm by Harold Sanderson, who was losing considerable money on the victualling of many of his ships serving as troopers.[77] On 20 January 1916 White Star had written to the Admiralty Transport Division, stating that although they had been given £6,953 4*s* 9*d* for the cost on *Olympic*'s first trip, £9,667 12*s* 7*d* had actually been spent on food alone, resulting in a loss of £2,713 17*s* 10*d*. On *Megantic* they had lost £419 and *Northland* £582 11*s* 9*d*. They suggested new rates of 6*s* 6*d* per officer per day, 3*s* per non-commissioned officer and 1*s* 9*d* per day for normal soldiers. New rates had been under consideration in any case, but these were still not as high as requested. On 29 January 1916 the Transport Division pointed-out that the company's suggested rates were 'considerably in excess of those quoted by other companies as sufficient'. They said they could 'not concede preferential treatment to any one company'.

On 23 January 1916[78] it was suggested 'that it might be possible to use *Olympic* for the conveyance of troops to India via the Cape'. Upon investigation it was found that even at 18–19 knots she would need 485 to 550 tons of coal per day, economical for a ship her size, but it would certainly be preferable for her to be faster. Yet, even at these speeds, she would need 8,760 tons to reach Cape Town. (Maintaining a comfortable 22½ knots, she would have needed nearly 10,000 tons.) *Olympic* had been built for the short transatlantic run and so could only accommodate 6,060 tons of coal in her bunkers, 1,070 tons in her reserve coalbunker, and 300 tons on her stokehold plates, a total of 7,430 tons; or, in other words she was 1,330 tons short. However, if the reserve coalbunker was enlarged, sacrificing cargo space, she would be able to carry the amount of coal required. The double bottom would also have to be partly flooded to provide 5,400 tons of the necessary water (at nineteen knots, *Olympic* required 105 tons of boiler water and 75 tons of drinking water per day). Loaded this heavily, however, she would draw 38ft 6in, a displacement approaching 58,000 tons. Over the 15,000-mile journey it would be necessary to take on 18,300 additional tons of coal, a total of 27,000 tons.

However, there were further problems here. While coaling at Cape Town she would have to anchor some distance from the dock entrance with her heavy draught, but at Bombay the distance would be up to 3 miles and the anchorage exposed. Trincomali was suggested, but the facilities there were by no means sufficient. In any case, while the ship was anchored she burned 125 tons per day even without people on board, which only added to the fuel requirement.

Even if the journey was done at 16 knots, a dangerously slow speed as far as avoiding submarine attack was concerned, her draught would still be 36ft with the supplies needed, the ship consuming 370 tons of coal per day.

On 28 January 1916 the suggestion was quickly dropped, the Director of Stores writing: 'The whole matter appears to bristle with difficulties from a coaling point of view. I hesitate to say that the proposal is an impracticable one.'

An alternative use for the ship soon presented itself. Canada could provide many troops, but was unable to transport them in large numbers so *Olympic* was chartered for this task, starting in March 1916. On 23 March 1916 she pulled out of Liverpool on her first trip to Halifax, which was to become a favourite port.

Originally, it had been proposed that *Olympic* should sail home in an convoy, but with a convoy's speed being only 12 knots, Captain Hayes logically asked to sail unescorted and rely on his high cruising speed of over 22 knots.

During April 1916, she carried an important British mission delegation, headed by Mr A.J. Balfour, to Halifax and back. In recognition of the fact, Captain Hayes was awarded the CMG, commenting with his usual modesty; 'the honours were shared by every member of my crew…' On one run, *Olympic* departed from Halifax with over 7,000 crew and troops aboard, one of the largest numbers ever carried by a vessel of the White Star Line.[79]

There was a little excitement aboard in October 1916 when an anonymous letter received at Southampton told that a man of German descent was serving aboard her. Further investigation[80] revealed it was indeed true and Second Extra Baker Frederick William Repphun was taken into custody by aliens officer Henry Murphy.

When questioned, twenty-three-year-old Repphun told authorities that although his father was in Knockaloe Camp, he had lived in Liverpool and Manchester for thirty years, having been born in Stuttgart, Germany. His mother Alice Repphun was Welsh, born there of Welsh parents.

After the *Lusitania* disaster of May 1915 he had been dismissed from his job at Messrs Reece Ltd, but given a character and ability recommendation, enabling him to go to sea on the SS *Orissa*.

He was later found to be suffering from venereal disease, but *Olympic*'s surgeon had been unaware and Repphun hadn't been medically examined when he had signed on. Due to the illness he left the ship. The Director of Transports concluded: 'Though the man has been removed from the ship the possibility of a similar case might constitute a certain risk to troops on board a transport.' He recommended stricter inspections.

Olympic made eleven return crossings in 1916 – from Liverpool to Halifax – and continued to carry troops for most of 1917, following a refitting and commissioning under the White Ensign on 4 April 1917, during which time six 6in guns were installed and forty Naval ratings added under the charge of a mate gunner.

Although *Olympic*'s time on the Canadian run was immensely successful, Halifax was hardly an ideal port for such a large liner and while she was docked there, her stern actually protruded into the harbour for some length, necessitating a patrol vessel to cruise the area and prevent other ships from colliding with her stern. Supplying her with the necessary supplies of coal and water taxed Halifax's facilities to their limit.

While *Olympic* was at Halifax, the newspapers would devote much space to her arrivals and departures, often with the enormous headline: 'The Old Reliable In Port Again.' She became a great favourite. At Southampton the train that entered the docks was always audible as loud cheers went up whenever *Olympic* was visible.

Although carrying large numbers of troops for the war effort, *Olympic* also carried oil fuel in her tanks, certainly making efficient use of the available resources. The 'Big Four' were other vessels which carried oil, in their case up to 3,500 tons of the fuel each trip, bringing together some 88,000 tons over to Britain.[81]

One episode that happened to *Olympic* in the early summer of 1917 is rarely mentioned in histories of the ship. Departing Halifax on Sunday 29 April 1917, she carried a full load of troops. As Lieutenant Harry Hanan[82] of the 176th Battalion, Canadian Expeditionary Force, recalled:

> We started out slowly at 6.00 p.m. I was at the stern and as it backed out slowly we came very close to the French cruiser *Conde*. They had all the crew on deck and a guard paid us the compliment of their country which was followed by three great cheers.

Soon *Olympic* was proceeding down the harbour, receiving loud cheers from the other vessels. 'Then we were out in the open sea going at full speed,' he wrote. At first *Olympic*'s voyage was marred by bad weather, but that slowly improved. By Thursday 3 May 1917 *Olympic* had steamed some distance into the so-called 'danger zone' around the British Isles and all troops on board had their revolvers ready. 'Every day the alarm was sounded and a drill test made which was for practice in case of trouble.' At 4.00 a.m. on Friday 4 May 1917 he was on deck when Ireland was sighted. Owing to worries about submarine attack, *Olympic* soon put in to Lough Swilly and she remained there for some time; eventually she was escorted to Liverpool, and docked there at 6.00 a.m. on Monday, 7 May 1917.

Sergeant James Alexander McGeachie, another of the troops belonging to the Battalion, recorded the voyage for the 'folks back home':

…Over 6,000 troops were transported to England, and it is certainly surprising how arrangements were carried out in regard to feeding, sleeping accommodations, etc. It is practically a floating city. Zigzagging across the Atlantic at full speed we evaded the submarines, the presence of which made the voyage exciting, but nothing eventful occurred as the British Navy saw to that…

Unsurprisingly, everyone on board seems to have been impressed by the huge ship. It was not uncommon for her to be highly praised, even without her luxury fittings.

It was the entry of the United States of America into the war in April 1917 that made further demands on transportation, as the authorities were eager to get their troops across the Atlantic as quickly as possible.

However, although America had entered the war in April, it was not until 25 December 1917 that *Olympic* arrived in New York to transport her first load of American soldiers and she would continue this routine for the remainder of the war.[83] Captain Hayes recalled that the authorities had initially wanted to transport two or three thousand more troops than was usual aboard *Olympic* – about 8,000 troops – before he persuaded them that they would not arrive in good condition as there was not comfortable accommodation for such a large number aboard the ship. In fact, it was not until 11 January 1918 that *Olympic* could be got ready for sea, as the Hudson River was frozen over for some time, preventing coal being supplied; the delay proved a blessing, as Captain Hayes recalled that it gave the authorities time to think about and agree to his request that the usual complement of troops be carried.

Hayes' suggestion was certainly a sound one and *Olympic*'s time on the New York run would be in many respects as successful as the time she spent on the Halifax run. Although from spring 1918 the majority of her crossings served New York, there were several visits to Halifax during the period, whose residents cheered *Olympic* whenever she came into sight.

The final year of the war was perhaps the finest of *Olympic*'s trooping career, but it does not seem to have been a bad year for Richard Bradley either, who seems to have been a slippery character.

It seems that after signing on he cashed an advance note of payment, but then failed to join. He was initially summonsed for desertion, but through a loophole in the system the case against him was dismissed.

Bradley had been prosecuted under Defence of the Realm regulation 39A,[84] but in order to prove that he had been lawfully engaged under section 115 of the Merchant Shipping Act he must have signed the articles in the presence of a witness. However, as no witnesses were forthcoming, the Board of Trade Solicitor J. Paxton noted 'there was really no strict proof of lawful engagement'. It was not proved either that he had personally cashed the advance.

Proving Bradley's identity would not have been difficult as he had had on him an allotment note with his signature on from the Cunarder *Mauretania*, while further evidence from that ship could have been obtained with little difficulty, but it was really the major difficulty in proving that he had ever been lawfully engaged in the first place. Of course, if this could not be proved, the prosecution had to be dismissed.

A practice had been adopted of taking photographs of seamen claiming to be British subjects, to be attached to either a certificate of nationality or the discharge, but this did not apply to vessels owned, chartered, requisitioned or hired by the Admiralty. Even if it had applied, a photograph might have proved that it was the seaman's certificate or book, but it would hardly be foolproof as he could declare that his book had been stolen and used by someone else.

There were real difficulties, the Board of Trade Solicitor writing: 'if it once gets known amongst Solicitors practicing in the Police Court, that such a difficulty exists, they will advise their clients to plead not guilty and contend that there was not strict proof against them.' He thought it unlikely a seaman would deny his signature on articles if there was additional evidence, but stated: 'if he does so successfully the proper course would seem to be to prosecute him for perjury.'

On one voyage, Lord Reading was aboard the ship. He had previously been Sir Rufus Isaacs.[85] During this time he asked Captain Hayes his opinion of the *Olympic-Hawke* case. Hayes recalled that Reading had been acting for the Admiralty at the time, and cleverly replied: 'The Admiralty must have had the better lawyer as they certainly hadn't the better case.'

While *Olympic* was returning from a trooping run, on 6 March 1918 she was instructed to meet her escort off the French coast, but owing to fog she could not and was forced to steam in curves at 17 knots for eight hours. Although her officers were worried about enemy vessels, she was lucky and ended the voyage safely.[86] Any number of near misses or perceived threats did not seem to harm *Olympic*. In fact, she became the only passenger liner to sink an enemy submarine during the conflict, although several other merchant ships could claim the accolade of destroying a U-boat. Her victim was the *U103*.

Olympic was just off the entrance to the English Channel – around position 49° 16' north 4° 51' west – at 3.55 a.m. on 12 May 1918, heading at full speed, when a submarine was spotted off the starboard bow, half a mile away.[87] During 1917 several 6in guns had been fitted to *Olympic* for self-defence, and these were put to good use. Opening fire on the submarine, the guns missed and the submarine got under way, but *Olympic*'s bow swung round as the helm was turned at Hayes' order and *Olympic*'s bows smashed through the submarine, the ship suffering no damage other than a twisted stem.[88] It was a memorable event. 'The shock of the impact,' Captain Hayes recalled in his memoirs, 'was much greater than I expected. I had always thought of submarines as being frail things, but it jumped us off our feet on the bridge.'[89]

'I heard our 6in guns in action and felt the shock of the collision,' Engineer C.W. McKimm would recall nearly eighteen years later, 'little but the tail of the U-boat remained by the time I scrambled on deck'. Thirty-one survivors were picked up by the passing American destroyer USS *Davis*,[90] to be landed at Queenstown.

In Southampton, a diver discovered the stem bent 8ft to port with several dented hull plates, but some dry-dock repairs allowed a rapid return to service.[91] £1,000 from the Admiralty was distributed among the crew and some American soldiers paid for a plaque to commemorate the event.[92] It read:

> This tablet presented by the 59th Regiment United States Infantry commemorates the sinking of the German submarine U103 by the *Olympic* on May 12th 1918 in latitude 49 degrees 16 minutes north longitude 4 degrees 51 minutes west on the voyage from New York to Southampton with American troops…

Captain Hayes heard at Southampton that two of the lookouts on duty at the time of the sinking had disagreed about who had spotted the submarine, so being aware that the White Star Line paid a £20 bonus to the lookouts for sighting a submarine which was avoided, he thought he would try and settle the matter. The man at the stem had called out when he had seen the submarine, whom Hayes had heard; but the lookout

Olympic's passengers had a good view of the stricken *Audacious*. One of the '*King George V*' class, she was one of the largest battleships in the navy. Just under 600ft in length, her service speed was 21 knots and she had entered service in October 1913. (Nigel Aspdin collection)

in the starboard side of the crow's nest maintained that he had been phoning the bridge at the time.

'Why didn't you sing out?' Hayes asked.

'To tell you the truth, sir, I thought he [*U103*'s captain] would hear me and go under again.'

Although Hayes decided to give the reward to the man on the stem, the two men later shared the money.

After the Armistice of November 1918, the Canadian Government chartered *Olympic* to carry their troops home. Her post-war Halifax arrival was 'simply indescribable' according to Captain Hayes:

> Every ship in the harbour, moving or stationary, was decked with flags, and every one of them kept their whistles blowing all the time we were in sight of them. The ends of the piers we passed on our way up town were crowded with people who added to the noise by their shouts of welcome. Banners of welcome were stretched along the sheds, and perhaps what touched me most was that our ship was not forgotten in the general welcome to the troops. "Welcome to the Old Reliable" was prominently displayed. In addition to the crowds of people on our pier there were three bands of music, wind instruments predominating, and all blowing their hardest, at different tunes, I should say, by the noise they made.

Owing to the noise, it was impossible to give docking instructions even by megaphone, so orders were given by hand, the operation being made difficult by the ship's severe list owing to the presence of so many people on the upper decks, which was corrected when some were moved.[93]

Captain Hayes was pleased when, in February 1919, the White Ensign was lowered and the 'Red Duster' for the Merchant Service was added in its place; several months after the war had ended, after which time *Olympic* had been able to run at night without being blacked out.

Olympic eventually returned home to Liverpool and then to Harland & Wolff in August 1919 for a much-needed refitting. During her war service *Olympic* had steamed 184,000 miles and burned 347,000 tons of coal, earning the nickname, 'Old Reliable'.[94] This coal consumption figure seems very high compared to that consumed in peacetime service, yet even so the vessel undoubtedly consumed a large amount. She had carried on trooping and return voyages during the hostilities some 41,334 passengers, 24,600 troops destined for the Mediterranean, 80,088 Canadian troops, 42,835 United States soldiers, plus some 12,000 members of a Chinese labour unit; a grand total of 200,857 people.[95] In fact, the smaller *Mauretania* had carried less than 80,000 people, while the similarly-sized *Aquitania* had transported around 145,000 people, less than three-quarters of *Olympic*'s total.

Of the major liners, *Olympic*'s war service was surely the longest and most strenuous, as she had been in virtually continuous service, yet she had stood up to it remarkably well. *Mauretania* and *Aquitania* by comparison had spent the whole of 1917 laid up with more lengthy service breaks, while the *Leviathan* had only entered troop-carrying service in 1917, following America's entry into the war, carrying 100,000 troops in all.[96] *Leviathan*'s record was that she had carried 10,860 troops on one voyage, but *Olympic* was the next best with a record of 6,148, beating *Aquitania* by fifty-eight people, although *Mauretania* carried 5,162.[97]

Despite her distinguished service, however, during which she suffered no mechanical failure whatsoever and avoided many enemy attacks, *Olympic* did not finish her war service unscathed. Early in 1919, a dent and sprung hull plates were discovered during a routine dry-docking, forming a hole shaped little like a football, in all probability caused by a torpedo that had fortunately failed to explode, with the result that part of the outer skin had been flooded. The damage had previously gone unnoticed and the frustration of the U-boat commander can only be imagined when the torpedo he had fired at the enormous liner failed to explode.★

★   ★   ★

Olympic's second major refit would ensure that she remained in tune with the times. She had already seen years of arduous service, yet it was only in the 1920s that she would settle into an enduring, largely uninterrupted passenger schedule.

During the early 1920s oil was introduced to fire the large ocean liners' furnaces; oil was cheaper and cleaner than coal and the showers of soot from the funnels became a thing of the past – in many ways, oil may have seemed the 'perfect fuel' until the 1970s oil crisis.[98] *Olympic* was in fact the first of the big liners to be converted, the first to move with the times or even ahead of them.[99] There were many more advantages to the new fuel. With oil fuel, time was reduced when refuelling because there was not any need for the thousands of tons of coal to be shovelled into the bunkers and there was no need for the fireman and trimmers. This reduced personnel in the engineering department from around 350 people down to sixty.

Conversion to oil meant that strict attention was paid to fire prevention. Valves were fitted outside the machinery spaces to shut off steam to the oil pumps, extension rods operated the suctions to the oil fuel tanks, while steam admission to the stokeholds,

---

★ For further information, see my article 'Target *Olympic: Feuer!*', *Titanic Commutator*, *Titanic* Historical Society, 2008. It examines the available evidence, with considerable assistance from other researchers, providing a fairly conclusive answer as to the identity of the U-boat and the timing of the attack.

water hose and spraying nozzles, and sand, were carefully monitored. Additionally, main 34-gallon and 2-gallon 'Foamite' extinguishers were fitted. Captain Hayes recalled that passengers, prior to the war, had always been worried that oil was dangerous and easily flammable compared to coal, but it is a fact that the temperature had to be increased and the oil vaporised in order for it to ignite. However, it was admittedly a danger in that condition.

Olympic's oil fuel was carried in twenty-six side bunkers in the double skin, with a capacity of 1,658 tons, while two overflow tanks flanking the turbine engine room held a further 100 tons; ten bunkers contained 2,528 tons, and six settling tanks (one for every boiler room) each held 882 tons, for no fewer than 5,168 tons. After the initial conversion, by early 1921 additional oil was stored in holds 1 and 3, to be transferred to the other bunkers while in port – for a total oil fuel capacity of 7,631 tons. A proposal to store a further 1,805 tons in parts of the double bottom was not carried through. Ample oil-pumping power was provided for delivering it to the furnaces: firstly, the oil was pumped into the settling tanks where the water was separated from it, at this stage the oil temperature being 100° Fahrenheit; then the oil was drawn through suction filters by the fuel pumps which discharged it, through various heaters and filters, to the burners (one burner was fitted for each boiler furnace) in the furnaces at 210° Fahrenheit, at a pressure of about 80psi.

One other alteration was a new central propeller, driven by the turbine, which was four-bladed and replaced the probable three-bladed design installed during the 1913 refitting, although it does not seem that the wing propellers were replaced.

Changes were made to the liner's life-saving apparatus during the refit, an entirely new arrangement of lifeboats and davits in fact being installed. Twenty-four Welin davits were installed, to hold the new complement of Murray's nested boats: two nests consisting of 30ft, 28ft and 26ft boats (the latter an emergency boat); two nests composed of a 30ft lifeboat and 28ft motor boat inside; and twenty nests of 30ft and 28ft lifeboats, with a capacity totalling 3,428 people, or thirteen more than the total number of passengers and crew that the ship was authorised to carry. The two 28ft motor boats were made by Gouk & Nisbet, Glasgow, equipped with their own wireless and powered by Gardner four cylinder 4in x 4½in stroke engines, which delivered 7 knots. Subsequently, between 1925 and 1927 the boats' wireless installation was reconstructed by the Marconi company to meet new requirements, searchlights being part of the boats' equipment.

Although attention was focused on the lifeboats, another interesting change occurred. The means of closing *Olympic*'s watertight doors throughout the boiler and engine room spaces was improved and the new arrangement was similar to that of the new Harland & Wolff ship *Arundel Castle*. As before, there were arrangements for them to be closed manually, but the doors could now be closed by means of a new system employing electric power: 'From the time the switch is put in circuit for closing all doors, about seven seconds elapses, before the first door commences to move, and from then until the last door is shown closed about another 29 seconds; altogether 36 seconds from the start,' reported a surveyor after tests proved satisfactory.

Olympic's passenger accommodation was restored and she was registered to carry 750 first-class, 500 second-class and 1,150 third-class passengers, which combined to show a moderate reduction on the number she had been able to carry in 1911. As always, the enduring provision of interchangeable accommodation meant that there was room to be flexible if there was a greater demand in any one class. Several former third-class passenger areas on the lower decks were improved and allocated to the ship's crew and engineering staff.

Audacious' crew evacuate the ship as her condition deteriorates. *Olympic's* lifeboats look fragile on the open sea. (Günter Bäbler collection)

But now that the *Olympic's* refit was complete, the ship was opened to the public for inspection. Proceeds went to the Royal Victoria Hospital, as they had done when the *Olympic* had been opened to the public in 1911, before her maiden voyage. Several photographs exist today of visitors looking around the ship on 12 June 1920.

On Thursday 17 June 1920, at 10.30 a.m., the *Olympic* pulled out of the deep water wharf. She then proceeded down the Victoria Channel, 'her passage being watched by crowds of interested spectators'. Satisfactory running trials were completed in Belfast Lough. Then the tug *Musgrave* brought out to the ship Lord Pirrie, Lord Inchcape (Chairman of the P&O and British India Lines), Lord Inverforth (Minister of Munitions and Supply), Field-Marshal Sir William Robertson and Sir Joseph Barclay (Shipping Controller), among others, who were to travel to Southampton. At 6.00 p.m., with journalists also on board, *Olympic* left for the nearly 600-mile run to Southampton. After nine years, she remained the largest British ship in terms of tonnage and was ranked fourth largest in the world, the largest vessel (HAPAG's *Bismarck*) still being under construction.

During the running trials, particular attention had been paid to the Parsons low pressure turbine engine, which had actually been under close inspection since 1913. The binding metal strips on the blades of the rotor casing had originally been of ordinary soft brass, which had turned-out not to be an ideal material as it wore too heavily, although there had never been any serious problems with the turbine and it had proved reliable. After the war, the first and second binding strips on all the blades of the rotor casing were replaced with new material (the composition being 70 per cent copper and 30 per cent zinc, an improvement on the original soft brass composition). The thousands of blades were all examined, new material being fitted on this occasion, while internal parts of the casing and rotor, along with the inlet and exhaust steam valves, were cleaned and scaled, to be covered with 'Apexior' non-corrosive paint. The Board of Trade surveyor had observed the turbine running on 11 June 1920 with the ship in dock, finding everything to be in order, and, following the actual trials in the Lough, he was able to state that the 'turbine was worked under all conditions. It manoeuvred and worked satisfactorily.'

'The passenger accommodation of the big liner has been completely overhauled and redecorated,' the *Belfast News-Letter* recorded. '...For nine months an army of workmen, numbering over 2,000, were employed continuously on the vessel, and for some time past an increased staff was busily engaged so as to have her completed in time to fulfil her engagement to sail from Southampton on the 25th...'

As she returned to service, celebrations were held in the first-class dining saloon, during which Harold Sanderson called her the company's 'one ewe lamb', adding 'owing to the world condition, I cannot see such a large vessel being built for some time to come'.[100] Field-Marshal Sir William Robertson, Hayes recalled, changed the wording to 'our one ewe ram', recalling the sinking of the *U103*.

During the voyage to Southampton the ship was only steaming at a moderate speed and the oil-fired machinery was working well, although there was one unfortunate accident. In boiler room 6, one of the attendants thought he was opening one of the oil-regulating valves to the burner of one of the boiler furnaces, but unfortunately the valve cover was slack and unscrewed completely. Oil heated to the usual high temperature and at a pressure of nearly 80psi began escaping into the stokehold, and another attendant happened to be lighting at that time one of the other burners with a torch, with the result that the escaping oil caught fire and the stokehold was immediately ablaze. One of those in the stokehold was badly burned when his clothes caught fire. Owing to the flames, the shutting off valve in the boiler room could not be operated; so that had to be done in the next stokehold. Fire-control efforts then went into effect, sand, steam and pyrene (tetra-chloride) being used to quell the blaze. Much pyrene was used especially, without hurting those fighting the fire, and the fire was extinguished within fifteen minutes. It turned out that the defective valve, supplied by Messrs Brigham & Cowan, was badly designed and all the valves were to be replaced to prevent such mishap in the future; otherwise, as a temporary measure they would be secured by pins to make them quite safe.

Olympic departed Southampton on schedule at noon on 25 June 1920, with a 'remarkably long passenger list', carrying 511 first-class, 575 second-class and 1,163 third-class passengers, for a grand total of 2,249 passengers; in fact, second and third classes were

An interesting postcard of *Olympic*. She is shown taking on coal. A number of the ship's windows had been painted over, although some of the B-deck windows are visible because they were open. On the reverse, it was noted that *Olympic* arrived in Halifax on 14 November 1917. By that time, her paint scheme had changed considerably and she was 'dazzle' painted. (Ioannis Georgiou collection)

more than fully booked, some interchangeable cabins being utilised to exceed the normal capacities. Her crew numbered 787, which helped to demonstrate the reduction in stokehold personnel following the conversion to oil fuel. All in all, there were a total of 3,036 people on board. Among the passengers were the violinist Jascha Heifetz; George Engles, on his world tour with the New York Symphony Orchestra; famous New York Opera singers Miss Braslau and Messrs Murphy and Werrenrath; Princess Olga Hasson; the Honourable Mrs Campbell; Sir Percival Perry and Sir William de C. Wheeler.

Described by the *Southampton Times* as 'refitted and resplendent', it was almost nine years since the liner's maiden voyage, yet 'the *Olympic* looked even better than when she made her first voyage'. It was reported that a 'safety steering device' had been fitted to *Olympic*, apparently one of the first aboard a ship, which had the effect of rendering 'additionally sure the absolute control of the ship's course by the officer in command of the bridge'. Captain Hayes had made it clear that he had no intention of 'driving' the new oil-fired fuel installation, and he did not. The statistics for *Olympic*'s 'Voyage Number 43 West' (the count resuming from the interruption of her peacetime service in 1914) showed the highest day's run at 533 miles. She encountered 'hazy weather at times' as well as a few hours of fog, but as she approached New York the weather was fine and clear. She passed the Ambrose Lightship at 6.45 a.m. on 2 July 1920, having covered 3,233 miles at an average speed of less than 21 knots. All passengers were pleased with the ship, including Mr White, the designer of the low-pressure burning system, who declared that when the crew were more used to the machinery the ship would easily be able to average 22 knots with a daily consumption of some 500 tons of oil.

When *Olympic* arrived, a reception committee appointed by Mayor Hylan went down the bay to greet the New York Symphony Orchestra after their successful tour. President Harry Flagler was among those greeting the ship, as reception boats surrounded the liner amid loud cheers and the ship's band played music. Unfortunately the docking was delayed owing to some suspected cases of typhus among 180 Serbians and other third-class passengers, as was the docking of the liner *Dante Alighieri* with her 1,198 passengers; both ships were held at Quarantine and the third class and steerage passengers held for five days at Hoffman Island, while 'cabin' – first and second – class passengers who were willing to go ashore with hand luggage were able to disembark in the afternoon as the other passengers stayed aboard for the night. The *New York Times* reported: 'The drastic action taken today by the authorities was the result of…advice received from Health Commissioner Royal S. Copeland and former Surgeon General Blue, both of whom are in Europe.' The paper concluded, 'Doctor Blue crossed on the *Olympic* from Southampton to Cherbourg and it was because of a message sent by him to Washington that this liner was held here…' Dr J.C.H. Beaumont, *Olympic*'s surgeon, declared that there was not a single case of illness on board and it would be impossible for a ship to have a cleaner bill of health, while many of the passengers were irritated by the delay. Otherwise, however, the voyage had been satisfactory in every respect, the ship's performance being most acceptable; the next decade would see continuing popularity, the liner in her maturity also being faster than ever before.

'I do not remember having ever seen more smiling faces amongst the ship's company on a sailing day, on any ship, than there were on the *Olympic* when we sailed from Southampton in June 1920,' Captain Hayes recalled. The liner was 'spick and span' he said, 'like a new ship, and our passengers had happy faces, as if they, too were glad to see her in commission again'.

Above left: Olympic at Southampton. Designed by artist Norman Wilkinson, the 'dazzle' paint schemes are often described as 'camouflage'. While they may resemble that military look, the purpose of the several 'dazzle' paint schemes that *Olympic* wore towards the end of the war was not to camouflage her entirely. Rather, the intention was to make it difficult to identify the ship's course and speed, reducing the chances of an effective torpedo hit. (J.&C. McCutcheon collection)

Above right: Olympic's additional lifeboats and the 6in guns are clearly visible in this illustration, based on an aerial photograph taken towards the end of the war. The colour version depicts *Olympic* painted in bright colours including yellows, blues and reds; in fact, the geometric shapes were generally duller and included greys, blues and browns. (J.&C. McCutcheon collection)

All had gone well and, finally, with *Olympic* back in service she would have the chance to maintain a regular schedule to New York. Unfortunately, the White Star Line were faced with the lack of a suitable running mate. *Oceanic*, the only vessel in the fleet that was capable of matching *Olympic's* speed and her sole running mate in 1914, had been lost shortly after the war's outbreak. *Britannic's* loss had been a particularly severe blow.★

★   ★   ★

Fortunately, there was a solution. After the war, the punishing Treaty of Versailles demanded the confiscation of practically the entire German commercial fleet. The pre-war competition from HAPAG's *Imperator* and *Vaterland*, plus the challenge posed by the

---

★ *Adriatic* and *Lapland* were placed on the Southampton to New York service in September 1919, but *Lapland* departed in January 1920, six months before *Olympic's* refit was complete. It fell to *Olympic* and *Adriatic* to maintain the service until replacement tonnage could be found.

incomplete *Bismarck*, would no longer be damaging to the British companies on the North Atlantic. Instead, they would work for them.

If the solution appeared too good to be true, then perhaps it was. There were concerns within the British government regarding the White Star Line's own position. IMM had got into considerable financial difficulties:

> It never prospered, and at the outbreak of war, as a result of the inability of the British companies to pay such dividends as were needed by the American company to meet its fixed charges, the American company went into the hands of a receiver. During the receivership the earnings of the British and American companies increased enormously with the result that in 1916 the receivership ended and the American company found itself in a strong position.

Unfortunately: 'New American interests had acquired control of the company [IMM] and these… very largely acquired their holding in the belief that all the earnings and assets of the British companies were available for use by the American company.'

Harold Sanderson, as the chairman and managing director of the Oceanic Steam Navigation Company (White Star Line) and chairman of IMM's board of directors, visited New York in May 1916 and obtained 'the assent of the American stock holders to a proposition stipulating that the effective control over the vessels should be vested in the London boards and that a proportion of the directors of the International mercantile Marine Corporation, as well as of the British companies, should be subjected to the approval of the British government.' The Ministry of Shipping was satisfied 'as far as it went, but in 1917 difficulties began to arise from a conflict of policy' between the British directors and the American financial interests: 'An attempt to secure formal confirmation of the understanding reached in 1916 was unsuccessful.' Wisely, companies such as the White Star Line were 'accumulating large reserves to replace tonnage lost in the war, and by refraining from declaring large dividends were limiting the return received by the American bondholders on their capital.' The agreement confirming that vessels such as the White Star Line's fleet would remain on the British registry was due to expire in September 1922, and the British government was worried that the bond holders would 'assert their position and secure the transfer of the vessels to the American flag and the investment of the reserves in American shipping.'

It was made clear to Sanderson by the American investors in IMM that 'their investment was no longer attractive' and they requested that the British government either acquire their holdings in the British companies; or authorise the transfer of 'all earnings and liquid assets… for use by them in America for such purpose as they may think fit.' The British government sought to put together a buyer. A British syndicate, including Lord Pirrie and Sir Owen Philipps (later Lord Kylsant), secured the approval of the British government and made an offer to the American bond holders. The offer was 'virtually accepted, but, at the last moment, the United States government, although they had been kept advised of the progress of the negotiations, vetoed the transaction.' The British government had rightly feared 'a state of irritation' between the American and British interests 'because of the refusal of the British directors to comply with the wishes of their American associates that they should be paid exorbitant dividends to the prejudice and serious weakening of the British companies.' They were similarly concerned with the possibility that German tonnage awarded to the White Star Line would ultimately be transferred to

American control. It was only when the original agreement, including the stipulation that the British liners would remain on the British registry, was extended in September 1919 that the issue was dealt with, but in the long term IMM wanted to dispose of its interests in the White Star Line and its other British companies.

The White Star Line were allocated the North German Lloyd liner *Columbus*, which would be completed and renamed *Homeric*. Although her gross tonnage was greater than *Mauretania*'s, her speed was significantly lower at 18½ knots and she had a significant third-class capacity. Her first-class interiors were particularly impressive. The real prize was the world's largest liner, *Bismarck*, still lying incomplete at Hamburg after being launched in June 1914. On the same day that *Olympic* arrived in New York on her first westbound crossing after the war, Harland & Wolff's representatives, Messrs Wilding and Rebbeck, gave a verbal report of the vessel's condition following an inspection on 30 June 1920. A summary noted: 'The ship is 85 to 90 per cent completed. Dr Blohm [from the German builders, Blohm & Voss] estimated that the ship would be completed in Germany in about nine months with from 2,000 to 2,500 men,' but the estimate proved optimistic and there were other issues ('the propellers, which are not yet fitted, are being made of cast steel, in light of the shortage of bronze'). As the White Star Line did not have their own technical staff, the German builders raised no objection to officials from Harland & Wolff inspecting the ship or ensuring that she met the required standard for her new owners.

Homeric arrived at Southampton on 31 January 1922 and made her maiden voyage on 15 February 1922, but *Bismarck*'s completion had been delayed by fire in October 1920, reported to have 'started in a coal bunker used as a store room and worked upward until fireproofing arrested its progress'. By May 1921 her funnels were in place and she underwent an 'official steaming trial of six hours duration' on 31 March 1922. Her engines demonstrated that they could produce at least 70,000hp and with her engines reversed from 'full ahead' to 'full astern' she proved capable of coming to a stop in 'four minutes from the time the telegraph rang'. Her maiden voyage from Southampton as the White Star Line's *Majestic* took place on 10 May 1922.

Cunard were in a slightly better position insofar as they still had *Mauretania* and *Aquitania*, but with the loss of ships including *Lusitania* they were allocated *Bismarck*'s older sister ship, *Imperator*, which they renamed *Berengaria*. (The middle sister, *Vaterland*, was renamed *Leviathan* and joined the American fleet after the war.) The purchase of *Imperator* and *Bismarck* was a joint one between Cunard and the White Star Line, and its arrangement was finalised in January 1921. Its total price came to £1,500,000 (£1,000,000 for *Bismarck* and the remainder for *Imperator*) and the payments were to be made in ten equal instalments. While each company would operate one ship as its own, by virtue of their joint ownership half of each vessel's profit would be distributed to the other company.

★ ★ ★

Olympic's machinery was working well and 'she had a great reputation for regularity and as a really excellent sea boat'.[101] On an eastbound crossing several months after her return to service she logged an average speed in excess of 22½ knots. In November 1921 she completed her fastest ever round trip: from 26–31 October 1921 she covered 2,931 miles westbound at fractionally over 22 knots in 5 days, 12 hours and 38 minutes; and she returned eastbound between 5–10 November 1921 in 5 days, 12 hours and 39 minutes at an average somewhat under 22¾ knots. Although she had not been pushed, taken together her speed for the entire round trip was about 22½ knots, but she would better both the westbound and eastbound crossings later in her career.

According to a newspaper report in July 1922, *Olympic*, 'on its voyage from New York to Cherbourg, maintained for several hours a speed of 27.81 knots, which is a world record for a passenger liner.' She had made 'the burst of speed' in the English Channel towards Cherbourg, covering about 190 miles in fine weather and smooth seas. There were sometimes other similar reports in the papers, for instance relating to *Aquitania*, but the reality was that if *Olympic* even came close to such a speed it could only have been by the assistance of an exceptional current and in ideal conditions. Her machinery simply did not have the power to drive her through the water at such a high rate of speed. The reality was impressive enough, whether it was the fact that she had maintained 24.2 knots over a twenty-four-hour period before the war, presumably with another obliging current, or the numerous instances where she recorded speeds well in excess of 23 knots.

On one occasion in August 1923, claims of a race between *Olympic* and *Leviathan* led to White Star Line officials issuing a denial:

> That a race between the *Olympic* and any other ship was thought of by the *Olympic*'s commander, Captain Hugh F. David, or any official of the White Star Line in connection with the voyage of the *Olympic* ending today at Cherbourg is a fantastic implication. No White Star captain would race his ship, for as experienced and careful seamen they know the folly and risk of racing, or of trying to force a ship beyond her normal speed.
>
> The White Star Line admits that the *Olympic* is at least a knot slower than the ship she is reported to have raced with across the Atlantic. Its fastest ship, and the world's fastest, is the *Majestic*, which made the existing New York–Cherbourg record in five days six hours thirteen minutes without racing or being forced. It is suggested that the beating of this record would be better evidence of speed than an imaginary race with the *Olympic*.

Majestic was not the fastest in the world, but the company's denial of a race did have a ring of truth about it, as *Olympic*'s speed had been slower than usual. *Leviathan* arrived at Cherbourg fourteen-and-a-half hours before *Olympic*, prompting one passenger to send a telegram to their friend on board *Olympic*: 'I will be in Paris when you reach Cherbourg.'

Olympic did better the following summer. On 5 July 1924 she left New York on the same day as *Leviathan*. It took her 5 days, 22 hours and 47 minutes to cover 3,241 miles at an average speed of 22.7 knots. She was not driven at full speed, although one day's run was a record 550 miles: extremely good for an eastbound crossing and apparently closer to 24 knots than 23. It was her fastest eastbound crossing. There was no doubt that *Leviathan*'s average speed came in at a lower 22.65 knots, but the American liner covered fewer miles, which meant that her voyage time was shorter even though her average speed was lower.

'*Olympic* would remain a profitable and fashionable ship, attracting her share of wealth and celebrity.'[102] On Saturday 3 September 1921 *Olympic* left New York carrying none other than the actor Charlie Chaplin, not to mention members of the British Davis Cup tennis team; Charles Mitchell, president of the National City Bank; Martin Ansorge, Congressman of New York; W. Bigelow, the editor of *Good Housekeeping* magazine; Edward Knoblock, the playwright; and Percy Rockefeller of New York, to name just a few of the more than 400 first-class passengers. There were numerous reports about Chaplin in particular, stating how he had enjoyed extensively using the squash court, gymnasium and smoke room, but he had not taken part in any card games, which was probably for the best considering the large number of professional gamblers frequently found on the prestigious express liners. Chaplin was a success in a ship's concert, which he had appeared in despite his underlying shyness. In fact, due to fog *Olympic* arrived at Cherbourg four hours late, at 5.00 p.m., and so much of the crowd there had dissipated, but when Chaplin landed at Southampton he was met by the Mayor and Mayoress, while Councillor Hood – of a local cinematographic association – extended 'a hand of welcome on behalf of the trade'.

Olympic left Southampton on 14 September 1921 with a healthy first-class passenger list, including bishops, generals, judges, senators, diplomats, actors and numerous American society people. Two of many notables were Dr Nicholas Butler, 'eminent head of the Columbia University', and Iroquois Indian Chief Deskaheck who was returning to America after visiting the Colonial Office.

It was reported that actress Mary Pickford and actor Douglas Fairbanks, who had crossed on the liner before, would be making the return eastward crossing for a visit to Paris and a Continental tour, then going to London before returning from Southampton. With so many famous people regularly crowding her first-class accommodation, *Olympic* was soon nicknamed: 'the Film Star liner.'

Olympic was returning eastbound to Southampton via Cherbourg on 12 December 1921 when she encountered one of the Atlantic's worst storms for many years with 120mph winds of 'exceptional strength', at cyclonic pressure for several hours, which forced Captain Hayes to reduce speed. Early that morning the waves' strength was so great that several D-deck portholes of the first-class reception room were smashed. Yet worse would follow: early that afternoon the ship gave several quick rolls, which were severe enough to move several watertight doors that trapped passengers as they closed. In third class, Domenico Serafini was killed after suffering a fractured spine and John Onsik suffered a crushed left leg; Chief Surgeon John Beaumont and Assistant Surgeon Robley Browne were forced to amputate it. Onsik later went to hospital at Cherbourg, 'with £200 collected by the passengers to cheer him up'. By the end of 13 December 1921 the weather had improved and fifteen covered starboard portholes on the ship's side were all that indicated that the storm had taken place. *Olympic* had behaved relatively well and she docked with a large shipment of Christmas mail, but first-class passenger Albert Bemis would remember the crossing for some time to come:

> About nine o'clock Monday morning a great comber struck the ship just forward of the main saloon. I was taking my bath at the time, on the lee side, and felt it strike but thought little of it. The wave broke through all the portholes of the music room [reception room] and flooded the room and a part of the dining saloon and put six or eight inches of water in the cabins on the deck below. Splashing upward on the side of the ship, it tore away a piece of steel railing two hundred feet long, not to mention the after-housing of one of the lifeboats on the boat deck, probably seventy feet above the *waterline* [original emphasis]. Fortunately, only a few passengers were about at the time… Two of the three Marconi wires were at some time in the night torn apart, and for several hours the loose ends whipped about dangerously from the masts…As noon approached the wind began to abate and by one o'clock the captain put on more power

and headed easterly. He started somewhat too soon, for as we were finishing luncheon we struck some big combers and in about ten great rolls all the loose furniture and some that had been 'fast' was sliding from one side of the ship to the other, with an intermingling of china, food, and man. After two or three oscillations, I made for the piano, which was well anchored down, and perched upon its keyboard and watched the fun, for such it proved to be, as nobody was hurt. Some furniture fell down the gangway. Staterooms were in a medley. In one the bed was found in the middle of the floor quite upside down. But 'all's well that ends well' and we passed on into better weather and calmer seas…'[103]

The Prince of Wales boarded *Olympic* in New York on 25 October 1924, with his staff members General Trotter, Captain Alan Lascelles and Major Metcalfe. He made good use of the squash court most days, playing various deck games and dancing in the evenings, despite a 'rather stormy' crossing, 'but the ship behaved finely and passengers were quite unaffected by the rough seas'. He followed the General Election results with 'great interest', later telling Harold Sanderson that he had had an 'extremely happy' trip. Despite the rough weather, *Olympic* docked at Southampton early on the afternoon of Friday 31 October 1924.[104] Captain Howarth had allowed the Prince on the bridge while in pilotage waters and received a reprimand from White Star when the photograph appeared in the press.[105]

On a sad note, one well-known passenger that year was Lord Pirrie. Four years earlier, it had been said that he was 'extremely active for his age and takes long walks every day and devotes several hours to business', but he died on board the Pacific Steam Navigation

Olympic at the Thompson Wharf, Belfast, on 9 September 1919, undergoing a thorough overhaul and refitting after her war service. (Photograph reproduced courtesy the Trustees of National Museums Northern Ireland)

Company's *Ebro* on 7 June 1924 and his body was carried home by *Olympic*, his favourite ship.

★　★　★

As early as May 1921, barely a year after *Olympic* had re-entered service, the United States Government had passed the 'Three Percent Act', limiting the number of immigrants entering the country to that percentage of foreign born citizens according to the 1910 census; meaning that only 360,000 people per year would now be allowed in.[106] By means of comparison, in 1913 there had been 1,141,000 immigrants.[107] Yet, if this was thought drastic, in 1924 the limit was altered to 2 per cent of the foreign-born population of America, but according to the smaller census of 1890, indicating a total of only 160,000 immigrants. In fact, by 1931, the number of immigrants had decreased to fewer than 100,000 people. The effects of the dramatic reduction were felt by the major Atlantic liners, as although they competed as luxurious vessels and were advertised as such. the German liner *Vaterland* of 1914 had been designed with a capacity of some 2,500 immigrants.

Another change in America later affected the North Atlantic liners, prohibition. 'That meant American liners could not offer one of the most wonderful aspects of an ocean voyage – the long bars, you know…brandies and all that kind of stuff. So the foreign lines were really able to capitalise on this,' explained liner expert Bill Miller. The situation grew worse after the 1929 Wall Street crash. 'When the depression set in, the general trade fell tremendously. Cunard and White Star Line were really desperate for passengers. They had to turn away from what once was the lucrative Atlantic trade to run booze cruises – $10 trips overnight where you left New York city docks at 5.00 p.m., sailed outside the three-mile-limit, on board say, *Mauretania* or *Majestic*. They would open the bars and the Americans could drink themselves into oblivion until 8.00 a.m., come back, and go ashore, and it all worked beautifully…'[108]

New York's Treasury Agents were instructed to seize any but 'medicinal supplies' of liquor that liners were carrying inbound; wine had to be poured overboard, on some occasions personally by the chief steward, before the *Olympic* had penetrated the three-mile-limit.[109]

'We were called upon as if it were part of our daily task, to help, advise, and often assist passengers to conceal their "hooch",' Stewardess Violet Jessop would recall in her memoirs. 'Often our men obliged, at a price, and even our women too. One ample-bosomed stewardess found she could carry off a quart of champagne in her "balcony", and no Customs Official…had the nerve to tap the offending bottle… so she got away with it!'[110]

★　★　★

Prohibition may have been in force, but, in the early and mid-1920s, the economic problems following the Wall Street crash were very much in the future. *Olympic* left Harland & Wolff on Thursday 7 February 1924, following 'undergoing overhaul and tuning-up in anticipation of a brisk season'. It was reported that she was 'steadily increasing her well-established popularity with all classes of passengers for comfort and reliability'. She was rightly described as 'an outstanding unit in the British mercantile marine during the World War' and had 'enhanced this fine reputation since her conversion to peaceful pursuits'. There was 'no more sought-after vessel on the North Atlantic service'.

There was much truth in the report, but inevitably exaggerations crept in. *Olympic* did well, but there was a good share of challenges even after the war and they were certainly evident in 1924. From her return to service in June until the end of 1920, *Olympic* was practically full whenever she left for New York. She carried an average of 1,076 third-class passengers to America on each crossing; by 1923, the first tightening of the immigration laws had already reduced that figure to 322. The completion and introduction of *Homeric* and *Majestic* by the spring of 1922 and Cunard's own express service, which was moved to Southampton after the war and consisted of *Berengaria*, *Aquitania* and *Mauretania*, meant that there were an even greater number of ships competing for a smaller number of passengers.

In 1921, *Olympic* did even better than she had in 1913 and carried almost 38,000 passengers; the following year it fell to 28,000 and her new running mate *Majestic* exceeded 26,000 passengers. Moreover, *Majestic* carried a higher average passenger list and by 1923 she was the most popular liner afloat. All that was good news for the White Star Line, as they were part of the same fleet, but Cunard were in a slightly better position with their own express ships. *Majestic* was certainly a match for *Berengaria* and *Olympic* did better than *Mauretania*, but in turn *Aquitania* quite naturally had an edge over her; and *Homeric*'s passenger lists, the lowest of the 'Big Six', peaked in 1922.

If it was unsurprising that newer vessels had the edge over *Olympic* in passenger numbers, then she remained one of the most popular liners afloat. Her strength in first class, in particular, demonstrated the attractions behind the company's policy of comfort rather than speed. First-class passenger numbers were at their highest in 1921, but throughout the 1920s they remained at a similar level to what they had been prior to the war and for the most part second class also held up relatively well. It was the reduction in third-class passenger lists that was the most noticeable, but if it had an impact on the average number of passengers carried then perhaps its influence on the ship's profits was less noticeable. First-class ticket prices were far higher in comparison and on ships of *Olympic*'s ilk it was usually the revenues from first-class that contributed the greatest proportion of her income.

Unfortunately, although *Olympic* had shaken off the jinx of petty accidents that had troubled her otherwise sunny childhood, it was during 1924 that one of her serious collisions occurred.

Saturday 22 March 1924 began normally enough. *Olympic* prepared to sail from New York for Southampton via Cherbourg with a quite respectable complement of 1,170 passengers, while the Bermuda rivals *Arcadian* and *Fort St George* left their piers within a short time of one another thirty blocks upriver of *Olympic*'s pier.

At exactly 11.00 a.m. *Olympic* began to back out of her pier and as she reached midstream her whistles began sounding, her stern moving upriver and her bow pointing towards the bay. But by this time, *Arcadian* and *Fort St George* were racing each other. The former easily passed *Olympic*, but the *Fort St George* was heading across *Olympic*'s stern, and although she quickly steered westward, collision was unavoidable.

Olympic's stern hit *Fort St George*'s aft port quarter with a terrible groan. Six women, of 275 tourists aboard the smaller vessel, fainted as the deck railing crumpled and the roof over the promenade stove in. Ventilators were torn out, a lifeboat was smashed, wireless

'Here, among the palms, one may take after dinner coffee, or watch the evening's dancing, in an atmosphere of social smartness'. An evening view of *Olympic*'s first-class reception room, published in a post-war brochure. (Author's collection)

antennae destroyed and the aft mast crashed down, with damage extending over more than 150ft. One of *Fort St George*'s steel derricks, 50ft high, was demolished in the collision and both vessels lost their stern flag staffs. Amazingly, the glass-covered smoke room was unscathed in the accident, although when part of the deck collapsed three people were injured. Damage to *Fort St George* was estimated to be in the region of $150,000, although *Olympic*'s damage initially seemed confined to the loss of part of her name and some paintwork underneath her counter stern.

However, it was soon realised that *Olympic*'s sternpost had been fractured and therefore during the winter of 1925/26 the liner's stern frame was completely replaced, the first time a repair of the sort had ever been carried out.[111]

In fact, time would tell that the new stern frame was not as sound as the old; the Board of Trade later stipulated that it should be specially inspected along with the surrounding hull for the next few annual surveys. In the 1928 annual survey, it was observed that the frame was generally satisfactory, but following increasing signs of 'pitting' in 1929 it was sheathed in light metal, 80 per cent tin, in order to protect it.

Adding insult to injury, *Arcadian* was soon wirelessed and subsequently she took on *Fort St George*'s passengers, as their ship was now totally incapable of continuing on her journey. Meanwhile, *Olympic* continued to Quarantine and stopped for her steering gear to be tested. Fortunately, it proved to be fine and at 1.30 p.m. she was able to resume her journey, after a delay of some two-and-a-half hours.

If collisions were not causing threats to the schedule, then the hostility of the North Atlantic ocean could always be relied upon to create its own challenges. On 27 February 1925 a 70ft wave hit *Olympic*, engulfing the bridge, smashing a window and twisting a steel compass pedestal, among other things. Captain William Marshall described 'one of the worst voyages he had ever made across the Atlantic' when *Olympic* docked in New York on the evening of 3 February 1926. Already thirty hours behind schedule, she had to be docked in 'a driving snowstorm' and the river was 'filled with floating ice.' One evening, Marshall told a reporter, winds of 90 miles per hour had been accompanied by waves at least 45ft high:

> We were only making six knots, and then she kept falling off [course] through the force of the wind and the tremendous sea. Early Sunday morning one tremendous sea that was as high as the crow's nest came over the starboard bow and carried away thirty feet of the rail on the forward deck, the two ladders leading down from the boat deck, four glasses [windows] on the bridge and the clear screens and about ten feet of the planking on the after part of the bridge.

Six months later, *Olympic* arrived in New York after battling fog and heavy seas, carrying 1,059 passengers and 6,500 sacks of mail. Unfortunately for the 200 'aliens' in first and second class, the immigration doctor could not give them the all clear because it was after 7.30 p.m. The film actress Gloria Swanson's husband, the Marquis de la Falaise, was invited by White Star Line officials to stay on board *Olympic* for the evening, because his friend could not be cleared.

On another occasion, in February 1927, *Olympic* suffered damage while she was ploughing 'through heavy seas'. One of the portholes in the firemen's quarters towards the bow was smashed, causing flooding. The ship had to be stopped for half an hour while the porthole was plugged and other repairs were made.

Her running mate *Majestic* had her share of storms, as well. On 14 January 1929 she experienced a particularly bad incident during a westbound crossing that resulted in a fatality. The ship's log recorded:

> 3.20 p.m.: Heavy sea broke on board, No.1 hatches D and E decks stove in, forward third-class passenger accommodation flooded (passengers moved to Tourist class aft) and various extensive damage done on forward decks. Engines dead slow. Wind: WNW, force 9.

Homeric suffered damaged forecastle rails, broken promenade deck windows and smashed hatch covers during heavy weather in November 1928; again, 'promenade deck windows were smashed in December 1929 and the ship's orchestra hurled off its platform' in bad weather as she approached Southampton.[112] Such storms were part of life on the North Atlantic run.

★ ★ ★

The White Star Line itself saw some substantial changes as the 1920s drew to a close. After a quarter of a century, the company's shares were acquired from IMM by Lord

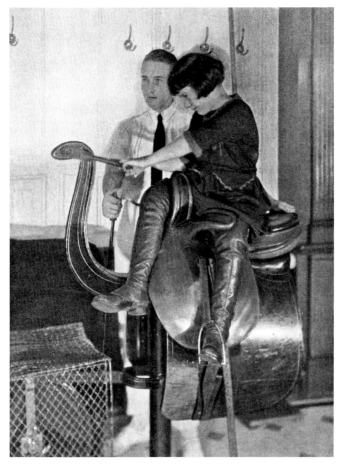

'Each of the Magnificent Trio [*Olympic*, *Majestic* and *Homeric*] has a perfectly appointed gym, which is popular with passengers of all ages.' (Author's collection)

Kylsant's Royal Mail Group. The purchase price, once interest was taken into account, exceeded £7,000,000 and was payable in instalments stretching to 1936. To complicate matters, the Oceanic Steam Navigation Company (or White Star Line's) shares were held by a new company that Kylsant created, named White Star Line Ltd. Kylsant used it as a vehicle for his ambitious plans to expand his shipping empire. White Star Line Ltd, itself only one of many companies in the large and complex Royal Mail Group, acquired two ships from the Royal Mail Steam Packet Company for £1,150,000 in April 1927; purchased shares in Shaw Savill & Albion Company Ltd to the value of £910,000 in March 1928; and seven ships from the Australian Commonwealth for £1,900,000 in April 1928. The Oceanic Steam Navigation Company began to suffer as its profits were milked by Kylsant. Following a dividend payment of £450,000 in 1927, the figure was reduced to £400,000 in 1928, but an identical payment of £400,000 was declared in 1929 even as the company increased its overdraft. This represented two thirds of the year's £613,062 profit, and with mounting liabilities there was no scope for an economic downturn. In fact, what was required to help restore fortunes was a substantial improvement in the economic situation.

That Kylsant's grandiose plans were in jeopardy became increasingly apparent. Plans to construct a magnificent new ship for the express service, to be named *Oceanic*, were well advanced and the keel was laid at Harland & Wolff in June 1928. She would be much larger than *Olympic* or *Majestic*, incorporating their best features combined with numerous improvements. Construction did not progress very far before it was abandoned the following year. Kylsant tried to explain that he was not actively proceeding with the vessel until the design of the propelling machinery had been finalised, but the reality was that there was no money available.

After sixteen years in service, efforts were made to maintain and improve *Olympic*'s popularity, as well as adapt her to changing circumstances on the Atlantic. Although long thought to have occurred during one major refit in 1928, in fact a number of changes were made to *Olympic* at the turn of 1927–28 and a year afterwards from 1928–29.

By 1929, the inside staterooms forward on A-deck had largely been converted into private bathrooms while the outside rooms were enlarged and refurbished; amidships on C-deck many staterooms were converted into private bathrooms.

Early in 1929, forward of the grand staircase on B-deck the original first-class staterooms were removed and sixteen new, spacious suites with private facilities were installed – extending right to the liner's side. A number of styles were used, including Adam, Queen Anne, Tudor, Colonial and Chippendale. In retrospect, it does seem strange that these alterations were carried out so late in *Olympic*'s career, although it is possible in earlier years that White Star had not wished to reduce the enclosed promenade space on B-deck. Whtever the reason, they represented an increased earning capacity compared to the original staterooms they had replaced. Another change evident on B-deck by this time was the Café Parisien, redecorated in 1927–28.

Another change was evident in the first-class dining saloon, by 1929. In the central section a parquet dance floor was installed, dividing the carpeted areas, and the chairs were fitted with new slipcovers as part of the new look.[113] The saloon became a kind of 'pseudo-nightclub' with passengers at each sitting being able to dance between courses, while an orchestra provided music on a raised platform with piano.[114]

Some of *Olympic*'s second class became 'tourist' class following the 1927–28 refit, after the introduction of 'tourist third class' in 1925. Although second was usually referred to as 'tourist' class after the late 1920s, in fact tourist-class passengers were carried in tandem with second-class passengers until *Olympic*'s 19 September 1931 New York departure. This class became popular with leisure travellers.

While a dance floor had been fitted in the first-class lounge in 1927–28, one year later cinema apparatus was installed and also in the second-class library on C-deck. One report said *Olympic* was on a par with 'the most modern picture houses in new York and London'. 'Talkies' followed in 1931.

Adding to *Olympic*'s attractions was a new ladies' hairdressing salon on C-deck, in addition to the origial men's barber and souvenir shop. After hours, it doubled as the two hairdresser's sleeping quarters! It was described as being 'painted in soft apple green' and having 'the quaint bow-fronted windows of the eighteenth-century style'.

Aft on C-deck, the after part of the enclosed promenade from the original second-class configuration was divided and became an area for tourist-class passengers in 1927–28. It was accessed via the doors leading from the landing for the original second-class stairway aft of the library.

The original D-deck second-class dining saloon, as it had been known, was divided during this refit by a new bulkhead; the port third of the original saloon now had accom-modation for 166 diners, while the starboard two-thirds accommodated 192 seats. Another of many improvements made to both the tourist and third classes was the addition on the port side, aft of the saloon, of a 'tourist-class dance floor', also equipped with ninety-five seats, that took the place of what had previously been second-class cabins and added much to the facilities of the new tourist class, enhancing *Olympic*'s reputation. The old third-class public rooms aft on C-deck were refurbished and became part of 'tourist' class, while an airy 'gramaphone lounge' and 'spacious new smoke room' were constructed for third class in place of the original third-class open space on D-deck.

As a consequence of the improved accommodation, *Olympic*'s passenger capacity had been reduced. On 11 February 1928 she was registered with a net tonnage of 21,726 tons, although her gross tonnage remained the same. She could now carry 675 first-class pas-sengers, 561 passengers in 'tourist' class and 819 passengers in third class, a total of 2,055 passengers. *Olympic*'s average passenger lists continued their rise every year from 1926 to 1929. The combined second and 'tourist' class carried more than the second class of 1920 – both were recorded as 'tourist' on the British registry papers.

White Star's Southampton manager Philip Curry ran a competition in September 1929 for a group of Pangbourne College boys who had visited *Olympic* at Southampton, for the best essay describing the visit. Cadet V. Paget won, describing his visit in detail – from the 'huge engines' which 'were a source of amazement' to the 'palatial fittings': 'Some [Cadets] found their way to the bridge, some to the massive engine rooms; others explored the cabins and smoking rooms, wondering at the palatial fittings, which include not only a swimming bath but also a Turkish bath…' *Olympic* never lost her ability to impress.

On Monday 18 November 1929 *Olympic* experienced one of the most unusual events of her career. Steaming westwards at 22 knots, *Olympic* was in position 42° 12' north 56° 56' west when at 3.30 p.m. a violent tremor and sustained vibration was felt for two minutes. Captain Walter Parker left the chartroom and came onto the bridge; there was a calm sea and gloomy sky, but nothing had been sighted ahead or in the ship's wake and the engines were still running smoothly, allaying fears of a lost propeller blade.

Parker immediately sent for the carpenter to sound the ship, or check for flooding, but apart from the loss of electric lighting in the mail room the ship was undamaged; he concluded that an underwater earthquake was responsible and soon reports coming into the radio room confirmed it. Half of the twenty-one transatlantic cables had in fact been severed.

Many of the first-class passengers, including Senior Purser J. Shepherd, were watching movies in the first-class lounge and so did not feel anything; but Anita Lobs, an author, was in her cabin and immediately recognised the earthquake because she had become used to them at her home in California.

Cunard and White Star's 'Big Six' had effectively dominated the North Atlantic for nearly a decade, with little or no competition from the Germans and French, but by 1930 there was some serious competition.

★ ★ ★

Germany's North German Lloyd launched two new 50,000grt 'superliners', the *Bremen* and the *Europa*, entering service in 1929 and 1930 respectively; they were planned to dominate the Atlantic and capture the 'Blue Riband'.[115] Indeed, *Bremen* showed what she was capable of on her maiden voyage, which was completed at an average speed of nearly 28 knots.[116] Britain's national pride was dented: Cunard's *Mauretania* made her best ever crossing that year, logging 27¾ knots, but simply could not keep up with the new 'greyhounds'.[117] The 43,000grt *Ile de France* entered service in 1927 and proved a huge hit with first-class passengers, while more tonnage was on the way from Italy and France, and the dominance of the 'Big Six' on the Atlantic was under serious threat; then the Wall Street crash of 1929 reduced passenger numbers. Quite simply, there were not enough passengers to sustain the great number of ships, forcing ship owners to employ their vessels in other ways, such as cruising. In fact, the combined effect of new tonnage, the depression and immigration restrictions soon turned even the mightiest company's profit into loss despite their best efforts.

In 1930 it was still possible to deny the severity of the decline in passenger traffic. For example, in June 1930 *Olympic* was still sailing from New York with more than 1,000 passengers, including many tourist-class travellers; but likewise in December that year she had carried only 265 passengers. Yet her schedule continued to be hectic and even in 1931 she completed a full schedule of round trips. Aside from the continuing number of celebrities on board, such as the famous soprano Madam Amelita Galli-Curci, in October 1930 *Olympic*'s surgeon, Dr A. Elder, was able to lend his expertise to people on other vessels by wireless. On the ship's westbound voyage of 24 September 1930 a wireless call was received from the SS *La Crescenta*, bound for Liverpool, whose chief engineer had been taken ill with malaria. Elder was able to advise on his treatment. Returning to Southampton early the following month, the SS *Ventura de Larrinaga*, also bound for Liverpool, asked for advice, because her chief officer was suffering from asthma and another crewman was suffering from a mild form of paratyphoid.

By 1932 the depression was showing its drastic effects. White Star's *Homeric* was switched to full-time cruising that year after a number of cancelled crossings,[118] while *Olympic* and *Majestic* sustained the express service. However, while at New York, the two ships ran brief cruises to Halifax in 1931. An announcement in late July 1931 read:

> The White Star Line are planning a series of short cruises from New York in trans-atlantic liners, mostly at weekends. These American cruises have been planned with the idea of catering for those who do not wish to be away from home for any great

Olympic's first-class lounge was described by the company during the 1920s: 'A distinguishing feature of this splendid ship is the wood carving in her lounge, the beauty of which is here suggested.' The figure on the mantelpiece is Artemis of Versailles. An identical figure on board *Titanic* was discovered at the wreck site, but an artist's impression of *Britannic*'s first-class lounge appears to show a clock on the mantelpiece instead. (Author's collection)

length of time, of whom there appear to be large numbers in the United States at present.

The *Majestic*, sailing on July 30th 1931 to Halifax, opens the program; followed by the *Olympic* on August 6th 1931; the *Majestic* on August 20th 1931; the *Britannic*, August 24th 1931; and the *Olympic*, August 27th 1931.

Between September 26th and October 31st 1931 the *Homeric* will make six-day cruises to Nassau. The rates for these cruises range from forty to sixty dollars, according to the ship.

Cunard withdrew *Mauretania* from full time Atlantic service and increasingly sent her cruising; *Aquitania* combined an increasing number of cruises with a busy express schedule that included an amazing eighteen round trips to New York in 1931; and *Berengaria* was also employed on a significant number of cruises.

Olympic's passenger schedule in 1932 saw a considerable reduction from the number of round trips she had made in 1931. However, she made fewer cruises as well and did not return to Halifax. Instead, she made one weekend cruise out of Southampton and

Cherbourg in the middle of May 1932 at a sedate eleven knots; and another 'around the Scilly Islands via Cherbourg' over the first weekend in August 1932. They coincided with the Whitsun and August Bank Holidays. Only first- and tourist-class tickets were sold and the public rooms were open to all: 'The first-class restaurant and Café Parisien will be available for *á la carte* meals, snacks, refreshments, tea and supper dances at moderate charges.' Deck games, swimming galas, dances and 'talkie' film shows were also advertised. Passengers were told to expect 'the finest weekend holiday of your life', but they would be the last 'pleasure' cruises *Olympic* made.

It was not an ideal time for Cunard or White Star to modernise their existing tonnage or to order new ships, or to keep all of their 'Big Six' in service as their profitability decreased.

Shipping companies were faced with other worries as their older liners needed extra attention and maintenance, but there were other concerns for the larger liners such as *Olympic*. Although part of a long line of larger and more luxurious liners, they had been a considerable leap forward in terms of their size and tonnage. Naval architects applied theoretical knowledge to their designs, which was complemented by their practical experiences once the ships were in service. As time passed, those designs were tested. In the early 1920s, one ship surveyor working for the Board of Trade noted:

> It is not an uncommon experience in these large vessels, which may be driven at speed through heavy seas, to find defects revealed by dry docking which otherwise would not be brought to light, and if not made good, might seriously affect the seaworthiness of the vessel. Two cases in point are *Aquitania* and *Empress of Britain*. In other cases serious defects of lesser importance have been revealed, for instance when *Majestic* was last dry docked, many thousands of rivets in the flat of [her] bottom were caulked… it is well recognised that these big ships, which are quite outside anything catered for by the classification societies rules for building cargo ships, require very careful watching in the early stages of their careers, for any signs of stress due to the severe conditions of their service.

Majestic provided an example of that requirement. In June and August 1924, minor cracks were seen in the ship's hull plating, but in December 1924 she experienced a sudden and dramatic fracture the night before she arrived in New York. It was a fracture that extended from the starboard funnel uptake across the deck, through the ship's thick plating on C-deck and down the ship's side. There were several causes, in particular the design of the ship's funnel uptakes: 'The German method in both these vessels [*Majestic* and her sister ship *Leviathan*] of separating the funnel uptakes into two parts and carrying them up on opposite sides of the vessel involves cutting into the stiffer parts of the strength deck plating,' noted one observer. Unfortunately, stresses could be concentrated at the corners of these openings, and sufficient strengthening measures to compensate had not been provided. Another problem was that ventilator and other deck openings had been placed at the corner of funnel uptakes. To make matters worse, tests revealed *Majestic*'s steel was not as strong as it should have been, invalidating the usual calculations of strength used in the ship's design. Even the positions of the ship's expansion joints were not ideal: 'While it is not expected that the superstructure should take any material stress of the main [hull] structure, it is unfortunate, I think, that the positions of the expansion joints should coincide with the weakest portion of the strength deck.' The design had 'proved insufficient to withstand the heavy stresses due to excessive speed in bad weather.' The White Star

Line's proposals, developed by Harland & Wolff, involved 'not only restoring the vessel's strength but increasing it materially' and in future *Majestic*'s commanders were appraised of the need to take special precautions in severe weather conditions.

One qualified and informed observer believed that her running mate, *Olympic*, 'has, I think, proved to be a successful ship in the matter of strength'. Harland & Wolff had not experimented with such radical concepts like split funnel uptakes, unlike *Majestic*'s German builders. Their design that was very much in keeping with previous ships such as *Adriatic*, introducing additional strengthening commensurate with her greater size and numerous refinements based upon their experience of building large vessels. *Olympic*'s funnel uptakes each required a single opening in the deck where adequate compensation was provided. When *Majestic* suffered her failures, she had only seen two years' service, whereas *Olympic* had been in service for thirteen years and been satisfactory.

After *Olympic* struck a fender while undocking in January 1926, six small cracks were discovered extending from the bottom of portholes along C deck through the small drainage hole immediately below and 'extending in several cases to the rivet holes in the shell plating and doubling below'. Further cracks would be noted on the other side of the ship the following year, but they were simply incipient fractures and no immediate alarm was felt: 'It is probable therefore that the fractures commenced at these small holes and spread to the larger, and that the concentration of stress has been relieved by the fractures which may not proceed further.' In March 1927 Senior Ship Surveyor F.W. Daniel wrote: 'A careful examination was made of the shell [plating] and decks, in way, for signs of working or strain, but none was found, and even the rivets to which the fractures extend, appear quite tight.' Nevertheless, the Board of Trade had responsibility for surveying passenger ships and decided to keep a close eye on *Olympic* as well. In 1928, Daniel wrote: 'No extension of these fractures can be observed and the shell riveting in way remains sound. No other sign of working is apparent.' In general, the hull's condition was satisfactory 'and the original scantlings [thickness of shell plating and structural members] are so well maintained that drilling was considered unnecessary'. The position remained the same the following year, except that:

> Opportunities for a more extended survey have shown that most of the side scuttles [portholes] in the forward half of the bridge erection [the doubled hull plating at the sides of C-deck] are affected, to a similar or lesser degree. All the fractures appear to be of about the same age and, judging from the plating in way of a port [hole] removed for examination, originated from corrosion in way of the small drainage hole.

As late as 18 November 1930, 'no extension' was visible in the fractures.

Unfortunately, after a heavy winter *Olympic* underwent her annual overhaul and a large number of the fractures had extended, which caused considerable alarm for the Board of Trade. Some of them were still less than a quarter of an inch long, but a large number of them extended up to 1 or 2in beyond the drainage hole. On 7 January 1931, the White Star Line's superintendent engineer, assistant superintendent engineer and one of Harland & Wolff's representatives were among the men who visited *Olympic* to make their own examinations and confer about the repairs that needed to be completed. As a result, the company's general manager's committee advised that 'it was decided to fit strengthening plates [doublers] over the cracks which have developed on the ship's side plating in way of the ports, which, it is felt, should prevent a recurrence of the trouble.'

Two days later, Daniel reported: 'Extensive tests have been made for other signs of straining in the upper structure, but with negative results…' He wrote: 'All ports fractured beyond the first row of rivets to have welded doublers fitted below and riveted doublers fitted above the ports internally, and fractures welded'; 'All ports fractured down to the first row of rivets to have welded doublers fitted below the ports internally, and fractures welded.' Daniel was not convinced that the repairs would 'prove permanently effective, but as the really efficient method would entail the redesign and renewal' of the affected shell plating 'which would be extremely lengthy and costly, the present method must be accepted as being reasonably satisfactory, and affording sufficient security against any sudden and important failure of the hull.' A particular concern was that 'the working stresses have been such as to cause failure in parts of the structure, but it is likely that other adjacent parts, as yet showing no signs… may give way under heavy weather conditions now that local stiffening has been applied elsewhere.' He recommended continuing to keep a close eye on the ship and limited *Olympic*'s certificate of seaworthiness to a period of six months rather than the usual twelve, although the White Star Line felt that 'it is not anticipated that any difficulty will arise when the certificate requires renewing'. Another observer wrote: 'From pure theoretical considerations the position is alarming, but in light of practical experience derived from serious and extensive structural breakdowns in the *Majestic* and *Leviathan* I do not anticipate any sudden disastrous failure…'

In July 1931, Daniel reported that the repairs were 'in perfect condition' so far and the passenger certificate was extended as the White Star Line had anticipated. After that, it was again issued for twelve months every year. The repairs had been satisfactory except for a couple of fractures which had 'occurred through the welds' beneath several portholes and needed repairing, it was noted in February 1932. Chief Ship Surveyor J. Sheriff believed that 'the local concentration of stress below the sidescuttles [portholes] occurs over a short length of plating not more than 3 inches or 4 inches long immediately below the centre.' He was interested because 'the plating adjacent to the weld on either side could not have been suffering very much from fatigue or it would have given way long before the weld.' If Sheriff's theory was correct, 'it is considered that the doubling fitted on the inside will considerably reinforce the weak spots and will probably prove efficient for a few years.' It might also have gone some way towards allaying Daniel's concerns the previous year that adjacent areas of the structure would fail, since their observations indicated that 'the very localised concentration of stress' below the portholes was 'the cause of the trouble'. In November 1932, Daniel wrote that 'it is considered that further defects will give sufficient warning of their presence to allow of their being dealt with before they become serious.' Happily, the observations helped naval architects and ship surveyors gain further experience before ships grew even larger still, and particular attention was paid to the design of the new Cunard liner *Queen Mary* based on *Olympic*, *Berengaria* and other vessels. Their service revealed specific aspects of their designs that could be improved upon for the future. The repairs endured for the remainder of *Olympic*'s career.

Undoubtedly the White Star Line were pleased by that and, following an extensive overhaul of the ship's reciprocating engines, they were better placed than they had been in 1911. *Olympic* arrived back at Southampton on 14 October 1932 after a satisfactory eastbound crossing, but defects were found in crankshafts for both the port and starboard engines while a routine adjustment was being carried out. In consequence, although the company had already scheduled engine work to take place during the annual overhaul, they had to cancel the ship's next crossing and bring it forward. The double bottom beneath the engines was 'very carefully examined' and with the exception of a few defective rivets its condition was satisfactory. The engine bedplates themselves were strengthened, while parts were renewed and additional balance weights were fitted to improve the working of the engines. By the time the work had been completed, it was clear that it had done the job.

Olympic's engines were tested for twelve hours and the revolutions increased to a maximum of 73rpm. According to the surveyor, 'everything went satisfactorily, there being practically no movement of the bedplates, and the chief engineer, who has been in the vessel since she was new, is definitely of the opinion that at no time in the vessel's history have the engines and thrust blocks been so free from movement.' He reported on 10 May 1933 that *Olympic* had completed three round voyages to New York 'and on the last voyage the engines were run at 77.1 revolutions port and 75.5 revolutions starboard, giving an average speed of 21.3 knots without the slightest trouble.' He 'made a careful inspection' of the repairs, including the engine bedplates, and was 'unable to find any indication of movement', adding, 'I am of the opinion that these parts are substantially as good as ever they were.'

★   ★   ★

While *Olympic* was out of service, the White Star Line took the opportunity to try and bring her into step with the times. The improvements were handled by Ashby Tabb, of Heaton Tabb & Co:

> The entrance halls and grand staircase have been redecorated and the staterooms modernised. There are now 127 staterooms with private baths, large numbers of outside rooms on B and C decks at minimum rates, and the tourist accommodation includes many rooms with private baths.
>
> After much thought it was decided to build up a background of soft, Georgian green with attractive harmony of colour in quiet tones relieved with the rich bronze balustrade and some touches of gold on the more prominent carved cornices, and thus lead up to a number of decorative panels of classical landscapes which had been specially painted and form points of unusual interest in the design.[119]

One of the original designers, probably Edward Croft-Smith, was less than pleased with the changes. He was said to be 'appalled'.[120] A number of the staterooms were brightened up. Stateroom A55 (numbered B57 in 1911), one of Harland & Wolff's own 'Bedroom B' designs with oak dado and white panelling, had pink colouring added to the panelling; another stateroom, A63 (numbered B65 in 1911), had blue and cream. The first-class lounge and smoke room remained unchanged, but when she arrived in New York early in March 1933 she was described as 'looking brand new'. *Olympic*'s passenger list fell below three hundred, including Lord Revelstoke, head of Baring Brothers, and his son, Rupert Baring. Meanwhile, the ship's officers were reported as saying that vibration had been further reduced following the engine work. An optimistic assessment by one reporter was that *Olympic*'s 'new service speed' was now 23 knots. While the engines performed well, they were eased in gradually, but the White Star Line were more concerned with reducing fuel costs than increasing them.

Aquitania and *Olympic*, photographed from *Leviathan*'s bow. The American liner arrived at Southampton, after her first eastbound crossing for her new owners, in July 1923. Sometimes described as an unpopular ship, in fact she established a strong following. In 1926, she carried over 36,000 passengers; *Aquitania* lagged with 26,000 and *Olympic* suffered a poor year with 24,000. *Leviathan* was withdrawn from service in 1934. (J. Kent Layton collection)

Indeed, following the engine work *Olympic* proved herself a ship that could shrug off age easily, for between 26 July 1933 and 6 September 1933 she completed three consecutive westbound crossings at 22 knots, beating her 1911 record; each was 3,094 miles long, proof of her excellent steering capabilities and testament to her officers' superb navigational skills, and her average speed hardly varied by a decimal point. The crossing times varied by only half an hour. Had the current been in her favour, going eastbound, her averages would have been a solid 23 knots. It would have been interesting to see the averages that she could have achieved had she truly been driven at full speed; certainly it is not inconceivable that they would have been much higher.

As of 24 July 1933, *Olympic* was registered with a capacity of 618 first-class passengers, a reduction due to further improvements and the fitting of additional private bathrooms, 447 tourist-class passengers, and only 382 third-class passengers, a total of 1,447 passengers. Her net tonnage had further been reduced to 20,994 tons, although her gross tonnage still remained the same as that given following her 1920 refit. Similar changes and reductions in capacity were taking place on the ships of other companies, as they struggled in the depression with diminishing passenger numbers.

In fact, with many conditions on the North Atlantic worse in 1933 than 1932, it would be the last year of the White Star Line's existence. The Oceanic Steam Navigation Company's balance sheet went from bad to worse. Even in 1929, the directors reported that the company's profit was 'somewhat disappointing' and attributed it to 'increased competition in the North Atlantic trade', but at least it was making a profit. For the first time in its history, the company carried a loss of £379,069 to its balance sheet in

'The old fashioned idea that going tourist meant "roughing it" has been dispelled by the complete, suave comfort of tourist cabins on White Star Line ships,' advised the company in 1932: 'This stateroom on the *Olympic* with twin beds and running hot and cold water proves the point. It was formerly first class.' (Author's collection)

1930; £450,777 in 1931; £152,045 in 1932; and £353,552 in 1933. Although there was an improvement in 1932, when the company actually made an operating profit, interest charges and other liabilities pulled it into the red, and any hopes of a sustained improvement were dashed when it went into reverse the following year.

Cunard had halted construction of its planned new liner, yard number 534, in 1931, and the British government saw an opportunity to combine the two companies to establish a single strong entity. 'My own aim,' Chancellor Neville Chamberlain wrote in his diary, 'has always been to use the 534 [yard number for the *Queen Mary*] as a lever for bringing about a merger between the Cunard and White Star Lines, thus establishing a strong British firm in the North Atlantic trade.'[121]

In October 1932, he asked Lord Weir to 'conduct a confidential enquiry' into 'the trading and financial position of the British shipping companies carrying on mail and passenger services in the North Atlantic, with special reference to the New York–European berth...' He examined White Star and Cunard in detail. On the express service, it was apparent that both companies' passenger carryings were suffering as foreign competition intensified, so that newer ships gained an increasing share of a declining market. Weir produced a table 'showing the trend of trade to the new express vessels from their older competitors in terms of total passengers carried of all classes in the last four years':

'Sprightly music draws lovely young couples forward, and nice middle-aged couples, and grand old couples. Cards are played, amusing chatter is chatted…and so the merry-making goes on.' A dance floor was available to tourist class passengers in the original second-class library. (Author's collection)

	1928	1929	1930	1931
Berengaria	37,062	36,853	23,472	13,408
Aquitania	28,033	29,363	27,895	21,992
Mauretania	16,992	18,842	15,805	12,560
Bremen		24,960	49,759	42,157
Europa			38,123	43,291
Columbus	24,911	13,426	15,706	5,717
Majestic	37,949	34,894	28,978	16,345
Olympic	26,221	25,775	19,282	13,975
Homeric	13,072	13,837	12,397	5,897
Ile de France	27,115	33,881	27,706	20,605
Paris	22,510	12,103	16,169	12,365
France	11,456	12,707	9,093	4,850

Weir wrote:

> Due to progress in naval architecture and marine engineering, it has now become pos-
> sible to operate a weekly service from Southampton by Cherbourg to New York by
> the provision of two vessels in place of three. Such vessels require to have a sea speed
> of about 29 knots, and would be of 75,000 tons… The alternative form of investment
> in say three modern vessels of the '*Aquitania*' type would neither meet the competition
> nor yield the same economic return.

Cunard's new liner, yard number 534, was expected to require only 10,100 tons of fuel
for each round voyage, but *Berengaria* required 9,400 tons even though she was far slower.
Weir was 'driven to the conclusion that every step should be taken to utilise existing
British tonnage as a whole in the most efficient and effective manner and to avoid duplica-
tion of overhead costs and wasteful inter-British competition'. As he saw it, 'this can best
be secured by the merging of the Cunard and Oceanic interests on the North Atlantic, so
that the fleets may be operated under a single control and with a single progressive British
policy.'

Weir's report caused some concern for Lord Essendon, the Oceanic Steam Navigation
Company's chairman:

> The impression I obtained from a perusal of the report was, that its author started out
> with the preconceived idea of the superiority of the Cunard, probably, perhaps not
> unnaturally, influenced by the association of the Oceanic with the Royal Mail Group.
> They have been made to appear like a naughty boy who should be removed to the
> bottom of the class. Altogether it has created an unfortunate atmosphere…

He disputed some of Weir's conclusions, even while acknowledging: 'For the past thirty
years the Oceanic Company has been part of a large combine [IMM and then the Royal
Mail Group], and as a result its liquid resources have been depleted in order to provide
dividends far in excess of what, under ordinary circumstances, would be regarded as prudent.' He pointed out that White Star's ships were, on average, younger, faster and larger
than Cunard's, while the new *Britannic* and *Georgic* had earned substantial profits in 1932:
'They are undoubtedly the best paying ships of either of the groups today.'

Unsurprisingly, Weir in turn disputed some of Essendon's statements. On 6 April 1933,
he wrote: 'The plain business facts made available by both companies are the elements on
which I have based my judgement as to their respective positions and I cannot but accept
the conclusions to which they lead me… Put in the simplest words, I feel that… a company which has and is meeting its full obligations stands and is justified in regarding itself
as standing in a superior position to a company which has not met and is not meeting is
obligations.' The same month, an official pondered:

> Not long ago the Cunard and the White Star were both great and prosperous compa-
> nies. The Cunard was the greater of the two, without, however, in any way dominating
> its rival.
>
> The misfortunes which affected the Kylsant group were due to an almost incred-
> ible financial incompetence, and the White Star suffered as much as any. But it has
> since been taken care of: its physical assets are unchanged and I doubt very much

whether its goodwill as a North Atlantic line is permanently impaired in a serious degree.

From the financial point of view the Cunard has for some time been running fast downhill from the top (just as a painfully large number of other great businesses in different classes of trade have done at various times before now). Recently, the White Star, despite its misfortunes and because it possesses two profit earning assets [*Britannic* and *Georgic*] (unusual things for shipping companies to possess just now) has been laboriously but surely climbing up from the bottom. They certainly have not yet passed each other in their opposite courses: but I am not clear that they will never do so.

The White Star Line was at a relative disadvantage, particularly given its worrisome liabilities, and by 30 December 1933 the company's directors had agreed a merger with Cunard; the government agreed financial support to complete the new express liner. Cunard White Star Ltd was registered on 10 May 1934, with Cunard interests accounting for 62 per cent of the new company.

During summer 1934 the *Olympic*'s survey was perfectly satisfactory, the surveyor noting that 'the bedplates of the main engines have been very carefully and minutely examined and in no case could any movement or defect be discovered'. In fact, the ship had never performed better for the same period. She remained the 'Old Reliable', running like a regular express train, only letting the infamous North Atlantic storms cause any serious disruption to her schedule. In this respect *Olympic* shared the *Oceanic*'s reputation for regularity established thirty years before. Encountering days of rough seas and wind on her 240th westbound crossing, *Olympic* averaged a shade under 21 knots; her 242nd eastbound crossing left New York on 28 April 1934 with her best day's run of 523 miles showing an average speed rising towards 22¾ knots.

However, 1934 would prove 'the most disastrous year in living memory' for Atlantic travel; until 1930 there had generally been a total of 1 million passengers, but it had now shrunk to 460,000,[122] many of whom were choosing newer vessels. To help judge the effect on *Olympic*, not to mention her contemporaries, during her total peacetime service to 1924 she had averaged 1,165 passengers per crossing and 951 passengers throughout the 1920s, but this declined by more than half by 1932 and on her May 1934 crossing to New York she carried 233 passengers.

Olympic's worst collision, in many people's opinion, occurred in 1934. It was after the Cunard White Star merger, but before the merger actually came into effect on 1 July 1934.

The Nantucket Lightship – number 117, as she was known officially – had been one of six sister-ships built for watching off the shoals off Nantucket. She was 'the newest thing in lightships, a great advance over the sailing vessels that stood watch…for over seventy years.' Constructed of steel in Charleston, South Carolina, and with two decks, the two-masted single-funnel ship displaced 630 tons and was 133ft 3in in length with a beam of 30ft. However, she was tiny compared to the express passenger vessels of the day sailing to and from the busy port of New York. By 1934 she had been on station for four years at the 'windy corner, forty-one miles south-east of Nantucket and about 200 miles from New York'. It was a dangerous station, where she was moored using 2in cast steel chain cables attached to two 7,000lb 'mushroom' anchors. One particularly notable incident had happened on 6 January that year. *Washington*, a 24,500-ton liner, had sideswiped her in a fog, carrying away a lifeboat davit, mast grating and some wireless rigging. *Washington* had hit the ship three times and it was surprising that she had not sunk in the 200ft deep waters…

Captain Edgar Lukeman Trant took over command from Captain George Ernest Warner in December 1930. Trant served as *Olympic*'s commander for almost a year and then joined *Majestic*; in turn, he handed over to *Olympic*'s penultimate commander, Captain John William Binks, in December 1931. (Günter Bäbler collection)

Radio operator John Perry, of Provincetown, was quite worried that if a liner rammed them head-on much worse would happen. 'But some day we are going to get it head-on, and that will be the finish,' he told friends, 'One of those big liners will just ride through us.'

Meanwhile *Olympic* was nearing the lightship on Tuesday 15 May 1934 in thick fog, under the command of Captain John Binks. Described as 'a veteran who had commanded ships for more than twenty years', Binks had 'a good record' and so far there had never been any accidents involving a ship under his command. He 'would not take any risks' unnecessarily, said Captain Thompson Lyon, the United States Lines' marine superintendent. It was on 31 December 1934 that he planned to retire, aged sixty, after a distinguished career.

By 5.00 a.m., due to thickening fog, *Olympic*'s speed was further reduced from 19½ to 16 knots; she later slowed to 12 knots as conditions worsened further.[123] Her whistles sounded periodically, as did the lightship's.

In fact, despite thick fog, which had clouded all but one day of the crossing after leaving Southampton the previous Wednesday, Binks still hoped that the *Olympic* could be brought into New York by midnight. In New York, Marine Superintendent Captain James Thompson expected her to reach Quarantine by about 10.00 p.m. for a midnight docking, but still waited for a wireless report to confirm the time.

On board *Olympic*, wireless transmissions went dead at 10.56 a.m. although the lightship's foghorn was audible; speed was reduced to ten knots.[124]

It was a few minutes past 11.00 a.m. when the red-hulled lightship – 'Nantucket' white-painted on her plates – became visible right up ahead, only a short distance away. Captain Binks ordered the helm hard over for a port turn, and then 'full astern' was ordered on the port engine. As *Olympic* began the turn, the starboard engine was reversed as well.[125]

Passengers began to arrive on deck as the engines' reversal became apparent. *Olympic*'s whistles blasted in warning to the lightship, but it couldn't move. Then there came the shrill ringing of the watertight door alarm as they began to close.

One of the passengers had been speaking to an assistant engineer when they heard the lightship's horn. The assistant engineer began explaining that the horn was magnified in the fog and was actually a long way off. The engines were now pounding in reverse. *Olympic*'s speed was decreasing: 9 knots, 8, 7, 6, 5… But a collision was inevitable.

Aboard the lightship Captain Braithwaite was in his bunk reading a novel that had been a present from one of his crewmen. Then a sailor ran in. '*Olympic*'s on top of us,' he yelled. Men ran for the deck, but there was little time.

Olympic smashed into the lightship and the impact was so forceful that the lightship's hull completely separated into two; she began settling and soon oil began to leak into the sea and a sickening smell of acetylene became apparent. Debris of all sorts – deck fittings, a red fishing dory and a red hatch cover – filled the sea. A shark began to nose around.

By this time, although *Olympic* was still very slowly moving, the port side 'emergency cutter' was in the water and the starboard counterpart followed three minutes later at 11.09 a.m.

Captain Binks wirelessed the company's New York office with his brief report:

> Please inform all concerned. In collision with Nantucket lightship and sunk same. Standing by to save crew.

It was hardly the liner's speed, but rather her huge weight that had been devastating; she was over seventy times heavier than the lightship.

Almost immediately after touching the water, the port boat's crew rescued one man from the water. Both cutters were lost for forty-five minutes in the fog.

Olympic had anchored at 11.30 a.m., while the starboard motorboat had been lowered to help with the search. When the starboard cutter returned, observers from the liner's decks could only see a motionless figure; but the port cutter returned a minute or two later, carrying five or six men, two of whom were 'lifeless'. In total, seven people were rescued from the sea, but three died in *Olympic*'s hospital.

Captain Braithwaite was later observed there; 'he was badly cut about the head, and lay there quietly smoking a cigarette, the first one that had touched his lips in thirteen years…'

Ironically, the fog cleared a little over half an hour after the collision. It was 12.29 p.m. when *Olympic* weighed anchor and resumed her journey to New York, with all hope of rescuing anybody else abandoned. However, by sundown the fog had returned 'denser than ever', forcing *Olympic* to proceed at 'dead slow ahead'.

It was on the morning of Wednesday 16 May 1934 that *Olympic* docked, somewhat later than the midnight arrival originally expected. The *New York Times* reported:

> An investigation of the collision will be started by the United States Steamboat Inspection Service at the Custom House this afternoon if the four survivors on the *Olympic* are in a condition to testify at that time. Captain John W. Binks, Master of the liner; the officers who were with him on the bridge, and the lookout men in the crow's nest, it is expected will be called…

In the event, the inquiry opened at 10.00 a.m. on Thursday 17 May 1934. White Star accepted responsibility for the collision (although the company would later dispute the claim of damages against them) and *Olympic* was allowed to sail at midnight on Thursday 17 May/Friday 18 May 1934,[126] as scheduled originally.

Liners had, in fact, previously had trouble with picking up wireless signals in the region, although an official statement had reported:

> ...in approaching, it is possible by radio cross bearings to obtain the distance off, at least approximately; thus in the case of the Nantucket lightship, with similar bearings on either Pollock Rip or Cape Cod, radio beams will give a position, and the signals are so operated that there should be no difficulty in obtaining radio bearings at suitable intervals regardless of weather conditions.

Although this had not been the case, as related many liners had frequently passed at inappropriately high speeds, homing-in on the radio beams. There had been 'a false sense of security', the Department of Commerce had recorded in its statement after *Olympic* docked, because of the ability to pick up long-distance radio signals, even in fog.

Olympic's bow damage was limited to a dent in her prow and scarred paintwork, a detailed hull inspection found after her return to Southampton on 24 May 1934.[127] But the loss of life was irreparable, especially to the families of those killed. However, 'through the United States Employees' Compensation Act, dependants of those lost received remuneration.'[128] Of the eleven-man crew, seven were killed: engineer William Perry, oiler John Richmond, cook Alfred Montero, first cook I. Pinna, seaman E. George, seaman John Fortes, and seaman John Rodriques, all of Massachusetts. In addition to Captain George Braithwaite, mate C. Mosher, radio operator John Perry and oiler Robert Laurent survived. Yet those who had survived would still remember the collision. 'At the time of the smash I was in the radio cabin. I had barely time to get on deck and swim for my life,' John Perry told the press. Robert Laurent recalled: 'It all happened so quickly, you had no chance to panic. We all had our life preservers and it was a good thing that we did.'[129]

The newly formed company was faced with claims of $500,000 in damages.[130] In the event, White Star paid for the United States Coastguard Lightship number 112, as a replacement for the doomed 117.[131]

★   ★   ★

In October 1934 the company decided that the *à la carte* restaurants on both *Olympic* and *Majestic* would be closed as an economy measure, although a similar service to that previously offered by the restaurants would be available in the first-class dining saloons 'without additional cost'. It was a far cry in the depression from the *Olympic*'s restaurant receipts totalling £1,730 on her first round voyage. However, in spring 1935 some new equipment was installed in the main galleys of the dining saloons, improving service.

The numerous efforts to save money could only go so far. In 1931, the average expenses for each round trip *Olympic* made came to £31,234, which had been reduced to £26,390 by 1935. Unfortunately, the revenues from passengers and cargo carrying had

---

★ A number of caveats need to be applied to such data. Where financial statements have survived, it is often a comparison between records compiled by the White Star Line prior to the merger and then the combined Cunard White Star company afterwards. There may be accounting discrepancies and other difficulties making a comparison. In this case, the data seems to be broadly comparable and in line with what might be expected: for instance, the fall in revenues shows a similar trend to the ship's passenger numbers. However, even the combined company's records are not always clear and provisional figures can show slight variations from one document to another.

fallen even more sharply, so that a gross profit of almost £5,000 on each round trip in 1931 declined sharply in 1932; from 1933 it appears *Olympic* was running at a loss.* On a net basis, including allowance for office and advertising expenses, depreciation charges and so forth, the figures would be even worse. In 1934, the combined company's four express ships all ran at a loss on both a gross and a net basis and passenger numbers were low: only *Aquitania* even came close to making a gross profit, with an average loss of £255 on each round trip, while *Majestic's* figures were the worst and showed a loss of £4,924.

By the end of 1934, it was not hard to see why *Adriatic*, *Homeric* and *Mauretania* had been withdrawn from North Atlantic service. The total number of passengers carried by *Olympic* rose that year, the first increase since 1928, but it was only because she made more crossings than she had done in 1933. Her 249th round trip in September 1934 generated a gross profit of £6,139, but over the ten round trips from her 248th to 257th she only made a gross profit half of the time; and on a net basis she continued to run at a loss. There were signs of encouragement by the beginning of 1935: her passenger numbers compared to the same period in 1934 rose by nearly 40 per cent; her gross loss of £4,729 on each round trip improved to £1,342; and on a net basis her performance improved as well.[132] Unfortunately, there were too many ships in the fleet. *Olympic's* running mates still had the edge in terms of their passenger carryings. If, in 1934, she had been able to earn as much as *Berengaria* then *Olympic* would have made a gross profit and been the best performing of the four ships on a net basis, due to her lower running costs. As it was, she was the oldest of the four and perhaps the passenger figures were more important.

During March 1935 the revised insurance value for *Olympic* was given as £740,000, *Majestic's* being £900,000, *Homeric's* £550,000, *Aquitania's* £730,000 and *Berengaria's* £830,000, but *Mauretania*, had already been withdrawn from service and was not valued.[133] By this time, *Olympic* bore a number of signs of the merger with Cunard, for her officers' rank titles had been changed (as one example): Captain Peel was in command, but below him were the new ranks of staff captain, staff captain & chief officer, senior first officer, junior first officer, senior second officer, junior second officer, senior third officer and two

Olympic at New York, March 1931. Her impressive profile remained in her twentieth year of service. (Günter Bäbler collection)

A unique snapshot of *Olympic* at Southampton in the 1930s. (Author's collection)

junior third officers. These positions were filled respectively by Mr Foyster, Mr Sharp, Mr Moughton, Mr Devlin, Mr Williams, Mr Law, Mr Shaw, Mr Anson and Mr Jones.

On 5 April 1935 *Olympic* left New York on what would be her final eastbound crossing, arriving back at Southampton at 2.06 p.m. on 12 April 1935 to be laid up. It was not a good week for the new company, as the previous day *Aquitania* had gone aground at Southampton with 270 passengers while returning from a Mediterranean cruise.

Although on the return leg of her penultimate round trip *Olympic* had averaged 22¼ knots, she made the westbound leg of her final voyage at 21½ knots, covering the 3,159-mile distance in 6 days, 3 hours and 9 minutes. She returned eastbound in 6 days, 2 hours and 42 minutes at an average of 21¾ knots. *Olympic* had logged 257 round trips to New York, carrying in excess of 430,000 passengers on her commercial voyages and the occasional cruise. It was a testament to her enduring popularity, even though passenger numbers had declined sharply after the depression set in.

It had been announced in late January 1935 that *Olympic* would undertake a number of cruises during the summer season from the end of June. The company hoped that cruising would be a profitable activity. At the end of March, the many intended cruise destinations were announced, including Halifax, the St Lawrence and Caribbean. The company drew up a schedule: on 29 June 1935 *Olympic* would make a westbound crossing to New York, followed by five cruises, and then on 28 September 1935 she would leave New York for Southampton. There would be two further round trips, leaving Southampton on 20 November 1935 and 11 December 1935, which would take her to 1936 and her twenty-fifth year of service. On Sunday 14 April 1935, twenty-three years to the day from her doomed sister's fatal accident, it was announced that the cruise programme had been cancelled.

Olympic must have covered close on 1.8 million miles including her war service, equivalent to about seventy circumnavigations of the earth, which had been clocked up without any significant mechanical failure; she had given safe, reliable service throughout 24 years, transporting not only passengers but military personnel as well. As an indication of the hard work she had done, the reciprocating engines must have each revolved some 51 million times, while the turbine likely achieved some 108 million revolutions during its lifetime. Although the ship was certainly now physically capable of giving many more years' service, times had changed. The planned refitting before July 1935 to modify some of her accommodation for cruise passengers, particularly tourist class, was cancelled.

Late in April 1935, Cunard White Star's board noted of *Olympic*: 'The cruising programme of this ship in United States waters advertised for the coming summer has been cancelled and the ship is now laid up at Southampton. We have no further employment in sight for her.' If the cruises had been cancelled, then by July 1935 it appeared that *Olympic* might be reprieved. Among other proposals, a syndicate had proposed to purchase her 'for operation as a floating hotel in the South of France'. Unfortunately, it came to nothing.★ On 20 August 1935 *Olympic* had been laid up for five months at Southampton and she was opened up for inspection by potential buyers. Sir John Jarvis – a Member of Parliament – bought the *Olympic* on 10 September 1935 for the sum of £97,500 for scrap; she was to provide employment for his constituents in the Tyneside town of Jarrow.

News of *Olympic*'s sale for scrapping brought many protests. In New York, the Prince of Wales spoke highly of her seagoing qualities, while Passenger Manager Charles Fecke opined that the *Olympic* had twenty-four of the finest cabins that he had ever seen on any ship. On the day following the liner's sale, the *Southern Daily Echo* reflected: 'Although the news of the sale of the famous White Star liner *Olympic*, 46,439 tons, did not come as a surprise, it has most certainly occasioned a feeling of regret in the minds of a large number of local residents…' *Olympic* had 'come to be regarded as an old favourite', it reported, continuing: 'She was a ship in the true sense of the word. There was somewhat quiet dignity as opposed to the modern bizarre tendency in ship decoration.' One opinion asked: 'First *Mauretania*, now *Olympic* [are to be scrapped] – what next?'

It was a good question. Carpet tiles from *Mauretania* and *Olympic*'s quality restaurant carpets were transferred to *Aquitania* in September, whose equivalent fittings were worn.

On 11 October 1935 *Olympic* departed Southampton for the final time under sad gazes. Numerous small craft escorted her down Southampton Water as her siren blew farewell; she looked stately and magnificent, smoke billowing from her third funnel, the ensign fluttering at her stern. The late afternoon had proved cloudy but bright and her funnels cast shadows over the water. Meanwhile, preparations were underway at Jarrow's shipbreaking yard to receive the liner; 'scores of workmen reached fever pitch activity in preparing for the liner's reception'. Along the 1,000ft jetty, mooring positions had been established at 200ft intervals, signal codes arranged and final, careful instructions delivered for the docking.

But although *Olympic*'s arrival at Jarrow was scheduled for early on 13 October 1935, a Sunday, in the event she performed well and arrived early.

'It is almost sacrilege to destroy her after the performance she put up on this last voyage from Southampton,' Chief Engineer C.W. McKimm complained, who had served on *Olympic* since May 1911, initially as a junior second engineer, and was the only remaining member of the original crew. 'I could have understood the necessity [of scrapping] if the "Old Lady" had lost her efficiency,' he would tell a reporter, 'but the engines are as sound as they ever were. Better, in fact, than when they were first installed in 1911.'

★ See '*Olympic*: A Floating Hotel' in *Titanic Commutator*, Titanic Historical Society, 2007.

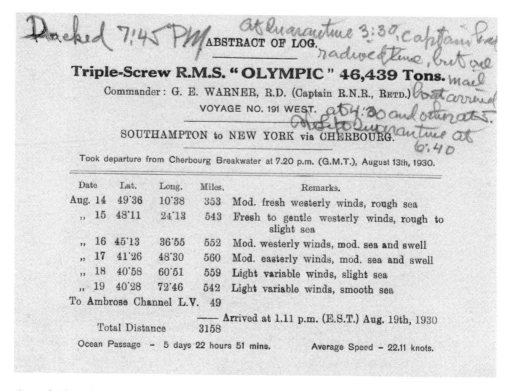

Docked 7:45 PM ABSTRACT OF LOG. *at Quarantine 3:30, captain pilot radioed time, but one mail boat arrived at 4:30 and others at 5.*

Triple-Screw R.M.S. "OLYMPIC" 46,439 Tons.

Commander: G. E. WARNER, R.D. (Captain R.N.R., RETD.)

VOYAGE NO. 191 WEST.

SOUTHAMPTON to NEW YORK via CHERBOURG. *and to Quarantine at 6.40*

Took departure from Cherbourg Breakwater at 7.20 p.m. (G.M.T.), August 13th, 1930.

Date	Lat.	Long.	Miles.	Remarks.
Aug. 14	49'36	10'38	353	Mod. fresh westerly winds, rough sea
,, 15	48'11	24'13	543	Fresh to gentle westerly winds, rough to slight sea
,, 16	45'13	36'55	552	Mod. westerly winds, mod. sea and swell
,, 17	41'26	48'30	560	Mod. easterly winds, mod. sea and swell
,, 18	40'58	60'51	559	Light variable winds, slight sea
,, 19	40'28	72'46	542	Light variable winds, smooth sea
To Ambrose Channel L.V.			49	

Arrived at 1.11 p.m. (E.S.T.) Aug. 19th, 1930

Total Distance   3158

Ocean Passage – 5 days 22 hours 51 mins.   Average Speed – 22.11 knots.

One of *Olympic*'s passengers kept their Abstract of Log card as a souvenir, complete with their own annotations about the delay when she reached New York. She finally docked at 7.45 p.m. on Tuesday evening. (Author's collection)

'Three miles out to sea, the *Olympic* had to wait until late afternoon before there was sufficient water to permit navigation of the channel,' the *Shields Gazette* reported. Early in the morning the liner was shrouded in haze, which gradually cleared. 'Vantage points were well-used during the morning, but as the day wore on the crowds assumed huge proportions.' The road on Lawe Top was scarcely passable, while hundreds of people thronged the South pier, South Marine Park, and there was an enormous crowd on the Groyne pier. 'The crowd was much larger than that which saw the *Mauretania* pass the Tyne on 2 July [1935].' Many people wore binoculars and carried telescopes. She waited outside the harbour, 'her funnels resplendent in the sunshine'.

At 2.55 p.m. her bow was turned westward and, under her own steam, she entered the Tyne. 'Leaning over the rails were a hundred British seamen, maritime pall bearers as it were, conducting an old warrior to the last resting place.'

'Once abreast of The Narrows the escort of tugs closed in. As if firmly resolved not to stand any nonsense, the *Hendon* and the *Joffre* moved under bows, each taking a thick hawser aboard her, while the *Wearmouth* jostled fiercely against the *Olympic*'s starboard flank so that the hemp buffers groaned in protest. Meanwhile the tugs *Plover* and *George V* had taken hold at the stern. Holding a watching brief, the sixth tug, *Great Emperor*, sped alongside in readiness for any emergency.'

A plane followed her, while numerous cameras on the T.I.C. ferryboat *Tynemouth* recorded the event. *Olympic*'s whistles now sounded continuously. Numerous craft surrounded her. 'The convoy sped at a steady two knots.'

R.M.S. "MAJESTIC"
THE LARGEST STEAMER IN THE WORLD
R.M.S. "OLYMPIC"

FIRST CLASS À LA CARTE RESTAURANT.

In addition to the regular First Class Dining Saloon there is, on board the R.M.S. "MAJESTIC" and R.M.S. "OLYMPIC," a large modern *a la carte* Restaurant, with Reception Room, where meals may be obtained at any time at fixed charges, as shown on the bill of fare issued from day to day.

The Restaurant is under the Management of the Company.

If passage is taken entirely without meals in the regular Dining Saloon, an allowance will be made from the advertised rates of £6. 10. 0. per adult when the passage fare is paid in sterling, and $25.00 per adult when the passage fare is paid in dollars.

First Class Passengers wishing to use the Restaurant should apply on board to the Manager for the reservation of tables.

R.M.S. "MAJESTIC"	R.M.S. "OLYMPIC"
PALM COURT—Adjoining the Restaurant is the Palm Court, a magnificent apartment where light refreshment may be obtained at fixed prices.	CAFÉ PARISIEN—Adjoining the Restaurant and with large windows overlooking the sea, is a charmingly decorated Café, where light refreshment may be obtained at fixed charges.
The Palm Court is also, as in the case of the Restaurant, under the Company's management.	The Café, is also, as in the case of the Restaurant, under the Company's management.

One of the last sailing lists issued in the name of the White Star Line contained information about the extra tariff restaurants on board *Olympic* and *Majestic* in summer 1934. It is interesting to compare the rebate figures with those before the war. Cunard had always had a different attitude than the White Star Line to such facilities, believing they created two tiers of first-class passengers: when *Majestic*'s sister ship *Berengaria* was taken over by Cunard after the war, her restaurant was closed; *Aquitania* had a grill room but, contrary to popular belief, it did not function as an extra tariff restaurant. The restaurants on board *Olympic* and *Majestic* were closed within months. (Author's collection)

It was 3.50 p.m. when she reached the Palmer's Yard and stopped abreast her berth. Fifty minutes were needed to secure her in, an operation providing 'the most spectacular display of seamanship the Tyne has seen for years'.

'Gently, with infinite slowness, the *Olympic*'s stern was brought nearer the quay. Scarcely a ripple disturbed the surface of the water as the tugs hauled her in inch by inch.'

At 4.45 p.m. the final mooring ropes were secured, but by 5.15 p.m. the tide had fallen and *Olympic* had firmly settled, despite previous extensive dredging.

Sir John Jarvis and Mayor Dodds of Jarrow boarded to welcome Captain P.V. Vaughan and South Shields Pilot J. Ramsey, who had guided the ship from Southampton.

The temporary crew of 100 was officially discharged, while Chief Engineer McKimm left for his Southampton home late that evening. Many crew were particularly sad to see the ship's life end, for she had been their home for years; many had stayed on her for more than a decade. As one crewman put it, 'she got you for good.' Another lamented that she was such a fine ship, particularly since 1933, and she had many years left in her.

Olympic was awaiting her fate, her ghostly interiors toured by curious visitors in a brief afterlife. On Tuesday 5 November 1935 auctioneers Knight, Frank & Rutley began to sell some of the 4,456 lots, completing the auction in good time thirteen days later; the first-class purser's office became the auctioneer's office, 'open daily from 10.00 a.m. to 5.00 p.m'.

Cunard White Star maintained their express service with *Majestic*, *Berengaria* and *Aquitania*. Although initial plans envisaged *Berengaria*'s retirement, in a change of mind *Majestic* was withdrawn from service instead. She was sold for scrapping but then was called into government service as the training ship *Caledonia*, serving until the outbreak of war in September 1939. *Queen Mary*'s arrival in May 1936 marked an improvement in the company's fortunes and for a period she operated with *Aquitania* and *Berengaria*. Passenger numbers were recovering and the average passenger lists for the older ships increased even as *Queen Mary* carried large numbers, bringing them into profit, although they never quite reached the levels of the 1920s. Unfortunately, increasing electrical problems and maintenance issues dictated *Berengaria*'s withdrawal from service earlier than planned in 1938. She was no longer seaworthy and it was prohibitively expensive to make her safe for passenger service. While the retirements of *Olympic* and *Majestic* were planned, the company had no choice with *Berengaria*; perhaps, in hindsight, they regretted not keeping one of the White Star liners in reserve. *Aquitania* herself was expected to be retired in 1940, on the arrival of the new *Queen Elizabeth*, but the outbreak of war prolonged her life by another decade of war and austerity service.

Meanwhile, *Olympic*'s scrapping continued and her superstructure had been dismantled by August 1936. It was reported that workers at Thomas Wards noted that her twenty-seven-year-old hull was 'surprisingly sound'. The remnants of her lower hull were towed to Inverkeithing for final demolition in September 1937. Weeks later, J. Bruce Ismay passed away at his home in London.

Olympic's registry was cancelled over a year later, recorded in red scrawl in the register: 'Certificate cancelled and Registry closed February 4th 1939. Vessel broken up at Inverkeithing. Advice received from the beneficial owner.'

'She will always be remembered for her magnificent war service and as a very fine-looking, reliable, comfortable and steady "old lady" – even though she was only twenty-four when taken out of service,' J.H. Isherwood wrote in *Sea Breezes*, February 1956. He continued:

Olympic's paintwork shows a decline in her appearance while she lies at Southampton's 'Berth 108' in the summer of 1935. (Author's collection)

> Four years more and she might have been of enormous value to her country in the Second World War. Her hull was still as sound as a bell. But the great and rapid strides in marine engineering had made her uneconomical by modern standards and the slump rendered her redundant. The dreary flattened hulk towing up to Inverkeithing was, I think, rather specially pathetic. Besides being all that remained of a very proud ship, it brought back memories of the terrible disasters that had befallen her two sisters and was a symbol not only of the end of a ship but also of one of the greatest of transatlantic shipping companies.

At the time she was conceived, few people foresaw that she would outlast the company she served, but *Olympic* did. Nobody, surely, imagined that she would be the only one of the three sister ships to complete even a single commercial voyage. *Olympic* was the first liner to exceed 40,000grt; the first vessel to displace over 50,000 tons. Even if competitors sought to better her, she retained her own qualities with luxurious and comfortable accommodation, a regularity and reliability of service, economy of operation and as a good sea boat. The proof was her long and successful career, in peace and war.

6

RMS *TITANIC*

After the collision with the *Hawke*, *Olympic* required a new propeller shaft. Therefore the shafting for the *Titanic* was put into her and the second vessel had new parts installed, fatefully delaying her maiden voyage.[1] *Titanic*'s maiden voyage was originally scheduled for 20 March 1912 and her second Southampton departure for 10 April 1912; in the event, her maiden voyage took place on what should have been her second round trip.[2]

On Monday 27 March 1912 Captain Herbert James Haddock was signed on as *Titanic*'s master at Southampton.[3] First Officer Murdoch and Second Officer Lightoller were aboard by 20 March 1912, while *Titanic*'s junior officers signed on on 27 March 1912 and there was an inspection of the immense new liner by the British Board of Trade. Originally, trials were scheduled for 1 April, but strong winds caused a postponement because it would be harder to handle the ship in the confines of the river and lough. It was on this date, 1 April 1912, that Captain Edward J. Smith formally took command of the new vessel from Captain Haddock.[4]

Titanic's trials were completed successfully on 2 April 1912, a day that was generally fine and clear. The ship left Belfast for Southampton shortly after 8.00 p.m. and she averaged about 20 knots for the approximately 570 miles she had to cover. During a short period, according to Edward Wilding, she attained a speed of 23¼ knots. If this was the case, conditions must have been ideal given that a number of boilers remained unlit.[5]

Titanic's accommodation was also improved: there were more lavish B-deck suites, an enlarged *à la carte* restaurant and new 'café parisien'. The forward third of the promenade deck was also enclosed in glass. Her tonnage was also slightly larger partly because of these additions, with her net tonnage being 21,831 tons and the gross tonnage being 46,328 tons – the new ship was therefore 1,004 tons larger than *Olympic*. However, it remains a mystery why the addition of the enclosed promenade was made at so late a stage in construction. Possibly the B-deck enclosed promenade, which had been eliminated by additional first-class suites, had only left the open A-deck promenade and it had not been fully realised until the last minute. After all, the A-deck screens were never fitted to the *Olympic*, but they were fitted to the third liner, which had two-thirds of B-deck occupied by suites. Then again, *Olympic* was given a row of lifeboats which blocked out the sea view from the boat deck, and *Britannic*'s advanced davits allowed an open sea view.

Forward on B-deck, just aft of the forward grand staircase, were two 'millionaire's suites', that were similar to the parlour suites here on *Olympic*'s B-deck. They had private bathrooms and wardrobe rooms, plus a sitting room and two bedrooms: a private enclosed promenade was also available (where part of the first-class promenade was situated on *Olympic*). These suites cost up to £870 ($4,350) for a single crossing, compared to £450 ($2,250) for the best suite on *Mauretania*, which was somewhat inferior. Other suites were similar to *Olympic*'s, but were slightly larger, with private bath and wardrobe rooms, and some had inner cabins for servants. All rooms were interconnecting and could be transformed into suites of any size if necessary – all suites extended to the sides of the ship and were decorated in an array of different styles and colours. As well as oak or white-panel-covered walls, many suites were white with coloured panels.[6]

The *Shipbuilder* magazine described the new reception room for the *à la carte* restaurant:

> Friends and parties will meet prior to taking their seats in the restaurant. The elegant settees and easy chairs are upholstered in silk of carmine colour, with embroideries applied in tasteful design. The breadth of treatment and the carefully proportioned panels on the walls, with richly-carved cornice and surrounding mouldings, from an impressive *ensemble*, which is distinctly pleasing to the eye. There is accommodation for a band in this room.[7]

Shortly after midnight on 4 April the new ship berthed in Southampton for provisioning and the start of her maiden voyage. Other last minute outfitting was still to be completed owing to the shorter time left for construction after *Olympic*'s February 1912 return to the shipyard.[8] To emphasise the hurry, when the ship had left Belfast much of the décor was incomplete. The ornate forward grand staircase panel's clock was not installed until the final minutes; initially, a mirror had been fitted before the clock so that the gap was less noticeable.[9]

The following morning, Good Friday, saw flags fluttering from the ship's masts and rigging – the only time that *Titanic* would ever wear her flags. During her stay in the port many supplies would be loaded, among them were forty tons of potatoes, 75,000lb of meat, and many items of linen, around 75,000 separate pieces, not to mention the cutlery.

Assistant emigration officer Maurice Clarke, under the British Board of Trade, had the duty to clear the immense liner to sail under the Merchant Shipping Act. Over three days he visited the ship to inspect the accommodation, safety and provisioning.

★ ★ ★

Wednesday 10 April 1912, Sailing day.

At 7.00 a.m. Captain Smith left his detached redbrick twin-gabled house on Southampton's Winn Road;[10] he boarded *Titanic* half-an-hour later. It was his duty to see the ship's articles and make his report to the company before the liner went to sea.

Maurice Clarke also came aboard at 7.30 a.m., wishing an early start. He would stay on board until noon when the ship sailed. All crew were mustered and Captain Benjamin Steele checked the articles; the crew were medically inspected by the Board of Trade. Two boats – numbers 11 and 15 on the starboard side – were raised and lowered to the water under the direction of Fifth Officer Lowe and Sixth Officer Moody.

Titanic's hull lies beneath the gantry at Harland & Wolff's Queen's Island yard. (J.&C. McCutcheon collection)

There was something of a last minute change to the ship's senior officers before *Titanic* sailed. Henry Wilde came aboard as the new chief officer, replacing William Murdoch★ who moved down to first officer; in turn, Charles Lightoller became second officer; and David Blair, the original second officer, left the ship. The remaining officers in Smith's team, Third Officer Hebert Pitman, Fourth Officer Joseph Boxhall, Fifth Officer Harold Lowe and Sixth Officer James Moody retained their original roles. Wilde and Murdoch both had experience of *Olympic* and Wilde's was perhaps a temporary appointment. (Following *Olympic*'s maiden voyage, Joseph Evans, her original chief officer, left the ship

---

★ It is interesting to note one incident nine years earlier on board the White Star liner *Arabic*, related by the author Geoffrey Marcus in his classic book *The Maiden Voyage* (published in 1969). He described Murdoch as 'an officer of ripe experience, cool and steady judgement, and instant presence of mind':

> When serving in the *Arabic*, he had displayed all these qualities in consummate degree in coolly, skilfully, and, in the nick of time successfully averting a collision. It happened one night on the outward passage, one day from Nantucket Light, with a fresh north-westerly breeze and a light impalpable mist (known as 'a Scotchman'), which rendered visibility difficult and set up a false horizon. Just after 10 o'clock Murdoch came up on the bridge to relieve Fox, the OOW [officer of the watch]. Before taking over, the former as usual took a few turns while accustoming his eyes to the darkness. There came a sudden warning from the lookout: 'Light on the port side!' Fox, without observing the light himself, promptly shouted 'Watch your port helm' (i.e. *be ready to alter course to starboard*). He moved over to the side, Murdoch following; then, seeing the light, gave the order to port the helm. At the same instant Murdoch also suddenly saw, almost under the *Arabic*'s bows, a single red [port side] light. Realising there would be no time to alter course, he acted with swift decision: already the quartermaster had begun to port the helm when Murdoch, rushing to the wheel, shoved the man aside, brought the wheel back a few spokes, and held on.

Arabic narrowly avoided colliding with the sailing vessel.

and was replaced by Wilde.) All were highly competent and would have had Smith's confidence as final preparations were made for departure.

On the bridge, Captain Smith completed the document entitled 'Master's Report to Company':

> I herewith report this ship loaded and ready for sea. The engines and boilers are in good order for the voyage, and all charts and sailing directions up-to-date – Your obedient servant, Edward J. Smith.

The other great masses of paperwork were signed and checked. The 'Report of Survey of an Emigrant Ship' was signed by F. Carruthers, W. Tarrant and P.J. Atkey for the Board of Trade. Enough coal was on board: '5,892 tons…sufficient to take the ship to her next coaling port'… 'I am satisfied that the hull, boilers and machinery are in good condition and fit for the voyage.' There was enough water aboard, which was: '…certified to amount to 206,800 gallons…contained in seven tanks.'*

Due to the recent coal strike, 4,427 tons of fuel had been taken from the *Majestic*, *New York*, *Oceanic*, *Philadelphia* and *St Louis* – all of them lying idle in port.[11] Some 1,880 tons had been in the bunkers before the additional 'pirated' fuel and 415 tons had been used in port to provide heating and lighting.[12] Although this was less fuel than would normally be carried, there was still enough to maintain a good speed to New York.

Titanic's officers were now all at their stations: Chief Officer Wilde at the forecastle head – in charge of moorings – with Second Officer Lightoller seeing to the forward spring lines and offering general assistance; First Officer Murdoch at the aft docking bridge over the poop deck – in charge of the moorings there – next to Third Officer Pitman, who passed instructions to Murdoch pertaining to the bridge's orders; Fourth Officer Boxhall was on the bridge with Pilot George Bowyer and Captain Smith – he operated the gleaming engine room telegraphs and logged each command; Fifth Officer Lowe was also on the bridge – manning the telephones – and Sixth Officer Moody was stationed at the aft port side gangway on F-deck to supervise its withdrawal.[13]

On time, *Titanic* departed. She drifted from the dockside once the lines were released, with six tugs assisting her. One observer wrote:

> It is doubtful whether the *Olympic* has ever cleared the new dock in such a splendid manner as did the *Titanic* on this occasion. From the moment she began to move from her berth in that dock she was under absolute control, and she passed out of the dock not only majestically, but also smoothly and calmly. If anything, she was proceeding

---

* Captain Maurice Clarke, assistant emigration officer with the Board of Trade, was unaware that a fire had been smouldering in the forward starboard coal bunker of boiler room 5. When he learned about it subsequently, he believed that 'it is not an uncommon thing to have these small fires in the bunkers' and the fact that it was not reported to him was not unusual or untoward. The fire started prior to *Titanic* reaching Southampton and continued to smoulder until it was finally extinguished three days after she had left Southampton. Chief Engineer Bell was aware of it, as were personnel from Harland & Wolff including Thomas Andrews, who wished to make an inspection. The watertight bulkhead itself was 'dinged' as a result of the fire. Leading Fireman Charles Hendrickson observed: 'You could see where the bulkhead had been red hot…all the paint and everything was off, it was dented a bit.' He 'got some black oil and rubbed over it'. The bulkhead was a little less than half an inch thick and 'specially stiffened and strengthened' so that it could 'stand the necessary pressure in the event of [an] accident'.

more slowly than the *Olympic* usually does, and she turned her nose towards the sea with the greatest ease… the tugs seemed to be working magnificently, and once she had turned round and straightened herself for the channel a few of the people standing by began to move homewards, some of them being heard to make exclamations of surprise at the ease with which a 46,000 ton steamer could be shaped for the sea. Indeed, matters were going so well that some of the tugs were able to slacken off. One or two, at least, had left the vessel, and were merely following in her wake until she had cleared the dock head.

Unfortunately, any hopes that *Titanic's* so far impressive departure would be hassle-free were about to be dashed. As she continued forward into the channel, she had to pass White Star's own *Oceanic*, which was tied up at Berth 38; and the American Line's *New York* was moored alongside *Oceanic*. One by one, the lines holding *New York* parted as *Titanic* drew abreast, and she began to drift towards *Titanic* stern first. There was a grave danger that the liner, adrift and without steam up, would touch *Titanic's* port side with her stern and make contact with *Oceanic* with her bow.

Quick thinking averted a collision. Captain Gale, in command of the tug *Vulcan*, made an important contribution. He recalled:

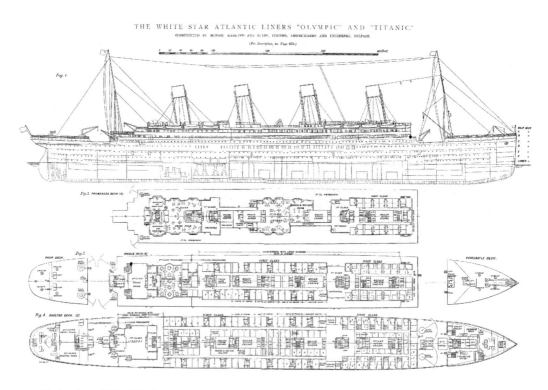

Engineering published deck plans of *Olympic* and *Titanic* in 1911. They were accurate generally for *Olympic* when she entered service, but by the time of *Titanic's* completion numerous alterations had been incorporated: including additional first-class staterooms near the aft grand staircase on A-deck; the expansion of the *á la carte* restaurant, first-class staterooms and the addition of two private promenades on B-deck; and the new Café Parisien. (J.&C. McCutcheon collection)

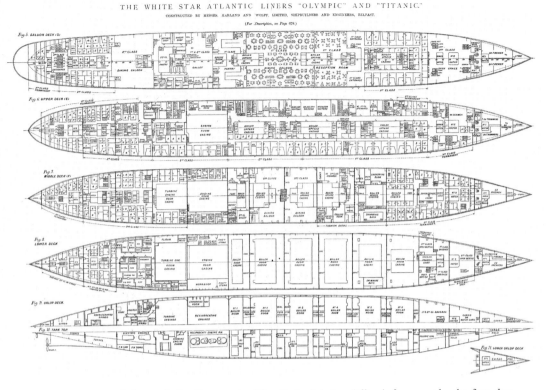

THE WHITE STAR ATLANTIC LINERS "OLYMPIC" AND "TITANIC."

CONSTRUCTED BY MESSRS. HARLAND AND WOLFF, LIMITED, SHIPBUILDERS AND ENGINEERS, BELFAST.

(For Description, see Page 678.)

Olympic and *Titanic*'s lower decks. Once again, *Titanic*'s final design differed: for example, the first-class reception room was expanded at the expense of the first-class entrance either side of the grand staircase; and the Turkish bath establishment's layout was altered compared to *Olympic*. (J.&C. McCutcheon collection)

> Someone sang out to me to get up and push the *New York* back, but such a thing was impossible. Had I got between the two ships we would almost certainly have been jammed. Instead, I turned the *Vulcan* round and got a wire rope on the port quarter of the *New York*. Unfortunately, that rope parted, but our men immediately got a second wire on board, and we got hold of the *New York* when she was within 4ft of the *Titanic*. Our movements were all the more trying because the broken mooring ropes from *New York* were lying in the water, and we stood a good chance of fouling our own propeller. Every line on the *New York* snapped, the stern lines being the first to go…[14]

Meanwhile, *Titanic*'s engines had been reversed and checked her forward momentum. The same observer believed that 'only once in a hundred times would three ocean liners escape from such a perilous situation without sustaining damage'. Unlike *Olympic*'s early mishaps, it may have seemed to some that *Titanic* was destined to be a lucky ship; others thought it was an unfortunate start to her maiden voyage.

    New York was secured and attention was paid to *Oceanic* to ensure that she did not drift from her berth. Although delayed, *Titanic* was able to continue safely. She covered 89 miles on the run from Southampton to Cherbourg via the Nab lightship, averaging a leisurely speed of over 16 knots and arriving early that evening. The new tenders *Nomadic* and *Traffic* ferried passengers out to the ship. Shortly after 8 p.m. she left Cherbourg and vanished into the night. Her speed increased gradually until she was making around 20 knots and this enabled her to reach Queenstown shortly before noon the following day. Just like the procedure at Cherbourg, passengers would be ferried out to the ship.

While she lay off Queenstown, J. Bruce Ismay called Chief Engineer Bell to his suite. One of the questions that Ismay asked related to the amount of coal on board. He believed that there was sufficient to reach New York 'with two days spare consumption'.

Chief Engineer Bell also found the time to write a brief letter to his son Frank during the Queenstown stop:

> We have made a good run from Southampton everything working "A1", we nearly had a collision with the *New York* and *Oceanic* when leaving S'ton the wash of our propellers made the two ships range about when we were passing them this made their mooring ropes break and the *New York* set off across the river until tugs got hold of her again no damage was done but it looked like trouble at the time...
>
>   Your Loving Father
>   J. Bell.[15]

As the two men were discussing the new ship, several passengers who were not taking the ship all the way to New York disembarked. One of the passengers who left at Queenstown recorded their thoughts about the new ship, from her first day in commercial service:

> 'Look at how that ship is rolling. I never thought it was so rough.'
>
> The voice was a lady's, and the place was the sun deck of the *Titanic*. We had just got well clear of the eastern end of the Isle of Wight, and were shaping our course down the English Channel towards Cherbourg. The ship that had elicited the remark was a large three-masted sailing vessel, which rolled and pitched so heavily that over her bow the seas were constantly breaking. But up where we were – some 60 feet above the water line – there was no indication of the strength of tossing swell below. This indeed is the one great impression I received from my first trip on the *Titanic* – and everyone with whom I spoke shared it – her wonderful steadiness. Were it not for the brisk breeze blowing along the decks, one would have scarcely imagined that every hour found us some 20 knots farther upon our course. And then this morning, when the full Atlantic swell came upon our port side, so stately and measured was the roll of the mighty ship that one needed to compare the moving of the side with the steady line of the clear horizon.
>
> After a windy night on the Irish Sea, when the sturdy Packet boat tossed and tumbled to her heart's content – by the way; have ships a heart? – the lordly contempt of the *Titanic* for anything less than a hurricane seemed most marvellous and comforting. But other things besides her steadiness filled us with wonder. Deck over deck and apartment after apartment lent their deceitful aid to persuade us that instead of being on the sea we were still on *terra firma*. It is useless for me to attempt a description of the wonders of the saloon – the smoking room with its inlaid mother-of-pearl – the lounge with its green velvet and dull polished oak – the reading-room, with its marble fire place and deep soft chairs and rich carpet of old rose hue – all these things have been told over and over again, and only lose in the telling. So vast was it all that after several

hours on board some of us were still uncertain of our way about – though we must state that with commendable alacrity and accuracy some 325 found their way to the great dining saloon at 7.30 when the bugle sounded the call to dinner. After dinner as we sat in the beautiful lounge listening to the White Star orchestra playing the *Tales of Hoffman* and *Cavalleria Rusticana* selections more than once we heard the remark: 'You would never imagine you were on board a ship.' Still harder was it to believe that up on the top deck it was blowing a gale, but we had to go to bed, and this reminds me that on the *Titanic* the expression is literally accurate. Nowhere were the berths of other days seen, and everywhere comfortable oaken bedsteads gave place to furniture in the famous suites beloved by millionaires. Then the morning plunge in the great swimming bath, where the ceaseless ripple of the tepid seawater was almost the only indication that somewhere in the distance 72,000 horses [sic] in the guise of steam engines fretted and strained under the skilful guidance of the engineers, and after the plunge a half-hour in the gymnasium helped to send one's blood coursing freely, and created a big appetite for the morning meal.

But if the saloon of the *Titanic* is wonderful no less so is the second class and in its degree the third class. A word from the genial purser acted as the open sesame of the Arabian Nights, and secured us an English officer and his son, whose acquaintance I had made at lunch, and myself a free passage through all this floating wonder. Lifts and lounges and libraries are not generally associated in the public mind with second class, yet in the *Titanic* all are found. It needed the assurance of our guide that we had left the saloon and were really in the second class.

On the crowded third-class deck were hundreds of English, Dutch, Italian and French mingling in happy fellowship, and when we wandered down among them we found that for them, too, the *Titanic* was a wonder. No more general cabins, but hundreds of comfortable rooms, with two, four or six berths each, beautifully covered in red and white coverlets. Here, too, are lounges and smoking rooms, less magnificent than those amidships to be sure, but none the less comfortable, and which, with the swivel chairs and separate tables in the dining-rooms, struck me as not quite fitting in with my previous notion of steerage accommodation.[16]

The passenger could not have anticipated at the time just how lucky they were to be getting off the ship.

Once the passengers had come aboard from the tenders, *Titanic* was on her way. She passed Daunt's Rock at 2.20 p.m. and gathered speed. *Titanic's* course was set and she followed the usual route for the time of year:

Outward track between 15 January and 14 August (since 1899) followed the circle between the Fastnet Light and a point in latitude 42 degrees north 47 degrees west (the "corner"), and from thence by Rhumb line so as to pass just South of the Nantucket light vessel and from this point onto New York...

Passengers busied themselves with their daily routines. 'First-class passengers studied the printed passenger list, looking for old friends or familiar names.'[17] The very neatly printed list displayed all of the 'big names'; most of them millionaires of the time.

First-class passengers included Colonel & Mrs J.J. Astor; Major A.W. Butt, President Taft's aide-de-camp; Mr Benjamin Guggenheim, of the well-known banking firm; Mr C.M.

Hays, the president of the Grand Trunk Railway, Mrs & Ms Hays; Scotland's Countess of Rothes and her cousin Gladys Cherry were aboard; Mr W.T. Stead; Mr Clarence Moore; Mr & Mrs Isidor Straus; George D. Widener and Mr W. Roebling, J. Bruce Ismay...

Although many passengers looked up old friends, others formed new acquaintances. Friendship groups formed – inseparable on an Atlantic crossing, but only casual acquaintances afterwards. Mrs Helen Candee dazzled Colonel Archibald Gracie, Messrs Hugh Woolner, Edward Kent, Clinch Smith, Björnström Steffanson and E.P. Colley; she felt 'divinely flattered to be in such company'.[18] They formed a group, 'Our Coterie', who frequently spent time together. Woolner was the son of a well-known sculptor, Kent was a well-connected architect, Smith a Long Island socialite, Colley a laughing 'roly-poly' Irishman and Steffansön was a reserve lieutenant in the Swedish Army.[19]

In third class, Frank Goldsmith soon made friends with other boys the same age. They were soon running up and down stairs and through crowded corridors, and even peered into some of the boiler rooms and watched the stokers; some of the stokers even waved at them.[20]

One problem had, however, already presented itself. The storage box in the port side corner of the crow's nest for the lookouts' binoculars was empty. Although the binoculars had been available from Belfast to Southampton, they were not seen after leaving the busy port.

Aboard White Star vessels, it was common practice for the second officer to lend his company-issued binoculars to the lookouts. Indeed, the binoculars were marked 'Second Officer, *Titanic*'. Before Lightoller was demoted to second officer, David Blair who had held the position had locked the binoculars away in his cabin, then left the ship and neglected to inform anybody. Lightoller was blissfully unaware and so was unsuccessful in finding binoculars for the lookouts when he was asked by George Symons.

Symons went to the officers' mess and asked Second Officer Lightoller about the missing binoculars, or glasses as they were often called. Lightoller went to an officer's cabin, which Symons thought was Murdoch's cabin, and came out, saying merely 'Symons, there are none.' If Lightoller had looked in his own cabin, he would surely have found them.

Symons told the other lookouts, who were all naturally irritated about the matter. Symons had previously had binoculars on the *Oceanic* and recalled that he had found them 'very useful'.

Lightoller told Murdoch about the missing binoculars and he said he knew and would deal with the matter.

Symons went so far as to ask Chief Officer Wilde about the binoculars. 'There is none,' he confirmed. Lightoller also asked the chief officer and was told that the matter was 'in hand'. It wasn't. The binoculars were never found...

'I asked for the glasses several times,' Symons recalled. 'It is always customary to have glasses in the crow's nest.' He had served for over three years as a lookout on the *Oceanic*, during which time binoculars had always been supplied.

But not to have binoculars in the crow's nest was usual for a White Star vessel. Lookout Hogg said that he had only ever had binoculars supplied on ships of the line. White Star Line practice to supply binoculars to the lookouts had stopped in 1895, seventeen years before the *Titanic* sailed, after which time it was left to an individual captain's discretion. It must be emphasised, however, that binoculars would probably not have helped sight the iceberg sooner in the circumstances that did occur, contrary to popular belief. They may be useful for identifying an object seen in the distance, but binoculars extremely limit a person's field of view.

During the spring of 1912, ice had been reported numerous times in the North Atlantic shipping lanes. Cunard's *Carmania* had encountered ice during her mid-April crossing, which her captain reported as 'an immense icepack of ragged surface'. It was then that she had received a distress call from the French steamship *Niagara*, damaged in ice 20 miles away. In fact, the ice field was 35 miles wide and 100 miles long according to one report. The ice was 'certainly at the time further south than it had been seen for many years'. *Titanic*'s course took her right into the ice field which contained *icebergs*…detached portions of polar glaciers; *'growlers'*…icebergs of small mass, with little of them above the surface; *pack ice*…floating ice covering wide areas of the polar seas, kept together by wind and current, often frozen from seawater; *field ice*…lighter than pack ice…

Already on Friday 12 April ice warnings were received, among them the *La Touraine*'s. Senior wireless operator John ('Jack') Phillips, aged twenty-five – he had celebrated his birthday on 11 April – and junior wireless operator Harold Bride, aged twenty-two, manned the wireless equipment.

Titanic's wireless set received many messages. At 9.12 a.m. on 14 April Captain Smith acknowledged receipt of the following message:

> Captain, *Titanic*, westbound steamers report bergs growlers and field ice in latitude 42 degrees north from 49 degrees to 51 degrees west, April 12th. Compliments, Barr.

Titanic's aft grand staircase on B-deck opened into the *á la carte* restaurant's reception room, as depicted in an artist's impression of how the completed space would appear. The double doors in the background accessed the Café Parisien. (J.&C. McCutcheon collection)

Fourth Officer Boxhall noted the warning and marked it on the chart. Captain Smith also showed it to Second Officer Lightoller on the bridge at 12.45 p.m., while First Officer Murdoch was eating lunch. When Murdoch returned, Lightoller told him of the message, which placed ice near *Titanic*'s track, some 300 miles ahead and somewhat to the South of her then current course. The sighting was two days old, however, and it was quite possible that the ice had drifted since then, further away and to the South...

It was 11.47 a.m. when the Dutch liner *Noordam* reported that there was 'much ice' in roughly the same position.[21] Captain Smith acknowledged receipt of the message, but it seems not to have been noted by any of the other officers on the bridge, and certainly none of the surviving officers read it.

A message from *Amerika* arrived at 1.47 p.m.:

> *Amerika* passed two large icebergs in 41 degrees 27 minutes north 50 degrees 8 minutes west.

It was not handed to any officer and another message arrived from *Baltic* at 1.54 p.m., warning of ice in the same vicinity:

> Captain Smith, *Titanic*; have had moderate, variable winds and clear, fine weather since leaving. Greek steamer *Athenai* reports passing icebergs and large quantities of field ice today in latitude 41 degrees 51 minutes north longitude 49 degrees 52 minutes west. Last night we spoke [to the] German oil tank steamer *Deutschland*, Stettin to Philadelphia, not under control, short of coal, latitude 40 degrees 42 minutes north 50 degrees 11 minutes west. Wishes to be reported to New York and other steamers. Wish you and *Titanic* all success – Commander.

Smith handed the message to J. Bruce Ismay, who retained it all afternoon and into the evening. It was not until 7.10 p.m. that the captain retrieved it from Ismay, who was in the first-class smoke room. He explained that he was going to post it in the chart room.

More warnings were received that evening, although not all specifically addressed to *Titanic*. Harold Bride intercepted one from the Leyland liner *Californian*, which he jotted down and handed to an officer on the bridge.

> To Captain, *Antillian*, 6.30 p.m. apparent ship's time; lat. 42 degrees 3 minutes N., long. 49 degrees 9 minutes W. Three large bergs five miles to southward of us. Regards. – Lord.

At 9.52 p.m. a message was received from *Mesaba*:

> From *Mesaba* to *Titanic* and other eastbound ships. Ice report in latitude 42 degrees north 41 degrees 25 minutes north, longitude 49 degrees to 50 degrees 30 minutes west. Saw much heavy pack ice and great number large icebergs. Also field ice. Weather good, clear.

The Leyland liner *Californian* sent a message at 11.07 p.m.: 'We are stopped and surrounded by ice.' Phillips cut off the message, which would have told *Titanic*'s officers that *Californian* was stopped to the north, because of ice. He was busy with the volume of passenger traffic and tapped back: 'Shut up, shut up. You're jamming my signal. I'm working Cape Race…' Unfortunately, *Californian*'s wireless operator, Cyril Evans, had not been given an official message by his commander, and so he only sent an informal warning. Consequently, Phillips was not obliged to pay it the attention he would have done had it been an official message.

★   ★   ★

Steward Henry Etches brought a shiny silver tray and service, loaded with fruit and tea, to cabin A36, just off the aft grand staircase, at 7 a.m. on Sunday 14 April. A36 was thirty-eight-year-old Thomas Andrews' cabin, Harland & Wolff's on board representative and *Titanic*'s chief designer. The handsome cabin was spread with plans, maps and drawings. Charts were rolled by the side of the bed and blueprints covered the table, along with Andrews' observations and notes of improvement for the passenger accommodation. Indeed, it seemed to Etches that Andrews never stopped working except for meals. Andrews took pleasure in noting every aspect of the ship, from the machinery and structure, to the luxurious compartments. Wearing a blue engineer's suit, he frequently visited the boiler and engine rooms. He had conversed with Chief Engineer Bell regarding the general working of the machinery and the engines' performance, which was proving to be better than ever hoped for. That morning and for most of the night, the engines had been running faultlessly at 75rpm, indicating 22 knots in the perfect weather conditions with only 21 of the boilers alight. He had noted various improvements to the ship regarding the *à la carte* restaurant hot press, stateroom coat hooks, pebble-dashing on the promenade of the port 'millionaire suite', the over-sized first-class reading and writing room and had a plan to stain some of the wicker furniture green on the port side of the ship.

Perhaps the most serious problem lay with the second-class heating system – one thing that was not 'working A1', as Chief Engineer Bell put it. For much of the time it refused to work, and there had also been trouble with the heating plant for some third-class areas.

Colonel Gracie also rose early on Sunday morning, for the purpose of finally getting some healthy exercise. Usually it was his custom, but for the past three-and-a-half days he had spent more time relaxing and socialising; 'I enjoyed myself as if I were in a summer palace on the seashore surrounded by every comfort,' he later wrote. But this morning he spent a half-hour session with Fred Wright, the squash pro., followed by a swim in the pool. He booked the squash court, gymnasium and swimming pool for early the next morning.[22]

Following a delicious breakfast, he attended the Church of England service in the first-class dining saloon at 11.00 a.m., led by Captain Smith as the ship's commander. Lunch followed shortly afterwards. Few people noticed that the morning boat drill had been cancelled. Second class had their own hymn-sing organised for 8.30 p.m. in their dining saloon, to be led by Reverend Carter.

Although there was little in the way of organised entertainment, one good source was music. *Titanic*'s band provided entertainment for passengers throughout the day: Bandmaster Wallace Hartley, second violinist Jock Hume, pianist Theodore Brailey, cellist Roger Bricoux, bass-viola player Fred Clark, George Krins playing the viola, cellist J.W. Woodward and pianist P.C. Taylor.[23] They usually played in two separate groups: 'one of three musicians, piano, violin and cello, played in the second-class dining saloon or lounge, while the others played in first class.' Each member was expected to know all of the 352 tunes in White Star's songbook by number.[24] Outside the *à la carte* restaurant and café parisien on B-deck – in the restaurant's reception room off the aft first-class grand staircase – providing entertainment, was the special trio added to *Titanic*. All part of White Star's efforts to plant a little corner of Paris in the heart of a British liner.[25]

But although everyone – or nearly everyone – was full of confidence in the new ship, Charles M. Hays felt uneasy. He apparently remarked that afternoon:

> The White Star, the Cunard and Hamburg-American Lines, are now devoting their attention to obtaining the most luxurious appointments for their ships, but soon the time will come when the most appalling of all disasters at sea will be the result.[26]

Throughout the afternoon the weather got colder and many passengers sought comfort in the spacious interior apartments. Second-class passengers sought their enclosed C-deck promenade, flanking the library. 'The library was crowded that afternoon,' recalled Lawrence Beesley, 'but through the windows we could see the clear sky with brilliant sunlight that seemed to augur a fine night…'

Many passengers indulged in letter-writing. These could be posted outside the second-class library, first-class lounge or be given to stewards to be taken to the mail sorting room near the bow at regular intervals.

Of those who did not write, reading was a common occupation. Colonel Gracie finished reading Mary Johnston's *Old Dominion* that afternoon and returned it to the library. He also spent much time chatting with Mr and Mrs Isidor Straus, who had communicated with their son and his wife on the *Amerika* by wireless.[27]

There was much talk throughout the ship of her steady progress and faultless running. Every day had seen an increasing number of miles posted and the engines had been running three revolutions faster than at any other time in the voyage, according to a report at noon, which had accompanied the posting of the ship's best daily run.

Some heard of an encounter between prominent Philadelphian Emily Ryerson and Mr Ismay. A first-class passenger, Mrs Mahala Douglas, later heard the rumour. Mrs Ryerson was quoted as saying; 'Mr Ismay, whom I know very slightly, passed me on the deck. He showed me, in his brusque manner, a Marconigram, saying "We have just had news that we are in the icebergs."

"Of course, you will slow down", I said.

"Oh no", he replied, "we will put on more boilers and get out of it."'

Curiously, Mrs Ryerson later didn't mention the encounter in her affidavit to the Senate inquiry. When Ismay was later asked, he denied that the encounter had taken place. However, in 1913 she recalled they had spoken and that Ismay had given her the impression 'that "we are going to get in [to New York early] and surprise everybody." I don't know whether he used the word "record", but that was left on my mind.'[28]

A second-class passenger, Imanita Shelley, heard rumours of ice warnings from other ships, warning of icebergs nearby, and as the afternoon became the evening she noticed the dropping temperature. She had also heard rumours that the ship would 'be speeded through' the ice region.

To the main of *Titanic*'s passengers, however, the liner seemed the utmost in luxury, comfort and safety, the greatest ship yet built.

Second Officer Lightoller would later recall, 'it was clear to everybody on board that we had a ship that was going to create the greatest stir shipping circles had ever known.' He continued: 'Each day, as the voyage went on, everybody's admiration of the ship increased; for the way she behaved, for the total absence of vibration, for her steadiness even with the ever-increasing speed, as she warmed up to her work.'[29]

At 5.00 p.m. on 14 April *Titanic* should have turned at a location called 'the corner', to take her to New York; the corner was at '47 degrees west and 42 degrees north'. Captain Smith ordered this course change to be delayed which caused the ship to travel further south than normal, perhaps 4 or 5 miles. This precaution might have been taken because of the ice messages the captain had seen, but certainly if he had realised the extent of the ice field ahead a sharp, decisive swing to the south would have been expected. He was well-aware that they were heading into an ice field, but the ice field was much larger than he thought; in fact, it extended for some 78 miles. It was 5.50 p.m. when *Titanic* turned from 'south 62 degrees west' to the new course 'south 86 degrees west', with the compass heading of 'north 71 degrees west'.

That evening, many passengers enjoyed dinner. In the *à la carte* restaurant, the diners included J. Bruce Ismay and Dr William O'Loughlin; Sir Cosmo Duff Gordon and his wife 'Lucile'; and a table that included Captain Smith, as well as the Thayers and Carters.

Captain Smith 'didn't drink a drop' of alcohol, in accordance with company regulations, but rumours later circulated that he was drunk. At about 8.55 p.m., or perhaps a little later, Captain Smith bade his companions 'good night' and left for the bridge.

Daisy Minahan enjoyed a gorgeous dinner followed by coffee, then her party listened to the orchestra for some time, before retiring at about 9.30 p.m., at her brother's suggestion. Major Peuchen enjoyed 'an exceptionally good dinner', coffee, and then went up to the smoke room.

High in the crow's nest, Lookout Archie Jewell remarked to George Symons about the continuing drop in temperature. 'It is very cold here.'

'Yes,' Symons confirmed. 'By the smell of it there is ice about.'

'Why is ice about?'

'As a rule you can smell the ice before you get to it,' Symons explained.

Meanwhile, Captain Smith arrived on the bridge with Lightoller.

'It is very cold,' he remarked.

'Yes, it is very cold sir. In fact,' Lightoller replied, 'it is only one degree above freezing. I have sent word down to the carpenter and rung-up the engine room and told them it will be freezing during the night.'

They began to discuss the weather. 'There is not much wind,' Smith observed.

'No, it is a flat calm,' Lightoller agreed.

'A flat calm,' repeated Smith.

'Yes. Quite flat; there is no wind.'

Lightoller said that it was a pity the breeze had not kept up with them while going through the ice region, as there would be no ripples breaking against an iceberg's base, making the berg harder to spot.

Smith said though that 'it seems quite clear'.

'Yes, it is perfectly clear,' Lightoller agreed.

Then the two men discussed indications of ice. Lightoller mentioned of the icebergs, 'In any case, there will be a certain amount of reflected light.'

'Oh, yes,' Smith agreed.

Between them it was said that even if the blue side of a recently turned-over 'blue' iceberg was presented towards them, they would still be able to see it at a good distance and have time to take sufficient avoiding action.

'If it does come on in the slightest degree hazy we shall have to go very slow,' Lightoller remembered Smith saying.

Leaving the bridge, Smith ordered: 'If it becomes at all doubtful, let me know at once, I will be just inside.'

The temperature had in fact been steadily dropping from 5.30 p.m. when it was 43° Fahrenheit and had dropped to 33° Fahrenheit at 7.30 p.m., indicating the possibility that the ship was approaching ice. The explorer Sir Ernest Shackleton later stated: 'if there was no wind and the temperature fell abnormally for the time of the year, I would consider that I was approaching an area which well might have ice in it.'

Although some ice warnings had not reached the bridge, *Titanic*'s senior officers were well-aware of the ice threat. At 7.15 p.m. First Officer Murdoch was on the bridge while Lightoller was eating, and he ordered lamp trimmer Samuel Hemming to 'go forward and see the forecastle hatch closed as we are in the vicinity of ice and I want everything dark before the bridge.'

Lightoller took precautions as well. At 9.30 p.m., a few minutes after the captain's departure, he sent word to the lookouts, Jewell and Symons, to 'keep a sharp lookout for ice, particularly small ice and growlers'. He told them to pass on the word at the end of their watch.

Quartermaster Hichens was then ordered to find the deck engineer and get the keys for the heaters from him for the chartroom, wheelhouse, and officers' quarters so that they could be heated.

Lightoller had also ordered at 8.10 p.m. the carpenter to watch the fresh water tanks in the ship's double bottom and take care that they shouldn't freeze.

After dinner had finished, many second-class passengers had gathered in their dining saloon for hymns, led by the Reverend Ernest Carter, while Douglas Norman played the piano.[30] In a far less secular society than today's, the saloon was quite full.

'It is the first time that there have been hymns sung on this boat on Sunday evening,' Carter told the crowd as he closed shortly after 10.00 p.m., 'but we trust and pray it won't be the last.'[31]

The previous day, first-class passenger Elisabeth Lines had sat down after lunch to enjoy coffee in the first-class reception room. J. Bruce Ismay and Captain Smith entered after her and sat down nearby, at the same table where she had seen them the day before. She recognised Ismay from when they had both lived in New York years earlier, and her steward confirmed the man's identity. At first, she did not pay much attention to their discussion, but her attention was drawn when she heard the two men discussing *Titanic*'s performance. 'Well,' Ismay said, 'we did better today than we did yesterday, we made a better run today than we did yesterday, we will make a better run tomorrow. Things are working smoothly, the machinery is bearing the test, the boilers are working well.'

Smith nodded in agreement and she noticed a great deal of repetition. 'You see they are standing the pressure, everything is going well, the boilers are working well, we can do better tomorrow, we will make a better run tomorrow,' Ismay said. They discussed *Titanic*'s performance with the corresponding stage of *Olympic*'s maiden voyage and believed she was doing equally well. She had covered 1,003 miles by noon on Saturday compared to *Olympic*'s 962 miles, although the improvement was due to the fact that *Olympic* had been late leaving Queenstown. Nevertheless, *Titanic* had ample time to better her sister by increasing speed. The two men 'seemed to think a little more pressure could be put on the boilers and the speed increased so that the maiden

'*Titanic* the night before she sailed on her fatal trip'. At the stern, the notice reads: 'Notice This Vessel Has Triple Screws Keep Clear of Blades'. She dwarfed the other ships at Southampton. (Chirnside/Klistorner/Layton collection, restoration © Steve Hall)

trip of the *Titanic* would exceed the maiden trip of the *Olympic* in speed.' Ismay concluded: 'We will beat the *Olympic* and get in to New York on Tuesday.' They then headed down to look at the squash court.

By Sunday evening, *Titanic*'s speed had reached the highest yet. From the time she left Queenstown and passed Daunt's Rock until noon on Friday, she logged 484 miles at an average speed of about 21 knots. Her engines were running at 70rpm and only twenty of her boilers were lit, giving ample power in reserve to increase her speed. The revolutions increased to 72rpm after another boiler was brought into operation and *Titanic* covered 519 miles at an average a little under 21 knots, working against the current. Another increase in speed to 75rpm enabled *Titanic* to log 546 miles when the figure for the last day was reported at noon on Sunday, showing an average speed in excess of 22 knots. It had taken *Olympic* until the fifth day before she showed a day's run that averaged over 22 knots, but *Titanic* had exceeded that already and her run was a mere 2 miles short of *Olympic*'s highest.

Fireman John Thompson recalled 'a bulletin was posted in the hole [sic] at 3 o'clock Sunday afternoon which stated that we were making seventy-seven revolutions a minute.' During the 4 p.m. to 8 p.m. watch that Sunday, Second Engineer James Hesketh informed Fireman Charles Hendrickson that the engine revolutions were averaging 76rpm. The final two or three of the twenty-four double-ended boilers had been lit earlier that morning and they were connected to the engines around 7 p.m. The ship's speed increased further from that time onwards.

One first-class passenger, Helen Candee, understood that it was hoped *Titanic*'s next run would be as high as 570 miles.[32] It seems unlikely it would have been that high, since seven hours had already elapsed before the additional boilers had been connected, but *Olympic* had achieved 560 miles on her second westbound crossing and exceeded even that figure during her first year's service. There was still time for *Titanic* to squeeze in the extra miles. A run of 570 miles would have required an average speed around 23 knots. Trimmer William McIntyre noticed that the steam pressure in the boilers had increased to 220lb and Trimmer George Cavell was 'quite sure' that the gauge showed a steam pressure of 225lb in boiler room 4. Fireman George Kemish recalled that an order had been received for 23 knots before the collision. Although he had gone off watch at 8 p.m., Thompson 'was told the ship was making close to 23 knots when she hit.'[33]

Olympic had completed her maiden voyage without any of the five single-ended boilers being lit, but preparations were also being made to light *Titanic*'s and bring them online. Undoubtedly, part of the reason was the intention for a 'full speed' run to be accomplished either on Monday or Tuesday, which would enable additional data to be gleaned about the new ship's performance. However, it seems clear that it was hoped that *Titanic* would do better than her sister had, completing her own maiden voyage in a shorter time and with a higher average speed. It could even be argued that it might have been disappointing had she been unable to match her older sister's performance.

There seems little danger that would have been the case. *Olympic*'s maiden voyage had been the fastest of any White Star liner and she had reached the Ambrose Lightship at 2.24 a.m. on the Wednesday; if *Titanic* had simply matched her average speed then she would have arrived at 12.22 a.m. on Wednesday, and even this would have required her to slow down in the time remaining. In fact, she was increasing her speed further and she was well on the way to arrive at the Ambrose Lightship late on Tuesday evening.

Lightoller's watch finished uneventfully and when First Officer Murdoch came on duty at 10.00 p.m. he told him, 'we might be up around the ice any time now,' but it seems he did not mention the captain's instructions. Leaving the bridge, Lightoller went on his rounds before going to bed.

Quartermaster Hichens took over the helm from Quartermaster Olliver and noted the ship's heading, while the ship had accomplished about 45 knots in the past two hours. Olliver remained on the bridge as standby quartermaster. Two new lookouts came on duty at 10.00 p.m.: Frederick Fleet and Reginald Lee, who were informed of Lightoller's orders.

Second-class passenger Lawrence Beesley read in his stateroom from 11.15 p.m. and noticed:

> The increased vibration of the ship, and I assumed that we were going at a higher speed than at any other time since we sailed from Queenstown… as I sat on the sofa undressing, with bare feet on the floor, the jar of the vibration came up from the engines below very noticeably; and… as I sat up in the berth reading, the spring mattress supporting me was vibrating more rapidly than usual: this cradle-like motion was always noticeable as one lay in bed, but that night there was certainly a marked increase in the motion.

First-class passengers Walter and Mahala Douglas retired for the night, after dining in the *á la carte* restaurant: 'As we went to our stateroom − C86 − we both remarked that the boat was going faster than she ever had. The vibration as one passed the stairway in the centre was very noticeable.' When Henry Stengel retired around 10.00 p.m., he called his wife's attention 'to the fact that the engines were running very fast… I could hear the engines running when I retired, and… I said I noticed that they were running faster than at any other time during the trip.'

George Rheims and his brother-in-law, Joseph Loring, were discussing the ship's speed in the first-class smoke room. They wanted to work out what the next day's run might be. One of the ship's stewards approached and suggested that they increase their estimate. They asked why, and he replied, 'Because we are making faster speed than we were yesterday.'

Loring asked: 'What do you know about it?'

'I got it from the engine room,' the old steward replied.

'That don't [sic] mean anything,' Loring responded.

'Gentlemen, come out and see for yourself.' They went out into the passageway outside the smoke room and the steward commented: 'Now you will notice the vibration.' Loring had never noticed such vibration and remarked: 'We are evidently making very good speed.' Even though Rheims had been in the smoke room every night, he had never noticed it before: 'The vibration… was very strong.'

★ ★ ★

At 'seven bells', 11.30 p.m., Fleet and Lee noticed a slight haze developing ahead, a few points on either side, Fleet would later recall to Lord Mersey. It was 'on the waterline, but nothing to talk about', he said, as it was not preventing them seeing clearly and so not worthy of reporting to the bridge. Lee described it as 'a haze right ahead' and stated: 'in fact it was tending more or less round the horizon.' He said that Fleet had remarked that they would be lucky to see through it, but Fleet flatly denied the remark. Fleet described seeing 'a black mass' ahead of the speeding liner, 'just after' 11.30 p.m., which initially did not look very large, perhaps the size of 'two tables' put together when sighted; it rapidly grew larger, materialising into an iceberg.

'There is ice ahead,' he remarked. He rang the crow's nest bell three times to indicate an object ahead, then he snatched the crow's nest phone and rang the bridge. The phone was picked up by Sixth Officer James Moody and there was a quick exchange of words:

Fleet: 'Are you there?'

Moody: 'Yes, what do you see?'

Fleet: 'Iceberg right ahead.'

Moody: 'Thank you.'

Murdoch may have heard the sound of three bells as he sighted the iceberg himself. As Sixth Officer Moody repeated Fleet's warning, Murdoch yelled the order 'hard a starboard'. He rushed to the telegraphs to order the engines stopped. Hichens spun the wheel hard over and Moody shouted to Murdoch to confirm, 'the helm's hard over, sir.'

While the iceberg drew nearer, Fleet realised that the ship might collide with it head on, possibly bringing down the foremast and the crow's nest. He ordered Lee to climb down, but although he made a start down the ladder inside the foremast he returned to his station.[34]

As the bow began to swing, Murdoch ordered 'hard a port', to swing the stern, which was moving toward the iceberg as the bow swung to port, away from the danger, but the bow drew level with the iceberg and the wall of ice advanced along the bow, there was no obvious collision, although some brittle ice lumps crashed onto the forecastle and forward well decks. Quartermaster Olliver, a twelve-year veteran of the sea, having gone to sea aged sixteen, was entering the bridge and he noticed what he described as: 'a long grinding sound, like… I knew we had touched something.'

Some people were immediately aware of what had happened. James McGough, travelling first class and a buyer for the Gimbel Brothers department store, watched chunks of ice come into his stateroom on E-deck through the open porthole. [35]

Others felt that something was amiss. Able Bodied Seaman Joseph Scarrott, near the forecastle head, felt the vibration of the collision, which felt to him as though the engines 'had been suddenly reversed to full speed astern.' He observed the ship's stern clear the iceberg as the helm had been put hard to port. Steward Samuel Rule awoke in his berth on the port side in the after part of E-deck near the engine room when he felt the engines stop and then what he thought was them slowly begin to go into reverse, before quickly stopping. Trimmer Thomas Dillon, in the main engine room, heard the telegraphs ring and then observed engineers rush to their stations to change the engine settings.

Leading Stoker Frederick Barrett had been talking with Second Engineer James Hesketh on the forward starboard side of number 6 boiler room when the red warning light came on, indicating 'stop'. As the man in charge, Barrett issued his own order, 'Shut all the dampers.' Clearly, less steam would be needed for the stopping of the engines. But before all the dampers had been closed, there came a 'roar of thunder' and about 2ft above the stokehold plate water burst in through the ship's side. To Barrett it seemed as though the whole side of the ship had caved in; 'the ship was torn right through,' he would recall. The two men leapt through the watertight door leading to boiler room 5, which was closing, to be greeted by a gash running through the forward starboard coalbunker and a jet of icy water.

Greaser Frederick Scott, forward in the turbine engine room, thought something had gone wrong in the main engine room when he felt a shock. He looked into the main engine room through the open watertight door and saw 'stop' indicated on the port, starboard and 'emergency' telegraphs, before the watertight doors closed up to thirty seconds after impact as Murdoch activated the switch on the bridge.

Fourth Officer Boxhall was approaching the bridge when he heard the sound of the telegraphs. He arrived on the bridge, seeing Sixth Officer Moody and First Officer Murdoch.

Captain Smith appeared. 'What have we struck?' he asked Murdoch.

'We have struck an iceberg,' he replied.★

'Close the emergency doors,' Smith ordered.

'The watertight doors are closed, sir.'

'And have you rung the warning bell?'

'Yes, sir.'

The three officers rushed to the starboard bridge wing to try and glimpse the iceberg, but only Boxhall thought he could see it.

Returning inside, Smith told Quartermaster Olliver: 'Find the carpenter. Get him to sound the ship forward.' He ordered Fourth Officer Boxhall to go below to check for signs of damage in the ship's forward third-class accommodation. Checking the commutator inside the wheelhouse, he saw that the ship had a slight 5-degree starboard list.

Daniel Buckley, a third-class passenger, soon noticed water coming into his room forward on G-deck. 'I heard some terrible noise and I jumped out on the floor, the first thing I knew my feet were getting wet; the water was just coming in slightly,' Buckley recalled. He told the others in his room to get up as the room was flooding, but someone yelled 'Get back to bed. You're not in Ireland now.'

Ignoring this, Buckley quickly decided to get dressed. Two seamen came along, yelling. 'All up on deck! unless you want to get drowned!' He quickly obeyed, but soon decided to return for his lifebelt. When he did reach the stairs leading below, he could see greeny-blue seawater rising, which covered the bottom three or four steps. He decided logically not to wade through it to his cabin.

Lawrence Beesley, a second-class passenger in cabin D56, was reading when he noticed 'what seemed to be nothing more than an extra heave of the engines and a more than usually obvious dancing of the mattress on which I sat.'[36]

Stewardess Violet Jessop awoke in her E-deck cabin to 'a low, rending, crunching, ripping sound'. She and her room-mate looked at each other. 'Sounds as if something has happened.'[37]

★ Fourth Officer Boxhall then recalled Murdoch explaining: 'I put her hard a' starboard and run [sic] the engines full astern, but it was too close; she hit it. I intended to port around it, but she hit before I could do any more'. However, there is no corroboration for the statement that the engines were ordered 'full astern' prior to the collision.

Quartermaster Hichens described a briefer exchange of words: 'The skipper came rushing out of his room… and asked, "What is that?" Mr Murdoch said, "An iceberg." He said, "Close the emergency doors."' Similarly, Quartermaster Olliver testified: 'When he [Captain Smith] first came on the bridge he asked the first officer what was the matter, and Mr Murdoch reported, sir, that we had struck an iceberg, and the captain ordered him to have the watertight doors closed, and Mr Murdoch reported that the watertight doors were closed'.

Titanic cleared the dock (on the right) and moved into the river. A number of interested spectators can be seen in particular on the forward well deck, the first-class promenade on A-deck and the second-class promenade aft on B-deck. It appears that several of the rectangular windows belonging to J. Bruce Ismay's private promenade were open. (J. Kent Layton collection)

Major Peuchen had just reached his cabin when he felt something unusual. 'I felt as though a heavy wave had struck our ship. She quivered under it somewhat.' He donned an overcoat and, as he entered the forward grand staircase, met a shipboard acquaintance. 'Why, we have struck an iceberg,' he was told, 'if you will go up on A-deck, you will see ice on the forepart of the ship.' Peuchen did so.

In cabin C51, Colonel Archibald Gracie awoke and believed that the ship had struck something. He went out into the corridor and noticed that there was the noise of steam far above being blown-off after the engines had stopped; Gracie hurriedly dressed and went to see what the matter was.[38]

Emily Ryerson lay awake in her luxurious B-deck suite when she heard the engines stop. As her husband was sleeping soundly, she rang the bell for her steward, Bishop. When she asked what the matter was, he told her, 'there is talk of an iceberg ma'am, and they have stopped not to run into it.' After asking Bishop to keep her informed of any orders, she wrapped up warmly, then looked out of the large square window. The stars shone brightly over the quiet calm sea.

Other passengers were awakened, but many did not get-up and see what the matter was, although stewards' bells began ringing and some curious passengers made sure that they knew what was going on.

J. Bruce Ismay awoke in his suite. He lay in bed for a few moments before putting on his dressing gown and slippers. Then he went out into the corridor and asked a steward the matter. 'I do not know, sir,' he was told. Donning a coat, he left for the bridge, where he found Captain Smith.

'What has happened?' he asked.

'We have struck ice,' replied Smith.

'Do you think the ship is seriously damaged?

'I am afraid she is,' Smith replied. The two men probably continued to discuss what had happened, Ismay anxious for the ship not to be delayed, before he left the bridge.

Quickly he ran into Chief Engineer Bell in the main companionway. Perhaps not believing Smith, he again asked 'Do you think the ship is seriously damaged?'

'I think that she is,' came the reply. Not wishing to alarm Ismay – the managing director of the line – he added 'I am quite satisfied the pumps will keep her afloat.'

Having found the carpenter already taking a draft of the water, Quartermaster Olliver returned to the bridge quickly. Captain Smith telegraphed 'half ahead' to the engine room, then noticed Olliver and wrote-out a note on a slip of paper, instructing him to take it to Chief Engineer Bell.

Boxhall returned to the bridge, reporting to Smith and Murdoch that he had seen no damage. Still worried, Smith told him to find the carpenter and get him to sound the ship. The fourth officer left the bridge and descended the crew stairway, where he met the ship's carpenter.

'The captain wants you to sound the ship,' Boxhall explained.

'The ship is making water fast,' said Carpenter John Hutchinson, as he rushed to the bridge.

Boxhall headed below where he met one of the mail clerks, Jago Smith. Smith asked where the captain was and Boxhall replied that the captain was on the bridge.

'The mail hold is filling rapidly,' explained Smith in an excited tone.

'Well, you go and report it to the captain and I will go down and see,' Boxhall ordered.

He went far down and found the mail clerks. Boxhall looked through an open door and he saw that the clerks were working quickly to save the mail from the water that was now 2ft below G-deck. For a while he stayed there.

In the wireless room, Bride had just sat down at the set and Phillips made a move to his bunk. Phillips told him that he feared that the ship had been damaged and would need to go back to Belfast. Now, Captain Smith came in. 'We've struck an iceberg,' he said, 'and I'm having an inspection made to see what it has done to us. You'd better get ready to send out a call for assistance, but don't send it until I tell you.'

Having escaped the quickly rising water in boiler room 6, the firemen were ordered to draw the fires, in order to prevent any boiler explosion. Feverishly, they hurried to get the job done as the freezing water rose higher. When the water was up to their waists, Fireman George Beauchamp heard somebody shout down from above. 'That will do!' He rushed up the escape ladder.

It seems likely Thomas Andrews had noticed the collision, as he left his stateroom on A-deck and descended below decks, where he was seen heading in the direction of the engine room. Meanwhile, hearing the reports of Carpenter Hutchinson and Jago Smith, Captain Smith was gaining a clearer picture of the damage below. Deciding on a personal inspection, Smith left the bridge.

Forward, Lamp Trimmer Samuel Hemming had been investigating the hissing noise coming from the forepeak tank when Chief Officer Wilde appeared.

'What is that, Hemming?'

'The air is escaping from the forepeak tank,' he replied, 'She is making water in the forepeak tank, but the storeroom is quite dry.'

'Alright,' Wilde said, before leaving.

Stewardess Annie Robinson had earlier seen the carpenter taking a draft of the water forward, looking alarmed, 'absolutely bewildered and distracted', then Jago Smith hurry up to the bridge, but now she saw Purser McElroy and Captain Smith appear. She was quite alarmed by the state of the flooding.

Thomas Andrews had earlier gone to the engine room and now Captain Smith followed him, but the two returned within minutes to the mail room, now entirely submerged, while the squash court was now awash.

It was clear that the flooding was beyond pumping and the officers returned to the bridge, Andrews remaining behind for some minutes assessing the ship's situation. As Andrews hurriedly ascended the forward grand staircase, he could not disguise the look of terror on his face.

Major Peuchen ran into Charles M. Hays.

'Mr Hays, have you seen the ice?'

'No.'

Both went to the foremost end of the A-deck promenade. The ice had fallen some way inboard. *Titanic* was also listing to starboard, Peuchen noticed.

'Why, she is listing,' he remarked, 'She should not do that; the water is perfectly calm and the boat has stopped…That is rather serious.'

'Oh, I don't know; you cannot sink this boat,' Hays assured him. 'No matter what we have struck, she is good for eight or ten hours.'

★   ★   ★

Captain Smith would soon know differently. At some point, the order 'slow astern' appears to have been given to bring the ship to a complete halt. In discussion with Thomas Andrews, the two men reviewed the situation. Although the pumps in boiler room 5 were keeping ahead of the water, boiler room 6 was flooding uncontrollably, along with all the compartments ahead of it. The extent and severity of the flooding overwhelmed the ability of the ship's watertight subdivision to contain it. Nor were *Titanic*'s pumps capable of handling the vast quantities of water: their combined capacity was less than 2,000 tons per hour, but following the collision water was entering the ship at an average of that rate every few minutes. As the bow settled lower into the water, the flooding would gradually overwhelm each deck, eventually creating further openings for the sea to penetrate. It was only a matter of time before the ship sank as the flooding grew progressively worse.

It is likely that Smith asked how long the ship might remain afloat. Only a few words from their conversation have survived: 'From an hour to an hour and a half,' Andrews estimated.

Captain Smith ordered Boxhall to call Second Officer Lightoller and Third Officer Pitman. It was at some point after midnight that he gave orders to the ship's officers to organise the evacuation. J. Bruce Ismay left the bridge, calling to one of the officers on deck as he walked aft along the starboard side: 'Get the boats out.'

Hutchinson had taken another draft of the water as requested and could only report to Captain Smith that *Titanic* was continuing to flood below, settling quickly lower and lower into the water. Having been running 'slow astern' for the previous five minutes to take the way off the ship, quite possibly backing the ship a small distance, Smith now finally telegraphed for the engines to stop.

Lightoller met Chief Officer Wilde on the boat deck who ordered him to see to the boats, also saying that all hands had been called. Lightoller went to the port side with Chief Officer Wilde and began to uncover the boats; Pitman also helped with the boats

Titanic clears the dock. Some observers were impressed with her graceful departure. On the aft docking bridge, First Officer Murdoch and Third Officer Pitman were stationed. Moments later, they would have a good view of the threatened collision between *Titanic* and *New York*. (*Titanic: The Ship Magnificent/* R. Terrell-Wright collection)

on the starboard side and went to view the ice on the foredecks when Moody told him the ice was there. First Officer Murdoch also got to the boat deck and ordered several crew, including Lookout George Symons, to assist with the boats. Captain Smith now ordered Fourth Officer Boxhall to work-out the ship's position to include in a distress signal.

Chief Officer Wilde found Quartermaster Olliver and told him to find the boatswain. He was to pass on the order to get the oar lines and uncover the lifeboats, getting them ready for lowering.

Then as soon as Olliver had taken the message and got back to the bridge, Sixth Officer Moody intercepted him. He ordered him to find the list of boat assignments and Olliver found it, giving it to Moody on the boat deck. Olliver then went to assist with the boats.

Titanic lay stopped on the ocean, listing slightly, her funnels' exhausts blowing off steam with a deafening roar and there were knots of the deck crew working around each lifeboat, who were hurriedly uncovering and swinging the boats out, as well as preparing them. Down slightly at the head, but not noticeably, the G and F-deck portholes forward glowed under the surface of the black sea.

Around 12.15 a.m., Fourth Officer Boxhall gave Captain Smith his position of the ship: '41 degrees 44 minutes north 50 degrees 24 minutes west.' Smith took it to the wireless room personally, ordering the distress call sent out at once. 'Be sharp about it,' he told the operators. Phillips took over from Bride at the radio set. Fourth Officer Boxhall appeared shortly after Smith with his corrected position of 41° 46' north 50° 14' west. He didn't know it, but his position was 13 miles off.

Soon, *Titanic*'s signals spread. At 12.15 a.m. *La Provence* heard... then *Mount Temple*... Cape Race... at 12.18 a.m. *Ypiranga... Frankfurt...*

At 12.25 a.m. *Carpathia* heard Phillips, now sending Fourth Officer Boxhall's corrected position: 'Come at once. We have struck a berg. It's a CQD old man. Position 41 degrees 46 minutes North 50 degrees 14 minutes West.' *Carpathia* advised that she was 'coming hard'.

'I require assistance immediately,' Phillips continued to send, 'Struck by iceberg in 41 degrees 46 minutes north 50 degrees 14 minutes west.'

Bride had previously found Smith on the starboard boat deck to report that their calls had reached the *Frankfurt*, but after hearing *Carpathia*'s news he returned and found the captain in the wheelhouse. Smith returned to the wireless room with him and asked what ships they were in contact with. *Olympic* was now chiming in, as well, although she was some distance away.

'What are you sending?' Smith wondered.

'CQD.'

Bride suggested, 'Send SOS.' It had recently been introduced and Bride joked, 'it may be your last chance to send it.'

In his head, Smith would have worked out *Carpathia*'s distance: some 58 miles… 15 knots… about four hours… He knew *Titanic* might only last for another hour. He left without comment.

Far below, water was flooding onto E-deck forward, about 16,000 tons having come aboard since the collision. *Titanic* was drawing about 50ft of water, contrasting with the usual draught of 34ft.

★ ★ ★

Thomas Andrews' steward, Henry Etches, was sleeping down on E-deck, along with nineteen others in the same space. Etches awoke and called to his mate 'What time is it that they are going to call us next?'

'I don't know,' came the laconic reply. Etches rolled over, and was going to sleep again when he heard the boatswain yelling 'Close the watertight bulkhead doors!' He was referring to some of the non-automatic doors on the higher decks within the hull. The boatswain was running along the E-deck working alleyway with a seaman (the E-deck alleyway was also called 'Park Lane' and 'Scotland Road'). It was 11.47 a.m. Etches soon decided to get dressed and he walked forward along E-deck, he saw third-class passengers all going aft; he walked thirty yards and a third-class passenger threw a piece of ice at him. 'Will you believe it now?' the passenger said to Etches, chucking the ice on the floor. He hadn't even met the passenger before. Etches went back to his cabin and went up on deck. He was going through a door when he met Steward Stone. Stone was the E-deck bedroom steward, and Etches asked him 'What is the time?'

Stone replied: 'Never mind about that; there is something else for you to do. I saw them [the mail clerks] pull up bags of mail, and the water was running out of the bottom of them.'

Etches went up to A-deck and he noticed the bedroom steward assisting passengers, and observed that most of the doors were open. He asked 'Have you called all of your people?' and the man whom Etches was to relieve replied 'Yes, but I can't get them to dress.'

He ran into Thomas Andrews. Etches went down the pantry stairs to C-deck and Andrews instructed Etches to assist the passengers in any way that he could. The two men walked along the first-class corridors on C-deck and came to the pursers' office. The purser was telling a large group of ladies to go back to their cabins, perhaps to put lifebelts on, and to ask their stewards to give assistance. Andrews remarked, 'That is exactly what I have been trying to get them to do.'

Indeed, many passengers were now aware that something had happened, but few seemed to take the situation seriously.

While *Titanic* lay off Cherbourg, the night drew in. (*L'Illustration*, 1912/Author's collection)

Lawrence Beesley asked a steward 'Why have we stopped?'

He replied, 'I don't know, sir, but I don't suppose it is anything much.'

After hearing this, Beesley went to see what the matter was, but later continued reading. He finally realised that something was quite wrong and went to the boat deck at about 12.20 a.m.[39]

At 12.10 a.m., Emily Ryerson looked into the corridor outside her suite and saw people heading for the boat deck. 'Put on your lifebelts and come up on the boat deck,' said a passenger passing.

'Where did you get those orders?' she demanded.

'From the captain.'

She roused her husband and children, then her maid Victorine who had an inside cabin adjoining the suite. Almost 'paralysed with fear' that they would not all get on deck in time, she only allowed her younger daughter to put on a night-gown. Her husband cautioned her to keep the family together and they went up to the A-deck landing of the forward grand staircase. They chatted there for half an hour with a group they knew – the Carters, Thayers, Astors and Wideners. Everyone was wearing a lifebelt, but people were cheerful. Chief Second Steward George Dodd then appeared at the head of the stairs, telling everyone to go up to the boat deck.

They walked up to the boat deck forward and were then ordered down to A-deck, to wait for lifeboat number four to be lowered to the glass-enclosed deck.

Major Peuchen was now waiting in the A-deck foyer of the forward grand staircase. Many ladies and gentlemen were coming back in from the freezing boat deck, looking serious. They didn't want to go out in the freezing cold for a stupid boat drill on an 'unsinkable' ship.

Strains of music could be heard from the lounge. Occasionally, remarks were heard such as, 'It is really too tiresome; everybody knows this ship cannot sink' or, 'This ship could hit a hundred icebergs and not feel it. It is ridiculous.'

Certainly it seemed better to stay inside. The beautiful glass dome and chandelier overhead, the magnificent balustrades, oak panelling and the cherub at the foot of the stairs had a look of permanence.

Peuchen met another acquaintance, Mr Beatty. 'What is the matter?' he asked. 'Why, the order is for lifebelts and boats.'

Peuchen recalled, 'I could not believe it at first, it seemed so sudden.'

Soon he decided to head for the boat deck.

Looking down the well of the stairs, E-deck could be seen far below. Forward of the staircase on this deck it was flooding rapidly.

A bedroom steward that Violet Jessop knew knocked on her door as he awoke many cabins and stunned her with the words, 'You know the ship is sinking?'

Jessop recalled, 'my mind…could not accept the fact that this super-perfect creation was to do so futile a thing as to sink.'

Soon they headed for the boat deck.[40]

Second-class passenger Winnie Troutt had no illusions about the ship's condition. She bumped into her table companions who asked her what the matter was. She replied, 'a very sad parting for all of us', and then, with emotion, 'This ship is going to sink!'[41]

At cabin C78, Etches could not get the occupants to open the door. Etches knocked 'What is it?' asked a voice within; a lady's voice said 'Tell us what the trouble is.'

'It is necessary that you should open the door, and I will explain everything, but please put the lifebelts on or bring them in the corridor,' Etches replied.

'I want to know what is the matter.'

'How the *Titanic* struck the iceberg. The blow was received forward on the starboard side, and tore open the ship's side and bottom…' It was difficult for many to envisage such a large ship being sunk by anything but an enormous gash. (*The Deathless Story of the Titanic*, 1912/Author's collection)

'Kindly open the door,' repeated Etches.

Etches gave up. The next cabin was empty, but then he came to a next cabin, occupied by an American couple, who were standing in the door swinging their lifebelts. Etches did not see this couple again, and he went to the pursers' office. 'It is necessary to go up on the boat deck,' said the purser, 'tell the other bedroom stewards to assemble their passengers on the boat deck and stand-by.' Etches went up to the boat deck and assisted getting lifeboat number 7 ready.

Colonel Archibald Gracie bumped into Fred Wright, the *Titanic*'s squash pro, at about this time, and suggested 'Hadn't we better cancel that appointment for tomorrow morning?'

'Yes,' he replied, neglecting to tell Gracie that the court was deeply submerged.[42]

Hudson Allison awoke in his C-deck suite after a knock on the door from his wife's maid, Sarah Daniels, who was worried that the engines had stopped; he reassured her, 'Oh, Sarah, you are so nervous. Go back to bed. This ship's unsinkable.'[43]

After helping with some of the lifeboats, Poingdestre went down to the forecastle to get his boots on at about 12.45 a.m. Water was coming in to the forecastle and a cabin bulkhead gave way, letting water surge in; the water seemed to be coming mostly from the starboard side. Gushing, gurgling water was rising quickly and he had to wade through the icy water that was up to his waist to get out.

About twenty minutes after Wheat had come up, Johnson spoke to Second Steward George Dodd, who said, 'I think it's serious.' Now he went to his quarters, 'The Glory Hole', on E-deck, to change his clothes.

As passengers arrived in greater numbers on the boat deck, many of them were soon driven inside by the freezing cold and deafening noise of steam blowing from the towering funnels. Many stayed indoors or explored…

Hugh Woolner, a first-class passenger, was walking with Mrs Churchill Candee and they passed on of the entrances to a corridor on one of the higher decks, people were wearing lifebelts and Woolner asked 'Is this orders?'

'Orders' was the short reply. Woolner and Mrs Candee went to Mrs Candee's cabin and Woolner took her lifebelt out of the top of the wardrobe and tied it to Mrs Candee. Mrs Candee picked a few small things from her luggage that she could put into her pocket and Woolner returned after a short visit to his cabin, 'We will now go up on deck and see what has really happened.' A rug was taken up because of the cold weather, Woolner wanted to get Mrs Candee away in the first lifeboat and they waited on deck observing the preparations needed to get the lifeboats ready for lowering. On the boat deck on the port side, lifeboat number 4 was being readied for lowering and Captain Smith ordered 'I want all the passengers to go down on A-deck because I intend they shall go into the boats from A-deck.'

Woolner remembered that the forward A-deck promenade was glass-enclosed, and he walked to the captain: 'Haven't you forgotten, sir, that all those glass windows are closed?'

Smith remembered and exclaimed, 'By God, you are right. Call those people back!' Not many people had actually moved but those that had came up from A-deck.

Second Officer Lightoller was forward on the port side of the boat deck near the officers' quarters. He had asked the captain: 'Hadn't we better get the women and children into the boats, sir?'

'Yes, put the women and children in and lower away,' came the reply.

Third Officer Pitman was in his cabin dressing when Fourth Officer Boxhall arrived: 'What is happening?' asked Pitman. 'We['ve] struck an iceberg,' replied Boxhall. Then

Pitman put on his coat and went on the boat deck. He saw the lifeboats being uncovered and cleared away. He was far aft on the boat deck when he met Sixth Officer Moody and asked Moody if he had seen the iceberg. Moody said he hadn't, but that 'There is some ice on the forward well deck.' Pitman was curious so he went down to the forward well deck himself to see; he saw a little ice there and went further to the fo'c'sle head, where he did not see any damage. He met a crowd of firemen coming up from below with their bags, and asked 'What is the matter?'

'The water is coming in our place,' he was told.

'That is funny,' Pitman remarked, and he looked down number 1 hatchway and saw water flowing. He then left for the boat deck.

Fifth Officer Lowe woke up and saw people with lifebelts on outside his window so he went on deck. He went on to the boat deck and took his revolver with him. 'You never know when you may need it,' he later explained.

At 12.23 a.m. Quartermaster Robert Hichens was relieved at the wheel in the enclosed wheelhouse by Quartermaster Perkis, then one of the officers said, 'That will do with the wheel; get the boats out.' Hichens went to the boats forward on the port side.

Fourth Officer Boxhall was now back on the bridge. He noticed two masthead lights of a steamer 5 or 6 miles away, about half a point off the port bow.

Joseph Thomas Wheat ascended the steep crew stairway that led from E-deck to the boat deck. He walked onto the open area of B-deck forward and he met there Chief Steward Andrew Latimer, who was wearing a lifebelt over his coat. Wheat advised Latimer to wear the coat over the lifejacket – it made it easier to swim. As Wheat left for the boat deck he did notice the slight starboard list.

Chief Baker Charles Joughin woke up in his quarters on the port side of E-deck, amidships. He got up immediately, but it was not until 12.15 a.m. when he heard that provisions (bread and biscuits), were needed for the lifeboats that were being readied. Joughin sent the thirteen bakers, who worked under him, to the boat deck with four loaves – about 40lb – of bread each. He stayed below, then he climbed the second-class stairway, past the D-deck second-class dining saloon, the C-deck lounge-library, and the B-deck smoke room, all the way to the boat deck. He watched the activity around him as the boats were readied and passengers stood around.

Steward Henry Etches was assigned to lifeboat number 5. The passengers hadn't got any boat assignments at all, but by 12.30 a.m. quite a few passengers had appeared on the boat deck and they waited around, waiting to be told what to do. The crew were hurriedly taking the covers off lifeboat 5 and number 7 was prepared; First Officer Murdoch, J. Bruce Ismay, Third Officer Pitman, Quartermaster Alfred Oliver, two stewards and Etches were around boats 7 and 5 on the boat deck. Etches helped clear the falls and Ismay helped him. Murdoch thought there was danger, but Third Officer Pitman thought that the ship would stay afloat. Lifeboat number 7 was lowered to boat deck level so that passengers could easily board it, the boat swung slightly clear of the deck due to the very slight starboard list. First Officer Murdoch was giving the orders and Fifth Officer Lowe was also there.

Ismay called: 'Kindly make a line here and allow the ladies to pass through,' to the gentlemen who stood nearby. The Bishops, a Mr Greenfield and his mother, the aviator Marechal, Mr and Mrs Harder, some couples and many single men got in. 'Any more ladies before this boat goes?' called Murdoch. None appeared, so he ordered the lifeboat lowered away with approximately twenty-eight people aboard, or quite possibly less.

Etches had thought that the boat was three-quarters full of ladies; he also observed a baby boy in the boat, with a small woollen cap over his head.

The ship's orchestra, led by Wallace Hartley, had assembled initially in the first-class lounge to play selections such as *Great Big Beautiful Doll* and *Alexander's Ragtime Band*. They moved up to the first-class entrance on the boat deck and subsequently out onto the deck itself, the intention presumably being to try and help to calm the passengers.

Far below them, boiler room 5 remained dry. Although most of the firemen and stokers had been ordered up on deck, Leading Stoker Frederick Barrett and Second Engineer James Hesketh continued their work. The pumps continued to keep ahead of the flooding, but Barrett noticed an increasingly worrying problem: the ship was down by the head and the angle was increasing as her condition deteriorated. He did not remark upon it. Even after 1.00 a.m., the pumps were doing their work, but suddenly 'a rush of water' came through between the boilers, from the forward end of the boiler room. It appears that the coal bunker door – which was not designed to hold back an enormous head of water – eventually gave way under the pressure. Barrett 'did not stop to look' behind him as he abandoned the boiler room, following Junior Assistant Second Engineer Herbert Harvey's instruction to head up.

Titanic's distress call had now become SOS, although she still sent CQD as well. 'I require immediate assistance,' her signals pleaded, 'going down fast at head.'

James Johnson, the nightwatchman, now headed for the boat deck. He noticed Chief Steward Latimer, Purser McElroy and a few others on the C-deck landing of the forward grand staircase as he came up.

After checking the list of boat assignments, Johnson headed for emergency boat number 2, on the port side directly aft of the port bridge wing bulwark. Checking that the plug was in the boat, Johnson stood by the boat for 'a bit'; the second steward, Dodd, asked him to look after his dustcoat, but Johnson never saw Dodd again.

Confirming with Chief Officer Wilde that number 2 was his boat, Johnson went below to collect his coat and a few other things; as he got to the bottom of the companionway Chief Steward Latimer told him to go back up because the water was now washing in.

On the bridge, Fourth Officer Boxhall had already fired at least one distress rocket before the telephone rang. Far aft, on the docking bridge, Quartermaster Rowe had noticed a lifeboat in the water and rang to report it. Boxhall instructed him to bring to the bridge some detonators that were used for firing the distress signals. Rowe, as well as Quartermaster Bright who had come to relieve him, took a box each.

Lawrence Beesley described the firing of the first rocket:

> ...Suddenly a rush of light from the forward deck, a hissing roar that made us all turn from watching the boats, and a rocket leapt upwards to where the stars blinked and twinkled above us. Up it went, higher and higher, with a sea of faces upturned to watch it, and then an explosion that seemed to split the silent night in two, and a shower of stars sank slowly down and went out one by one. And with a gasping sigh one word escaped the lips of the crowd: 'Rockets!' Anybody knows what rockets at sea mean...[44]

As Pitman assisted clearing away number 5, Ismay told him quietly: 'There is no time to waste,' clearly implying that Pitman was moving too slowly. Pitman didn't know Ismay at the time so he just continued as they were; he was surprised at how easily the boat swung

Although its layout differed from its counterpart on board *Olympic*, *Titanic*'s cooling room was furnished in an identical manner. It is not known how many passengers used the Turkish Baths during *Titanic*'s maiden voyage, however twenty-three women and sixty-two men used it during *Olympic*'s first west-bound crossing. Perhaps the trend that men used it more than women was reflected on *Titanic*. At least one female passenger, Mrs Spedden, is known to have disliked the experience. (*The Illustrated London News*, 1912/Daniel Klistorner collection)

out, a great improvement over the davits on the older ships. The lifeboat was ready for lowering in only two minutes; a few people had been needed to lower it using the new davits, whereas a dozen people were needed to operate the older davits on the older ships.

Ismay said that the boat had better be loaded with women and children, and Pitman replied that he waited for Captain Smith's orders. 'Very well,' said an anxious Ismay. The third officer realised that this man might be J. Bruce Ismay and he told the captain that a man who he thought was J. Bruce Ismay wanted him to get the boat away with women and children. 'Go ahead; carry on,' replied Smith. Pitman asked for the ladies to board the lifeboat and shouted if there were any more women who wanted to board, the boat soon had over thirty-six women in it and Ismay helped in every way. Pitman allowed a few men in until the lifeboat contained about forty-one people.

Murdoch ordered Steward Etches to get in and he assisted with one of the falls.

Then a stewardess came running up. 'Come along; jump in,' Ismay instructed.

'I am only a stewardess,' she replied.

'Never mind,' Ismay told her, '– you are a woman; take your place.'

She got in.

Murdoch approached the third officer: 'You go in charge of this boat,' he told Pitman, 'you go away in this boat, old man, and hang around the after gangway.' Pitman got into the boat, although he thought he was better off on the ship and that the *Titanic* wouldn't sink.

'Good-bye, good luck,' Murdoch wished Pitman, ordering the crew at the davits to 'lower away'.

As boat 5 was being lowered, Dr Frauenthal and his brother Isaac jumped into it. As a result, Mrs Stengel suffered two broken ribs when one of them landed on her.[45]

Fifth Officer Lowe was lowering the boat. But Ismay was anxious and a bit excited: 'Lower away! Lower away! Lower away! Lower away!' he yelled.

Lowe couldn't stand the interfering. He swore at Ismay, although he didn't know the stranger in pyjamas and slippers: 'If you get the hell out of that I shall be able to do something.'

'Do you want me to lower away quickly? You will have me drown the whole lot of them!' Ismay walked away to number 3 lifeboat.

As number 5 descended to the flat, calm, ocean many feet below, a call from the boat deck was heard. 'Be sure and see the plug is in that boat.' There was a call to stop lowering but the boat still descended and Quartermaster Olliver managed to put the plug in as the boat settled on the sea. A bit of water came in, but not much. Oliver had had trouble getting the passengers to move out of the way. He had had to crawl right at the bottom of the boat to reach the plug.

As lifeboat 5 pulled away, the ship was down about 20ft at the bow and the E-deck portholes gleamed, although they were now going under the water's surface. The ship had sunk a long way, although this was not obvious to those on board.

On the port side no lifeboats had left yet, but lifeboat number 6 was loading under Lightoller's direction, as was number 8.* Lightoller did not think that the situation was serious, but he still loaded the boat with women and children, not allowing any men into the boat.

When Lightoller first called for women and children the response was unenthusiastic to say the least, many women refused to leave the apparent safety of the ship and others refused to go without their husbands. The thought of being lowered so far down in a boat in the dark and then rowing around all night didn't appeal to many when they could just remain on the 'unsinkable' ship, which still seemed as solid and safe as ever.

Some progress was made, however, and twenty-four women and children boarded the lifeboat. Quartermaster Hichens was ordered into the lifeboat as a crewmember, Lookout Frederick Fleet was also told to get in, and Captain Smith himself ordered a 'young Italian' into the boat. As it began to descend, first-class passenger 'Molly' Brown was bundled 4ft into the descending lifeboat, which was very under-filled.

Number 6 reached C-deck when a call came up, saying that not enough seamen were in the lifeboat. Lightoller leaned over the boat deck and looked down at the lifeboat. 'We will have to have some more seamen here,' he said. Fifty-three-year-old Major Arthur Godfrey Peuchen, of Toronto, Canada, was standing near Lightoller.

'Can I be of assistance?' he asked.

'Are you a seaman?' asked Lightoller.

'I am a yachtsman and can handle a boat with an average man.'

Lightoller replied, 'Why, yes. I will order you to the boat in preference to a sailor. If you are seaman enough to go down that fall (rope) you can go.'

Captain Smith was quite nearby and suggested 'You had better go below and break a window and get in through a window, into the boat.'

---

* Although it is popularly believed that lifeboat number 8 left after number 6, in fact there is considerable evidence that the opposite was the case and lifeboat number 8 left first.

'Sir, I do not think that would be feasible, I could get in if I could get hold of a rope,' replied Peuchen.

They got hold of the rope and Peuchen swung out from the ship and climbed down into the lifeboat. As Peuchen left Lightoller wished him 'Good luck.'

Once in the lifeboat, Major Peuchen asked Quartermaster Robert Hichens, 'What do you want me to do?'

'Get down and put that plug in,' came the reply. It was very dark in the lifeboat so Peuchen had to feel around in the bottom of the lifeboat for the plug; he told Hichens, 'Now you get down and put in the plug and I will undo the shackles.' Hichens rushed to assist Peuchen after putting the plug in. 'Hurry up, this boat is going to founder,' he said in a loud voice. Peuchen at first thought that the plug wasn't in, but realised that Hichens was referring to *Titanic*. Hichens got out the lifeboat's rudder and steered, Peuchen and Lookout Fleet rowed as Hichens warned to row away from *Titanic* as fast as possible.

Number 6's oars splashed and bumped in the glassy-smooth sea as the lifeboat glided away from the sinking liner, which was now very low in the water. Another distress rocket burst loudly overhead sending out a shower of white stars.

Hugh Woolner stood with Mrs Candee watching the boats prepared, as lifeboat number 6 was loaded, he helped Mrs Candee into the lifeboat, and gave her the steamer rug that they had brought up from her cabin and he stepped back and watched as the boat was lowered away.

Fourth Officer Boxhall thought that the light he could see was moving closer, but after attempting to Morse the stranger using the powerful lamps on the bridge wing cabs, he realised it wasn't. She was slowly turning, he observed. Captain Smith looked at the ship as well. They concluded it was just a masthead light flickering.

As lifeboat number 8 was being filled, Mr and Mrs Straus approached with Ellen Bird, Mrs Straus' maid. Ellen Bird got into the boat and Mrs Straus went over to the boat, before returning to her husband.

'We have been living together for many years, Isidor. Where you go, I go.'

People were shocked. Hugh Woolner approached Mr Straus, 'I am sure nobody would object to an old gentleman like you getting in, there seems to be room in this boat.'

'No, I will not go before the other men,' Mr Straus insisted. He and his wife moved over to some deck chairs and sat down together.

The Countess of Rothes, and her cousin, Miss Cherry, boarded the lifeboat. There were now more than twenty women and children on board, Seaman Jones who was in charge, another seamen, Steward Crawford and another steward. First-class passenger Mrs White carried a cane with an electric light in the end of it which would later prove useful in the dark night.

Captain Smith ordered Seaman Jones, 'Row for that light, leave your passengers on board of her and return.' Smith obviously believed the light was quite close. The lifeboat was then safely lowered away, another boat loaded far below capacity.

Fifth Officer Lowe had finished helping with number 5 and he went forward to boat number 3, not enough people could be found or persuaded to board the lifeboat. Everyone there was calm and quiet, but eventually a good complement was persuaded to board. After the women had boarded number 3, men were allowed in if there was nobody else. The boat deck forward was pretty much deserted, although little knots of people hung around the boat deck a bit farther aft. A small crowd was near the gymnasium doorway; people were also inside the gymnasium because it was warmer than the cold boat deck and there was the exercise equipment to keep people entertained. The Astors were both inside the gym and Mr Astor was showing his wife a lifejacket.

Number 3 contained over forty people when First Officer Murdoch ordered, 'That will do,' then – moments later – 'Lower away' as another distress rocket lit up the sky. J. Bruce Ismay had assisted with number 3 and now watched as it was lowered. Seaman Moore was put in charge, although Moore thought that only thirty-two people were aboard the lifeboat.

Lowe and Murdoch now focused on an emergency cutter, number 1 lifeboat, which had a forty-person capacity.

Cosmo Duff Gordon, Lucile and Miss 'Franks', Lucile's secretary, stood on the starboard side of the boat deck and watched three lifeboats leave. Number 1, right forward, was still hanging from the davits. Lucile refused to go in a boat without her husband, and her secretary refused to go alone, so Sir Cosmo asked Murdoch if they could all go, and Murdoch replied, 'Oh certainly do, I'll be very pleased,' according to Sir Cosmo, but simply, 'Yes, jump in,' according to George Symons, a lookout nearby. Two American passengers got in the lifeboat, one tripping and rolling into the boat. Murdoch remarked, 'That's the funniest sight I've seen tonight,' and then Murdoch added six firemen and Lookout Symons who was in charge, and ordered, 'Stand off from the ship's side and return when we call you.' The boat was then lowered, probably at about 1.10 a.m.

Once in the water, Sir Cosmo shared out cigars and the lifeboat stood 200 yards off the starboard bow. Murdoch had probably sent the boat away with only twelve people hoping that the boat's occupants would later pick up survivors after the ship had sunk, but in the event they didn't.

Many third-class passengers had not even had the chance to get into the boat. Gates barred access to second and first-class areas in order to segregate the classes, but even now many were still closed. They did not actually bar access to the upper decks, but certainly by preventing access to other areas they made access considerably harder. Some stewards were even keeping passengers below decks behind locked gates. Even many who did not get stopped by closed gates had trouble finding the boats on their own. The poop deck and aft well deck were crowded with passengers, waiting for word on what to do. At one point, an officer came along and told them to be calm as a ship was coming. Like ants, people were climbing over cranes and then crawling over the railings and into second-class territory.

In lifeboat 8, the Countess of Rothes volunteered to steer; she took the tiller and her cousin rowed along with the lifeboat's crew. The forward well deck was still dry, so was the forecastle deck, but the openings in the bulkheads at the sides of the well deck were only a matter of feet above the water.

Those below decks knew how serious the situation was. Down in boiler room number 4 Trimmer Thomas Dillon noticed that water was entering the room; it was seeping-in through the floor plates and the men worked the pumps, although they could not quite keep ahead of the water. Perhaps the iceberg had in some way punctured the double bottom. The order was given, 'All hands on deck, put your life preservers on'; the flooding boiler room was then deserted. Dillon went up past the well deck, where he noticed some passengers had gathered, he then continued up to the boat deck.

Lifeboat number 9 on the starboard side – the furthest forward of the aft four boats – was lowered level with the boat deck not long past 1.10 a.m. First Officer Murdoch and Sixth Officer Moody then loaded it.

Joseph Thomas Wheat approached number 9, and he found at the boat Murdoch and 'a load of stewards' helping to pass the women and a few children into the boat. The boat was half-full when Murdoch ordered the stewards down to A-deck, where they could pass the women into the boat. A ring was formed 6ft around the boat, and Wheat had one foot on the gunwale and one on the bulwark as he helped passengers in. There were forty women and two children in the boat, six male passengers and eight crew when Murdoch said, 'You've enough there.' Then he ordered, 'Lower away together.' The boat was lowered quite safely.

The team of stewards went aft to number 11 that was loading, again under the provision of Sixth Officer Moody and First Officer Murdoch.

Hudson Allison had realised something was very wrong and he left to investigate – leaving Alice Cleaver, their nanny, with his wife, two-year-old Loraine and baby Trevor.[46] Panicking, Alice Cleaver took baby Trevor and rushed on deck, escaping in boat 11; Hudson Allison returned to his wife and Loraine.[47]

Sarah, the Allisons' maid, was pulled into boat 8; she was reassured by a sailor that he would see that the Allisons were safe and she stayed in the boat – she didn't know that the Allisons had got to the boat deck or that she would never see them again.[48]

Hudson Allison, Mrs Allison and little Loraine ascended the forward grand staircase to the boat deck, but once there they would not be separated and would stay until the *Titanic* sank beneath them.[49]

In lifeboat number 6 an officer's whistle was heard. Quartermaster Hichens ordered people to stop rowing so that he could hear. Using a megaphone, Captain Smith was ordering the half-filled lifeboat to return to the ship so that it could be filled to capacity. Many women thought that they should go back, particularly those who had left husbands on the sinking ship. 'No, we are not going back to the boat,' Hichens responded. 'It's our lives now, not theirs.' He also insisted in rowing further away, and although there were cries of protest from many, lifeboat number 6 did not return. Major Peuchen later said that, 'if we [had] wanted to go back, while he [Hichens] was in possession of the tiller, I do not think we could have done so.' In fact, not one of the half-filled lifeboats responded to the command.

Wheat helped load lifeboat 11 with Moody and Murdoch. He checked the plug was in and when the boat was full Murdoch ordered 'lower away'. Stepping into number 11, Wheat looked around and estimated nearly eighty people on board.

The Beckers were on the boat deck and Ruth's brother and sister stepped aboard number 11, then someone called: 'That's all for this boat.'

Ruth's mother pleaded, 'Please, those are my children, let me go with them,' and she was allowed to step into the boat; she called to Ruth to 'get into the next lifeboat',[50] as number 11 began its jerky descent.

Leading Stoker Frederick Barrett arrived on the promenade deck, A, where boat 13 was being loaded; it was pretty full when he got there. Barrett boarded the boat along with Fireman Beauchamp; 'Let no more in that boat, the falls will break! Now lower away,' ordered Murdoch. Boat 13 was then lowered with sixty-four people – one man, five crew and fifty-eight women and children; Lookout Reginald Lee, on duty at the time of the collision, was on board the lifeboat.

Ruth Becker asked if she could get into number 13, 'Sure,' was the reply, and an officer picked her up and 'dumped her in' to the boat.[51]

Lawrence Beesley did not ask if he could board number 13, but a crewman asked him if there were any more women near him. He replied, 'No,' and the crewman advised him, 'then you had better jump'; Beesley jumped in at the stern.[52]

Titanic's first-class gymnasium was largely identical to *Olympic's*, yet it was one of her few public rooms that were photographed. On the night of the disaster, some passengers went inside to shelter from the cold of the boat deck. (*L'Illustration*, 1912/Author's collection, restoration © Daniel Klistorner)

After ordering the lowering of number 13, Murdoch stepped aft to number 15, which was full of mainly third-class women and children. Some people were trying to rush the boat, and after stopping them Murdoch ordered 'lower away'. The boat was lowered with up to seventy people. Sixth Officer Moody went over to the port side to help with the boats there. Turning around and walking down the steep deck forward, Murdoch sighed to a steward, 'I believe she's gone, Hardy.'

Number 13 was lowered to the waterline and a discharge of water from the side of the ship caused it to drift aft, the falls tightened up, and it was impossible to detach the boat, and lifeboat number 15 was heading down straight for them.

Using a knife, Leading Stoker Barrett tried to cut the taught ropes, he eventually succeeded and the lifeboat pulled away just in time.

Opposite, on the port side of the ship, lifeboats 16, 14 and 12 were loading, assisted at various times by Sixth Officer Moody, Fifth Officer Lowe, Chief Officer Wilde and Second Officer Lightoller. Lifeboat 16, the furthest aft, was filled without trouble under Sixth Officer Moody. Violet Jessop, glancing forward, suddenly noticed that the ship's bow had sunk very low into the water when she felt someone tug her arm. She turned to see Sixth Officer Moody, looking 'weary and tired', but he smiled as he helped her in, throwing a baby into the boat with her. First-class bathroom steward Frank Morris went to boat 14 as 16 was lowered away.

Lifeboats 12 and 14 remained, nearly ready for lowering, yet panic was appearing on deck. People were surging around the boats while 'officers and men were yelling and cursing at men to stand back and let women into the boats', passenger Daisy Minahan recalled. At lifeboat 14, which was nearly full following Chief Officer Wilde's orders, some 'foreign passengers' who did not appear to understand English, were trying to rush the boat and Able Seaman Joseph Scarrott had to keep them back with the boat's tiller. When Fifth Officer Lowe took charge of the boat he was worried that it was overloaded and when Scarrott told him of the trouble, Lowe pulled out his revolver.

'How many are in the boat?' he asked.

Scarrott replied about fifty-four women and four children, as near as he could tell.

'Do you think the boat will stand it?' Lowe asked, worried.

'Yes, she is hanging alright.'

'Alright,' Lowe ordered; 'Lower away 14.' As the boat started down, Lowe was worried about the crowd on deck jumping in. He fired his revolver several times between the boat and the ship as a warning.

The boat stopped when the after fall jammed, leaving the stern 10ft above the sea and the bow touching the water. Lowe was worried about the distance, but using the release gear the boat was released, albeit landing 'with a terrific thud'. Scarrott checked that the plug was still in, but time would tell that the boat had sprung a small leak elsewhere which would need baling.

Lifeboat 12 had probably started down just after number 14, with up to forty occupants, although second- and third-class men had also tried to rush the boat. 'They were trying to rush number 12 and number 14,' Able Seaman Poingdestre recalled. He and Second Officer Lightoller had trouble keeping them back, but as the boat was lowered and reached B-deck a passenger jumped in. Further trouble occurred when the boat reached the water, as the falls had to be cut using a third-class passenger's knife.

It appears that lifeboat 10 remained on deck and had not been prepared for lowering. By the time it was, *Titanic's* increasing list to port opened up a gap between the boat and the edge of the deck that had not been such a problem when the previous three boats left the ship. Although they had left the ship within a matter of minutes of each other, from around 1.20 to 1.30 a.m., lifeboat 10 does not seem to have left until as late as 1.45 a.m., about the same time as preparations were being made on the forward end of the boat deck to lower lifeboat 2.[53]

Before official loading began, 'about sixteen or eighteen stokers' had got in the boat. An officer – identified as Murdoch, but more likely to have been Lightoller – bellowed: 'Get out, you damned cowards; I'd like to see everyone of you overboard.' Then they got out.[54] Loading started and eventually twenty-one women and children boarded the boat, two crew got in and Fourth Officer Boxhall boarded. He wisely took with him some green flares. The time was now slightly past 1.45 a.m.

Remaining on board the ship was collapsible D, forward on the port side, and lifeboat number 4, directly aft of collapsible D, on top of the officers' quarters were collapsibles A and B on the starboard and port sides respectively.

Number 4 had been lowered to the promenade deck more than an hour earlier and the socially prominent group of passengers still waited. The Ryersons, Astors, Wideners, Thayers, Mrs Carter, her maid and children… the glass-enclosed promenade was now open because the key had been found to open the windows. Lightoller was loading the boat with Steward Dodd and he had one foot in the window and one on the lifeboat.

Rough steps had been rigged to bridge the gap between the lifeboat and sinking ship using coaling wires, as there was a list to port.

Emily Ryerson boarded the boat with her husband and maid, although her son was briefly prevented from going in the boat by Lightoller.

'That boy can't go!'

'Of course that boy goes with his mother; he is only thirteen,' Arthur Ryerson protested.

Jack was allowed to board, but Steward Dodd uttered, 'No more boys.'

Hearing this, Lucile Carter put a hat on ten-year-old Billy Carter's head. Nobody noticed.

Mrs Ryerson kissed her husband goodbye. As she climbed into the boat through the window, it impressed her of the darkness outside compared to the lit deck. 'It was as if you stepped out into the dark,' she would recall, meaning the unknown.

Another drama played out before the boat was lowered. Pregnant Mrs Astor was helped into the bat by Colonel Gracie and her husband. 'Can I go in the boat to protect my wife?' asked Mr Astor, 'as my wife's condition is delicate.'

'No, sir; no man is allowed on this boat or any of the boats until all the ladies are off,' Lightoller replied, standing firm with the unwritten law of the sea.

'Well, tell me the number of the boat so I may find her afterwards,' Astor insisted.

'Number 4, sir.' Lightoller was sure, albeit illogically considering the circumstances, that Astor would later file a complaint.

Someone asked from the boat deck above, 'How many women are there in the boat?'

'Twenty-four.'

'That's enough. Lower away,' came the order.

The davits' tips flexed and the pulleys began to shriek. The boat jerked and began to descend. It tipped as the ropes kept sticking briefly. Someone called out for a knife to cut the falls, but there was no answer.

After a terrifying journey, boat 4 touched the water a mere 15ft below.

Mrs Ryerson watched water washing into the deluxe suites, sea pouring onto the forward end of B-deck. Greeny-blue water had covered the C-deck ports. The ship was shaking noticeably.

Looking up, she saw her husband, Mr Widener, Mr Thayer and some other men standing quietly on the boat deck. She was now certain that *Titanic*, and quite possibly her husband, was doomed.

'How many seamen have you?' asked Lightoller through one of the A-deck windows.

'One, sir.'

'That is not enough,' Lightoller advised. 'I will send you another.' Storekeeper Foley and some other crewmen climbed down.

The lifeboat made slow progress away from the ship, aft. Barrels, deckchairs and other objects were being thrown overboard and littered the sea.

Number 4 received some more occupants as it rowed aft, before rowing away from the sinking ship. Greaser Thomas Ranger and Greaser Frederick Scott climbed down the vacant falls of one of the boats aft on the port side and were able to get into the boat. Patrick Dillon went down a little when the ship sank and swam for twenty minutes before being recovered by number four; he was unconscious and when he awoke in the boat, Seaman Lyons was on top of him, dead. Dillon had a bottle of brandy in his pocket, which was thrown overboard by quartermaster Perkis. As he was drunk, Dillon was left in the bottom of the boat.

Well forward on the starboard side, collapsible C was being loaded and prepared for lowering by Chief Officer Wilde and First Officer Murdoch. Purser McElroy assisted.

Initially, there had been a large crowd rushing the boat. Many men from third class had climbed aboard. 'There was a large scramble,' recalled Hugh Woolner. Murdoch was forced to fire two pistol shots overhead. 'Get out of this boat. Clear out,' Murdoch was yelling.

First-class passengers Björnström Steffanson and Hugh Woolner heard the shots and ran to the boat. They helped clear the stowaways from the lifeboat. Many were now leaping out after the shots had been fired. But the crowd dispersed and women and children could be loaded.

J. Bruce Ismay was assisting to load the boat with women and children and he later stated that he saw no passengers in the boat's vicinity. When it started jerkily down to the sea not far below just a few minutes before 2.00 a.m., J. Bruce Ismay stepped into the lifeboat and so did a first-class passenger, Mr William Carter. Quartermaster Rowe had left the bridge after Captain Smith ordered him to join boat C and he was put in charge of it. Thirty-nine people were on board including five crew, Ismay and Carter, and four stowaway 'Chinamen'; the remaining twenty-eight were women and children. Among those aboard the boat were Frank Goldsmith and his mother.

Collapsible D was directly forward of the davits vacated by boat 4, hanging several feet away from the ship's side owing to the list to port, which was now about 8°. Before loading began, Lightoller was forced to draw his pistol because 'men from steerage', as he later said, 'rushed the boat'.[55] Before him, on the deck, were hundreds of desperate souls, with the knowledge that nearly all lifeboats had left and that within minutes the ship would sink. Lightoller was now quickly loading collapsible D with many women and children – through a ring of crew and some male first-class passengers who were stopping people 'rushing the boat' – and the boat was lowered at around 2.05 a.m., or perhaps up to five minutes later.

Hugh Woolner and Björnström Steffanson were on the port side A–deck promenade forward after leaving collapsible C a few minutes before, no doubt they noticed that the ship's lights were now beginning to glow red. Walking forward, they noticed a collapsible boat being lowered, at the same moment the sea was washing onto the deck with a loud noise. 'There's nobody in her bows. Let's make a jump for it. You go first,' Woolner said to Steffanson. Then they both jumped, but Woolner fell out of the boat and was pulled in once the boat was on the sea, then a male passenger was seen floating in the water and he was pulled into the boat by both of them. Forty-four people were in the lifeboat as they quickly rowed away.

At 2.05 a.m. Captain Smith entered the wireless cabin. Phillips was still working the apparatus, although power was fading. 'Men, you have done your full duty,' he advised. 'You can do no more. Abandon your cabin. It's every man for himself. You look out for yourselves. I release you. That's the way of it at this kind of time.' But as the captain left, both operators remained at their posts. While there was power, they were not leaving.

Collapsible B was on the port side of the officers' quarters and it fell down to the boat deck upside down when the crew attempted to ready it. Lightoller, Greaser Hurst and Samuel Hemming were among those trying to right it.

On the starboard side collapsible A fell to the boat deck upright. The crew having tried to get it down from the roof of the officers' quarters with some oars positioned there, but the oars buckled. It had been harder to get it down because of the port list and the crew had to push it 'uphill' to the edge of the roof and onto the boat deck.

Phillips continued to work even after he had been released, but eventually the two men abandoned the wireless room and the long list of communications came to an end:

One of *Titanic*'s new features was the addition of the Café Parisien. It proved so popular that a practically identical café was installed on *Olympic* after the disaster. (*L'Illustration*, 1912/Author's collection, restoration © Daniel Klistorner)

New York Time	*Titanic* time	Communications
10.25 p.m.	12.27 a.m.	*La Provence* receives *Titanic*'s distress signals
10.25	12.27	*Mount Temple* hears *Titanic* sending CQD; says require assistance. Gives position. Cannot hear me. Advise my Captain his position 41° 46′N 50°24′W
10.25	12.27	Cape Race hears *Titanic* giving position on CQD 41°44′N 50°24′W
10.28	12.30	*Ypiranga* hears CQD from *Titanic*. *Titanic* gives CQD here. Position 41°44′N 50°24′W, require assistance (repeated about ten times)
10.35	12.37	CQD call received from *Titanic* by *Carpathia*. *Titanic* states 'Come at once, it's a CQD old man, position: 41°46′North 50°14′West. Calling him, no answer given.
10.36	12.38	MGY (*Titanic*) says CQD, here corrected position 41°46′N 50°14′W. Require immediate assistance. We have collision with iceberg.

New York Time	*Titanic* time	Communications
		Sinking. Can nothing hear [sic] for noise of steam. Sent fifteen to twenty times to *Ypiranga*.
10.37 p.m.	12.39 a.m.	*Titanic* sends following: 'I require immediate assistance. Struck by iceberg in 41°46′North 50°14′West'.
10.40	12.42	*Titanic* gives his position to *Frankfurt*, and says, 'Tell your Captain to come to our help. We are on the ice.'
10.40	12.42	Caronia sent CQ message to MBC, *Baltic* and CQD: 'MGY (*Titanic*) struck iceberg, requires immediate assistance.'
10.40	12.42	*Mount Temple* hears MGY (*Titanic*) still calling CQD. Our Captain reverses ship. We are about fifty miles off.
10.46	12.48	DKF (*Prinz Friedrich Wilhelm*) calls MGY (*Titanic*) and gives position at 12 a.m. as 39°47′N, 50°10′W. MGY (*Titanic*) says, 'Are you coming to our aid?' DFT (*Frankfurt*) says, 'What is the matter with you?' MGY (*Titanic*): 'We have collision with iceberg. Sinking. Please tell Captain to come' DFT (*Frankfurt*) says, 'OK, will tell'
10.48	12.50	*Mount Temple* hears *Frankfurt* give MGY (*Titanic*) his position 39°47′N, 52°10′W.
10.55	12.57	*Titanic* calls *Olympic* SOS
11.00	1.02	*Titanic* calls CQD and says, 'I require immediate assistance. Position 41°46′N, 50°14′W' received by *Celtic*
11.03	1.05	*Caronia* to MBC (*Baltic*) and SOS 'MGY CQD in 41°46′N 50°14′W wants immediate assistance'
11.10	1.12	MGY (*Titanic*) gives distress signal. DDC replies MGY's position 41°46′N 50°14′W, assistance from DDC not necessary as MKC (*Olympic*) shortly afterwards answers distress call.
11.10	1.12	*Titanic* replies to *Olympic* and gives his position 41°46′N 50°14′W, and says, 'We have struck an iceberg.'
11.12	1.14	*Titanic* calls *Asian* and said 'Want immediate assistance' *Asian* answered at once, and received *Titanic*'s position as 41°46′N 50°14′W which he immediately takes to the bridge. Captain instructs operator to have *Titanic*'s position repeated.
11.12	1.14	*Virginian* calls *Titanic* but gets no response.

New York Time	*Titanic* time	Communications
		Cape Race tells *Virginian* to report to his captain the *Titanic* has struck iceberg and requires immediate assistance.
11.20 p.m.	1.22 a.m.	*Titanic* to MKC (*Olympic*) 'We are in collision with berg. Sinking head down. 41°46′N 50°14′W. Come soon as possible.'
11.20	1.22	*Titanic* to MKC (*Olympic*) Captain says 'Get your boats ready. What is you position?'
11.25	1.27	*Baltic* to *Caronia* 'Please tell *Titanic* we are making towards her.'
11.30	1.32	*Virginian* hears MCE (Cape Race) inform MGY (*Titanic*), 'That we are going to his assistance. Our position 170 miles North of *Titanic*.'
11.35	1.37	*Caronia* tells *Titanic* '*Baltic* coming to your assistance.'
11.35	1.37	*Olympic* sends position to *Titanic* 4.24 Greenwich Mean Time as 40°52′N 61°18′W 'Are you steering Southerly to meet us?' *Titanic* replies 'We are putting the women off in the boats.'
11.35	1.37	*Titanic* and *Olympic* work together.
11.37	1.39	MGY (*Titanic*) says, 'We are putting the women off in lifeboats.'
11.40	1.42	*Titanic* tells *Olympic* 'We are putting passengers off in small boats.'
11.45	1.47	*Olympic* asks *Titanic* what weather he had. *Titanic* replies 'Clear and calm.'
11.45	1.47	*Baltic* hears *Titanic* say 'Engine room getting flooded.'
11.45	1.47	*Mount Temple* hears DFT (*Frankfurt*) ask, 'Are there any boats around you already?' No reply.
11.47	1.49	*Baltic* tells *Titanic* 'We are rushing to you.'
11.50	1.52	*Olympic* to *Titanic* 'Am lighting up all possible boilers as fast as can.'
11.50	1.52	Cape Race says to *Virginian* 'Please tell your Captain this: "*Olympic* is making all speed for *Titanic* but his (*Olympic*'s) position is 40°32′N 61°18′W. you are much nearer *Titanic*. The *Titanic* is already putting women off in the boats, and he says the weather there is calm and clear. The *Olympic* is the only ship we have heard say, 'Going to the assistance of the *Titanic*.' The others must be a long way from the *Titanic*"'.
11.55	1.57	Last signals heard from *Titanic* by *Carpathia*

New York Time	*Titanic* time	Communications
		'Engine room full up to boilers.'
11.55 p.m.	1.57 a.m.	*Mount Temple* hears DFT (*Frankfurt*) calling MGY – no reply.
11.57	1.59	Caronia hears MGY – although MGY's signals are unreadable.
11.58	2.00	*Asian* hears *Titanic* call SOS. *Asian* answers *Titanic* but receives no answer.
12.00 a.m.	2.02 a.m.	*Caronia* hears *Frankfurt* working to *Titanic*. *Frankfurt*, according to position, is 172 miles from MGY (*Titanic*).
12.05	2.07	Cape Race says to *Virginian* 'We have not heard *Titanic* for about half an hour. His power may be gone.'
12.10	2.12	*Virginian* hears *Titanic* calling very faintly, his power being greatly reduced.
12.20	2.22	*Virginian* hears two V's signalled faintly in spark similar to *Titanic's*. probably adjusting spark.
12.27	2.29	*Virginian* hears *Titanic* call CQ but is unable to read him. *Titanic's* signals end very abruptly as power is suddenly switched off. His spark rather blurred or ragged. Called MGY (*Titanic*) and suggested that he tried emergency set, but heard no response.
12.30	2.32	*Olympic*, his signals strong, asked him if he had heard anything about MGY (*Titanic*). he says, 'No. keeping strict watch, but hear nothing more from MGY. No reply from him.'★

Captain Smith appears to have returned to the bridge, where he was seen by first-class passenger Richard Williams. If he looked ahead, as Williams did, he would have seen the bow entirely submerged: the water was almost level with the bridge and only the ship's foremast could be seen sticking out of the dark black water. Harold Bride believed that he saw the *Titanic's* commander dive into the ocean as the bridge was inundated by the sea.[56]

It is not known with any certainty what happened to Thomas Andrews. One account was reported by Shan Bullock: 'An assistant steward saw him standing alone in the smoking room, his arms folded over his breast and the [life] belt lying on a

---

★ The original list of messages compiled by the British investigation assumed a time difference of 1 hour 50 minutes between New York Time and *Titanic* Time. However, modern research has shown that the time difference was twelve minutes greater, so that *Titanic* Time was 2 hours 2 minutes ahead of New York Time. Consequently, *Titanic* Time has been adjusted twelve minutes further ahead. It must be noted that this places two messages logged by *Virginian* at 2.22 a.m. and 2.29 a.m., after the ship sank. However, they were only assumed to come from *Titanic*: the first sounded 'similar to *Titanic's*' and the second seems to be an assumption that the 'blurred or ragged' transmission came from the doomed ship. It appears the final message that was really from *Titanic* was logged at 2.12 a.m., the ship's wireless power 'greatly reduced'. (For further reading, see Sam Halpern's article 'Time and Time Again' in *Voyage*, *Titanic* International Society, 2010.)

table near him. The steward asked him: "Aren't you going to have a try for it, Mr Andrews?" He never answered or moved, "just stood like one stunned."[57] Whether he was there when the ship's end came is unknown. There is no evidence that he tried to save himself.

Collapsible B floated off the submerging deck and the 60-ton forward funnel collapsed, causing the collapsible to wash clear of the ship. Lightoller was pinned against a forward grate as water poured into it and he was washed clear when a blast of hot air blew him away from it. He swam to the crow's nest on the mast and realised it was useless before getting to the boat. A large crowd of people continued to move aft as the ship started to sink even more quickly.

The minority of her passengers and crew who had boarded lifeboats watched in horror. Lookout George Symons noted:

> You could see her starboard sidelight [on the bridge], which was still burning, was not so very far from the water, and her stern was well up in the air... You could just see the propellers... I stood and watched it till I heard two sharp explosions in the ship. What they were I could not say... she took a heavy cant and her bow went down clear... Head down, and that is the time when I saw her lights go out, all her lights. The next thing I saw was her poop. As she went down like that so her poop righted itself and I thought to myself, 'The poop is going to float.' It could not have been more than two or three minutes after that that her poop went up as straight as anything; there was a sound like steady thunder as you hear on an ordinary night at a distance, and soon she disappeared from view... It righted itself without the bow; in my estimation she must have broken in half.

Able Seaman Edward Buley saw that: 'She went down as far as the after funnel, and then there was a little roar, as though the engines had rushed forward, and she snapped in two, and the bow part went down and the after part came up and stayed up five minutes before it went down. It was horizontal at first, and then went down.' Quartermaster Olliver saw: 'The after part righted itself and made another plunge and went right down. I fancied I saw her black form. It was dark, and I fancied I saw her black form going that way.' Steward Crowe described:

> After getting clear of the ship the lights were still burning very bright, but as we got away she seemed to go lower and lower, and she almost stood up perpendicular, and her lights went dim, and presently she broke clean in two, probably two-thirds of the length of the ship... She broke, and the after part floated back... then there was an explosion, and the aft part turned on end and sank.

'*Titanic* was upright like a column: we could see her now only as the stern, and some 150ft of her stood outlined against the star-speckled sky, looming black in the darkness,' Lawrence Beesley recalled. '...She slid slowly forwards and dived slantingly down.'[58]

The ship vanished. More than 1,000 people were left in the freezing waters. Cries from the mass of humanity slowly faded into lonely cries from the darkness. Emily Ryerson heard the cries: 'They seemed to go on forever,' she recalled. 'Someone called out, "Pull for your lives or you'll be sucked under!" and everyone rowed like mad.'

The Captain of the "Titanic" and some of his Officers:—1. W. M. Murdock, first mate, who was in charge on the bridge when the ship struck. 2. Captain Smith with his pet dog. 3. H. W. McElroy, chief purser. 4. H. F. Wilde, chief mate 5. Dr. J. E. Simpson, the ship's surgeon. 6. H. J. Lowe, fifth mate. 7. F. Evans, one of the look-out men. 8. H. J Pitman, third mate.

'The captain of the *Titanic* and some of his officers'. There are a number of small errors in the captions: for instance, Murdoch's surname was spelt incorrectly and Lowe's middle initial was wrong. (*The Deathless Story of the Titanic*, 1912/Author's collection)

In boat 3, one crewman yelled 'She's gone, lads. Row like hell or we'll get the devil of a swell!'

Violet Jessop in boat 16 recalled an 'awful moment of empty, misty blackness enveloped us in its loneliness,…an unforgettable, agonising cry went up from 1,500 despairing throats, a long wail and then silence and our tiny craft…at the mercy of the icefield.'[59]

A 'cork carpet' lay on the sea and explosions could be faintly heard from somewhere far below. The stern section had been submerged when it was still quite full of air; it had not already filled with water like the bow section. Now air ripped through the hull with enough force to level a square mile of houses and the cork-insulated refrigerated food storerooms disintegrated.[60] The ship's stern was now a total wreck, the ship submerged and hidden, corroded, as it would be for seventy-three years.

J. Bruce Ismay had turned his head on the ship as soon as collapsible C left. In the same boat were Frank Goldsmith and his mother who would never see Tom Theobald or Frank's father again, or Alfred Rush, who had also died when the ship sank, by his own sacrifice.[61] Bravely, he had refused to even get to the upper decks because he had turned sixteen that day. In later years when Frank was living in Detroit, the cries from the baseball field whenever the home team hit a run reminded him of the awful noise.

150 yards from the site of the sinking, boats 14, 12, 10, 4 and collapsible D floated together. Fifth Officer Lowe had approached in boat 14.

'Are there any seamen there?' he asked.

'Yes, sir.'

'Alright; you will have to distribute these passengers among these boats. Tie them all together and come into my boat to go over into the wreckage and pick up anyone that is alive there.'

Lowe also helped with the transfer, but was irritated by the length of time needed. 'Jump, damn you, jump!' he cried to one woman. On the other hand, one figure wrapped in a shawl seemed too fast. He grabbed the shawl and found himself looking at a man, pale with terror. Without comment, Lowe pushed him hard into one of the other boats.

By the time boat 14 was ready to return, with eight or nine crew aboard to man it, there were few alive in the water. Seaman Evans was afraid to look over the boat's side at the dead bodies frozen, fearing he would break down.

Among the dead was a woman with a child held above her, frozen…three men frozen clinging to a piece of wreckage as though in their last struggle for life…

Four people were picked up from the water, but one of these – William F. Hoyt – died. Nobody else was living; more than 1,000 people had frozen to death in the near-to-freezing 28° Fahrenheit water.

Bath steward Harold Phillimore, determined to survive, was pulled onto a piece of wreckage by a man he didn't know.[62] For a moment the two were face to face. 'What a night!' exclaimed his companion in extreme understatement before falling dead into the sea.

Around twenty minutes after the sinking, while 800 yards from the wreck, lifeboat number 4 – under Quartermaster Walter Perkis' command – was stopped on the water. Searching for survivors, eight people were picked-up from the water, but two were unlucky: Sidney Siebert, who later died in the boat and William Lyons, who later passed away on the *Carpathia* according to one account, but Trimmer Dillon had thought that he was dead when in the boat.

'It is 2.20 a.m.,' remarked Third Officer Pitman, in boat 5, as the ship vanished under the sea. This boat's crew started back to the wreck but they stopped at several female passengers' requests.

In boat 6, Quartermaster Hichens refused to return to the wreckage for survivors, fearing the boat would be swamped. Some of the women, including Molly Brown, urged him that they should return. After a while, Major Peuchen, who had had an argument with Hichens earlier, told them, 'It is no use you arguing with that man, at all. It is best not to discuss matters with him.'

Boats 6 and 16 later tied together during the night, with lifebelts in between so that the hulls did not rub against each other, which could cause damage.

Boats 1 and 2 drifted and no attempts were made to return.

Lifeboats 7 and 5 were tied together and several passengers redistributed to keep the two boats level.

Many men scrambled aboard collapsible B, including Colonel Gracie, Harold Bride, Second Officer Lightoller and Greaser Walter Hurst. A crowd of swimmers surrounded the boat. Some claimed that Captain Smith had actually reached the collapsible and laid a hand on it, before saying: 'I'll follow the ship.' Walter Hurst said that among the swimmers was a man with a voice of authority, who never asked to climb aboard and offered encouragement. 'Good boy! Good lads!' he cried. Hurst held out an oar, but by this time the swimmer was gone. All his life, he was convinced that the swimmer was actually Captain Smith. Although he never asked to come aboard, someone told the swimmer there was no room. Colonel Gracie heard the swimmer say: 'Alright boys; good luck and God bless you.'[63] Constantly whenever someone tried to get aboard, there came the cry 'Hold on to what you have old boy. One more of you would sink us all.' Nobody in the water protested.[64]

Thirty men were eventually aboard the low-floating collapsible. Lightoller took charge of the boat and gave orders to balance it. 'Lean left, right, left...' he repeated at intervals. Throughout the night lay a trying ordeal. It was a battle to stay afloat that was ultimately won. People waited to die, to live, to starve, waited for a rescue that seemed impossible. In such small boats floating on the dark Atlantic, the situation seemed all too real.

Nearing 5.00 a.m., Collapsible A still floated, with its sides still down and its occupants standing in water. Lowe ordered their rescue and collapsible A was set adrift with seacocks open. Lifeboat 12 had had people transferred to it from collapsible D and now collapsible B, which was still floating upside down with Second Officer Lightoller in command. He was blowing his whistle and boat 12 took aboard all of collapsible B's occupants, making a total of nearly eighty people on board. With the sea becoming 'choppy', the lifeboat safely made it to *Carpathia*. Second Officer Lightoller was the last survivor to board the rescue ship, at 8.30 a.m.

★   ★   ★

Cunard's 13,600-ton twin-screw *Carpathia* was placed under Captain Arthur Rostron's command on 18 January 1912. On 11 April 1912 she departed New York with 125 first-class ('saloon') passengers, sixty-five second-class passengers and 550 third-class passengers, bound for Gibraltar. 325 crew were aboard – there were also eighteen lifeboats with a far lower capacity than the number of people that the liner could accommodate – even a ship of this moderate size did not always have lifeboat accommodation for all on board. Proceeding down the river, the Ambrose Channel's lightship was passed at 2.00 p.m. and the voyage was uneventful for the first three days, steaming at a speed of fourteen knots across the calm sea 'in clear, fine weather'.

Planning to retire soon, twenty-one-year-old wireless operator Harold Thomas Cottam was waiting for acknowledgement from a wireless message he had sent earlier to another ship. He had taken off his coat and was untying his shoe laces, waiting...still waiting... Hearing *Titanic*'s signals momentarily stopping, Cottam called him: 'I say, old man, do you know there is a batch of messages for you from Cape Cod?'

Titanic broke in with her own message: 'Come at once...we have struck an iceberg. It's a CQD old man, position 41 degrees 46 minutes north 50 degrees 14 minutes west.'

'Shall I tell my captain? Do you require assistance?' Cottam asked.

'Yes at once, come quick!' came the reply.

Running to the bridge, Cottam burst in and yelled out the distress message to First Officer Dean; with Cottam in front, the two men went to the captain's cabin and went

'The Terrors of the North Atlantic: Our photograph shows a typical iceberg in the North Atlantic…the vast bulk of ice concealed beneath the water.' (*The Deathless Story of the Titanic*, 1912/Author's collection)

in without knocking. Irritated, Rostron asked the matter and Cottam quickly told him of the distress message.

Working out the distance of 58 miles and the course 'north 52 degrees west', Rostron ordered the ship turned around and asked for all possible speed. Rostron then assembled many department heads on the bridge.

Many orders were exchanged:

> I then sent for the Chief Engineer. In the meantime I was dressing and seeing the ship put on her course. The Chief Engineer came up. I told him to call another watch of stokers and make all possible speed to the *Titanic*, as she was in trouble.
>
> He ran down immediately and told me my orders would be carried out at once.
>
> After that I gave the First Officer, who was in charge of the bridge, orders to knock off all work which the men were doing on deck, the watch on deck, and prepare all our lifeboats, take out the spare gear, and have them all ready for turning outboard.

Many things needed doing, while the quick-thinking Rostron ordered that:

> English doctor, with assistants, to remain in first-class dining room.
>
> Italian doctor, with assistants, to remain in second-class dining room.
>
> Hungarian doctor, with assistants, to remain in third-class dining room.
>
> Each doctor to have supplies of restoratives, stimulants, and everything to hand for immediate needs of probable wounded or sick.
>
> Purser, with assistant purser and chief steward, to receive the passengers, etc., at different gangways, controlling our own stewards in assisting *Titanic* passengers to the dining rooms, etc.; also to get Christian and surnames of all survivors as soon as possible to send by wireless.
>
> Inspector, steerage stewards, and master at arms to control our own steerage passengers and keep them out of the third-class dining hall, and also to keep

them out of the way and off the deck to prevent confusion. chief steward: That all hands would be called and to have coffee, etc., ready to serve out to all our crew.

Have coffee, tea, soup, etc., in each saloon, blankets in saloons, at the gangways, and some for the boats.

To see all rescued cared for and immediate wants attended to. My cabin and all officials' cabins to be given up. Smoke rooms, library, etc., dining rooms, would be utilised to accommodate the survivors.

All spare berths in steerage to be utilised for *Titanic*'s passengers, and get all our own steerage passengers grouped together.

Stewards to be placed in each alleyway to reassure our own passengers, should they inquire about noise in getting our boats out, etc., or the working of engines.

To all I strictly enjoined the necessity for order, discipline and quietness and to avoid all confusion.

Chief and first officers: All the hands to be called; get coffee, etc. Prepare and swing out all boats.

All gangway doors to be opened.

Electric sprays in each gangway and over side.

A block with line rove hooked in each gangway.

A chair sling at each gangway, for getting up sick or wounded.

Boatswains' chairs. Pilot ladders and canvas ash bags to be at each gangway, the canvas ash bags for children.

Cargo falls with both ends clear; bowlines in the ends, and bights secured along ship's sides, for boat ropes or to help the people up.

Heaving lines distributed along the ship's side, and gaskets handy near gangways for lashing people in chairs, etc.

Forward derricks, topped and rigged, and steam on winches; also told off officers for different stations and for certain eventualities.

Ordered company's rockets to be fired at 2.45 a.m. and every quarter of an hour after to reassure *Titanic*.

Normally *Carpathia* attained a top speed of 14½ knots, meaning that she would take four hours to get to the distress position – but nobody dreamed how fast the ship could go… Slowly, very slowly, speed increased to 15 knots… then 15½ knots per hour…16 knots…

Adding a man to the crow's nest, two more on the bows, and a pair on each wing of the bridge, all chosen for their keen eyesight, there were seven pairs of eyes scanning the horizon.[65] This would prove a good precaution: five icebergs were dodged later that night,[66] the helm's sudden turn pointing the bows in another direction and the old ship heeling and heeling again, returning to her original course.

Captain Rostron spotted a flare in the water about half a point off the port bow at 2.40 a.m., he thought that the *Titanic* was still afloat because they were a long way away and the flare had seemed to be high in the water. He soon realised that it could not have been.

Rostron ordered rockets to be fired at intervals to reassure the people in the lifeboats. The *Carpathia* soon reached the position where the *Titanic* would have been, if afloat.

4.00 a.m. Rostron rang down to the engine room 'stop engines'. Ten minutes later the first of the lifeboats was alongside, lifeboat number 2. Ringing down 'full speed astern', Rostron slowed the ship further and then rang down 'stop', not long afterwards, as *Carpathia* came to a halt.

Among the first to board the rescuer was Fourth Officer Boxhall. He was asked to appear on the bridge, where he confirmed to Rostron what had happened. *Titanic* had sunk.

Fortunately daylight's arrival revealed the lifeboats, contained in an area of about 4 square miles.

★   ★   ★

Icebergs were also revealed, scattered all over the sea, as dawn broke.

Young Douglas Spedden exclaimed to his mother in boat 3, 'Oh muddie, look at the beautiful North Pole with no Santa Claus on it!' Many peopled laughed, in spite of the recent tragedy, which was indicated merely by the pathetic fleet of small lifeboats and insignificant wreckage.

Slowly, each boat reached the small Cunarder's side. Survivors boarded the rescue ship by climbing rope ladders to the gangways. Canvas ash bags were used to hoist up younger children. Pursers took survivors' names and class. Then brandy and coffee was available. Even before the last survivors were aboard, *Californian*, a small steam vessel of the Leyland Line, was seen by the rescue ship at 8.00 a.m. Using semaphore, Rostron informed her of the sinking. He wasn't sure that all of the lifeboats had been accounted for, and so advised: 'Think one boat still unaccounted for.'

Captain Lord of the *Californian* asked, 'Shall I search around?'

'Yes, please.'

Second Officer Lightoller was the final survivor to board, at 8.30 a.m.

Rostron, a religious man, told the purser he wanted a service held for the survivors. 'A short prayer of thankfulness for those rescued and a short service for those who were lost.' It was soon arranged.

As the service was being held, Rostron saw to the lifeboats. *Carpathia*'s boats were still swung out, so he ordered them swung inboard and secured on their blocks. Then the davits were swung out and falls attached to *Titanic*'s boats. These were raised to the boat deck and taken aboard. Thirteen boats were taken aboard in total: seven were on the boat deck davits and the remaining six were stowed on the forecastle head with the forward derricks.

At 10.50 a.m., *Carpathia* headed to New York with the lost liner's survivors. The total '712 saved' brought home the chill reality that 1,496 people had died.

For many survivors aboard, the next days would be a challenge before life could return to normal; for some, life would never be the same again; for others, a rapid downward spiral began.

Jack Thayer was reunited with his mother on board the *Carpathia*; she was naturally overjoyed to see him, but sad to discover that her husband hadn't survived.[67]

Helping with wireless messages was Harold Bride, who had agreed to help the exhausted Cottam who had been on duty continuously for over twenty-four hours. Bride was himself suffering from severe frostbite.

Colonel Gracie was another of the many survivors who suffered physically; he had severe bruising and cuts on his legs. In fact, even those who had only been in the freezing waters very briefly had suffered considerably.[68]

Rostron personally controlled all outgoing messages and *Olympic* assisted with sending the long list of survivors to New York, having a much more powerful wireless apparatus than *Carpathia*. The cruiser *Chester* had been ordered to act as a relay for the wireless traffic, but Bride later complained of *Chester*'s wireless operator's slowness.[69]

When Ismay boarded the ship, he stood against a bulkhead quietly. Then *Carpathia*'s Dr McGee approached him.

'Will you not go into the saloon and get some soup, or something to drink?'

'No, I really do not want anything at all.'

'Do go and get something,' McGee persisted.

'No. If you will leave me alone I will be very much happier here. If you would get me in some room where I can be quiet, I wish you would.'

Ismay went to the doctor's own cabin along with Jack Thayer. For the rest of the voyage, he would live on soup.

J. Bruce Ismay notified White Star's New York offices about the disaster, scribbling out a telegram at Rostron's suggestion.

'Don't you think, sir, you had better send a message to New York, telling them about this accident?'

'Yes,' Ismay replied.

He wrote the message on a slip of paper, then asked Rostron, 'Captain, do you think that is all I can tell them?'

Glancing at the message, Rostron replied 'Yes.'

The message's transmission was delayed until 17 April, by which time the offices knew of the lost ship's sinking:

> Deeply regret [to] advise you *Titanic* sank this morning after collision with iceberg, resulting in serious loss of life. Full particulars later – J. Bruce Ismay.

To take home the surviving crew Ismay wanted the *Cedric* detained – the *Cedric* being due to leave New York on 18 April. He sent several wireless messages, but the *Cedric* sailed as previously intended:

> Most desirable *Titanic* crew aboard *Carpathia* should be returned home earliest moment possible. Suggest you hold *Cedric*, sailing her daylight Friday unless you see any reason contrary. Propose returning in her myself. Please send outfit of clothes, including shoes, for me to *Cedric*. Have nothing of my own. Please reply. – YAMSI.

> (To) ISMAY, *Carpathia*:
> Have arranged forward crew *Lapland*, sailing Saturday, calling Plymouth. We all consider most unwise delay *Cedric*, considering circumstances.
> Very important you should hold *Cedric* daylight Friday for *Titanic* crew. Reply. – YAMSI.

> (Again) Very important you should hold *Cedric* daylight Friday for *Titanic* crew. Answer. – YAMSI

> Think most unwise keep *Titanic* crew until Saturday. Strongly urge detain *Cedric* sailing her midnight if desirable. – YAMSI.

1. *Adriatic* maintained successfully her schedule on the Southampton express service for four years before *Olympic*'s completion. Although she was the company's largest liner in 1907, *Adriatic* and her older sister *Celtic* together were about the same in gross tonnage as *Olympic*. (Author's collection)

2. When she was completed in 1909 at a cost of £377,599, the performance of *Megantic*'s quadruple-expansion reciprocating engines, compared to her sister *Laurentic*'s combined triple-expansion reciprocating engines and low-pressure turbine, confirmed the decision to use the combination machinery on a much larger scale for the '*Olympic*' class ships. This postcard is one of a series of 'Celebrated Liners' by Raphael Tuck & Sons. By the time this card was posted to Master Arthur Potter at the Children's Ward of Croydon General Hospital, in January 1920, *Laurentic* had been on the ocean floor for three years after being sunk by two mines. The White Star Line had hoped that *Megantic* could take *Olympic*'s place on the Southampton express service while she was being reconditioned, but the government required her services instead. *Megantic* made her final Atlantic crossing in 1931 and was sold for scrapping two years later. (Author's collection)

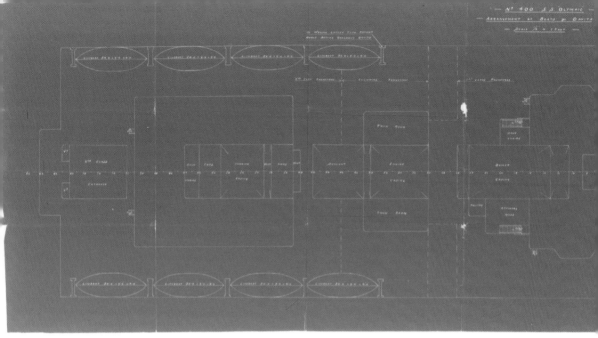

TRIPLE SCREW STEAMER "TITANIC."

2ND. CLASS

APRIL 14, 1912.

DINNER.

CONSOMMÉ TAPIOCA

BAKED HADDOCK, SHARP SAUCE

CURRIED CHICKEN & RICE

SPRING LAMB, MINT SAUCE

ROAST TURKEY, CRANBERRY SAUCE

GREEN PEAS   PURÉE TURNIPS

BOILED RICE

BOILED & ROAST POTATOES

PLUM PUDDING

WINE JELLY   COCOANUT SANDWICH

AMERICAN ICE CREAM

NUTS ASSORTED

FRESH FRUIT

CHEESE   BISCUITS

COFFEE

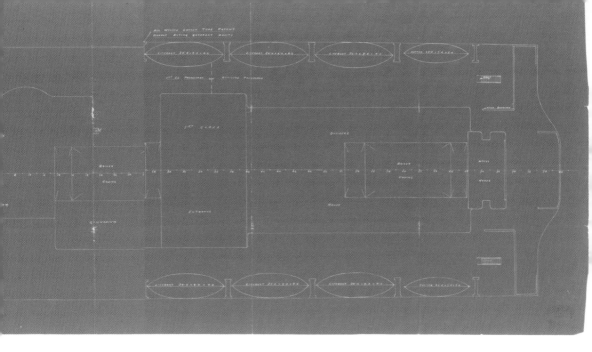

Above

3. Early in March 1910, when the designs for the Welin davits were approved, the Board of Trade believed that '*Titanic* and *Olympic* are each to be fitted with 32 boats'. On 30 June 1910, the same day that Alexander Carlisle retired, Harland & Wolff stamped the prints for submission that showed the planned arrangement of *Olympic's* lifeboats and davits: fourteen lifeboats and two emergency 'cutters', reverting back to the same number envisaged in the Design 'D' concept of July 1908. Early in June 1911, they were informed by the shipbuilder that an additional 'four collapsible boats with a total cubic capacity of 1,584ft were fitted on board in such a position that they can readily be put into the water by the forward davits'. It increased the capacity of the lifeboats by around 16 per cent, but it was still far short of the earlier understanding. (National Archives)

Opposite

4. Second-class passenger 'Bertha' Watt kept the menu for dinner on 14 April 1912, which was the last meal for many of *Titanic's* second-class passengers. Travelling with her mother, she was twelve years old at the time of the disaster and passed away in 1993. (National Maritime Museum, Greenwich, London, F5245)

No. 433, TRIPLE S.S. "BRITANNIC"   Oceanic S. N Co Ltd

72

1911			
Oct.	23	Contracted for	850' x 92' x 64' 6" (93.6)
June	28	S. M. & E.W. Ordered to proceed	54" 84" 97" 97" x 75"
Nov.	30	Keel laid, 2 slip	L. P. turbine
May	12	Framed to height of D.B.	5 SE 11' 9" (3 Jan 12)
Feb.	27	Fully framed	24 DE 20' 0" (24) x 15' 9" diar
	20	Plated	W.P. 215 lbs.
1914 Feb.	26	Launched	

B/D. for Pass. Cert. &c
comply with American
Emigration Laws.

97
(69)

Harland & Wolff Ltd   Belfast
February 20th 1912

No. 433
Gigantic
Britannic

1 330 fathoms 3⅜ NETHERTON SPECIAL BEST BEST.
Stud Link Chain Cable, shackled
complete, in 15 fathom lengths, with
one end shackle fitted with two steel
pins for each cable to suit large
links in anchors
Studs in links of cables to be all of forged steel at 16/- extra.
All connecting shackles fitted with two
tapered Greenheart Pins
To   Napiers   Windlass
2 Lengths each, consisting of 3 large links
for 155 cwt. Bower Anchors
1 Length, consisting of 3 large links
for 16 Ton Anchor
Detailed plans of these attachments to be
submitted for approval
1 Spare Anchor Shackle to suit large links
2 Spare Cable Shackles
2 Joining shackles for Locker
2 Halls Latest Improved Patent Stockless
Anchors each weighing 155 cwts.
No webs required on heads
Pins of shackles to be secured with nuts
to suit large links
1 Halls Latest Improved Patent Stockless
Anchor. weighing 320. cwts. the overall
dimensions not to exceed those supplied for
Nos. 400 + 401, so as to suit their stowing arrangements
Scantlings to be increased as necessary to make
up difference in weight
1 Trotmans Anchor 20 cwts ex stock
Anchor Stocks fitted with keys instead of forelocks
All tested as required by Lloyds, the Board of Trade +
in accordance with Act of Parliament

MAR 1 9 1913

Above
5. Harland & Wolff's order book records the order for 'Yard Number 433'. The ship's original breadth was crossed out and amended, a change which had occurred by October 1911, indicating that her specification had been recorded before that time. The increase in the size of her boilers is also noted on 3 January 1912. There is no indication of any change of name or amendment; consequently, it seems clear that the name *Britannic* was the only one formally recorded by the shipbuilder. (Public Records Office Northern Ireland/Harland & Wolff)

Left
6. The anchor outfit for 'Yard Number 433' was ordered from Messrs Noah Hingley & Sons Ltd at Netherton, Dudley. The company's chain and anchor order book, covering August 1911 to June 1914, recorded the order using the name *Gigantic*. It also documented the ship's complete anchor outfit in February 1912, using the name again before it was subsequently crossed out and amended to *Britannic*. (Dudley Archives and Local History Service)

Transcript of Register for Transmission to Registrar-General of Shipping and Seamen.

Official Number	Name of Ship	No., Date, and Port of Registry
137490	Britannic	9³/1915 Liverpool

No., Date, and Port of previous Registry (if any)	new vessel

Whether British or Foreign Built	Whether a Sailing or Steam Ship; and if a Steam Ship, how propelled	Where Built	When Built	Name and Address of Builders
British	Steamship Triple screw	Belfast	1915	Harland & Wolff Ltd Belfast

				Feet	Tenths
Number of Decks	five & 2 partial decks	Length from fore part of stem, under the bowsprit, to the aft side of the head of the stern post		852	5
Number of Masts	two	Length at quarter of depth from top of weather deck at side amidships to bottom of keel		849	2
Rigged	schooner	Main breadth to outside of plank		94	
Stern	Elliptical	Depth in hold from tonnage deck to ceiling at midships		31	6
Build	clencher	Depth in hold from upper deck to ceiling at midships, in the case of three decks and upwards		59	6
Galleries	none				
Head	none	Depth from top of beam amidships to top of keel			95
Framework and description of vessel	Steel	Depth from top of deck at side amidships to bottom of keel		65	33
Number of Bulkheads	sixteen	Round of beam			25
Number of water ballast tanks eleven and their capacity in tons 5843 tons		Length of engine room, if any		434	6

PARTICULARS OF DISPLACEMENT.

Total in quarter the depth from weather deck at side amidships to bottom of keel	78956	Ditto per ton [immersion at same] depth	73	Tons.

PARTICULARS OF PROPELLING ENGINES, &c. (if any)

No. of sets of Engines	Description of Engines	Whether British or Foreign made	When made	Name and address of makers	Reciprocating Engines.		Rotary Engines.	N.R.P. I.H.P. Speed of Ship.
					No. and Diameter of Cylinders in each set.	Length of Stroke.	No. of Cylinders in each set.	
two sets	Inverted Direct acting Triple expansion condensing			Harland & Wolff Ltd Belfast	1 @ 54	75"	one Turbine	7150
Turbine		British	1915		1 @ 84			50000
Three Shafts					2 @ 97			21 Knots

PARTICULARS OF TONNAGE.

GROSS TONNAGE.		No. of Tons	DEDUCTIONS ALLOWED.	No. of Tons
Under Tonnage Deck		18176·65	On account of space required for propelling power	23060·07
Space or spaces between Decks	upper etc	6866·08	On account of spaces occupied by Seamen or Apprentices, and appropriated to their use, and kept free from Goods or Stores of every kind, not being the personal property of the Crew. These spaces are the following, viz:—	
	lower	5612·37		
Turret or Trunk		5143·85		
Forecastle		218·86		
Bridge space		3699·67	Crew spaces in upper Forecastle	6·05
Poop or Break	Poop	4480·27		
Side Houses	Promenade Deck	2664·48		
Deck Houses	Poop	333·46	Deductions under Section 79 of the Merchant Shipping Act, 1894, and Section 54 of the Merchant Shipping Act, 1906, as follows:—	
Chart House	Deck Houses	799·21		
Spaces for machinery, and light, and air, under Section 78 (2) of the Merchant Shipping Act, 1894		1214·78	Cubic Metres. Masters Accommodation 29·58	444·54
Excess of Hatchways			Boatswain's Store 75·00	
	Gross Tonnage	48197·90 136,000·06	Chart Space 7·78	
Deductions, as per Contra "next page"		23565·66 6690·82	Navigating Room 6·68	
	Register Tonnage	24633·24 67,709·24	Water & Ballast spaces 325·50	23565·66
			Total	

NOTE.—1. The tonnage of the engine room spaces below the upper deck is 11962·40 tons, and the tonnage of the total spaces framed in above the upper deck for propelling machinery and for light and air is 1214·78 tons.

NOTE.—2. The undermentioned spaces above the upper deck are not included in the cubical contents forming the ship's register tonnage:

Open space between Bridge & Poop Length 55·3 ft Tonnage – 328·03
Open space Promenade Deck Length 42·0 ft Tonnage – 139·58

Name of Master		Certificate of { Service No. { Competency No.

Names, Residence, and Description of the Owners, and Number of Sixty-fourth Shares held by each, viz.,	
Oceanic Steam Navigation Company Limited having its principal place of business at 30 James Street Liverpool — Sixty four shares.	Colonel Henry Concanon of 30 James Street, Liverpool designated the person to whom the management of the vessel is entrusted by and on behalf of the owners. Advice received 6th December 1915 under the seal of the owning Company

Dated 6th December 1915.

               Registrar.

NOTE.—Registrars in the Colonies are requested to distinguish the Managing Owner by placing the letters "M.O." against his name.

N.B.—To be sent in an envelope addressed to the Registrar-General of Shipping and Seamen, Tower Hill, London, E.

No. 345. Instructions to Registrars of British Ships, para. 26.—Sec. 15801/1914

7. *Britannic* was entered on the British registry with the official number 137,490. Her gross tonnage was subsequently calculated at 48,157.9 and her net tonnage 24,592.24. The red writing across the first page explains that she foundered 21 November 1916. (National Archives)

WHITE · STAR · LINE

Rec'd 10/1/16

S.S. Britannic

9 - 1 - 16

Dear Dad,

Just a line to let you know
that I am within a few miles of
England. I left P. Said on the 26th
Dec. and travelled to Alexandria
by train, and then embarked on the
H/S Dunluce Castle, which sailed that
night for Mudros Bay, the naval base
of the Eastern front, we waited there
for two days for the above hospital
ship, a magnificent boat of 50,000 tons
larger than the "Aquitania"; thus

44

is her maiden voyage, so you
see I have the privilege of saying
that I am one of the first passengers
to sail on the sister ship of the
ill fated "Titanic".

We have had a splendid voyage,
so smooth has been the passage,
that one would scarcely realize
that you were afloat.

Rumour has it that the
enteric patients are going to Croydon.

Will write again as soon as I
arrive ~~a~~ at my destination.
I remain
Your affectionate son
Wallie

8. Private Walter Alexander Goodwin wrote home to his father. He enjoyed the experience of being on board *Britannic*'s maiden voyage, describing her as a 'magnificent boat'. (Imperial War Museum)

9. *Britannic* began to develop a serious list to starboard shortly after the explosion, as she settled at the bow. The lifeboats were made ready for lowering and Captain Bartlett attempted initially to beach the ship, but the portholes along much of E-deck were soon underwater. When this painting was commissioned, it was believed that her hospital ship designation remained 'G608'; however, it is now known that it had been changed to 'G618' by the time of the ship's loss. (Painting © Stuart Williamson, 2004/Author's collection)

WHITE STAR LINE.

HOSPITAL SHIP. BRITANNIC

WARD

COT No.

NUMBER & RANK

NAME

REGIMENT

DISEASE

DATE AND PLACE OF ORIGIN OF DISEASE

TREATMENT

10. Goodwin kept the postcard, giving the details of his ward, cot number, and military position, as a souvenir. Although stamped 'hospital ship Britannic', the ship depicted was *Olympic*; on the reverse, *Britannic* was described as 'the largest British steamer'. (Imperial War Museum)

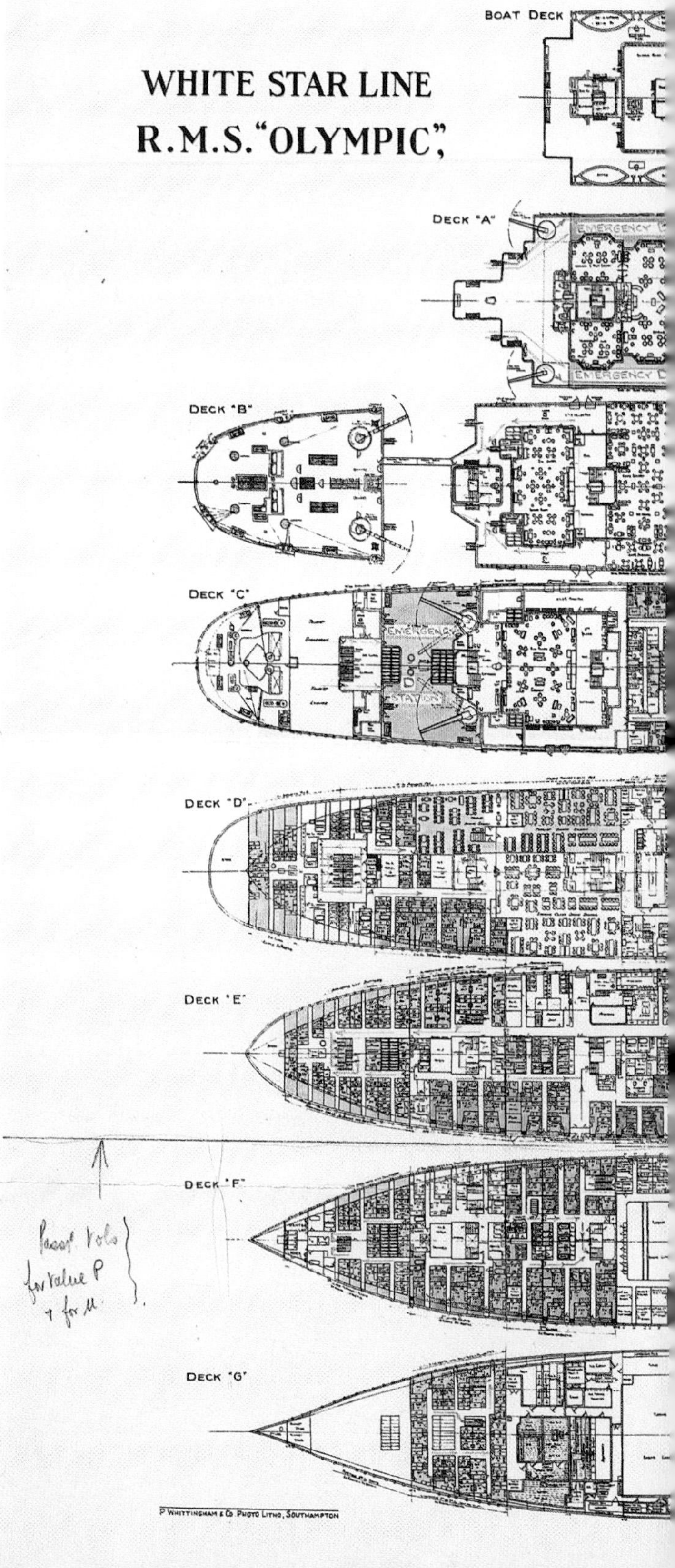

WHITE STAR LINE
R.M.S. "OLYMPIC",

BOAT DECK

DECK "A"

DECK "B"

DECK "C"

DECK "D"

DECK "E"

DECK "F"

DECK "G"

P. WHITTINGHAM & CO. PHOTO LITHO, SOUTHAMPTON.

11. This emergency stations plan –
'P. Whittingham & Co. Photo Litho,
Southampton' – was one of a number
issued by the White Star Line in the
1920s. It is interesting in that it dates
from 1928: after the overhaul and refit
of 1927–28, which included adding the
tourist third cabin public rooms; but
before the overhaul and refit of 1928–29,
which included expanding the first-class
staterooms forward on B-deck. The deck
letters have been altered after the plan
was produced, reflecting a change that
occurred when *Olympic* returned to
service at the start of 1929. As the plan
indicates, a scheme of colour-coding
was used to direct passengers to the
appropriate station. Although many of
the details are hard to make out due to
the scale, the plan's intended purpose was
to outline these escape routes. (National
Archives)

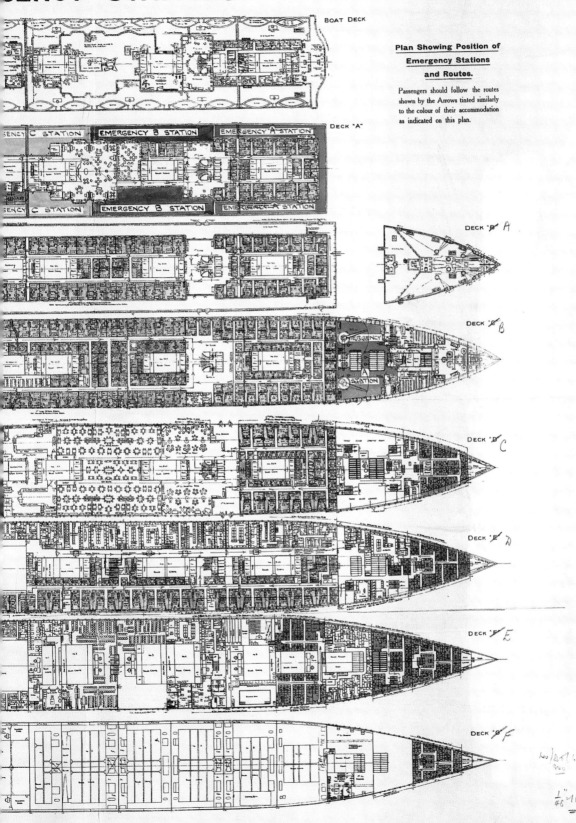

GENCY STATIONS

BOAT DECK

DECK "A"

**Plan Showing Position of
Emergency Stations
and Routes.**

Passengers should follow the routes
shown by the Arrows tinted similarly
to the colour of their accommodation
as indicated on this plan.

GENCY C STATION   EMERGENCY B STATION   EMERGENCY A STATION

GENCY C STATION   EMERGENCY B STATION   EMERGENCY A STATION

DECK "B" A

DECK "C" B

EMERGENCY
A STATION

DECK "D" C

DECK "E" D

DECK "F" E

DECK "G" F

1"/48"=1F.

CUNARD WHITE STAR — TOURIST CLASS PLAN

S. S. OLYMPIC

LENGTH 882½ FEET   GROSS TONNAGE 46,439   BREADTH 92½ FEET

KEY FOR SYMBOLS

- PUBLIC ROOMS
LC — LINEN CLOSET
W — WARDROBE
DT — DRESSING TABLE
B — BUREAU
S — SEAT
D — CHEST OF DRAWERS
W — WASHBASIN
B
WC — TOILET

ODD NUMBERS LOWER BERTHS
EVEN NUMBERS UPPER BERTHS

ROOM NUMBERS IN RED
BERTH NUMBERS IN BLACK

Fittings in rooms approximately correct, but may be changed without notice.

A DECK

B DECK

FRESH SEA AIR IS DRAWN
DOWN THIS VENTILATOR
TO YOUR
INSIDE
STATEROOM

Up on deck, these huge ventilators such in lungfuls of fresh, sparkling sea air, with powerful blower fans acting as lungs. This fresh air is passed your stateroom in a stream that may be regulated suit yourself.

C DECK AFT

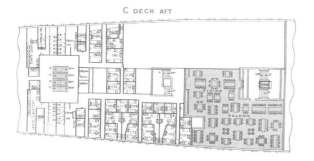

C DECK FORWARD

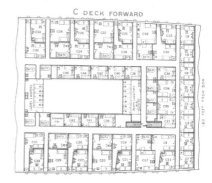

D DECK

E DECK

F DECK

D DECK AFT

CUNARD WHITE STAR
FOREIGN REMITTANCES

—By Draft
  —By Cable
    —By Money Order

The safe way to carry
    or send money abroad

CUNARD WHITE STAR
BAGGAGE INSURANCE

Inexpensive, comprehensive and world-wide in its scope, Cunard White Star Baggage Insurance is a boon to the traveller. Sponsored by Cunard White Star Limited, it assures remarkably broad protection at lowest cost, and covers the baggage in ships, trains, automobiles, aeroplanes, hotels, boarding houses, and other buildings anywhere in the world. Apply to your local agent or any Cunard White Star Office.

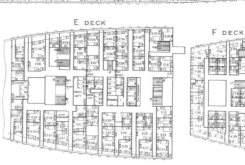

NOTE : FOLDING GUIDES AT TOP, BOTTOM AND SIDES

Opposite
12. This tourist-class plan for *Olympic*'s accommodation was issued by Cunard White Star in January 1935, replacing an earlier April 1932 issue by White Star. It was one of the last, if not the last, issued for the ship. The deck letters reflect the changes in 1929: A-deck is the original B-deck, and so on. The first class staterooms forward on the original D-deck had by this time been allocated to tourist class; while the same was true for the first- and second-class staterooms the deck below. Consequently, a number of the tourist-class staterooms had access to their own private bathrooms. (Author's collection)

Above
13. *Britannic*'s organ was intended to impress. The original plan apparently envisaged an Aeolian organ, but the White Star Line placed the final order for the largest Philharmonie organ available from the prestigious firm of Welte, in Freiburg, Germany. As well as being played by an organist, it could play pre-recorded music using perforated paper music rolls. This particular model had not been available when *Olympic* and *Titanic* were under construction and the increasing competition from Cunard and the German companies gave added impetus to making *Britannic*'s interiors all the more impressive. It seems unlikely that it was ever shipped to Belfast or installed, nor is there any documentation of it among the ship's fittings ashore that survived the war. In 1920, it was installed in a Stuttgart home. It was subsequently returned to the manufacturer and installed in the reception room of the Radium lighting company seventeen years later, where it remained until the 1960s. Heinrich Weiss, founder of the Swiss *Museum für Musikautomaten*, acquired the organ and moved it at the end of the decade. It was fully restored at its new home, the Swiss National Museum, Seewen; here is a magnificent view of the completed organ in the museum's *KlangKunst-Saal* in October 2007. (*Museum für Musikautomaten*, Seewen, Switzerland)

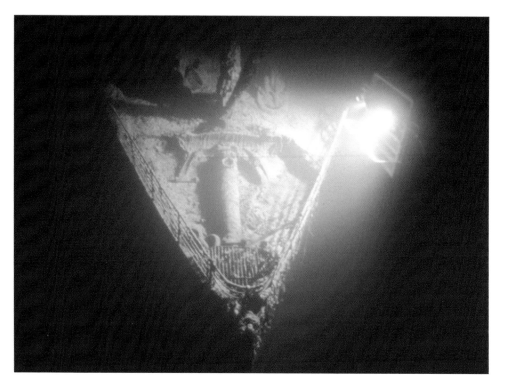

14. *Titanic's* bow, hidden in darkness for seventy-three years, appears out of the gloom. (© 1987–2010 RMS Titanic, Inc., a subsidiary of Premier Exhibitions, Inc.)

15. *Titanic's* port propeller is partially visible. When the stern landed on the seafloor, it hit with such force that the port and starboard wing propeller shafts and their supports were wrenched upwards. However, the mud line is almost as the waterline would be if the ship was floating on the ocean's surface; consequently, the centre propeller is hidden from view. (© 1987–2010 RMS Titanic, Inc., a subsidiary of Premier Exhibitions, Inc.)

16. A remarkable sight: deep inside *Britannic's* bow, one of the two spiral staircases leading down to the firemen's tunnel is photographed at F-deck level. Situated between the number 1 hatchway on one side (forward) and a watertight bulkhead on the other (aft), the ship's original construction plans envisaged accommodation for fifty-three firemen, fifteen leading firemen and ten leading greasers on this deck. (© Leigh Bishop)

17. A well-preserved bathtub located inside the officers' quarters on the port side of the ship. It is interesting to note the configuration of four taps, for salt water and fresh water. Captain Bartlett's personal bathtub, situated on the starboard side, was identical and photographed in 1998. (© Leigh Bishop)

18. The *Titanic* Engineers' Memorial, Southampton. In June 1913, *The Marine Engineer and Naval Architect* reported: 'The selected design is circular in plan, with the centre forming an architectural treatment of a Roman altar, with a grouping in two panels on the frontal piece, the sculptor suggesting in two bas reliefs, groups of engineers, firm in courage and duty during moments of danger, sacrificing themselves to certain death for others.' Several designs were submitted for consideration. The chosen one was by Joseph Whitehead, 'of Messrs J. Whitehead and Sons Ltd, Imperial Works, Kennington Oval, London.' The same firm designed the Queen Victoria Memorial outside Buckingham Palace. (Author's collection)

19. The Thompson Graving Dock today. Although its great length is not apparent from this angle, it remains a remarkable structure. It continued in regular use until 2002. If it were possible to look behind and to the left, the vast open space where the '*Olympic*' class ships were built would be visible, the slipways and overhead gantry long gone; ahead and to the right, where the cranes are, was where they were fitted out. The pumping house alongside the dock is out of sight to the immediate left. Harland & Wolff completed their last ship, *Anvil Point*, in 2003, but they continue to undertake design work and ship repairs. (Trevor Ferris Photography)

Incoming wireless messages were ignored because of *Carpathia*'s operators' exhaustion. The world would have to wait for the story and relatives would have to wait until the printed lists.

Ruth Becker recalled many children eating sugar lumps from the dining room tables. She slept with her family in the officers' quarters, which scared her because on *Carpathia* the officers' accommodation was deep below.[70]

Second Officer Lightoller and Third Officer Pitman spent much time discussing the disaster with Colonel Gracie and Huge Woolner. It was the topic of most conversations.

Lifeboat number 1's occupants, meanwhile, posed – at apparently Lady Duff Gordon's suggestion – for a group picture. Sir Cosmo had honoured his £5 promise to the crew, as if tipping some loyal servants. One can easily question his bad taste.

Carpathia's voyage was made partly in bad weather. A severe storm accompanied her soon after rescuing the survivors. 'The crowded public rooms, the dismal weather, and the incessant, grating beat of the ship's foghorn got on nerves that were already on edge.'[71]

★ ★ ★

On shore, the *Daily Mirror* of 16 April stated:

> Disaster to the *Titanic*: World's Largest Ship Collides with an Iceberg in the Atlantic During her Maiden Voyage

Although wireless messages had been received stating that *Titanic* had collided with an iceberg, no papers stated that she had foundered, and the *Daily Mirror* reported:

> Though she smashed into an iceberg, a collision that would have meant the foundering of any liner a few years ago, the *Titanic* still floats, she is indeed practically unsinkable… all the beams, girders… in the *Titanic*'s [hull] framework were specially forged and constructed… to make the hull a monument of strength.

New York Time's 16 April issue told a very different story – its headline shocked the public:

> Titanic sinks four hours after hitting iceberg; 866 rescued by *Carpathia*, probably 1,250 perish; Ismay safe, Mrs Astor maybe, noted names missing.

The paper told:

> Captain Haddock's wireless message from the *Olympic*…strongly indicated that none but the 655 taken from lifeboats by the *Carpathia* had been saved. This message was relayed immediately to the White Star offices, but Mr Franklin positively declined to make the message public… Mr Franklin said the message… 'neglected to say that all of the crew had been saved'… 'Loss likely 1,800 souls.' 'We can replace the money loss, but not the lives of those who went down.'

Gradually Franklin said that, 'probably a number of lives had been lost'… then 'we very much fear there has been a great loss of life'; at 9.00 p.m. on the night of 15 April, Franklin broke down – there had been a 'horrible loss of life', he stammered, 'Gentlemen, I regret to say that the *Titanic* sank at 2.20 this morning.'[72]

★ ★ ★

Before *Carpathia*'s New York arrival, news was incomplete or inaccurate – or both. The *Daily Mirror* reported on 17 April, 'only 868 alive of 2,200 on sunken liner *Titanic*'. Lord Pirrie was not well and news of the sinking was kept from him for a long time – as the *Daily Mirror* reported:

On a sick bed – Lord Pirrie, father of the *Titanic* is told sad news at last: 'Because he's worried.'

Lord Pirrie knows the worst. Lying on his bed of sickness at Witley Park, near Godalming. The father of the *Titanic*, the man whose great comprehensive brain made it possible to build the greatest ship the world has ever known, has had to be told the dreadful news of what has befallen her on her first trip.

As was pointed out in the *Daily Mirror* newspaper of Tuesday last night, the tragic tidings were being kept from him as long as was humanly possible to do so. To tell him might have killed him.

But no man of Lord Pirrie's stamp is content to lose touch with the doings of the world for long; even on a bed of sickness, even against doctor's orders, at vital risk to himself, he must know what is going on.

So long as he is in the world he must be one of the world.

And so Lord Pirrie has learned the awful truth. The chairman of the great shipbuilding firm of Harland & Wolff knows that the wonder ship which he conceived and his company carried out, is lying, a broken, battered mass of iron, steel and wood, two full miles under the grim Atlantic.

The news could not be kept from him any longer, The *Daily Mirror* was told last night by a member of Lord Pirrie's household.

He wanted to know how the *Titanic* was progressing; and somehow – one knows how bad news has a way of coming instinctively to those mainly concerned in it – he began to get an inkling that all was not well with her.

And so, because he worried, the truth had to be broken gently to him. Not the whole, dreadful truth – for the newspapers are still kept away as much as possible from him – but the salient points of it.

Lord Pirrie knows the *Titanic* has sunk, and that many of the human beings who entrusted themselves to her keeping have been lost.

'Some of the newspapers had to be shown to him,' said the *Daily Mirror*'s informant. 'We kept the news from him as long as we could, but it could not be kept from him forever.'

He might have been a passenger – 'How it has affected him is not easy to say at present. Tonight he is not perhaps quite so well as he has been recently.'

'I believe that he has not said a great deal on the subject yet, but that he has expressed a great hearted sympathy concerning the dreadful loss of life and the many poor people who have been affected by the loss of the *Titanic*.'

'What Lord Pirrie is told rests mainly with Lady Pirrie. Messages are continually coming for him, but they all go to Lady Pirrie first.'

But for the fact that he had to undergo an operation, Lord Pirrie might have been a passenger on the *Titanic*.

Hitherto it has been his invariable habit to take his personal share in the triumphs of the first voyages of the great ships which his brain has enabled his firm to turn out at Belfast.

It is a curious and sad coincidence that a brother of Mr J. Bruce Ismay, the chairman of the White Star line, is at present lying ill and forbidden to know the fate which has come upon the great ship which a week ago sailed forth in all the splendour and pride of her new life.

Two closely-spaced columns were filled with mention of the millionaires on board; but third- and second-class passengers scarcely had a mention.

18 April's *Daily Mirror* told how a relief fund was being set-up for the survivors:

Relief Funds Opened…
The King and Queen have once more shown their practical sympathy with their distressed and suffering subjects by subscribing handsomely to a fund which the Lord Mayor of London opened yesterday on behalf of those who have suffered by the *Titanic* disaster.

At the Easter banquet at the Mansion House last night the Lord Mayor announced that he had received the following telegrams: –

'York Cottage, Sandringham.
I am commanded to inform your Lordship that the King subscribes five hundred guineas and the Queen two hundred and fifty guineas to the Mansion House Fund your Lordship is so kindly raising for the relief of those who are in need through the awful shipwreck of the *Titanic* – William Carrington.'

'Sandringham.
Queen Alexandra will give £200 towards the fund which your Lordship is raising for the relief of the relatives of those who have lost their lives in the terrible disaster to the *Titanic* – Colonel Streatfield.'

By last night, the Lord Mayor, to use his own words, had 'within a few hours, a considerable sum, amounting to thousands of pounds', in hand – a tribute to the generosity of the British public.

Questions were asked, among them: 'Why were there only twenty lifeboats for 2,207 people on board the ill-fated *Titanic*?' The *Daily Mirror* pointed out that *Mauretania* could carry 2,972 people but carried lifeboats for 962; that *Adriatic* could accommodate 2,225 people but only had lifeboats for 1,038 and that even a small ship, *Orama* – which could only carry 1,261 people – had lifeboats for fewer than the number aboard.

The same issue printed a short 'Survivors' Description of Catastrophe', given to the press the previous day when the *Carpathia* docked:

We, the undersigned surviving passengers of the *Titanic*, in order to forestall any sensational or exaggerated statements, deem it our duty to give the press a statement of the facts which have come to our knowledge, and which we believe to be true.

On Sunday, April 14, at about 11.40, on a cold, starlit night, the ship struck an iceberg which had been reported to the bridge by the lookouts, but not early enough to avoid a collision.

SOME FACTS OF THE DISASTER.

The iceberg, from 50 to 100 feet high, was struck at 11.35 p.m.

The blow was a glancing one on the starboard side, which was ripped open, rendering useless the essential water-tight compartments.

The "Titanic" sank in two miles of water, two hours and forty-five minutes after she struck.

Jack Phillips, the "Titanic's" wireless operator, remained at his post flashing out signals for assistance until the deck was awash.

Captain Smith, indifferent to his own safety, worked till the very last moment to save as many as possible. "Be British" was his word to one and all.

The "Carpathia's" wireless operator, by a lucky chance, was up ——— and heard the "Titanic's" call for help.

The White Star liner "Olympic," on hearing the "Titanic's" wireless call for assistance, covered 400 miles at twenty-four knots, the highest speed the liner has ever attained.

| ••• S | ——— O | ••• S | How the wireless call for help was sent. |

(1.) Jack Phillips, the chief Marconi operator on the "Titanic," who flashed out his messages till the ship went down.

| —•—• C | ——•— Q | —•• D 4 | (2.) The wireless cabin on an ocean liner, the operator receiving a message. |

(3.) Harold Bride, the second Marconi operator on the "Titanic," who was saved.

"Going up on the deck again, I saw that there was an unmistakable list downwards from the stern to the bows, but knowing nothing of what had happened I concluded that some of the front compartments had filled and had weighed her down.

(4.) The wireless signal of distress, "S. O. S." in the Morse code. Formerly the signal "C. Q. D." was used.

Titanic's wireless operators, John ('Jack') Phillips, and Harold Bride, were responsible for the distress messages that brought *Carpathia* to the rescue. Jack turned twenty-five on the day *Titanic* left Queenstown, but his memorial plaque at Farncombe church gave his age as twenty-six. It seems to have been common at the time to quote the year of life, so he was in his twenty-sixth year. His photograph was taken by a local Godalming photographer, Jennie Steadman, whose brother George was at school with Jack and whose family were longstanding friends of the Phillips family. Some of the 'facts of the disaster', published in a number of newspapers or journals at the time, were incorrect. (*The Deathless Story of the Titanic*, 1912/Author's collection)

Steps were taken to ascertain the extent of the damage and to save the passengers and the ship.

Orders were given to put on lifebelts, the boats were lowered, and the usual distress signals were sent out by wireless telegraphy and rockets were fired at intervals.

Fortunately, a wireless message was received by the *Carpathia* about midnight. She arrived on the scene of the disaster about 4.00 a.m. on Monday.

The officers and crew of the *Carpathia* had been preparing all night for the rescue work and for the comfort of the survivors. These were received on board with the most touching care and kindness, every attention being given to all, irrespective of class.

Passengers, officers and crew gladly gave up their staterooms, clothing and comfort for our benefit. All honour to them.

The English Board of Trade passengers' certificate on board the *Titanic* allowed for a total of approximately 3,500. The same certificate called for lifeboat accommodation for approximately 950 in the following boats: – Fourteen large lifeboats, two smaller boats, four collapsible boats. Life preservers were accessible in apparently sufficient numbers for all on board. The approximate number of passengers carried at the time of the collision was: –

First class	330
Second class	320
Third class	750
Total	1,400
Officers and crew	940
Total	2,340

Of the foregoing about the following number were rescued by the *Carpathia*:

First class	210
Second class	125
Third class	200
Officers	4
Seamen	39
Stewards	96
Firemen	71
Crew	210
Total (about)	775

The number saved was about eighty per cent of the maximum capacity of the lifeboats.

We recommend that the boats at all time[s] to be properly equipped with provisions, water, lamps, compasses, lights, etc. Lifesaving boat drills should be made frequent and thoroughly carried-out.

A greater reduction of speed in fog and ice, as the damage if a collision actually occurs is liable to be less.'

We feel it our duty to call the attention of the public to what we consider the inadequate supply of lifesaving appliances for modern passenger steamships and recommend that immediate steps be taken to compel passenger steamers to carry sufficient boats to accommodate the maximum number of people carried on board.

The following facts were observed and should be considered in this connection: – in addition to the insufficiency of lifeboats, rafts, etc., there was a lack of trained seamen to man the same; stokers, stewards, etc., are not efficient boat handlers.

There were not enough officers to carry out the emergency orders on the bridge and to superintend the launching and control of the lifeboats and an absence of searchlights.

The Board of Trade rules allow for entirely too many people in each boat to permit the same to be properly handled.

On the *Titanic* the boat deck was about 75ft [sic] above water, and consequently the passengers were required to embark before lowering of the boats, thus endangering the operation and preventing the taking of the maximum number of people the boats would hold.

In conclusion we suggest that an International Conference should be called, and we recommend the passage of identical laws providing for the safety of all at sea.

We urge the US Government to take the initiative as soon as possible.

The orchestra belonging to first cabin assembled on deck as the liner was going down and played *Nearer My God To Thee*…by the time that most of the lifeboats were some distance away, only a faint sound could be heard…she was "Hogbacked" and… was breaking in two.

It was reported that Mr Guggenheim had intended to sail on *Lusitania* on 6 April, but the liner's sailing was cancelled and *Carmania* was to sail instead; Mr Guggenheim didn't care to sail on her and he decided to go on the next fast ship. He booked passage on the *Titanic*, went over to Paris on business for a few days and boarded the *Titanic* at Cherbourg.

Mr Walter Harris was having tea with friends and had his palm read by somebody who practised palmistry; she said she 'did not like it', and Harris' little son asked, 'Is Daddy going to be drowned?' Harris had sailed on *Titanic* and perished.

★ ★ ★

Preparations for the burial of *Titanic*'s deceased passengers and crew began. On 17 April the cable-laying ship *Mackay Bennett* departed from the Canadian port of Halifax carrying coffins and the necessary tools – tons of ice, embalmers tools and fluids – and an Undertaker was aboard. She reached the wreck site on 20 April.

306 bodies were recovered and of these 116 were buried at sea and 190 were taken back to Halifax; *Minia* relieved the *Mackay Bennett* on 25 April and the *Montmagny* set off for the site on 6 May.[73] Colonel John Jacob Astor's badly-crushed body was recovered with $2,500 in cash,[74] £225 in English bank notes, £5 in gold, seven silver shillings, 50 Francs, plus a gold pencil and pocketbook.[75]

Mackay Bennett's crew carved some picture frames and cribbage boards – among other things; as did *Minia*'s crew and *Montmagny*'s.

Halifax's Fairview cemetery, situated at the end of Windsor Road, near Halifax's centre, contains the graves of 122 of the victims. Some of the headstones do not bear a name, just a number. Few are ornate, but these include J. Bruce Ismay's stone for his late secretary, Ernest Edward Samuel Freeman, and the stone erected by the crew of the *Mackay Bennett* for an 'unknown child', a blonde two-year-old boy pulled from the water. The 'unknown child' is now believed to have been the youngest son of Mrs Paulson, whose grave is adjacent.[76] Also here are the graves for Jock Hume, the violinist, and Luigi Gatti, late manager of the *à la carte* restaurant.

Twenty-four-year-old Trimmer Everett Edward Elliott's gravestone bears the simple but suited inscription:

Each man stood at his post
While the weaker ones
Went by, and showed once

More to all the world
How Englishmen should die.[77]

★   ★   ★

Carpathia arrived in New York late on 18 April. After dropping off the *Titanic*'s lifeboats at the White Star pier, she docked at Cunard's pier 54 at 9.30 p.m.[78] 30,000 people had come to watch the arrival, and relatives were reunited with loved-ones – but sadly, many would not be.

Ismay was met by Phillip Franklin and shortly afterwards Senator William Alden Smith of Michigan boarded *Carpathia* and subpoenaed J. Bruce Ismay to testify at a 'formal investigation' into the disaster – all hope of quickly going home had left Ismay.[79] He later told the press, 'We welcome the fullest investigation, the company has nothing to conceal.'

One member of Congress, Republican Luther Mott, sent a telegram to each director of IMM, asking their views about an investigation. J.P. Morgan junior responded that he was 'much in favour of [the] fullest investigation and any suggestion looking to safety which can be made'; Philip Franklin telegrammed:

> You can rest assured that the White Star Line will cooperate with the authorities in any movement toward practical regulations which will be calculated to guard against a repetition of the horrible loss of life resulting from the *Titanic* catastrophe. It always has been and always will be our anxiety to protect to the utmost the lives of those entrusted to our care, and we cannot convey to you how inexpressibly shocked and deeply grieved we are at this fearful calamity.

★   ★   ★

Senator Smith was an opponent of J.P. Morgan's business interests. He 'favoured small independent businesses over the east-coast monopolies and was a strong believer in the spirit of competition that the trusts had sought so hard to crush. In the past, Smith had spent many hours in Congress contending with Morgan's steel and railroad trusts.'[80] Under the provisions of the Harter Act, in response to an earlier maritime disaster, 'if a company owning a steamship had privity of negligence aboard, then individual passengers or their surviving kin could sue the company for damages. Though the *Titanic* may have been a British ship, she had nevertheless been owned by an American trust [IMM] indictable under the Harter Laws.'[81] The investigative body was a sub-committee of the Committee on Commerce, pursuant to a Senate resolution 'directing the Committee on Commerce to investigate the causes leading to the wreck of the White Star liner *Titanic*.' Its hearings got underway on a Saturday, 20 April 1912: the day *Titanic* had been scheduled to leave New York on her first eastbound crossing, and for which more than six hundred passengers had originally booked first-class accommodation.

J. Bruce Ismay took the stand first, expecting a short questioning, but he soon realised that he was in for much more than he had expected. Giving his full name as 'Joseph Bruce Ismay', he indicated that his fiftieth birthday would be on 12 December 1912. As managing director of the White Star Line, he had boarded the doomed *Titanic* at Southampton at 9.30 a.m. on 10 April 1912. He opined that she was 'the latest thing in the art of shipbuilding; absolutely no money was spared in her construction. She was not built by contract. She was built on a commission.' Revolutions had been 70 from Cherbourg to Queenstown, he said, then the first full day's run had been either '464 or 484 miles'. On the second day revolutions had risen to 72 for 519 miles, and 546 or 549 miles had been logged on the third day, he recalled. Denying that the ship had been proceeding at full speed, he said that the ship had never to his knowledge exceeded 75 revolutions. He had been in bed when the accident occurred; the ship had sunk at 2.20 a.m.; 'that, sir, I think is all I can tell you.'

After this brief statement, Ismay's testimony before Senator Smith filled many pages as he endured many questions put to him.

He described that after the collision Captain Smith had told him the ship was badly damaged, then he had gone below and encountered Chief Engineer Bell, who also thought the damage was bad, but thought the ship would stay afloat.

'I think I went back to the bridge. I heard the order given to get the boats out,' he recalled.

'Did you have any talk with any officer?' Senator Smith asked.

'Not that I remember.'

'Did you have occasion to consult with the captain about the movement of the ship?'

'Never.'

'Did he consult you about it?'

'Never, but what we had arranged to do was that we would not attempt to arrive in New York before five o'clock on Wednesday morning,' Ismay told him.

Smith didn't question him further about the matter, as he was unaware about the speed needed to reach New York from the point of the accident. Smith was also unaware that a notice had appeared in a shipping column stating that the liner had been due in on Tuesday, signed by the 'White Star Line'. From the point of the collision, *Titanic* needed to maintain 20 knots to reach New York at the time on Wednesday, but she had actually been doing over 22½ knots.

Ismay was asked about his departure from the ship.

'…the Officer called out asking if there were any more women…there were no passengers left on the deck…as the boat was in the act of being lowered away, I got into it,' Ismay said.

Senator Smith's inquiry lasted eighteen days. During this time eighty-two witnesses were called and many statements given. Twenty-one of these were passengers, but only three were from third class.[82] Hearings were at New York's Waldorf Astoria Hotel and at Washington.

Second Officer Lightoller, Third Officer Pitman, Fourth Officer Boxhall and Fifth Officer Lowe testified. Harold Bride and Harold Thomas Cottam – *Titanic*'s and *Carpathia*'s wireless operators – testified as did Captain Rostron and many others.

Lightoller answered many questions. Third-class passengers had not been kept below, he said; the ship had 'forty or fifty' watertight compartments, but he must have been aware there were only sixteen in the main hull. Between 6.00 p.m. and 10.00 p.m. on 14 April the ship had been steaming at about 21 or 21½ knots he said, but he surely would have been aware that the ship was going over one knot faster. He had not used his revolver, he said.

Wireless operator Thomas Cottam – sometimes referred to as 'Harold Thomas' or just 'Harold' – of the rescue ship was next to testify. He described in detail hearing the distress call and what subsequently happened.

Harold Bride then testified. He recalled Phillips telling the *Frankfurt*'s operator that he was a 'fool', and saying 'keep out'. Bride admitted selling his 'exclusive' story to the *New York Times*, for which he had received several hundred dollars.

Phillip Franklin of IMM testified. He described the company in some detail, the fall in its market value, and described hearing the news of the sinking. Franklin said, 'We considered the ship unsinkable, and it never entered our minds that there might have been anything like a serious loss of life.' The lost liner had been insured for two-thirds of her construction cost and five or six watertight compartments must have been flooded, he correctly estimated.

Fourth Officer Boxhall described all he had done on the night of the sinking and how he had worked out his distress position, based on a speed of 22 knots from 7.30 p.m. Pitman described what had happened that night. He had taken charge of boat 5 and rowed for a while from the ship. After being in the water some time, thinking that three compartments were flooded, he realised that the ship would sink. After the sinking, he had wanted to return to the wreck, but some other passengers in the boat opposed him.

Major Peuchen described boarding boat 6, then quartermaster Hichens' behaviour during and after the sinking. He had refused to return to the ship, even when ordered.

Fifth Officer Lowe described waking up and seeing passengers outside his cabin in lifeboats, then what he had done with regard to the lifeboats. He had told Ismay, who was present when he testified, to 'get the hell out', after he had been yelling orders at boat 5. Then he mentioned the lowering of boat 14, when some 'Italians'★ had tried to 'rush the boat'. After the sinking, he returned for survivors in boat 14. Senator Smith asked him what an iceberg was composed of, and Lowe went in for the kill: 'Ice, sir.'

Quartermaster Hichens described what had happened during the collision, boarding boat 6 and his conduct in the boat. After the sinking, he denied that he had refused to return for survivors, or that he had been asked to. He denied remarking, 'We are to look out for ourselves now, and pay no attention to those stiffs.'

'I have never made use of that word,' he said, 'never since I have been born...'

Hichens said he had had 'a bit of trouble' with Major Peuchen, who had been trying to take charge of the lifeboat. 'I am put here in charge of the boat,' he admitted saying to the Major. 'You go and do what you are told to do.'

Steward George Crowe said that the ship had 'broke clean in two' before disappearing. After the collision, many people had been making jokes about it. They knew the danger was exaggerated.

Lamp Trimmer Samuel Hemming testified. After the collision, he had awoken and investigated a loud hissing noise from the forepeak tank. Then Chief Officer Wilde had come along. Both had had a brief discussion before Wilde headed to the bridge.

'What is that, Hemming?' Wilde had asked.

'The air is escaping from the forepeak tank,' he had explained. 'She is making water in the forepeak tank, but the storeroom is quite dry.'

'Alright,' Wilde had replied.

Able Seaman Evans testified that soon after the collision, 'the Fifth or Sixth Officer' had spoken to him. Fourth Officer Boxhall was more likely to have spoken to him though, from previous testimony.

★ He later substituted the words 'people of Latin races,' having been forced to by the Italian ambassador, and apologised, saying he meant no offence to the Italian people.

'Go down and find the carpenter and sound all the wells forward, and report to the bridge,' he had been ordered. He had gone down the engineers' alleyway on E-deck and met the boatswain.

'Who are you looking for?' he had been asked.

'The carpenter.'

'He has gone up.'

'What is the matter, then?'

'I do not know. I think we have struck an iceberg.'

He had soon afterwards seen water rising in one of the forward cargo hatches.

Evans had been in boat 12 and helped Fifth Officer Lowe with the rescue attempt. When it was daylight, a woman passenger in the boat had passed around a welcome flask of whiskey.

Next to testify were a parade of people from the *Californian*. Their stories are told in the later appendix.

An affidavit of Ernest Gill had drawn attention to the *Californian*'s Captain Stanley Lord and his officers' actions on the night of the sinking. At midnight, Gill had 'looked over the rail on the starboard side and saw the lights of a very large steamer about ten miles away.' He said: 'I watched her fully for a minute…going full speed.' After going below, at 12.40 a.m. he was on deck when he 'saw a white rocket…about ten miles away…I thought it must be a shooting star…in seven or eight minutes I saw distinctly a second rocket…I said to myself "That must be a vessel in distress."' Gill recalled: '…it was not my business to notify the bridge or the lookouts…I turned in immediately after.'

Captain Henry Moore of the *Mount Temple* testified. Giving his account of what had happened on board his ship, he was then asked his technical opinion about the *Titanic*'s unfortunate collision.

'My theory would be that she was going along and touched one of those large spurs from an iceberg,' he explained, '…they are very sharp and pointed. They are like a jagged rock. My idea is that she struck one of those on her bilge, and that she ran along that, and that opened up her [hull] plates, the lining of her plates…; and so much water got in that I think her bulkheads could not stand the strain.'

Senator Smith explained that he had asked if passengers might have sought refuge in the sinking ship's watertight compartments, and people had expressed humour about the matter. He realised people thought he was a fool, but described that some years ago Captain Smith had shown him around the *Adriatic* and he knew what the compartments were. Smith said he had asked such questions to reassure the many people who were unaware about the watertight compartments' structure.

Steward Henry Etches described Thomas Andrews' daily activities working on his beloved ship, and his own escape shortly before 1.00 a.m. in boat 5, before being rescued by the *Carpathia*.

Huge Woolner described hearing Mr and Mrs Straus talking. She refused to part with him. He gave details of what had happened during the sinking and mentioned a 'scramble' and 'two flashes of a pistol' at the beginning of the lowering of collapsible C, forward on the starboard side. Woolner had helped clear the boat of stowaways.

Ismay was recalled. He thought the lost ship's top speed would be about the same as the *Olympic*'s, or perhaps a little faster.

'Did you have any talk with the captain with reference to the speed of the ship?' Senator Smith asked him.

M.S. "CARPATHIA."

J. W. Barker, Copyright.

Titanic's gross tonnage was about three-and-a-half times greater than that of the Cunard liner *Carpathia*, but she was a welcome sight to the survivors, out on the open sea hundreds of miles from land. *Carpathia* was also claimed by the sea, when she was torpedoed months before the war's end. Her wreck was discovered in 1999. (Günter Bäbler collection)

'Never, sir.'

'Did you, at any time, urge him to greater speed?'

'No, sir.' Ismay repeated.

Ismay also denied an account that he had told the passenger Mrs Ryerson about going through the ice '...we will speed up and get out of it'.

Henry Stengel said he had wagered in a pool about the ship's speed. At midday on 14 April the ship had been making 22 knots for the past day, and 'the report came from the engine room that the engines were turning three revolutions faster than any other time on the voyage'. This referred to 75rpm, which was increased further that day. 'When I retired...I could hear the engines running and I noticed that the engines were running fast,' he said, '...faster than at any other time during the trip.'

Then he described being woken by his wife when the collision had occurred and their later escape from the sinking vessel.

When the ship had gone down, 'there was an awful wail, like'.

He said he had heard some shots from the ship, but there was order on the ship before he boarded lifeboat 1, an emergency boat, and left. His wife had gone in an earlier boat forward on the starboard side.

Colonel Gracie described what had happened to him. He recalled Astor at boat 4 with his pregnant wife and the conversation that took place there, the loading of several of the boats and declared that the ship had sunk intact.

Mrs Stuart White recalled boarding boat 8. She said, 'before we were cut loose from the ship they took out cigarettes and lighted them; on an occasion like that!' The women had rowed and many of the boat's crew had difficulty in rowing, she recalled...

Senator William Alden Smith put forward his report to the Senate on 28 May 1912, five days after the inquiry had finished, before delivering a very colourfully worded speech.

Smith's report detailed the witnesses heard, *Titanic*'s ownership, IMM's structure, 'General Particulars' of the lost liner, trials, the Board of Trade Certificate, lifeboat particulars, the ship's departure from Southampton, and a listing of survivors, noting that 60 per cent of the first-class passengers had been saved and 42 per cent of the second-class passengers had survived, but only 25 per cent of third-class passengers and 24 per cent of the crew had come through the ordeal alive. The voyage was described in some detail, including the various ice reports, speed ('the speed of the *Titanic* was gradually increased...just prior to the collision the ship was making her maximum speed of the voyage...'), the collision, which had 'tore the steel plating' above the bilge, [sic] reports of the damage, flooding, and the watertight compartments. Distress calls were summarised, as were lights seen from the *Titanic*, the steamship *Californian*'s 'grave responsibility', the lowering of the lifeboats and the rescue and *Carpathia*. Quite briefly, the report recommended much the same as the British inquiry would some months later: it called for lifeboat places on passenger vessels for all the people on board; increased lifeboat drills; two electric searchlights to be carried aboard all steamships carrying over 100 passengers; continuous manning of the wireless equipment, with direct communication installed between the bridge and the wireless room, such as a speaking tube, and auxiliary back-ups compulsory; rockets at sea to be used in future only to indicate distress; watertight double skins; increased watertight compartmentalisation and the height of such bulkheads should extend to the uppermost continuous structural deck.

Testimony, letters and affidavits filled over 1,100 pages. Many aspects of the Senate inquiry would set the tone for a more formal British counterpart.

★   ★   ★

The Right Honourable Lord Mersey was appointed Wreck Commissioner for the Board of Trade's 'Formal Investigation into the Loss of the SS *Titanic*'. His inquiry began on 2 May 1912, while the American investigation was still in progress and a number of witnesses were as yet unavailable.★

The Right Honourable Rufus Isaacs KC MP was Attorney General;† Sir John Simon KC MP was Solicitor General; Mr Butler Aspinall, KC; Mr S.A.T. Rowlatt and Mr Raymond Asquith appeared as counsel on behalf of the Board of Trade. The solicitor to the Board of Trade, Sir R. Ellis Cunliffe, had instructed them to do so.

★ On the morning of 11 May 1912, J. Bruce Ismay arrived from New York. He returned to his Liverpool home ('Sandheys', Mossley Hill) and immediately wrote to the Earl of Derby, Lord Mayor of Liverpool. His father had established the Liverpool Seamen's Pension Fund twenty-five years earlier, to support British sailors; and, following his father's death, his mother had established the 'Margaret Ismay Fund' to provide for their widows. Now, he proposed a fund to provide 'for widows of those whose lives are lost while they are engaged upon active duty, in whatever capacity, upon the merchant vessels of this country'. He thought 'the necessity of such a fund is brought prominently into notice by the terrible disaster to the *Titanic*' and proposed to contribute £10,000 of his own money, as well as £1,000 from his wife. (When the press became aware of Ismay's proposal, Derby asked if he could 'publish it with [a] paragraph saying I have gratefully accepted your offer?' Ismay responded to Derby's telegram within half an hour: 'Please act in whatever manner you think best, [I] leave myself entirely in your hands.')

The Right Honourable Sir Robert Finlay, KC MP, Mr F. Laing, KC, Mr Maurice Hill, KC, and Mr Norman Raeburn appeared as Counsel on behalf of the White Star Line, having been instructed by Messrs Hill, Dickinson & Co.

Numerous others represented various interests, including several unions. The 'Order for Formal Investigation' was read out to the court:

> The Merchant Shipping Act, 1894.
>
> Order for Formal Investigation..
>
> Whereas, on or about the 14th day of April, 1912, the British steamship *Titanic*, of Liverpool, Official [Board of Trade] Number 131482, struck ice in or on latitude 41°46′North, longitude 50°14′West, North Atlantic Ocean, and on the following day foundered, and loss of life thereby ensued or occurred. And whereas a shipping casualty has occurred, and the Board of Trade have requested a Wreck Commissioner appointed under this act to hold a Formal Investigation into the said shipping casualty, and has consented to do so.
>
> Now the Board of Trade, in pursuance of the powers invested in them by Section 466 of the Merchant Shipping Act, 1894, do hereby direct that the Formal Investigation shall be held into the said shipping casualty in the Scottish Hall, Buckingham Gate, London, SW…

Twenty-five questions needed to be answered – these were orally summarised for Lord Mersey by Sir Rufus Isaacs:

> Questions 1 to 8 inclusive relate to what happened before the casualty and before there is a question or suggestion of a warning that the *Titanic* was approaching ice. Questions 9 to 14 relate to the suggestion of warning given to the *Titanic*, and ask what was done with regard to lookout or other precautions before the casualty, that is to say, it is suggested by those questions that those responsible for the navigation of *Titanic* were warned that they were approaching ice, and then the questions are put in order to ascertain what was done, and the court may answer what it finds as fact was done by those responsible for *Titanic* after they received such warning, if they did receive it. Then, my Lord, Question 15 is a question relating to the casualty itself. Questions 16 to 24★ relate to the events after the casualty, as to what steps were taken either to save the vessel or to save life. Then there is a general question, 25, which relates to the rules and regulations under the Merchant Shipping Acts and the administration of those Acts and the rules and regulations, invites such recommendations or suggestions as the court may think fit: to make with a view to promoting the safety of vessels and persons at sea…

---

† During the inquiry, Isaacs praised and emphasised the part wireless had played in the disaster. This was unsurprising for two reasons: firstly, wireless had played an important part, and second, Isaacs had £16,000 ($80,000) – £960,000 at today's prices – shares in Marconi. (Gardiner, page 240.)

★ Question 24 was later changed (insertions in italic), to read, 'What was the cause of the loss of the *Titanic* and the loss of life which thereby ensued or occurred? *What vessels had the opportunity of rendering assistance to* Titanic, *and, if any, how was it that assistance did not reach the* Titanic *until the steamship* Carpathia *arrived?* Was the construction of the vessel and its arrangements such as to make it difficult for any class of passenger or any portion of the crew to take full advantage of the existing provisions for safety?' Rufus Isaacs proposed the insertion on 24 June.

One of the many published tributes to *Titanic*'s 'brave bandsmen'. None of the orchestra survived the disaster. (*The Deathless Story of the Titanic*, 1912/Author's collection)

After various discussions, the first day ended. Nobody actually testified on the first day.

On the second day, 3 May 1912, Archie Jewell (Lookout) and Joseph Scarrott (Able Seaman) testified. Jewell earned a very rare 'thank you' from Lord Mersey before being dismissed.

7 May – day three – saw Robert Hichens (Quartermaster), William Lucas (Able Seaman) and Frederick Barrett (Leading Stoker) testify.

On day four Frederick Barrett's testimony concluded, and Reginald Lee (lookout on duty during collision), John Poingdestre (Able Seaman) and James Johnson (saloon steward) all testified.

Johnson's testimony concluded on the fifth day, and Thomas Patrick Dillon (Trimmer), Thomas Ranger (Greaser), George Cavell (Trimmer), Alfred Shiers (Fireman) and Charles Hendrickson (Leading Fireman) testified.

Day six saw Frank Morris (bathroom steward), Frederick Scott (Greaser), Charles Joughin (Chief Baker) and Samuel James Rule (bathroom steward) testify.

Captain Stanley Lord of the *Californian* testified on 14 May – day seven – as did James Gibson and Herbert Stone (Second Officer). Charles Groves (Third Officer), George Stewart (Chief Officer), Cyril Evans (Wireless Operator), James Henry Moore (captain of the *Mount Temple*).

John Durrant (the *Mount Temple*'s Wireless Operator) testified on day eight, and Groves was recalled.

During day nine, John Durrant's testimony was concluded, as was Samuel Rule's. John Edward Hart (third-class steward), Albert Pearcy (third-class steward and pantry-man), Edward Brown (first-class steward), Charles Mackay (bathroom steward) and Joseph Wheat (assistant second steward) also testified.

Charles Hendrickson was recalled on day ten when George Symons (Able Seaman), James Taylor (Fireman), James Barr (captain of *Caronia*) and Albert Horswell (Able Seaman) testified.

Symons received 'quite a grilling'. Mr Scanlan put it to him that it was cowardly for the crew of boat 1 not to make a rescue attempt after the sinking.

'No, I cannot see that,' said Symons. He was aware that if the boat had returned it could have been swamped.

'You admit it was cowardly?' Scanlan persisted.

'No, I do not admit it was cowardly.'

Then Lord Mersey broke in: 'Have mercy on the man!'

Mr Scanlan's questioning ceased.

Mr Clement Edwards asked about the £5 that had apparently been given to the crew of boat 1. Although it was some time since the sinking, Symons said he still had the banker's order.

'Have you not changed it?' Mersey asked.

'No, sir. I have not got to that yet.' Symons replied. He had money 'in the locker.'

'You are a pretty thrifty sort of man, are you?' asked Mr Edwards.

'Well, yes –'

'Do you ever pay money into the bank at all?'

'What do you mean?' Symons responded. 'Is that a question to put?' he asked. 'That is not right, sir!'

'Have you a banking account?'

Symons refused to reply, said it was not their business and then more appropriate questions were asked.

Sir Cosmo Duff Gordon's testimony on this day was of much interest: he denied any attempts to prevent boat number 1 going back to the sight of the sinking to save people in the water, he described how he came to be in a boat with only one-fourth of its capacity, and that he had given a £5 cheque to crew in the boat. He denied that this had been an attempt to bribe them to not go back and rescue people in the water:

> There was a man sitting next to me, and of course in the dark I could see nothing of him. I never did see him, and I do not know yet who he is. I suppose it would be some time when they rested on their oars, twenty minutes or half an hour after the *Titanic* had sunk, a man said to me, 'I suppose you have lost everything' and I said 'Of course.' He says 'But you can get some more,' and I said 'Yes.' 'Well,' he said, 'we have lost all our kit and the company won't give us any more, and what is more our pay stops from

tonight. All they will do is send us back to London.' So I said to them 'You fellows need not worry about that, I will give you a fiver each to start a new kit.' That is the whole of the five-pound-note story.

Sir Cosmo was asked by Mr Harbinson (representing third-class passengers), 'Would I accurately state your position if I summed it up in this way, that you considered when you were safe yourselves that all the others might perish?'

It was actionable outside a courtroom, and Lord Mersey interrupted, 'Do you think a question of this kind is fair to the witness? The witness' position is bad enough. Do you think it is fair to put a question of that kind to him? I do not!'

'If your Lordship says so I will not pursue it further,' responded Harbinson.

On day eleven, Sir Cosmo's testimony was concluded, and his wife took the stand. They convinced the court that they had not 'acted improperly'. Fireman Samuel Collins, Frederick Sheath (Trimmer), Robert Pursey (Fireman), Elizabeth Leather (first-class stewardess), Annie Robinson (first-class stewardess), Walter Winn (quarter-master) and Charles Lightoller testified, and Assistant Second Steward Joseph Wheat was recalled.

Lightoller's testimony concluded at the end of day twelve, after he had had to answer a total of over 1,600 questions! Throughout the inquiry, he defended the company admirably and he seems to have whitewashed many details – like the inquiry to which he was testifying.

Perhaps the worst 'grilling' he had endured had been from Thomas Scanlan, representing the National Sailors' and Firemen's Union:

14364. What maximum speed do you think you could have attained? – Well, just as a matter of hearsay, or rather, what we estimated roughly, for instance myself, I judged that the ship would eventually do about 24 knots.

14365. Did you say yesterday that you were going at as high a speed as you could in view of the coal you had on board? – Did I say so yesterday?

14366. Yes? – I was not on the stand yesterday.

The Solicitor-General: Yes, you were.

14367. (*Mr Scanlan.*) You were being examined yesterday? – Oh, yes; I beg your pardon. Not only with regard to shortage of coal, but I understand several boilers were off.

14368. Do you know any reason for those boilers being off? – Merely that there was no wish for the ship to travel at any great speed.

14369. There was no reason, I take it, why you should not go fast; but, in view of the abnormal conditions and of the fact that you were nearing ice at ten o'clock, was there not a very obvious reason for going slower? – Well, I can only quote you my experience throughout the last 24 years, that I have been crossing the Atlantic most of the time, that I have never seen the speed reduced.

14370. You were asked by my Lord this forenoon how an unfortunate accident like this could have been prevented in what you describe as abnormal circumstances? – Yes.

14371. Is it not quite clear that the most obvious way to avoid it is by slackening speed? – Not necessarily the most obvious.

14372. Well, is it one way? – It is one way. Naturally, if you stop the ship you will not collide with anything...

14398. I suggest to you it would have been a much safer thing to have believed the reports which you had from a number of sources as to the presence of ice, than to have acted in disregard of the warnings you had received from other ships, and goneahead at the rate of 21½ knots an hour until the collision occurred? – In the view of after events, of course, we form a totally different opinion. It would naturally have been safer, we can see now, not to have gone ahead at all.

14403. The warning you had had at half-past one led you to understand that you would be right up against the ice, so to speak, from 10 to 11? – The position where it had been reported.

14404. I could understand your going ahead at 21½ knots up to 10 or half-past 10: what I fail to understand is why from half-past 10, when you knew you were about the place where you were led to believe ice was to be found, you still proceeded at 21½ knots? – That I cannot answer for after 10 o'clock…

14414. What I want to suggest to you is that it was recklessness, utter recklessness, in view of the conditions which you have described as abnormal, and in view of the knowledge you had from various sources that ice was in your immediate vicinity, to proceed at 21½ knots? – Then all I can say is that recklessness applies to practically every commander and every ship crossing the Atlantic Ocean.

14415. I am not disputing that with you, but can you describe it yourself as other than recklessness? – Yes.

14416. Is it careful navigation in your view? – It is ordinary navigation, which embodies careful navigation.

14417. Is this your position, then: that even with the experience of the *Titanic* disaster, if you were coming within the near vicinity of a place which was reported to you to be abounding in ice, you would proceed with a ship like the *Titanic* at 21½ knots? – I do not say I should.

14418. At night time, and at a time when the conditions were what you have described as very abnormal, surely you would not go on at 21½ knots? – The conditions were not apparent to us in the first place; the conditions of an absolutely flat sea were not apparent to us till afterwards. Naturally I should take precautions against such an occurrence.

Day thirteen was filled with the testimony of Third Officer Pitman, Fourth Officer Boxhall and Fifth Officer Lowe, of the late *Titanic*; George Turnbull, the Deputy Manager of the Marconi International Marine Communication Company. Turnbull's testimony concluded the following day – 23 May, day fourteen of the inquiry.

Harold Bride, Charles Lightoller, Pitman, Boxhall, Lowe were recalled; Turnbull was recalled halfway through day fourteen.

Day fifteen was filled with the testimony of Harold Cottam (the *Carpathia*'s wireless operator), Frederick Fleet (Lookout on duty at the time of collision), George Hogg (Able Seaman), George Rowe (Quartermaster), Samuel Hemming (Lamp Trimmer) and Wilfred Seward (second-class pantry steward).

Fleet's testimony was quite long. He endured many repeated questions. Several times he did not answer.

When being questioned by Sir Robert Finlay, Fleet was uneasy. 'That gentleman is not trying to get round you at all,' Mersey told him.

'But some of them are, though,' responded Fleet.

Above: Collapsible D, on the left, is towed towards *Carpathia* by lifeboat 14, on the right. Lifeboat 14 was under the command of *Titanic*'s fifth officer, Harold Godfrey Lowe. (Library of Congress, Prints and Photographs Division)

Below: Titanic's survivors on board *Carpathia*. (Library of Congress, Prints and Photographs Division)

'They are not indeed,' Mersey replied, 'I can see you think most of us are, but we are not. We only want to get…your own story.'

Then Mr Harbinson began questioning the lookout.

'Is there any more likes to have a go at me?' asked Fleet.

'Well, I rather sympathise with him,' Mersey stated. 'Do you want to ask him anything more?'

'No.'

'A good job, too.'

'I am much obliged to you,' Mersey told Fleet, 'I think you have given your evidence very well, although you seem to distrust us all.'

'Thank you,' replied Fleet, perhaps with a hint of sarcasm.

On 4 June – day sixteen of the inquiry – Alfred Crawford (first-class bedroom steward), Edward Buley (Able Seaman), Ernest Archer (Able Seaman), Ernest Gill (Donkeyman on the *Californian*) and J. Bruce Ismay testified.

Ismay's testimony concluded the following day – he managed to convince the court that he had nothing to do with the late liner's navigation and that he had boarded collapsible C with no passengers or crew visible on the deck. Ismay admitted that he knew the ship was sinking as he got into the lifeboat.

Harold Sanderson told the court on 5 June – day seventeen – about the late liner's construction: that there was no specification with regard to lifeboats or a fixed price, that the ships equipment and construction exceeded Lloyds regulations… He gave details about the speed of *Olympic*, her fastest eastbound crossing being at 22½ knots and her fastest westbound crossing at between 21¾ and 22 knots. Sanderson said that from the point of accident, *Titanic* needed to maintain only 20 knots to reach New York at 5 a.m. on Wednesday – but there was still the fact that the speed of *Titanic* was 22½ knots and that preparations were being made to accelerate.

He strangely confused the lost liner with her sister-ship when being questioned about the lack of binoculars.

'We have been told by the lookout people that there were binoculars on the *Olympic*?'

'Coming from Belfast to Southampton.'

'On the *Olympic*, I am speaking of?'

'Oh, I beg your pardon; yes.'

Sanderson's testimony concluded on 6 June – day eighteen – and Edward Wilding (Naval Architect of Harland & Wolff) took the stand, giving the court details of *Titanic*'s construction and specification, and that the watertight bulkheads had been thought adequate. With two adjoining watertight compartments flooded the tops of the bulkheads would still be above the waterline by twice the amount recommended by the 1891 Bulkheads Committee, in what he termed 'the most severe' case with the ship fully loaded, easily making the ship able to float in that condition in moderate weather. (Three forward compartments flooded would not have sunk the ship, while if four forward compartments were flooded the ship would have still floated in good weather and conditions, such as at the time of the collision.)

On day nineteen, Paul Maugé (secretary to the chef of the late *à la carte* restaurant) testified and then Edward Wilding was recalled.

Wilding's long testimony revealed that if *Titanic* had maintained speed and hit the iceberg head on, she would still be afloat, although 80–100ft of the bows would be crushed and two forward watertight compartments would have been flooded. Wilding said that longitudinal watertight bulkheads could – in some cases – be a danger, and it was suggested that if the *Mauretania* (with her longitudinal bulkheads) had been flooded for a sufficient length, she would have toppled right over. Later during the inquiry, Wilding handed in a report made in conjunction with Cunard's Naval Architect, Leonard Peskett:

> We have considered by approximate methods the flooding of the *Mauretania* in the event of an accident similar to that met with by the *Titanic*. we have assumed the watertight doors and hatches to be closed and similar deductions for those calculations for the *Titanic*. From the calculations made, taking the vessel as damaged from the stem to after end of the forward boiler room (corresponding nearly – but not quite – to the length from stem to the after end of number 5 boiler room in the *Titanic*) the vessel would remain afloat with a considerable list, say fifteen to twenty degrees, which, no doubt, could (possibly) be slowly reduced by carefully flooding some after spaces on the opposite side. With the data available we do not think that we can satisfactorily discuss flooding corresponding to the damage extending into boiler room 4 in the *Titanic* – (signed) Ed. W.; L. Peskett.

If the equivalent damage to *Mauretania* had been as far aft as *Titanic*'s number 4 boiler room, then she would have had a heavier list and possibly completely capsized before there was a time to counter-flood for the purpose of correcting the list.

Wilding was recalled again on the inquiry's twentieth day. Watertight bulkhead stiffeners were spaced slightly less than 30in apart, he said, closer together than Lloyd's minimum 30in interval requirement; the watertight bulkheads' plating were also 10–20 per cent thicker (thus *stronger*) than Lloyd's requirements. Watertight bulkhead stiffening, in terms of strength, was 50 per cent in excess of Lloyd's requirements; Lloyd's rules did not extent to such large ships as *Titanic*, but would probably have required thirteen watertight bulkheads as opposed to the fifteen that she had.★

Cunard's Naval Architect Leonard Peskett was heard, giving technical details of their flagship's construction, and then the Right Honourable Alexander Carlisle took the stand to give information about the Merchant Shipping Advisory Committee of 1911.

Carlisle said that an interview with him in the *Daily Mail* was reported as it happened; he said that it was his view that such large liners did not have enough boats and that the davits he had proposed for the *Olympic* and *Titanic* were fitted with davits that could handle 'over forty' boats (sixty-four). Although these were his views, he admitted that he had never told representatives of White Star that his view was that the two liners should have more boats. Carlisle said that he had signed the 1911 Merchant Shipping Advisory Committee's report, despite the fact that he did not agree with it (the report did not recommend an increase in lifeboat accommodation and Carlisle wanted to increase such accommodation on giant new liners).

★ By means of comparison, the German-built *Imperator*, due to enter service the following year, was more than 900ft long but only had twelve watertight transverse bulkheads and thirteen compartments, carried to 20ft above the waterline and enabling the ship to float with any two compartments flooded, but was equipped with longitudinal bulkheads in the engine room spaces and an inner skin in the forward holds. *Titanic*'s D-deck bulkheads extended above the waterline when fully loaded to 20ft amidships, 33ft at the bow, and 25ft at the stern; the figures for the E-deck bulkheads were 11ft amidships and 24ft at the bow. (*Shipbuilder 2*, page 221, 251 (Fig. 3 Deck Plans).)

A crowd gathers, awaiting news, outside the White Star Line's New York offices. (Library of Congress, Prints and Photographs Division)

'Was that your view?' he was asked by Lord Mersey.

'It was not,' replied Carlisle.

He was immediately asked, 'Why on earth did you sign it?'

'I do not know… I am not generally soft… But I must say, I was very soft the day I signed that,' he weakly replied.

On day twenty-one – 11 June 1912 – Charles Alfred Bartlett (the White Star Line's Marine Superintendent, who was later to command the *Britannic*) testified and Bertram Fox Hayes (later to command *Olympic*) testified. Also testifying were Frederick Passow (Master of the Inman Line's *St Paul*), Francis Miller (an assistant hydrographer of the Admiralty), Benjamin Steel (White Star's Marine Superintendent – who had cleared the ship to sail), Stanley Adams (Wireless Operator of the *Mesaba*) and Sir Walter J. Howell (Assistant Secretary to the Board of Trade and Chief of the Marine Department).

Howell's long testimony continued through day twenty-two and part of the twenty-third day. During his testimony, Sir Edward Harland's 1891 Bulkhead Committee Report was put on the record, notable points including:

> The recommendation that vessels with longitudinal (as well as transverse) watertight bulkheads should not list sufficiently to bring the 'deck on either side below water level' with flooding in those compartments;

Various proposed grades of watertight subdivision, the highest 'first grade' applying to 'vessels subdivided throughout their lengths so that they may float in moderate weather with any two adjoining compartments in free communication with the sea;

A compartment between transverse bulkheads that was 'subdivided by one or more longitudinal watertight bulkheads' should only be treated by the Board of Trade as one compartment, unless the Board was convinced that the ship's stability with one longitudinal watertight compartment flooded would not be severely reduced.

During day twenty-three (13 June 1912), Sir Alfred Chambers (late Professional Member of the Marine Department of the Board of Trade) and Alfred Young (Professional Member of the Board of Trade) testified. Young's testimony concluded the next day, the inquiry's twenty-fourth.

Day twenty-four saw Richard Jones (captain of the SS *Canada*), Edwin Cannons (Master Mariner of the Atlantic Transport Company) and Francis Carruthers (engineer and Ship Surveyor to the Board of Trade) testify.

Both captains declared that in conditions like the *Titanic* had encountered, they would not have slowed down.

During day twenty-five (17 June 1912), Francis Carruthers' testimony was concluded, William Chantler (Ship Surveyor to the Board of Trade at Belfast), Alfred Peacock (engineer and Ship Surveyor to the Board of Trade at Glasgow) and Maurice Clarke (Assistant Emigration Officer to the Board of Trade at Southampton) testified. William Archer (Principal Ship Surveyor to the Board of Trade) was the final witness.

Archer said that the watertight bulkheads that separated the boiler rooms on *Titanic* did not reach as far as originally intended (to saloon deck, D); he said that he had seen a builders' calculation which made this height unnecessary. If the two foremost watertight

'Southampton, where the majority of the crew lived, was a city of sorrow as soon as news of the disaster became known.' Milbank Street was one of the 'streets of mourning' and several of the bereaved homes are marked. (*The Deathless Story of the Titanic*, 1912/Author's collection)

From the left, Philip Franklin, then vice-president of IMM; Charles Burlingham, who represented the company at the limitation of liability hearings; and J. Bruce Ismay. (Library of Congress, Prints and Photographs Division)

compartments and the firemen's tunnel were flooded, said Harland & Wolff, the liner would sink only 2½ft at the head. With the ship down like this, the top of the watertight bulkhead between the fourth and fifth watertight compartments would still be 15½ft above the waterline. Therefore there was no need to extend the watertight bulkhead's height.

Day twenty-six – 18 June 1912 – was filled with the testimony of Alexander Boyle (Engineer in Chief to the Board of Trade), Eber Sharpe (Surveyor to the Board of Trade at Queenstown and Emigration Officer), Joseph Harvey (Principal Examiner of Masters and Mates to the Board of Trade), Sir Norman Hill (Chairman of the Merchant Shipping Advisory Committee), Guglielmo Marconi (inventor of wireless) and Joseph Ranson

Carpathia's captain, Arthur Rostron, poses with his ship's officers. The cup on the deck in front of them was presented to Rostron on 29 May 1912 by surviving first-class passenger Margaret Brown, as a thank you to him and his crew. (Library of Congress, Prints and Photographs Division)

(Master of the *Baltic*). Other witnesses heard this day were: Sir Ernest Shackleton and Riversdale French (Surgeon of the *Oceanic*).

Twenty-seven days into the inquiry, 19 June 1912, a parade of captains testified that speed was always maintained in good conditions until ice was actually sighted. These were Captain Pritchard (formerly of the speedy *Mauretania*), Captain Young (retired from the Anchor Line), William Stewart (retired from the Beaver Line), John Fairfull (retired from the Allan Line) and Andrew Braes (also retired from the Allan Line). Edward Wilding was recalled briefly.

On 21 June – day twenty-eight – Arthur Rostron, *Carpathia*'s captain, Gerhard Apfeld (Marine Superintendent of the Red Star Line) and Arthur Ernest Tride (Master of the SS *Manitou*) testified.

During the remaining eight days of the British inquiry, counsels for the many interested parties presented arguments and statements on their behalf. There was also a detailed evaluation of the testimony.

It was stated that during the past decade British passenger ships had carried 3.5 million passengers and there had just been seventy-three casualties.

The inquiry concluded, minutes of testimony were studied and considerations were made. Mersey's commission presented its findings on 30 July 1912 in a seventy-three-page report.

In the report, Mersey voiced his opinion of the '*Californian* incident':

> There are contradictions and inconsistencies in the story as told by different witnesses. But the truth of the matter is plain. The *Titanic* collided with the iceberg at 11.40 p.m. The vessel seen by the *Californian* stopped at this time. The rockets sent up by *Titanic* were distress signals. The *Californian* saw distress signals. The number sent up by *Titanic* was eight. The *Californian* saw eight. The time over which the rockets from *Titanic* were sent up was from about 12.45 to 1.40 o'clock. It was about this time that the *Californian* saw rockets. At 2.40 a.m. Mr Stone called to the Master that the ship he had seen had disappeared. At 2.20 a.m. the *Titanic* had foundered. It was suggested that the rockets seen by the *Californian* were from some other ship, not the *Titanic*. But no other ship to fit this theory has ever been heard of.
>
> The circumstances convince me that the ship seen by the *Californian* was the *Titanic*, and if so, according to Captain Lord, the two vessels were about five miles apart at the time of the disaster. The evidence from *Titanic* corroborates this estimate, but I am advised that the distance was probably greater, though not more than eight to ten miles. The ice which the *Californian* was surrounded by was loose ice extending for a distance of not more than two to three miles in the direction of the *Titanic*. The night was clear and the sea smooth. When she first saw the rockets, the *Californian* could have pushed through the ice to the open water without any serious risk and so have come to the assistance of the *Titanic*. Had she done so, she might have saved the lives of many, if not all, of the lives that were lost.

J. Bruce Ismay and Sir Cosmo Duff Gordon were exonerated from allegations of 'improper' conduct:

> The attack upon Mr Ismay resolved itself into the suggestion that, occupying the position of managing director of the steamship company, some moral duty was imposed upon him to wait on board until the vessel foundered. I do not agree. Mr Ismay, upon rendering assistance to many passengers, found 'C' collapsible, the last boat on the starboard side, actually being lowered. There was room for him and he jumped in. had he not jumped in he would have added one more life, namely his own, to the number of those lost.
>
> The very gross charge against Cosmo Duff Gordon that, having got into number 1 boat he bribed the men in it to row away from the drowning people is unfounded. I have said that the members of the crew in the boat might have made some attempt to save the people in the water, and that such an attempt would probably have been successful; but I do not believe that the men were deterred from making the attempt by any act of Sir Cosmo Duff Gordon's. At the same time I think that if he had encouraged the men to return to the position where the *Titanic* had foundered they would probably have made an effort to do so and could have saved some lives.

Although Captain Smith was not judged to have been negligent, *Titanic* had maintained an excessive speed:

> The question is what ought the Master to have done. I am advised that with the knowledge of the proximity of ice which the Master had, two courses were open to him: The one was to stand well to the southward instead of turning up to a westerly course; the other was to reduce speed materially as night approached. He did neither. The alteration of the course at 5.50 p.m. …brought the vessel back to within about two miles of the customary route before 11.30 p.m. And there was certainly no reduction of speed. Why, then, did the Master persevere in his course and maintain his speed? The answer is to be found in the evidence. It was shown that for many years past, indeed, for a quarter of a century or more, the practice of liners using this track when in the vicinity of ice at night had been in clear weather to keep the course, to maintain the speed and to trust to a sharp lookout to enable them to avoid the danger. This practice, it was said, had been justified by experience, no casualties having resulted from it. I accept the evidence as to the practice and as to the immunity from casualties which is said to have accompanied it. But the event has proved the practice to be bad. Its root is probably to be found in competition and in the desire of the public for quick passages rather than in the judgement of navigators. But unfortunately experience appeared to justify it. In these circumstances I am not able to blame Captain Smith. He had not the experience which his own misfortune has afforded to those whom he has left behind, and he was doing only that which other skilled men would have done in the same position. It was suggested at the bar that he was yielding to influences which ought not to have affected him: that the presence of Mr Ismay on board and the knowledge which he perhaps had of a conversation between Mr Ismay and the Chief Engineer at Queenstown about the speed of the ship and the consumption of coal probably induced him to neglect precautions which he would otherwise have taken. But I do not believe this. The evidence shows that he was not trying to make any record passage or indeed any exceptionally quick passage. He was not trying to please anybody, but was exercising his own discretion in the way he thought best. He made a mistake, a very grievous mistake, but one in which, in face of the practice and of past experience, negligence cannot be said to have had any part, and in the absence of negligence it is, in my opinion, impossible to fix Captain Smith with blame. It is, however, to be hoped that the last has been heard of the practice and that for the future it will be abandoned for what we now know to be more prudent and wiser measures. What was a mistake in the case of the *Titanic* would without doubt be negligence in any similar case in the future.

Recommendations included that wireless should be installed on foreign and emigrant ships and be manned twenty-four hours a day and that a frequent lifeboat drills should be held. More watertight compartments should be fitted on ocean-going vessels and there should be better lookout procedures and the provision of lifeboats for all people on board. Britain's Board of Trade was criticised for its failure to update its 1894 regulations.

The commission found, very briefly, that the collision had been due to the excessive speed at which the ship had been navigated; that a proper watch wasn't kept; the lifeboats were lowered properly, but some of them were not manned sufficiently.

Perhaps the White Star Line's directors were relieved that the outcome had not been worse, especially if they thought back to the lengthy enquiries into the *Atlantic* disaster

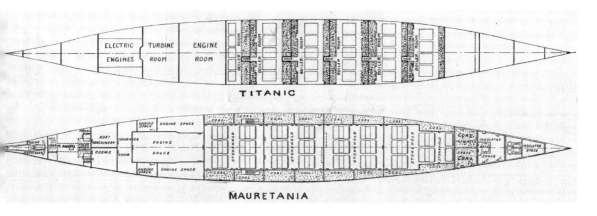

An interesting comparative diagram demonstrates *Titanic*'s arrangement of transverse watertight bulkheads; and *Mauretania*'s arrangement of transverse and longitudinal watertight bulkheads. Edward Wilding and Leonard Peskett each testified as to why they believed their design was superior. (*Scientific American*, 1912/Author's collection)

thirty-nine years earlier. Then, the company had fought back strongly to clear its name from the accusation that *Atlantic* had been dangerously short of coal. Following the Mersey report's publication, J. Bruce Ismay had been anxious to speak out and defend himself, perhaps mindful of the suggestion that he had been some sort of 'super captain'; however it was easier said than done. His solicitor, F.M. Radcliffe, referred to the correspondence that had taken place in the summer of 1911 regarding *Olympic*'s speed and schedule, when he wrote to him on 1 August 1912:

> I am strongly of the opinion that the incident of the *Olympic* has a double edge. If you seek to use it as showing that you personally do not press for high speed, you must not be surprised if other people use it as showing that you are prepared to acquiesce in a speed higher than you yourself think necessary when others press for it for business reasons, and since the determining vote is yours, as chairman, the responsibility is yours. Captain Smith was Captain of the *Olympic* as well as the *Titanic*. There is no evidence that he knew of the difference in the office on this question or of your individual views, but if he did, he knew equally that you waived those views. I know all that is to be said on the other side; but I think, if you start a correspondence, you would be giving any ill-disposed person pellets to fire at you, on such a doubtful basis; and I think you may well be content with the very clear finding of Lord Mersey in this matter.[83]

As Radcliffe had said in an earlier letter, any public reference by Ismay to the correspondence in 1911 would be 'not only unnecessary, but which at best, could only show that you at first opposed a Tuesday arrival for the *Olympic*, but yielded to that policy at the suggestion of your colleagues.' It was liable to worsen his case, not strengthen it.

Mersey was unaware of Elisabeth Lines' recollection of the discussion that she had overheard between J. Bruce Ismay and Captain Smith in the first-class reception room on the day before the disaster, because she was not called as a witness. However, if Ismay had voiced his approval of the new ship's performance and expressed the hope that she would do better than *Olympic* had done the year before, it is hard to see that Smith would not have shared those sentiments in any case. It was an entirely natural ambition and it is unsurprising that there would be such interest in the ship. If, in Smith's experience and judgement, there had been no need to reduce *Titanic*'s speed when she was proceeding through the water at over 22½ knots, then it raises the question as to whether a speed of 21½ knots would have been any safer. When he was in charge of *Adriatic* a couple of years earlier, that ship's highest speed in service was closer to 17 or 18 knots. Would it, therefore, have been safe for *Adriatic* to proceed at her utmost speed? What about the faster *Mauretania*? *Titanic* was undoubtedly performing well, but she was still not proceeding at the highest speed she was capable of. What rate of speed was too great in the circumstances was a subjective judgement, and if Smith misjudged the situation then there is no evidence that any of his senior officers had considered suggesting a reduction in speed.

Radcliffe also advised Ismay that Mersey 'seems to me to afford you complete exoneration from the charge or suggestion that you were responsible for the speed of the *Titanic* at the time of the disaster.' Smith was the ship's commander and he bore responsibility for her safe navigation:

> The only dissentient note is the ill-natured phrase in the leading article of the *Daily Mail*, obviously directed only to the incident of the boats. As I told you at the beginning, different people till the end of time will take different views on ethical questions. That you should have one dissentient voice only in all the respectable newspapers of England, is an extraordinary evidence of the fact that public opinion is on your side on the question of your leaving the vessel, and I have only heard the *Daily Mail* article mentioned to be disapproved.
>
> I suppose that when a good man is charged with an offence in a criminal court the verdict 'not guilty' always sounds a little cold to his friends. They would like something very much warmer – something which would embody their knowledge that he not only *was* [original emphasis] not guilty, but could *not have been guilty* [original emphasis]. That is not the way of the world...

Mersey had not been in charge of a criminal court, but the example appears to have been well taken. He wrote: 'To begin to supplement the judgement or dot its I's, or cross its T's, would only be to invite a correspondence in the papers, or in other words, to put out your head to be hit.' He concluded: 'You have taken the whole affair calmly and with dignity. Do nothing to lead people to suppose that you are not satisfied with a vindication which is recognised to be complete.'

★   ★   ★

Claims for damages against the White Star Line totalled £3,464,765 ($16,804,112).[84] According to the Merchant Shipping Act of 1894, *Titanic*'s owners were liable for $600,000 (£123,711); in America, 'limited liability' ruled that they were liable for losses of $97.772.02 (£20,159).[85] Claims included $1 million for loss of life, filed by Renée Harris for the loss of her husband; this compared to the average $1,500 claim for loss of life in steerage.[86] Eugene Daly filed a $50 claim for the loss of his set of bagpipes and William Carter filed a $5,000 claim for the loss of his 35hp Renault.[87] Håkan Björnström Steffanson filed a $100,000 claim for the loss of his painting, *La Circassienne Au Bain* by Blondel.[88] The claims' total was divided pro rata among all claimants; on 28 July 1916 Judge Mayer finally signed the decree ending *Titanic* lawsuits – £136,701 ($663,000) was distributed among all claimants.[89]

★   ★   ★

And so *Titanic*'s official history ended. With the disaster, thousands of lives had either been ended or devastated by the loss of a friend or loved one. Many people's hopes of a new life ended with the sinking. Today *Titanic* has become the most famous ship in the world. Sadly, she is remembered for the tragedy itself rather than her qualities as a ship and 1912's finest.

7

HMHS *BRITANNIC*

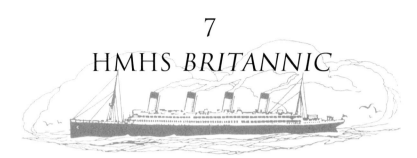

'The most wonderful hospital ship that ever sailed the seas...'

– Dr John Beaumont, Chief Surgeon.

*O*lympic's performance was so satisfactory that there was no hesitation on J. Bruce Ismay's part in confirming the order for the third sister ship before she had even reached New York. On 28 June 1911, Harland & Wolff ordered the shipyard and engine works to proceed with construction and the 'letter of agreement' was signed on 23 October 1911. The order for 'Yard Number 433' envisaged another steamship of identical dimensions to *Olympic* and *Titanic* and identical propelling machinery, but soon there would be changes that increased her size.

By the time the 'letter of agreement' was signed, the new ship's breadth had been increased from *Olympic* and *Titanic's* 92ft 6in to 94ft, which built in an additional margin of stability and passenger comfort.[1] *Titanic's* first-class accommodation had already been expanded and improved compared to *Olympic's*, marginally increasing the weight of her upper decks, and the younger sister would undoubtedly incorporate further improvements. On 3 January 1912, it was also specified that her twenty-four double-ended boilers would be increased in length by one foot, which would increase the amount of steam available for the new ship's engines. It seems probable that this alteration stemmed from the decision to increase the ship's engine power, which itself resulted from her increased breadth and displacement. As *The Engineer* put it: 'It is to this increase in beam that the rise in gross tonnage [and displacement]... is chiefly due. This again, reacts on the machinery.'

Following the launch of *Arlanza* on 23 November 1911, the keel for 'Yard Number 433' was laid seven days later on the same slipway where *Olympic* had been constructed. She was framed to the height of the double bottom by 12 March 1912, as work continued to complete *Titanic* for her maiden voyage the following month. When the disaster occurred construction came to a halt.

Unlike *Olympic* and *Titanic*, whose names had been announced publicly before the 'letter of agreement' had even been signed at the end of July 1908, their younger sister remained anonymous. However, there was plenty of rumour and speculation as to the new ship, her name and dimensions, from an early stage.[2] In July 1911, the *New York Times* reported:

NEW WHITE STAR GIANTESS?

The *Gigantic* Will Follow the *Olympic* and *Titanic* in 1913, It's Said.

Some of the men on the White Star liner *Baltic* which arrived yesterday brought in a rumour that the line contemplates building another gigantic steamship of the same type and size as the *Titanic* and *Olympic*. The vessel will be built in the yards of Harland & Wolff, Belfast, and the rumour had it that the new vessel will be launched in 1913. She will be called the *Gigantic*.

The new steamship, it is said, will contain improvements, the result of watching the operation of the *Olympic* and *Titanic*. The shipbuilders will carefully study the behaviour of both, and the proposed liner will be built to correct every shortcoming found in the other two.

The newspaper printed another report towards the end of November 1911:

London, Nov. 24. (by telegraph to Clifden, Ireland; thence by wireless) – Remarkable details are now known of the thousand-foot liner, the *Gigantic*, which the White Star Line has commissioned Harland & Wolff to build at Belfast.

The beam will measure between 111 and 112 feet; the displacement will be 70,000 tons, and the gross tonnage over 50,000. The levels [sic] will be a dozen or thirteen, with the highest over seventy-five [feet] above the water line. The passenger accommodation will be increased in the first class from 800 to 1,000 or more, and the total passengers that can be carried will number over 4,000.

The *Gigantic* will not be an ocean greyhound, but a seven-day boat. She will have both reciprocating and turbine engines. The cost is to be close on to £2,000,000, or $10,000,000. She will have a cricket field, a tennis court, golf links, and reception and ball rooms, and restaurant and veranda cafés, which will be placed forward instead of aft. There will also be a plunge and all kinds of baths, and a gymnasium.

There will be a most elaborate scheme of decoration.

This time the comments as to the ship's size were getting quite out of hand. Rather than a new ship 'of the same type and size', she had grown to 1,000ft long with plenty of other exaggerations. It was not the first time that the name *Gigantic* had been mentioned in connection with a new White Star liner. A report that the company were going to built a new express liner of that name was published in 1892; seven years later it was reported that they had considered that name for *Oceanic*, before discarding it in favour of the name which honoured their pioneer; and one report even asserted that the name *Gigantic* had been considered at one stage for *Olympic*.

Seven days after *Titanic*'s loss, it was reported:

CHANGE NEW WHITE STAR BOAT
Builders to Provide Double Bottom and Sides for the *Gigantic*.
London, April 21 – It is understood that the plans of the White Star Line steamship *Gigantic*, which is now being built at Belfast and was to have been 1,000 feet long, will be modified.

It is probable that the new plans will provide for double cellular bottom and sides, such as the *Mauretania* and *Lusitania* have, as a stipulated condition of receiving Government subsidy.

The reporter's comments as to the ship's length may have been inaccurate, but the speculation as to changes to the design was more believable, even if the reporter was unaware that *Titanic* already had a double bottom.

Although J. Bruce Ismay had seen some of the newspaper reports before the *Titanic* disaster and commented upon the inaccurate dimensions, he did not make any reference to the name and whether it was accurate or not. Nor does it appear that the White Star Line made any public announcement or comment until after *Titanic* sank. There were some references to a new liner that had not been assigned a name, including the *Shipbuilder*'s reference early in April 1912 to a 47,000grt ship that 'has not been named'.

In mid-May 1912, the *Southampton Times* recorded that:

> Mr Ismay has been written to on the subject, and he has replied that the managers never had any intention of calling the new ship *Gigantic*.

The paper recorded that they had first seen it 'in an American journal', and continued:

> It was shortly after the maiden voyage of the *Olympic*, and an enterprising journalist in the States waylaid one of the stewards of the new ship. Some leg-pulling ensued and the Steward unfolded all the secret plans of the White Star Line to the unsuspecting pen man. 'Vessels of extraordinary size and length were being ordered, in comparison with which the *Olympic* was a mere flea bite, and the name of the largest…was given as the *Gigantic*.' It was all a gigantic joke![3]

On 30 May 1912, Ismay, Imrie & Co., the White Star Line's management company, wrote to the Board of Trade and requested that the name *Britannic* be reserved for them.[4] The application for the use of the name was renewed after one year on 1 June 1913 and confirmed when 'Yard Number 433' was launched.

It is difficult to come to a definitive conclusion as to where the name *Gigantic* came from. Certainly, it was a pretentious name, but the same could be said of *Titanic*. It is certainly possible to consider that it had been discussed at an earlier stage, since it was very much in keeping with the theme of her sister ships' names, but then the new ship was not formally ordered until June 1911. It may be that she remained without an official name until *Britannic* was reserved at the end of May 1912. Edward Wilding stated that 'there is no name for twelve months' with some new ships being referred to by their yard number only, even though this had not been the case for *Olympic* and *Titanic*. In February 1912, Messrs Noah Hingley & Sons' chain and anchor order book contained reference to the ship, giving her name as *Gigantic* to accompany the order for her enormous anchor outfit. (The name was even used in November 1913.) However, Harland & Wolff's own order book contains only the name *Britannic*. The initial specifications had clearly been written before the amendments of October 1911 and January 1912 – before the keel was even laid – and there is no evidence that the name had then been altered.

Britannic was a sound choice and the *Belfast News-Letter* explained:

> It was a happy thought which induced the owners to adopt *Britannic* as the name of the new vessel, for that appellation was also applied to one of the earliest ships acquired by the White Star company. The first *Britannic*…was employed until the year 1901 [sic] and it is to be hoped that the second vessel to bear that honourable name will have an equally lengthy and prosperous career. The new *Britannic* is a twentieth century ship in every sense of the word, and in her machinery and fittings the builders are employing the latest scientific devices…

Harland & Wolff's builder's model of *Britannic*, photographed two months after the ship's launch, shows her profile. She appears radically different from how she was originally conceived, with the new lifeboat arrangements and deck features. (Photograph reproduced courtesy the Trustees of National Museums Northern Ireland)

The first *Britannic* had sailed on her maiden voyage from Liverpool to New York on 25 June 1874 and during her lifetime she made 271 round trips. She was destined to steam 2,232,999 miles, consuming 626,000 tons of coal, and carrying 112,711 first-class passengers with 282,685 third-class passengers. Her popularity 'was unexcelled by that of any of the renowned liners of her day'. In 1903 she was scrapped, having been in service for twenty-nine years; it had been specified by the line that the ship be broken-up, rather than continue service as a less prosperous vessel.

Her successor's name was now public knowledge and when construction resumed the influence of the *Titanic* disaster would become evident. Harland & Wolff had an added advantage with *Britannic* in that she was still under construction, so they were able to make the extensive changes to her watertight subdivision without much of the inconvenience associated with the changes to *Olympic*.

The changes were very much in keeping with those *Olympic* underwent. Five of the watertight bulkheads were extended to B-deck and their stiffening increased commensurate with their greater height; a new watertight bulkhead was fitted, dividing the electric engine room into two compartments; and a new inner (or 'double') skin extended for the length of the boiler and machinery compartments for the majority of the ship's length amidships. Several of the bulkheads towards the stern that were originally intended to reach D-deck were now only watertight to E-deck. Even if the first six compartments were completely flooded, it was expected that the ship would remain afloat, and modifications to the ship's hatchways and entrances were enacted because they would then have been below the ship's forward waterline in that condition. Taken together, the ship would be able to float in a number of situations with six watertight compartments flooded, while the inner skin was intended to contain flooding if the outer hull was pierced.

Britannic would have differed from her older sisters in some interesting respects even if *Titanic* had not been lost. Certainly, the disaster resulted in a marked change to her watertight subdivision, but there were other far smaller changes to which less attention was paid. As usual with a series of sister ships, Harland & Wolff had the advantage of practical experience gained in operation of the first two to further improve the design of the third. Although *Olympic*'s arrangement of two expansion joints proved generally satisfactory in protecting the superstructure from the stresses borne by the structural hull beneath, by March 1912 the shipbuilder was aware that the configuration could be improved further and it was decided to increase the number of expansion joints on *Britannic*.[5] As well as three expansion joints in the superstructure, which included an additional one amidships and the relocation of the after expansion joint, another one was needed further aft as a result of the enclosure of the ship's aft well deck.★ New requirements from the Board of Trade as to the access of third-class passengers to the upper decks would have impacted on her design in any case. These had not been in force when *Olympic* and *Titanic* were under construction and they caused some concern for Cunard in regard to *Aquitania*, even before the disaster. The company did not want their new liner to be placed at a competitive disadvantage from the new regulations. There were some necessary changes to *Britannic* as a result of the plans for a new system of lifeboat davits, which would concentrate weight and required strategic reinforcements to be included at the relevant locations throughout the superstructure.

All these technical details could easily be overlooked and the company's objective was to focus public attention on the new ship's extensive safety features. They published a detailed description of the ship, portraying the ship's strength and safety features as something that the travelling public could have absolute confidence in:

> The new vessel is about 900ft long and 50,000 tons gross register; and in general features will be similar to the *Olympic*, with various improvements introduced as a result of the experience gained in that vessel, which has proved so popular in service. Both in design and workmanship the element of strength has been kept steadily in view, and the most approved structural arrangements suggested by the latest experience have been adopted. From keel to truck the *Britannic* will be as perfect as the human brain, the highest skill, and the most powerful appliances can make a vessel. The double bottom extending the whole length of the vessel, the massive beams and close framing, the large shell plates, the steel decks, the double skin and watertight bulkheads, combine to make a structure of exceptional strength and rigidity. The hydrau-

---

★ *Olympic* encountered a severe North Atlantic storm, which was one of the worst Captain Smith had ever experienced, in January 1912. Her number 1 hatch cover, which weighed several tons, was ripped off and deck fittings damaged. As a result of observations during the passage, Harland & Wolff decided to make some changes to *Titanic*: along the side of boiler room 6 and further ahead, they fitted a one-inch-thick steel 'strap' over the landings at the upper turn of the bilge; and along the side of the turbine engine room and into the reciprocating engine room, they did the same, as well as drilling additional rivet holes above the landing in order to make it a quadruple-riveted joint. *Olympic*'s great length meant that the stresses at these points – about a quarter of her length ahead of the stern and abaft the bow – required some additional reinforcement, beyond what previous experience had suggested was necessary, to prevent rivets in these areas becoming gradually slack in severe weather conditions. *Olympic* had also been modified by May 1912 and *Britannic* would have incorporated similar improvements. Additional riveting was then seen in these areas on liners such as *Aquitania* and *Bismarck/Majestic*. It was an example of practical experience supplementing theoretical knowledge. (This information was first published in my online article, 'Olympic and Titanic: "Straps" and Other Changes' for the *Titanic* Research & Modelling Association [TRMA] website in summer 2005.)

lic riveting in the vessel is also an important factor, the whole of the shell plating up to the turn of the bilge being riveted by hydraulic power, and an immense amount of the riveting having been carried out in other parts of the vessel – shell, top sides, decks, stringers, etc. the rivets were closed by means of the powerful seven-ton riveting machines suspended from the travelling frames on the gantry; and, while making the sound, tight connection so essential in this mighty hull, it will be seen that the rivets studding the shell plating present a pleasing and symmetrical appearance.

Exceptional interest having been taken in the inner skin of this vessel and the *Olympic*, it may be well to state that the inner skin consists of heavy plating, well stiffened, extending for more than half the length of the vessel, from the watertight bulkhead in front of the forward boiler room to the after end of the turbine engine room, and being strongly connected by longitudinal plates and angles and specifically strong connections at bulkheads and watertight divisions. This reinforced structure also extends from the tank top, i.e., from the top of the double bottom, to above the middle, or F-deck, and the watertight bulkheads are carried right up to the Bridge deck. The strength and safety afforded by this method of construction will be easily appreciated when it is mentioned that the *Britannic*, like the *Olympic*, in which the inner skin and similar watertight divisions were introduced, besides having this extra protection against serious damage, will be able to float with *any six watertight compartments* flooded. The White Star Line and the builders believe that by this means they have solved the problem of carrying the passengers in these large and popular leviathans in absolute safety, as far as it is possible for human ingenuity to do so...

The passenger accommodation in the *Britannic* will be of a generally similar character to that so much admired in the *Olympic*, and naturally, the *Britannic* being a larger ship, still greater facilities for passengers are provided, such as additional private baths etc., there will be accommodation for over 2,500 passengers in all, besides a crew of 950. As some indication of the extent of the accommodation in this vessel, it may be remarked that there will be over 2,000 sidelights and windows in the ship. Full advantage is being taken of the enormous size and spaciousness of the vessel in the arrangement of both public rooms and private cabins; and the entrances, the magnificent staircases, promenades, and other features will leave nothing to be desired... Special suite rooms and an unusually large number of private baths will be the distinguishing features of the first-class stateroom accommodation. The second-class staterooms are large and comfortably furnished, and the third-class passengers will have a large number of enclosed berths, including two berth rooms...

An important feature will be the arrangements for handling the boats. The vessel is fitted with the latest and most approved type of electrically driven boat-lowering gear, by means of which a very large number of boats can, one after the other, be put over the side of the vessel and lowered to the waterline in much less time than was possible under the old system of davits. One of the advantages of the new system is that the passengers take their places in the boats expeditiously and with perfect safety before the boats are lifted from the deck of the vessel, and the gear is so constructed that the fully laden boats are lowered at a very considerable distance from the side of the ship, thus minimising risk in bad weather. Moreover, the whole of the boats on board can be lowered on either side of the vessel, whichever side happens to be clear, and the gear has been kept so far inboard as to give a wide passage at either

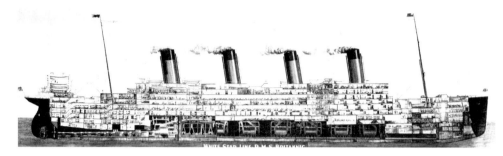

The plans for *Britannic*'s vast interiors are displayed in this cutaway. (Photograph reproduced courtesy the Trustees of National Museums Northern Ireland)

side of the ship for promenading, and for marshalling the passengers in case of emergency.

The following are also connected to the emergency circuit by means of change-over switches: – Five arc lamps, seven cargo and gangway lanterns, wireless apparatus, boat davits, mast, side, and stern lights, and all lights on bridge, including those for navigating and chart rooms, wheelhouse, telegraphs, compasses, and Morse signalling lanterns.

It will thus be seen how perfect and complete are the arrangements provided against any possible contingency.

Great and far reaching developments have taken place in the application of electricity to various purposes during recent years, and the installation in the *Britannic* will be probably the largest and most comprehensive yet placed on board ship. In addition to the lighting of the immense vessel from stem to stern, above and below, there will be lifting gear in the engine room, electrically controlled watertight doors, emergency sets, the electric heating and motive power for the fans, electric winches, boat-lowering gear, gymnastic apparatus, etc., etc.

In connection with the lighting it is interesting to note that on the Promenade deck special lamps are provided for the convenience of passengers in arranging dancing parties.

The arrangements for working the ship and cargo, the anchor gear, cranes, winches, and navigating appliances, are of the latest and most approved type, and specially arranged in view of the size of the vessel.

The post office and baggage accommodation will be arranged in the most suitable position for expediting the reception and despatch of the mails on the departure and arrival of the ship.

The refrigerating installation is of the best type, and fully adequate to all the requirements on board the vessel.

As already indicated, the *Britannic* is a triple-screw steamer, having a combination of reciprocating engines with a low-pressure turbine. By which two main objects are attained – the greatest comfort ensured to passengers by the smooth working of the ship, and, from an engineering standpoint, the utmost economy in the utilisation of the steam...

Generally, the *Britannic*, in design, construction, and appointments, represents the highest excellence, and passengers are assured the greatest comfort. The most expert knowledge, varied experience, and technical skill have combined to produce a vessel worthy of the name she bears, as representative of great twin industries, Shipping and Shipbuilding. The spacious entrances, public rooms, staterooms, promenades, facilities for recreation, unusually generous private bathrooms and lavatory accommodation, unfail-

An artist's impression of *Britannic*'s magnificent first-class grand staircase. The organ would have been accessed through the door at the foot of the stairs. (Photograph reproduced courtesy the Trustees of National Museums Northern Ireland)

ing supply throughout the passenger spaces of cool or warm air according to the season, by means of the exceptionally powerful appliances for mechanical ventilation, and other arrangements, added to the well-known excellence of the table and efficiency of the service, ensure the utmost comfort and enjoyment of the latest White Star leviathan.

Britannic's accommodation would be improved considerably, as the White Star Line observed increasing competition from Cunard, whose new *Aquitania* would be in service by the summer of 1914, and a great German rival. Albert Ballin, the Hamburg-Amerika Line's (HAPAG) managing director, had conceived a trio of monster liners of 50,000 tons. The 909ft *Imperator* was the first of his trio, and was launched in May 1912. Planned originally to accommodate 700 first-, 600 second-, 940 third- and a staggering 1,750 'fourth-class' passengers, she carried well over 5,000 people. Her first-class accommodation included a social hall, winter garden, Ritz-Carlton restaurant, veranda café, smoke room, ladies' saloon, reading and writing room, dining saloon, gymnasium, Turkish bath and swimming pool. Second class had a smoke room, drawing room, dining saloon and gymnasium. Although Ballin had planned an enormous emigrant 'village', the third-class dining room with its bolted benches, crammed-in long tables and slanting bulkheads – a result of it being in the ship's bow – was a throwback to an earlier time when compared with *Imperator*'s competitors. Nevertheless, by 1914 *Vaterland* even had stewards in the dining room, a laundry and band for her emigrant passengers. Frahm's anti-rolling tanks had been fitted to the new vessel, but 'as first completed by the builders the vessel did not prove satisfactory in regard to stability'; however, even with modifications she would earn the nickname 'Limperator'. On her maiden voyage *Imperator* was observed to be listing[6] and she was soon noted for her heavy-rolling motions.[7] Four Parsons steam turbines driving quadruple 16½ft screws were designed to produce 60,000hp, a predicted speed in service of some 22 or 22½ knots, and as things turned-out the engines performed admirably.

Vaterland, second of Ballin's class, similar to her older sister, was launched in April 1913. She accommodated slightly more people, owing to the 2,000 gross ton size increase; additionally, she was 950ft long and 2ft wider with a 100ft beam. She was also faster than her sister.

Bismarck was launched on 20 June 1914, as 'an improved and enlarged sister-ship', of 56,000grt, with accommodation to be 'practically identical'. But she would never serve Hamburg-Amerika.[8]

Starting on the *Britannic*'s boat deck, a large children's playroom was built on the port side of the second funnel casing, opposite the gymnasium on the starboard side of the funnel. The additional lifeboats did not take up as much space on the boat deck as they might have done, had it not been for the new 'girder'-type davits that could hold up to six lifeboats each. It was intended that one of these davit stations would be on either side of the officers' quarters; two stations on each side of the ship near the fourth funnel; and another station on each side of the ship near the stern. Although changes to the number of lifeboats appear to have been made throughout the design process, by the time of the ship's launch all the nautical journals were in agreement that *Britannic* was to be fitted with a total of forty-eight lifeboats, many of them the largest yet fitted on a ship.

Two of the 34ft-long boats were motor boats, built by Maynard on subcontract from John I. Thornycroft & Co.★ (Thornycroft Yard Nos 766 and 767) and were on board the ship late in August 1915, after receiving builder's trials on the River

Thames.[9] A single three-bladed propeller drove each motor boat.[10] Originally it had been planned that the two motor boats would both be situated on the large davit stations near the bridge: one on the port davit station and the other on the starboard. However, when the ship entered service, only the starboard davit station was fitted near the bridge; the two boats were therefore fitted on the aft sets of the four aft davit stations at the fourth funnel: one on the port side and the other motorboat to the starboard davit station, on the outboard 'stack' of boats. This distributed them evenly, which would not have been possible at the originally planned stations owing to the port davit station being omitted.

Contemporary press reports described the working of the new davits thus:

> The davits will be inclined inboard or outboard by means of powerful screw gear. From the stem of each davit there will extend inboard a built-up stay, the inner end of which will be secured to a nut mounted on a worm shaft on the deck. By electric motor the two worms for each pair of davits will be rotated, and as the worm screw rotates the nut will travel along it, and acting through a stay push the two davits from the vertical to a considerable angle outboard. The reverse travel of the two nuts on the worm will pull the davit from the vertical to a considerable angle inboard in order to lift the boats from their chocks on the decks. The height and outreach of the davit will enable the boats to be mounted one over the other in tiers, and will also facilitate the placing of several tiers in the width of the ship... Limit switches will be provided, so that in the event of any accident to...the man manipulating the gear, the motion of the davits or boats will be arrested before any damage will take place, thus making the gear practically mistake-proof.

Yet another advantage was that the forward and after falls were wound on separate shafts, and although they normally operated in unison, they could operate separately to keep the lifeboats on an even keel if the ship was down by the bow or stern.

Between the bridge and the wireless room was another safety feature – a pneumatic tube – which allowed communication between the two without the wireless operator leaving his post or any of the officers leaving the bridge. Pneumatic tube also linked the wireless room and the pursers' office, on the C-deck landing of the forward first-class grand staircase, so that any incoming messages that were received could be sent down to the purser and then distributed to the addressee without the wireless operator leaving his post. Messages left at the pursers' office by passengers for transmission could also be sent to the wireless room via pneumatic tube. (Despite the high prices to pay for sending such 'wires', many passengers would be prepared to pay for the privilege.)

There were improvements and changes on the promenade deck immediately below. Like *Titanic*, *Britannic*'s forward promenade was enclosed by a screen housing a number of large glass windows, which was similar in design. Inside, nearly all of the first-class staterooms enjoyed their own private bathrooms, which was a luxury not seen on *Olympic*

★ Thornycroft also constructed two motor boats for the *Aquitania*: 30ft in length, they bore Yard Numbers 731 and 732 and were fitted onto the ship late in May 1914. In fact *Aquitania* was equipped with a variety of boats: these two motor boats, some canvas-sided collapsible boats and clinker-built lifeboats. The motor boats were later replaced, in the 1920s, with some smaller 28ft motor boats. (National Maritime Museum, Greenwich. 'Historic Photograph Record: Aquitania (Br.)...1914.')

Britannic's first-class swimming pool was vastly improved compared to those on board her sisters. The ship's side plating and other metalwork were hidden behind the new scheme of decoration. It is probable that it was in response to the grand pools on board new German liners such as *Imperator*, which was two decks high and featured Pompeian columns. (Photograph reproduced courtesy the Trustees of National Museums Northern Ireland)

and *Titanic*. A number of additional staterooms were installed between the grand staircase and the reading and writing room, while further aft there were changes to the first-class smoke room. On the starboard side, the smoke room was slightly smaller than that on her sister ships because of the addition of the new accumulator room on the starboard side of the fourth funnel casing. It contained emergency batteries and generators which would supply the emergency circuit if needed. However, it was still a good size and its arrangement also differed because it had two rectangular bay windows rather than the arrangement on her sisters. The smoke room had the added attraction of a large dome over its centre portion, reviving a proposal that had been envisaged for *Olympic* and *Titanic* when one of the builder's initial design concepts was submitted for approval in July 1908. Unlike the familiar stained glass panels, which had also featured on earlier White Star lines such as *Adriatic* and *Megantic*, *Britannic*'s smoke room décor took a different approach. The surviving artist's impression shows a magnificent room, 'panelled in cedar of Lebanon with lime tree carvings after Grinling Gibbons', and apparently inspired by one of the state apartments in Hampton Court.★ The two veranda cafés followed the configuration of *Olympic* and *Titanic*, although they saw a number of improvements to their pantry facilities.

★ Although claimed at one time to have been 'a reproduction of one of the state apartments in Hampton Court', it is not an evident match for any of the rooms.

Far aft, the 'shade deck' marked the top of the new deckhouse at the stern, above the third-class accommodation, and housed the aft docking bridge and two 'girder' davit stations. It was accessible from their own accommodation without having to make the journey to the boat deck itself.

The deck altered the most was probably B-deck, the lowest non-continuous deck level. There was a promenade forward of the main grand staircase, and a bank of cabins – the majority of which had got private en-suite bath facilities. This promenade was enclosed by windows the same as those that were enclosing the forward end of A-deck, although doors led out onto an open promenade right at B-deck's forward end. Two 'millionaire suites' were available for passengers – these were the best accommodation on board. One suite, the suite foremost on the port side aft of the grand staircase, had a promenade, sitting room, two bedrooms, a bathroom and toilet, and two wardrobe rooms. The suite forward on the starboard side had two larger bedrooms, a large lounge/veranda, servant's room and a saloon and pantry. Each bedroom had its own bathroom, wardrobe room and toilet down a private passageway as well as access to the saloon and lounge/Veranda. These were described in much detail in the 'Specification Book':

> The suite on the port side to consist of two bedrooms and a sitting room, with lavatory accommodation and wardrobe rooms arranged between the bedrooms; the sitting room being at the fore end of the suite next [to the] first-class entrance. The after bedroom to be decorated by Harland & Wolff, the walls being oak panelled and the furniture of oak in the French style; this room to contain two cot beds one 6ft 9in by 2ft 9in and one 6ft 6in by 4ft 3in; a settee with an oval table in front; a two-basin washstand; a 3ft dressing table with chair; and an electric heater; the floor to be laid with blue carpet. The forward bedroom to have two brass cot beds of the same size as above, the other articles of furniture being as enumerated for the after bedroom, but the decoration of the room and style of the furniture to be to approval by A. Heaton & Co. The sitting room by A. Heaton & Co. to have round table in the centre of the room, with two armchairs and two ordinary chairs, a sideboard, a cabinet, a corner writing table with chair, two other lounge chairs, a fireplace and an octagonal coffee stool; the panelling, decoration and style of furniture to be to approval. The lavatory accommodation to consist of a bathroom and WC; the bathroom containing bath and shower, an open washbasin, a hinged grating seat and an electric heater. The floor of the bathroom, WC and communicating corridor between the bathrooms to be laid with lino tiles. A wardrobe room for each bedroom to be arranged with hat and coat hooks and suitable chest of drawers.
>
> ...Suite on the starboard side to consist of two sets of rooms each compromising bedroom, wardrobe room, bathroom and WC. Each set to be separately entered from the fore and aft passageway through a vestibule and private athwartship. Between the two sets of rooms a saloon and veranda to be arranged each communicating with the bedroom of either set of rooms. The saloon to have a small pantry at the fore end, and a servant's bedroom to be arranged adjacent to the forward set of rooms, with an entrance from the main fore and aft passageway. Each bedroom to have cot beds, one 4ft 6in and one 2ft 6in wide; a settee with small round table in front; an arm chair, writing table and chair; a combined dressing table and wash stand, with chair; an electric heater. The saloon to have round table in the centre constructed as to extend for the accommodation of four persons; four chairs to be supplied for the dining table; a sofa bed; four arm chairs; a corner writing

table and chairs; a small square table and chair; a sideboard and fireplace. Bathrooms to contain bath and shower; wash basin and hinged seat.

The veranda to have three settees with small square tables in front, two round backed chairs, two arm chairs, and two small round tables.

The servants' rooms to be finished in dark mahogany and fitted with bed having Pullman over, sofa, wardrobe, folding lavatory, electric heater and a red carpet.[11]

There were also suites aft of this that could be interconnected to form suites of any size – each had two bedrooms, a servant's room, wardrobe room, and bathroom and toilet, as on the previous sisters. Other additions on this deck were a gents' barber shop, ladies' barber shop, and an extra elevator that ran down to E-deck; this made a total of four elevators in first class and one elevator in second class. In fact, the ladies' barber shop was the first seen in an Atlantic liner.

The *Titanic*'s *à la carte* restaurant had been larger than *Olympic*'s, and *Britannic*'s restaurant was even larger than that, plus there was a separate large reception room that was entered by double doors leading to the B-deck landing of the aft grand staircase. Doors led from the reception room into the restaurant. Owing to the restaurant's increased size, there was a much larger galley, larger storage rooms, plus a cold room and wine storage rooms. There was a cash office because passengers using this restaurant had to pay extra; this was off the galley on the port side, near the storage rooms.

No Café Parisien was included on the starboard side, as there was no room now that the restaurant had been enlarged and a reception room added. It might have been possible to move the café forward, although this would have sacrificed first-class suites.

This 'sidewalk' café feature had proved so popular on *Olympic*, but it seems that a similar area for *Britannic* might have been planned elsewhere. In March 1914, *The Shipbuilder* reported: 'On the promenade deck,…a feature of the vessel is that the plating is carried up the side to enable either a winter garden to be arranged or a sheltered promenade with a complete view of the sea.'[12] Although no such area appears on plans of the ship before that date, it may have been a later decision like the glass enclosure of *Titanic*'s forward A-deck promenade and her new B-deck amenities in 1911. Similar amenities were appearing on *Aquitania* – two 'garden lounges' on her first-class promenade deck – while *Imperator* had a winter garden on her upper promenade deck like her sister *Vaterland*. Those vessels also had veranda cafés, which were becoming a standard feature aboard the Atlantic liners. For such an area on *Britannic*, the most convenient location would have been the starboard after end of the enclosed A-deck promenade; near the lounge, corridor and pantry, not to mention the forward grand staircase, but well away from the A-deck staterooms. The presence of a bulkhead at this end of the promenade when the ship was finally completed, but with no bulkhead on the port side, would seem to support this location and feature. It did not have any windows or a door, but this could easily be explained by the hurry to get the ship into service, including some of the first-class lounge windows which were not cut. Indeed, the installation of such a feature would be quite possible.[13]

Aft of the restaurant was the second-class staircase and smoking room, with an open promenade that was larger owing to an extra roof over the aft well deck which I shall describe later. Over the larger poop deck was a deckhouse containing the third-class smoking room, and the main third-class stairway led up to the smoke room. Another staircase led up to the 'shade deck' above.

The first-class smoke room was changed radically from that on board *Olympic* and *Titanic*. It appears to have been inspired by one of the apartments at Hampton Court and was panelled in Cedar of Lebanon. (Photograph reproduced courtesy the Trustees of National Museums Northern Ireland)

On C-deck level, the uppermost continuous deck, there were not as many changes as were made to the decks above. Like on the decks above, however, there were many extra private baths for the first-class staterooms; also there were larger and more luxurious suites that could be interconnected. Four of these were similar to the port side 'millionaire's suite' on B-deck, in the sense that they had the same rooms and similar accommodation, although these were all without promenades. The maids' and valets' dining saloon was relocated to D-deck, near the galleys. Aft of the first-class accommodation were the second-class main stairway and the second-class lounge/library; there was also a promenade enclosed by square glass windows that had gangways for the passengers' boarding. The smaller second-class stair-well was situated aft of the library, and to add to the facilities, a second-class gymnasium was fitted. The promenade for the second-class passengers was cut off from the third-class prom-enade (under the now-enclosed well deck) by the new extra watertight bulkhead dividing the electric engine room, which came up to this level, although watertight doors could be opened if necessary. Third-class accommodation aft of the promenade space on the enclosed well deck consisted of the general room, and main entrance; the new larger hospital took up the space where the smoking room had previously been (the smoking room was now on top of the poop deck). Forward, where the forward well deck was, four staircases led from third-class accommodation in the bow to give these passengers better access to the decks. The foremost watertight bulkhead penetrated the seamen's quarters and another watertight bulkhead made-up the division between the interior first-class accommodation and the open well deck. Forward of the grand staircase, another watertight bulkhead was situated, with watertight doors allowing access to the foremost first-class C-deck cabins. The watertight bulkhead that separated boiler room 1 and the main engine room separated the aft grand staircase and first-class accommodation, although there were many doors allowing for easy access.

On D-deck, the second most continuous deck, forward, the foremost 'collision' watertight bulkhead penetrated the firemen's quarters and there were extra third-class cabins in the third-class area here as well as the open third-class space. The third bulkhead from the bow separated the third-class and first-class accommodation forward, and the first-class staterooms had many extra en-suite facilities. The first-class reception room was entered from the grand staircase, and doors led into the first-class dining saloon. The galleys were situated aft of the saloon; these also served the second-class saloon, directly aft of the galleys – the galleys alone were the size of the first-class saloon. The second-class accommodation was aft of their saloon, and this second-class space could also become third class alternatively depending on differing passenger numbers on each voyage; third-class accommodation was at the very stern.

The third most continuous deck, E-deck, contained crew, first-class, second-class, and third-class accommodation. Forward were the firemen's quarters, pierced by the forward 'collision' bulkhead, then the second bulkhead from the bow divided the firemen's quarters from the further aft seamen's quarters. The third bulkhead divided the first-class accommodation and the crew quarters, although there were watertight doors so that crew could move around easily. A wide companionway that ran for three-quarters the length of this deck was on the port side, and was lined with crew accommodation; on the starboard side first-class accommodation prevailed. The watertight bulkhead separating boiler room 1 and the main engine room pierced this deck, dividing the forward first-class accommodation from the second-class accommodation. The bulkhead that divided the electric engine room separated the second-class accommodation from the third-class areas at the very stern of this deck. The extra elevator that ran from B-deck stopped at this deck, opening onto the first-class corridor on the starboard side; the elevators on the grand staircase forward also stopped at this level. First-class accommodation along the starboard side's companionway was alternative second or first class; this was the cheapest first-class accommodation or the best second-class. It partly accounted for the *Britannic's* larger second-class capacity, some of the staterooms here having private baths.

On the port side of the reciprocating engine's casing, just off the main companionway, the engineers' accommodation was improved: there was a separate passageway lined with their cabins and a larger mess room and lavatories were fitted.

Many additional small stairways were fitted in the third-class accommodation aft to make it much easier to get to the third-class main stairway that led up to the aft boats. Other small modifications were made to the second-class accommodation on this deck as well, including a second-class barber shop and the relocation of the Pursers' Office for second class.

All of the seventeen watertight bulkheads pierced F-deck, which, briefly described, contained crew accommodation forward, then third-class births, the first-class squash court and swimming pool, and an enlarged Turkish bath establishment. Working aft, the third-class dining saloon was the whole width of the ship amidships, and there were the galleys and some stewards' accommodation further aft. The reciprocating engine casings took up space next, then the turbine engine casing, there was then the cheaper second-class accommodation and some third-class staterooms, plus some interchangeable accommodation that was either second or third class.

G-deck contained much less accommodation than the deck above, being pierced by the boiler casings from the six boiler rooms, the casings of the reciprocating engines and turbine engine, and the coalbunkers. The double skin went through this deck, up to F-deck's underside. This deck was also pierced by all of the watertight bulkheads. Far forward, there were some firemen's quarters; then some portable third-class cabins that could become cargo areas if desired; then there were the boiler and engine room casings, and refrigerated storage rooms and other space for food. Aft of this was a fair

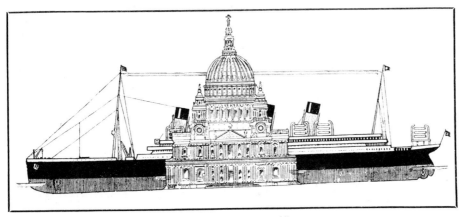

" SEEING IS BELIEVING ! "

St. Paul's Cathedral compared with the *Britannic*.

One of many interesting attempts to demonstrate the size of the '*Olympic*' class ships, *Britannic* is depicted in contrast to St Paul's Cathedral. (*Railway & Travel Monthly*, 1914/Author's collection)

amount of second-class accommodation that was interchangeable and could become third-class areas.

Britannic's twenty-four double-ended boilers, which had been increased in length by one foot compared to her sisters, contributed to an increase in the total heating surface from 144,142sq.ft on *Olympic* to 150,958sq.ft. The reciprocating engines were the same physical size, but they incorporated some further refinements and were intended to be more powerful. They produced 16,000hp while driving the wing propellers at 77rpm and the turbine would produce around 18,500hp at 169rpm. The additional power was achieved by the use of piston valves in all cylinders, whereas on *Olympic* the low-pressure cylinders had flat slide valves. When the steam was exhausted into the turbine, it was at a higher pressure of 10psi instead of 9psi. *Britannic*'s turbine was larger and heavier, with its weight increased from 420 to 490 tons, and it was undoubtedly a proud boast that it had been built by Harland & Wolff, whereas the turbines for her sister ships had been sub-contracted to John Brown & Co. on the Clyde. While running at full speed, the engines could produce substantial additional power, and there was little doubt that *Britannic* had the capability to maintain a service speed of 21 knots with ample reserve to enable her to make up for delays experienced on the hostile North Atlantic.[14]

History would dictate that *Britannic*'s 'hybrid' propulsion system – two reciprocating engines exhausting steam into a turbine – would soon be phased out as marine engineering advanced rapidly, particularly with regard to turbines. 'Overall, the plant was engineering on a massive scale, but the balance was precise and the performance unequalled by any ship afloat.'[15]

Numerous more tangible changes would be noticeable to passengers and crew. 'Instead of an enormous number of soil discharge pipes from lavatories, etc., on each side of the ship, the arrangement simulates in each compartment the conditions applicable to the best town planning system, with the assistance of electric pumps', it was reported.

The enormous number of private bathrooms was a feature further advanced by the improved plumbing, which had 'had special consideration'. In 1913 *Olympic* was equipped with almost fifty private bathrooms (with WCs); in 1914 *Aquitania* had seventy-one and *Vaterland* had 136; yet *Britannic*'s early design included 201 private facilities (including a small minority of private shower rooms without a WC, plus private WCs without a shower or bath). Contemporary sources stated of the new plumbing: '...the system adopted is such that immediately a tap is turned on hot water will be obtainable, instead of a large quantity of cold water preceding the flow of warm water. Thus there will be a great saving in the fresh water supply – an important consideration on board ship where any shortage must be made-up by distilling.'

As with the *Olympic,* every first-class room had an electric fan, and public rooms were certainly well-ventilated, but the ventilation was further improved. 'The dominant idea,' it was publicised, 'is to extract foul air from the interior and to pass fresh air – which may be heated in the winter time – through trunks along the side of the ship on each deck, having louvres at various points; there will be as many as 1,500 such louvres in the vessel.' In fact, the trunking was even sectioned to specially avoid the watertight bulkheads, further enhancing the hull's magnificent watertight integrity.

Although the use of electricity was not notably expanded from the *Olympic,* it was proudly stated that it was used 'down even to electric machines for clothes pressing and for heating the tongs in the staterooms, and in the ladies' hair dressing department...a new feature in Atlantic ships.'

Improvements particularly notable were made to the bridge, mostly with regard to outfitting but also to equipment. 'An interesting feature of the ship will be the complete control which the captain exercises,' over the ship from the bridge, it was said:

> From there orders can be given by telephone or telegraph to every working quarter of the ship, and instruments will be provided to demonstrate that most of the important orders have been carried out. Thus there will be an indicator to show the working of the main engines, the operation of the steering machinery, and the actual position of the bulkhead doors, the arrangement in this case being such that the progress in opening or closing the door will be automatically shown... The angle of the rudder will be electronically recorded, and the depth of the ocean sounded by electric machinery,

The *Railway & Travel Monthly* published an interesting view of *Britannic*'s construction, taken in October 1913. (*Railway & Travel Monthly*, 1914/Author's collection)

while electric submarine bells will indicate the proximity of lightships, etc., The look-out will have telephonic communication with the bridge, and the steering will be done through telemotor gearing direct. Telegraphs will indicate the necessary instructions to the men in charge of the anchors and capstans…

Britannic was to be equipped with no fewer than five anchors: 'one 11-ton and one 9-ton bower anchor of the "Dreadnought" stockless type, a 16-ton Hall's patent stockless anchor, a "Stream" anchor of 1 ton, and a Kedge anchor of ½-ton.'[16]

Her compass arrangement remained similar. Above the first-class lounge's raised roof was a compass platform where one Kelvin standard compass was situated 12ft above any iron or steel. This compass had an azimuth mirror on the platform, which was 78ft above the waterline. 'Compass number two' was a Kelvin standard steering compass inside the wheelhouse; a third compass was further forward on the bridge. One light card compass was supplied for the after docking bridge. This was identical to the compass arrangement on *Britannic*'s older sisters, but there was an additional compass situated on top of the bridge's roof, forward, which was indicated on the vessel's deck plans. In wartime, it may have housed a Morse lamp, or perhaps remained a compass, in addition to the single Morse lamps on the port and starboard bridge wing cabs.

Slightly aft of the bridge, around number one funnel, the vents and fans there were considerably different to those of the earlier two vessels. Owing to the new arrangement of 'girder' davits, it seems, the 'Sirocco' fans – made by Messrs Davidson & Co., of Belfast – were changed in terms of their layout, as shown by the builder's model.

By the time *Britannic* was ready for launching, the White Star Line had a firmer timescale in mind for when she would join their express service. Her hull was fully framed by 27 February 1913, then fully plated by 20 September 1913 and the launch date could be set for 26 February 1914. This was later than some people had expected. On 7 May 1912, the *New York Times* had reported that 'in view of the loss of [*Titanic*], the work of completing this new vessel will be accelerated. Every available man in the Queen's Island works is engaged in order to have the liner finished as soon as possible. It will be over a year before the new ship will be completed…' By month's end, the same paper reported that the White Star Line expected *Britannic* to be in service by autumn 1913, but that would have necessitated completing the ship and fitting her out less than two years after her keel had been laid. In August 1912, IMM's Phillip Franklin indicated that 'work was being pushed steadily forward on the new big liner *Britannic*, which was to replace the *Titanic*, and was expected to be ready for service in the beginning of 1914.' An estimate in May 1913 that she would be ready for launching in November 1913 proved optimistic.[17] However, the impression that her construction was beset by ongoing delays seems rather unfair, since from the laying of her keel to the day of her launch *Britannic* was completed at about the same rate as *Titanic*'s construction had proceeded. Now that she was ready, the company's publicity machine could get into gear. *Britannic* was hailed as 'as perfect a specimen of man's creative power as it is possible to conceive', and her launching '…may be claimed as an event of international importance'.

Perhaps the only unsatisfactory aspect of the launching was the weather; dull and drizzly, as seen from contemporary photographs.[18] Although *Olympic*'s hull had been painted white when she was launched, to aid photography, *Titanic*'s had been painted black.[19] *Britannic*'s hull had been painted grey, but had red anti-fouling paint at the waterline and below, like on the two earlier vessels.

Lord Pirrie was at the shipyard very early, at 5.00 a.m., ensuring preparations were completed. Indeed, a lot of work was necessary to ensure the launching's success. The 772ft-long sliding way was lubricated with in excess of 20 tons of soap, mixed tallow and oil: 15 tons of tallow were used, and more than 7 tons of mixed tallow and train oil plus soft soap. To halt a hull of this huge size after the launch required two piles of cable drags, each with over 80 tons of cable drags, attached to the hull using eye plates riveted onto the hull and thick hawsers, and three anchors in the river bed on each side of the ship, varying in weight from 5½ to 8 tons, connected with wire hawsers to the hull plating.

London journalists had left Euston aboard a special train at 5.50 p.m. the day before, reaching Liverpool at 9.25 p.m. There, at the Princes' Dock, they boarded the Belfast Steamship Company's SS *Patriotic*, specially chartered for the occasion, which arrived in Belfast on the morning of the launch.

In honour of the launching, the day was a public holiday, and, as the *Daily Telegraph* put it, 'Belfast is en Fête.' It was indeed.[20]

'From early morning spectators from across the Irish Sea and the surrounding districts of Belfast had been converging on the great shipyard, and by 11 a.m. not only was all the space in the yard completely filled, but there were many thousands of people on the opposite side of the river…in every place from which a view of the launch could be obtained'.

Long standing White Star tradition was not for any formal 'champagne bottle breaking' over the bows, but simply a row of signal flags on the gantry, spelling out the word 'Success', and the White Star Line pennant, with the American flag and the British Union Jack also flying.[21] Later recalling *Britannic*'s launch, a retired shipyard worker simply said, 'They builds 'em and chucks 'em in.'[22]

When entering the shipyard's gates, spectators were directed to a huge platform directly ahead of the stem. Distinguished guests of Lord Pirrie included Viscount Newry, Lord Trimlestown, Mr George Lambert MP, Civil Lord of the Admiralty, the Reverend A. Harland, Mr Harold Sanderson, Colonel Henry Concanon, Mr J.A. Shelley, Captain Bartlett, Mr Currie, Sir Alexander Dempsey, Sir John Byers and Sir Andrew Newton-Brady. From their platform could be seen *Britannic*; 'this mammoth represents the highest level of marine engineering that has yet been attained', wrote an impressed reporter, 'she marks another epoch in the conquest of the ocean.' The ship's long square bottom and the huge bilge keels were visible to other observers.

Fifteen minutes before the launch, Lord Pirrie made a final tour of inspection with Harold Sanderson and gave final instructions regarding the launch rams and hydraulic triggers.

At 11.05 a.m., a red flag was raised at the sternpost, signalling river craft to get clear. Five minutes later the first rockets went off, indicating that launching was imminent. The noise of loud hammering arose as the workmen knocked away the remaining keel blocks…gradually *Britannic*'s full 24,800-ton weight was carried onto the sliding ways. All that now prevented her moving were the pair of huge steel triggers held in place by hydraulic pressure. 'The gauge showed that the pressure which the rams attached to the triggers had to sustain in order to prevent movement amounted to 560 tons.'

Exactly on 11.15 a.m. the valve was opened which allowed the water to leave the ram cylinders, releasing the pressure so the pair of steel triggers fell back and released the ship. Hydraulic rams placed at the bows to give the vessel a push if she failed to move of her own accord were rendered superfluous as *Britannic* began to move down the slipway. After some seconds she quickened her pace, but never reached an exceptionally high speed. Eighty-one seconds later – having reached a maximum speed of 9½ knots

Lord Pirrie (eighth from right) poses for a photograph with a number of officials from the Belfast Harbour Commissioners. The photograph was taken on 25 February 1914, one day before *Britannic*'s launch. (Photograph reproduced courtesy the Trustees of National Museums Northern Ireland)

– her bow dipped from the end of the ways. The event was recorded for posterity by a man standing on the platform ahead of the bows and winding a motion picture camera. Although some shipyard workers were ready to let go of the centre anchor in the forecastle deck as a precaution, there was no need and they waved from the bow rails and cheered as the ship cleared the slip.

'Local patriotism was undoubtedly a strong element in the enthusiastic outburst that took place, the cheers of the workmen away up on the top deck of the *Britannic* were answered in a rousing manner by their comrades ashore, and the visitors joined in too, while above the din could be heard the raucous hooting of sirens and the deep sound of the horns of many steamers,' an observer recorded. 'The *Britannic* was instinct with life, the arduous work of many months had a fitting culmination, and Belfast once again led the way for all shipbuilding ports in the United Kingdom…'

Now fully water-borne, *Britannic* had made the irreversible transition from land to sea. 'A launch is always an impressive sight, but the present one was even more impressive than usual, because of the slowness with which the ship travelled throughout,' recorded *The Times*; '*Olympic*, which had a launching weight of 200 tons less…had the maximum speed of 12½ knots and the time of only 62 seconds.'

The various wire hawsers came into action when *Britannic* was 100ft from the end of the ways and were so effective that the ship was brought to a halt in much less than her own length, having slid through a total launch run of 2,000ft. As the same arrangements had worked for *Olympic* and *Titanic*, they worked just as successfully for the *Britannic*. She was drawing 15ft 4½in forward and 20ft 7in aft, a mean of some 18ft.

Launching completed, twelve tugs – including *Herculaneum, Hukisson, Hornby, Alexandra* and *Hercules* – towed the hull to a berth alongside the Belfast Harbour Board's wharf. These tugs, excluding *Hukisson*, had towed the *Titanic* after her launching on 31 May 1911.[23]

Meanwhile, the slipway *Britannic* had vacated was prepared for yard number 469, a 30,000-ton vessel for the Red Star Line.

But, with the ship ready for outfitting, reporters were able to board. 'Vast as the vessel appeared on the ways, she seems many times bigger when one is aboard,' recorded the *Daily Telegraph*'s reporter. He continued, describing the ship and his tour in detail:

> Here can be seen to full advantage the immensity of the space available for the passenger accommodation…A brief examination shows that the vessel has been constructed with a full inner skin throughout her most vulnerable sections. In fact, she is a ship within a ship and is subdivided with an unusually large number of watertight bulkheads. The preparations for the fitting of several sets of a new and most approved type of electrically-driven gear for [life] boats are well in evidence… This…gear is different from that of any other preceding ship, and at last the death-knell of the ancient system of davits is sounded.
>
> Looking through the opening on the after boat deck into the cavernous depths of the ship, some idea is gained of the enormous room which is required to install the colossal combination engines which are to drive the vessel. Further forward there are more openings, which shortly will receive the numerous boilers at which an army of men will toil, feeding the scores of hungry furnaces when the floating palace is in service… It is realised that this vessel will be more than a ship; she will be a city floating on the broad Atlantic.
>
> The passengers for all classes are excellently provided for, and the first-class promenade is a really magnificent esplanade. If there is a factor of the *Britannic* which more than any other compels attention it is the evident efforts spent to make everything as safe as possible… *Britannic* will be supplied with…forty-eight of the largest lifeboats yet made…two of these have powerful engines…

In fact, it was only on the day of launching that the leading details of the ship were released to the press. *The Times* recorded, 'the leading particulars of the ship – length, overall, about 900ft, breadth about 94ft, depth, moulded, 64ft 3in, total height from keel to navigating bridge, 104ft 6in, gross tonnage about 50,000…passenger accommodation for 2,500; crew accommodation over 950.' It also recorded a description of the vessel in some detail:

> The double system of construction is carried up the sides of the ship to a considerable distance above the load waterline. The framing throughout is exceptionally heavy... Hydraulic riveting has been introduced to a greater extent than formally... great longitudinal and vertical stiffening of the whole structure.
>
> Accommodation is provided for about 2,500 passengers, including 790 in the first class and 836 in the second class. A feature of the accommodation is that a large number of the first-class rooms are single berth rooms. In practically every case there is in connection with each a bathroom or a shower bath and lavatory. There are a larger number of special suites on the bridge and shelter decks...two suites...including sitting room, two bedrooms, servants' rooms, bathrooms, etc., with an isolated veranda [lounge] about 25ft long on the starboard side and on the port side an isolated promenade deck 50ft long...[List of numerous first-class accommodation features.] The second-class accommodation...is little inferior to first-class quarters...
>
> The system of davits used differs from that in any other preceding ship. They are of lattice girder construction with swan-necked tops turned towards each other in each pair. They are pivoted at their base and move from the vertical position to a considerable angle inboard or outboard...

After the razzmatazz of the ship's launching, the officials left for the reception at the Grand Central Hotel in Belfast.

Mr George Cumming, one of Harland & Wolff's managing directors, proposed a toast for 'the steamship *Britannic* and success to the White Star Line'. He hoped she would be as successful as the first 1874 ship of the name, but although recent White Star ships were magnificent, the new liner was 'the most excellent ship that he had ever seen'. He did not think that any vessel being built for the Atlantic would excel her in comfort, luxury and safety.

Colonel Henry Concanon, Joint Manager of White Star, apologised on Harold Sanderson's behalf that he had had to leave for Queenstown to catch *Baltic* for a trip to

Slipping down the ways, *Britannic* reaches the water for the first time. (J.&C. McCutcheon collection)

America on business. Without labouring with figures, he thought it remarkable that the new *Britannic* was twice as long as her predecessor and ten times larger in terms of her gross tonnage.

He declared of *Britannic*:

> Neither thought nor money has been spared and when you see the finished article we feel sure that we will have your approval, as we have your good wishes today.[24]

Many of the speeches were in truth repetitive, ending with the press wishing 'good luck to the *Britannic* and to all who sail in her'. Press and other guests later attended a dinner at the hotel at 7.00 p.m., given by White Star.

After the celebrations had been completed, at 9.35 p.m. *Patriotic* left Belfast for Liverpool, where a special train was to return the guests to London. They were scheduled to leave Lime Street for Euston at 8.10 a.m. the next day.

They left behind an empty hull, which Harland & Wolff now had to transform. As with *Olympic*, they would be guided by the specifications laid down in a specification book which amounted to around 300 pages, as well as numerous plans, drawings and diagrams that would be used in the installation and assembly of the ship's fittings. The vast boiler and machinery spaces would be filled with the boilers, lowered through the funnel casings into the depths of the hull; the engines, assembled, then disassembled, lowered into the engine rooms and reassembled; throughout the accommodation areas, interior bulkheads and stateroom partitions needed to be installed; wiring, plumbing and ventilation systems; and then the fixtures and furnishings that would make her accommodation so comfortable. Manufacturers took advantage of the situation to advertise their products, which were evidently good enough to be used on the largest British liner: Thomas Anderson Ltd's advertisements proudly displayed that their palladium bulkhead insulation would be fitted; J. Stone & Co. Ltd's patent hydraulic underline ash expeller had been 'adopted throughout'.

Hopes that *Britannic* would be in service by the end of September 1914, in time to accommodate the large numbers of passengers at that time of year travelling westbound, were dashed. The IMM annual report for 1913 was published on 15 June 1914, noting that *Britannic* was 'expected to take her position in the passenger and mail service of the White Star Line between New York and Plymouth, Cherbourg and Southampton early next year [1915]. This vessel will embody in her construction every modern improvement for safety and comfort.'*

★ ★ ★

---

* The IMM report for 1911 was published on 24 June 1912 and referred to a 'White Star Line steamer, approximately 50,000 [tons]' as one of six vessels under construction; the report for 1912 was published on 2 June 1913 and referred to her by name:

> There is also under construction at Belfast for the White Star Line the steamship *Britannic*, a vessel of about 50,000 tons gross register, which is expected to be launched early next year, and in due course will take her place in the Southampton and New York Mail and Passenger Service. This vessel will, generally speaking, be similar in type to the *Olympic*, and will embody in her design such alterations and improvements as experience has suggested, and it is confidently anticipated that this steamer will be a creditable and profitable addition to your fleet.

When *Britannic*'s propellers were fitted in September 1914, her future in peacetime service was already in doubt. After the outbreak of war, the White Star Line decided to withdraw *Olympic* from service, and there was hardly any hurry to complete her younger sister. While she remained incomplete, at least she was safe for the time being, and as the months passed it was harder and harder to see a swift end to the conflict.

In May 1915, Harold Sanderson was advised by Harland & Wolff:

> *Britannic* under ordinary conditions could be ready for service in say four weeks but with so many men of the principal trades engaged on government work the time for the necessary work would under present circumstances be extended probably to ten or twelve weeks unless priority is allowed by the government. In the foregoing estimate we assume the work would be limited to making the vessel seaworthy in all respects and fitting accommodations for officers, engineers and crew. Vessel has already had mooring trial of engines.

Olympic was available even earlier and, after she had entered government service along with *Mauretania* and *Aquitania*, then *Britannic* began to look even more attractive. By the end of July 1915, 'the landing at Sulva Bay and the subsequent heavy fighting (which increased the average number of casualties to 1,000 a day) made it impossible to carry out the scheme of carrying the serious cases from the Dardanelles to England, and it was necessary to live from hand-to-mouth by taking all cases first to Imbros (or later to Mudros) and subsequently evacuating them to Egypt, Malta or England as opportunity offered...' The pressing need for additional hospital ships to serve the Dardanelles led to *Aquitania* sailing as a hospital ship early in September 1915. On 6 October 1915 the War Office requested another twenty ships and *Mauretania* was converted from a troop transport to a hospital ship, leaving at the end of October 1915. Consideration was being given to *Britannic* ('whose capacity would equal that of eight ordinary hospital ships') and on 13 November 1915 it was confirmed that her services would be required.

Since the need for *Britannic*'s services had only been a matter of time, Harold Sanderson had already been considering the question of a commander, writing on 22 October 1915 that 'having regard to her importance it is essential that we put her in charge of the very best man available in our employ'. As he had with *Olympic*, he pressed the government as to whether Captain Haddock might now be made available, writing: 'I should be very glad to know that Captain Haddock's services could be placed at our disposal, in which case we would give him the command of the *Britannic*.' He was not available when the answer came a fortnight later, but Sanderson had plenty of able commanders at his disposal.

On 8 December 1915, *Britannic* completed her sea trials under Captain Joseph Ranson's command. His experiences included a number of years on such ships as White Star's *Baltic* and then *Adriatic*, but his command of *Britannic* would be temporary. The same day, the new ship was entered on the British register, with her official number as 137,490. She left for Liverpool on the evening of 11 December 1915 and arrived the following day, where final preparations would make her ready for service.

Sanderson had selected Captain Charles Alfred Bartlett, an experienced man with many years in the company's service. Born in London on 21 August 1868, he joined the White Star Line in 1894 and served on board ships such as *Doric*, *Gothic*, *Georgic*, *Teutonic*, *Celtic* and *Oceanic*. His first command was *Armenian* in October 1903 and he commanded

As *Britannic* entered the water, a number of spectators cheered and followed her down. (Author's collection)

various other ships, including *Gothic* when she experienced a serious fire on board in 1906. In April 1907, he was appointed to *Cedric*, one of the largest ships in the fleet, and he remained in command until he became the company's marine superintendent at Belfast in January 1912.★ He was appointed a captain in the Royal Naval Reserve on 22 June 1914 and then officially joined *Britannic* on 14 December 1915. Serving with him was Assistant Captain Harry William Dyke, who had been on board *Olympic* as her chief officer before the war, being promoted in September 1915 and then transferred to *Britannic*. Chief Officer Robert Hume also had experience of large ships, having been *Olympic*'s second officer when she made her maiden voyage in June 1911 and climbing steadily through the ranks. Completing the team were First Officer James Henry Callow; Second Officer Alfred Brocklebank;† Third Officer J.H. Walker; Fourth Officer J. Harris; Fifth Officer W. Walker and Sixth Officer Duncan Campbell McTavish.

The appointment of a chief engineer followed the same precedent on *Titanic*. After Chief Engineer Joseph Bell oversaw *Olympic*'s completion and her maiden voyage, he

★ In this capacity, Bartlett drafted a series of recommendations regarding the duties of an assistant commander on *Olympic* or *Britannic*, dated December 1913. The newly created post was partly a response to the *Titanic* disaster and followed similar innovations on the Cunarders *Lusitania* and *Mauretania*. The officer needed to be 'tactful and energetic' and would be assigned 'special quarters' 'near the commander and navigating room and he should have certain privileges in port as regards leave, etc.' As well as being 'responsible for the efficiency of all life saving appliances', the assistant commander would be required 'to assist the commander on the bridge whenever he considers it necessary'.
† See my article 'The Mystery of *Britannic*'s Second Officer', *Atlantic Daily Bulletin*, British *Titanic* Society, 2006; and Remco Hillen's article about *Britannic*'s officers in *Titanic Post*, Swiss *Titanic* Society, 2006.

subsequently transferred to *Titanic*; his replacement as *Olympic*'s chief engineer, John Fleming, was reassigned to *Britannic* in December 1913. Fleming had joined the White Star Line in July 1881 and was appointed sixth engineer of the first *Britannic* in April 1882. By the time of the Jubilee Review at Spithead in 1889, he was serving as the new *Teutonic*'s senior third engineer and his career continued to progress. Following a stint on other ships, including *Laurentic*, where he gained experience of her combination propelling machinery, and then *Olympic*, Fleming was undoubtedly proud to join the company's largest ship shortly before she was launched.

Britannic was soon ready for service, but inevitably there were some slight snags. The Admiralty had believed that the ship's X-ray room would be ready by 30 November 1915. However, on 14 December 1915 the contractors, Messrs F. R. Butt & Co., reported: 'Our representative on arriving found that the X-ray rooms, wiring, etc. were not quite ready for the erection of the apparatus but owing to the size of the ship and the rooms this did not cause any appreciable delay to the actual erection of the apparatus.'[25] John C.H. Beaumont, *Britannic*'s chief surgeon, was impressed with the new ship: 'What a fine vessel – the very latest word in everything new and the triumph of all that the science and art of modern shipbuilding could accomplish. The two large operating rooms, each with anaesthetic and instrument room attached; the X-ray rooms, dental cambers, dispensaries, research laboratories, lecture rooms, lofty and spacious wards to accommodate 4,000 [sic] sick and wounded; quarters for sixty doctors and 300 nurses, besides 800 of a ship's crew, galleys, staterooms, etc. all combined to make her a wonderful institution unsurpassed by any even on shore.'*

Her external appearance was rather different to that her designers had envisaged. At the time she was required for service, only five of the planned eight 'girder'-type davit stations had been installed: the station on the port side of the first funnel was omitted; and the two stations aft on the shade deck were not fitted. Consequently, *Britannic* was also fitted with a number of Welin davits along the length of the boat deck amidships, and aft on the shade deck, in order to provide enough lifeboats for her full complement.

Unlike her White Star Line livery, her hull was painted white, accompanied by a green band punctuated by red crosses. Her funnels were not painted black at the top, but instead a buff yellow throughout. Two glass panelled red crosses on the boat deck lit up at night, while there were many green lights along the promenade deck and some green lights were arranged in pairs amidships, beneath the Welin davits. Beneath the nine windows of the bridge was a painted red panel with *Britannic*'s transport number painted in white lettering: 'G608'.[26] (The number would change subsequently to 'G618'.) The authorities soon learned of the difficulties that the hospital ship lights could cause to navigation. In August 1915, the fourth officer of the transport *Drome*:

> Seeing a red light [port side navigation light] to starboard, turned to the right to show his light of the same colour, but to his astonishment he then perceived a second red light to the right of the first. Quickly warned I mounted the bridge and it was only in approaching that I recognised the shape of the cross, then from the placing of his navigation lights I saw that we were cutting across his bows at the risk of running him

---

* John H. Plumridge's research indicated that *Britannic*'s capacity was 3,310 patients. The figures given by Beaumont appear to have been from memory. By contrast, *Aquitania* could squeeze in 4,182. However, her capacity was given as 3,069 in a government minute in early October 1915. (See *Hospital Ships*, page 167.)

down had the night been less clear. The two ships thus crossed each other at about a hundred yards to port whereas by continuing their routes they would have passed to starboard without having to manoeuvre. But the side lights and in particular the green light, eclipsed by the glare of the red lamps, were only visible at the last moment.

When the account was forwarded from the French naval attaché, the authorities sought to prevent it happening again: 'In order that the light of the starboard red crosses on hospital ships may not be mistaken for a port side light in fog or misty weather, in the close vicinity of other vessels, all hospital ships not already thus fitted, are to be provided with a separate switch on the bridge capable of extinguishing the light of the starboard red crosses,' instructed the Director of Transports in December 1915.

As the ship's commander, Captain Bartlett received strict sailing orders. His attention – and that of Assistant Captain Harry William Dyke – was 'called to paragraph three of the "Instructions Regarding Hospital Carriers & Hospital Ships" as to [such vessels] being utilised for no other purpose than that of assisting the wounded, etc., as laid down in the Geneva Convention.' He was to 'report to the senior naval officer' upon arrival at Mudros in the Aegean Sea; and display ensigns as specified in the previous publication. Returning home, he was to report to Gibraltar the number of patients on board and all cases of dysentery and enteric diseases being carried; otherwise, it was specified 'the use of wireless telegraphy is to be reduced to a minimum'. Any transmissions overheard could be open to misunderstanding by the enemy. If any unnecessary delays took place, as captain he would be held responsible for them.

The handbook of 'General Instructions for Masters of Transports and Hospital Ships on Military Service' covered crew; navigation; signalling; cargo; hospital ships; efficiency of transports; and miscellaneous instructions for commanders. Instructions were given specifically for the maintenance of the hospital ship lights:

> Green Bands and Red Crosses. To prevent the illuminated green bands and red crosses of hospital ships showing white at night the following methods are to be adopted: –
>
> a) The glass shades of boxes containing the lights are to be washed clean, so as to remove the salt, and they are to be kept clean;
>
> b) A bottle of red mixture has been supplied for 'dipping' the lights of red crosses in. (The lamps should be alight when 'dipped' in the mixture.)

Another document that governed many of the actions on board *Britannic* was the 'Standing Orders and Instructions for Officers Commanding Troops in Hospital Ships'. It described in detail the responsibilities of the officer commanding troops: 'He is responsible for providing medical attendance for the ship's crew, if required, in the absence of the ship's surgeon…' The instructions covered everything from bottles of beer ('a daily issue of bottled beer is to be issued on repayment to all members of the RAMC who desire it'); diet ('he will exercise the closest supervision over hospital supplies and diets, and satisfy himself that they are sufficient and of good quality'); X-ray equipment ('orderlies engaged in X-ray work should be warned of the danger of undue exposure to X-rays and of the serious consequences likely to ensue…') and port procedure ('when hospital ships are in port the officer commanding troops or an officer representing him must always remain on board, with a detachment of NCOs [non commissioned officers] and men to look after stores, equipment…')

Britannic left Liverpool at 12.20 a.m. on 23 December 1915. Slipping away in darkness just before Christmas, it was very different departure to her sisters' maiden voyages. She was bound for Mudros on the Greek island of Lemnos and would stop at Naples on the way. It served as a good collection point for casualties from the Dardanelles and other military campaigns. During the day there was a set routine: at 6.00 a.m. patients were woken and wards cleaned, breakfast being served one-and-a-half hours later; staff cleaned the dining saloons after each meal and the captain made his daily inspection; lunch was served at 12.30 p.m. and tea at 4.30 p.m.; at 8.30 p.m. patients were put to bed, before Captain Bartlett inspected the ship again. Patients had their injuries or illnesses treated in between mealtimes and those who were well enough were allowed on deck to get some fresh air. Hospital suits, with blue trousers and jackets with brown facings, were needed if patients were to go on deck. If the enemy sighted people in military uniforms walking on the decks of a hospital ship, then they would arrive at the conclusion that the hospital ship was being abused. There was little in the way of organised entertainment, although there was the occasional concert, such as the one held on 8 February 1916.[27]

Britannic reached Naples on 28 December 1915, where she took on supplies of coal and water. It was not long before she was underway again and she left the following afternoon, arriving at Mudros on 31 December 1915. As she was such a large vessel, a number of smaller hospital ships were required to come alongside and transfer the wounded. They looked tiny in comparison. John Fleming would later write that *Britannic* '…seemed like a mother with two tiny infants in her great arms.'[28] After embarking a full load of wounded, *Britannic* left Mudros on 3 January 1916 and reached Southampton on 9 January 1916.[29] Unfortunately, three people did not survive the journey. On 2 January 1916, twenty-four-year-old Private Arthur Howe died of Tuberculosis; three days later twenty-four-year-old Sam Jones was lost overboard in position 37° 10' north 11° 25' east; and on the day *Britannic* reached Southampton twenty-one-year-old Private Charles Vincent succumbed to Tuberculosis at 49° 58' north 3° 12' west.

Once safely docked, the wounded were transferred via waiting hospital trains to hospitals ashore, such as the Royal Victoria Hospital, Netley;[30] where possible, they were sent to hospitals near their homes or to hospitals that treated a specific illness.[31] Indeed, patients on hospital ships were labelled with one of five areas corresponding to their home area: 'London & Southern'; 'West of England'; 'Midlands'; 'North England & Scotland' or 'Ireland'. Therefore there was always a probability that patients could be sent to a hospital that was in the vicinity of their homes. Sometimes the numbers of wounded were so high that two 'emergency' trains were available. Both used the 'trestle' system, whereby supporting movable stretchers were on movable trestles in vestibule vans; the London & North Western Railway provided the vans and the London & South Western Railway provided the trestles. These two trains proved of great use whenever *Mauretania*, *Aquitania* or *Britannic* docked.[32]

If *Britannic* had successfully completed her maiden voyage, unlike the doomed *Titanic*, there were further tasks ahead. She left Southampton shortly before noon on 20 January 1916 for another round trip to Mudros, but the voyage would not go as planned. She arrived at Naples at 7 a.m. on 25 January 1916 to take on 1,500 tons of water and 2,510 tons of coal. The authorities at Mudros were informed that she would leave early the next morning and arrive two days later, but that afternoon a telegram was received from the Principal Naval Transport Officer at Cairo. The British Consulate General was informed that *Britannic* would need to remain at Naples and embark invalids coming from Malta and

The size of *Britannic's* centre anchor was demonstrated by the presence of two officials from Lloyds Proving House, where the anchor was tested. (*Railway & Travel Monthly*, 1914/ Author's collection)

Egypt. Captain Bartlett, as well as Colonel Anderson of the Royal Army Medical Corps (RAMC), were soon informed of the new arrangements.

The Duke of Aosta made enquiries if any wounded were already on board, as he wanted to visit them. However, by the time the first of them arrived he had already returned to the Italian front. If a Royal visit was not on the cards, then the authorities asked Captain Bartlett to invite the commander of the American warship *Des Moines* on board. Him and his staff would be shown around *Britannic* and shown 'all hospitality possible', while the medical officers of *Des Moines* would be invited to assist in the transfer of invalids. Forty American naval personnel were entertained on board. Nelson Page, the American Ambassador to Rome, was also invited on board with his wife and daughter. They were given a tour of the ship and Page was very pleased that he had been able to go on board.

During her stay, *Britannic* took 436 patients from the hospital ships *Grantully Castle*, 393 from *Formosa*, 594 from *Essequibo*, 493 from *Nevasa* and 319 from *Panama*. Once the final patients had been taken aboard from *Panama*, shortly before noon on 4 February 1916, everything was ready and *Britannic* left for Southampton that afternoon, where she would arrive on 9 February 1916.

On 10 February 1916 Captain Bartlett submitted to Southampton's Principal Naval Transport Officer, Captain Wrey, RN, suggestions for the stop at Naples to be more efficient. He suggested that as there was no naval officer there, instructions be incorporated into the Sailing Orders of captains of smaller vessels to come alongside *Britannic* when she arrived, making the transfer of patients quicker and more comfortable for them than if the transfer was made using barges and boats. Through the Consul General there he had obtained permission to use *Britannic's* wireless for hospital work from the Italian Admiral, so he suggested that while *Britannic* was in Naples she could be used as a powerful station, able to receive messages from Malta and other ships, 'which would facilitate [communication] matters for all concerned'. The Consul General could be instructed to communicate by telephone with the ship on arrival, enabling him to be in constant touch. Bartlett pointed out: 'Painting the ship overside could be done at Naples by Italian labour cheaper than at home ports, the ship supplying the paint.' The Consul had forwarded an

£80 estimate to him, but in the end the offer could not be accepted. In fact, Bartlett's suggestions were communicated to the Cunard company with regard to the *Mauretania* and *Aquitania*.

Twenty-seven days later – as part of the regular boat drills held every voyage – boats numbers 2, 2a, 4, 4a, 6, 6a, 8, 8a, 10, 10a, 12, 12a, 14, 14a, 14b, 14c, 14d and 16 (one of the motor launches, the other launch being numbered 17) were lowered to the water and the crews were exercised. They were assisted by fifty members of the RAMC, who often took part in such drills. Another regular feature of life aboard the ship, although not as regular as the boat drills, were the tests of the fire-fighting equipment; such as the tests during the boat drill on 14 March 1916. All the fire hydrants and hoses were tested with the full pressure of water, as were five Fire Queens (a brand of fire extinguisher).[33]

It is likely that at this time some of the temporary canvas partitions hastily put-up on the upper decks to get the ship ready for service were replaced with materials 'of more substance'.[34] Some other small changes would be made later during the year to various parts of the ship.

Voyage No.3 commenced more than a month after her second trip on 20 March 1916 and *Britannic* reached Naples five days later. On 27 March 1916 she left for Augusta in Sicily; she departed thence on 30 March 1916, arriving back at Southampton on 4 April.[35] However, Chief Surgeon John Beaumont had been forced to leave the ship for medical reasons and so in his place went Dr D.W. Stevens Muir.[36] Sadly, twenty-one-year-old Private Robert Pask succumbed to Diabetes on the day *Britannic* arrived back at Southampton, when the ship was in position 49° 27' north 3° 37' west.

By April 1916, the Dardanelles had been evacuated,[37] and therefore *Britannic*'s service was discontinued. The majority of her crew signed off on 8 April 1916 and the Official

' THE NEW WHITE STAR LINER " BRITANNIC."

THE LARGEST BRITISH BUILT VESSEL.   GROSS TONNAGE 50,000.   LENGTH 900 FEET.   BREADTH 94 FEET   TOTAL HEIGHT FROM KEEL TO NAVIGATING BRIDGE 104 FEET 6 INCHES.   ACCOMMODATION 2,600 PASSENGERS. 950 CREW

An interesting period postcard depicts how the new liner would have appeared in service. Although the new lifeboat davits are visible, the ship featured is closer in appearance to *Olympic* as she appeared when she entered service in 1911. (Author's collection)

Log Book of crew was delivered later the same day to the Marine Superintendent at Southampton, Mr J. Doddy;[38] the document covered the past three voyages, the crew having differed little over the three voyages.

The fact that fewer hospital ships were now needed allowed some vessels to be dispensed with. On 16 January 1916 the War Office had asked for *Mauretania*, *Aquitania* and *Britannic* to be discharged from service,[39] but instead several smaller vessels were released that could be employed more usefully elsewhere. However, it had dawned on them that following the evacuation of the Dardanelles such large vessels were not needed. In February 1916 *Aquitania* was laid up at half-rate with her hospital fittings intact. On 17 February 1916 it was decided to discharge *Mauretania* and on 1 March 1916 Cunard were paid £60,000 to recondition her; while seven days later the War Office asked for *Aquitania* to be discharged, which was done on 10 April 1916, Cunard being paid £90,000 to cover reconditioning her as an ocean liner.

Britannic was laid up on 12 April 1916 at the half-rate of five shillings per gross ton, with her fittings intact to allow a rapid return to service if necessary. Meanwhile, the War Office proposed for her to be discharged, but the Ministry of Transport protested strongly against it. 'It was pointed out that in the event of an emergency arising, a shortage of hospital ships might occur and that in view of the very favourable terms arranged with the owners, the Army Council would be well advised to retain the ship for at least three or four months.' This would prove to be the time she was needed and recalled to service, as the Ministry of Transport had predicted quite sensibly, but the War Office persisted with their proposal and on 21 May 1916 *Britannic* was discharged from service, the White Star Line receiving the sum of £76,000 to cover the cost of reconditioning, three days after she had returned to Belfast.

Britannic's war was not over, and in the meantime, there was an overwhelming stream of casualties from the Somme and other theatres of war. Perhaps this is best illustrated by the figures for the week ending 9 July 1916, when 151 ambulance trains departed from Southampton with in excess of 30,000 patients; on 9 July 1916 alone, 29 trains transported over 6,000 patients.[40]

Although *Britannic* had been the last hospital ship discharged with more intact fittings than the other vessels, officials illogically called up *Aquitania* in July 1916. Her conversion to an ocean liner was nearly complete, but the government abruptly ordered the ship reconverted to a hospital ship; it was not until December 1916 that she was back in service.

On 28 August 1916 *Britannic* was recalled by the War Office to resume her service as a hospital ship. She returned to Southampton on 9 September 1916 and anchored off Cowes. Captain Bartlett remained in command and retained many of his officers. However, there were a few changes. John Chapman joined the ship as sixth officer; Duncan Campbell McTavish was promoted from sixth to replace J. Harris as fourth officer; Francis William Laws joined as third officer, replacing George Newlove (who had been appointed in May 1916); and Hugh John Hollingsworth joined as first officer, replacing James Henry Callow. However, Hollingsworth would not complete a single voyage to the Mediterranean on *Britannic*. He joined *Adriatic* on 22 September 1916 and was replaced with George Oliver.★ Two days later, *Britannic* would depart on her fourth round voyage.

The new chaplain, Reverend John Fleming, joined the ship in September. He enjoyed a tour of the vessel and was most impressed with the ship's propelling machinery. 'The engines were, perhaps, the most impressive thing in the ship,' he wrote. 'The Chief

Engineer was, of course, a Scot, a man of massive strength, adored for his grasp and resource by all the men who served him…One of the Junior Engineers, who took delight in showing us round, told us that in the engine rooms of the *Britannic* there was more power than in the whole of Birkenhead.'[41]

Also joining *Britannic* for her first of three voyages was a nurse Ada Garland.[42] Early on Saturday 23 September 1916 she was among the party of VADs who arrived at Southampton docks to board a tender for the one-hour journey to *Britannic*, anchored off Cowes on the Isle of Wight. In the event, they were early and had a couple of free hours before joining the tender, which they spent looking around the city.

As the tender approached the ship, Ada recalled, '*Britannic* made a beautiful picture anchored with the evening sun glistening on the waters around showing up her white paint and the deep green band around.' But once aboard, dinner was served early and many people 'retired for the night, rather cowed at the vastness of everything'.

On Sunday morning she and a friend began exploring the ship and after an endless walk they found the post office. 'I thought the boat beautiful from the outside but ten times more beautiful and marvellous on the inside,' she would later write.

The wards were divided into blocks, she soon found, and in Ada's block there were six wards, with some 500 beds, including the padded 'mental ward' of twenty beds. She discovered the patients' dining room (small, with a ten-person capacity), dispensary, laboratory, operating theatre, dental surgery and barber shop. 'Our quarters comprised the dining saloon which seated 250 at one sitting, lounge, music room, writing rooms, library [and] swimming bath,' she remembered. 'Our little cabins, which were fitted out for two, were lovely with bathroom and dressing room attached, all lit by electricity. I was fortunate to get a cabin on the outside with two portholes but some of the girls were less fortunate in getting inside cabins…they had to have electric light on all the time and the electric fans to keep it cool.'

That afternoon, the tender arrived with 200 more VADs and several hundred RAMC boys, bound as passengers for Malta, Salonika and Mesopotamia. Soon afterwards *Britannic* departed, 'escorted for several miles by destroyers with several seaplanes hovering over-head for a good distance'. The towers of Old Osborne, Ryde and Cowes could be seen in the distance.

Despite the boat deck being out of bounds, fellow VAD Vera Brittain went up and watched the receding shore, going down below soon after:

> On the deck below us the Royal Army Medical Corps orderlies were singing and dancing; we looked down upon them as though seeing a music hall stage from the front of the dress circle. One man who played a violin played Tosti's *Good Bye*; the plaintive familiar notes rang out into the mild September twilight.[43]

Although ropes divided the decks, separating the sexes – the Voluntary Aid Detachments and Royal Army Medical Corps – one or two couples were soon found in 'compromising positions'.[44]

---

* Although Hollingsworth might have been grateful for the transfer when *Britannic* sank, he did not escape drama entirely. He was on board *Justicia* when she foundered in July 1918. Sixth Officer John Chapman was replaced by Herbert Welsh on 10 November 1916. The twenty-four year old Welsh transferred from the older *Cedric*, but he served on board *Britannic* for eleven days.

Britannic's massive engines were a masterpiece of heavy engineering. They were the largest triple-expansion marine reciprocating engines ever made, photographed in Harland & Wolff's engine works on 1 April 1914. On their right are the engines of the Holland America liner *Statendam* (destined to be sunk under the name *Justicia* in July 1918). It is interesting to note that the ship's turbine engine was physically the largest ever to be constructed for marine use, if not the most powerful. (Photograph reproduced courtesy the Trustees of National Museums Northern Ireland)

Monday began with a boat drill. From various parts of the ship people had to reach the boat deck, alerted by three blasts of the ship's whistles. Nobody was allowed to go below decks as the drill took place, which happened every morning. Once on deck, lifebelts were worn and many lifeboats readied for lowering. 'In these drills everything was carried out just as if it was real danger,' Ada described, 'only we didn't get in the boats and have the rides.'

By Tuesday, the ship was in sight of Portugal and by 6 p.m. *Britannic* passed Cape St Vincent, 'which looked very beautiful with its high rugged cliff in the setting sun'.

Most evenings after dinner the RAMC held concerts on deck in 'brilliant moonlight' singing old favourites. 'On some of the evenings there would be concerts all over the ship…it seemed as though there was music everywhere for there were heaps of pianos.'

When the liner steamed through the waters off the Sardinia coast, shoals of porpoises could be seen, 'which looked so fascinating jumping out of the water by leaps and bounds'.

It was roughly 2 a.m. on Friday 29 September 1916 that *Britannic* encountered 'an awful storm' with dense fog; all whistles were blown at intervals and 'the engines slowed down to just a creeping pace'. Thunder and lightning abounded. 'I never beheld such lightning before, it lit up the whole sky in one beautiful terrific glare,' remembered Ada. Nevertheless, shortly after 7.30 a.m. *Britannic* entered Naples.

Countless small craft and fishing boats came out to welcome them, while many young-sters swam out to dive for money that some people threw overboard.

Breakfast was served, but everyone was exited about going ashore. Ada joined the trip to see much of the town, which became a feature every time the ship was in Naples. They returned late that evening.

Throughout Saturday 30 September 1916 to the afternoon of Sunday 1 October 1916 coaling continued. Divine service was held on Sunday morning, but through the after-noon all time was spent making beds. At 5.30 p.m. *Britannic* left for Mudros.

Monday was another day of work, which did not finish until 10.30 p.m.

'We were travelling at a terrific rate on Monday doing 24 knots,' at one point, recalled Ada. The day's run was 480 miles, an average of about 21 knots.

At 1.00 p.m. on Tuesday 3 October 1916 eight smaller hospital ships were waiting as *Britannic* anchored at Mudros. Two of them immediately came alongside – one on each side – and the wounded came aboard. 'Our wards seemed swarming with men and the orderlies bringing down their kits, baskets, flaskets and stretcher loads of hospital clothing. Every patient had to exchange his kit for hospital clothing,' Ada wrote.

She was allowed on deck at 9.00 p.m.:

> I, for one, was glad to get on deck for a breath of air. What a magnificent sight, the huge bay was full of ships and they were giving a search light display, one could see every boat in the bay and the hills were lit up for miles. The hospital ships looked like fairy palaces with all their hundreds of red and green lights reflected in the water and last but not least the dear old moon making a path of gold across the water. It was indeed a perfect picture.

There was actually an outbreak of food poisoning at Mudros, resulting in the ship being detained for several days, longer than usual.[45]★

From 8.00 a.m. on Wednesday 4 October 1916, more patients began coming aboard. They were followed by a large group of sisters returning home on leave. *Britannic* departed for Southampton the following day with a near-full capacity of over 3,000 patients, a total of 'well over 4,000 people on board'. Unfortunately, thirty-eight-year-old Corporal Joseph Seddon died at 3.40 p.m. of nepticitis uraemia in position 38° 5' north 24° 41' east. The remaining patients were 'landed…all safely in due time at Southampton without any adventures', on 11 October 1916.

On 13 October 1916 the War Office requested that the Transport Division arrange for 115 officers, 386 other ranks of the RAMC, 161 nurses and 311 tons of medical stores to be carried on board her fifth voyage: a total of 662 additional people. The Transport Division decided that they could proceed 'as being arranged prior to the decision'. Three days later it was noted to 'agree [to the transportation of personnel] as a special case' ('on

---

★ HMHS *Galeka* was also checked at the same time because of a food poisoning outbreak; she was thoroughly disinfected, although this later proved to be a waste of time: *Galeka* was torpedoed in the English Channel on her voyage home. (*Testament of Youth*, Vera Brittain, 1943, fifteenth reprint, William Clowes & Sons Ltd, London and Beccles.)

the grounds of expediency rather than illegality') but 'in future cases it might be well to allow the women to go on hospital ships and bar the men. It would add to the safety of the women nurses and no question is likely to arise about the legality of conveying them [in hospital ships].'

Southampton's Principal Naval Transport Officer was informed on 17 October 1916 by the Transport Division that the extra personnel would embark on the morning of sailing, but that the medical stores would be alongside *Britannic* for loading the following morning.* It was expected she would leave on 20 October 1916 to reach Naples five days later (at about 8.00 a.m.), where 3,000 tons of coal and 2,000 tons of fresh water would be required for the remainder of the journey out and the return trip home, to Mudros and back to Southampton.

Britannic's departure was on schedule,[46] carrying thirty-three officers, chaplains and other ranks of the RAMC (plus 1,865 packages of medical stores) for Egypt; twenty personnel including female doctors and British Red Cross members (plus ninety-six packages) for Malta; 349 people for Salonika (with 795 packages and 165 tons of medical stores); eighty-two people for India; and fifteen packages of stores for Mesopotamia – 484 extra personnel and 2,711 packages of stores for transhipping at Mudros (actual figures vary somewhat, although these are taken from a War Office summary of 23 October 1916).†

Britannic's fifth voyage was recorded through the eyes of Nurse Mrs E.B. Moor.[47] Having travelled down to the docks by train with some others she knew, the train stopped right beside the ship. With nobody to assist with their luggage, there was a 'dreadful scramble to get at our luggage', she wrote in her diary, and once everybody boarded the ship – possibly through the D-deck gangways below the second funnel or perhaps through the aft gangways on decks E, C or B – 'all the Sisters were collected at the foot of the stairs waiting to sign-on.' She continued, 'it was a very tedious affair. We stood in a perfectly awful crush from 2.30 till 4.30 p.m., before it was possible to get anywhere near the table to sign.'

Eventually, everyone had signed on and all were sent to report to the Matron, Mrs Dowse. Mrs Moor was allocated a place to sleep in Ward Y, which contained forty-eight cots and several bathrooms. Dinner was served at 6.00 p.m. and she recalled, 'The cooking was excellent. The dining room was a pretty sight.'

The day after boarding, *Britannic* departed Southampton. Soon everybody settled into the shipboard routine. During the days that passed, lazy times were spent on the boat deck, lying in deck chairs in the sun. 'The *Britannic* is just splendid. A lovely swimming bath, gym...,' Mrs Moor recalled. 23 October 1916 dawned a bright, clear day. Earlier that morning, at 3.00 a.m., *Britannic* had passed through the Straits of Gibraltar. Many of the nurses got up and went on deck to see. She remembered, 'you could only see the lights, of course, but that was something. The [other] coast has been splendid, so wild and rough looking.'

---

* *Britannic* was not the only hospital ship carrying such personnel; *Glengorm Castle*, *Lanfranc* and *Panama*, much smaller vessels, were also carrying such stores and personnel, although in fewer numbers.

† In detail, the exact medical personnel carried consisted of:

For *Egypt*: fifteen officers; sixteen chaplains; two other ranks.

For *Malta*: five officers; one chaplain; ten lady doctors; one nurse; two British Red Cross members; one other rank.

For *Salonika*: ten officers, 181 other ranks (both of No.33 Statny Hospital); 156 nurses; two British Red Cross members.

For *India*: seventeen officers; fifty-two nurses; four assistant surgeons; eight dentists; one other rank.

On 1 August 1914, the day Germany declared war on Russia, *Britannic*'s turbine engine rotor was lifted on board as her propelling machinery was assembled. The turbine's upper casing, which enclosed the rotor, was lifted on board three days later: the same day that Great Britain entered the war against Germany following the invasion of Belgium. (Photograph reproduced courtesy the Trustees of National Museums Northern Ireland)

Early on 25 October 1916 at roughly 6.30 a.m., *Britannic* entered Naples harbour, about an hour and a half ahead of schedule. 'Everyone, of course, was up and on deck watching the proceedings. The moment the great ship came to anchor, the coal barges came at once alongside and coaling commenced,' she wrote later.

'The Chaplain,' possibly Reverend Fleming, 'organised a trip to Pompeii.' At 11.15 a.m. the party boarded both of *Britannic*'s 34ft motor boats for the trip to the quay, across the harbour.

Immediately a group of Italian traders presented themselves, offering exchanges for currency and various other items. They 'were a perfect nuisance to everyone'.

Three guides were hired and the party divided into three groups. Each took turns to do various things: a visit to the local museum, a tour of Pompeii… Unfortunately it began to rain hard and the train journey from the quay to Pompeii took nearly two hours, for a fifteen-mile journey. Ultimately all enjoyed the trip; but everyone boarded *Britannic* late. According to another nurse, Miss W. Greenwood, '*Britannic* was a glorious sight from the other side of the harbour. She was dazzling white with a broad band of green round her hull, and twinkling with innumerable lights all over.'[48]

On 27 October, the next day, nobody – except the officers and eleven lady medical officers – was allowed off the ship. So from the crowded decks everyone watched the day's proceedings: the busy motor launches ferrying people around the harbour, coalers on barges shovelling the fuel through the F-deck coal scuttles, far below…

At 5.00 p.m. four tugs strained to pull the enormous *Britannic* out of the harbour. They cast off, leaving the liner alone, before she moved under her own power.

Britannic's course took her past Stromboli, Gallipoli…the Dardanelles…

Early on 28 October 1916 the ship passed Messina. She soon arrived at Mudros. As the afternoon began, the boat deck was crowded with people and at 3.30 p.m. *Britannic* anchored, careful, skilled navigation having allowed her to enter the harbour through the narrow mouth, delimited by two large booms.

Many smaller ships were waiting to transfer their patients, which began in good time and continued until 11.00 p.m. According to Nurse Miss W. Greenwood, 'these ships of 10,000 or 12,000 tons looked like playthings by the side of our floating town.'

Although *Britannic* was due to leave Mudros at noon on 31 October 1916, *Grantully Castle* had engine trouble next to the *Britannic*; it was 4.30 p.m. when she moved, and shortly afterwards *Britannic* departed, forty minutes before the booms at the harbour entrance were closed.

The run to Southampton reversed the outbound course. Sadly, thirty-four-year-old Corporal George Hunt died of dysentery at 12.05 p.m. on 2 November 1916 at position 36° 30' north 2° 35' west. *Britannic* was due to arrive on Sunday 5 November 1916, but bad weather forced a reduction in speed.[49]

Nurse Greenwood recorded, 'There was a terrific storm in the Channel and we had to "hang about" outside, as the ship was too large to be navigated safely in a small space… During the few moments we were on deck I saw two waves go right over our bridge.' But on 6 November 1916 *Britannic* safely got into port.

Some of the nurses were 'doomed to disappointment' when they were told to transfer to the Cunarder *Aquitania*, but as fate would have it they eventually were told to stay put on *Britannic*. She had to start her sixth voyage on 12 November 1916, only six days following her arrival at Southampton. She departed from Southampton for the final time at 2.23 p.m.

Violet Jessop had been summoned to present herself to sign the articles, the 'signing-on' list, for *Britannic*'s sixth voyage; this was her first voyage on *Britannic* and she looked forward to seeing her brother in the Mediterranean.[50] Violet wrote that, 'It was like a new world …to board that stately hospital ship. For all the world, she looked like a great white swan. Soon renewed friendships made me feel more at home, for at sea you always meet someone you know.'[51]

Britannic passed the Needles and headed for the Cornish coast…through the Bay of Biscay, Portugal's red-brick coast…past the low grey rock of Cape St Vincent… Gibraltar… the arrogant peaks of Sierra Nevada could be seen…the grey and purple rocks of Sardinia… Now there was a forty-eight-hour stop at Naples for coaling.[52] The giant Mount Vesuvius was visible, towering very high, not far away.

Nurse Sheila Macbeth was among a party of eight who hired two cars and a guide for the day when they disembarked for an excursion. In Naples, she did some Christmas shopping.[53]

It was hoped that *Britannic* would be able to depart the following morning, but a violent storm broke during the night and it proved impossible; all anchors and twenty hawsers at the stern were needed to hold the huge ship to the quay. However, on Sunday afternoon a 'short lull came' and the ship put to sea, dropping off the pilot with much difficulty as the mountainous seas began to rise again.[54]

Through the straits of Messina…the sapphire sea of the Mediterranean gleamed with the jewels of the golden, purple-shadowed islands… *Britannic* continued into the Aegean, gliding smoothly across the waters.

Sunday night was enjoyable. 'It happened that this was the chief steward's birthday,' remembered Nurse Greenwood, 'and he gave us an extra special dinner to celebrate it. It was "some" dinner too!'

On Monday morning Nurse Sheila Macbeth was able to observe the Straits of Messina, her 'favourite bit of the voyage' which 'looked nicer than ever'. That day, she wrote, 'from breakfast time until our afternoon swim we worked like factory hands, tying up all the kits ready for the next evening so that we might rest the day before the patients came on board.'

'Our days are well-filled. One of the sergeants gives us a gymnastic class each morning on the boat deck, much to the amusement of the medical orderlies who come-up and take snap shots of us when looking most ridiculous and unable to retaliate. Each afternoon we have a lecture by the bacteriologist, and, as soon as we can get away, we fly down to that precious hour in the swimming bath. After our swim, we have tea and then either play cricket or some other game on deck.' That night, at a regular church service, Reverend Fleming and Violet Jessop were among a congregation singing one of the final hymns, *There is a Green Hill Far Away.*

★   ★   ★

Early on Tuesday 21 November 1916 Reverend Fleming was awake and on deck to watch 'the loveliest and quietest sunrise of the voyage. The waters were as glass, and the sun shone on them with dazzling brilliance.' He looked for a village he had previously seen, with 'closely packed houses with all their variety of colouring, and the turrets with their windmills standing out against the sky.' 'The beauty was so absorbing,' he later wrote, that he hardly heard the gong for breakfast.[55]

It was about 7.30 a.m. that Nurse Ada Garland was called, but she felt tired and stayed in bed until the last minute, before leaving for breakfast.

When the time reached 7.52 a.m., Captain Bartlett altered course to north 48° east, a more direct heading into the Kea Channel. Chief Officer Robert Hume and Fourth Officer Duncan Campbell McTavish were on the bridge with Captain Bartlett, while Lookout J. Murray relieved J. Conelly in the crow's nest.[56] By 8.00 a.m. the watch was changing, which involved the opening of the watertight doors, kept closed normally in a war zone as a precaution. The firemen needed the doors open for moving from the boiler rooms to their quarters and vice versa. However, the doors would remain open for a while after the watch had changed.

Everyone in the dining room was laughing and joking, enjoying breakfast time, which was always the happiest time on board.[57] In a minute, their happiness would be shattered.

Captain Bartlett surveyed the beautiful coast and sparkling sea from *Britannic*'s bridge when the ship shook violently, going over to port as an enormous explosion occurred on the starboard bow. He soon 'felt the ship trembling and vibrating most violently fore and aft' as the ship rapidly took on thousands of tons of water.

Private J.W. Cuthbertson was in the forward barrack room of G-deck when the explosion occurred, wrecking the stairs that led above. He was carried by the flood and eventually escaped uninjured.

Stewardess Violet Jessop heard a 'dull, deafening roar', then felt *Britannic* shuddering from 'stem to stern', rattling and breaking crockery around her. People in the pantry with

Britannic at Belfast, 1915. *Olympic*'s four funnels can be seen behind her. In front of *Britannic* are *Michigan*, disguised as HMS *Collingwood*, and *City of Oxford*, disguised as HMS *St Vincent*. (Photograph reproduced courtesy the Trustees of National Museums Northern Ireland)

her immediately stopped what they were doing, leaving for the dining room, while she froze, clutching a teapot in one hand and a pat of butter in the other.[58]

Nurse Ada Garland recalled: 'I had to rush in time for breakfast which was at 8.00 a.m., as it was I was five minutes late. I had just sat down and started on some stewed pears when we heard a loud report, an indescribable noise; it appeared we had come into collision with something. Everybody jumped up, trays dropped from the stewards' shaking hands and there was a clatter of broken glass.'

Major Priestley quickly took control of the situation in the dining room. 'Keep your seats, it's alright.' They resumed their meal in 'a most unnatural silence'.[59]

Sea Scout James Vickers watched crewmen run onto the foredecks below from his viewpoint on the bridge.[60]

When the explosion occurred, it was 8.12 a.m. *Britannic* had moved three points – 33¾° – to port, a distance of over 200ft. Captain Bartlett ordered the engines stopped, the alarm sounded throughout the ship, lifeboats made ready for lowering, and a radio distress call in an immediate flurry of orders. He had the bridge's switch activated that closed the liner's watertight doors, then requested a report of the damage.

The explosion had opened up a large gash in the hull plating, damaging the watertight bulkhead between holds 2 and 3 and allowing both compartments to flood. The firemen's tunnel extending along the ship's bottom and through the two holds took on water. To make matters worse, hold 1 began to flood. As the flooding progressed, even the forepeak would be flooded, as the bow settled and water was able to penetrate additional openings.

Since the firemen's tunnel was flooded, it was especially important that the two watertight doors leading from it to boiler room 6 were closed. But this was not the case. The forward watertight door of the pair was wide open, leaving an unwelcome opening. To make matters even worse, the second door also failed to close. Perhaps the force of the explosion had affected their mechanisms.

The result of the open watertight doors was evident when catastrophic flooding was observed, the opening allowing thousands of tons of water to swamp boiler room 6. Owing to the high water pressure, a jet of the frothy Aegean burst into the space. In less than two minutes the water was so deep that the firemen abandoned the compartment and the boilers were inoperable. After an interval probably in the region of ten or fifteen minutes, perhaps longer, the water had risen to E-deck.

Boiler room 5 was separated from the forward boiler room 6 by a watertight door, which failed to close completely, so this area flooded soon afterwards. However, the watertight bulkhead between boiler rooms 5 and 4 was undamaged and extended up to B-deck. This bulkhead's watertight door was successfully closed, sealing the forward six flooding compartments, the maximum number that could be flooded without sinking the ship.

However, although the ship at this point was in no danger of foundering, she took-on a strong starboard list and settled at the head, where the list was very noticeable. As *Britannic* sent out her distress signal, other vessels soon responded. 'SOS. Have struck mine off Point Nikola.' [sic: Port St Nikolo.]

Only three minutes after the explosion, *Britannic*'s distress signal reached HMS *Scourge*,[61] under the command of Lieutenant Commander Henry Tupper. The previous day, the Greek steamer *Sparti* had struck a mine and was then beached on the north side of the island of Phleva. *Scourge* had embarked her passengers and mails, taking them to Piraeus, and when she received *Britannic*'s distress call she was arranging for a tow for the *Sparti*. However, the tow would have to wait. Tupper ordered the French tugs *Goliath*, *Polyphemus* and Trawler 258 to follow him as he ordered *Scourge*'s 7½-knot speed increased to 'full speed ahead' – about 24 knots – and set a course for the Kea Channel.

HMS *Heroic*, under the command of Lieutenant Commander Percival Ram RNR, had earlier that morning passed *Britannic* and, having turned onto a course of

Britannic arrives at Southampton. She is escorted by tugs, who will assist her into berth. (Imperial War Museum, Q22770)

North 62° west at 7.48 a.m., immediately turned around to go to her assistance after the SOS signal was received at 8.28 a.m. Ram quickly ordered *Heroic*'s speed increased from 12 knots to the maximum of 18 knots. In fact, although *Heroic* was slower than *Scourge*, she was closer and would arrive a few minutes earlier at the distress position.

On board *Britannic*, Reverend Fleming felt the explosion and snatched his lifebelt from his cabin before heading to his assigned ward for emergencies. He was greeted with empty beds, as no patients were to board until Mudros, later that morning. Then the alarm sounded: he snatched his bible and headed for the boat deck.[62]

Sheila Macbeth had only just sat down to breakfast and ate two spoonfuls of porridge before the explosion. When the alarm sounded, she and the other nurses headed for their cabins and then for the boat deck[63] when Major Priestley instructed them: 'You had better go to your cabins for your lifebelts.' Many remarked how lucky it was that no sick or wounded were on board.[64] In fact, despite the severe explosion, most of them didn't realise the serious nature of the damage and merely thought the ship had hit another vessel.

The valuables that people collected from their cabins illustrated the strange workings of minds under pressure: Reverend Fleming fetched his bible; Violet Jessop collected her toothbrush, remembering how she had missed one after leaving the sinking *Titanic* four years earlier; and one girl snatched her fountain pen, leaving £30 on her pillow, a substantial sum in 1916.[65] As everyone reached the boat deck, many of the boats were ready for lowering.

Lieutenant R.A. Shekleton had charge of the only patients on board (men of the RAMC personnel) and at once assembled them with their life jackets on the boat deck.

Captain J.L. Renton gathered the nurses on the boat deck compass area, the raised roof over what would have been the first-class lounge, with lifebelts and blankets. Fortunately, it was a warm morning of nearly 70° Fahrenheit, a contrast to the near-freezing temperatures in the isolated Atlantic for *Titanic*'s survivors four years earlier.

Major Priestley paraded the RAMC detachment with their lifejackets at the after end of A-deck, then went down the stairs – second-class stairs in peacetime – and checked the aft barrack rooms on F and G-decks, ensuring that nobody had been left behind.

Back on the boat deck, 'the crew were working with frantic speed swinging out the lifeboats.'[66] Although Captain Bartlett had only ordered the boats *made ready for lowering*, *Britannic*'s strong list caused urgency and the boats began to be lowered while the bridge was unaware.

Owing to the 20-degree starboard list, the powerful steering gear was unable to control the 101¼-ton rudder properly. Only a slight movement resulted when helm commands were given. So when Captain Bartlett decided to beach the ship – unaware of the flooding in boiler rooms 5 and 6, which would still not have been enough to sink the ship – he ordered the port engine astern and the starboard engine ahead for the turn to port, towards Kea island's sandy shores. The ship turned in a small area and then Captain Bartlett rang down for 'full speed ahead'.

Britannic's hard working engines helped develop a reasonable forward momentum and she was soon leaving a large 'V' in her wake, despite the fact that she had already taken on considerable quantities of water. Unfortunately, it soon became clear that her condition was worsening. Bartlett recalled 'the forward holds filled rapidly and water was reported in Nos 5 and 6 boiler rooms, so I stopped the engines and ordered all boats possible to be sent away, but to stand by near the ship.' At this stage, the key problem was that the ship's list to starboard had submerged much of E-deck, where a number of portholes had been left open to assist in ventilating the ship's lower decks. Gordon Fielding, *Britannic*'s fifth officer, recalled 'it was impossible to stop the rush of the sea through these holes, and soon every section of the ship on the low side was awash below the waterline, and the watertight bulkheads were now useless.'[67] Fifteen minutes after the explosion, E-deck was underwater between the first and second funnels and 'water was coming along this deck from forward'.

Nurse W. Greenwood had got her lifebelt and joined a party of nurses heading up the main stairs to the boat deck. They met an officer, who hailed them. 'You had better hurry up, ladies.' When they reached the boat deck, Miss Greenwood recalled, 'we realised that something dreadful had happened'. Everybody was 'lined up on deck', waiting calmly to get into the lifeboats.[68]

Assistant Captain Harry William Dyke was stationed at the aft starboard 'girder' davit stations; Fifth Officer Gordon Fielding and First Officer George Oliver on the aft port 'girder' davit stations; Sixth Officer Hebert Welsh worked the smaller Welin davits on the starboard side; and Third Officer Francis Laws the Welin davits on the port side.

Meanwhile, Sea Scout James Vickers remained on the bridge, having supplied Captain Bartlett with his megaphone from the locker[69] in the officers' quarters. Sea Scout George Perman had been operating the elevators when he felt the explosion and, on appearing on deck, a passing crew member handed him a spare lifebelt. Then he waited his turn for the lifeboats.

Violet Jessop had been preparing a breakfast tray for a sick nurse when the explosion occurred and she had delivered the breakfast and saw her charge safely to the boat deck before she headed for her cabin, aft on C-deck, near the RAMC mess, which would have been used as the doctor's cabin in peacetime. Then she went onto the boat deck forward and boarded lifeboat four on the port side, one of the boats served by the smaller 'Welin' davits, which was lowered with difficulty owing to the gradually increasing starboard list that was developing at the time. In fact, the lifeboat splintered part of the green glass lighting on the line along *Britannic*'s hull, as well as hooking itself on a porthole.[70] But as they cast off *Britannic* was still underway, causing their boat to move nearer and nearer the stern…

There were several boats in the water on the port side and the irresistible pull by *Britannic*'s propeller, whose blades were breaking the surface, led to tragedy. Jessop watched bemused as her lifeboat's occupants abandoned the boat and she found herself almost alone. Then, to her horror, she looked behind and saw the monster propeller breaking the frothy surface, sending up lashings of spray. Her lifeboat was being inexorably drawn into the 'mincing,…glittering, relentless blades'. A quick jump and a dear struggle for life followed. She was spun around by the propeller underwater and hit her head on the keel of another lifeboat before being rescued.[71] Two boats were pulled in and dashed to pieces, their occupants killed and injured. It was simply by luck that the situation was not even more serious, by virtue of Bartlett's decision to stop the engines when he gave the official order for *Britannic* to be abandoned. The propeller stopped before a third boat was pulled in. Captain T. Fearnhead of the RAMC was among the boat's occupants, who were able to push off from the propeller's stationary blades.

Seventy people had been killed or wounded by the blades and many lifeboats managed to assist with rescue attempts. Brandy flasks, aprons and bandages were given to the wounded. At the time of the accidents, Matron Mrs E.A. Dowse did not draw anybody's attention to the terrible sights as she saw them from her lifeboat.[72]

From the compass deck amidships, Major Priestley was among those who threw life-belts, rafts and deckchairs overboard to those in the water. Nurse W. Greenwood recalled her evacuation from *Britannic*:

> We climbed in [to the lifeboat] in double quick time, and were at once lowered over the side of the ship,…to the water below. As soon as we got a little distance away, we could see our glorious ship was going down at the head…many other lifeboats had been lowered and we were pulling away from the ship we had been so happy on.

On the bridge, Captain Bartlett realised that the flooding was progressing and, with *Britannic*'s bows down heavily, many of the lifeboats having left and the Kea island only a short distance away, he moved the engine telegraphs to 'full speed ahead' at 8.45 a.m. Although having taken on enormous quantities of water, the ship still managed to make quite good headway.

At the same time, the starboard list had increased a little and no more boats left from the port side, despite the advanced 'girder'-type davits aft, which finally lowered the port side motor launch, whose occupants included Lieutenant Colonel Anderson. He noticed the ship had been moving and that her wake stretched far back.

Earlier, Fifth Officer Fielding had stopped some seamen and stewards rushing the boats here, then lowered the boats nearly to the water to get the group out of the way, not releasing the boats as a precaution against the deadly port propeller.[73] His precautions were wise: were it not for this action, then these boats would almost certainly have been drawn in, adding to the list of casualties.

Another lonely example of bad discipline belonged to a group of fifteen firemen, who had commandeered one of the boats on the 'shade deck', above the stern poop.[74]

Nurse Sheila Macbeth recalled that as her lifeboat was hanging over the ship's side, from the aft starboard 'girder' davits, *Britannic*'s Assistant Commander, Harry William Dyke, rushed from his station and ordered the firemen to rescue those who had already jumped overboard.[75]

Reverend Fleming told of the RAMC men paraded aft on A-deck. 'They maintained a quiet, resolute and courageous demeanour throughout,' he later wrote. He helped draft them to the boat deck and the lifeboats in groups of fifty.[76] *Britannic* was soon deserted by all but a few, those in her lifeboats watching as she battled to stay afloat and reach the shore.

VAD member Ms B. Mattison 'stood-up in her boat and controlled the rowing'. In fact, a number of the lifeboats were undermanned. Many nurses rowed and others cared for the wounded, picked up from the lifeboats wrecked by the port propeller. 'Our brandy flasks were invaluable, also aprons and pillow cases, which were torn-up as bandages,' recalled Sheila Macbeth. 'Some boats had only men in them and if any of these contained wounded, we always went alongside and gave them Sisters to help.'[77]

Captain H. Slater (Orderly Officer), Sergeant Major G. Pottinger and Sergeant P. Nichols had helped with the filling of the lifeboats and finally left *Britannic* at 8.55 a.m., in the last lifeboat but one. Sergeant S. Halliday and Corporal S. Ogden saved pay books and many records from the ship, also leaving at the eleventh hour.

Reverend Fleming emerged from the forward staircase, having been below for bread for the lifeboats, to the starboard boat deck, which 'seemed quite deserted'. He noticed Major Priestley there, before being called into the heavily-loaded last-but-one lifeboat.[78]

On the bridge, Captain Bartlett ordered Sea Scout James Vickers to abandon ship, which he did by boarding the same crowded lifeboat as Reverend Fleming.[79]

It was now painfully clear that his command could not be saved. The seas washed over the foredecks and the bows sank deeper as the liner's now-sharp angle increased. But the ship still had some headway. Moving in a large circle to starboard, owing mostly to the list, *Britannic* had now reversed her heading to the south-west by west with the strong surface currents 'twisting' the ship's head around – and was heading briefly back to where she had come from.[80]

Reverend Fleming recalled that as his crowded lifeboat moved away from *Britannic*, he 'could see the waves splashing already well over the bows and playing with them, as waves play with the sand dreadnoughts of the children on the beach'.[81]

Major Priestley had a final look around the boat deck to see that nobody remained on board before boarding the final lifeboat to leave the ship, along with Purser Claude Lancaster, who carried the precious ship's log. Eight men of the RAMC – Privates Bateson, Brelsford, Busson, McDowell, Jacklin, Netherway, Radcliff and Ward – had been with the Major, assisting, and he made sure that they were in the boat first. In particular, Busson and Netherway had 'carried out their police duties in an exemplary manner'. Their lifeboat left at 9.00 a.m.

All hope had gone and the bridge was almost level with the water. Captain Bartlett telegraphed 'Finished with Engines' and received an acknowledgement from the engine room. He then blew the ship's whistles 'for the last alarm'. Assistant Commander Harry William Dyke reported that it appeared everyone had left the ship, so Captain Bartlett told him to leave. He followed shortly afterwards: 'walking into the water by the forward boat gantry on [the] starboard side, the third funnel falling a few minutes later.' The ship's engineering staff, including *Britannic's* assistant chief engineer, Joseph Wolfe, were on board until the final moments. Wolfe recalled: 'When we reached the deck the foremost of the four funnels was touching the water, and the bows were completely submerged. We jumped eighty feet into the sea from the second-class quarters on C-deck and after swimming clear we watched the awesome sight of the mighty liner sinking.'★

Lieutenant J. Starkie had earlier left the boat deck to 'procure as much bread as possible' for the lifeboats, but when he re-emerged on deck after his odyssey through the tilting, flooding interiors, he was in for a shock. The decks were deserted. Lifeboats had departed, with the exception of some twenty-three lifeboats that remained on their davits and were never launched… He saw that the bridge was submerged and swam with all his might 100 yards from the ship before it disappeared. Even now, the vessel's propellers turned, but as they were above water, they had no effect over the enormous hulk.

As the bows now sank ever-deeper and the waters washed up the boat deck, *Britannic* gave up her efforts to remain upright and gave a heavy thunderous roll to starboard, completely capsizing. Deck fittings, exposed to an angle their mountings were not designed to cope with, 'fell into the sea like a child's toys', Violet Jessop would later remember.[82]

★ Joseph Wolfe served on board a succession of White Star liners, culminating in *Olympic*, before he joined *Britannic*. He was a respected engineer, known to be modest and reliable. Awarded the OBE (Order of the British Empire) in 1917, he travelled to Germany after the armistice to oversee the completion of vessels that would be handed over as war reparations. These included *Bismarck*, which entered White Star's service as *Majestic* in May 1922. Wolfe met King George V and Queen Mary when they toured the ship in the late summer of 1922 and he served as the ship's chief engineer for eight years. He retired after reaching the compulsory age limit and passed away in 1933.

Left and opposite: Private John Riddell, of the Royal Army Medical Corps (RAMC), was serving on board the hospital ship *Panama*. He took these unique photographs at Naples when *Britannic* called to collect the wounded. People watched and waved from her crowded decks; and then she departed for Southampton at 3.15 p.m. on 4 February 1916. (Mark Chirnside/Michail Michailakis collection)

Three of the four enormous funnels, through which two steam locomotives could have been driven side-by-side, could not stand the strain and toppled from the ship, but incredibly the partly submerged forward funnel remained in position, although vertical. 'They smashed off like matchwood.'[83]

Through the mysterious smokescreen that now hung around the sinking ship could be seen the figures of some of the engineers, abandoning ship finally. But now *Britannic*'s stern rose again slightly as she suddenly dived by the bow and slid forward into the sea.

From his crowded lifeboat, James Vickers watched in horror. 'She went bow first,' he described, 'the propellers came out of the water and I felt pretty flabbergasted.'[84] 'With a final roar,' Violet Jessop later wrote of the mesmerising finale, 'she disappeared into the depths, the noise of her going resounding through the water with undreamt-of violence.'[85] *Britannic* disappeared under 'a pitiless whirlpool'.[86]

Britannic's stern plates were covered by the sea at about 9.07 a.m. Captain Bartlett swam out to the starboard motor launch to order them to make for Port St Nikolo with the wounded, remaining himself aboard a raft.

Swimming in the water, Violet Jessop saw one of *Britannic*'s motor boats racing towards her, which slowed when it got nearer, and she was hauled on board, along with some other survivors from the water.[87] A local fisherman, Francesco Psilas, rescued several survivors from the water; he was later paid £4 by the Admiralty in gratitude.[88]

From the lifeboats was sighted 'smoke from two ships which seemed to be coming towards us at a terrific speed'. Immediately, people were worried that they were enemy vessels, but then they saw 'to great joy' the British Ensign.

Heroic sighted objects ahead of her in the water at 10.03 a.m., speed being reduced and the ship stopped three minutes later. Her boats were lowered to pick up survivors as the *Scourge* arrived at 10.10 a.m., having sighted *Britannic*'s thirty-five floating lifeboats ten minutes earlier. *Scourge*'s boats were all lowered to pick up survivors and over the next one-and-a-half hours sixty-four nurses, three stewardesses, three RAMC officers and 269 other ratings were taken aboard, a total of 339 survivors.

Having been on a raft since the sinking, Captain Bartlett was able to board the port motor launch at about 10.30 a.m., with Lieutenant Colonel Anderson in it, and then proceeded to Port St Nikolo as the rescue ships continued their work.

Meanwhile, *Heroic* took aboard about 493 survivors, including several wounded, and one dead person. One of the wounded would later die as *Heroic* travelled to Piraeus.

After *Scourge* had raised her boats and then proceeded to Piraeus at 11.30 a.m., her year-younger sister-ship *Foxhound* arrived at 11.45 a.m., having been signalled by *Scourge* sometime earlier while on patrolling duties. She had then proceeded at 10.30 a.m. at full speed for the sight of the sinking. *Foxhound* – under Lieutenant Commander William Shuttleworth's command – was left searching for survivors in the water after *Heroic* had left for Piraeus at 11.55 a.m.

However, with many survivors at Port St Nikolo on Kea island, including many injured and taken there by *Britannic*'s two motor boats, more help was on the way in the form of the vessels *Foresight* and *Chasseur*. It was fortunate that the local residents were especially helpful, showing 'much practical sympathy' and freely 'opening their homes'. Having rescued three or four survivors from the water, the local fisherman Francesco Psilas then took them into his home, while the local doctor came as fast as he could to assist the wounded, at least ten of whom were in a 'serious' condition.

Foxhound proceeded to Port St Nikolo on Kea island after searching the sea, arriving there at 1.00 p.m. *Foresight* and *Chasseur* arrived there forty-five minutes later. Here *Foxhound*, which had already taken-on wounded, took aboard twenty-two wounded survivors and 171 uninjured survivors. From *Foresight* were sent several medical officers to assist the wounded, and she remained behind with *Britannic*'s lifeboats after *Foxhound* departed at 2.20 p.m. for Piraeus at 20 knots, or about 455 revolutions.

At Piraeus's Bay of Salamis, *Heroic* and *Scourge* transferred over 1,000 survivors to the 15,000-ton HMS *Duncan*, moored alongside. Fortunately, however, due to the thoughtful consideration of the French fleet's Admiral Darrieus, many of the uninjured survivors were able to board the French vessels to relieve *Duncan*'s situation.

The reunion was moving, as after 'an excellent tea' the ship's company lined up on deck for a roll call, which proved that some people were missing. All of the *Duncan*'s officers were 'almost falling over each other' to look after the survivors, especially the nurses, as there was the common rule that no ladies were allowed aboard any warships.

Violet Jessop was offered a hot bath on HMS *Foxhound* before joining the *Duncan* and she enjoyed the bath, but had a fright when she spotted a sign on a nearby door, reading 'Magazine Room,' and fled.[89]

Leaving the *Duncan*, Violet Jessop stayed at the Aktaion hotel in Piraeus with many of the sisters, VADs and stewardesses, although she thought some of the food 'the rankest thing I have ever tried to eat'.[90]

Sheila Macbeth had been rescued by *Scourge*, but she then boarded the *Duncan*. She reached Piraeus aboard a French vessel, then when she reached the quay was driven to Phaleron with other survivors, to go to the hotel Aktaion. The medical orderlies and officers went to another hotel not far away, which unfortunately proved to be anti-Venizelist, but at the Aktaion it was very crowded as the hotel had prepared rooms for eighteen instead of eighty. At the hotel, it was not until 10.00 p.m. that dinner was served, but shortly afterwards messages arrived from the Russian Hospital that nurses were needed for night duty, and several who spoke French travelled there by car for the night.

As she spoke French, Sheila quickly made friends and was able to act as a nurse/interpreter at the local Russian hospital. Although some of the Greeks seemed to resent them being there, the stay and accompanying work seems ultimately to have been enjoyed and appreciated.[91]

Vera Brittain and her previous room-mate on the *Britannic*, Betty, visited a once cheerful sister at the Floriana hospital in Valletta, whom she had made friends with on *Britannic's* fifth voyage, but who was now changed following her ordeal and nervous.[92]

The days following the sinking would reveal a mercifully small loss of life, but there were still funeral services to be conducted. At 1.20 p.m. on 22 November 1916 the bodies of Private Arthur Binks, Fireman Charles Phillips and Fireman Joseph Brown were landed from the flagship *Duncan* (flying her half-masted colours) at the grain quay. (Lookout George Honeycott, who passed away at the Russian hospital, was buried at the same time.)

Reverend Fleming recalled:

> We gathered in the afternoon amid glorious sunshine on the grain quay of Piraeus. The friends on the flagship had added to their many kindnesses the gift of lovely wreaths inscribed: "To the heroes of Britain." The allied fleets were represented there, and a firing party was furnished from the flagship. Greek sympathisers joined and our fellow countrymen whose homes were in these parts came down...
>
> The streets were densely packed with men who looked on with strangely conflicting expressions; but all were reverent towards us as we carried our burden to the tomb. The great wreaths which had been sent in sympathy our orderlies carried in front of the coffins. These men and the other orderlies who followed were a touching sight, dressed in all varieties of uniform, Naval and Military, French and British, a strange reminder of the losses and the trials of the day before; and so we wended our way to the quiet cemetery on the hill...[93]

Thirty people had died in the sinking (see appendices), but 1,032 had survived, including two *Titanic* survivors: Fireman John Priest and Violet Jessop (both had also been on *Olympic* when the *Hawke* collision occurred).[94] Two medical officers from the torpedoed *Galeka* had also survived the sinking.[95]

On 22 November 1916, at 4.00 p.m. the *Duncan* received four of *Britannic's* lifeboats from the ship *Verité*, sending in all seventeen lifeboats to the Salamis dockyard at 9.30 a.m. the following day. Other lifeboats had been distributed somewhat, although a photograph exists today of at least one boat secured alongside the *Heroic*.[96]

Foresight departed Port St Nikolo at 4.00 p.m. on the day of the sinking, while *Foxhound* and *Scourge* were back on patrol the following morning and *Heroic* left Salamis

An interesting perspective of *Britannic*, with hints that she was photographed beneath ominous skies. The smaller hospital ship on the port side is hard to identify, but she may be one of the Union Castle ships. (Digital restoration by Eric Keith Longo, © 2011/Author's collection)

early that morning at 6.55 a.m. *Duncan* remained at Piraeus and on 23 November 1916 at 1.15 p.m. she witnessed the discharge of various ratings from the French vessels to the HMT *Ermine*, near the *Royal George*.

Surviving officers and orderlies were shipped home via a troop transport to Marseilles, which was followed by an arduous three-day journey by train to Le Havre; the nurses remained at Malta until the *Valdivia* could take them home.[97] Archie Jewell, having boarded the HMT *Royal George* for the five-day journey to Marseilles, remembered the train journey home as being uncomfortable, due to the cold conditions and bad condition of the carriages,[98] which contrasted with Reverend Fleming's recollection of a good journey. Most of the survivors did not reach home until Christmas.

The hospital ship *Grantully Castle* was packed with wounded when she called to take some of the staff to Malta. Before she went home, Violet Jessop finally met up with her brother.[99]

Vera Brittain's friend said that she would remember the sinking for the rest of her life. For Reverend Fleming, too, the sinking had a profound effect on the rest of his life as he relieved the last moments on board; but for many years after the event he and Sheila Macbeth kept in touch.[100]

Two weeks after the sinking, Captain Bartlett recorded in the crew log the welcome news to some that: 'All fines and forfeitures imposed on those who were members of the crew on 21 November are cancelled on account of their excellent conduct when the ship sank.'

As the authorities struggled to cope with the worsening situation in the Mediterranean, the hospital ships *Warilda*, *Herefordshire*, *Wandilla*, *Llandovery Castle*, *Dover Castle* and *Glenart Castle* were returned to England with wounded as soon as was possible. The

General Headquarters at Egypt requested that the *Neuralia* be taken over as a hospital ship and that other vessels would be sent to ease the burden.

On 24 November 1916 the War Office's Director of Transports informed Cunard that orders had been issued for the *Aquitania* to be despatched to the Mediterranean port of Augusta as soon as possible and that she would leave in early December 1916.

It was 5 December 1916 when Lieutenant Colonel Anderson's report, written at Hamrun Hospital, was completed. In it he detailed the many examples of heroics during the sinking, noting specifically Major Priestley's actions, which Priestley had modestly described as 'a mere picnic compared with a day in a prisoners' camp'. He had also assisted the injured when they reached Port St Nikolo. Others mentioned especially included the Serbian Relief Committee, Mr and Mrs Anastasiali, and other local residents who had helped the survivors at the Russian Hospital. The commanders of the rescue vessels and their staff were thanked 'for their exceeding kindness'.

★ ★ ★

Britannic's loss was announced in the press of Thursday 23 November 1916. Unsurprisingly, information was often incomplete and inaccurate. *The Times* published a brief statement from the Secretary of the Admiralty:

> British Hospital Ship *Britannic* was sunk by mine or torpedo yesterday morning (21st) in the Zea [Kea] Channel, in the Aegean Sea.
>
> There are 1,106 survivors, 28 of whom are injured, and it is estimated that about 50 are lost. Full particulars will be published as soon as they are received.

The newspaper went on to say that *Britannic* had sunk 1½ miles from shore, listed that the ship had been carrying wounded, incorrectly, and noted, 'this new act of German barbarity excites profound indignation'. *Britannic* has been 'the largest British vessel afloat' and 'lowered all her boats'.

The *Daily Mirror* repeated the Admiralty's statement and noted that the liner had 'been sunk by a mine or torpedo'.

However, with over-imagination the paper stated 'every effort was made to save the sick and wounded, who are said to have numbered upwards of a thousand'.

The *Daily Telegraph* also published the Admiralty's statement, gave a description of the *Britannic* – including her designed passenger accommodation – and said the liner had been 'a veritable ship of mercy'.

Its New York correspondent said that a despatch was being prepared for Germany stating 'that the failure of the U-boats to respect the laws of nations must entail the severance of diplomatic relations'. This appears to have been untrue.

By 24 November it was made clear that the ship had not been carrying wounded, but the propaganda continued.

The Times' Naval Correspondent said that a 'deliberate opportunity was made by the Germans' to display the country's 'disregard for the laws of nations and…get rid of a vessel likely to be a formidable competitor' after the war had finished.

The *Daily Mirror* corrected that no sick or wounded had been aboard the hospital ship. But the paper speculated about the weapon of the ship's fate. It told of a talk in the House of Commons:

The Premier, replying to Sir E. Carson, said there was no further information… as to the suggestion that the attention of neutral governments should be drawn to this latest act of barbarism, the matter was receiving the most careful consideration.

Sir W. Byles: 'Is it yet ascertained whether the *Britannic* was torpedoed or mined?'

Mr Asquith: 'Not yet.'

Additionally, the ship's red crosses and lights were mentioned, making it clear that if the ship had been torpedoed, the Germans knew it was a hospital ship.

The *Daily Telegraph* called the sinking 'a dastardly crime'. Captain Bartlett was falsely reported as saying, 'I am convinced that she was sunk by torpedoes.' But the paper did note that mines could have since been laid, and in the deep channel. 'It appears also that the Germans can now anchor mines up to a depth of 200 yards.'

One story relayed by the paper stated that an enemy submarine had attempted to 'block' the distress signals. As with The *Daily Mirror*, it was reported 'every effort was made to indicate the character of the vessel'.

On 25 November the *Southampton Times & Hampshire Express* reported of the crew's survival, 'for the fact that the loss of life among them is comparatively small, no thanks are due to the enemy, to whose ghoulish malignity and utterly unscrupulous tactics the magnificent vessel fell victim.'

'Throughout Wednesday evening and the whole of Thursday,' numerous enquiries were made at the Offices of the British Seafarers' Union and the White Star Line's Southampton offices in Canute Road, before the Admiralty's initial list of casualties appeared late on Thursday.'

The February 1915 German attack on the hospital ship *Asturias* was mentioned, as well as the Kaiser's false statement that troops had been aboard at the time of the attempted torpedoing. Clearly, the Germans had struck before and would not have had hesitation in trying again.

It was reported that the hospital ship *Braemar Castle* had been sunk near the area of the *Britannic*'s sinking on 23 November 1916, two days afterwards; but in fact this hospital ship had been beached after striking a mine. In all fairness, even the Admiralty did not have the full details.

'There is only one kind of language that Germany understands, and we, who are at war with her, must employ it to the utmost of our capacity.'

A list of the dead and the missing was also published, which was riddled with inaccuracies. The paper noted that Fireman J. McFeat, among the missing, had played for Southampton's reserve football team. Another comment was: 'It is stated that about a dozen of the firemen on the ship were on the *Titanic* when she sank in the Atlantic on her maiden voyage.'

'In the full list there are four dead and twenty-seven are described as missing…,' the paper said.

Britannic had foundered in fifty-five minutes. 'Three of the boats launched were caught by the screws and cut to pieces.'

The Times exclaimed: 'War on Hospital Ships!'

'Within days of the sinking of the *Britannic* in the Aegean Sea another British hospital ship – the *Braemar Castle* – has been sunk in the same waters.'

Germany's government had given a statement on *Britannic*'s loss, which was published. They understood that the £2 million liner had carried over 1,000 people, of whom twenty-eight died:

> According to reports so far to hand, the ship was on its way from England to Salonika. For a journey in this direction the large number of persons…is extraordinarily striking, which justifies the forcible suspicion of the misuse of the ship for the purposes of [troop] transport.

Because *Britannic* carried hospital ship markings, there could 'naturally be no question of a German submarine in connection with the sinking'.

Published below the German statement was the British statement, justifying the number of people on board. There had been roughly 625 crew and 500 Medical Staff aboard, a total of 1,125 people. The medical staff had consisted of '25 officers, 76 nurses' and 399 'others' – sergeants, hospital orderlies, clerical staff, operating room attendants…

One interesting statement appeared in the *Kieler Zeitung*: 'The *Britannic* was transporting fresh troops for our enemies. If she had not been doing so, our submarines would never, of course, have torpedoed her.' The subject of much interest, the statement could be construed as an admission that she had been torpedoed. In fact, there was a more prosaic explanation. The Admiralty intercepted a message from Berlin to the German Embassy in Washington, sent on 29 November 1916:

> *Kieler Zeitung* November 23rd published report of English Admiralty about loss steamer *Britannic*. British report gave two causes 'mine or torpedo'; of these two first and most probable one however omitted in *Kieler Zeitung* by mistake. Newspaper thus only took notice of torpedo as cause, therefore added comment signed by editor that if hospital ship in any case most certainly had troops on board since otherwise would not have been torpedoed by submarine. For submarine unconditionally observe laws of nations. English wireless Carnarvon [sic] uses this publication of *Kieler Zeitung* and misinterprets it in fashion which characteristic for means used by British Press service. English wireless says: *Kieler Zeitung* declares that British hospital ship was torpedoed. *Zeitung* adds following apparently inspired comment: *Britannic* was transporting troops for our enemies. If she had not done this our submarines of course would not have torpedoed her. This comment – admits English wireless – is signed by editor of *Kieler Zeitung*. This interesting publication characterises attitude maintained International law by staff German navy. Carnarvon wireless than adds that German navy already torpedoed six hospital ships without warning which is absolute untruth. Declaration of German Admiralty November 24th already proved that nor sinking of *Britannic* German torpedo out of question.

★   ★   ★

When *Titanic* foundered, the loss of such a major ship in peacetime and during her maiden voyage prompted a huge number of questions. *Britannic*'s loss was perceived differently. She was one of many war losses by enemy action, however useful it may have been for wartime propagandists. Nevertheless, the authorities were keen to investigate the cause of her loss, even if the investigation would be cursory by comparison. On 24 November 1916 two of *Duncan*'s officers, her captain, Hugh Heard, and engineer commander, George Staer, submitted their own report to Rear Admiral Hayes Sadler, based upon interviews with a number of witnesses, but they freely admitted 'the difficulty in finding witnesses scattered over the whole fleet'.

They noted as a possible reason for the ship's loss and rapid foundering that the open portholes and scuttles on decks F and E had been submerged some fifteen minutes after the explosion, allowing considerable quantities of water into the ship. On E-deck, 'water was coming along this deck from forward', they wrote. In fact, the water flooding E-deck and F-deck deck would have slowly seeped below into the four dry boiler rooms, and likely accounted – certainly to an extent – for the ship's heavy starboard list, as much of the flooding was concentrated on the starboard side. As the ship sank further, the flooding increased continually and so did the list before the ship sank.

The question of what had caused the explosion was harder to fathom. On the surface, there seemed to be a great deal of evidence indicating that she had been torpedoed. One of the ship's bakers, Henry Etches, reported seeing the track of a torpedo on the port side and according to his subsequent written statement:

> I was at the after poop [deck], when the crash occurred, starboard side. I at once ran over to port and standing just forward of [the] after bridge I saw small jimps [sic] in water approaching at great speed about four hundred yards from side of ship, where I was standing, but what caught my eye most was, a long straight line following it reaching as far as my eye could follow, causing a slight displacement of a darker coloured water, no one being near me at the time…

Thomas Walters, a deck steward, also reported seeing a torpedo, but to starboard:

> …between the hours of 8 to 8.15 I was standing on the starboard side of the ship forward on A-deck looking over the rail in a forward position when my eyes caught sight of a white stream coming at a great speed towards the ship's bow. The thought flashed to my brain that this was a torpedo on the instant I gripped the rail and leaned inboard to await the explosion, which seemed to occur immediately, I then looked down at the water but had to hold my nostrils on account of the fumes which were stifling. I could see what appeared to be a great disturbance of water aft.

Another interesting account came from Thomas Eckett, whose sighting occurred after the explosion:

> …About twenty minutes after the *Britannic* was hit I was standing on the poop deck, starboard side, alongside my boat (No.19) when, on looking across the water, I saw, about a quarter of a mile away (or at the most no more than half a mile) about five or six points off the starboard bow, what appeared to be a small narrow mast sticking out of the water about three or four feet, there was a wash of water both fore and aft of this object – the wash being greatest at the after end – as if something was just awash, it was also moving along slowly. The direction it was going in would take it across the course the *Britannic* was then making.
>
> I called the attention of this to a fireman (E. Biffen) who was standing alongside me, remarking at the same time that 'it looked as if the submarine had come up to shell us'. After watching it for about two minutes I noticed it was being submerged – moving at the same time, after which it was gradually lost to view, the wash and mast having disappeared. I should say that from the time I first saw it until it was submerged would be about four minutes. The sea was very smooth at the time, there was not the smallest of

> waves breaking, it was this smoothness of the sea that enabled me to note the wash and
> wake of the object so plainly, compelling me to conclude that it must be a submarine.

Heard and Staer noted their evidence. Walters, in particular, was an impressive witness.
He had previously served as an officer's steward in the Royal Navy and observed torpedo practice. However, Etches' sighting had been on the port side of the ship and aft.
Assuming both men were correct, surely the only way to account for the discrepancy was
that a torpedo had been fired forward on the starboard side and another torpedo, from
another submarine, aft on the port side. Ultimately, they found it hard to give them cre-
dence.★ Although they wrote that 'the water was deep, probably over 100 fathoms' and
there was a current through the channel, which they felt argued against the mine theory:
'On the other hand there is no evidence of a column of water having been thrown up
outside the ship.' However severe the explosion, the characteristics of a torpedo hit were
missing: 'The effects of the explosion might have been due to either a mine or torpedo.
The probability seems to be a mine,' they concluded.

Vice Admiral Cecil Thursby also sent Commander C.G. Brodie to Salonika to interview some of *Britannic*'s survivors 'with a view to obtaining further evidence as to the
cause of her sinking'. Brodie was 'unable to obtain any further evidence of a conclusive
nature; but was much impressed by Deck Steward F. [sic] Walters, who gave his evidence very clearly… There was nobody near him at the time, everyone having gone
down to breakfast.' Thursby himself spoke with Thomas Walters, Henry Etches, lookouts
J. Murray and J. Conolly (both promoted in October 1916), Chief Officer Robert Hume
and Fourth Officer Duncan Campbell McTavish, but 'could obtain no fresh evidence
from them bearing on the case'. Nor did he convene a formal court of enquiry 'as to
do so, would have entailed detaining the officers and crew of *Britannic* at Salonika, and I
presumed that the sinking would form the subject of a thorough investigation in England.'

Reverend Fleming's own published account noted: 'numbers of the ship's people
agree that they saw what they took to be a torpedo miss the rudder and a second one
find us in the bow.'[101] It is difficult to substantiate such statements. Fleming's statement
was undoubtedly correct as far as it went, but how many of those people were on deck at
the time? Thomas Walters reported that nobody had been near him, as most people were
at breakfast, nor did Henry Etches mention anybody else. When Thomas Eckett spoke
to Fireman Biffen, he did so after the explosion. Perhaps the statements of Walters and
Etches became general knowledge as people spoke following the sinking, but then none
of the ship's officers or lookouts reported seeing the track of even one torpedo, although
conditions of visibility seem to have been ideal. When Conolly handed over to Murray,
the lookout reported to his relief that 'two suspicious objects were in sight'. Fleming
learned that 'moving objects resembling barrels' had been reported, but the significance of
the sighting is unclear since mines were usually found further below the surface. Although
Captain Bartlett reported the 'good evidence that the tracks of two torpedoes were seen',
again the issue came back to the characteristics of the explosion. His first impression was
that they had 'struck a mine'. The inevitable water column accompanying a torpedo hit

---

★ Sightings of torpedo tracks or submarines were far from uncommon during the war, but they were not always real.
It may be recalled, for example, that on 1 October 1915 numerous witnesses attested to seeing a torpedo or its track
miss *Olympic*'s stern, even though there was only one submarine in the vicinity. She did not report firing one, yet all
torpedoes needed to be accounted for.

had not existed: 'The damage was most extensive, probably the whole of the fore part of the ship's bottom being destroyed and in my opinion penetrating to No.6 boiler room. Water was seen to be thrown up to E or D-deck forward at the time of the explosion, and a cloud of black smoke was seen, the fumes for some time being suffocating.' The force of the explosion explains how water could have been thrown up as far as D-deck, but a water column from a torpedo hit would have extended far above the ship's bow.

The probability that a mine had been responsible was increasingly recognised. *Lloyd's War Losses, The First World War: Casualties to Shipping through Enemy Causes, 1914–1918* records that *Britannic* was sunk by a mine. One of the prisoners rescued from *UB109* when she was lost in August 1918 reported that he had been serving in the Mediterranean at the time and that she had 'struck on a German mine within an hour of its being laid by the submarine *U73*, then under the command of Kapitan-Leutnant Siess'. One of the class of *U71* to *U80*, she was far from reliable. Although a minelayer, she had the capability to fire torpedoes, but needed 'to go into dock for repairs after nearly every trip'. If his evidence was interesting, *U73* was not in the area one hour before *Britannic*'s loss, nor is there a record of any other submarine. Nevertheless, *U73* had been active the previous month. She reached the Gulf of Athens on 27 October 1916 and the following day, after he had observed the route of a number of steamers passing through the Kea Channel, Siess laid a number of mines where he thought they would be most effective. Although Captain Bartlett could not have known at the time, when *Britannic*'s course was changed twenty minutes before the explosion she was heading in precisely the direction of the mines Siess had laid. One barrier of six mines, laid on 28 October 1916 from 37°41´5 North, 24°17´ East to 37°41´7 North, 24°16´8 East, was remarkably close to where she sank, with the last of the six mines less than half a mile to the south-east according to Siess's positions. His submarine returned to port in early November 1916. When he learned of *Britannic*'s loss and the location, Siess claimed responsibility and counted her as part of the 75,000 to 80,000 tons of shipping that *U73* had succeeded in sinking. His report also noted the 'remarkable number of hospital ships' that had been observed.[102]

According to one intelligence report, covering mines laid in October and November 1916, a number of mines had been laid in the archipelago: '10 have exploded or have been swept in the Zea Channel (1 struck by *Burdigala*, 1 struck by *Britannic*, 8 raised and destroyed); 4 have been discovered in the Mykoni Channel (1 struck by *Braemar Castle* and 3 swept); 1 was struck by *Minnewaska* at the entrance of Suda, but we do not know the result of the sweeping in this last zone. In all 15 mines…' Another seven mines had been found in the Gulf of Athens, near the island of Phleva.

Lessons were learned from *Britannic*, as they had been with her sister four years earlier. There was no procedure to inform the wireless operators periodically as to the ship's position, which meant that one of the operators had to go and find it out from one of the ship's officers, while 'the position actually signalled was "Off Point Nikola" and con-siderable doubt existed at first as to the true position, owing to the number of points so named in the Aegean.' Another problem was that 'a defect in the receiving apparatus, possibly caused by the explosion, prevented *Britannic* from receiving the repeated enquiries from HM ships as to her true position, and occasioned a number of wireless signals at a moment when silence was particularly desirable.' Vice Admiral Thursby recommended that large and valuable hospital ships such as *Britannic* 'should carry at least three wireless operators and, in the event of emergency, special messengers should be detailed to attend on the wireless office.' On board ships faster than 12 knots, it would be required that the ship's position be reported every half hour to the wireless office, while 'a simple "stand by" receiving circuit, tuned to 600 metres, and capable of being immediately connected to the aerial, shall be supplied, since it is improbable that defects in the main receiving circuit will be readily located in moments of emergency.'

It is interesting to note the concerns about merchant ships during war time. In *Britannic*'s case, the fact that the watertight doors were still open and the opening of a number of portholes made all the difference. The Institution of Naval Architects appointed a committee to look into the effects of mines or torpedoes on merchant ships, so that they could make recommendations that would render existing ships less likely to sink if they were damaged. Large passenger vessels differed from ordinary cargo steamers in that they had a greater number of watertight doors; numerous portholes to ventilate accommodation on the lower decks; and 'relatively small' hatchways which 'do not afford such instantaneous relief from air and gas pressure resulting from an explosion as in the case of the larger hatchways of cargo vessels'. The committee's preliminary report noted 'devices for closing [watertight] doors from the bridge are likely to fail, both by reason of the… distortion [to watertight bulkheads and doors] and because of the probable destruction of the hydraulic or electric mains provided for the purpose in the region of the explosion' in May 1917. They considered a number of suggestions, including 'the disuse of all firemen's passages and the closing up of all doorways in bulkheads transversed by them when below the bulkhead deck, the firemen passing to and from their quarters by way of an upper deck, where a temporary screened passage could be provided if necessary'; 'all side scuttles situated below the first deck above the bulkhead deck should be closed up and sealed. Special fan ventilation is to be provided if necessary'; and 'all watertight doors in transverse bulkheads on decks below the bulkhead deck to be closed and so secured that they cannot be opened, additional exists to the decks above being provided when necessary.'

Following *Britannic*'s loss, it was increasingly clear that hospital ships were in danger. There was concern on the Allied side that hospital ships should obey, and be seen to obey, international requirements. At the end of July 1916, the hospital ships *Nevasa* and *Oxfordshire* arrived at Port Said, but they 'both carried such a number of RAMC men in khaki as to make it appear that they had troops on board'. *Nevada* was ordered into Algiers by a French patrol, showing how seriously the incident was taken. Although *Britannic* had been given 'special permission' to take RAMC officers, other ranks and nurses as passengers when she left Southampton on 20 October 1916, after that it was directed: 'no passengers other than invalids, nurses and no medical stores other than medicines, instruments, surgical appliances, bandages and the like are to be conveyed in hospital ships.' On 12 December 1916, the director of transports noted 'the remarks of the Germans as to the large numbers of souls on board the *Britannic* and the inference drawn therefrom that the ship was conveying passengers other than invalids'.

In January 1917, the American ambassador in Berlin forwarded to the British government a list of complaints from the German government which alleged numerous abuses of the status of hospital ships. Some of them referred to *Mauretania*, *Aquitania* and *Britannic*. The Germans referred to the allegations of Adalbert Messany, who had been transferred from *Wandilla* to *Britannic* prior to her final Mudros departure. His most serious allegation was that:

> In the ship's hold there were about 2,500 English soldiers wearing their ordinary
> uniform. These were strictly forbidden to go up on deck, and if they did so in spite

of orders they were sent back to their quarters by the medical orderlies. There was an emergency call to quarters every day when the men from the ship's hold were assembled inside the promenade deck. These men did not receive the same food as the patients on deck. In the ship's hold, also, there were no nursing sisters, but only medical orderlies, who did the work of the whole ship.

Two of the medical orderlies, Reg Tapley and Harold Hickman, spoke with Messany during the voyage and he alleged that 'from what these two men told me, and from my own observations, I came to the conclusion that there were about 2,500 men in the ship's hold, *not sick men, but men on leave or being transferred or something of that sort* [author's italics].' When *Britannic* docked at Southampton, Messany watched as 200 stretcher cases were disembarked, and eventually he saw 'the soldiers out of the ship's hold' leaving 'the ship in military formation'. In response, the British government noted a number of errors in Messany's statements, from the ship's departure date to the fact that *Britannic*'s cargo had been transferred to *Wandilla*, not vice versa as he had claimed. The number of invalids on board consisted of two 'non-cot' (or 'walking wounded') naval officers, three naval officer ratings who were 'cot cases' and nineteen naval officer ratings who were 'non-cot cases', fifteen military officers who were 'cot cases', 144 military officers who were 'non-cot cases', 349 military officers of other ranks who were 'cot cases', and 2,490 military officers who were 'non-cot cases'. As for the 2,500 soldiers wearing khaki uniforms, the government quoted paragraph 14 of the 'Standing Orders and Instructions to Officers Commanding Hospital Ships' which read:

> When on the Mediterranean service he will obtain from ordnance stores sufficient home-pattern khaki serge clothing, shirts, underclothing, etc., to fit out, on the homeward voyage, the maximum number of sick and wounded the ships are equipped to carry. Hospital clothing will be used for all cot cases.

Since 'it has never been deemed necessary to clothe walking cases on hospital ships with hospital clothing,' that explained the men's uniforms. It was pointed out that 'a very large proportion of these patients are always convalescent from dysentery, enteric, and malaria, and are quite able to walk about, though unfit for military service.' No restrictions existed on 'the movement of patients to the upper decks of British hospital ships other than those reserved for officers and nursing sisters. The food for all on board is the same, subject only to the medical requirements of cot or other special cases.' Hickman and Tapley refuted Messany's assertions. Hickman denied telling Messany that there were 2,500 troops on board who were not sick; he did not know how many men were on board; and he denied saying anything which implied that *Britannic* 'was being used for illegitimate purposes'.

However comprehensive the British authorities' denials, the war at sea was becoming more dangerous by the day. On 1 February 1917, the German government completed its decision to introduce unrestricted submarine warfare by confirming that they would no longer 'tolerate' hospital ships in certain defined areas such as the Mediterranean, so they were now a legitimate target. Five days later America declared war on Germany.[103] On 17 April 1917, the authorities noted: 'The *Aquitania*, owing to her size, is not only a magnificent target for torpedoes, but is unable to use most of the harbours in the Mediterranean. Since the German notice, she cannot use unprotected anchorages, and if she should still be employed on hospital service, her loss would simply be a matter of time… she must be withdrawn from hospital service.' *Britannic* would not have served much longer as a hospital ship even if she had survived the explosion.

Many hospital ships suffered after the German announcement. *Asturias* had already had a narrow escape when a torpedo missed her in February 1915,★ but she was torpedoed and beached on 21 March 1917 with the loss of fifty crew and RAMC staff; *Gloucester Castle* was torpedoed and beached on 30 March 1917 with the loss of four lives; *Salta* was mined and sank with the loss of 132 people on 10 April 1917; *Lanfranc* was torpedoed and sunk on 17 April 1917; *Dover Castle* torpedoed and sunk on 26 May 1917 with the loss of six lives; *Rewa* was torpedoed and sunk on 4 January 1918 with the loss of four people; *Glenart Castle* was torpedoed and sunk on 26 February 1918 with the loss of 153 RAMC personnel and crew; *Llandovery Castle* was torpedoed and sunk on 27 June 1918 with the loss of 234 crew and RAMC personnel. The war's end prevented any further deliberate attacks.

★ ★ ★

On 27 January 1917, several survivors arrived in New York as members of *Adriatic*'s crew. One steward, who had served on board *Arabic* when she sank in August 1915 as well as *Britannic*, 'said that he preferred the Aegean Sea because it was so much warmer to swim in'. Many of *Britannic*'s crew were assigned to the requisitioned Holland America liner *Statendam* (renamed *Justicia*). *Justicia* became a casualty of war herself in July 1918, although there was no doubt in her case that she had been struck by multiple torpedoes.

The one consolation for the White Star Line regarding *Britannic*'s loss was that as she had sunk in the government's service they were due for compensation. On 23 January 1917 the government paid them the sum of £1.75 million, but on 19 February 1917 Harland & Wolff certified the lost vessel's value as £1,920,963 0s 10d, which included £23,000 'covering payments that may have to be made to subcontractors for materials on order not yet delivered, and also in respect of the cancellation of contracts'. It also included the cost of materials and some luxury fittings in storage at the Belfast works. On 12 March 1917 White Star modified Harland & Wolff's figure, adding £15,042 2s 7d 'for interest during construction' and another sum of approximately £12,000 representing expenditure 'incurred…for equipment and outfit including furniture, fittings, electro plate, linen, bedding, etc'., which brought *Britannic*'s total value to £1,947,797 5s 10d.† Harold Sanderson wrote to the government on 31 May 1917, pointing out that the line had not received any further money since January's payment, while money was still owing on the lost *Laurentic* and *Afric*. No doubt other shipping

★ On 4 February 1915, the Principal Naval Transport Officer reported:

At first I must say that I was inclined to doubt the reality of the attack as the reports were made by officers who had never seen a torpedo fired or knew little about a submarine. Yesterday I spent a considerable time on board the *Asturias* and personally interviewed several of the witnesses. I now feel justified in saying that an attack was made but I am not quite convinced that the submarine did it knowing that the ship was a hospital ship…

† *Britannic* had originally been insured for £1,902,124 10s 10d, but on 20 October 1916 White Star modified figure to £1,930,981 1s 9d to account for additional expenses. It seems that this figure was then accepted as the ship's value prior to her loss a month later.

U73 was commissioned in October 1915, just over a year before *Britannic*'s demise. Her first commander, Kapitan-Leutnant Gustav Siess, remained in charge until May 1917. During the war's closing stages, she was commanded by a succession of other men, and she met her fate at the end of October 1918. One of the Pola Flotilla, a German naval formation whose purpose was to sink Allied shipping in the Mediterranean, she was scuttled. (National Maritime Museum, Greenwich, London, N00243)

lines were still pressing for payments, but in June the government did advance further funds. However, their inefficiency was only exacerbated by 'red tape', while on 4 June 1917 the White Star Line further complicated matters by another letter to the government. They had found that a £45 Steinway piano was still being held by contractors Smith & Son, although it had mistakenly been included in the original valuation, and was thus now government property, but they stated that they were willing to purchase it if the government did not have a use for it. Unfortunately, the reply seems to have been lost in time.

Although some of the ship's furnishings, retained in storage, were used on board *Olympic* after the war, *Britannic*'s interior panelling and other fixtures were auctioned off. In June 1919, the *Belfast News-Letter* announced that the well-known Belfast auction firm, Messrs W.P. Gray & McDowell Ltd, would conduct a sale of 'her palatial furnishings':

> The sales offer a unique opportunity to shipbuilders, hotel and entertainment concerns, contractors, furniture manufacturers, and others to acquire decorations and furnishings of a class rarely met with before the war, and which will certainly not be obtainable for a long time to come. The wood is almost exclusively solid mahogany and oak, and has been seasoning for a period of at least thirty to thirty-five years, while the rich carving and magnificent decorative work are the very highest and most artistic production of the craftsman's art. The furnishings of the various compartments of the great liner are all en suite, and represent various periods, and while being eminently suitable for ships, hotels, &., both the furniture and the paneling – the latter of exceptional quality and design – would be equally suitable for, and would greatly enhance the appearance and value of, large private residences.

Over 300 lots were listed and the sale included '4,000 fitment wardrobes, dressing chests, sideboards, bookcases, and other furniture easily convertible for utility purposes'. The children's playroom was 'panelled in walnut, modern design'; the *á la carte* restaurant panelling 'in Italian walnut, relieved with gold, Louis XVI period' and its reception room 'panelled and framed in the same period, but finished white'; the main first-class reception

From left to right: Sir Bertram Hayes, Captain F. Summers and Captain Charles Bartlett. Hayes, as commander of the White Star Line's first *Britannic*; Summers, as commander of the third ship of the name; and Bartlett, as the commander of the second, posed for this photograph on board the new motor ship *Britannic* in 1930. One of the company's final vessels, the economical and innovative new 'cabin' liner had a long and successful career under White Star, Cunard White Star, and then Cunard, which lasted until 1960. (Günter Bäbler collection)

room 'panelled and framed Jacobean period, handsomely carved and finished white, special stained glass to windows'; 'about seventy decorated bedrooms';★ the second-class library 'panelled and framed in sycamore'; while there was '70,000 square feet' of 'mahogany corridor panelling; 50,000 square feet oak panelling…'[104]

★   ★   ★

Britannic's life was all too short. If she made a number of voyages in productive service for the war effort, then less than a year passed between her completion and sinking. It is all the more unfortunate that she was lost, given the extensive improvements to her watertight subdivision compared with her doomed sister. If almost everything that could have gone wrong did go wrong, the more likely scenario in the event of her hitting a mine was what happened to *Olympic* after the *Hawke* collision in 1911: serious damage, with flooding contained to the damaged compartments and the ship remaining afloat and stable. The White Star Line lost a formidable vessel to serve alongside *Olympic* after the war, but her loss in 1916 resulted in her presence as the largest and most intact liner on the ocean floor today.

★ One of *Britannic*'s improvements that sometimes passes without mention, two additional sitting rooms were included among the first-class staterooms amidships on C-deck, in addition to the 'parlour' suites on B-deck (with their own promenade or veranda) and C-deck, which had their own sitting rooms. There were therefore six rooms that were furnished solely as sitting rooms.

8
THE WRECK OF *BRITANNIC*

Almost 400ft below the sea's surface (about 120 metres), *Britannic* rested largely forgotten for more than half a century. The person to locate *Britannic* was the famous French underwater explorer Captain Jacques Cousteau, aboard his faithful vessel *Calypso*. *Calypso* was of 350 tons and capable of a speed of 10½ knots with her two engines driving twin screws. She was built in 1942 as a minesweeper for the British (Cousteau had bought her after the war) and being designed as a minesweeper she had a double hull with double planking and narrowly spaced timbers. While she was not an ideal vessel for the purpose of underwater exploring, some small modifications were done to her after Cousteau bought her; a viewing space was installed on the lower hull, permitting underwater viewing even when the ship was moving, and sonar was fitted as well as steel decking being fitted forward.[1]

In the autumn of 1975, Captain Jacques Cousteau was working in the Aegean Sea, trying to locate the lost continent of Atlantis. It was then that the Vice-President of the American *Titanic* Historical Society, William Tantum, contacted him and enquired if it would be possible to locate the sunken *Britannic* and verify its position. Cousteau was interested and to help him with his search the society sent him copies of the Admiralty chart that showed the ship's estimated position.

For some time, the wreck proved elusive. But Cousteau called on the services of the Massachusetts Institute of Technology's Dr Harold Edgerton's side-sweeping sonar, which allowed the sea to be explored far quicker than previous sonar systems. After three days, Edgerton's sonar came up trumps. *Britannic* was located on 3 December 1975, but the cost had been in the region of $15,000 (about £5,000); however, all agreed it was certainly worth it. *Britannic* had been located 'in satellite navigation position 37°42′05 North 24°17′02 East' according to the Cousteau team's report. The location itself was interesting. Captain Bartlett reported that she had gone down about 3 miles north-west of Port St. Nikolo, which was where she was found, but her position had been recorded on Admiralty charts over 6 miles to the south-west.★ Unlike *Titanic*, she was in relatively confined waters and close to identifiable landmarks, so perhaps it was unsurprising that Bartlett's own report was correct, but it did give rise to questions as to why her location had been incorrectly marked, arousing conspiracy theorists' suspicions.

★ *Heroic*, one of the rescue vessels, was in the wreckage following the sinking and noted her noon position as 37°42′ North 24°18′ East. Her position was 0.8 miles to the west of *Britannic*'s wreck. By contrast, the incorrect position reported by the Admiralty charts was 37°39′10 North 24°09′42 East.

Because he needed the permission to dive on the ship from the Greek government (the Kea Channel was, after all, a busy shipping lane in Greek waters), Cousteau was unable to return to the ship until September 1976.

William Tantum set out to join Cousteau on 3 October 1976 and he was flown to the *Calypso* from Athens by the ship's helicopter. Later that day, Tantum and Cousteau boarded the tiny saucer submarine. After the pilot touched the submarine down on the port side of the ship, the bright lights were turned on.

'There is your *Britannic*,' Cousteau told Tantum.

Before actual diving commenced, the submarine explored the ship. As had been observed in 1916, the ship lay on her starboard side. Much of the hull was covered with a layer of coral, protecting the metal from corrosion; but other areas seemed quite untouched. Technological advances over the coming decades would allow a better picture of the ship's condition, but Cousteau's team did very well.

Although the starboard side was hidden and the explosion damage could not be seen, there was a huge hole in the port side of the ship below the forward well deck, which seemed to have been caused by the explosion, as some of the hull plates were clearly bent outward. Later analysis would prove this was not the case. It was 'large enough to drive a trailer truck through', Tantum observed. The bow was bent forward, the cause being the heavy weight of the ship bending the bow, especially beneath the forward well deck, as it came into contact with the seafloor.

Much of the wooden decking was gone, but in some areas the ship was preserved remarkably well. On the bridge, Cousteau only discovered one telegraph, but more would be seen at a later date. He raised the base, which found its way to the museum at Monaco. Cousteau recovered one of the brass-rimmed insets of the ship's helm from the wheelhouse[2] and one of the ship's bells, amongst other things.

'The glass is broken out of the dome over the grand staircase,' it was reported.

Since Cousteau's expedition, there have been many theories as to whether there was a second explosion and, if so, what caused it. If it was the case that the hull plating on the port side had been 'blown out' by an explosion of some sort, then even a mine or torpedo alone should not have caused damage on such a large scale. Although they did a good job with the resources available to them at the time, further exploration would help to shed light on the ship's demise.

Cousteau did find coal samples near the ship; they could have fallen out as the vessel sank, but the possibility of a coal dust explosion seemed strong, especially bearing in mind that the reserve coalbunker was in the vicinity of the explosion, cargo hold 3. For such an explosion to occur, the conditions have to be quite precise. What is often put forward as an argument against such explosions is that the bunker has to be quite dry; for example, if a coal bunker in a hot boiler room had been in contact with the outer skin of a ship, it is likely, especially if a ship is navigating in cold waters, that condensation would eliminate any dust and render the possibility of an explosion highly unlikely. But this was not the case on *Britannic*: the reserve coal bunker was not in contact with the outer skin of the ship and, not being situated in a hot boiler room, bearing in mind that in any case the sea temperature was in the region of 67° Fahrenheit,★ it is unlikely that condensation would have occurred. If it did, surely not all of the coal dust would have

---

★ This figure is based on the logs of the rescue ships.

been eliminated in pools of water. However, for an explosion to occur there also needs to be a good supply of air, while it is likely that coal dust needs to be disturbed, billowing into the air rather than remaining settled on the bunker floor, for ignition; certainly, it is an argument against the coal dust theory, for the reserve coalbunker, not in use, would hardly have a good, fresh supply of air to aid an explosion. Coal dust might well have been disturbed by the violent initial explosion, but evidence from the 1999 expedition to *Britannic* appears to put the coal dust explosion theory to rest. Video footage of the area of the reserve coalbunker and hold below number three hatch apparently indicated that 'no explosion or damage was done in the coalbunker'.[3] Despite the severe damage to the bow in this area, such a survey does inflict a severe blow on the coal dust theory's credibility.

Another possible reason for the severity of the explosion presents itself when we stop to consider what the *Britannic* was at the time of her sinking: a Hospital Ship, not only carrying patients but also medical supplies. The cargo manifest for *Britannic*'s 'Voyage 6 eastbound' cannot be consulted, but medical supplies frequently included ether, which was a common anaesthetic at the time. 'A horrible, vile smelling substance,' as a former nurse once described it to me, it was good as an anaesthetic, but also highly volatile. At the temperature it would have been stored at on *Britannic*, ether would have been in the form of a liquid, perhaps with a small amount of fumes. It will be recalled that all of the cargo holds were damaged by the explosion and it would be hardly surprising if the initial explosion had ignited the coal dust in the reserve coalbunker, and also ether in the ship's hold. Ether would have alone created 'a terrific explosion'. As with the coal dust theory, however, there is important evidence against the possibility that ether exploded: *Britannic*'s cargo holds have been reported to be practically empty of any cargo. It still might be possible that limited quantities of supplies including ether were being carried, but it does seem unlikely.

The accusation that *Britannic* was carrying arms, in violation of her status as a hospital ship, was perhaps reinforced for some people by the knowledge that her wreck was a number of miles from the position reported on Admiralty charts. However, all the indications are that this was a simple error made a number of years after the sinking. There is no evidence whatsoever that she was carrying such weapons. Not a trace has been found within or near the wreck. In fact, all the indications from contemporary documentation are to the effect that the authorities were keenly aware of the need for hospital ships to obey the international requirements and to be seen to do so. The debate as to whether *Britannic* should carry medical supplies or passengers on her fifth voyage is an important example of this concern.

It has been speculated that the initial explosion opened a gash of 20 x 30ft in *Britannic*'s forward hull,[4] therefore presumably totalling some 600sq.ft. If *Titanic*'s flooding of some 400 tons per minute had resulted from a mere 12sq.ft opening, then it is not hard to see why *Britannic*'s flooding would have been catastrophic. The immediate damage area of the two cargo holds 2 and 3 would have been flooded extremely rapidly, causing the settling of the bow, and from that point onward the partially closed watertight doors could only slow down the rapid flooding by limiting the flow of water into other areas of the ship, and not prevent water penetrating throughout the ship's forward main watertight compartments. (Had the watertight doors been closed at the time of the explosion, it is possible that the otherwise catastrophic flooding would have been restricted to perhaps three of the forward watertight compartments.) Once *Britannic* settled at the head and began to list to starboard, a number of open portholes were exposed to the sea and this allowed water into areas further aft that would otherwise have remained dry. Her fate was sealed.

There is one further interesting point to consider. Alone, a mine or torpedo was certainly enough to create some serious damage and flooding, but in *Britannic*'s case we should also consider that the explosion appears to have occurred unusually low down. Indeed, the ship fell off from her course three points, while her bow rose as a result of the explosion and the firemen's tunnel was pierced. There is also good evidence as to the double bottom being badly damaged. A mine explosion at this level of the ship's hull would have been more powerful than one at a higher level, such as just beneath the waterline; for the force of the explosion would surely be far more concentrated, and not so easily dispersed.

The American Society of Naval Architecture & Marine Engineering (SNAME) Marine Forensic Panel paper of 1998 speculates further as to why the primary explosion damage might have been increased. The paper concludes that a 'hull whipping response' might have resulted from the explosion, 'loosening rivets all around the point of detonation'[5] and enlarging the gash in the ship's hull, further speeding up the flooding of the forward holds. Numerous witnesses reported severe vibration following the explosion, and while the rapid flooding may partly account for this, certainly the vibration might also corroborate the theory of 'hull whipping'. We can still conclude that the explosion might have been more severe than normal merely because it occurred lower down than was usual.

One theory that has been put forward in the past relates to the *Britannic*'s inner watertight double skin. There has been ill-informed speculation that water might have entered the skin, having been damaged by the explosion, and then flooded along the ship's entire length, eventually causing her to capsize. Unfortunately for the theory, the watertight subdivision of the skin renders it physically impossible; the main transverse watertight bulkheads pierced the inner skin, while there was also significant horizontal and additional transverse watertight subdivision built into the vessel's design to prevent such an occurence. If water did penetrate the inner skin following the explosion, for which we have no evidence, then it would have been contained in a small area forward and could not possibly have spread, as has been suggested.

Despite the conspiracy theories, *Britannic*'s loss was more mundane. As a victim of war, she was a victim of circumstances and some very bad luck. If it was Cousteau's expedition that located her and provided the first glimpse of the ship in sixty years, then another twenty years would pass before further explorations took place and more became known about the lost ship.

★ ★ ★

In July 1995 Kostas Thoctarides, Greek commercial diver and underwater explorer, made a twenty-minute solo dive to the liner. Two years had been spent planning the short dive, which no doubt seemed all too brief. Thoctarides' dive was an important milestone in that he became the first visitor to the wreck since Cousteau's 1976 expedition, and that he was the first to use open circuit technical diving techniques.

★ ★ ★

During August 1995 explorer and oceanographer Dr Robert Ballard set sail from Crete, heading for the Kea Channel. He aimed to discover what had sunk the ship.

Dr Ballard brought with him a nuclear-powered United States Navy submarine, the Nr-1, and two remotely controlled underwater vehicles. Nr-1 was 145ft in length, 12½ft in width and could dive to 3,000ft – she had a speed of 3½ knots and was half as long as a naval attack submarine.[6] *Voyager* – provided by Perry Tritech Ltd – was the primary ROV (Remote Operated Vehicle), which would be connected up to the sophisticated three-dimensional imaging system, while the other vehicle was *Phantom* – provided by the University of Connecticut's National Undersea Research Program.[7] Their support ship was the *Carolyn Chouest* – a vessel with a striking bright-orange painted hull.

On 29 August 1995 – one day after arriving – the submarine descended into the Aegean. They only had the approximate position of the ship, but an hour after diving the Nr-1's Submergence/Obstacle Avoidance Sonar locked onto the *Britannic*. Nr-1 was approaching the ship from the north-east when the rudder and propellers came into view.[8]

In order to get an accurate map of the ship, the modern version of Dr Harold Edgerton's side-sweeping sonar was used: 'Look at that! Unbelievable! Oh, wow! Look at that!' Ballard was elated as he saw the printout of the scan. Every minute detail was shown of the ship, intact and magnificent.[9] Ken Marschall, acting as the expedition's visual historian, made a 48-hour dive to *Britannic*, followed by historian Eric Sauder.[10] '*Britannic* is this Walt Disney dream shipwreck,' Marschall would later relate, '– just this huge ocean liner looking way too good to be anything but a Hollywood creation.' He was deeply moved by the experience.[11] 'Except for the rent in the bow, it seemed only to need a good scrubbing to set out to sea again,'[12] Ballard would later observe.

While the Nr-1 illuminated the *Britannic* with its powerful lights, Ballard and his team focused on the ROVs as they watched the video monitors in the *Carolyn Chouest*'s control room. Ballard directed the ROV pilot to drive *Phantom* along the hull to the bow. Simon Mills and Ken Marschall watched through special glasses the amazing three-dimensional the images from *Voyager*. However, it proved too dangerous to send in the ROVs very deep and no evidence of the actual explosion damage could be seen.[13]

Even though the explosion did not cause the damage on the port side, much of the keel could still not be located. The hull had buckled below the forward well deck and partly separated; the bulwarks at the side of the well deck had also parted. After the mine explosion on the starboard side in the same general area, the hull was severely weakened, and when the bow came into contact with the bottom of the sea this part of the hull was at its weakest, causing it to buckle – a 'stubbed toe'.[14] As the bow settled onto the seafloor, the remaining hull settled at a different angle; the hull forward of the well deck is turned to starboard. The muddy bottom of the Channel has been disturbed by the foremost part of *Britannic*'s bows, the stem was also partly crushed and the foremost plating twisted; all visibly caused by the impact with the bottom.

Aside from this the ship is completely intact, most of the panels in the glass dome over the grand staircase are intact, while the railings and promenade deck windows look perfect.[15]

Confirming evidence given at the original inquiry, the ROVs spotted several lower deck portholes wide open. Before leaving on 5 September 1995 a plaque was placed at the wreck site:

Piraeus Municipal Cemetery at Drapestona houses several graves belonging to victims of the sinking. The cemetery is well maintained and the graves themselves are in surprisingly good condition. (Michail Michailakis, www.hospitalshipbritannic.com)

> In the memory of those who perished in the sinking of HMHS *Britannic* November 21st, 1916 and dedicated to all those who lost their lives in the war of 1914–1918 not in battle, but still in service to their country.[16]

Time was running short as the ROVs searched for evidence of mine anchors or other debris as they proceeded to cover *Britannic*'s presumed course, but as nothing was found it seemed possible that the reported position of the mines may have been in error.

★   ★   ★

'Project *Britannic* 1997' was the fourth visit to *Britannic* since her discovery.

Kevin Gurr – who runs the International Association of Nitrox & Technical Divers (IANTD) – led the nineteen-strong international team of divers and support staff for the early-1997 expedition to the *Britannic*.

The team of mixed-gas divers consisted of Kevin Gurr, Alan Wright, John Thornton, Dan Burton, Uffe Eriksson, Richard Lundgren, Ingemar Lundgren, Dave Thompson, Alexander Sotiriou and Kerk Kavalaris.[17]

The team's aim was to make a complete video survey of the sunken ship – concentrating on the bow damage – their operation was unique because it used Diver Propulsion Vehicles (DPVs) and non-commercial sport-diving techniques.[18]

Despite many unforeseen problems – including gale-force winds – the expedition was a great success. Excellent film was shot and many great photographs in full colour were obtained, showing the sunken ship to be alive with colour, rather than the normally visualised monotonous monochrome wash.

Forty dives were completed and more than 800 minutes were spent below 100 metres. All of those who took part in the expedition had a great experience seeing the largest liner ever to sink. Project Leader Kevin Gurr described his experiences:

She comes into sight when you are 75 metres down. The first of her deck rails are at 90 metres, though nearer the bow they are a little deeper. She lies on her starboard side, almost as though sleeping. When you reach the sand of the seabed at 120 metres and look up, she towers above you. If you land on the hull, it is so big that you think it is the seabed![19]

On the final dive a plaque was placed near funnel 4's original position, on the ship's port side:[20]

In honour of Jacques Yves-Cousteau – Pioneer/Technical Diver. One of the many frontiers he touched. His example had enticed many of us to follow him and experience 'The Silent World.'

★ ★ ★

During September 1998 a British team of divers completed 'the most detailed close-up survey' of the sunken ship. This was the first visit to the ship by a team of amateur divers and by the first female diver, Christina Campbell. The team hoped to clear up the mystery of what caused the sinking, or at least the initial explosion. As Geraint Ffoulkes-Jones, a member of the expedition, explained:

Something caused her to sink very quickly, and we intend to find out… If there were any military supplies on board, they would be in the inner depths of the hull.

The expedition leader was Nick Hope; there were twelve lead diving members; three expedition support divers – who dived during the expedition's second week; four full-time expedition support divers; surface supporter Jenn Samulski, and four people from the Greek Diving Centre at Piraeus.

Previously, the team had visited many shipwrecks – such as the famous *Lusitania* and *Andrea Doria* – and the not-so-famous *King Edward VII*, SS *Carolina*, a U-boat not identified until after diving (*U869*) and His Majesty's Submarine *Affray*.

As with previous dives to the sunken vessel, a single twenty-minute dive involved up to four-and-a-half hours in-water decompression; four large cylinders and two surface supplied gas cylinders for shallow in-water decompression; five mixtures of helium, oxygen and nitrogen (for the different depths), plus 100–140kg (220–300lb) of equipment.

Everybody was impressed by the sunken liner's condition ('awesome…without doubt this is the world's most magnificent shipwreck,' 'the wreck is unbelievably magnificent' and 'the wreck is an absolute beauty'). On 17 September 1998, *Britannic*'s condition proved a hindrance rather than a blessing, because the intact cover over the dome for the forward grand staircase prevented easy access to her interior. The elevator housings and gear at the top of the shafts proved another stumbling block. The port bridge wing running light, wing cab's intact glass and brass fitting remained intact.

During his fourth dive, John Chatterton tried locate the 18in lettering of *Britannic*'s name on her port bow, but was unsuccessful due to marine growth. Later dives saw the largest anchor sitting in its recess on the forecastle, while the port anchor remained stowed but slightly out of position. Divers were able to penetrate the fourth funnel casing, passing various deck level landings. At the bottom one diver faintly saw the forward ends of the enormous engine cylinder heads, indicating that the engines were still upright on their bedplates and intact.

Inside the second-class smoke room, just inside the back door, empty bottles could be seen and a floor covering similar to that discovered on the bridge. John Yurga was able to enter the area of the aft grand staircase, but the stairs themselves seemed to have vanished.

Coverage of the expedition was 'not limited to the diving industry but…distributed to a much wider audience'. Talks were given at various places, including a talk at the London International Dive Show, late in April 1999. Presentations were also made at the International Association of Nitrox & Technical Divers (IANTD) conference, while there was also coverage on BBC Radio.

Nick Hope described many of his experiences the following year in an issue of *Diver* magazine.[21] 'I set off across the foredeck towards the break, and made a brief examination of the devastation caused presumably by a combination of the mine that probably sank her and the force of the impact as she hit the seabed. Other than this chasm the *Britannic* is remarkably intact for her age. Quite why she is so well preserved is a little puzzling. Low oxygen levels due to sheer depth undoubtedly play their part, though her intactness is no doubt owed in part to the double skin that runs for much of her length…' His third dive to the ship stood as his favourite.

'In the middle of the bridge hangs one of the helms, the square spoke holes in its hub the only reminders of where the wheel would have been. Further aft where the wheel-house once stood is the telemotor, still standing perpendicularly to the deck. Again the wheel has rotted away, although the sharp stubs of the wheel spokes are left on this one. Simon Mills…had asked us to inspect the colour of the attractive tiles that covered the floor of the bridge. A good sample of this floor covering still remains around the base of the telemotor. On close inspection we found it actually to be red and white linoleum, not tiles.

'The partition between the bridge and the senior officer's quarters has also rotted away, and in there, just yards from the bridge itself, we found a large metal bath complete with pipe work and taps. If only removing the plug would get rid of a bit of this water and give us more time on the wreck.

'It was a joy and a privilege to witness the majesty of HMHS *Britannic* like no paying passenger ever did. This is the world's best wreck and she's beckoning me back.'

★ ★ ★

'Expedition *Britannic* 1999', organised by Global Underwater Explorers (GUE) and the Greek Diving Centre, with Jarrod Jablonski as expedition organiser, arrived at the wreck site for on-site organisation on 19 August 1999.[22] Team members included GUE instructors, Woodville Karst Plain exploration and support divers, plus Baltic Sea Tech divers.

It was planned that over the course of ten diving days, twelve gas divers would conduct eight dives each for a total of over ninety manned dives to the sunken liner, while every third day divers rested, also completing documentation.

Project goals included extended exploration of the ship to allow 'detailed structural surveys' to help 'illuminate the circumstances that contributed to the sinking of both the *Titanic* and *Britannic* by identifying the cause of the explosion and possible structural defects', the use of side-scan sonar to try to locate evidence of the explosion's cause, and the collection of small hull samples from the bow for metallurgic analysis.

Actual diving began on 21 August 1999, each diver being equipped with one 250-watt video light, while every diving team had one video diver. Although bad weather forced the postponement or cancellation of some dives, the expedition was very successful.

On 28 August 1999, a team was able to penetrate deeply into the ship's interior, looking for damage on the starboard side, but a second team surveyed extensively the bow damage; they were 'able to gather the first recorded measurements of the split between the bow and the rest of the ship'. Open portholes were filmed from the wreck's interior, while amazingly well-preserved flooring was seen over the following days. However, many interior spaces were cluttered by wiring and other loosened fittings.

Everyone was highly impressed by the ship, as all the previous expeditions had been.

★   ★   ★

Two years from the 1999 expedition, Kostas Thoctarides returned to the wreck with colleague Giorgos Avgeropulos to make their own dives to see *Britannic*. However, it was not until September 2003 that another full-scale expedition took place. Carl Spencer led an ambitious team, whose efforts and discoveries would be documented by programmes for Channel 5 in the UK and National Geographic. Particular interest was focused on the status of the watertight doors leading to *Britannic*'s forward boiler rooms. At great personal risk, diver Richard Stevenson would investigate them, as Leigh Bishop explained:

> Diving officer Geraint Ffoulkes-Jones and overall expedition leader Carl Spencer had requested him to dive deep into the wreck to check on the watertight doors. Successfully Richard would make a remarkable and historic dive on *Britannic* making his way deep into boiler room number 6! …With the wreck on its side orientation in an unfamiliar surrounding made for steady progress, Richard carefully negotiating his route over and through fallen obstacles to his final destination. Inside the boiler room his digital film clearly shows the gantry's walkways running around the boilers and firemen's coal barrows stacked in corners…[23]

Stevenson's camera recorded an important finding. The watertight doors between the firemen's tunnel and boiler room 6 were wide open. Confirmation of this fact brings to mind stoker Bert Smith's vivid description of being pinned against a boiler by the sheer force of the water. Stevenson also believed that the next watertight door, leading from boiler room 6 into boiler room 5, was partially closed, as suspected in 1916, but it was not possible to document that finding on video. It is interesting to note that the boilers remained *in situ* even though *Britannic* lay on her side.

Another exciting find came from beyond the wreck. Bill Smith and his team on the expedition were tasked with searching for any remains of the mines laid by *U73*. This time, the search was successful. Several remaining and identifiable mine bases were found precisely where the German records had claimed they had been laid. 'Clear as a bell,' Bishop wrote, 'they could be seen on the sonar scans, some with anchoring chains still attached. The sonar readings even gave light to an exploded mine still with its cradle and chain intact.'

Spencer was pleased with the expedition's accomplishments and proud of the team. He had some interesting observations. *Britannic*'s superstructure 'in general is in amazingly good condition considering its years underwater. There is very little marine growth

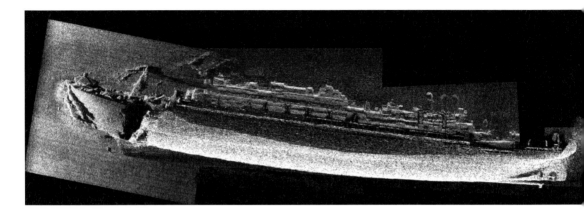

During the 2003 expedition, *Britannic*'s impressive profile was evident. This marvellous composite image is made up of three separate side scan sonar images: one shot down either side of the hull and the third at ninety degrees to the centreline of the ship. It is interesting to note that the first funnel can be seen on the seafloor close to the bridge. Unlike wrecks such as *Lusitania*, whose hull has largely collapsed along its length and lost much of its original breadth, *Britannic* retains her shape and integrity. (© Bill Smith, 2003)

internally, however externally the superstructure is covered in mussels and hard fauna which is helping preserve the steel structure.' As far as it was possible to tell, the forward hatches were all intact, contrary to accounts in some newspapers at the time that at least one of them had been blown off by the explosion. He was keen for further exploration of the boiler rooms, while an attempt had been made to reach the reciprocating engine room. Although debris had hindered his progress, diver Zaid Al-Obaidi observed one of the crankshafts and a connecting rod of one of the reciprocating engines. In particular, Spencer was impressed by 'the fact that the wreck is so intact in beautiful crystal clear warm water. *Britannic* was a beautiful ship and in many ways she is even more beautiful now with all of the colourful marine growth on her... The wreck is in exceptional condition, with the exception of a few wooden internal partitions that have long since rotted away, she is almost complete.'[24]

★   ★   ★

Three years later, another expedition came to see *Britannic*. In September 2006 a number of divers explored the wreck, part of an expedition that was a collaboration between the History Channel and Lone Wolf Documentary Group and led by the presenters of *Shadow Divers and Deep Sea Detectives*, Richie Kohler and John Chatterton, a previous expedition veteran. The team used high definition studio television cameras from Woods Hole Oceanographic Institute that were 'so expensive' and large that 'they had to be lifted into the water for the cameramen'. There were practical difficulties, as John Chatterton explained:

> The problem was that we could not anchor to or near the site, so dropping the camera, deploying the divers, disconnecting the camera, and then navigating the large camera in the current to the shot line, turned out to be a dance exercise in timing and toler-

ance. Some of the cameras needed a tether to the surface, where the video was actually recorded. Since the dive vessel could not anchor, we had to run the tether to a topside video station set up in a zodiac tied to the shot line, which was in turn tied into the wreck. The cameras that could run without a tether, were easier to navigate but pushing any big object through a sporty current is not easy.

On one dive, Richie and John were able to reach boiler room 6. They attempted to reach even further, to examine the watertight door between boiler rooms 5 and 6, but it was not safe to proceed and a wheelbarrow was lodged firmly into one of the accesses between the boilers. The next day, they planned to examine the design of *Britannic*'s forward expansion joint, but John Chatterton was taken ill and another diver, Mike Barnette, took his place alongside Richie Kohler.

The dive revealed changes to *Britannic* that had not been incorporated into the surviving plans, including the addition of a door on the B-deck promenade. The expansion joint, just forward of the first-class grand staircase, revealed an interesting change. Once the necessary marine growth had been cleared, it was clear that its base had been reshaped from the rectangular into a 'lightbulb' shaped curve. It was not surprising that numerous aspects of *Britannic*'s design had been improved compared to her older sister ships, but the discovery was an important one in that it had not been known before.★

Unfortunately, an attempt to reach the wireless room was thwarted by the discovery of what appeared to be 'a solid steel bulkhead bisecting the officers' quarters deckhouse', reported the *Belfast Telegraph*. Although the tuner for *Britannic*'s Marconi apparatus had been found lying on a beam in the area of the grand staircase three years earlier, visiting the wireless room itself had been a key target. And so another expedition concluded, having made new discoveries and added to our collective knowledge of *Britannic*.

★ ★ ★

In September 2007, a team whose project 'focused on the mapping of coralline algae' undertook work at the wreck site. It was part of a broader habitat-mapping project covering the Cyclades Islands (from the southern Aegean Sea to the eastern Mediterranean Sea), which was a collaborative effort between the Laboratory of Marine Geology and Physical Oceanography (MGPOL) and the Marine Biology Research Group of the Department of Geology and Biology of the University of Patras.[25]

They carried out a 'side scan sonar survey' of *Britannic*'s wreck, in two phases: 'During the first phase, a systematic side scan sonar survey of the seafloor at the reported vicinity of the wreck location was carried out'; and 'once the wreck of *Britannic* was successfully relocated' they sought to capture 'the highest resolution shipwreck imagery possible'. All together, an area covering 2½ kilometres squared was surveyed, centred on the wreck site, and 'a total of 5½ kilometres of digital side scan data were acquired.' A summary was published of the sonar imagery that related to *Britannic*:

> *Britannic* rests on her starboard side. The resulting sonographs seem to confirm that the wreck lies on a heading of 253° and on her side at an approximate angle of 85°. The

---

★ A discussion and analysis of this finding can be found in the following chapter.

Diver Richard Stevenson inspects *Britannic*'s propellers. This image helps to give an idea of the enormous scale of the ship. (© Leigh Bishop)

tip of the bow sits slightly more upright than the other part of the hull of the ship… The first 40 metres of the bow, which bore the brunt of the collision on hitting the bottom, are heavily twisted and contorted. However, sonographs show that the hull still remains in one piece.

The 253° heading of the wreck seems to indicate that during the last half-hour, the ship sailed in the opposite direction from which it was approaching prior to the explosion.★ The course of the ship during the sinking may have been affected by two factors: (i) the list to starboard which initiated a wide turn to the right; and (ii) the intensity of the currents in the area with prevailing currents flowing south-south-west. Sonographs show that the original superstructure of the ship, including deckhouses, mast, cargo cranes, giant lifeboat davits and Welin [sic] type davits, remains in remark-ably good condition.

★ The ship had originally been steaming in a north-easterly direction, prior to the explosion. The direction that *Britannic* is pointing on the seafloor is west-south-west, whereas Captain Bartlett's intended course when he tried to beach her was to the south-east. However, when he tried to work *Britannic* towards the shore on two occasions, he would hardly have resumed steaming had she been facing what was obviously the wrong direction: *away* from land. It seems probable this final change of direction occurred towards the very end, when her commander had abandoned hope of saving the ship and she was incapable of manoeuvring. (Although the term 'heading' has been used to describe the direction the wreck is pointing, in fact the navigational term applies to the direction that a moving vessel is travelling.)

The only exceptions are the funnels, since none of the four smokestacks are in position... The first funnel lies only a few metres from its original position just aft of the bridge of the ship, suggesting that it probably fell off only on impact. The poop deck and stern of the ship are almost perfectly preserved with the giant propellers still in place. There is only a few debris [sic] around the main wreck as the *Britannic* sank intact in shallow waters. The other three funnels were detected away from the wreck, the nearest (probably the second funnel) is about 50 metres... Sonographs show that the funnels retain some of their original elliptical-cylindrical shape although they have been flattened.

★   ★   ★

During four days from 18–22 September 2008★ the Hellenic Centre for Marine Research (HCMR), known in Greece as Elkethe, and the ship's owner explored the site and 'sought to investigate the impact of the sunken liner-cum-hospital ship on its immediate marine environment' as well as searching for yet more evidence of the minefield. They were on board the largest research vessel of the National Centre of Maritime Research (NCMR) in Greece, MV *Aegaeo* (Aegean), and had the use of the centre's *Thetis* submarine.

Samples of marine growth from the ship's hull were retrieved for further examination for analysis by HCMR, while the other side of the expedition focused on evidence of mines and gathering photographic evidence. The ROV was sent to 'mow the lawn' and try to find further evidence of the mine barrier laid by *U73*. While they did not locate any remains near the expected location, since no mine anchors were located, they did discover an object that seemed to be a fragment of 'the casing of a First World War moored mine. The object was [too] heavily covered by marine growth to enable an easy identification but the ROV retrieved a small cable from its interior for further study. The first results showed that it was from the First World War era...' In fact, on the completion of tests in a Belgian laboratory it was shown to be of German manufacture from the relevant period.

Although *Britannic*'s superstructure remained remarkably intact, the difficulty in exploring some areas of the ship was highlighted by the fishing nets that hung from some of the boat deck houses and the 'girder' type davits overhead. As Michail Michailakis explained, they were 'a potential safety threat for ROVs and submersibles'. The submarine could not explore the length of the superstructure, moving from the bow to the stern, because of the potential danger.

Vangelis Papathanassiou, one of the Hellenic Centre for Marine Research's oceanographers, relayed his experience of seeing the wreck with his own eyes from the submarine to the *Athens News*: 'As you close in, it is like seeing a mountain appear. Imagine that the propeller is 7.5 metres in diameter – more than the length of the submersible. You could see fish, algae, sponges, different fish on the hull and the superstructure of the ship. It was like an oasis in the desert. The rest of the surroundings were sandy. We even saw a plaque dedicated to Jacques Cousteau, who first discovered the wreck in 1975.' His first impressions were that the marine life was 'a very different substratum of biodiversity than expected at that depth' and Papathanassiou looked forward to studying further all the photographs that had been taken.

★ Early in September 2008, a team of Belgian divers explored the site, while a Canadian team was scheduled to visit later the same month.

There were a number of interesting observations even for the casual observer. The yellow sponges were observed growing almost exclusively on the ship's railings, rather than other areas of the ship. Simon Mills explained: 'Rather than following a relatively random pattern, the abundant life (flora, fauna and fish) is surprisingly structured, with certain species being dominant in certain areas of the wreck and yet almost completely absent in others. *Britannic* actually appears to have become an extremely complex ecosystem in its own right and the subsequent ecological environment has even surprised some of the directors at the HCMR.'

As a report for BBC Northern Ireland concluded, *Britannic* 'has become a "living" artificial reef in what is a very empty part of the Aegean Sea. Taken over by a wide variety of marine life, it is turning into a natural laboratory for scientists who want to learn more about how such reefs might benefit the marine biodiversity of the seabed.' Film from the expedition's dives was used in a BBC documentary, *In the Shadow of Titanic* and, as reporter Mike McKimm explained: 'We were able to film the three huge propellers on the ship and understand the sheer scale of these things. On *Titanic* they are all but inaccessible and are in a very dangerous part of the wreck. But on *Britannic* they are very visible.' He concluded: '*Titanic* captured the fascination of the public with the huge loss of life and her "unsinkable" tag but *Britannic*, supposed to be the ultimate ocean liner, having learnt many lessons from what happened to *Titanic*, ended up forgotten with no such emotional attachment.'

★   ★   ★

What are *Britannic*'s future prospects? Following her loss and the government's compensation to the White Star Line, her ownership passed to the government. The Board of Trade established the War Risk Insurance Office to administer the War Risks Insurance Scheme which compensated shipping companies for vessels lost during both world wars. The office became part of the Department of Transport in 1983, when responsibility for shipping passed from the then Department of Trade and Industry. However, following increasing interest in the ship following the Cousteau expeditions, the wreck passed into private ownership in 1977. Two offers were received by the government to purchase the wreck and, although no information is available on the criteria that were used to value her, there is one intriguing reference to the fact that a ship of her size would be expected to fetch £3,000. In the event, the higher bid came to £2,500 and from that point *Britannic*'s ownership rested with purchaser Mark Bamford, as the government retained no further interest in the wreck. Almost twenty years passed before she was purchased by maritime researcher and historian Simon Mills in 1996. Her future certainly seems safe, in that her owner recognises *Britannic*'s historical significance in her own right; and the importance of preserving, protecting and exploring the wreck site.

Even if that were not the case, there are a number of legal protections in place for shipwrecks such as *Britannic*. The Greek government certainly takes a keen interest in its cultural heritage. *Britannic* and other wrecks over fifty years old were declared as historic monuments in an act approved by parliament on 3 September 2003 and published on 19 November 2003. The Department of Underwater Antiquities, under the Ministry of Culture, has relevant jurisdiction. She is subject to the Law for the Protection of Antiquities and of the Cultural Heritage which is 'in force without prejudice to [the shipwreck's] legal status at the time of their sinking or to any proprietary or salvage rights on shipwrecks, and aims solely for their protection.' The Ministry of Culture 'exercises control over the wreck site from the part of the archaeological law and is one of the competent ministries, which are involved in the procedure for obtaining clearance to investigate the wreck.' No artefacts can be retrieved without the permission of the Greek authorities and the difficulties experienced by some recent expeditions in securing the appropriate diving permits illustrate all too well the strict care and attention that they bestow on the site, even for exploration that does not involve any sort of artefact retrieval. Any attempt to retrieve artefacts without permission is likely to end in the imposition of 'an extremely large fine and guaranteed loss of equipment, but in more severe cases could even earn a prison sentence of up to fifteen years!'[26]

If the past few years are anything to go by, then interest in *Britannic* is steadily increasing and technological progress is making exploration and discovery ever more achievable. She remains remarkably intact and compares favourably with the observable deterioration of *Titanic*'s wreck in recent years. *Britannic*'s future seems bright.

9
THE WRECK OF *TITANIC*

T he wreck of *Titanic* lay undiscovered 2½ miles under the North Atlantic Ocean's surface for over seventy years. At an approximate depth of 12,460ft in position 41° 43′ north, 49° 56′ west, the liner lies at rest.

Although out of sight, *Titanic* was not out of mind. Perhaps interest had faded somewhat between the wars, but it was in the 1950s that films such as *Titanic* (1953) and *A Night to Remember* (1958) brought her story to public prominence once again. It took a number of expeditions to locate the ship, but eventually she was found and seen for the first time since 1912.★

★　★　★

During the summer of 1953 Risdon Beasley Ltd – a Southampton salvage firm – attempted to locate *Titanic*'s wreck.[1] At the location of 43° 65′ north 52° 04′ west, explosives were used to obtain echo profiles of the seabed, but the firm's efforts were not successful.[2]

Little effort was being made until the 1970s. Many groups had been set up, including an alliance between Walt Disney Productions and *National Geographic* magazine.[3]

Since the sinking, many unfeasible plans had been made to raise the liner. These included encasing the ship in liquid nitrogen before raising her; attaching magnets to the hull and via chains to drained oil tankers on the surface, bringing the ship up; filling the ship with Vaseline, or even ping pong balls, which would lighten the ship and allow her to float. But every plan was considered too expensive; in addition, few had any ideas of what to do with the ship once she had been raised…

Jack Grimm – a very wealthy Texan oilman – mounted several expeditions during the early 1980s.[4] His first expedition departed from Port Everglades, Florida, in July 1980 aboard the *H.J.W. Fay*.[5] Continuous bad weather hampered the expedition. Searching area 41° 40′/41° 50′ north to 50° 00′/50° 10′ west, they found nothing and went home.[6] Similar attempts during the early 1980s did not find anything, although an object was photographed that Jack Grimm claimed was one of the *Titanic*'s massive 38-ton wing propellers.[7]

★ *Titanic*'s wrecksite lay some 13 nautical miles to the eastward of Boxhall's final calculated position. Although it has been suggested that she was, therefore, proceeding up to two knots slower than had been reported at the time, in fact this was not the case. (For the reasons behind this difference, see Sam Halpern's article, 'It's a CQD Old Man', *Atlantic Daily Bulletin*, British *Titanic* Society, 2008; and also printed in *Voyage*, *Titanic* International Society, 2008.)

On 5 July 1985 a joint expedition by America's Woods Hole Oceanographic Institution and the French Institution *IFREMER* arrived on the site.[8]

Their two-phase expedition would spend about 1½ months on site – aboard the French vessel *Le Suroit* and the American vessel *Knorr*.[9] The French team – led by Jean-Louis Michel – was to conduct the first phase of the expedition aboard *Le Suroit* and the American team – led by Dr Robert Ballard – were to conduct the second phase, aboard the *Knorr*.[10] Two photographic vehicles – *Argo* and *Angus* – equipped with state-of-the-art side-scanning sonar, would assist with their quest.[11]

Ballard's dream to help locate and photograph *Titanic* was about to come true. William Tantum, who had encouraged Jacques Cousteau to find and explore *Britannic*, had been an example to Ballard during his quest, dating from the early 1970s. After six weeks on site the French had covered 80 per cent of the search area without any success; it was now up to the American team to find *Titanic*.[12]

In the *Knorr*'s control van the monotonous sight on the video monitors of the muddy seafloor ended when definite fragments of debris began to appear. In a couple of minutes, there was a loud exclamation as a large object appeared – 'It's a boiler!' The cook was sent to rouse Ballard, who rushed into the control van, and the tape was replayed. Whoops and shouts erupted as even larger items appeared. It was 1.05 a.m. on 1 September 1985.

Twisted hull plating, portholes and pieces of railing came into view. Eight minutes after the boiler had been spotted – at 1.13 a.m. – Ballard ordered *Argo* raised 80–100ft as a precaution. Unwittingly, they were approaching the wreck from the most dangerous point, and were only 12ft above the deck.

By now, word of their discovery had spread throughout the ship. Paper cups of Mateus wine – the closest thing that was available to champagne – were drunk.

It was nearly 2.00 a.m., and quite a few people went to the fantail, where Ballard raised Harland & Wolff's flag. The sky was clear and filled with stars, the sea was also calm: as it had been when the *Titanic* had foundered. Ballard recalled, 'I imagined I could see the *Titanic* as she slipped nose first into the glassy water. Around me were the ghostly shapes of lifeboats, the shouts and screams of people in the water.'

Argo was sent down the next morning for a more extensive exploration of the site: cameras revealed *Titanic* sitting upright, seemingly intact, her bow appearing well-preserved – although lodged in the seafloor's silt.[13] It initially appeared that the second and third funnels were still standing, and it was noted that the liner had a very slight list to port.[14] *Titanic*'s hull was then found to have separated between the third and fourth funnels.[15] *Titanic*'s hull had split at the weakest point, where the main engine room – containing the reciprocating engines – and the aft grand staircase, created much open space. Good-quality images of the bow section were obtained, although there was not enough time to survey the stern section before *Knorr* departed for home on 4 September 1985.[16] The entire ship was covered lightly in anaerobic bacteria – what Ballard dubbed 'Rusticles', a fitting name to the structures that has stuck ever since. *Titanic* had sunk in an area of the ocean with higher levels of oxygen and salinity than average for the depth, it was found. 'The *Titanic* was unlucky to the last… She couldn't even sink in the right place!' Ballard exclaimed.[17]

With loads of videotape and still photographs, Ballard returned to Woods Hole, receiving a 'tumultuous welcome' and great international publicity.[18] Once again, *Titanic* was headline news all over the world.

The *National Geographic* devoted pages and pages to the expedition in its December 1985 journal (Vol.168, No.6), as it would for later expeditions. The 1985 journal article bore the title: 'How We Found *Titanic*', by Robert D. Ballard in association with Jean-Louis Michel. Their expedition was covered in some detail.

Photographs were included of much of the ship, which was still slowly building a picture of what the vessel looked like. However, it was noted that the bridge wing on the starboard side had collapsed, the cab splitting in two and much of the bulwark hanging over A-deck's forward end of the promenade directly below.

Although there had not been time to properly survey the stern section, some images of it existed. These included an engine room telegraph, a cargo crane foundation, detached from the crane tower, and some other items: a silver platter, from the first or second-class galleys situated near the break; 'Orex' spring mattress used in third class, and an elegantly cut glass window, which proved to be from the door to the second-class smoking room, aft on B-deck. A photograph of the aft end of the poop deck revealed traces of the wooden decking still intact, capstans and other deck fixtures in small quantities, and some of the stern railings. 'Whether *Titanic*'s entire stern lies within the debris field is still unknown,' Ballard wrote next to the large photograph, 'but identification of this fragment and the items associated with it is confirmed by a photograph taken in 1912 of the ship's stern area. Even more conclusive are pieces of equipment photographed in the area of the stern fragment.'

Ballard explained, 'Over the space of four days our undersea cameras shot more than 20,000 frames of film covering some 8,000 different scenes. Yet we have only sketched in the bare outline of *Titanic*; the full portrait is still to come.'

At a Washington press conference, Ballard closed with his prepared formal statement:

> The *Titanic* itself lies in 13,000ft of water on a gently-sloping alpine-like countryside overlooking a small canyon below.
>
> Its bow faces north and the ship sits upright on the bottom, its mighty stacks pointing upward.
>
> There is no light at this great depth and little light can be found.
>
> It is a quiet and peaceful and a fitting place for the remains of this greatest of sea tragedies to rest.
>
> May it forever remain this way and may God bless these found souls.[19]

Unfortunately, French–American co-operation was severely weakened when Woods Hole released video images to American television networks before the agreed simultaneous release to the French and American networks.[20]

Many announcements were made to salvage the ship or artefacts, and to prevent this, the 'RMS *Titanic* Memorial Act of 1985' was finally signed into American law on 21 October 1986.[21] The Bill's subtitle read, 'To encourage international efforts to designate the shipwreck of the RMS *Titanic* as an international maritime memorial and to provide for reasonable research, exploration and, if appropriate, salvage activities with respect to the shipwreck.'[22] Whether this bill had got any authority for a sunken ship lying in international waters was open to question. (A later bill was introduced on 3 August 1987, 'To prohibit the importation of objects from the RMS *Titanic*.'[23])

★　★　★

Mainly owing to the legal dispute (between Woods Hole and *IFREMER*) regarding the film release, the French team cancelled their plans to accompany the American team on the second expedition in July 1986.[24]

Aboard the Navy vessel *Atlantis II*, Ballard's 56-strong crew arrived at the wreck site in July 1986.[25] Accompanying the team was the submersible *Alvin* and a remotely controlled vehicle named *Jason Junior*. Occupying its own cage outside *Alvin*, the robot was controlled from the submarine and had its own still and video cameras. *Alvin* was launched from a crane at the *Atlantis II*'s stern, and both the submarine and the ROV *Jason Junior* could be monitored from the research vessel.

'Dive number one' commenced on 13 July 1986.[26] Ballard and two other crew boarded the submersible for the descent to the wreck – equivalent in depth to 10½ Empire State buildings – a journey two-and-a-half hours long.[27] After a brief glimpse of a towering black wall of steel covered in 'rusticles', the dive terminated due to technical trouble with the submarine.[28] Over the next twelve days, eleven dives were completed and many photographs were taken.[29] At the end of this, Ballard said that, 'I can almost say now that there is not a square inch of the *Titanic* that has not been photographed in beautiful detail in colour.'[30]

Titanic's stern section lay 1,970ft (600 metres) south of the bow and it was explored on the eighth dive.[31] Ballard saw the stern and described it as 'a carnage of debris. It looked violent and torn, fragmented and jumbled like a rat's nest.'[32] Much of the hull plating was gone from the stern's starboard side and sections lay twisted among debris on the ocean floor.[33] The port side had fared a bit better, although much of the ship's side was badly damaged. One of A-deck's cargo cranes remained intact, as did some of C-deck's aft second-class promenade.[34] A small area of the A-deck first-class promenade remained and the boat deck's second-class entrance still stood, although the area where the first-class smoking room had been situated was flattened.[35]

Titanic's bow had ploughed deep into the ocean floor, by as much as 50ft, so that the mud was almost up to the anchors.[36] Directly below the forward end of the superstructure was a large hole where the ship's plating had been forced outwards.[37] The bow was angled down forward of the well deck, while the fore mast had fallen and lay across the well deck and superstructure. The bridge was largely flattened and damage was evident to the officers' quarters, while the decks towards the after end of the bow section were compressed downwards. The boat deck entrance of the first-class grand staircase had been badly damaged. Unlike *Britannic*, the dome cover and the dome itself were completely gone, while the roof of the entrance itself had collapsed. There appeared to be no trace of the remains of the staircase itself.

Although much of the bow section was buried in mud, Ballard observed some split seams, popped rivets and sprung plates on the starboard side.[38] In 1912, a number of publications had pictured an enormous gash in the ship's side, even though Harland & Wolff's Edward Wilding had testified that he believed the damage was intermittent. There seemed to be no trace of such a gash, although given the force of the bow's impact with the seabed it would be folly to rule out further damage on top of that which had been caused by the collision with the iceberg.

Before the expedition left, time was found to place a plaque on the ship's stern, reading:

> In memory of those souls who perished with the *Titanic* April 14/15th 1912. Dedicated to William Tantum IV whose dream to find the *Titanic* has been realised by Dr Robert Ballard. – The officers and members of the *Titanic* Historical Society Inc., 1986.[39]

★   ★   ★

Although Jack Grimm began negotiations with *IFREMER* to mount an expedition the following year, nothing came of the plans,[40] and so the participants in 'Expedition *Titanic* 1987' were: Oceanic Research & Development Ltd (partner to Titanic Ventures Ltd., run by George Tulloch); Westgate Productions; Taurus International; LBS Communications Inc. and Compagnie Generale Maritime.[41] On 22 July 1987, aboard their support-ship *Nadir*, the French team reached the position of the wreck site.[42] They brought with them the submersible *Nautile* – which was designed and engineered at considerable large cost of £13 million ($20 million) and weighed nearly 19 tonnes (40,800lb).[43]

In a time shortly over seven weeks, thirty-two dives to the ship were completed and 1,800 artefacts were recovered.[44] Small items such as crockery, bridge equipment, fittings – such as portholes – and mast-head lights were included in this number. Many of the recovered items were exhibited during a tour of Scandinavia in 1991 and 1992.[45] Electricité de France's careful preservation of the objects partly ensured the exhibitions' successes: 293,000 people flocked to see the exhibitions.[46]

★   ★   ★

Participants of a 1991 'IMAX *Titanic*' expedition included Moscow's Institute of Oceanography, Underseas Research Ltd and *Titanic* Films.[47] The expedition's purpose was to film footage for a new film, entitled *Titanica*. Aboard the vessel *Akademik Keldysh*, two three-person submersibles – *Mir 1* and *Mir 2* – were to assist in the quest.[48] The IMAX® process – using cameras with very wide-angle lenses and requiring 70mm film – needed underwater lights capable of producing 150,000 watts of illumination and withstanding a 6,000psi pressure.[49] Twenty men spent 139 hours on the bottom and 40,000ft of film was shot;[50] the result was a 'remarkable film which, when seen on a huge IMAX screen, gives viewers the feeling they are…at the bottom of the sea.'[51] For the purpose of analysis, *Mir 2* recovered five pieces of metal and some 'rusticles' from the ship to be examined by Canadian laboratories in Dartmouth, Nova Scotia.[52]

After the 1991 expedition, during the summer of 1992, the company Marex-*Titanic* Inc. laid claim to salvage rights to the wreck; they stated that the company *Titanic* Ventures had not visited the site since 1987 and therefore no longer had rights to the wreck.[53] Marex-*Titanic* Inc.'s claim was dismissed by a US District Court late in 1992;[54] *Titanic* Ventures was reorganised as 'RMS *Titanic* Inc.' and was granted the legal rights to the shipwreck.[55]

★   ★   ★

IFREMER and RMS *Titanic* Inc. visited the liner's wreck site during the summers of 1993 and 1994, raising in the region of 1,000 and 1,750 items, making a 'grand total' of 3,600 items brought up.[56]

Following these expeditions, the company joined forces with the National Maritime Museum at Greenwich in 1994 to create the '*Titanic* International Advisory Committee', whose members included some historians. The committee was: 'concerned that these objects [salvaged from the wreck] are kept together in a secure way…documented, conserved, and… go on public exhibition'., as Chief Curator of the museum Dr Eric Kentley explained.[57] There was wide public interest and 'The Wreck of the *Titanic*' was the most

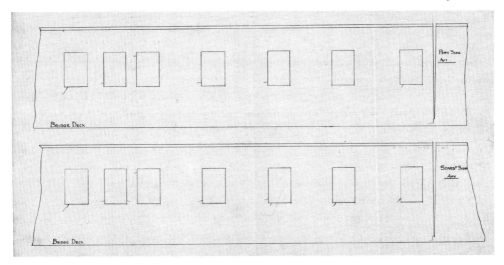

A simplified sketch depicts *Olympic*'s aft expansion joint in the side of the deckhouse plating on B-deck in March 1912. Her configuration was the same as *Titanic*'s, but on board *Britannic* there were a greater number of expansion joints. The forward expansion joint, presumably like her others, had a curved base. (National Archives)

popular exhibition ever presented by the National Maritime Museum; after an extension of the closing date, it ended, having had in excess of 720,000 visitors.

★   ★   ★

During 1995, aboard the Russian research vessel *Akademik Mstislav Keldysh*, Canadian film-maker James Cameron visited *Titanic*'s wreck to film footage for his movie, *Titanic*.[58] ROVs were sent deeper into the ship than ever before. The team captured some remarkable footage of the first-class reception room on D-deck and there were clear traces of the ship's former elegance.[59] They saw traces of the panelling, the ornate columns and the elaborate pattern of one of the doors.[60] Cameron's hypothesis as to why the area was so well preserved was that the white paint which covered the woodwork contained a high amount of lead that organisms could not digest.[61]

★   ★   ★

'*Titanic* Expedition 1996' was undertaken by RMS *Titanic* Inc. and *IFREMER* with support from many companies; the vessels *Nadir*, *Nautile*, *Ocean Voyager*, *Jim Kilabuk*, and *Ballymena* all took part in the expedition.[62]

Two cruise ships accompanied the expedition. George Tulloch had offered the berths to raise money to contribute to the dives' cost of more than $100,000 per dive. Passengers were able to view the salvage expedition.

Members of the expedition's 'mission team' included David Livingstone of Harland & Wolff, 'the first person from the firm to ever view the wreck'; Paul Matthias of Polaris Imaging; Naval Architect William H. Garzke of Gibbs & Cox; Dr Roy Cullimore, a Microbiology expert; the Historians were John Eaton, Charles Haas and Claus-Göran Wetterholm,[63] who had been on the 1993 expedition. Wetterholm had also gone on the 1994 expedition.

Sonar scans conducted by Paul Matthias revealed some starboard bow damage: a 'small stab' in the forepeak, 4 and 5ft holes in hold 1; 15ft of damage in hold 2; a 32ft opening from hold 2 to hold 3 and a 45ft gash through boiler room 6 and partly into boiler room 5, which it was concluded was caused by the iceberg.[64] Any damage to the double bottom, such as underneath boiler room 4, could not be detected, as it was completely underneath the ship.

A small section of *Titanic*'s hull plating – dubbed the 'Big Piece' – once the outer bulkhead of first-class cabins C79 and C81 – was to be raised,[65] but attempts failed and the piece crashed back down into the depths. Passengers on the cruise vessels were declared 'naturally very disappointed'.

'The ocean gives us no quarter. We failed on this attempt because we neglected to carefully co-ordinate twenty-first-century technology of deep ocean recovery with the nineteenth-century technology of winching and rigging,' expedition leader George Tulloch later reflected. 'We won't make that mistake again!'[66]

★   ★   ★

'Research and Recovery expedition of RMS *Titanic* Inc.' took place in August 1998; among the participants are *IFREMER*, and many of the vessels used took part in the 1996 expedition.[67] Although the previous attempt to raise the 'Big Piece' had failed, the twenty-ton section of hull was raised successfully.

Dr Roy Cullimore, a microbiologist, reported that several types of bacteria are devouring the hull at the rate of up to one-tenth of a ton per day.[68] In 'a matter of possibly 90 years, the RMS *Titanic* will biologically implode, and…become an iron ore deposit on the floor of the ocean.'[69]

He later calculated that during the intervening two years between the 1996 and 1998 expeditions, the rusticle growth had increased by 30 per cent,[70] while noting several examples of deterioration on the shipwreck: for example; the aft end of the A–deck promenade on the bow section is moving forward at about 1ft per year and some of the decking has slid away. 'There appears, to be evidence not of a catastrophic structural failure about to occur in the future, but rather of a gradual collapse that would follow a somewhat predictable pattern,'[71] he would later write.

★   ★   ★

Early in September 1998, the first of a number of paid trips to the wreck by Deep Ocean Expeditions took place. *Mir 1* and *Mir 2* were used for the descent, piloted by Anatoly Sagalevitch and Genya Cherniaev. At a cost of $32,000, fourteen tourists dived to the wreck, including four German citizens (Antje Steglich, Oliver Hesse, Heike Schnellbach and Brigitte Saar) who had won the chance to dive through radio and television promotions. Richard Garriott, who would go on to visit the International Space Station, and Anne White, then the oldest person to dive to the wreck were among the other visitors. Although an American court had ruled against such visits to the ship, Anne White's opinion was similar to many: 'What right has an American court to stop me from visiting a piece of history on international seas? After all, the British built the ship.'

When asked: 'How can a US court claim jurisdiction over a wreck site in international waters?' RMS *Titanic* Inc. maintained: 'Under customary international law, as reflected in Article 77 of the 1982 United Nations Convention on the Law of the Sea, coastal states are permitted to exercise sovereign rights over the continental shelf for the purpose of exploring and exploiting its living and non-living resources.'[72]

★   ★   ★

In July 2000, the RMS *Titanic* Inc. mounted the company's sixth expedition to the wreck, meeting up at the site on 27 July 2000 and continuing into the following month. Three vessels were used; *Akademik Mstislav Keldysh*, a veteran of many previous expeditions, *Ocean Intervention*, 'a vessel from the company Oceaneering that has dynamic positioning capabilities', and the third vessel *S/V Explorer*. Two mini-submarines, *Mir 1* and *Mir 2*, the ROV *Magellan 725*, and two more ROVs were also used for this expedition.[73]

The expedition members were many and was made-up of many experts, including: historical advisers Bill Sauder and Denis Cochrane; technical historian and marine artist Ken Marschall; president of RMS *Titanic* Inc. Arnie Geller; salvage consultant Ralph White; director of submersible operations Dr Anatoly Sagalevitch; operations manager for RMS *Titanic* Inc. David Walker; and Expedition 2000 operations manager Dik Barton. In round numbers, the expedition members numbered a total of nearly 150 people; eleven people on the *Explorer*, over eighty people on the *Keldysh*, more than twenty *ocean intervention* crew and twenty-five observers and media.

Although beset with weather problems, 'the 2000 expedition to *Titanic* proved to be one of the most successful to date', in the words of Michelle Turman, curator of collections at RMS *Titanic* Inc.

A grand total of 853 artefacts were raised during the four-week expedition's hectic schedule. Some of the artefacts raised included the ship's wheel from the wheelhouse and the stand of the wheel from the open bridge; a whistle control timer; the steering wheel cable from the main bridge; parts of a watertight door; the base of a main telegraph complete with cable and electric switch; the telephone from the aft docking bridge and finally a capstan controller.

Additionally, personal artefacts included a pair of binoculars, opera glasses, a leather case with sixty-five intact perfume ampoules belonging to first-class passenger Mr Adolphe Saafeld, a bowler hat, first-class Stonier & Co. dinner plate, a camera with eleven bits of nitrate film and some silver-plated dishes possibly used for the collection during the first and last Sunday morning service on the *Titanic*.

Historian Bill Sauder gave descriptions of some of the 'highlights' of the technical items recovered. The 'robust stand' of the wheel from the open bridge 'formed the base to the ship's auxiliary wheel located on the navigating bridge. This second wheel was used to steer the ship in fair weather and during docking operations when hearing commands correctly was crucial.' In fact, the wheel on the open navigating bridge had no direct control over the rudder. 'It simply operated by "remote control" through gearing and shafts and so was nothing more than a slave to the main wheel [in the wheelhouse].'

A landing sign from the aft first-class staircase's C-deck landing was recovered; the brass letters were originally screwed to the oak panelling of the aft wall, and part of the wood was indeed still attached. Among the other interesting objects were: 'a lead wrench and plumbing gooseneck with the number 401' – *Titanic*'s yard number given to her by Harland & Wolff – 'stamped on their respective handles; a lavatory slate with the number 401 etched onto the reverse side; a watertight shaft with the embossing of 401, Watertight

Door A16T; and a marble public lavatory splash that has the number 401 written on the reverse side of the stone.'

Michelle Turman said of the expedition:

> During Expedition 2000, every dive had a mission, every passenger a job, and in the end, every artefact tells a significant story. To the credit of the team, the lab. aboard *Keldysh* was never back-logged. We worked hard to be on schedule and to be ready for each day's new batch of historical artefacts. Despite the close quarters, pontificating Historians, rigid lab practices and computer set-backs, each person pulled together to preserve, protect and properly interpret the artefacts of *Titanic*... This year's expedition is sure to generate controversy, which is nothing new to this endeavour. But in years to come, when the wreck is too unstable to explore, the tragedy of *Titanic* and the triumph…may not only be told through this collection... I truly believe that what was accomplished this summer will be remembered as a historical success.

★   ★   ★

Six years after exploring the ship for the first time, film-maker James Cameron returned with a team whose goal was to examine the ship's interiors in greater depth. Following the enormous commercial success of his movie, there was a keen interest in what the team would discover during their seven weeks in August and September 2001. Aboard the *Akademik Mstislav Keldysh* with its two submersibles *Mir 1* and *Mir 2*, the team brought two smaller ROVs to help them penetrate further than any previous attempts. Designed and built by Cameron and his brother Michael, they would prove invaluable.

The first-class reception room and dining saloon's leaded windows proved to be remarkably intact; in a first-class stateroom on A-deck, a gleaming headboard was one of a number that were remarkably preserved, with its brass and gilded inlays; on an upright wash cabinet's outer shelf, an intact water carafe still stood, with a drinking glass on the shelf beneath; the fireplace in J. Bruce Ismay's sitting room was clearly recognisable; and even some of the decorative woodwork on the private promenade deck.[74] There were some interesting changes between *Olympic* and her sister that had not been noted before: from changes to the design of the grillwork doors for the first-class elevators, to the ceiling lights outside; and additional columns were seen in the first-class reception room.[75] (The decorative columns throughout the dining saloon and other passenger areas were used to hide the structural pillars which supported the decks. Perhaps these columns were a consequence of the enlargement of *Titanic*'s reception room by repositioning the interior bulkheads to reduce the size of the entrance foyers, which would have exposed the pillars.)

As well as exploring areas of the ship that had not been seen since 1912, there were also comparisons between areas that had been seen on previous expeditions. The deck at the bridge front had collapsed further onto A-deck below, revealing the windows to the first-class staterooms that had previously been hidden; there was increasing damage on the boat deck and the deckhouses, from a further collapse of the roof on the starboard side of the grand staircase, to the continued settling of the boat deck at the after end of the bow section, which was 'caving in to A-deck on both the port and starboard sides, taking the gymnasium with it'. There were further signs of deterioration at the stern section, where the team had hoped to explore the remnants of the veranda café and the *á la carte* restaurant. Unfortunately, when they tried to access these areas from the more intact port side, it appeared that there had been a substantial collapse: 'the space between the boat deck and B-deck' had 'simply disappeared'. In the debris field, a number of tile sections from the first-class smoke room and dining saloon were visible. It had been noted previously that *Titanic*'s smoke room was decorated with red and blue tiles rather than the grey and buff coloured tiles of *Olympic*, while a dining saloon tile showed a consistent rich blue colour. It contrasted to recovered tile sections that indicated a much lighter blue, opening the possibility that it might have faded following its recovery or restoration.[76]

★   ★   ★

Rumours circulated in November 2002 that an expedition to *Titanic* was taking place. Although the sole salvage rights were awarded to RMS *Titanic* Inc. in 1994, a judgement that was intended to be recognised worldwide, an investigation by a Portsmouth maritime lawyer, Mark Davis, indicated that there might be some truth in the rumours.[77] An unmanned French submarine, one of a few worldwide with the capability to reach *Titanic*'s wreck, had been at the wreck site, while a government satellite image was reported to show a ship in the vicinity. It was unclear if the ship had been 'passing through or was stationary over the shipwreck'.

★   ★   ★

On 22 June 2003, *Akademik Mstislav Keldysh* left port to return to *Titanic*. On board were a number of groups working together to document *Titanic*: a seven-member team working under the American National Oceanic and Atmospheric Administration's (NOAA) Office of Ocean Exploration; six people participating at the invitation of Deep Ocean Expeditions; and a third group of eleven scientists 'conducting ongoing scientific research projects under the auspices of the P.P. Shirshov Institute of Oceanology of the Russian Academy of Sciences'.

The Deep Ocean Expeditions team included David Concannon, Kevin Gurr, Leigh Bishop, Carl Spencer, Larry Daley and Richard Robol. Concannon had helped organise the expedition led by RMS *Titanic* Inc. three years earlier, while Daley had provided logistical assistance to at least six expeditions and Robol was present to 'assess the condition of the *Titanic* and photograph the wreck'. Gurr, one of the leading technical divers worldwide, had visited *Britannic* in 1997, while Bishop and Spencer were also preparing for the *Britannic* expedition that would take place later that year.

Part of the National Oceanic and Atmospheric Administration team, Dr Roy Cullimore and Lori Johnton (from Droycon Bioconcepts, Inc.) 'organised microbiological and rusticle observations', while the Russian team focused on research of geophysics, marine biology, physical oceanography and microbiology, 'adding to the unique body of scientific knowledge that has been obtained by studying and exploring the *Titanic* site.' The expedition accomplished its mission and helped prepare for the first digital photo mosaic of the wreck, although there was another sign of the ship's deterioration. The foremast, which previously lay across the well deck, had 'now completely collapsed – like a pretzel stick that has been hit with a hammer'. Plans were afoot for further examination of the wreck the following year and they returned to port on 2 July 2003.[78]

★   ★   ★

Less than a year passed before those plans came to fruition. Returning to the ship nine-teen years after its discovery, Dr Robert Ballard and a team of scientists from the National Oceanic and Atmospheric Administration were on board the organisation's research ship *Ronald H. Brown* for an eleven-day expedition to *Titanic*. Dr Dwight Coleman, from the University of Rhode Island and the Mystic Aquarium and Institute for Exploration (MAIFE), was the expedition's lead researcher, while marine archaeologist Jeremy Weirich oversaw the archaeological component of the expedition.

They worked at the site from 30 May 2004 to 9 June 2004 and 'utilised high-defi-nition video and stereoscopic still images to provide an updated assessment of the wreck site.' The National Oceanic and Atmospheric Administration's focus was 'to build a baseline of scientific information from which we can measure the shipwreck's processes and deterioration, and then apply the knowledge we gain to other deep water shipwrecks and submerged cultural resources.' As well as a programme, *Return to Titanic*, which was broadcast by National Geographic and included a live underwater telecast from the wreck, MAIFE 'enabled thousands of children to experience the *Titanic* mission as it occurred'. Four shows were transmitted by satellite daily over five days from 4 June 2004.[79]

By all accounts, the expedition was a success but it 'was not an easy one':

> The explorers and the crew of NOAA ship *Ronald H. Brown* battled weather so difficult it sometimes kept the remotely-operated vehicles (ROVs) lashed to the deck of the tossing ship when they should have been relocating *Titanic* or gathering scientific data and images of the wreck. When the sea state did allow operations, technical problems with the underwater robots or electrical glitches in their long umbilical cords caused further delays.[80]

Shortly after the expedition's conclusion, another positive step for the ship's preserva-tion was taken. In November 2003, the shipping minister, David Jamieson, had signed an international agreement on behalf of the British government. It 'recognises the liner and its surrounding areas as a memorial to those who lost their lives as well as "a historical wreck of exceptional international importance". It means dives will have to be licensed by all the participating governments.'[81] The intention was that it would become a four-party international agreement between the British, Canadian, French and American governments, and when the American ambassador in London signed it in June 2004 it came into force. It served as an 'international extension' of the 'Guidelines for Research, Exploration and Salvage of RMS *Titanic*' that NOAA published in April 2001.

★ ★ ★

Another expedition took place in the summer of 2004. RMS *Titanic* Inc., whose last expedition had been four years earlier, returned to the site to conduct their 'seventh research and recovery mission'. The team left Halifax on 25 August 2004 on board *Mariner Sea* with their goal 'to recover artefacts for exhibition, identify objects for future recov-ery, inspect the wreck site for alleged harm caused by previous visitors, and, if necessary, to establish guidelines for future visitations.' When they arrived at the site, the company 'promised that the mission would be conducted with reverence and respect for the tragedy that had taken place on the location in 1912'.

The team returned to Halifax on 8 September 2004, having recovered 'a variety of artefacts': 'Each rescue documented as to time and location by video, still photographs, and written notations.' They included a gilded wall sconce from the *á la carte* restaurant. RMS *Titanic* Inc.'s president and the leader of the expedition, Arnie Geller, was pleased to note the discovery, saying: 'several important artefacts were located and those rescued will certainly fascinate visitors attending the company's public exhibition program.' One month later, on 15 October 2004, the company underwent a reorganisation and restructuring and it was announced that a new holding company, Premier Exhibitions Inc., would:

> Create an organisational framework that tends to be more flexible and conducive to future expansion. As a result of the new framework, Premier Exhibitions Inc., will continue the company's overall business of developing and touring museum quality exhibitions throughout the world, while RMS *Titanic* Inc., will be limited solely to touring the company's *Titanic* exhibitions.

RMS *Titanic* Inc. continued to maintain its rights to the wreck under its status as salvor-in-possession, while investors' shares were converted on a one-for-one basis from RMS *Titanic* Inc. to Premier Exhibitions Inc.[82]

★   ★   ★

Titanic's wreck site was humming with activity from June to August 2005. There was barely a day when nobody was at the site. For the third and, he claimed, final time, James Cameron returned to explore further the ship's interiors. The expedition generated a lot of interest and was documented for the Discovery Channel's *Last Mysteries of the Titanic*. The first leg of the expedition, on board *Akademik Mstislav Keldysh* and led by Dr Anatoly Sagalevitch, took place between 24 June 2005 and 7 July 2005; and then the team returned from 19 July 2005 to 29 July 2005.

Four 'highly manoeuvrable unmanned explorers, called X-bots, capable of reaching depths of 23,000 feet' were on board and were 'the smallest deep sea wreck penetration vehicles ever built'. Designed and built by Phoenix International, they were 24in long with a height and width of 13in. Their size was a great advantage in exploring deep inside the ship. The team's efforts were largely successful and they made some remarkable findings, examining areas such as the wireless room's interior; first-class staterooms; Scotland Road, the long E-deck corridor that served as a thoroughfare for the crew; and the Turkish Baths.

One the twelfth day, the expedition diary reported:

> Cameron immediately piloted the 'bot to F deck on the *Titanic*, to an area that has never been explored. In a half hour or so, the ROV entered the Turkish Baths, a tile-walled room that, to our knowledge, had not been seen since 1912. Cameron brings the hardy souls who are still awake to greet him down to mission control to watch the 'bot footage. Remarkably, the [cooling room] tile is still in place. The team of historians is outwardly giddy with excitement.[83]

★   ★   ★

During the interlude, another expedition took place from 7 July 2005 to 17 July 2005. Deep Ocean Expeditions, in conjunction with P.P. Shirshov Institute of Oceanology of the Russian Academy of Sciences, offered a number of fee-paying passengers the opportunity to visit the wreck. It was the sixth such expedition to the wreck, following from the first in September 1998 and similar visits in 1999, 2000 and 2003. There were a number of educational lectures on board and the company's interest was 'in educating by adventure' and working with others to 'expand opportunities for deep ocean research and documentation as a way of increasing the knowledge and understanding of our planets' major geographical feature'.

Passengers would see: 'her huge anchors, larger than the submersible, and the capstans, the bridge and the famous grand staircase, all nestled amongst rivers of rust as the ocean slowly consumes the grand old lady. You'll see the ship's telemotor, the massive boilers, the propellers and the Marconi Room....'[84] For those lucky enough to make the dive, including one prize winner, it was the trip of a lifetime.

Another group returned after the second leg of Cameron's expedition finished, led by G. Michael Harris, former chief operating officer of RMS *Titanic* Inc. They arrived at the end of July and stayed until 9 August 2005. Thirteen-year-old Sebastian Harris warranted a mention in the *Guinness Book of Records* when he became the youngest person to dive to *Titanic* on 5 August 2005.

★   ★   ★

On 10 August 2005, *Akademik Mstislav Keldysh* left St John's, Newfoundland, with a team led by David Concannon. They planned to search for additional clues about *Titanic*'s sinking and examine a new debris field to the south of the known wreck site. The expedition would be covered by the History Channel documentary *Titanic's Final Moments: Missing Pieces*. Among the expedition's participants were Dr Anatoly Sagalevitch, from the P.P. Shirshov Institute of Oceanology of the Russian Academy of Sciences; Ralph White, an experienced underwater cameraman; John Chatterton, who had dived to *Britannic*; and a host of other advisers, researchers and technicians.

Each dive day was focused on a particular objective. The first was to 'search for and relocate a new debris field' that had been discovered more than half a mile to the south of the southernmost part of the main wreck site, that had first been observed in August 2000; and explore the bow and stern sections of the wreck to 'look for evidence to support the "grounding theory"'.★ David Concannon described seeing 'the awesome devastation caused by the force of the ship tearing in half before it sank. Steel hull sections are torn like paper; massive hull plates are stacked like cards in a deck, one on top of the other; portholes are blown open; and decking is folded back on itself.' On the second day 'detailed high definition images of the bow and stern sections' were obtained as further exploration was undertaken. By the third day, *Mir 1* and *Mir 2* were in action and venturing to the east of the stern section:

★ In a nutshell, the grounding theory consists of 'the argument that *Titanic* grounded on an underwater shelf of the iceberg, compromising her double bottom structure. The combination of direct impact damage suffered along the ship's bottom and subsequent racking damage which parted plates along her starboard side allowed enough water into the hull so that the internal subdivision was overwhelmed.' For further reading see David G. Brown and Parks Stephenson, 'White paper on the Grounding of *Titanic*', presented for consideration by the Marine Forensic Panel on 31 May 2001. It is also available online at Parks Stephenson's website, Marconigraph.com.

This area to the east is the last truly unexplored area of the *Titanic* site, and Concannon, Sagalevitch and [Bill] Lange knew it contained large hull sections based on their earlier dives to this area in 2000 and on other expeditions. Shortly after leaving the stern section on an easterly course, [Richie] Kohler and [John] Chatterton in *Mir 1* came upon two large sections of the *Titanic*'s double bottom hull, almost 90m in length and in almost pristine condition. These hull sections had been observed on previous expeditions, including by Concannon and Sagalevitch in 2000, but they had never been closely studied. *Mir 1* was soon joined by *Mir 2*, containing Bob Blumberg and Kirk Wolfinger, and both submersible teams spent several hours analysing these hull sections and obtaining high definition digital imagery for later study.[85]

That later study and analysis would reveal a number of interesting facts, but the expedition's accomplishment in extending their search of the wreck site and its boundaries beyond what had been seen before was noteworthy.

★   ★   ★

Almost five years passed before another expedition returned. On 27 July 2010, Premier Exhibitions Inc. announced:

That its wholly owned subsidiary RMS *Titanic*, Inc., as salvor-in-possession of the RMS *Titanic* and its wreck site, in partnership with Woods Hole Oceanographic Institution and the Waitt Institute, will conduct a ground-breaking expedition to *Titanic* 25 years after its discovery, to do what no one has ever attempted before: take innovative measures to virtually raise *Titanic*, preserving the legacy of the ship for all time.

The Waitt Institute, an American organisation based in California, had only been founded five years earlier and sought to 'advance human understanding of the past and secure the promise of a better future through exploration and discovery'. In what was 'arguably the most technologically advanced scientific expedition to *Titanic* ever organised', Premier Exhibitions Inc. had 'brought together a team of leading archaeologists, oceanographers and scientists including The Institute of Natural Archaeology, The National Oceanic and Atmospheric Administration's Natural Marine Sanctuaries Program, and The National Park Service's Submerged Resources Centre.'[86]

Using acoustic technologies to complete two- and three-dimensional maps of the site, the expedition leaders hoped to compile a comprehensive image of the wreck site and debris fields. 'The equipment we'll be using will be able to plot each large section, as well as many of the smaller artefacts that are visible on the ocean bed, so it will give us almost a complete picture [of] the condition and location of everything associated with *Titanic* at this moment in time,' the expedition's chief conservator, Alex Klingelhofer, told one news organisation.[87] One of the joint expedition co-leaders, David Gallo, explained: 'We'll map the debris field and the bow and stern, both with sonar to get the shape of the objects but also with very special high-dimension 3D cameras that we've got on board. And that will do two things: we have an archaeological type base map to work with in the future and a virtual *Titanic*, so we can share that with the public.'

The team left port on board *Jean Charcot* on 23 August 2010, one day later than planned. News organisations and an interested public were kept informed every step of the way. The company had set up a website dedicated to the expedition and its progress, while periodic updates were posted online each day. As usual for the North Atlantic, the weather proved a challenge. Hurricanes Danielle and Earl forced a temporary suspension of the expedition and contributed to a week's delay, causing the second phase of the expedition to be rescheduled. Nonetheless, the team made progress and a number of stunning photographs were released.

Undoubtedly, the company plans further expeditions in the future, while other organisations' interest in the wreck shows no sign of abating.

★   ★   ★

What has been learnt from the wreck, and what may be discovered in the future? There is certainly new information about *Titanic's* anatomy. Although she is one of the most documented liners in history, there is surely a lot more to learn; and for all the substantial similarities there are also a number of interesting differences compared to *Olympic*.

What of the iceberg damage? It is a key question. Unfortunately, since *Titanic's* bow ploughed into the seafloor it is quite plausible that some of the damage to the bow section was caused by this impact, which would make it impossible to tell precisely what the pre-existing damage from the collision with the iceberg was. While Ballard had noted damage on the starboard side – split seams and popped rivets – most of the bow section at this level was hidden in the mud. An attempt to examine the issue was made in 1996. Using a technique known as 'sub bottom profiling', sonar imaging was used to try and examine the hidden areas of the hull. It revealed six openings on the starboard side below the waterline. While the finding appeared to confirm Edward Wilding's own calculations back in 1912, given that similar damage was also found on the port side it is difficult to make a definitive assessment.[88] Two years later the Discovery Channel reported that the starboard side of the hull had been examined and they also noted 'undeniable proof of a parted seam plus what looked like several empty rivet holes'.[89]

From a scientific viewpoint, new information has come to light through studying the ship. The subject of widespread publicity, undoubtedly many people today subscribe to the 'brittle steel' theory as one of the reasons for the ship's loss. In fact, the truth is rather different. Based upon a sample of material recovered in 1991, scientists at the Defence Research Establishment Atlantic (DREA) in Halifax and the Canada Centre for Mineral and Energy Technology (CANMET) in Ottawa conducted a series of tests and analyses. Their results indicated that the steel had undesirably high quantities of sulphur and therefore became brittle when subjected to the cold water temperatures that were seen on the night of the disaster. However, media coverage did not necessarily reflect the subjective interpretations of the results: 'It was a neat, clean package: too much sulphur, bad steel, cracks, sinking. The media couldn't have asked for a more oversimplified, easy to digest story. It was picked up everywhere, and over the years, it has become something of an assumed "fact" – it was the steel, wasn't it?'[90]

Further tests were conducted five years later from another steel sample, by a team of metallurgists led by Professor H.P. Leighly, of the University of Missouri-Rolla, who were assisted later by Tim Foecke's laboratory at the American National Institute of Science and Technology (NIST), in Gaithersburg, Maryland. Chemical tests were assisted by Dr Harold Reemsnyder of Homer Laboratories, Bethlehem Steel in Pennsylvania. Mechanically, the steel's properties fell within the requirements laid down by Harland & Wolff and in force in 1911. In fact, the tensile test results in 1996 showed the *Titanic* hull plate with a yield stress about the same as Harland & Wolff required.★

To test the toughness of the steel in resisting fracture, Foecke:

> Performed a slow three-point bend test on six samples of *Titanic* hull steel, three at room temperature (25°C) and three at 0°C. The data demonstrated that the hull steel was by no means a brittle material. In fact, the results show indisputably that *Titanic's* hull steel is a very tough material under slow loading rates…
>
> These results seem to prove that the steel was not of inferior quality – it had sufficient fracture toughness, well within typical *modern* [original emphasis] fracture toughness values, even at ice brine temperatures…[91]

Titanic was built before the time that ships' hulls were entirely welded. Drawing upon past experience, Harland & Wolff were aware that riveting was a potential weakness in big ships and they sought to make sure that the ship's design guarded against it: 'We adopted, to an unusual extent, hydraulic riveting wherever possible, to insure the rivets being thoroughly well closed,' explained Edward Wilding. 'This was of course a slow and expensive affair, but it was done.' Generally speaking, rivets were made of steel and hydraulically driven for three-quarters to three-fifths of the ship's length amidships, where the greatest stresses were borne by the hull, with the iron rivets towards the bow and stern hand-riveted. The seams between the plates were treble riveted for three-fifths of the length, while the iron rivets towards the bow and stern were generally double riveted. (Some particular joints had as many as five rows of rivets.) The long, straight joints amidships could be hydraulically riveted much more easily than the narrow and often confined areas of the bow and stern. In turn, by using iron instead of steel in these areas it was easier for hand riveters to do the job. When Francis Carruthers reported to the Board of Trade on *Titanic's* completion, he noted: 'The workmanship is of the highest class throughout,' and confirmed that she had been constructed in accordance with the design specifications and plans submitted by the shipbuilder.

A small number of the ship's three million rivets have been subjected to analysis by Jennifer Hooper McCarty, studying for a PhD, in conjunction with Tim Foecke and supervised by Professor Timothy Weihs, at John Hopkins University. Forty-eight rivets were recovered and nineteen of those had lost their mushroom-shaped heads. Since they had been found on the ocean floor and had already failed, it is likely that they were already a weaker sample; yet five steel rivets were retrieved from the 'Big Piece' and four from a riveted section of bulkhead, intact and *in situ*. One of the iron rivets was a hull rivet. The steel rivets were clearly superior to the iron, while the iron rivets had an excessive quantity of slag, a residue from smelting that could make them more prone to fracturing under stress. Some rivets were better than others: one iron rivet averaged only 1.1 per cent slag, substantially better than the required standard, whereas another reached as high as 12.8 per cent. Comparison with rivets from *Arabic*, built in 1903 and a casualty of the

---

★ The 'ultimate tensile strength' of the steel came in at 62.6 ksi. (Ksi stood for kilopounds per square inch; a kilopound being equal to 1,000lb).

war twelve years later, showed that the *Titanic* rivets 'do not represent an anomaly of the era'.

Their findings included the conclusion that the 'installation of wrought iron rivets from variable, and often inferior, feedstock would result in a distribution of different seam strengths along the hull'; that 'the installed substandard rivets could not have been detected unless they were loose after they cooled, since the quality control and certification procedures used at the time of construction were insufficient to the task'; that 'the nature of the impact between the hull and the ice (bumping, scraping over a significant distance) was very unusual and happened to stress the rivets in a manner that exposed their weakness'; and that 'at least some of the rivets would have failed no matter their quality or strength'.[92] They concluded: 'This analysis does not mean that the quality of rivets was a deciding factor as to whether the ship would have sunk. Any quality [of] rivets would probably have failed under the load of the initial impact and opened a number of compartments to the sea, potentially dooming the ship to sink eventually…'[93]

It is interesting to note that while Cunard's *Lusitania* and *Mauretania* used steel rivets throughout, even then there was room for improvement. They were built under naval supervision and would run with a government subsidy, but the rivets that were specified were mild steel rivets. It caused some comment because they also used high tensile steel plating in the ships' upper structures, which enabled some weight to be saved. It was stronger than mild steel and therefore less material needed to be used. Nevertheless, some observers felt that silicon steel (superior to mild steel and more costly) should have been used for the riveting of the high tensile steel plating, as the concern was that 'the rivets were softer than the high tensile plates they connected'.[94] When *Aquitania* was built several years later, she did not have the benefit of a government subsidy and Cunard bore this in mind during the design process: she needed to earn a dividend. Her hull plating consisted of the traditional mild steel, as the White Star liners did, and so there was no issue in using mild steel rivets.* Practically any design could be improved if enough money was spent, but a commercial ship needed to be capable of generating a profit for her owners as well as operating in her anticipated service conditions with an ample margin of strength and safety. There will always be judgements to make as to the right balance to strike, but if *Titanic* was particularly unlucky in how the collision unfolded – it seemed to stress the rivets in a manner that precisely exposed their weakness – then *Olympic*'s rivets did their intended job over a period of a quarter of a century. Anecdotally, it appears that *Aquitania*, *Berengaria* and *Majestic* required more repairs and replacement of rivets during their annual overhauls than *Olympic*. It is also interesting to note that *Titanic*'s bow is one of the most intact sections of the wreck, yet was riveted with iron. There are numerous seams where rivets remain in place despite considerable distortion of the hull plating itself.

The wreck's discovery put to rest any doubts as to whether the ship broke apart in the final stages of the sinking. However, for all the evidence that is available, the break-up was an extremely complex series of events, involving enormous forces that are hard to comprehend. As *Titanic* readied for her final plunge, progressive flooding over more than

---

* When Thomas Andrews explained that mild steel was used throughout, he noted *Olympic* and *Titanic*'s stability 'would be so much greater than that of the *Lusitania* and *Mauretania* that lightness in the upper works was not a vital necessity with them as it had been in the case of these two ships.'

two-and-a-half hours meant that she had lost longitudinal stability, while the list to port can only have contributed to an unusual distribution of stresses.

Following closer analysis of the double bottom sections for the History Channel's *Titanic's Final Moments: Missing Pieces*, the team's efforts evolved into what became known as the 'shallow angle' break theory. Roger Long, a naval architect, led the development of the theory by examining the physical evidence and discussions with the other researchers and team members. They believed that:

> The damage patterns in the steel appear more consistent with a slow and progressive break followed by grinding together of the separated hull sections by still tenuously connected hull portions. The double bottom sections themselves show tension breaks at the tank top and compression in the hull shell, indicating that the double bottom was bent and broken as a separate unit. If the entire hull had broken as a unit then both the inner bottom tank top and the hull shell should show compression failure.
>
> The sudden clean break depicted in high angle scenarios should have produced a great deal of crushing and structural deformation in the double bottom, while the topsides and superstructure showed fairly clean tension breaks and minimal secondary damage due to being pulled apart and away from each other...[95]

While the description may sound overly simplistic, the theory envisaged *Titanic's* hull structure failing from the top down: the failure potentially beginning on the starboard side, partly in consequence of the ship's list to port; progressing irregularly towards the ship's bottom; and then as the sides of the ship separated the double bottom broke loose. It seems possible that the two double bottom sections were held together by the remains of the keel, but they eventually landed separately and only a relatively short distance apart.

Parks Stephenson, a naval systems engineer who assisted with the post-expedition analysis, observed: 'It has often been stated that "steel doesn't lie", meaning that the wreckage itself should reveal impeachable truths, but as we were to discover... sometimes the seemingly benign "steel" speaks different languages to different people.'[96] While he examined the same evidence, his interpretation and conclusions differed from Roger Long's in some important details. His interpretation came to be referred to as the 'traditionalist' break up scenario, in that it envisaged the hull failing at a greater angle. Whereas the 'shallow angle' break theory envisaged the hull failing at an angle of around ten degrees or more, Stephenson's analysis saw an angle closer to thirty degrees as more appropriate.

He believed that there was less buoyancy in the bow. Therefore, the ship would have settled further into the water, with the hull 'rotating around its centre of buoyancy – and subsequently failing – at a much greater angle'. Drawing upon eyewitness testimony and the input of others, such as Ken Marschall and James Cameron, who were intimately acquainted with the wreck, the hypothesis was developed. With the ship's bow deeply submerged and water having reached the third funnel, the enormous and increasing stresses concentrated on the upper starboard side plating, beginning a progressive failure as cracking propagated vertically to the double bottom structure and then lengthways along the ship's bottom. The failure would have spread to the port side shortly afterwards as the decks failed progressively and the main bow and stern sections came apart, but with the ship low in the water much of the failure of the decks would have occurred at and below the waterline. As the stern section developed a greater list to port, the 'twisting motion caused an approximate seventy foot section of the double bottom to tear transversely from starboard to port'. The flooding from the damaged forward end prevented any chance of the stern remaining afloat, but as it plunged to the ocean floor the double bottom sections still attached would have separated.

Another interpretation differed from both the 'shallow angle' and 'traditionalist' break up theories in that it envisaged the failure progressing from the bottom up rather than the top down. It was developed in a paper by Roy Mengot and Richard Woytowich for the Marine Forensics Panel of the Society of Naval Architects and Marine Engineers (SNAME).[97] They envisaged a failure beginning in the double bottom, just forward of the engine room, while the ship was at an angle of some fifteen degrees. The double bottom's depth was increased beneath the engine room and was nothing to cause any concern in normal service but, with the ship's bow deep in the water and enormous stresses acting upon the hull, the slope where it narrowed back to its normal depth became a problem. The failure would have rapidly propagated 'across the full breadth of the ship', around the riveted joints at the turn of the bilge where the ship's bottom rounded to meet the sides, and then along the ship's side for 60 or 70ft. As the failure progressed upward, the last part to fail would have been the hull plating around C-deck level: 'The two layers of plate were heavily riveted together, so as to approximate, as nearly as possible, the strength of a continuous strake of 2 inch steel plate…'

They noted that some of the plating on C-deck projected 'farther aft than any other elements of the bow section of the wreck, suggesting that the uppermost shell strakes and the associated decks were among the last – if not *the* last – elements to fail. The portions of the hull and deckhouse that might have interfered with the flexing of the ship are either missing or collapsed.' Photographic evidence of the double bottom sections showed 'the bar keel bent into an "S" shape, consistent with bending under a large compressive load'.

While there are many theories as to the exact manner in which the ship's hull failed, the knowledge that it did raised the question in some people's minds as to the strength of the ship. The question was assessed for the History Channel documentary *Titanic's Achilles Heel*, which was aired in June 2007. As part of the assessment, the naval architectural firm JMS was approached by Roger Long and the Lone Wolf Documentary Group to assist with their research for the History Channel documentary. The firm produced 'a digital model of the *Titanic*'s hull and superstructure using HECSALV salvage engineering software'. They then determined the 'hull girder bending moment' under a series of different wave patterns and calculated the 'progressive flooding according to the scenarios specified by RLMA [Roger Long Marine Architecture] and up to a trim angle of ten degrees forward'. The firm found:

> That the predicted flooded bending moments exceeded the predicted 'design' bending moments in excess of two times. If damage to the hull girder occurred as a result of the flooding condition and associated bending moment, this would not necessarily indicate the vessel was insufficiently designed, disproving the hypothesis of the documentary.[98]

Titanic's hull failed in the final stages of the sinking when it was subjected to stresses that were more than two times greater than the worst stresses she was expected to encounter in normal service, such as a severe North Atlantic storm.★

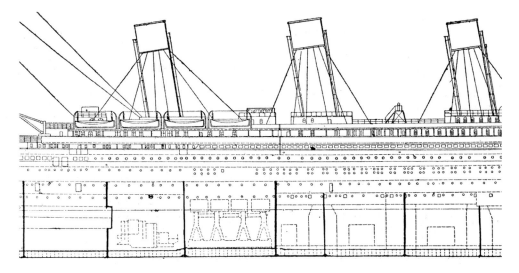

The 'double bottom is 5ft 3in deep, and is increased to 6ft 3in in the reciprocating engine room.' In normal service, it was not a problem: other liners such as *Aquitania* had a similar feature; and *Olympic* never showed any sign of weakness. However, the theory that *Titanic* broke from the bottom up envisages a failure beginning immediately forward of the engine room, where the depth graduated down to the usual 5ft 3in. (*The Sphere*, 1912/Ioannis Georgiou collection)

The question came up in a discussion before Lord Mersey in 1912. During one exchange between Clement Edwards, representing the Dock, Wharf, Riverside and General Workers' Union of Great Britain and Ireland, and William David Archer, principal ship surveyor to the Board of Trade, Archer tried to explain that the Board had looked at *Olympic* and *Titanic*'s greater size compared to previous ships and assessed their strength accordingly. His explanation sounded rather technical, but was a broad comparison of stress borne by each vessel:

> 24355. What I want to get at is this. Take the case of the plates: by what system do you
> test the efficiency of the plates of extra thickness for a ship of this size as compared
> with the plates of a given thickness for a ship of 10,000 tons? – I do it in the man
> ner I have already described. I treat the ship as a beam or girder. I assume that the
> tendency to bend the ship is equal to the displacement of the ship multiplied by her
> length and divided by 30, and I work out the stress in tons per square inch on the
> gunwale. Shall I give you the figure I arrived at, Sir?

---

* Unfortunately, these findings were misinterpreted in press reports and elsewhere. For instance, an article entitled '*Titanic* was Doomed Before it Set Sail', appeared in the *Daily Telegraph* shortly before the documentary aired. It asserted: 'The *Titanic* faced disaster from the moment it set sail' and went on to note: 'even if the ocean liner had not struck an iceberg during its maiden voyage, structural weaknesses made it vulnerable to any stormy sea.' The statements were baseless.

A series of comparative diagrams depicted the stages of *Titanic*'s sinking, including one that showed the expansion joints extending right down through the structural hull and to the keel at the very bottom of the ship, rather than merely in the deckhouses of the superstructure, which was not part of the structural hull. It then showed the ship breaking directly at the aft expansion joint, almost as a hinge opening up.

> 24356. If it will help, certainly do so, please? – I arrived at a figure of 9.9 tons per square inch on the sheer strake [plating] of the bridge [deck] of the *Olympic*. As I endeavoured to describe I drew out a smaller vessel having the scantlings of Lloyd's Rules, and I treated her in exactly the same way, and I arrived in that case at a figure of 12.2 tons per square inch for a vessel having Lloyd's scantlings, the inference being that the *Olympic* was stronger than the Lloyd's vessel.

The term 'scantlings' simply referred to the dimensions and thickness of the ship's structural components: whether it was the beams that ran across the ship and the pillars that helped support the decks; the frames that served as the 'skeleton' of the ship; or the steel plates that formed the watertight skin. While the White Star liners were not built under the supervision of Lloyd's, Harland & Wolff was familiar with the society's standards and they were built to a similar standard of strength. According to Archer's assessment, in a comparison of stresses *Olympic* appeared to be significantly stronger in that the stress was markedly lower. However, his testimony drew the attention of Dr Thearle, chief surveyor of Lloyd's Register of Shipping. Thearle contacted him because he was concerned that Archer's statement would be damaging to the classification society, and worried about:

> Evidence that what you call 'a Lloyd's vessel' – but which it appears from your letter to me… is not an actual but only an imaginary vessel – is so much inferior in strength to the *Olympic* or *Titanic* as represented be the foregoing figures.
>
> I am not concerned with the strength of the *Olympic* and *Titanic*, and am quite prepared to accept the figure which you quote for these vessels, but I am very much concerned that the standard of this society's classification for any vessel which can be fairly compared with those vessels should not be depreciated by misrepresentation. That is the sole point of my complaint…

Thearle was further concerned that Archer had used an assumed vessel based on the requirements of Lloyd's rules from 1885, rather than use the society's most recent revision from 1909 or a comparison with an existing vessel built to the society's supervision. Archer told him that he had 'nothing to *correct* [original emphasis] in my evidence' but that he was willing to offer clarification as to his testimony and the methods he had used. He defended his use of the older rules, stating that they were 'the standard of comparison adopted by the Board of Trade for the purpose' after 'conference with representatives of Lloyd's Register and other classification societies…' The relevant instructions for surveyors using the rules from 1885 had been updated as recently as 1906.[99] Nevertheless, it is quite easy to see Thearle's concern, in that an observer might have assumed that a large ship such as *Mauretania*, which had been built under the society's supervision, was significantly inferior in strength to *Titanic*, whereas the reality was that they were designed to a very similar standard.

It is interesting to examine this measure of strength using other large vessels. *Lusitania* and *Aquitania* were built under Lloyd's supervision and *Imperator* was built to the standards of the German classification society, *Germanischer Lloyd*:

	Lusitania (1907)	*Olympic* (1911)	*Imperator* (1913)	*Aquitania* (1914)
Stress (tons per sq.in.)	10.1	9.9	10.2	8.5

While *Lusitania*'s design included high tensile steel in her upper hull structure, which enabled her to bear safely a higher stress,★ all the other ships were constructed throughout of the usual mild steel. The stresses varied depending on a ship's displacement at any given time, but with calculations based upon the normal state of loading it is quite clear that they were all built to a very similar standard. Shipbuilders of the period sought to keep this particular measure of stress to around 10 tons or below for mild steel vessels and Harland & Wolff's design figures fall within those of comparable ships.

These figures of stress are merely one of many aspects of the ships' structural designs. While there were marked differences between liners such as *Aquitania* and *Olympic*, in terms of their watertight subdivision and machinery layout, there were also striking similarities. In a number of instances, aspects of *Olympic*'s structure could be considered somewhat superior to the Cunarder's and vice versa. That a number of different naval architects, shipbuilding companies and classification societies working to the highest standards of the time should develop designs exhibiting such similarities is telling. While practical experience led to further improvement as liners grew larger, *Titanic* and her peers were built to an ample overall standard of strength.†

There is certainly a lot of misunderstanding about the ship's expansion joints and their role in the ship's design. While B-deck formed the top of the structural hull, the deckhouses at this level, A-deck and the boat deck above were comparatively lightly constructed and formed the superstructure. The two expansion joints divided the super-structure into three separate sections so that they could move as the structural hull beneath flexed in a seaway. They protected the superstructure from the higher stresses that were borne by the structural hull beneath; stresses that the superstructure, which was essentially placed on top of it, was not intended or designed to bear. Expansion joints were not a perfect solution. On board a number of large liners such as *Aquitania*, *Berengaria* and *Olympic* they did not prevent some localised stress fractures, for example at the corners of deckhouse windows adjacent to the expansion joints. However, in general they did their job and, as one Board of Trade surveyor noted: 'It is practically impossible to prevent working [movement] in the plating of long superstructures of this nature and further [sic] the seaworthiness of the ship is not involved.'★★ This is an important point. In fact, the

---

★ Another source recorded *Lusitania*'s figure at 11.4 tons, with the explanatory note that her design included high tensile steel.

† It is also interesting to note some figures produced in a modern analysis of *Titanic* and other large liners that were constructed in the late 1920s and 1930s. This compared the 'bottom bending stress' in tons per square inch, with results ranging from *Manhattan* 7.9 tons; *Titanic* 9.1 tons; *Conte di Savoia* 9.8 tons; *America* 9.9 tons; *Rex* 9.9 tons; *Normandie* 11.1 tons and *Europa* 12.1 tons. While *Europa* and *Normandie* were constructed of high tensile steel and could 'exploit the properties of their steel for higher stresses than other ships,' the authors concluded: '*Titanic* does not stand out among this group as a ship with a highly stressed hull.' She was one of the least stressed. (See Garzke and Woodward, page 468.)

★★ *Olympic* and *Titanic* were the first liners that Harland & Wolff built with expansion joints. In 1905, they completed *Amerika*. Her superstructure was designed to be so flexible as to relieve it from any stresses imparted by the structural hull beneath, yet by the 1920s there were numerous 'spider webs' of cracks propagating from deckhouse windows and openings, some of which extended for 30in. The hull itself was of ample strength and showed no sign of weakness, but the superstructure required considerable modifications. Although she spent a number of years laid up, she served in both world wars and was not scrapped until 1957. Nonetheless, her example illustrates the advantage of the expansion joints. (See Carl Petersen and Lorentz Hansen's 'The Design of Superstructures for Large Passenger Ships' which was published by the Society of Naval Architects and Marine Engineers in 1927.)

superstructure could have been removed entirely and the structural hull beneath would retain its strength and integrity.

Titanic's expansion joints *did not cause* the ship's hull to break apart. They did not penetrate below the superstructure to the structural hull. The superstructure plating near an expansion joint would not be under tension stress: that would only be acting on the deck below, which formed the uppermost part of the hull girder. However, it would create a slight stress concentration point. Once the ship's hull was stressed to the point of failing then an initial failure had to begin somewhere. Therefore the areas in close proximity to the expansion joints would be more likely to experience failure, regardless of whether the ship broke initially from the top down or the bottom up. (It does not follow that the failure necessarily began there.) One of the questions raised during the production of *Titanic's Achilles Heel* centred on the expansion joints. Following the discovery of changes to *Britannic*, which showed the base of an expansion joint altered from the rectangular to a curved 'bulb', there was some speculation as to whether Harland & Wolff had amended the design in light of *Titanic's* loss. In fact, given the numerous smaller improvements to *Titanic* based on experience with *Olympic* – whether it was changes to the passenger accommodation, adjustments to the ship's propellers or minor structural refinements – and the knowledge that Harland & Wolff were already aware that *Olympic's* expansion joint configuration could be improved in March 1912, it is highly likely that it was simply a result of the company's progressive improvement of their designs. By the time *Titanic's* hull failure began, she was on the verge of foundering due to the sheer quantity of water she had taken on; and with the enormous and increasing stresses upon her hull, the failure was inevitable. It is difficult to imagine an unluckier ship on her maiden voyage.

★   ★   ★

If the past is any indication, then it is inevitable that interest in *Titanic* will continue. The ongoing interest and debate, from research into the passengers and crew to her technical design and foundering, seems to ensure that. What can be said for certain is that *Titanic* has not given up all her secrets, but there is more that can be learned before she is given up to the sea.

APPENDIX ONE
THE 'OLYMPIC' CLASS

	Olympic	Titanic	Britannic
Yard Number	400	401	433
Contracted for	31 July 1908	31 July 1908	23 October 1911
Order to proceed	17 September 1908 shipyard and engine works ordered to proceed 'except with [propelling] machinery'; 26 February 1909 shipyard and engine works ordered to proceed 'with boilers'; 20 April 1909 shipyard and engine works ordered to proceed 'with remainder of machinery'		28 June 1911 shipyard and engine works ordered to proceed
Keel laid	16 December 1908	31 March 1909	30 November 1911
Framed to height of the double bottom	10 March 1909	15 May 1909	12 March 1912
Fully framed	20 November 1909	6 April 1910	27 February 1913
Fully plated	15 April 1910	19 October 1910	20 September 1913
Launched	20 October 1910	31 May 1911	26 February 1914
Delivered	31 May 1911	2 April 1912	8 December 1915
Gross Tonnage	45,323.82	46,328.59	48,157.90
Net Tonnage	20,894.20	21,831.34	24,592.24
Length, between perpendiculars	850ft	850ft	850ft
Breadth, moulded	92ft	92ft	93ft 6in
Depth, moulded	64ft 6in	64ft 6in	64ft 6in
Displacement	52,310	52,310	53,170
Registered displacement	77,780	77,780	78,950
Nominal horsepower	6,906	6,906	7,150
Indicated horsepower	50,000	50,000	50,000
Boilers	24 double ended, 5 single ended	24 double ended, 5 single ended	24 double ended (enlarged), 5 single ended
Pressure	215lb per sq. in.	215lb per sq. in.	215lb per sq. in.
Speed	21 knots	21 knots	21½ knots
First-class passengers	735	787	790
Second-class passengers	675	676	836
Third-class passengers	1,030	1,008	953
End of Service	Completed final westbound crossing 12 April 1935	Foundered 15 April 1912	Foundered 21 November 1916

The 'moulded breadth' specified was a measurement that did not include the outer extremities of the hull plating, while the 'extreme breadth' did and was the usual measurement given: 92ft 6in for *Olympic* and *Titanic* and 94ft for *Britannic*.

Although *Britannic*'s service speed was half a knot higher than her sisters according to Harland & Wolff's order book, perhaps the figure reflects that her engine power had been increased to enable her to maintain the same rate of speed with a good quantity of power in reserve. All other sources are in agreement that no effort had been made to increase her speed further.

Olympic's passenger figures were taken from the entry on the British registry as amended in 1913; *Titanic*'s were based on a room-by-room, berth-by-berth count of the accommodation, undertaken by Daniel Klistorner for *Titanic: The Ship Magnificent*; and *Britannic*'s were those as reported by *Engineering* in 1914. The variations over time, interchangeable staterooms that could be assigned to more than one class, and the numerous contradictions in reliable sources mean that there will always be disagreement on the precise totals. In the case of *Britannic*, for example, even the figures from February 1914 might have seen some changes during the outfitting process. However, it is hoped that these figures form a reasonable basis of comparison. They reflect, in particular, the increase in first- and second-class accommodation and the decrease in third class.

The '*Olympic*' class ships' propeller specifications saw a number of changes over time, as Harland & Wolff sought to find the most efficient configuration. In 1911, *Olympic*'s wing propellers were adjusted during her repairs following the *Hawke* collision; *Titanic*'s were altered further, while her centre propeller specification changed; in 1913, *Olympic* saw more changes and a new centre propeller; and *Britannic*'s wing propellers were the largest fitted to an '*Olympic*' class liner, while her centre propeller reverted to the same design as *Olympic*'s original.★

		Olympic Wing propellers	*Olympic* Centre propeller	*Titanic* Wing propellers	*Titanic* Centre propeller	*Britannic* Wing propellers	*Britannic* Centre propeller
June 1911	Diameter	23ft 6in	16ft 6in				
	Pitch	33ft	14ft 6in				
	Blades	3	4				
	Area (sq.ft)	160	120				
November 1911	Pitch	34ft 6in					
January 1912	Diameter			23ft 6in	17ft		
	Pitch			35ft	14ft 6in		
	Blades			3	3		
	Area (sq.ft)			160	120		
March 1913	Diameter	22ft 9in	17ft				
	Pitch	36ft	14ft				
	Blades	3	3				
	Area (sq.ft)	165	125				
September 1914	Diameter					23ft 9in	16ft 6in
	Pitch					35ft	14ft 6in
	Blades					3	4
	Area (sq.ft)					160	120

★ The table is extracted from my article, 'The Mystery of *Titanic*'s Central Propeller', in *Voyage*, *Titanic* International Society, 2008. It was compiled from a number of sources which are explored in the article and it covers the period from *Olympic*'s completion to the fitting of *Britannic*'s propellers. Therefore, it neglects to mention further changes to *Olympic*, such as the fact that her centre propeller reverted to the original four-bladed configuration after the war, or that the wing propellers were adjusted again and the pitch increased further. The article focused on the entry in a Harland & Wolff engineering notebook which specified that *Titanic*'s centre propeller had three blades instead of the assumed four.

APPENDIX TWO
NOMADIC & TRAFFIC

Since 1907, the tiny thirteen-year-old 461-ton paddle-wheel tender *Gallic* had been stationed to serve White Star liners at Cherbourg, when they began to call there. With a length of 150ft and a breadth of 28ft 3in, she was by no means well suited to serve the forthcoming *Olympic* class.[1] Two new tenders were therefore ordered from Harland & Wolff in 1910: *Nomadic* and *Traffic*.

Nomadic had a designed tonnage of 1,273grt, was 220ft long by 37ft 2in wide, and was a twin-screw vessel capable of 12 knots.[2] *Nomadic* was designed to carry in the region of 1,000 first and second-class passengers plus their luggage.[3] She was launched on 25 April 1911 to be followed by the *Traffic* two days later.[4]

Traffic was a twin-screw 12-knot vessel like *Nomadic*, but she was smaller at 175ft 7in long by 35ft 2in wide, with a tonnage of 675grt.[5] She could accommodate fewer passengers than *Nomadic* and was designed to carry third-class passengers and mails, being fitted with heavy-duty conveyers for the latter purpose.[6]

Both tenders accompanied *Olympic* on her trials,[7] before heading to Cherbourg to begin their duties there as tenders servicing the new class of vessels. However, when the two tenders serviced *Olympic* on her maiden voyage, the baggage handling and subsequent transfer 'left a lot to be desired'.[8] On 10 April 1912, when *Titanic* called at Cherbourg, the transfers were completed without a hitch.[9] Thomas Andrews wrote home to his wife: 'The two little tenders look very fine. You will remember [that] we built them last year.'[10]

They were to enjoy reasonably long and successful lives, but were to suffer several mishaps. On 13 November 1911 *Nomadic* collided with the liner *Philadelphia*, crushing her bow and twisting many hull plates.[11] 5 June 1929 saw *Traffic* bump into the liner *Homeric* and damage her rail and two hull plates on her starboard quarter.[12] *Traffic* hit the liner *Minnewaska* on 9 December 1929 in stormy weather, some of her bows and bulwarks suffered damage; *Nomadic* later collided with the same liner on 29 November 1931, twisting her stem and denting four hull plates, as well as denting one of the liner's starboard plates.[13]

During the war, logs reveal that *Nomadic*'s main duties from 1917 to 1919 were sweeping mines around the area of Saint-Nazaire, although there are also records that she ferried American troops at Brest and passengers from the French liners.[14]

'In 1927 they were sold to the Compagnie Cherbourgeoise de Transbordement,' but their names and duties remained unchanged; in 1934 they were sold again,[15] this time to the Société Cherbourgeoise de Remorquage et de Sauvetage. *Nomadic* became *Ingenieur Minard* and *Traffic* became *Ingenieur Riebell*.[16]

During 1940, *Traffic* was scuttled at Cherbourg, but was raised and refurbished by the Germans; on 17 January 1941, while in the English Channel in German Naval Service, she was torpedoed by a British torpedo boat and sunk.[17] The vessel does not appear on any German naval lists, but there are two blanks which are listed under FC19★ and FC20, so *Traffic* was in all probability one of these vessels.[18]

Nomadic survived the war in British naval service and was returned to her French owners after the war's end. Following the creation of Cunard White Star in 1934, the company continued to use the White Star name, but it would be dropped several years after the war. By 1960, the third *Britannic*, last of the White Star liners, had been withdrawn from service. *Nomadic* served *Queen Mary* and *Queen Elizabeth* for years when they were a tremendous success, but by 1968 both had been withdrawn from transatlantic service. After fifty-seven years, *Nomadic*'s future was in doubt.

★ Frankreich (France) Cherbourg.

Fortunately, she survived. Although *Nomadic* was sold for scrapping in 1969, she was bought by Ronald Spinnewyn. She was towed from Cherbourg to Conflans-Sainte-Honorine and he made a start on plans to transform her into a floating restaurant, but it was only when she was sold again to Yvon Vincent that the project became a reality. She arrived in Paris in the early 1970s and remained there for over thirty years under his ownership.

There were efforts to preserve the ship by Yvon Vincent and Philippe Delaunoy, involving collaboration with organisations such as Belfast Industrial Heritage and the Belfast City Council. The intention was that *Nomadic* would return to the city where she had been built. However, by the late 1990s new European Union regulations required that any ship moored on the River Seine needed to be examined in dry dock. *Nomadic*'s superstructure had been modified since she arrived and it was not possible to move her beneath the river's bridges for examination. Although her owner paid for divers to examine the hull, the Paris harbour authorities were not satisfied. To make matters worse, *Nomadic*'s license expired so that she could not be open to the public, resulting in financial problems for her owner who could not pay the mooring fees. A number of options were explored, but in 2005, she was seized and auctioned.

Belfast Industrial Heritage had requested assistance from White Star Memories⋆ and the 'Save the *Nomadic*' campaign was launched with the goal of raising €250,000. They had only raised one-fifth of their target by the time of the auction in January 2006 but, fortunately, the Department for Social Development (DSD) in Northern Ireland had become aware of the campaign and decided to purchase *Nomadic*.

In July 2006, the ninety-five-year-old vessel returned to her birthplace. The Department for Development created the *Nomadic* Charitable Trust (NCT) to oversee the management of the restoration; the 'Save the *Nomadic*' campaign became the *Nomadic* Preservation Society (NPS).†
The following year, the society undertook maintenance and restoration work before *Nomadic* was opened to the public and, as the owner of a number of significant historical artefacts, is making the case for a complete historical restoration to take her back to her 1911 configuration.

Whatever happens in the years to come, *Nomadic*'s future is hopefully secure.

⋆ International *Titanic* Exhibition Specialists owned by John White and operated with David Scott Beddard.

† The *Nomadic* Preservation Society was created 'to promote the history, research and restoration of the SS *Nomadic*, one of the world's most important historic ships'.

APPENDIX THREE
LUSITANIA VOYAGE NOTES

Cunard were interested in *Olympic* when she entered service, in order that they might examine her for any suggestions that might improve their new *Aquitania*. Their interest was an enduring tradition whereby one shipping line observed their rivals' newest ships and sought to improve upon them. The White Star Line also had the chance to observe *Lusitania* and *Mauretania* while *Olympic* and *Titanic* were being designed and constructed. J. Bruce Ismay himself travelled on board *Mauretania* and it is known that he was impressed by the design of the deckhouse windows on her bridge deck. One passenger, on board *Lusitania* during her first year in service, made some interesting typewritten notes about the Cunarder. They appear to have been connected with Harland & Wolff or the White Star Line, but their comments appear to be those of an interested professional observer.★

Regardless of the author's identity, he brings a useful perspective from a passenger interested in the ship's comfort and performance, whether it was the inadequacy of some of the ship's door springs, to the arrangement of the electric light switches in first-class staterooms, or first-class ladies enduring passengers from second and third class smoking while they waited to access the purser's office:

> During the first two days when we had moderate to fresh westerly gales with rough head seas there was a certain amount of vibration in various parts of the ship, but nothing to fuss about. In smooth weather, such as we have had since, the vibration is very little, except possibly in the Second Saloon quarters right aft, but I do not think it would be very noticeable there, were some of the entrance doors and windows properly secured. The constant jarring of these doors makes the vibration seem much worse than it really is; and in my room – B73 – I have noticed nothing at all.
>
> In some of the staterooms which are panelled with hard woods, there is a lot of creaking and noise when she is steaming into a head sea, and I should think that this is attributable entirely to the binding of the woodwork, as I remember quite well we had the same trouble in the *Majestic* and the *Teutonic* years ago, and only overcame it by putting rubber strips between the panels of the woodwork.
>
> There are, I think, a good many minor matters which might with convenience be attended to, for instance: –
>
> 1. Electric Lights. The switches for these lights are all over the place, sometimes most difficult to find being hidden behind doors, curtains, &c. In my comparatively small room there are no less than four switches in different corners; while in the two parlours of the Regal Suites, there are five, all of which are of course unnecessary.

★ It shows an interesting attention to detail characteristic of a ship designer and the author's reference to the White Star Line's earlier ships *Teutonic* and *Majestic* indicates someone interested in their design and construction. He further refers to the trouble 'we had' with the creaking noises attributed to the binding of their woodwork, which may suggest that he was a representative of their builder. The obvious person to spring to mind is Alexander Carlisle, as he was involved in their construction; however it has been difficult to ascertain if he sailed on *Lusitania* at the relevant time. Thomas Andrews had travelled on board *Majestic* as an apprentice, including once with William John Pratten, the manager of Harland & Wolff's engine works, in October 1896, but he was only seventeen when *Majestic* entered service and it seems probable that any problem with the binding of her woodwork might have been observed then, rather than years later. Edward Wilding made a round trip on board *Lusitania* in January and February 1908, the right time period, but the reference to *Teutonic* and *Majestic* is again puzzling because he did not join Harland & Wolff until February 1904. Perhaps the writer had been alerted to those two ships by a colleague, but their wording seems to make that unlikely.

2. In the Dining Room of the Regal Suite there is no heating apparatus at all, and in cold weather this room would not be nearly warm enough.

3. Smoking on Deck B. I do not think any smoking should be allowed on this particular deck forward of the expansion joint. To my knowledge, on several occasions ladies have had to leave their seats because men have been smoking pipes to windward of them, blowing ashes and smoke in their faces. There is any amount of smoking accommodation on the ship, and it seems to me most unnecessary that ladies who are not feeling particularly well should be bothered by inconsiderate men on practically the only bit of sheltered deck they have, i.e., leading from the Regal Suites aft.

4. None of the lavatory doors, as far as I have seen, have any hooks, a patent spring being supposed to always hold the door. This spring is quite useless when the ship is rolling, consequently all these doors have to be tied back by towels round the handle of the door and hand rail. These doors, I think should be supplied with hooks, and the best I have seen are those used in the White Star Line which automatically catch the door when pushed back, and merely require lifting to release.

5. Doors in Library, &C. The same remark replies to these doors. The springs are not strong enough to hold them, and the draught of the ship constantly keeps these doors open, making it very uncomfortable in the room.

6. Baths, &C. I suppose that they have placed all that they can on the different decks, but I think one or two more amidships, round say B73 and so on, would have been an advantage, as one has to make a long journey now to reach the baths. I have also noticed that on two or three occasions there has been no bathroom Steward. This morning, for instance, he being away for his breakfast at about half past nine o'clock, when he should of course have been attending to the baths.

7. In some of the staterooms, which have their own bathrooms, there is a good deal of violent noise, especially noticeable during the night, apparently caused by the sea rushing up the discharge pipe from the bath or basin when the ship rolls. I have heard this noise, and it is quite enough to seriously inconvenience a seasick lady passenger. I imagine a trap valve might possibly be fitted which would obviate this.

8. The water arrangements have not been quite so good as they might. The first morning we could get no cold salt water in the baths, only red hot, and cans of cold water had to be brought. Sometimes the fresh water in the basins in the bathroom and staterooms has been turned off, so that no fresh water has been available. But these of course are all matters of detail which can be easily attended to.

9. The Dining Saloon arrangements are excellent, and the small tables most comfortable, and the boon of being permitted to smoke after dinner, to ladies and gentlemen alike, is great. The music is very good and much appreciated, but the band leaves the First Class Saloon at 8.10 or 8.15 to go into the Lounge at nine. This, I think, is too early, as many passengers do not dine till half past seven or eight, and they like the music. I should say the musicians should have their food before dinner, and play certainly up to half past eight, or a quarter of an hour longer than they do at present, before going into the Lounge.

10. A great many of the windows want overhauling. The inside windows jamb [sic], and are very difficult to open. In my room I had to get the Joiner to work, and in very hot Gulf Stream weather, such as we have been having, it is very disagreeable if one cannot open ones window and get fresh air when required. The same remark applies to the bathroom I have been using where the heat has been terrific because although the outer window would screw down the inner window has been immovable.

11. One peculiar feature about this ship is – and in a way rather unfortunate – that is [sic] such a wind as we have today, practically due south and strong, the spindrift curling round the stem is caught up by the wind and blown all over the lee decks, from the Boat Deck down, so that they are wringing wet, obliging passengers to sit on the weather side. I have never noticed this in any ship before. It is of course attributable to the great speed.

12. I think it would be worth the Company's considering carrying a Masseur on board these two ships. I have heard two or three people asking if such a person existed, and I should say that he would be welcomed by a great many Americans especially.

13. Door Latches. Almost all through the ship the latches of the doors are bad. They are much too small, are not heavy enough, and do not catch, resulting in the constant swinging and banging of doors, to the damaging of the latter and inconvenience of the people.

14. I do not think 2nd and 3rd Class Passengers should come – some of them smoking – to the Purser's Office on B Deck to change money, &c. It is not agreeable for first-class ladies to be mixed up with them.

15. The W.C. Pans are in my opinion much too narrow and too shallow. I have seen one flush right over, and when the ship is moving in a heavy sea the water in the plans 'sluices up'.

APPENDIX FOUR

THOMAS ANDREWS' MAIDEN VOYAGE NOTES

Thomas Andrews kept himself busy throughout *Olympic*'s maiden voyage, monitoring the ship's progress and making notes for improvements that would be incorporated into *Titanic* during her outfitting.★ His eye for detail comes across in the notes that he made, ranging from the permanent fitting of the propeller notice boards, to the mirrors fitted to wardrobe doors in some of the first-class staterooms:

In Liverpool when docking or undocking stern first, the Pilot is always on the Docking Bridge aft, think this practice should be carried out in Southampton .

Would suggest propeller notice boards being permanently fitted on outside of ship's side rails in way of after Docking bridge, as is the practice in other Company's Steamers. Thus saving the placing & stowing away of these boards every voyage with corresponding destruction to the painting and printing.

Propose ACQUIRING SOME additional Accomd. In officers' acc. [accommodation, or officers' quarters] As per plan for [unreadable]. And [unreadable]. Converting their present Accomd. into staterooms.

Propose dispersing [sic] with 1st class stateroom C144–146 placing the Chief Steward in this position & enlarging the Asst Doctor's room.

The hat and cloak room on C deck 1st class entrance is not sufficiently used to warrant this loss of earning power space, would suggest substituting SAME to berth as staterooms with athwartship passage, as per plans fitting hooks for hats & cloaks across the bulkhead facing elevators on D deck.

Would propose fitting eleven additional four seated tables in 1st class restaurant as per plan, this room being short of table accommodation.

A screen to be an improvement if fitted on the side of the restaurant/buffet SUPT entrance door so as to prevent passengers from seeing behind the buffet.

The two single serving doors P&S [port and starboard] from the pantry to the 1st class saloon do not appear to be necessary for service and are better kept shut owing to noise. The space in way of these doors will provide accommodation for one additional four seated table P&S in the saloon.

The 1st class Reception Room being the most popular room in the 1st class passenger accommodation being more or less crowded after lunch & dinner also for afternoon tea 4.30 p.m. It was found necessary to bring up all the spare caine [sic] chairs from the baggage room to provide temporary seating accommodation, would strongly recommend additional permanent caine [sic] furniture being ordered. As smoking is allowed at all times in the Reception Room an exhaust fan drawing from the fore and after girder P&S as in the saloon.

Captain Smith strongly recommends protective windows with round bulls eye lights to be fitted in way of square windows on centre shelter navigating bridge as in *Adriatic*.

To prevent the excessive draught in the steward's stairway leading from 1st class pantry to working passage on E deck which is also used by the stewardess on E deck, suggest a fore & aft wood bulkhead with sliding doors be fitted at foot of stairs as shown on plan.

★ The notes are presented with their original spelling and grammar, although the original notes were numbered 5 to 20. There were several carbon copies, presumably intended for the White Star Line, Harland & Wolff, and another for Thomas Andrews himself. This is not a complete set: some of the notes are separated and the additional pages have either not survived or are retained in private collections.

The numbering of the promenade dk. chairs to be altered in accordance with the terms on lithographic plans. H&W to enquire if any change was made on the numbering of the approved plan to which they were supposed to work.

Linoleum tiles not to be fitted in Captain's sitting room in which a full room carpet has been provided.

Sponge holders to be fitted in the private bathrooms on B and C decks where these have been omitted.

The mirrors in the wardrobe doors adjoining the entrance doors into inside staterooms on C deck to be dispensed with as when the entrance doors are left open on the deck anyone in the passage can see the occupant of the room dressing or undressing.

Back plates for electric reading lamps to be fitted over beds etc. in Suite Staterooms on B and C decks same as ordinary staterooms.

He performed the same task for *Titanic*, making suggestions even before she left Southampton. According to Shan Bullock's *Thomas Andrews: Shipbuilder*:

One of the last letters he wrote records serious trouble with the restaurant galley hot press, and directs attention to a design for reducing the number of screws in stateroom hat hooks.

Another of earlier date, in the midst of technicalities about cofferdams and submerged cylinders on the propeller boss, expresses agreement with the owner that the colouring of the pebble dashing on the private promenade decks was too dark, and notes a plan for staining green the wicker furniture on one side of the vessel.

Undoubtedly, Andrews would have performed the same function when *Britannic* entered service. She incorporated all the improvements from *Olympic* and *Titanic* combined and some of these had been considered before the *Titanic* disaster. Andrews did not live to see her maiden voyage.

APPENDIX FIVE

FINANCING THE 'OLYMPIC' CLASS

T he construction of the 'Olympic' class ships represented a tremendous financial undertaking for the White Star Line. Between 1901 and 1907, Celtic, Cedric, Baltic and Adriatic (the 'Big Four') had been completed at a total cost of £2,332,175, with each ship's price rising from Celtic's £556,442 to Adriatic's £632,464. However, the company's most expensive ship was Oceanic, reputed to have cost more than £1,000,000 when she entered service in 1899. Olympic's cost would comfortably exceed that on its own, even when adjusted for inflation over the intervening decade.

Although it is popularly believed that J.P. Morgan's money was made available for the project, in fact the company mortgaged their existing fleet. It was estimated initially that the construction costs of Laurentic, Megantic, Olympic and Titanic would amount to some £3,600,000.★ There were three main possibilities: either financing it from earnings; raising money by issuing additional shares; or issuing debt against the company's assets in the form of bonds. Although the company's profits were rising, it would have taken the entirety of a number of years' profits to pay for the projected cost of the new ships. In 1908, the White Star Line's capital consisted of £750,000 in 750 shares.† All but eight of them were held by the International Navigation Company (Liverpool), whose shares in turn were held by IMM (New Jersey). If the company was to issue further shares, then the necessary new shares would have required substantial further investment from the shipping combine, unless it was prepared to allow its proportion of the company (and entitlement to its share of the profits) to decline. In that context, the choice was fairly clear.

The company's directors decided to authorise an issue of £2,500,000 in bonds paying 4½ per cent interest. In October 1908, the company issued the first series of bonds – totalling £1,250,000 – for public subscription, with the new tonnage and its existing fleet of twenty-three ships (valued at £4,850,000) as security for these 'First Mortgage Debentures'. The interest was payable on 30 June and 31 December each year. There was little difficulty with the issue, as the White Star Line recorded increasing profits:

★ Olympic's cost was given at £1,764,659 on a valuation of the company's fleet at December 1916. Information obtained by researcher Mark Warren put Titanic's cost at £1,564,606. It seems probable that the figure for Olympic included £156,000 for the safety improvements completed during the 1912–13 refit and an additional, smaller sum, for the alterations to her accommodation. Britannic's final cost was put at £1,947,797 5s 10d. On a cash basis, the 'Olympic' class ships cost more than the entire fleet had been valued at in September 1908.

† The Oceanic Steam Navigation Co. (White Star Line's) capital consisted of £400,000 in £1,000 shares when it came into being in 1869; this increased to £500,000 in £1,000 shares in April 1872; and to £750,000 in £1,000 shares in December 1872. The capital was increased dramatically to £3,750,000 by the issue of 3,000 new £1,000 shares in August 1916; it increased – for the final time – to £5,000,000 in £1,000 shares four years later.

It is interesting to note Edwin Green and Michael Moss's comments in their book A Business of National Importance: The Royal Mail Shipping Group, 1902–37:

> During the war the cost of replacing tonnage rose by a factor of five or six. The value of second hand tonnage… increased correspondingly. Consequently shipping and shipbuilding companies found that the value of their assets was considerably in excess of their balance sheet entry. Moreover, because of wartime inflation, the earning power of these assets in cash terms was greatly expanded. For public companies this increased the risk of a takeover. A solution to this difficulty was to raise the ordinary share capital…

These comments help to demonstrate some of the changes wrought by the war on the shipping business.

Year	1907	1908	1909	1910	1911	1912	1913
Profit	£848,486	£298,941	£613,054	£1,057,519	£1,073,752	£885,332	£1,080,918

Following *Titanic's* loss, 'Yard Number 433' was added as security in July 1912. By July 1914, the company was ready to issue a second series, but decided to increase the total authorised to £3,375,000 – an increase of £875,000 over the original £2,500,000. They then issued a further £1,500,000 in 4½ per cent bonds, taking the total to £2,750,000 and giving them leeway to create a further issue of £625,000 if required. However, following the war's outbreak the very next month, the White Star Line had other things to concentrate on and they never did issue further bonds to the entire authorised total.

Several months after *Britannic* was lost, the initial £1,750,000 payment from the government was lodged with trustees for the bond holders, in addition to payments totalling £630,000 which resulted from the loss of other vessels including *Oceanic*. While the first issue of £1,250,000 from October 1908 was not due to be redeemed in full until 30 June 1922, the second issue of £1,500,000 from July 1914 was not due to be redeemed until 30 June 1943, demonstrating the long-term liability on the company's books.

The annual interest payments due to the bond holders began at around £56,000 in the first full year of their issue, 1909; rising with the second issue to £65,000 in 1914 and over £104,000 in 1916; they declined to less than £50,000 in 1925 and fell to £23,000 in 1930. The decline reflected a fixed rate of interest and a declining number of bond holders as the outstanding bonds were gradually redeemed, leaving fewer bond holders who were owed interest payments. By 1926, the total liability from these issues had fallen below £1,000,000; the outstanding sum was reduced to less than £500,000 in 1930. However, with the company recording a loss for the first time in its history, the debt remained on the books until the company's end.

APPENDIX SIX
TITANIC: DESCRIPTION OF THE SHIP

Harland & Wolff's Edward Wilding supplied a lot of information about the ship when her loss was being investigated. A detailed 'Description of the Ship' was included in the British enquiry report into the ship's loss and forms a useful reference tool for researchers. Generally accurate for both *Olympic* and *Titanic*, it is worth quoting selected extracts. They include descriptions relating to the ship's decks and accommodation; structure; life-saving appliances; pumping arrangements; electrical installation; machinery and general information:

DECKS AND ACCOMMODATION

The boat deck – was an uncovered deck, on which the boats were placed. At its lowest point it was about 92ft 6in above the keel. The overall length of this deck was about 500ft. The forward end of it was fitted to serve as the navigating bridge of the vessel and was 190ft from the bow. On the after end of the bridge was a wheelhouse, containing the steering wheel and a steering compass. The chart room was immediately abaft this. On the starboard side of the wheelhouse and funnel casing were the navigating room, the captain's quarters, and some officers' quarters. On the port side were the remainder of the officers' quarters. At the middle line abaft the forward funnel casing were the wireless telegraphy rooms and the operators' quarters. The top of the officers' house formed a short deck. The connections from the Marconi aerials were made on this deck and two of the collapsible boats were placed on it. Aft of the officers' house were the first-class passengers' entrance and stairways, and other adjuncts to the passengers' accommodation below. These stairways had a minimum effective width of 8ft. They had assembling landings at the level of each deck, and three elevators communicating from E to A-decks, but not to the Boat deck, immediately on the fore side of the stairway.

In addition to the main stairways mentioned, there was a ladder on each side amidships, giving access from the A-deck below. At the forward end of the boat deck there was on each side a ladder leading up from A-deck, with a landing there, from which, by a ladder, access to B-deck could be obtained direct. Between the reciprocating engine casing and the third funnel casing there was a stewards' stairway, which communicated with all the decks below as far as E-deck. Outside the deckhouses was promenading space for first-class passengers.

On the decks was provided generally, in the manner above described, accommodation for a maximum number of 1,034 first-class passengers, 510 second-class passengers and 1,022 third-class passengers. Some of the accommodation was of an alternate character, and could be used for either of two classes of passenger. This makes total accommodation for 2,566 passengers.★

Accommodation was provided for the crew as follows: about seventy-five of the deck department including officers and doctors; 326 of the engine room department including engineers and 544 of the victualling department including pursers and leading stewards. (Total 945.)

★ Figures for numbers of passengers and crew vary enormously. Interchangeable second- and third-class berths, conversion of first-class single berths to two-berth rooms, movable partitions of some third-class berths and differences regarding crew accommodation do not help. In 1913 *Olympic*'s British registry papers showed her passenger figures at 735 first-class, 675 second-class and 1,030 third-class passengers.

If the highest alternative class figures with interchangeable berths were counted, *Olympic*'s 1911 accommodation totalled 1,054 first-class, 510 second-class and 1,020 third-class passengers, according to her entry on the British registry: 2,584 passengers in total. *Titanic*'s 1912 accommodation would total 1,034 first-class, 510 second-class and 1,022 third-class passengers, or 2,566 passengers in total. Each vessel could carry a maximum crew of 944, according to the passenger certificate.

ACCESS OF PASSENGERS TO THE BOAT DECK

The following routes led directly from the various parts of the third-class passenger accommodation to the boat deck: from the forward ends of A, B, C, D and E-decks by the staircase in the forward first-class entrance to the boat deck. The elevators led from the same decks as far as A-deck, where further access was obtained by going up the top flight of the main staircase. The same route was available for first-class passengers forward of amidships on B, C, and E-decks.

First-class passengers abaft amidships on B and C-decks could use the staircase in the after main entrance to A-deck, and then could pass out onto the deck, and by the amidships stairs besides the house ascend to the boat deck. They could also use the stewards' staircase between the reciprocating engine casing and boiler rooms 1 and 2 casing, which led direct to the boat deck. This last route was also available for passengers on E-deck in the same divisions who could use the forward first-class main stairway and elevators.

Second-class passengers on D-deck could use their own after stairway to B-deck, and could then pass up their forward stairway to the boat deck, or else could cross their (dining) saloon and use the same stairway throughout.

Of the second-class passengers on E-deck, those abreast of the reciprocating engine casing, unless the watertight door immediately abaft them was closed, went aft and joined the other second-class passengers. If, however, the watertight door at the aft end of their compartment was

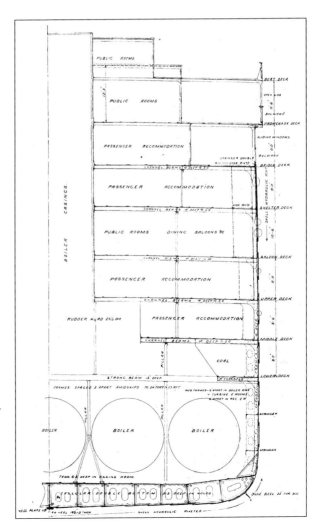

A simplified midship section of *Olympic* and *Titanic* as built. An improvement compared to earlier White Star Line ships, such as *Oceanic*, was that the double bottom extended to the turn of the bilge. The complete version included the instruction 'shell [plating] to be hydraulic riveted to upper turn of bilge'. Harland & Wolff's specifications included additional strengthening commensurate with their greater size and the incorporation of features employed in such ships as *Laurentic*. (J.&C. McCutcheon collection)

closed, they passed through an emergency door into the engine room and directly up to the boat deck, by the ladders and gratings in the engine room casing.

The second-class passengers on E-deck in the compartment abreast the turbine casing on the starboard side, and also those on F-deck on both sides below could pass through the watertight bulkhead to the forward second-class main stairway. If this door was closed, they could pass by the stairway up to the serving space at the forward end of the second-class saloon, and go into the saloon and thence up the forward second-class stairway.

Third-class passengers at the fore end of the vessels could pass by the staircases to C-deck in the forward well and by ladders on the port and starboard sides at the forward end of the deck-houses, thence direct to the boat deck outside the officers' accommodation. They might also pass along the working passageway on E-deck and through the emergency door to the forward first-class main stairway, or through the door on the same deck at the forward end of the first-class alleyway and up the first-class stairway direct to the boat deck.

The third-class passengers at the after end of the ship passed up their stairway to E-deck, and into the working passage, and through the emergency doors to the two second-class stairways, and so to the boat deck, like the second-class passengers. Or, alternatively, they could continue up their own stairs and entrance to C-deck, thence by the two ladders at the after end of B-deck, and thence by the forward second-class stairway direct to the boat deck.

Crew – from each boiler room an escape or an emergency ladder was provided direct to the boat deck by the fidleys, in the boiler casings, and also into the working passage on E-deck, and thence by the stair immediately forward of the reciprocating engine casing, direct to the boat deck.

From both the engine rooms ladders and gratings gave direct access to the boat deck.

From the electric engine room, the after tunnels and the forward pipe tunnels, escapes were provided direct to the working passage on E-deck, and thence by one of several routes already detailed from that space.

From the crews' quarters they could go forward by their own staircases into the forward well, and thence, like the third-class passengers, to the boat deck.

The stewards' accommodation being all connected to the working passage on E-deck or the forward main first-class stairway, they could use one of the routes from thence.

Engineers' accommodation also communicated with the working passage, but it was possible for them to be shut between the two watertight bulkheads, they also had a direct route by the gratings in the engine room casing to the boat deck.

On all the principal accommodation decks the alleyways and stairways provided a ready means of access to the boat deck, and there were clear deck spaces in front of all first-, second- and third-class main entrances and stairways on boat deck and all decks below.

STRUCTURE

The vessels were built throughout of steel and had a cellular double bottom of the usual type, with a floor at every frame, its depth at the centre line being 63in, except in the way of the reciprocating machinery, where it was 78in. For about half the length of the vessels, this double bottom extended up the ships' sides to a height of about 7in above the keel. Forward and aft of the machinery space the protection of the double bottom extended to a less height above the keel. It was divided so that there were four separate watertight compartments in the breadth of the vessels. Before and abaft the machinery space there was a watertight division at the centreline only, except in the foremost and aftermost tanks. Above the double bottom, the vessels were constructed on the usual transverse frame system, reinforced by web frames, which extended to the highest decks.

At the forward end the framing and plating was strengthened with a view to prevent panting (crumpling) and damage when meeting thin harbour ice.

Beams were fitted on every frame at all decks, from the boat deck downwards. An external bilge keel, about 300ft long and 25in deep, was fitted along the bilge amidships.

The heavy ships' plating was carried right up to the boat deck, and between the C and B-decks it was doubled; this doubled plating was hydraulically riveted. All decks were steel plated throughout.

The transverse strength of the ships were in part dependent on the fifteen transverse watertight bulkheads, which were specially stiffened and strengthened to enable them to stand the necessary pressure in the event of accident, and they were connected by double angles to the decks, the inner bottom, and the shell plating.

The two decks above B-deck were of a comparatively light scantling, but strong enough to ensure their proving satisfactory in these positions in rough weather.

WATERTIGHT SUBDIVISION

In the preparation of the design of these vessels it was arranged so that the bulkheads and divisions should be placed so that the ships would remain afloat in the event of any two of the adjoining watertight compartments being flooded. They should also be so built and strengthened that the ships would remain afloat in this condition; the flooding of two compartments would not affect the ships' safety in any way. If the first four of the watertight compartments forward were flooded, the ships would still float. The minimum freeboard that the ships would have, in the event of any two compartments being flooded, was between 2ft 6in and 3ft from the deck adjoining the top of the watertight bulkheads (under the worst condition). With this object in view, fifteen watertight bulkheads were arranged in each vessel (these bulkheads were designated, from the bow, A, B, C, D, E, F, G, H, I, J, K, L, M, N and O). The lower part of C bulkhead was doubled, and was in the form of a cofferdam. So far as possible the bulkheads were carried up in one plane to their upper sides, but in cases where they had for any reason to be stepped forward or aft, the deck, in way of the step, was made into a watertight flat, thus completing the watertightness of the compartment. In addition to this, G-deck in the after peak was made a watertight flat. The orlop deck between bulkheads that formed the top of the firemen's tunnel was also watertight. The orlop deck in the fore peak tank was also a watertight flat. The electric machinery compartment was further protected by a structure some distance in from the ships' side, forming six separate watertight compartments, which were used for the storage of fresh water.

Where openings were required for the working of the ship in these watertight bulkheads, they were closed by watertight, sliding doors which could be worked from a position above the top of the watertight bulkhead. Those doors immediately next to the inner bottom were of a special automatic closing pattern, as described below. By this sub-division there were in all seventy-three compartments, twenty-nine of these being above the inner bottom. Sixteen of these were the main large-sized compartments.

WATERTIGHT DOORS

The doors (twelve in number) immediately above the inner bottom were in the engine and boiler room spaces; they were of Messrs Harland & Wolff's latest type, working vertically. The doorplate was of cast iron of heavy section, strongly ribbed. It closed by gravity, and was held in the open position by means of a powerful electromagnet controlled from the captain's bridge. In the event of accident, or any other time when it may be considered advisable, the captain or officer on duty could, by simply moving an electric switch, immediately close all of these doors.★ The time required for the doors to close was between twenty-five and thirty seconds. Each door could also be closed from below by operating a hand lever fitted alongside the door. As a further precaution floats were provided beneath the floor level, which, in the event of water accidentally entering any of the compartments, automatically lifted and thus released the clutches, thereby permitting the doors in that particular compartment to close if they had not already been dropped by any other means. These doors were fitted with cataracts which controlled the speed of closing; due notice of closing from the bridge was given by a warning bell.

A ladder or escape was provided in each boiler room, engine room and similar watertight compartment, in order that the closing of the doors at any time should not imprison the men working therein.

The watertight doors on E-deck were of horizontal pattern, with wrought steel doorplates. Those on F-deck and the one aft on the orlop deck were of similar type, but had cast-iron doorplates of heavy section, strongly ribbed. Each of the 'tween deck doors,

★ '...Practically making the vessels unsinkable' stated contemporary White Star Line publicity.

The 'Olympic' Class Ships

and each of the vertical doors on the tank-top level could be operated by the ordinary hand gear from the deck above the top of the watertight bulkhead, and from a position on the next deck above, almost directly above the door. To facilitate quick closing of the doors, plates were affixed in suitable positions on the sides of the alleyways indicating the positions of the deck plates, and a box spanner was provided for each door, hanging in suitable clips alongside the deck plate.

COMPASSES

Compasses were supplied as follows: one Kelvin standard compass, with azimuth mirror on compass platform (on the raised roof of the first-class lounge); one Kelvin steering compass inside of wheelhouse; one Kelvin steering compass on captain's bridge; one light card compass for (aft) docking bridge and fourteen spirit compasses for lifeboats. All the ships' compasses were lighted with oil and electric lamps. Messrs C.J. Smith, of Southampton, were to later adjust them.

DISTRESS SIGNALS

These were supplied of number and pattern approved by the British Board of Trade, i.e., thirty-six socket signals in lieu of guns, twelve ordinary rockets, two Manwell Holmes deck flares, twelve blue lights and six lifebuoy lights.

PUMPING ARRANGEMENTS

The general arrangement of piping was designed so that it was possible to pump from any flooded compartment by two independent systems of 10in mains having cross connections between them. Rods controlled these from above and wheels led to the level of the bulkhead deck. By these it was possible to isolate any flooded space, together with any suctions in it. If any of these should accidentally happen to be left open, and consequently out of reach, it could be shut off from the main by the wheel on the bulkhead deck. This arrangement was specially submitted to the Board of Trade and approved by them.

The double bottom of the vessel was divided by a total of fifteen transverse watertight divisions, including those bounding the fore and aft peaks, and again sub-divided by a centre fore and aft bulkhead, and two longitudinal bulkheads, into forty-six compartments. Fourteen of these compartments had 8in suctions, twenty-three had 6in suctions, and three had 5in suctions connected to the 10in water ballast main suction; six watertight compartments were used exclusively for fresh water.

An interesting image demonstrating the arrangement of the enormous stern castings. *Olympic*'s rudder and stern castings were manufactured by the Darlington Forge Company and made of Siemens-Martin mild cast steel, although the rudder stock was forged ingot steel. The stern frame, in two pieces, weighed 70 tons, while the rudder was 101¼ tons. (*The Shipbuilder*, 1911/Ioannis Georgiou collection)

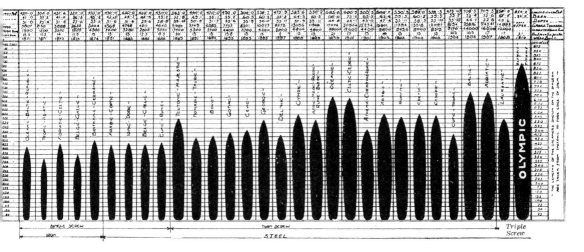

An interesting diagram, used in several publications at the time, demonstrated the increase in size from the White Star Line's *Oceanic, Baltic* and *Republic* in 1871 to *Olympic* in 1911. (Georgiou/Chirnside/Klistorner/Layton Collection)

The following bilge suctions were provided for dealing with water above the double bottom, in number 1 hold were two 3½in suctions, in number 2 hold were two 3½in suctions and two 3in suctions. In bunker hold 2 were two 3½in suctions and two 3in suctions.

The valves in connection with the forward bilge and ballast suctions were placed in the firemen's passage, the watertight pipe tunnel extending from number 6 boiler room to the after end of number 1 hold. In this tunnel, in addition to two 3in bilge suctions, one at each end, there was a special 3½in suction with valve rod which led up to the lower deck above the load line. This was so as always to have been accessible should the tunnel be flooded accidentally.

There were three 3½in suctions, one 4½in suction and two 3in suctions in boiler rooms 6 and 4. In the remaining boiler rooms (5, 3, 2 and 1), there were three 3½in suctions, one 5in suction and two 3in suctions.

In the reciprocating engine room there were two 3½in, three 3in, two 18in and two 5in suctions.

In the turbine engine room there were two 3½in, three 3in, two 18in, two 5in and one 4in suction.

The electric engine room had four 3½in suctions. Storerooms above the electric engine room had one 3in suction; the forward tunnel compartment had two 3½in suctions; the watertight flat over the tunnel compartment had two 3in suctions. The tunnel after compartment had two 3½in suctions; in the watertight flat over the tunnel after compartment there were two 3in suctions.

SUBMARINE SIGNALLING

The Submarine Signal Company's apparatus was provided for receiving signals from the submarine bells. Small tanks containing the microphones were placed on the inside of the hulls of the vessels on the port and starboard sides below the waterline, and were connected by wires to receivers situated in the navigating room on the port side of the officers' quarters.

VARIOUS

The whistles were electrically actuated on the Willett Bruce system. The boiler telegraphs, stoking indicators, rudder indicators, clocks and thermostats were also electrical; the watertight doors, as previously mentioned, were closed by electromagnets.

VENTILATION

There were twelve electrically driven fans for supplying air to the stokeholds; six electrically driven fans for engine and boiler room ventilation. There were fans for engine and boiler rooms.

MACHINERY

Boilers – All of the boilers were 15ft 9in in diameter, the twenty-four double-ended boilers being 20ft long, and the single-ended 11ft 9in long. Each double-ended boiler had six furnaces, and each single-ended boiler three furnaces (159 furnaces in total), with a total heating area of 144,142sq. ft and a grate surface of 3,466sq.ft. The boilers were constructed in accordance with the rules of the Board of Trade for a working pressure of 215psi, (although they could stand a much higher pressure). They were arranged for working under natural draught, assisted by fans, which blew air into the open stokehold.

...Bilge and ballast pumps – The ships were also fitted with the following pumps: – five ballast and bilge pumps, each capable of discharging 250 tons of water per hour; three bilge pumps, each capable of 150 tons per hour capacity.

One ash ejector pump was placed in each of the large boiler compartments to work the ash ejectors, and to circulate or feed the boilers as required. This pump was also connected to the bilges, except in the case of three of the boiler rooms, where three of the ballast and bilge pumps were placed. The pumps in each case had direct bilge suctions as well as the connection to the main bilge pipe, so that each boiler room might be independent. The remainder of the auxiliary pumps were placed in the reciprocating and turbine engine rooms. Two ballast pumps were placed in the reciprocating engine room, with large suctions from the bilges direct and from the bilge main. Two bilge pumps were also arranged to draw from bilges. One bilge pump was placed in the turbine room and one of the hot salt-water pumps had a connection with the main bilge pipe for use in an emergency. A 10in main ballast pipe was carried fore and aft through the ship with separate connections for each tank, and with filling pipes from the sea connected at intervals for trimming purposes. The five ballast pumps were arranged to draw from this pipe. A double line of the main bilge pipe was fitted forward of number 5 boiler room and aft of number 1 (boiler room).

GENERAL

There were four elliptical-shaped funnels; the three forward ones took the waste gases from the boiler furnaces, and the after one was placed over the turbine hatch and used as a ventilator. The galley funnels led up this funnel. The uptakes by which the waste gases were conveyed to the funnels were united immediately above the watertight bulkheads that separate the boiler rooms.

All overhead discharge from the circulating pumps, ballast pumps and bilge pumps, etc., were deep below the load line, but above the light line (when the ships are loaded or not loaded).

The boilers were supported in built steel cradles, and were stayed to the ships' sides and to each other athwartships by strong steel stays. Built steel chocks were also fitted to prevent movement fore and aft. Silent blow-offs from the main steam pipes were connected direct to both condensers.

APPENDIX SEVEN
'...SHORT OF COAL?'

It has sometimes been claimed that *Titanic* was short of coal on her maiden voyage, to the extent that she would only have been able to arrive in New York on Wednesday morning. However, as with many claims surrounding the doomed liner, it can be shown to be false.

When Third Officer Pitman testified in New York following the sinking, he was asked by Senator Smith: 'Were you trying to reach twenty-four knots?'

'No; we had to study the coal. We had not the coal to do it,' Pitman replied. This is usually taken to mean that there would be no attempt to maintain maximum speed for the remainder of the crossing due to a lack of coal; however Pitman explained later in more detail:

'I understood we had not quite sufficient; there was not sufficient there on board to drive her on at full speed,' he said to Senator Fletcher. Pitman stated he had heard that from an engineer. Fletcher asked, when referring to the speed on Sunday:

'You were told, you say, by the engineer, that you did not have enough coal to go at a faster rate of speed than that?'

'He remarked,' Pitman replied, 'we had not sufficient coal on board to drive her full speed *all the way across*.' [Author's italics]

This was an important detail, as the ship's engines had been turning at 70 and 72rpm for the first two days of the maiden voyage, delivering speeds of about 20½ and 21 knots, which was nothing like the ship's maximum speed. Even on Sunday 14 April 1912, the ship's final day afloat, her last full daily run had been 546 miles at about 22 knots. Considerable fuel would have been saved on these three days compared to the consumption if the ship had been moving at full speed. These three days marked a substantial part of the anticipated duration of the crossing.

J. Bruce Ismay confirmed that about 6,000 tons of coal was on board when leaving Southampton, which was 'sufficient coal to enable her to reach New York, with about two days' spare consumption'. If there had not been this substantial reserve, then it would have been in Ismay's interest to say so in order to dispel the contention that the ship was being driven hard. Ismay himself said that he had asked Chief Engineer Bell how much coal was on board *Titanic* and that Bell had told him. He was in a good position to answer.★

★ Ismay explained before Lord Mersey:

> 18387. With whom would you discuss this question of driving her at full speed on the Monday or Tuesday? – The only man I spoke to in regard to it was the chief engineer in my room when the ship was in Queenstown.
>
> 18388. Is that Mr Bell? – Yes.
>
> 18389. The chief engineer? – Yes.
>
> 18390. Can you tell me on what day it was that she first made the 75 revolutions on this voyage? – I think it would be on the Saturday.
>
> 18391. And when was it that you discussed the question of putting her at full speed on the Monday or the Tuesday? – On the Thursday when the ship was at anchor in Queenstown Harbour.
>
> 18392. Will you explain that. It is not quite clear why you should discuss the question in Queenstown? – The reason why we discussed it at Queenstown was this, that Mr Bell came into my room; I wanted to know how much coal we had on board the ship, because the ship left after the coal strike was on, and he told me. I then spoke to him about the ship and I said it is not possible for the ship to arrive in New York on Tuesday. Therefore there is no object in pushing her. We will arrive there at 5 o'clock on Wednesday morning, and it will be good landing for the passengers in New York, and we shall also be able to economise our coal. We did not want to burn any more coal than we needed.

Second Officer Lightoller was questioned by the fierce Thomas Scanlan at the British enquiry, during which he maintained that 'several [five auxiliary] boilers' were off, the reason being 'merely that there was no wish for the ship to travel at any great speed.' He maintained that there could not have been such a desire for even higher speed, stating: 'Not only with regard to shortage of coal, but I understand several boilers were off.'

To find out whether there was enough coal on board for *Titanic* to increase her speed further and maintain that higher rate of speed, it is necessary to examine the amount of coal on board when she left Southampton; the amounts likely to have been burned at different speeds; the size of the required reserve; and *Olympic*'s own coal consumption during her maiden voyage the year before.

On sailing day, Maurice Clarke completed the mandatory 'Reports By Board of Trade Officers': 'The coal on board is certified to amount to 5,892 tons, which is sufficient to take the ship to her next coaling port.' It is known that some 415 tons had been used in port following the bunkers being loaded with coal from other ships, but the figure given in the above report is surely indicative of the coal on board at the time of sailing. *Titanic* had carried 1,880 tons left over from Belfast before being loaded with 4,427 additional tons, a total of 6,307 tons of coal; subtracting the 415 tons of coal used in port gives a total of 5,892 tons of coal on sailing day, fitting perfectly Clarke's figure.

It is a little more complicated to gauge the quantities of coal burned at various speeds. *Titanic* was hardly in service for long enough to establish any sort of definitive picture. However, *Olympic*'s performance is recorded. Since the two ships were so similar then it is entirely reasonable to examine *Olympic*. Ismay was certainly pleased at her maiden voyage performance, as he understood that she had consumed an average of around 620 tons of coal per day, which was significantly lower than anticipated. (Since the time that *Olympic* took to complete her maiden voyage was reported incorrectly in 1911, this figure can be adjusted to conform with this newfound knowledge, which changes it very slightly to 629 tons. However, the average speed was also higher and so the relationship between the coal consumed and the rate of speed is essentially the same.)

What is particularly interesting is to compare *Olympic*'s performance on her maiden voyage with the figures given for her coal consumption at various speeds by Harold Sanderson. Sanderson supplied these figures in January 1916, as part of ongoing discussions as to whether *Olympic* was suitable to convey troops to India:

Knots per hour	Consumption per 24 hours
22.5	850 tons
22	800 tons
21	710 tons
20	630 tons
19	550 tons
18	485 tons
17	425 tons
16	370 tons

In each case includes 100 tons per day for auxiliary purposes.†

Ascertaining the coal consumed by *Titanic* during a single day is complicated by the fact that westbound and eastbound days at sea are not the same length. On the westbound crossing, the clocks

---

It was not true that *Titanic* was incapable of arriving on Tuesday evening. She was well on course to make the Ambrose Light Vessel. However, Ismay's comments in regarding to landing the passengers on Wednesday morning are more plausible. While his comments about the need to conserve coal might imply that there was a concern about the amount on board, in America he said:

Senator PERKINS. She had about 6,000 tons of coal?
Mr ISMAY. She had about 6,000 tons of coal leaving Southampton.
Senator PERKINS. Sufficient to make the voyage to New York and return to Southampton?
Mr ISMAY. No; but sufficient coal to enable her to reach New York, with about two days spare consumption.

were adjusted in keeping with the ship's progress so that a day was more than twenty-four hours; on the eastbound crossing, the situation was reversed, so that the length of a day was less than twenty-four hours. Sanderson's figures simply refer to consumption during a twenty-four-hour period. When Ismay stated that he was pleased with *Olympic*'s coal consumption during her maiden voyage, were his figures for a twenty-four-hour period or the slightly longer westbound day? It is quite plausible that they were for the former, although the variation would probably only be in the range of a couple of per cent.

Sanderson's figures are certainly higher than Ismay's. While it is possible that they accounted for *Olympic*'s originally anticipated coal consumption, as we have seen she proved more economical once she was in service. However, there is another explanation. When it was being considered whether *Olympic* would be able to convey troops to India, it was anticipated that she would require so much coal and other provisions for this long voyage that she would be loaded down to a draft of 38ft 6in. Not only would this increase her displacement far beyond the requirements of her normal peacetime service, but it could only serve to increase her coal consumption. It would therefore be entirely sensible for Sanderson to have taken that into account in providing figures for her anticipated coal consumption. American researcher Sam Halpern has investigated this possibility and produced a series of calculations which indicate strongly that this was the case.★ On that basis, Sanderon's figures can then be adjusted for the normal service conditions:

Sanderson's Coal Consumption Figures (adjusted for a draft of 34ft 6in):

RPM	Knots	Speed ratio	Ratio cubed	Coal used	Plus 100	Rounded
	16	1.000	1.000	243.0	343.0	345
	17	1.063	1.199	291.5	391.5	390
	18	1.059	1.187	346.0	446.0	445
	19	1.056	1.176	406.9	506.9	505
	20	1.053	1.166	474.6	574.6	575
70	**20.6**	**1.030**	**1.093**	**518.6**	**618.6**	**620**
	21	1.019	1.059	549.4	649.4	650
	22	1.048	1.150	631.7	731.7	730
	22.5	1.023	1.070	675.8	775.8	775
80	**23**	**1.022**	**1.068**	**721.8**	**821.8**	**820**

In his American testimony, Ismay was asked about *Titanic*'s daily coal consumption at 70 revolutions and replied that it was 'perhaps 620 to 640 tons'. He did not know how far consumption would increase at 75 revolutions, but believed that at 'full speed she burns about 820 tons'. It is more than likely that he was simply quoting figures for *Olympic*. These figures are remarkably close to the calculations presented in the table above (marked in bold for 70 and 80 revolutions). They

---

† Since the first edition of this book was published, further evidence has come to light regarding Sanderson's figures. The figures, given in a telephone message from Liverpool, were marked 'in each case include 100 tons per day for auxiliary purposes'. This indicated potentially that each figure for the tons of coal consumed needed to be raised by 100 tons. However, the resulting figures seemed far too high, and another copy of Sanderson's table has surfaced which had been amended by hand so that the description read 'in each case include*s* [author's emphasis] 100 tons per day for auxiliary purposes.' The confirmation that each figure already included 100 tons within the total consumption figure is in line with other evidence.

★ The calculations presented in these tables may seem quite complex, however it is important to record them. Halpern recognised that the required power to move a ship through the water is directly proportional to the cube of a vessel's speed. He noted that the power required to move it at a certain speed also depends on the cross-sectional area of the vessel's hull below the waterline. Deeper draft vessels of the same hull form require more power to move them at a certain speed than a shallower draft vessel of the same form and speed. On a ship like *Olympic*, the cross-sectional area below the waterline – approximately a product of the vessel's draft and breadth – will tend to increase in proportion to the draft because its breadth will not significantly change for small changes in draft. Therefore, the amount of power required is approximately proportional to the vessel's draft as well as the cube of the vessel's speed through the water. Fuel consumption is directly proportional to the power required to move the ship.

can be adjusted further, since neither *Olympic* or *Titanic* was loaded to the designed 34ft 6in when they left Southampton on their maiden voyages. The coal consumption model can be tested against *Olympic*'s own maiden voyage. Her average speed and coal consumption are a matter of record. When the model is used independently to calculate what her coal consumption would have been for her speed and draft, the result is accurate to one per cent of the actual figure: an extremely strong indication of its accuracy.

We can, therefore, illustrate *Titanic*'s probable coal consumption. Her average speeds for the first few days are known, while an assumed rate of speed can be used for the remainder of the voyage if the iceberg had not intervened:

Sanderson's Coal Consumption Figures (adjusted for a mean draft of 32ft 8in):

RPM	Knots	Speed ratio	Ratio cubed	Coal used	Plus 100	Rounded
	16	1.000	1.000	229.1	329.1	330
	17	1.063	1.199	274.8	374.8	375
59	18	1.059	1.187	326.2	426.2	425
63	19	1.056	1.176	383.6	483.6	485
67	20	1.053	1.166	447.5	547.5	550
69	20.5	1.025	1.077	481.9	581.9	580
71	21	1.024	1.075	518.0	618.0	620
73	21.5	1.024	1.073	555.9	655.9	655
75	22	1.048	1.150	595.6	695.6	700
77	22.5	1.023	1.070	637.1	737.1	735
79	23	1.022	1.068	680.5	780.5	780
81	23.5	1.022	1.067	725.9	825.9	825
83	24	1.021	1.065	773.2	873.2	875

An illustration of the entire voyage can be produced using these figures, using assumptions of the ship's performance if the collision with the iceberg had not taken place. By assuming higher speeds for the final stages of the voyage, the ship's average speed would be a little greater than that achieved on *Olympic*'s first four westbound crossings, thereby raising the coal consumption figures and making the illustration even more cautious:★

	Run	Hours	Average Speed	Coal Consumed
Southampton, Cherbourg and Queenstown (approximate)	408	21.47	19	434
	484	23.61	20.5	570
	519	24.71	21	638
	546	24.82	22	724
	560	**24.72**	**22.7**	**804**
	570	**24.73**	**23.1**	**804**
	211	**9.17**	**23**	**298**
Daunt Rock to Ambrose Lightship	2,890	5 days, 11 hours, 46 minutes	21.93	
Totals	**3,298**			

Coal Loaded 5,892
Unusable Coal 550
Coal Available 5,342
Coal Consumed 4,272
Coal Reserve 1,070

★ It should be noted that the figures for coal consumption are approximate. For example, a figure of 804 tons is given for one day with an average speed set at 22.7 knots, and again for another day with a higher average speed at 23.1 knots. It is derived from the coal consumption for a round figure of 23 knots.

Olympic arrived in New York on her own maiden voyage with more than 1,300 tons of coal remaining on board, even though she had consumed significantly less than originally anticipated, which indicates that Captain Smith and Chief Engineer Bell would have initially expected to arrive with less than that. It is not known whether this was the total figure or the amount of usable coal, however the figures for *Titanic* on our calculations would be a total figure of 1,620 tons or a usable reserve of 1,070 tons, which seems very much in keeping with what was an acceptable reserve for *Olympic* during Captain Smith's command. To put it in context, as she was nearing New York we can assume a slightly lower draft for *Titanic* than the mean draft for the entire voyage: on that basis, the usable reserve was enough for around 1.3 days steaming at 24 knots (749 miles); 1.8 days steaming at 21 knots (907 miles); or 3.4 days steaming at 16 knots (1,305 miles).★ It is interesting that these calculations for 21 knots dovetail nicely with Ismay's belief that there was enough coal in reserve for about two days steaming.

When Captain Smith brought *Olympic* into New York less than a month earlier, it was reported that the coal surplus when she arrived was 'not more [than] 500 tons'. The figure is less than half the usable reserve projected for *Titanic* and is compelling evidence that, according to Smith's judgement with *Olympic*, then *Titanic* had an ample reserve even if her speed had been increased to around 23 knots for the remainder of the crossing.

Tragedy intervened.

> 'As long as the weather is clear I always go full speed. Twenty-six knots.'
> – John Pritchard, former captain of *Mauretania*.

> 'I believe every captain will give you the same answer; they will not slow down unless it becomes thick or hazy.'
> – Gerhard Apfeld, Red Star Line Marine Superintendent.

> 'This practice, it was said, had been justified by experience, no casualties having resulted from it. I accept the evidence as to the practice and as to the immunity from casualties which is said to have accompanied it. But the event has proved the practice to be bad. Its root is probably to be found in competition and in the desire of the public for quick passages rather than in the judgement of navigators.'
> – Lord Mersey, Report on the Loss of the S.S. *Titanic*, 1912.

★ It is interesting to note the following observations made at the wreck site: 'The amount of coal distributed around the debris field is testimony to the fact that there was *plenty of coal in boiler room 1 and the adjoining bunkers on either side of the bulkhead between this boiler room and boiler room number 2.* [Author's italics] These two spaces were the only boiler rooms which could yield coal in the amount found in the debris field. The coal in other boiler rooms would have stayed with the ship.' Boiler room 1 housed the single-ended auxiliary boilers. *Olympic*'s remained unlit throughout her maiden voyage, yet it was planned that *Titanic*'s would be brought online and her speed increased. (See: *Titanic, The Anatomy of a Disaster*, A Report from the Marine Forensic Panel (SD-7), 1997, page 40.)

APPENDIX EIGHT

CALIFORNIAN: 'THE SHIP THAT STOOD STILL'

'The Ship That Stood Still'... 'The *Californian* Incident'... Since 1912, perhaps the most heated historical debates relating to the *Titanic* disaster have focused on the actions – or inactions – of the Leyland liner *Californian* and her commander, Stanley Lord. The two investigations in America and Britain both concluded that she failed to respond to the sinking liner's distress signals by taking appropriate action. It is not possible or desirable to examine the numerous aspects of the saga in this brief appendix. There are others with far greater expertise and relevant skill. However, it is possible to highlight a few interesting issues and offer a general description of what happened that night, while referring the interested reader to the detailed works that have been published about the subject.★

The SS *Californian*, of the Leyland Line, was a ship of 4,038 net tons and 6,223grt. Her maximum speed was 12½–13 knots on a full consumption of coal, and she usually made about 11½ knots.

On 5 April 1912 the SS *Californian* departed from London, bound for Boston (where she arrived at 4.00 a.m. on 19 April 1912), she was carrying no passengers although she had accommodation for forty-seven and had a passenger certificate; she carried during this voyage a full crew complement of fifty-five. Therefore the most people likely to be aboard at one time numbered 102 persons. To cope with these, the ship carried four lifeboats, one gig, and a pinnace – these six boats could hold 218 people altogether. *Californian* was under the command of Captain Stanley Lord.

At 6.30 p.m. (which was the ship's apparent time for longitude 47°25′), on 14 April 1912, *Californian* sent a wireless message to *Antillian*, warning that there were icebergs 5 miles to the South of *Californian's* position. The icebergs' position was 42°5′N 49°9′W.

At 8.00 p.m. Lord doubled his lookout by stationing a man on the forecastle head in addition to the existing lookout in the crow's nest. He took charge of the bridge himself. There had been reports of ice ahead and the captain wanted to ensure his ship's safety – although Lord had not had any experience of field ice so far in his career.

Field ice was spotted ahead; it stretched as far to the North and as far to the South as the eye could see.

Captain Lord pulled the engine room telegraph to 'full astern', he also ordered the helm hard over, there was a little vibration of the engine's reversal as *Californian* swung around to a stop at 10.21 p.m.,† her bows pointed east-north-east by compass. During the time she lay drifting, *Californian* slowly turned to starboard throughout the night on account of the helm being hard over to port.

When a steamer's light was seen approaching from the east a little prior to 11.00 p.m., Captain Lord asked Evans, the Wireless Operator, 'What ships have you got?'

'I think the *Titanic* is near us, I have got her,' Evans replied.

'You had better advise the *Titanic* we are stopped and surrounded with ice,' said the captain. Evans did this but did not address his message properly and was cut-off: 'We are stopped and surrounded by

---

★ A number of excellent analyses have been published. See, for instance: Dr Paul Lee's *The Titanic and the Indifferent Stranger: The Complete Story of the Titanic and the Californian*, privately printed, 2009, and Leslie Reade and Edward P. De Groot's *The Ship That Stood Still: Californian and Her Mysterious Role in the Titanic Disaster*, Patrick Stephens Ltd, 1993.

However inappropriate the label may be, authors more sympathetic to Captain Lord's case are often said to write from a 'Lordite' perspective. See: Leslie Harrison's *A Titanic Myth: the Californian Incident*, 1992; Senan Molony's *Titanic and the Mystery Ship*, the History Press, 2006; Peter Padfield's *The Titanic and the Californian*, Hodder & Stoughton, 1965; and Thomas Williams and Rob Kamps' *The Titanic and the Californian*, The History Press, 2007.

† All times are *Californian's* time, *Titanic* time would be approximately ten minutes later.

ice.' *Titanic's* operator was working Cape Race and he was too busy for interruptions. Evans listened to the *Titanic*, turning in at 11.30 p.m.

Lord observed the approaching steamer and at 11.00 p.m. he thought she was about 6 or 7 miles away. As she got nearer he saw more lights, some deck lights, and a green (starboard) side light; the steamer was bearing 'south ½ west'. At 11.30 p.m. the steamer stopped; Lord thought that she was, 'a medium-sized steamer... like ourselves'.

Lord was not on the bridge at this time according to Third Officer Groves;★ Groves saw two masthead lights, as the steamer continued to approach, then he went to the chart room and reported this to Captain Lord: 'She is evidently a passenger steamer' and he later said that there was no doubt about it, in his mind at least. Lord replied to Groves, 'Call her up on the Morse lamp and see if you can get any answer.' Groves went to the bridge and started using the Morse lamp, Lord following him up not long afterwards. He remarked, 'That does not look like a passenger steamer.'

'It is, sir,' Groves replied, 'when she stopped, her lights seemed to go out, and I suppose [that] they have been put out for the night.' The red (port) side light of the steamer was visible. Groves thought that the time was 11.40 p.m., because 'one bell had been struck to call the middle watch'.†

Groves continued Morsing and he thought that he had got a reply at one point, but he squinted through binoculars and concluded that it was just the flickering of a masthead. Just after midnight, Second Officer Stone came onto the bridge for his watch. Groves pointed-out the steamer. 'She has been stopped since 11.40; she is a passenger steamer. Coming up on the starboard quarter. At about the moment she stopped she put her lights out.' He later said:

> Well, at the time her lights disappeared I thought in my own mind she had put them out because in the ships I was accustomed to before I joined this company it was the custom to put all the deck lights out, some at 11 p.m., some at 11.30 p.m., and some at midnight – all the deck lights except those absolutely necessary to show the way along the different decks. But when I saw the ice I came to the conclusion that she had starboarded to escape some ice.

Before heading up to the bridge, Lord met Stone and pointed out to him the other steamer to the south-east that had resisted attempts to make contact with the Morse lamp. Lord ordered that he be advised if the other ship came any nearer and told Stone that he was going to lie down in the chart room on the settee. Stone went to the bridge just before 12.10 a.m. and relieved Groves.

Ernest Gill, a twenty-nine-year-old making his first trip on the *Californian* as Donkeyman, went up on deck about midnight after going off duty in the engine room. Looking over to starboard, he saw 'the lights of a very large steamer about 10 miles away. I watched her for fully a minute.'

Going down to his cabin, his mate William Thomas had heard ice crunching along the ship's side and asked 'Are we in the ice?'

'Yes,' Gill replied, 'but it must be clear off to the starboard, for I saw a big vessel going along full speed. She looked as if she might be a big German.'

He turned in but could not sleep and at about 12.30 a.m. he went back on deck for a smoke, as he wasn't allowed to smoke between decks owing to the cargo. He was there ten minutes when he noticed a white rocket on the starboard side, about 10 miles away. Initially, he thought it was a shooting star, but then saw another shortly afterwards. 'That must be a vessel in distress,' he said to himself.

'It was not my business to notify the bridge or the lookouts,' he recalled. 'I turned in immediately after, supposing that the ship would pay attention to the rockets.'

Third Officer Groves did not go straight to bed. He went to the Marconi house to see Cyril Evans, the radio operator. 'What ships have you got Sparks?'

'Only the *Titanic*,' Evans replied laconically. 'You know, the new boat on its maiden voyage, I got [sic] it this afternoon.' Groves listened at the set to see if he could pick up a message. He listened for half a minute and heard nothing so he left at 12.15 a.m. and went below.

★ Groves was on the ship's articles as second officer, but he took the duties of third officer.
† The lights of the other steamer going out could be explained by the stranger turning sharply to port, or by the drifting of *Californian* to starboard, the time the vessel's lights seemed to go out would have been about 11.50 p.m. *Titanic* time.

During the middle watch, Stone's watch, apprentice Gibson was also on the bridge. His attention was first drawn to the lights of the mystery steamer at around 12.20 a.m. Gibson could see a masthead light, also some afterdeck lights with unaided eyes, and her red (port) side light with binoculars. Gibson thought that the stranger was Morsing. He replied, but then concluded that it was a flickering masthead light.

Around 12.40 a.m., Captain Lord used the speaking tube to enquire if the mystery ship had changed position;[1] Stone replied that the ship hadn't and that he had not received any reply to his Morse signalling.[2]

Over the mystery ship at 12.45 a.m., Stone observed a flash over the ship – probably a shooting star.[3] He saw four more white flashes, but did not hear any sounds like the noise of a rocket exploding.[4] Stone called Captain Lord via the speaking tube, informing him. Lord asked if they were private company signals.[5]

'I do not know, but they appear to be white rockets,' Stone replied.

'Go on morsing…when you get an answer let me know by Gibson,' Lord replied.[6] The time was around 1.10 a.m.

Gibson Morsed at Stone's orders, but he was not receiving any reply. Stone and Gibson both observed three more white rockets – a total of eight rockets. Between 1.00 a.m. and 1.40 a.m., (most probably closer to 1.40 a.m.) Stone remarked to Gibson: 'Look at her now, she looks very queer out of the water, her lights look queer.' The strange ship appeared to be listing, and at 1.40 a.m. the rockets ceased; Gibson noticed that her stern light seemed to be higher out of the water than it had been before – as if the stern was higher out of the water and the bow was settling – although he didn't tell Stone. 'A ship isn't going to fire rockets at sea for nothing,' Stone remarked to Gibson.

'I told Gibson to go down to the Master, and be sure to wake him, and tell him that altogether we had seen eight of these white lights like white rockets in the direction of this other steamer; that this steamer was *disappearing* [author's italics] in the Southwest, that we had both called her up repeatedly on the Morse lamp and received no information whatsoever,' Stone later described.

According to apprentice Gibson, he went and told the Master. Captain Lord replied, asking if all the rockets were white: 'were there any colours in the rockets at all?'[7] Gibson said no.

'Alright,' Lord acknowledged, asking the time,[8] which was now nearly 2.05 a.m.

Stone subsequently explained:

> Naturally, the first thought that crossed my mind was that the ship might be in trouble, but subsequent events showed that the ship steamed away from us; there was nothing to confirm that the rockets came up from that ship, in the direction of that ship, that is all I observed…It would be very difficult to express an opinion of the speed at which she steamed away from us, [but] I should say that at different times she was doing different speeds.

At 2.05 a.m., Gibson reported to Stone about his conversation with Captain Lord. Stone continued to observe the ship's lights: 'a gradual disappearing of her lights which would be perfectly natural with a ship steaming away from us'. It would also be 'perfectly natural' with a sinking ship's lights fading until the generators failed. The stranger's last bearings were south-west ½ west – the last position that he had seen the lights.

Later, Captain Lord stated that during his 1.10 a.m. conversation with Stone he had been informed of *one* white rocket. He also said that during Gibson's 2.00 a.m. visit, Gibson had not said anything, Lord had no recollection apart from Gibson opening and closing the chartroom door.

'I have recollection of Gibson opening the chartroom door and closing it immediately. I said "What is it?" *but he did not reply.*'[9]

There would seem to be three possibilities: either Gibson gave a faulty recollection, or Captain Lord was not fully awake and therefore did not remember the rest of the conversation, or that Captain Lord was mistaken. Gibson thought that the Master was fully awake the whole time.[10]

Around 2.40 a.m. Second Officer Stone called Lord by voice pipe to tell him that the ship had gone, bearing south-west ½ west; when Lord asked, he was assured the rockets had been 'just white'.

By about 3.40 a.m. three rockets had been recently sighted by Gibson, who had reported 'a white light' to the South, according to Stone, who did not think of a rocket; but Gibson recalled rockets, stating he had told Stone, who did not report them to Captain Lord. Gibson stated he had seen one, then himself and Stone had seen two more. These sightings took place around about 3.20 a.m. to 3.40 a.m., indicating the likelihood that *Carpathia*'s rockets had been sighted as she was firing them to reassure *Titanic*'s survivors.

Chief Officer Stewart relieved Second Officer Stone at 4.00 a.m. for his four-hour watch. Stone informed Stewart that at midnight he'd seen a ship about 5 miles off, that at 1.00 a.m. he had seen white rockets, and that the mystery ship then started to steam away.

A steamer was not in sight with two white masthead lights and a few lights amidships. Stone was asked by Stewart if he thought that this ship had been the ship that earlier fired the rockets; Stone replied that he did not think that it was.

It was 4.30 a.m. when Stewart woke up Captain Lord. Stewart informed the Master of the rockets seen by Stone and Lord replied 'Yes, I know, he's been telling me.'

Lord began talking of getting under way.

'Will you go down to look at that steamer to the southward?' Stewart asked.

'Why, what is the matter with it?'

'He might have lost his rudder,' Stewart suggested.

'Why?' Lord asked, 'he has not got any signals up.'

'No,' Stewart replied, 'but the Second Officer in his watch said they fired several rockets.'

'Go and call the Wireless Operator,' Lord ordered.

Stewart didn't tell the captain that this was a different steamer. Coming back to Captain Lord from the wireless room, Stewart said, 'There's a ship sunk. The *Titanic* has hit a berg and sunk!.'

Captain Lord later questioned Second Officer Stone regarding Stone's sightings of the mystery ship. He would later state:

> He [Stone] said that he had sent down and called me; he had sent Gibson down, and Gibson told him that I was awake and I had said 'Alright, let me know if anything is wanted.' I was surprised at him not getting me out, considering rockets had been fired. He said that if they had been distress rockets he would most certainly have come down and called me himself, but he was not a little bit worried about it at all…that was apparently his view.

Confirmation of *Titanic*'s sinking arrived from the Allan Liner *Virginian*, about 5.20 a.m. Captain Lord ordered that *Californian* proceed slowly, at first, through the ice. By 6.30 a.m., he had asked for 'full speed ahead' and she proceeded at full speed along the western edge of the ice field, around 13 or 13½ knots.

Between 6.00 a.m. and 6.30 a.m., *Californian* was spotted from *Mount Temple* in close proximity to the site of the disaster, perhaps 6 miles north, according to *Mount Temple*'s Captain Moore. He estimated that his own ship was about 7 or 8 miles to the west of *Carpathia* and, in turn, *Californian* was 7 or 8 miles to the north.

Ernest Gill was woken at 6.40 a.m. by the Chief Engineer, who told him, 'Turn out to render assistance. The *Titanic* has gone down.'

Going down to the engine room, Gill heard Second Engineer Evans and Fourth Engineer Wooten talking. Evans was telling Wooten about the rockets that had apparently been seen from the bridge. 'I knew then that it must have been the *Titanic* I had seen,' he later said.

He overheard someone ask, 'Why in the devil didn't they wake the wireless man up?'

Mount Temple was stopped in the vicinity of the distress position. *Californian* passed her at 7.30 a.m. and no wreckage could be seen, Captain Lord would recall, but wreckage was spotted when *Californian* neared *Carpathia* in position 41°33′ N 50°1′ W at about 8 a.m.

Third Officer Groves, however, provided a different time estimate of when his ship reached the *Carpathia* to Lord Mersey's inquiry:

> Mr Rowlatt: 'Now it is getting on for 7 [a.m.]?'
>
> Groves: 'I suppose by the time I got on the bridge it would be 6.50 [a.m.]; but you understand the time is only approximately.'
>
> Mr Rowlatt: 'I quite understand that. Were there any other vessels in sight?'
>
> Groves: 'Yes.'
>
> Mr Rowlatt: 'What were they?'

Groves: 'There was a four-masted steamer abeam on our port side.'

Mr Rowlatt: 'What steamer was that?'

Groves: 'I did not know at the time, but afterwards she was the *Carpathia*.'

Mr Rowlatt: 'Abeam on your port side?'

Groves: 'Abeam on our port side.'

Mr Rowlatt: 'In what direction were you going?'

Groves: 'That I could not say.'

Mr Rowlatt: 'You did not notice?'

Groves: 'No.'

Mr Rowlatt: 'How far off was she? [*Carpathia*]'

Groves: 'I should think she would be about five miles – possibly more, possibly less, but about five.'

Mr Rowlatt: 'Did you look at her with the glass[es]?'

Groves: 'I did.'

Mr Rowlatt: 'Who asked you to do that, anybody?'

Groves: 'The captain.'

Mr Rowlatt: 'Did you make out anything about her?'

Groves: 'After I had been looking at her I made out she had her house flag half-mast. She had a red funnel with a black top.'

Lord Mersey: 'She had what half-mast?'

Groves: 'Her house flag.'

Mersey: 'What is that?'

Groves: 'Her company's flag.'

Mersey: 'Is there any significance in its being half-mast?'

Groves: 'It is half-mast for death, my Lord.'

Mr Rowlatt: 'That is how you understood it at the time?'

Groves: 'That is what I understood it to mean.'

Mr Rowlatt: 'It was because of the disaster to the *Titanic* that this vessel was flying her house flag half-mast?'

Groves: 'Yes.'

Mr Rowlatt: 'What did your vessel do then?'

Groves: 'We continued on our course for a little time after I had told the captain she had a red funnel with a black top and the house flag half-masted, and the next thing that was done we starboarded.'

Mr Rowlatt: 'You made straight for her?'

Groves: 'We made practically straight for her.'

Mr Rowlatt: 'Did you see any other vessel?'

Groves: 'Yes, I saw two other vessels.'

Mr Rowlatt: 'At this time?'

Groves: 'Yes. I fancy one of them was in sight at the same time as I noticed this four-master.'

Mersey: 'Do you know what they were?'

Groves: 'I know what one of them was…*Mount Temple*.'

Mr Rowlatt: 'Where was she?'

Groves: 'She was ahead, a little on our starboard side when I saw her first.'

Mr Rowlatt: 'Before you changed your course?'

Groves: 'Before we headed for the *Carpathia*.'

Mr Rowlatt: 'How far off was she, do you think?'

Groves: 'Well, when I noticed her first – I had been paying particular attention to this other steamer – I should think she would be perhaps a mile and a half away from us.'

Mr Rowlatt: 'Nearer than the *Carpathia*?'

Groves: 'Much nearer than the *Carpathia*.'

Groves went on so say that *Mount Temple* was stopped in the ice. *Californian* reached *Carpathia* at 7.45 a.m. *Carpathia* headed south, skirting around the ice field at about 9.00 a.m. and leaving *Californian* to continue to search for any more survivors.

The plodding *Californian* got into Boston early on 19 April 1912. Shortly afterwards, a 'press conference' as it would now be called was held; Captain Lord explained that his ship had been stopped in ice with her wireless off on the night of *Titanic*'s peril, receiving the first news of the sinking from the *Virginian* at 5.30 a.m.[11] Nobody had seen any rockets, lights or anything unusual.[12]

It was on 23 April 1912 that the Clinton *Daily Item* published an article based on an interview with the ship's Carpenter W.F. McGregor,[13] which briefly explained that the *Titanic*'s distress rockets had been seen from *Californian* and that Captain Lord had 'failed to pay any attention' to them. Apparently, when Lord had found out the news about the *Titanic*, he 'had the appearance of being twenty years older'.[14] Then on the morning of 25 April 1912 the Boston *American* carried a sworn affidavit by crewman Ernest Gill.[15] It was later put fully on the American inquiry record, although there is no need to quote it in its entirety here. However, there were a number of interesting details in the statement, especially what Gill believed had happened on board the ship during the continuation of the voyage to Boston.

'…The next remark I heard… was, "Why in the devil didn't they wake the wireless man up?" The entire crew of the steamer have been talking among themselves about the disregard of the rockets. I personally urged several to join me in protesting against the conduct of the captain, but they refused, because they feared to lose their jobs.'

A day or two before the ship reached port the skipper called the quartermaster, who was on duty at the time the rockets were discharged, into his cabin. They were in conversation about three-quarters of an hour. The quartermaster declared that he did not see the rockets.

> I am quite sure that the *Californian* was less than twenty miles from the *Titanic*, which the officers report to have been our position. I could not have seen her if she had been more than ten miles distant and I saw her very plainly.
>
> I have no ill will toward the captain or any Officer of the ship, and I am losing a profitable berth by making this statement. I am actuated by the desire that no captain who refuses or neglects to give aid to a vessel in distress should be able to hush up the men.
>
> ERNEST GILL.

Gill's statement is sometimes questioned on the basis that he had received payment for his story, but it is hard to draw any conclusion on that basis as to whether his statement was reliable or not. If he had made it for the payment, it does not necessarily follow that his statement was not accurate. Certainly, there was a lot of interesting testimony from *Californian*'s officers and crew at both investigations, particularly before Lord Mersey.

As day twenty-seven – 19 June 1912 – opened, the formal draft was submitted for question 24, which had been famously altered to ask about *Californian*. The Attorney-General explained to Lord Mersey, 'It is quite simple, I think. The only one [vessel] that gives us any difficulty is the *Californian*. As to the *Mount Temple*, you have the evidence about that. That question will cover the *Californian*.' Mersey had initially asked about question 24, saying 'Will that involve dealing with the *Frankfurt*?' He remembered evidence about the German ship's Wireless Operator having trouble understanding the sinking liner's messages.

Lord had previously stated that he thought the mystery ship had sent up a rocket in reply to his ship's Morse lamp. When questioned about his actions after asking that Gibson be sent down to report the results of again Morsing the mystery ship, Lord replied: 'I remained in the chart room.'

'Then, as far as you were concerned, you did not know at all what the rocket was for?'

'No.' Lord was departing from his original position that the rocket might have been a reply.

'And you remained in the chart-room?'

'Yes, I remained in the chart-room.'

'And you did nothing further?'

'I did nothing further myself.'

'If it was not a company's signal, must it not have been a distress signal?'

'If it had been a distress signal the officer on watch would have told me,' Lord replied.

'I say, if it was not a company's signal, must it not have been a distress signal?'

'Well, I do not know of any other signals but distress signals that are used at sea,' Lord buckled.

'You do not expect at sea, where you were, to see a rocket unless it is a distress signal, do you?'

'We sometimes get these company's signals which resemble rockets; they do not shoot as high and they do not explode,' Lord responded, a little more robustly.

Suspicious testimony was given by apprentice Gibson, as one example. Questioned as to how he interpreted Second Officer Stone's report to Captain Lord that the ship they had seen had 'disappeared', Gibson remained silent.

'...Did you not understand him to mean [that] she had gone to the bottom?'

'No.'

'Then what did you understand, that she had steamed away through the ice?'

[*No answer.*]

When Thomas Scanlan asked him if he knew when the rockets were being observed that they were 'danger signals', Gibson replied: 'I thought they were some private signals.' However, *he admitted that nobody had told him so and he had not seen 'signals of that kind' personally.*

In many instances those from the *Californian* crumpled in the witness box. In one instance, Lord was questioned about his attitude towards the ice:

> 'You were treating the ice, so to speak, with great respect, and behaved with great caution with regard to it?'
>
> Lord: 'I was treating it with every respect.'
>
> 'May I take it that you were not anxious if you could help it, between 10 o'clock and 5 o'clock, to move your engines?'
>
> Lord: '*I did not want to move them if I could help it.* [But] They were ready to move at a moment's notice.'
>
> 'Was that the reason, perhaps, why you were not so inquisitive as to these signals as you might otherwise have been?'
>
> Lord: 'No, that had not anything to do with it.'

Questioned by Sir Rufus Isaacs, Lord had stated that he was 'very likely half awake' when he asked about the colour of the rockets at 2.05 a.m., but he had no reason to doubt Gibson's version:

> Sir Rufus Isaacs: 'Why did you ask whether they were white rockets?'
>
> Captain Lord: 'I suppose this was on account of the first question they asked, whether they were company's signals.'
>
> Isaacs: 'Do just think?'
>
> Lord: 'Company signals usually have some colours in them.'
>
> Isaacs: 'So that if they were white it would make it quite plain to you they were distress signals?'
>
> Lord: 'No, I understand some companies have white.'
>
> Isaacs: 'Do really try and do yourself justice.'
>
> Lord: 'I am trying to do my best.'
>
> Isaacs: '...Mr Lord, allow me to suggest you are not doing yourself justice. You are explaining, first of all, that you asked if they were white rockets, because companies signals are coloured. I am asking you whether the point of your asking whether they were all white rockets was not in order to know whether they were distress signals? Was that not the object of your question, if you put it?'
>
> Lord: 'I really do not know what was the object of my question.'
>
> Isaacs: 'And you think that is why you asked about it?'
>
> Lord: 'I think that is why I asked about it.'

Stone was questioned by Butler Aspinall about the rockets he had seen before 1 a.m. and buckled.

> Butler Aspinall: 'Now, what did you think at the time?'
>
> Stone: 'I knew they were signals of some sort.'
>
> Butler Aspinall: 'I know; of course – signals of what sort did you think?'
>
> Stone: 'I did not know at the time.'
>
> Lord Mersey: 'Now try to be frank?'
>
> Stone: 'I am.'

Mersey: 'If you try, you will succeed. What did you think these rockets were going up at intervals of three or four minutes for?'

Stone: 'I just took them as white rockets, and informed the master and left him to judge.'

Mersey: 'Do you mean to say you did not think for yourself? I thought you told us just now that you did think?'

Stone: [*No answer.*]

Butler Aspinall: 'You know they were not being sent up for fun, were they?'

Stone: 'No.'

Mersey: 'You know, you do not make a good impression upon me at present.'

Captain Lord's defence, Mr C. Robertson Dunlop, also got off to a bad start on day thirty-three, when the evidence was being discussed. Lord Mersey asked him: 'Now, Mr Dunlop, how long do you think you will take to convince us that the *Californian* did not see the *Titanic*'s lights?'

Dunlop began by explaining that the Leyland Line had asked him to appear on their behalf and Captain Lord's. Then he told the court, 'I desire at the outset to express their profound regret that the *Californian* was unable to, *or did not*, render any assistance to the *Titanic*.' He continued somewhat better, saying that Leyland had desired anxiously for their ship to render as much assistance as possible at the wreck site, reading out a telegram to that effect as proof.

He sought to make a number of arguments, pointing out that there were no 'grounds for the suggestion' that *Californian*'s logbook had 'been "cooked"'; that her reported position was correct and 'neither vessel could possibly have been at any time in sight of the other'; that the vessels seen from *Titanic* and *Californian* 'were different steamers'; and that rockets could have been fired from a vessel that had a broken rudder, no Morse lamp or wireless installation. Regardless of the logic of these assertions, Dunlop seemed to be making a gallant effort.

'What I wish to point out,' Dunlop said to Mersey about Second Officer Stone's actions when seeing the rockets, 'is that the conduct of the Second Officer is inconsistent with the conduct of a man who has seen rockets which he thinks to be signals from a vessel herself in distress.'

'I agree with you there,' Lord Mersey replied, '– it is.'

This also explained the absence of the rockets in *Californian*'s log, Dunlop explained; the signals were not entered because they were held to be unimportant.

However, Dunlop's defence was weak on the point; Lord Mersey's mind must have been clear regarding the Chief Officer's suspicious testimony on the matter:

Sir John Simon: 'Now, I should like to follow this. As far as your memory serves you, did you enter into that log book everything that you found on the scrap log sheet?'

Stewart: 'Yes.'

Sir John Simon: 'You observe there is nothing at all in your log book about seeing distress signals?'

Stewart: 'Yes.'

Sir John Simon: 'Is there anything?'

Stewart: 'No, nothing.'

Sir John Simon: 'Nothing at all?'

Stewart: 'No.'

Sir John Simon: 'No reference to any of these events of the night at all?'

Stewart: 'No.'

Lord Mersey: 'Does that convey to you that there was no reference to those events in the scrap log?'

Stewart: 'Yes, my Lord.'

Sir John Simon: 'Give us your views. Supposing you were keeping the scrap log on a watch when you were in ice, and supposing you saw a few miles to the southward a ship sending up what appeared to you to be distress signals, would not you enter that in the log?'

Stewart: 'Yes – I do not know.'

Mersey: 'Oh, yes you do.'

Stewart: 'Yes, I daresay I should have entered it, but it was not in our scrap log-book.'

Sir John Simon: 'That is not what I asked you. What I asked you was – apply your mind to it – supposing you had been keeping the scrap log in those circumstances and you saw distress signals being sent up by a ship a few miles from you, is that, or is not that, a thing you would enter in the log?

Stewart: 'Yes.'

Lord Mersey: 'How do you account for it not being there?'

Stewart: 'I do not know, my Lord.'

Mersey: 'It was careless not to put it in, was it not?'

Stewart: 'Or forgetful.'

Mersey: 'Forgetful? Do you think that a careful man is likely to forget the fact that distress signals have been going on from a neighbouring steamer?'

Stewart: 'No, my Lord.'

Mersey: 'Then do not talk to me about forgetfulness...'

Dunlop pointed out that it was not the inquiry's purpose to censure Captain Lord and that there was not the authority to do so. Captain Lord had not known of the allegations that had been made against him until he had left the witness box, so he had really been unable to defend himself. He had appeared in order to assist the inquiry. Question 24 had been altered without his knowledge and Dunlop pointed out that Captain Lord should have been able to hear other witnesses' evidence first.

'Captain Lord has already been sorely and severely punished for his apparent inactivity during those fatal midnight hours', Dunlop said. 'Whatever his conduct was it was conduct due to a want of appreciation of what the real circumstances at the time where, and certainly not to any wilful disregard of duty.' Lord had already suffered much public criticism, which would 'be a sufficient warning to him and to other Masters of the strict duty' they had at sea and to any vessels in distress.

'For all the reasons I have urged,' Dunlop concluded, '*I do ask your Lordship not to pass any censure on this man*, and I venture to think that if your Lordship does not censure him then truth and justice and mercy will meet together in your Lordship's report.'

Mersey's report concluded:

> The circumstances convince me that the ship seen by the *Californian* was the *Titanic*, and if so, according to Captain Lord, the two vessels were about 5 miles apart at the time of the disaster. The evidence from the *Titanic* corroborates this estimate, but I am advised that the distance was probably greater, though not more than 8 to 10 miles. The ice by which the *Californian* was surrounded was loose ice extending for a distance of not more than 2 or 3 miles in the direction of the *Titanic*. The night was clear and the sea was smooth. When she first saw the rockets, the *Californian* could have pushed through the ice to the open water without any serious risk and so have come to the assistance of the *Titanic*. Had she done so she might have saved many if not all of the lives that were lost.

It was the final conclusion that appeared so damaging: *Californian* 'might have saved many if not all of the lives that were lost'. It was also hard to credit. Even if it had been possible for her to proceed at full speed as soon as the first rocket had been seen, even if the distance had only been 5 miles, less than an hour remained for any sort of transshipment to take place. *Titanic* may have appeared stable and solid to some, even after 1 a.m., but she increasingly tipped by the bow and developed an increasing port list. The evident danger of bringing another vessel alongside is all too clear, while the practicalities of a ship-to-ship transfer in mid-ocean should not be overlooked. Three years earlier, there had been considerable time to evacuate the doomed *Republic*'s passengers and crew; time was not a luxury available on 15 April 1912. Nonetheless, an attempt should have been made.

How were distress signals defined at the time? As per the contemporary Regulations for Preventing Collisions at Sea, Article 31, Number 3 stated that night distress signals were: 'Rockets or shells, throwing stars of any colour or description, fired one at a time, at short intervals.' Those on *Californian* had seen eight white rockets, although there is some evidence that *Titanic* had fired more. Third Officer Pitman said of the number of rockets fired: 'It may have been a dozen or it may have been more.' Fourth Officer Boxhall recalled that he had fired 'between half a dozen and a dozen, I should say, as near as I could tell'. Steward Alfred Crawford said: 'I should say I saw about a dozen go up, probably more.' It is hard to imagine those aboard the sinking vessel counting the distress rockets. Boxhall was perhaps more likely to have paid attention, but even his estimate was varied. The Board of Trade records show clearly that they were white, but there are certainly variations in the recollections of witnesses. Quartermaster Hichens said: 'Some were blue – all kinds of colours – and some were white.' He did admit that he was by no means sure. Lookout Reginald Lee was later asked: 'Were they coloured rockets, or only white ones?' He replied: 'No, coloured rockets.' Even if that had been the case, they met the standard of 'throwing stars of *any colour or description* [author's italics]'; they were 'fired one at a time' and 'at short intervals'.

★ ★ ★

The *Titanic* disaster faded gradually from public memory, following the First World War, the depression of the 1930s and the Second World War. In 1958, the film *A Night to Remember* depicted *Californian*'s role and Captain Lord, long since retired, found himself the subject of unwelcome attention. Lord enlisted the assistance of the Mercantile Marine Service Association and its general secretary, Leslie Harrison. Several years later, Lord's death occurred at the age of eighty-four. Harrison continued to act as an advocate on Lord's behalf, submitting petitions to the government in 1965 and 1968. They were not accepted.

The continued urgings of a number of people sympathetic to Captain Lord lead eventually to a reappraisal of the case. They cited the discovery of *Titanic*'s wreck in a position some distance from where it had been accepted she foundered in 1912. By 1990, the Department of Transport was responsible for shipping matters. The Secretary of State for Transport, Cecil Parkinson, 'determined that the Marine Accident Investigation Branch should carry out a reappraisal of the role played by SS *Californian* at the time RMS *Titanic* was lost in 1912,' although the report was not published until 1992, when Malcolm Rifkind had succeeded him.

The terms of reference for the reappraisal were to take into account evidence unavailable in 1912: to establish where *Titanic* struck the iceberg and where she foundered; to consider 'whether *Titanic* was seen by *Californian* during that period, and if so, when and by whom'; to consider 'whether distress signals from *Titanic* were seen by *Californian* and if so, whether proper action was taken'; and to 'assess the action taken by Captain Stanley Lord, master of *Californian*, between about 10.00 p.m. ship's time on 14 April and the time on 15 April [1912] when passage was resumed.'

Chief Inspector of the Marine Accident Investigation Branch Captain Marriott appointed Captain Thomas Barnett to carry out the re-examination, but subsequently disagreed with a number of his conclusions and further appointed Captain James de Coverly, the deputy chief inspector. Marriott did 'not fully agree with all [of Barnett's] findings but this does not mean that I have any doubt at all as to either the thoroughness of his enquiries or the fair-mindedness of his approach. It rather serves to emphasise the difficulty of the task he was set...'

Captain Barnett had found that the 'two ships were between 5 and 10 miles apart whilst they lay stopped, and probably nearer five'; but Captain de Coverly believed the distance 'was substantially greater, probably about 18 miles'. Barnett thought the two ships were visible to each other, but de Coverly was less definitive. Regardless of further differences between them, they agreed *Californian* had seen *Titanic*'s distress rockets and that further action should have been taken:

– The master should have been called and if he did not immediately respond Mr Stone should have reported to him in person;
– Engine room should have been placed on immediate readiness by ringing 'Stand by engines';
– The wireless operator should have been called;
– Captain Lord on being called should have at once gone to the bridge, verified that the engine room was at readiness and the wireless operator at his post, and then got underway towards the apparent source of the rockets.

Of Stone's lack of action, the report stated: 'The impression... of Captain Lord is that, far from being slack as has sometimes been suggested, he was in fact something of a martinet, and [therefore] the young officer [Second Officer Stone] may have feared to leave the bridge... even though under the circumstances it would have been a safe and right thing to do':

A final word seems called for on the aftermath of the formal investigation and its findings so far as Captain Lord is concerned. He lost his post with the Leyland Line, but soon gained employment with another British company, Lawther Latta, quickly regaining command: he remained at sea throughout the Great War and into the 1920s with that company. He died in 1962. No formal action was ever taken against him, even though the conduct of his ship, as found by the court, seems clearly to call for inquiry into his fitness to continue to hold a Certificate of Competency. Examination of contemporary records shows that proceedings were considered but does not make it entirely clear why they were not pursued. Part of the reason may have been that, with the weight of a recent formal investigation headed by a very senior and distinguished judge, it was seen as difficult for there to be a completely unprejudiced inquiry. Be that as it may, it is difficult not to believe that some at least of those responsible at the Board of Trade felt a substantial measure of doubt as to the justice of the findings. It is not surprising if this were so: the case has continued to divide opinion to this day, and has been argued strenuously both on Captain Lord's behalf and against him. Some of the arguments have been well-reasoned but some – on both sides – have been absurd and scurrilous.

Neither party will be entirely satisfied with this report, but while it does not purport to answer all the questions which have been raised it does attempt to distinguish the essential circumstances and set out reasoned and realistic interpretations. It is for others if they wish to go further into speculation; it is to be hoped that they will do so rationally and with some regard to the simple fact that there are no villains in this story: just human beings with human characteristics.

APPENDIX NINE
GERMANIC: TITANIC'S REPLACEMENT?

'We can replace the money, but not the lives. It is horrible.' Philip Franklin, IMM's vice president, was deeply distressed as it became clear that there had been 'a horrible loss of life'. To make matters worse, he had to speak to enquiring reporters when he did not know the full facts. His comments were reported in a number of newspapers such as the American *Evening Tribune* in Minnesota on 16 April 1912.

The White Star Line had lost the finest vessel in their fleet. *Olympic* and *Oceanic* remained, while *Majestic* was called back into service from Southampton by the end of May 1912. *Britannic* would not be ready for service for several years. How, then, were they to maintain their passenger service?

They were able to make do for the time being. Although all three ships showed drops in passenger numbers in 1912, compared to 1911, and there were also fewer sailings, a good year was around the corner. Following her refit, *Olympic* did not return to service until April 1913, but even so she carried almost half of the White Star Line's passengers on the Southampton to New York service that year. *Titanic*'s loss undoubtedly held the company back; nonetheless, *Olympic*, *Oceanic* and *Majestic* together carried just over 68,000 passengers. It was the highest number that the White Star Line's express ships had carried since the service had been established at Southampton in 1907. Even better, the number of crossings was lower than in 1908, 1909 and 1910, so that the average number of passengers rose to 811. The figure was largely *Olympic*'s achievement: she carried an average of 1,325 passengers to *Oceanic*'s 710 passengers and *Majestic*'s 501 passengers.

Majestic was withdrawn from service the following year. When she left New York for the final time, on 30 January 1914, she did particularly badly and carried only five first-class, thirty-one second-class and eighty-eight third-class passengers. During the months before the war in 1914, *Olympic* and *Oceanic* continued to do well, but the gap between them widened; *Oceanic*'s average passenger lists were half those of *Olympic*. *Britannic*'s completion by 1915 would bring a welcome addition to the fleet.

What about a replacement for *Titanic*? The original plans envisaged three '*Olympic*' class liners maintaining the service and even with *Britannic*'s arrival it was clear that *Oceanic* would need replacing in time. It is sometimes asserted that the planned *Germanic* would serve as a smaller replacement for the lost ship, but according to IMM's annual report for 1913:

> Your directors have authorised the construction of a steamer of about 33,600 tons and 19 knots speed for the New York–Liverpool service of the White Star Line, to be named *Germanic*, and to be of the *Adriatic* type, with such alterations and improvements as experience has suggested and as are made possible by her greater size. It is expected the *Germanic* will be completed in time to enter the service in 1916, and that she will be an exceedingly attractive steamer.

Her speed would be a little slow for the express service, but as an improved version of the 'Big Four' she would be well suited for Liverpool. Harold Sanderson, the White Star Line's new chairman and managing director, explained in June 1914 that: 'We are building a new ship for the Liverpool–New York service, which is to be called the *Germanic*, and it will be a larger ship than the *Adriatic* but would be smaller than the *Olympic*.' He indicated that her length overall would be about 746ft.

Sanderson's comments bear out a record for an order with Harland & Wolff. Yard Number 470 was originally entered as *Germanic* and then renamed *Homeric*, probably with the outbreak of war, but her technical specifications are quite interesting. The length between perpendiculars, 720ft, matches Sanderson's description for a ship that was slightly longer overall; she was to be 88ft in breadth and her propelling machinery would consist of reciprocating engines driving a central propeller. *Homeric* was among a number of steamers listed as 'under construction' and on a list of the White Star fleet at 31 December 1915 there were payments of £103,041 14*s* 5*d* listed against her, but she was certainly not intended to be a replacement for *Titanic*.★

Was there a definite plan to directly replace her? According to Michael Moss and John Hume's excellent history of Harland & Wolff, 'by the close of the 1913–14 financial year the company had contracts for thirty steamers' including '*Ceric*, the replacement for the *Titanic*, of a projected 60,000 gross tons. The *Ceric* was allocated ship No.391, previously reserved for the cancelled Hamburg Amerika liner *Europa*. On 1 January 1914 Edward Wilding, who had already made designs for this massive vessel, was appointed a managing director of the company.'[1] The order for *Europa* was certainly cancelled and her yard number 391 was reassigned to *Belgenland*. However, there appears to be little further information. If design work had been undertaken, then there does not seem to have been any public announcement that the order had been placed, unlike previous vessels, and the war intervened in any case.

★ It appears that the circumstances of war led to the cancellation of the project, but there is an interesting reference indicating that some construction or assembly work had been undertaken. At one Harland & Wolff managing director meeting, it was proposed to draw 'No.470 farther up the slip to enable two standard ships class "D" 284ft long to be laid down.' Lord Pirrie 'approved the proposal'.

APPENDIX TEN
BRITANNIC & AQUITANIA COMPARISONS

Cunard's *Aquitania* entered service in May 1914, less than a year before *Britannic*'s anticipated maiden voyage. The two ships shared a number of similarities: both were four stackers; both were the third unit of a planned three-ship express service; and their respective owners claimed them to be the largest British ship. Using each ship's size in terms of gross tonnage, it is clear that *Britannic*, as completed, was larger than *Aquitania* (48,158grt verses 45,647grt); *Aquitania*'s dubious claim rested solely on the basis that she was almost 20ft longer overall.★

It is interesting to draw some comparisons:

	Britannic	*Aquitania*
Laid down	30 November 1911	5 June 1911
Launched	26 February 1914	21 April 1913
Maiden voyage	23 December 1915	30 May 1914[1]
Length (overall)	882ft 9in	901ft 6in[2]
Beam	94ft (maximum 95ft 6in)	97ft[3]
Beam/length ratio	1:9.4	1:9.3
Net tonnage	24,592	17,500
Gross tonnage	48,158	45,647
Displacement	53,170 tons	49,430 tons
Watertight bulkheads	16, up to 40ft above the waterline	16, up to 19ft above the waterline
Flotation capacity	6 compartments flooded forward or 7 compartments flooded aft	5 compartments flooded forward or aft[4]
Engine types	2 triple-expansion reciprocating engines; 1 low-pressure turbine	4 steam turbines
Service speed	21 knots	23 knots[5]
Maximum speed	24 knots	24-25 knots
Passengers – 1st	790	618
– 2nd	836	614
– 3rd	953	1,998
Crew	950	972
Total complement	3,529	4,202
Last voyage	19 November 1916	November 1949[6]
Length of service	1 year	36 years
Fate	Sunk: 21 November 1916	Scrapped: February 1950

★ Was *Aquitania* ever the largest British ship? Certainly she was longer than *Olympic* but, as we have seen earlier, by the time *Aquitania* was in service *Olympic*'s gross tonnage had been increased from its original 45,324grt to 46,358grt. *Olympic* and *Britannic* were both larger than the Cunard ship by that key measure. *Britannic* was the largest British-built ship until the advent of Cunard's *Queen Mary*; *Olympic* was the largest British-built ship in service from 1916 until 1935.

APPENDIX ELEVEN

BRITANNIC 'SUMMARY OF FIRST COST'

On 12 March 1917, the White Star Line received Harland & Wolff's 'final account' showing the 'total expenditure' or first cost of the ship and the interest incurred during construction. The White Star Line added their own expenses to reach the final figure. 'In arriving at this amount we have given credit for the outfit retained at Liverpool and Southampton, or which has been warehoused by the suppliers pending instructions to deliver. These goods we will use as opportunity occurs, either in connection with our present fleet or when constructing new vessels.'

RMS *Britannic*

No.433

Summary of First Cost

First Cost & Commission – per Messrs Harland & Wolff's account:		£1,920,963 0s 10d
Interest during construction:		£15,042 2s 7d
Expenditure incurred by owners:		
Cumberland Engineering Co.:		£1,335 17s 0d
Sundry stores & fittings:		£647 17s 6d
Electro plate, equipment and outfit:	£26,558 9s 5d	
Less retained on shore at Liverpool and Southampton, or with suppliers:	£18,784 9s 1d	£7,774 0s 4d
Furniture, fittings and sundries:		£567 19s 11d
Sundry expenses including supervision:		£1,446 7s 8d
		£11,792 7s 8d
		£1,947,797 5s 10d

APPENDIX TWELVE
OLYMPIC'S NEW RUNNING MATES

If everything had gone to plan, *Olympic* would have served her time on the express service operating in conjunction with two nearly identical sister ships. They were designed to operate the service together and make the same service speed; they had very similar accommodation; and their 'family resemblance' would encourage a feeling of comfort and familiarity to regular travellers. While the White Star Line were able to plug the gap with two ships acquired from Germany and create an acceptable express service, there were considerable differences between the ships.★ All details given here are accurate for 1924.

	Homeric	*Olympic*	*Majestic*
Length	774ft	882ft 9in	956ft
Breadth	82ft	92ft 6in	100ft
Draught	36ft	34ft 6in	38ft
Gross tonnage	34,351 tons	46,439 tons	56,551 tons
Engines	2 reciprocating engines, 32,000 horsepower[1]	2 reciprocating engines and 1 low-pressure turbine, 59,000+ horsepower	4 turbines, 100,000 horsepower
Service speed	19½ knots	21 knots	23½ knots
First class	529	750	875
Second class	487	500	725
Third class	1,750[2]	1,150	2,216[3]
Highest annual number of passengers carried	16,774 (1922)	37,535 (1921)	37,949 (1928)
Lowest annual number of passengers carried	5,897 (1931)	9,129 (1933)	13,573 (1933)
Years of North Atlantic express service	10 years	18 years	14 years
Total active service	14 years	24 years	14 years

★ Despite attempts to increase *Homeric's* service speed, she was never quite fast enough as a running mate for *Olympic* and *Majestic*. We can see this all too clearly in the figures for the three ships' average speeds during 1923, even though her two running mates recorded higher speeds in subsequent years: *Homeric*: 18.11 knots; *Olympic*: 21.44 knots; and *Majestic*: 23.29 knots.

APPENDIX THIRTEEN
NORTH ATLANTIC SERVICE 1931

B y 1931, the depression was taking its toll. The White Star Line's estimates* showed that only four of the ten ships listed for North Atlantic voyages that year were profitable:

	Number of Round Trips	Total Earnings	Total Disbursements	Profit
Britannic (1930)	8	£372,124	£227,119	£145,005
Olympic (1911)	16	£579,587	£499,572	£79,835
Majestic (1922)	13	£620,182	£546,486	£73,696
Baltic (1904)	11	£320,426	£274,652	£45,774

The remaining ships – *Homeric, Adriatic, Cedric, Laurentic, Doric* and *Megantic* – lost a total of £73,716 between them:

	Number of Round Trips	Total Earnings	Total Disbursements	Loss
Laurentic (1927)	10	£198,997	£205,015	£6,018
Megantic (1909)	1	£9,558	£17,863	£8,305
Homeric (1922)	8	£208,611	£217,337	£8,726
Cedric (1903)	6	£129,990	£139,447	£9,457
Doric (1923)	5	£81,318	£100,548	£19,230
Adriatic (1907)	8	£188,079	£210,059	£21,980

As well as indicating the increasing age of the fleet, the value of new motor ships such as *Britannic* was clear. By June 1932, the completion of *Britannic*'s sister ship, *Georgic*, meant that the company had two ships that were capable of generating a considerable profit. It is no wonder that Lord Essendon, the company's chairman, was enthusiastic about their performance.

---

* Described as the 'Results of Voyages – North Atlantic Service – (excluding weekend and other cruises) before charging office expenses, advertising and depreciation.' If these other charges were included then the profits would shrink even further or vanish altogether. Meanwhile, estimates could change as all the necessary information was compiled or depending on the relevant accounting treatments. (According to the results of *Majestic*'s voyages, for instance, which Cunard recorded as their half-share of her profits for their own accounts, she showed a deficit of £16,906 in 1931. See *RMS Majestic: The 'Magic Stick'*, Tempus Publishing, 2006.) The purpose of the figures is to illustrate a general trend.

APPENDIX FOURTEEN
BRITANNIC REMEMBRANCE

*B*ritannic's dead are remembered on various memorials throughout more than one country and four victims are buried in Piraeus Municipal Cemetery. Although there no individual memorials to the ship, many of her dead are mentioned on memorials from the Great War.

In Greece, the Mikra memorial – 'in the form of two groups of panels on the wall behind the Cross of Sacrifice' – contains names from various ships lost between 1915 and 1917; the Transports *Marquette*, *Ivernia*, *Arcadian*, Fleet Messenger *Princess Alberta*, plus the Hospital Ships *Britannic*, *Braemar Castle* and HMS *Sentinel*. It is at the south end of the Mikra British Cemetery, about 5 miles (8 kilometres) south of Thessaloniki, in the municipality of Kalamaria, on the road leading to the airport. Access can be made using the main entrance of Vryoylon Street, which is directly opposite the communal cemetery of Kalamaria. It contains the following eight names from *Britannic*:

> Cropper, Captain [sic: Lieutenant], John, RAMC. Drowned at sea, 21 November 1916. Son of Edward and Theodosia Cropper, of Fernhead, Great Crosby; husband of Anne E. Cropper, of Mount Ballan, Chepstow, Monmouthshire.
>
> Freebury, Private, Henry, 52640. RAMC. Drowned at sea, 21 November 1916. Age 31. Son of Mrs C. Freebury, of Clarence Cottages, Miserton; husband of Miriam Bilton (formerly Freebury), of High Street, Miserton, Doncaster.
>
> Jones, Private, Thomas, 84010. RAMC. Drowned at sea, 21 November 1916.
>
> King, Private, George William, 41692. RAMC. Drowned at sea, 21 November 1916. Age 24. Son of Herbert and Sarah King, of 21 Greenbank Avenue, New Brighton, Wallasey, Cheshire. Wounded in France in 1916.
>
> Sharpe, Sergeant, William, 12423. RAMC. Drowned at sea, 21 November 1916. Age 39. Son of Elizabeth Norah and the late John Sharpe. Served in the South African Campaign.★
>
> Smith, Private, Leonard, 40213. RAMC. Drowned at sea, 21 November 1916.
>
> Stone, Private, William, 35188. RAMC. Drowned at sea, 21 November 1916. Age 23. Son of Harry and Polly Stone, of 17, Dudley Street, Walsall, Staffs; husband of Anna Wilks (formerly Stone).
>
> Bostock, Private, George James, 81292. RAMC. Drowned at sea, 21 November 1916.

Another place is a fenced plot within Piraeus Municipal Cemetery at Drapetsona on the Western outskirts of Piraeus. From Piraeus' central port it is necessary to take Akti Kondila (west) into Kekropos (north), then to turn onto Anapafseos, following this west and north until the entrance is found. With only one exception, the war graves are situated in a group around the monument

---

★ Although Sergeant William Sharpe's name was recorded on the Mikra memorial, in fact it did not belong there, for the memorial was intended to list those who had been lost at sea and whose bodies had not been recovered. He passed away around noon on the day of the sinking and the French vice-consul arranged his burial in the cemetery of the church of Agios Trias, overlooking Port St Nikolo. Several years later he was moved to the New British Cemetery, which brought together all of the British war graves in the Cyclades and was 'established in June 1921 in the town of Ermoupoli on the Greek island of Syra (Siros)'. Unfortunately, he was mistakenly identified as 'Corporal Stephens' in October 1919 and it was only in 2009 that arrangements could be made to rectify the error. (The detective process is fascinating and involved a number of people, including *Britannic* researchers Michail Michailakis and Simon Mills. For the full story, see Mills' 'The Odyssey of Sergeant William Sharpe', *Titanic Commutator*, *Titanic* Historical Society, 2009.)

The Tower Hill Memorial in London, photographed in August 2007. It contains the names of eighteen of *Britannic*'s victims and was erected: 'To the Glory of God and to the Honour of Twelve Thousand of the Merchant Navy and fishing fleets who have no Grave but the Sea 1914-18.' (Author's collection)

to the marines and sailors of HMS *Exmouth* and the flagship *Duncan*, who were killed in December 1916 during gunnery. There are four *Britannic* graves at this site:

> Binks, Private, Arthur M. M., 33642. HMHS *Britannic*. RAMC 21 November 1916.
> Brown, Fireman, Joseph, HMHS *Britannic*. Mercantile Marine. 21 November 1916. Age
>   41. Husband of Ellen Brown, of 79, Bevois Street, Southampton. Born at Manchester.
> Honeycott, Seaman, G., HMHS *Britannic*. Mercantile Marine. 21 November 1916.
> Phillips, Trimmer, Charles James David, HMHS *Britannic*. Mercantile Marine.
>   21 November 1916. Age 23. son of Joseph and Bessie Phillips, of 'River View', West
>   End Road, Bursledon, Hants.

Many people are also remembered at the Tower Hill Memorial, London. It, as the name implies, stands on Tower Hill, London, on the south side of the pleasure garden of Trinity Square. An impressive monument, it is constructed of Portland stone, consisting of a 21½-metre-long corridor, 7 metres in width and a maximum of 10 metres high, being open at both ends. There are eighteen names from *Britannic*.

> Babey, Trimmer, Robert Charles, SS *Britannic* (Liverpool). Mercantile Marine. Died
>   21 November 1916. Age 24. Son of the late Robert Charles Babey and of Elizabeth
>   Babey, of Hook Lane, Warsash, Southampton.
> Crawford, 4th Butcher, Thomas Archibald, SS *Britannic* (Liverpool). Mercantile Marine. Died
>   21 November 1916. Age 27. Son of Elizabeth Jane Crawford, of 1, Argo Rd., Waterloo,
>   Liverpool, and the late Thomas Archibald Crawford. Born at Higher Tranmere.

Dennis, Trimmer, Arthur, HMHS *Britannic* (Liverpool). Mercantile Marine. Killed by mine, 21 November 1916. Son of Arthur and Emily Dennis, of Mansbridge Cottages, Swaythling, Southampton.

Earley, Fireman, Frank Joseph, HMHS *Britannic* (Liverpool). Mercantile Marine. Killed by mine, 21 November 1916. Age 47. Son of Catherine and the late William Earley; husband of Mary Ann Earley, of 6, Lower Back of Walls, Southampton. Born at Southampton.

Garland, Steward, Charles Claude Seymour, HMHS *Britannic* (Liverpool). Mercantile Marine. Killed by mine, 21 November 1916. Age 33. Son of Annie Romie Garland, of 150, Shirley Road, Southampton, and the late Alfred Garland. Born at Bristol.

George, Scullion, Leonard, SS *Britannic* (Liverpool). Mercantile Marine. Killed by mine 21 November 1916. Age 15. Son of Thomas and Catherine Elizabeth George (*née* Groves), of 15, Compton Walk, Southampton. Born at Southampton.

Gillespie, Second Electrician, Pownall, HMHS *Britannic* (Liverpool). Mercantile Marine. Killed by mine, 21 November 1916. Age 34. Son of Alice Matilda Gillespie (*née* Griffiths), of 7, Marine Terrace, Liscard, Cheshire, and the late William Gillespie. Born at Liverpool.

Godwin, Fireman, George William, HMHT *Britannic* (Liverpool). Mercantile Marine. Killed by mine, 21 November 1916. Age 28. Son of James and the late Ellen Godwin; husband of Charlotte Dorothy Madeline Godwin (*née* Woods), of 90, Belvoir Valley, Southampton. Born in Dorset.

Jenkins, Second Baker, Walter, HMHS *Britannic* (Liverpool). Mercantile Marine. Killed by mine, 21 November 1916. Age 39. Son of the late William and Margaret Jenkins; husband of Edith Jenkins (*née* Bates), of 260, Commercial Road, Liverpool. Born at Egremont, Cheshire.

McDonald, Taylor, Asst Ck Thomas, HMHS *Britannic* (Liverpool). Mercantile Marine. Killed by mine, 21 November 1916. Age 24. Son of Mary Taylor (formerly McDonald), of 5, Macqueen Street, Saint Oswald Street, Liverpool.

McFeat, Fireman, John George, HMHS *Britannic* (Liverpool). Mercantile Marine. Killed by mine, 21 November 1916. Age 27. Son of Jane and the late Mr McFeat; husband of Ellen Louisa McFeat (*née* Lewis), of 19, Bevois Street, Southampton. Born at Southampton.

Philps, Fireman, George Bradbury, HMHS *Britannic* (Liverpool). Mercantile Marine. Killed by mine, 21 November 1916. Age 41. Son of Harriett and the late Edward Philps; husband of Emily Louisa Philps (*née* Rose) of 4, Roman Street, Southampton. Born at Alton.

Rice, Steward, James Patrick, HMHS *Britannic* (Liverpool). Mercantile Marine. Killed by mine, 21 November 1916. Age 22. Son of James and Margaret Rice, of 13, Denbigh Street, Bootle, Lancashire.

Sherin, Greaser, George, HMHS *Britannic* (Liverpool). Mercantile Marine. Killed by mine, 21 November 1916. Age 42. Son of the late Joseph and Caroline Sherin; husband of Emily Sherin (*née* Pearce) of 4, West Place, Chapel Road, Southampton. Born at Southampton.

Smith, Fireman, William, HMHS *Britannic* (Liverpool). Mercantile Marine. Killed by mine, 21 November 1916. Age 29. Born in London.

Toogood, Steward, Henry James, HMHS *Britannic* (Liverpool). Mercantile Marine. Killed by mine, 21 November 1916. Age 48. Son of the late James and Henrietta Toogood; husband of Caroline Toogood (formerly Ramsey, *née* Davis), of 19, Chantry Road, Southampton. Born at Southampton.

★ The cemetery is known today as Ford Park Cemetery and 'contains 752 burials from the First World War, more than 200 of them in a naval plot, the rest scattered throughout the cemetery. All of the 198 Second World War burials are scattered, one of which is an unidentified airman of the Royal Air Force (RAF). There are a further four foreign national and one non world war service burials here.' There are a total of 955 burials, including the unidentified airman of the Royal Air Force.

> Tully, Steward, Thomas Francis, HMHS *Britannic* (Liverpool). Mercantile Marine. Killed by mine, 21 November 1916. Age 38. Son of the late Mr and Mrs James Tully; husband of Catherine Tully (*née* Woodall), of 49, Tennyson Street, Peel Road, Bootle, Lancashire. Born at Roscommon.
>
> White, Trimmer, Percival William Ernest, HMHS *Britannic* (Liverpool). Mercantile Marine. Killed by mine, 21 November 1916. Age 18. Son of James Albert and Nellie Elizabeth Mary White, of 28, College Street, Saint James, Southampton.

Although the ship's log recorded that twenty-one crew members and nine RAMC personnel had died in the sinking, for a total of thirty casualties, there are several instances where it appears possible or probable that people died as a result of the sinking in the following months and years. The Commonwealth War Graves Commission records contain the name of one crew member not listed in the log – Steward Genn – bringing the death toll up to 31. According to these records, in the United Kingdom there is one identified *Britannic* grave at the Plymouth Old Cemetery (Pennycomequick), Devon, England,★ where there are 200 graves in a naval plot:

> Genn, Steward, S., SS *Britannic*. Mercantile Marine. 9 May 1917. Church S. 5. 10.

Britannic's log records that Steward Genn had been injured during the sinking and subsequently admitted to the Russian Hospital at Piraeus. He was not included in the initial casualty list because his death occurred several months afterwards on 9 May 1917 and, although it is interesting to speculate that his death was accelerated or caused by the injuries and experiences of the sinking, the precise reason is currently unknown.

There is another interesting story relating to one of *Britannic*'s survivors:

> Rebecca McMurray Munro
> Royal Red Cross Sister
> Queen Alexandra's Imperial Military Nursing Service (Reserve)
> Died of wounds on 30 April 1920 as a result of the sinking of HMHS *Britannic* off the island of Kea in the Aegean Sea on 21 November 1916. Age 32.
> Daughter of John Munro and Elizabeth Shaw of Montrose.
> Montrose (Rosehill) Cemetery[1]

Rebecca Munro was born on 20 November 1887 in Montrose, Scotland, being educated at Southesk School. She soon went into nursing, beginning her training at the age of twenty-three. Having initially trained as a nurse at the City of Westminster Infirmary in London from June 1911 to October 1912, then from September 1913 until April 1915, she eventually joined QAIMNSR – Queen Alexandra's Imperial Nursing Service Reserve – and served on board *Britannic* from April 1916. During her time aboard ship, she nursed servicemen suffering from a number of illnesses, including those with tuberculosis on at least two voyages. Surviving the ship's sinking, Rebecca Munro was given leave and during her time ashore she became ill. Diagnosed with tuberculosis, she was discharged because she was 'permanently unfit for any Army service' following an Army Medical Board meeting in mid-March 1917. Entitled to an Army Pension and to wear the Silver War Badge (to show that she had been invalided out of active service), she was admitted to Noranside Sanatorium, near Brechin, Montrose, for urgent treatment that month, at the age of twenty-nine. Following her untimely death, Rebecca Munro's parents commissioned her gravestone to state that her wounds had been a result of *Britannic*'s sinking, possibly as an attempt to avoid the social stigma that tuberculosis used to bring. Although not recognised by the Commonwealth War Graves Commission (because she was a member of the QAIMNRS), Rebecca Munro's death occurred as a result of her active participation in the war. To this day she is the only woman on the Montrose War Memorial, among some three hundred names.

It is fortunate that the Hospital Ship *Britannic*'s sinking was not accompanied by the high death toll that it might have been, particularly had she been returning to Southampton, full from Mudros. But her victims are among the millions who were needlessly killed as a result of the First World War, and who lie overlooking a 'corner of a foreign field'.

APPENDIX FIFTEEN

UK HYDROGRAPHIC OFFICE DETAILS OF THE WRECK OF THE HMHS *BRITANNIC*

Details of the wreck of the *Britannic* held by the United Kingdom Hydrographic Office:*

Wreck Number: 39034
Symbol: NDW (Non-dangerous wreck)
Classification: Unclassified
Old Number: 101502722
Category: Non-dangerous wreck
World Geodetic System 1984: Latitude **37°42′083 North** *Longitude* **24° 17′033 East**†
Horizontal Datum: European 1950
Position Method: Satellite Navigation transit
Position Quality: Precisely known
General Depth: 110 metres
Vertical Datum: Mean low water springs
Depth Quality: Unknown
Existence Doubtful: No
Last Amended Details: 11 September 1991
Name: Britannic
Type: Steamship
Nationality: British
Dimensions: Length, b.p. 259.7 metres, (852ft 6in). *Beam* 28.7 metres, (94ft). *Draught:*** 18 metres, (64ft 3in).
Tonnage: 48,158 gross.
Date Sunk: 21 November 1916.
Circumstances of Loss: Vessel, built 1914 as a White Star Liner, was taken over by Admiralty for use as a hospital ship before completion. She was en-route to Salonika with 625 crew & 500 medical officers, to take on board wounded when she struck a mine in the Kea Channel. The mine had been laid only an hour earlier by German submarine *U73*. *Britannic* sank in a short time with loss of thirty lives. (*Dictionary of Disasters at Sea*)
Surveying Details
12 January 1960. European position: **37°39′10 North, 24°09′42 East**

   H3592/73. 4 December 1975 wreck located and identified by *Calypso* (Commander Cousteau and divers) in satellite navigation position **37°42′05 North, 24°17′02 East** (European). Lying in general depth 110 metres. Stated to have least depth of approximately 80 metres. (Telecom to W.O. dated 3 December 1975 and U.W.I. letter 12739/4/4 dated 3 December 1975)

   20 October 1993. Not shown on Greek chart 421 – no chart action. (Non-dangerous wreck at this depth below the sea's surface is not considered a hazard to surface shipping.)

   7 November 1995. Negotiations taking place between the Greek Government/Liverpool museums and Dr Robert Ballard to turn the wreck site into an underwater museum for 'Teletourists'. (*Daily Telegraph*, 24 October 1995)

   1 November 1999. Lying on starboard side. Bow section (forward of the bridge) separated from main body of ship by a break just in front of the bridge. Good visibility. Full description of wreck given. (*Diver*, January 1999)

APPENDIX SIXTEEN
GLOSSARY OF TECHNICAL ABBREVIATIONS

GRT   Gross registered tonnage: a measure of space and expresses the entire interior cubic capacity of the ship, as recorded on the register. Each ton is 100 cubic feet.

HP   Horsepower: a unit of power. One horsepower is 33,000ft lb of work performed in a minute.

IHP   Indicated horsepower: a term that is applied to the horsepower that is actually developed in the cylinders of an engine. In the case of the '*Olympic*' class ships, it refers to the piston-based reciprocating engines.

NHP   Nominal horsepower: a term of measurement of an engine's power. It is based upon the dimensions of the engine rather than its performance and the actual power developed. It was disregarded increasingly by the end of the nineteenth century.

NRT   Net registered tonnage: a measure of space and expresses the internal cubic capacity of a ship after certain specific spaces have been deducted from the figure of gross tonnage. These deductible spaces include areas such as the crew's quarters and machinery compartments. It is recorded on the register. Each ton is 100 cubic feet.

PSI   Pounds per square inch: a measurement of pressure. In this work, it will refer typically to the steam pressure in the boilers or engines on board the '*Olympic*' class ships.

RPM   Revolutions per minute: typically referring to the number of times a propeller revolves every minute.

SHP   Shaft horsepower: a term applied to the power of turbine engines, which is measured from the shaft by an instrument called a torsion meter. In the case of the '*Olympic*' class ships, it refers to the low-pressure turbine which drove the centre propeller.

ENDNOTES

CHAPTER 1

1 E & H TT, page 12.
2 Gardiner, page 18.
3 Marriott, page 10.
4 E & H TT, page 12.
5 Marriott, page 12.
6 E & H TT, page 12.
7 *Shipbuilder*, page 5.
8 Riddle, page 40.
9 *Merchant Fleets*, page 30.
10 *Merchant Fleets*, page 11.
11 E & H F S, pages 14–15.
12 E & H T T, page 12.
13 *Lost Liners*, pages 30 and 32.
14 Butler, page 5.
15 *Merchant Fleets*, page 31.
16 Butler, page 5.
17 *Merchant Fleets*, page 37.
18 *The Liners*, page 40; *Shipbuilder*, page 5.
19 *Merchant Fleets*, page 42.
20 E & H TT, pages 12–13.
21 *The Liners*, pages 39–43.
22 Marriott, page 14
23 *The Liners*, page 41.
24 *Shipbuilder*, pages 5–6.
25 Marriott, page 13.
26 See Günter Bäbler's article 'The Dinner at Lord Pirrie's in Summer 1907: Just a Legend?' in *Titanic Post*, Swiss *Titanic* Society, 2000.

CHAPTER 2

1 E & H DD, page 53.
2 Shipbuilders to the World, page 19. The book can be regarded as a definitive history of Harland & Wolff and is well worth reading for anyone with an interest in the shipbuilding firm.
3 E & H DD, page 53

CHAPTER 3

1 Many details taken from 'Table I: Large Atlantic Liners', *Shipbuilder*, page 18; and Report, pages 4–5.
2 *Mauretania*, pages 15, 21; *Lusitania*, page 23.
3 Report, page 5.
4 *Mauretania*, page 17.
5 E & H DD, page 171.
6 *The Liners*, page 46.
7 *Lost Liners*, page 45.
8 *Lost Liners*, page 44 (pictures and captions).
9 Report, pages 34–35 (deck plans).
10 *Lost Liners*, page 49.
11 *Aquitania*, pages 4–5.
12 (Length and Breadth). *Famous Ships of the Clyde*, Jack Webster, The Glasgow Royal Concert Hall, 1995; page 41.
13 *Aquitania*, page 5.
14 *Aquitania*, pages 35–36.
15 *Aquitania*, pages 23–29.
16 *Aquitania*, pages 29–31; *Shipbuilder 2*, *Aquitania* plans 'Plate VII'.

CHAPTER 4

1 E & H, page 20.
2 Gardiner, page 24.
3 Birth, page 116.
4 Voices, page 11.
5 Voices, pages 11–13 (three sentences).
6 Voices, page 32.
7 *Olympic*, page 8; E & H TT, page 51, footnote.
8 Hutchings, page 9; E & H TT, page 51.
9 Hutchings, pages 9–10;
Olympic, pages 8 and 15; Voices, pages 28, 32–33; E & H TT, pages 51–52.
10 E & H TT,
11 Voices, page 29.
12 Voices, pages 29, 30 and 31.
13 *Lost Liners*, page 78;
Olympic, page 8.
14 E & H JJ, page 26.
15 '*Titanic*', Peter Thresh,
Parkgate Books, 1998; page 11.
16 Article by Paul Louden Brown, '*Titanic*'s "Brittle" Steel?' *The Titanic Commutator*, *Titanic* Historical Society. My thanks to Paul Louden Brown, Mr Edward Kamuda and Mrs Karen Kamuda.
17 *Shipbuilder 2*, pages 95, 98–106.
18 E & H TT, page 33.
19 *Shipbuilder*, page 43.
20 *Shipbuilder*, page 129.
21 Power, page 106; Ismay Line, page 172.
22 Gardiner, page 48.
23 *Shipbuilder*, page 129.
24 Riddle, page 13.
25 Gardiner, page 50.
26 Birth, page 96.
27 Lord, page 25.
28 Gardiner, page 49.

29 Hutchings, page 9.
30 Hutchings, page 17.
31 Butler, page 21.
32 E & H TT, page 45.
33 Gardiner, page 49.
34 E & H TT, page 45.

CHAPTER 5

1 Voices, page 33.
2 Lost Liners, pages 77 and 81.
3 Shipbuilder, page 153.
4 Sea Breezes magazine, February 1956, 'The
  Great Olympic', by J. H. Isherwood.
5 Voices, page 33.
6 Voices, pages 50–51.
7 Voices, page 44; page 35.
8 E & H TT, page 65.
9 Jessop, page 102.
10 Jessop, page 103.
11 Marsh, page 67.
12 Lynch, page 40.
13 Marsh, page 13.
14 Jessop, page 102.
15 Voices, pages 34–35.
16 Voices, pages 34–35.
17 Riddle, page 15.
18 Butler, page 18.
19 Shipbuilder, page 81.
20 Shipbuilder, page 90.
21 Menu
22 Shipbuilder, page 100.
23 E & H DD, page 79.
24 Riddle, page 102–103.
25 Shipbuilder, page 68.
26 Shipbuilder, page 69.
27 Shipbuilder, page 69.
28 Shipbuilder, pages 91 and 95.
29 Shipbuilder, page 100.
30 Shipbuilder, page 100, bottom. (Several
   sentences.)
31 Shipbuilder, page 102, top.
32 Shipbuilder, page 102, middle.
33 Shipbuilder, page 102, bottom.
34 Shipbuilder, page 104, bottom.
35 Shipbuilder, page 105, top.
36 Shipbuilder, page 106.
37 Shipbuilder, page 106, bottom.
38 Shipbuilder, page 107, middle.
39 Ismay Line, page 175.
40 Ismay Line, page 172.
41 Hutchings, page 10.
42 Voices, page 35.
43 Olympic, page 15.
44 (Information about Deutschland, Lusitania,
   Mauretania.) Lusitania, page 22; Lost Liners,
   pages 48, 168; Liners, page 41.
45 Ismay Line, page 173.

46 Mills, page 6.
47 Lord, page 39.
48 Olympic, page 15.
49 Lord, page 39–40.
50 Wels, page 36.
51 Voices, page 35.
52 Wels, page 43.
53 Sea Breezes magazine, February 1956, 'The
   Great Olympic', by J. H. Isherwood.
54 Article 'Ismay and the Titanic' by Paul
   Louden-Brown, The Titanic Commutator,
   Titanic Historical Society. (Excerpted from
   'The White Star Line; An Illustrated History
   1869–1934'.); Merseyside Maritime Museum
   documents, DX/504/1/1-16.
55 Liverpool University Library, 'D42/S7/3/75'
56 Olympic, page 16.
57 National Archives files TS 36/175–195
58 George Behe's Titanic titbits: http://
   ourworld.compuserve.com/homepages/
   Carpathia/page2.htm
59 Olympic, page 22.
60 Atlantic Daily Bulletin, Journal of the British
   Titanic Society, number 1, 2001, page 10,
   quoting the Daily Mail, 2 April 1912.
61 Voices, page 221.
62 An interesting article by Maurice Weaver
   and Edwin Steel, with thanks from Brian
   Ticehurst. 'As Titanic's Sister Ship Headed
   for the Rocks' in Titanic Commutator, Titanic
   Historical Society, 1988. Captain Benjamin
   Steel, who remained White Star's marine
   superintendent at Southampton from 1909
   until the late 1920s, confided in his son Edwin
   and swore him to secrecy. It was only at the
   age of 82 that he felt that he was released from
   the promise to his father.
63 Sea Breezes magazine, February 1956, 'The
   Great Olympic', by J.H. Isherwood. (Whole
   paragraph.)
64 E & H TT, page 330.
65 Sea Breezes magazine, February 1956, 'The
   Great Olympic', by J.H. Isherwood.
66 Jessop, page 162–163.
67 Jessop, page 164.
68 E & H F S, page 139.
69 E & H F S, page 139.
70 National Archives file MT 10/1805
71 National Archives file MT 10/1805
72 National Archives file MT 23/781
73 Hull down, pages 177–179. Practically every
   mention of Hayes' personal experiences aboard
   Olympic at this point onwards are taken from
   his memoirs unless referenced otherwise; pages
   177–277.
74 Titanic and her Sisters, page 202.
75 National Archives file MT 23/470
76 National Archives file WO 95/4359
77 National Archives file MT 23/535

78 National Archives file MT 23/501
79 Bonsall, pages 57–58; White Star, pages 126 and 159.
80 National Archives file MT 23/615
81 E & H F S, page 195.
82 My thanks to Bill Smy, who generously shared his research on the 176th Battalion of the Canadian Expeditionary Force. Daily Record, 4 and 7 June 1917.
83 *Titanic and her Sisters*, page 206.
84 National Archives file MT 9/1146
85 *Olympic*, page 47.
86 *Four stackers*, page 136.
87 *Olympic*, page 44–45.
88 *Olympic*, page 45.
89 *Four stackers*, page 136.
90 *Four stackers*, page 136.
91 E & H F S, page 142.
92 *Titanic and her Sisters*, page 206; *Olympic*, page 45.
93 Although Captain Hayes' experiences are all taken from his memoir, this specific description is pages 240–
94 E & H JJ, page 175.
95 *Sea Breezes* magazine, February 1956. 'The Great *Olympic*', by J. H. Isherwood.
96 *Mauretania*, page 37; *Aquitania*, pages 41–45; *The Liners*, page 57.
97 *Titanic and her Sisters*, page 228.
98 *The Liners*, page 66.
99 *Olympic Titanic Britanic*, Fifth Avenue Films.
100 *Ismay Line*, page 233.
101 *Sea Breezes* magazine, February 1956, 'The Great *Olympic*', by J.H. Isherwood.
102 Bemis, pages 8–10.
103 *Lost Liners*, page 103. Inc. quote.
104 *White Star*, page 152.
105 *Shipbuilder*, page 180, top photograph, caption.
106 *Merchant Fleets*, page 20.
107 *The Mary: The Story of number 534*, by Neil Potter and Jack Frost, revised and updated by Lindsay Frost, Shipping Books press, 1998; page 7.
108 *The Liners*, page 65.
109 *Shipbuilder*, page 179.
110 Jessop, page 190.
111 *Olympic*, page 48; Gardiner, page 45.
112 E & H F S, page 215.
113 *Titanic and her Sisters*, page 176.
114 *Shipbuilder*, page 181.
115 *Shipbuilder*, page 174.
116 *The Liners*, pages 73–74.
117 *The Liners*, page 75.
118 *Glory Days: Cunard*, David L. Williams, Ian Allan, 1998; page 33.
119 Daniel Klistorner shared kindly a copy of *White Star Magazine* from April 1933, which described some of the changes.

120 Voices, page 52.
121 *The Mary: The Story of No. 534*, by Neil Potter and Jack Frost, revised and updated by Lindsay Frost, Shipping Books Press, 1998; page 46.
122 *The Mary: The Story of No. 534*, by Neil Potter and Jack Frost, revised and updated by Lindsay Frost, Shipping Books Press, 1998; page 68.
123 E & H F S, page 146.
124 *Olympic*, page 59.
125 E & H F S, page 147.
126 E & H F S, page 148.
127 *Olympic*, page 59.
128 E & H F S, page 148.
129 '*Olympic Titanic Britannic*' Fifth Avenue Films. Both quotes.
130 *Merchant Fleets*, page 72.
131 *Atlantic Daily Bulletin*, Journal of the British *Titanic* Society, Number 1, 1994; page 17.
132 See my article 'RMS *Olympic*'s Retirement', in *Titanic Post*, Swiss *Titanic* Society, published in three parts from September 2006 to March 2007. It was published in German, but a version in English is maintained online at Mark Chirnside's Reception Room (www.mark-chirnside.co.uk).
133 Liverpool University Library, 'B2/'

CHAPTER 6

1 Riddle, page 22.
2 E & H F S, page 153 & 155.
3 E & H JJ, page 40.
4 E & H JJ, page 41.
5 Butler, page 21.
6 *Inside the Titanic*, pages 4–5.
7 Birth, page 131.
8 E & H JJ, page 40.
9 Voices, page 25.
10 E & H TT, page 70.
11 Riddle, page 29.
12 E & H DD, page 70.
13 Butler, 40–41; E & H TT, page 75; E & H DD, page 83.
14 E & H TT, page 76.
15 Hutchings, page 37.
16 My thanks to George Behe, who generously shared with me a transcription of the newspaper article from the *Belfast Evening Telegraph* of 15 April 1912.
17 Lord, page 45.
18 Lord, page 51.
19 Lord, page 51; Butler, page 55.
20 *Inside the Titanic*, page 7–8.
21 Lord, page 58.
22 Gracie, pages 5–7.
23 Butler, page 49.

24 Gardiner, page 78–79.
25 Lord, page 120.
26 Gracie, page 4–5.
27 Gracie, pages 9–11.
28 Behe, page 25.
29 'Great Disasters: Dramatic True Stories of
   Nature's Awesome Powers', *Reader's Digest*,
   Reader's Digest Association, 1992; page 181.
30 Butler, page 65.
31 Lynch, page 82.
32 Behe, page 14.
33 Sam Halpern and I wrote an article, 'Speed
   and More Speed', in *Titanic Commutator*,
   Titanic Historical Society, 2007. It examines
   the question of *Titanic*'s speed during her
   maiden voyage and her intended arrival time.
   We are also indebted to the generosity of
   George Behe for sharing his research, including accounts from Trimmer William McIntyre
   and Fireman John Thompson, who were not
   called to testify at either subsequent investigation. It was George's book, *Titanic: Safety,
   Speed & Sacrifice* that was the first to examine
   all of the evidence in such detail, including
   Elisabeth Lines' statements.
34 Behe, pages 84–85, citing Leslie Reade's
   1964 interview with Fleet.
35 Lord 1, page 35.
36 Witness, page 41.
37 Jessop, pages 125–126.
38 Gracie, pages 14–15 (whole paragraph).
39 Witness, pages 42, 43, 44–45 and 49; (whole
   paragraph).
40 Jessop, pages 126–127.
41 Lynch, page 97.
42 Gracie, page 7 (whole paragraph).
43 Lynch, page 96.
44 Witness, page 50.
45 Gracie, pages 234, 244–245.
46 Lynch, page 117.
47 Lynch, page 118.
48 Butler, page 101.
49 Gardiner, page 119.
50 *Exploring the Titanic*, page 25.
51 *Exploring the Titanic*, page 25.
52 Witness, page 53, (whole paragraph).
53 See Bill Wormstedt, Tad Fitch and George
   Behe's article, 'The Lifeboat Launching
   Sequence' in *Titanic Commutator*, *Titanic*
   Historical Society, 2001. A revised and
   expanded version was made available online
   in 2009 and 2010 with contributions from
   researchers Sam Halpern and J. Kent Layton.
   These works followed George Behe's earlier
   publication, *Titanic Tidbits 1: The Launching
   of the Lifeboats: A New Chronology*, which was
   published in 1991.
54 Gracie, page 179.
55 Gracie, page 37.

56 Archie, pages 35–36.
57 Bullock, page 73.
58 Witness, page 57.
59 Jessop, pages 133–134.
60 Answers from the Abyss.
61 *Inside the Titanic*, page 30.
62 'Great Disasters: Dramatic True Stories of
   Nature's Awesome Powers', *Reader's Digest*,
   Reader's Digest Association, 1992; page 185.
63 Wade, page 128.
64 Wade, page 127.
65 Gracie, page 89.
66 Gracie, page 89.
67 Lord, page 159.
68 Lord, page 159.
69 *Exploring the Titanic*, page 61.
70 Gracie, page 77.
71 Riddle, page 171.
72 E & H DD, page 49.
73 Lynch, page 163.
74 Butler, page 169.
75 Lynch, page 176.
76 Lynch, page 175; Breaking new ground.
77 E & H DD, page 102.
78 E & H DD, page 104.
79 Butler, page 206.
80 E & H DD, page 50.
81 Lynch, page 171.
82 Butler, page 183.
83 See, *op. cit.*, 'Speed and More Speed' in
   Titanic Commutator, *Titanic* Historical Society,
   2007.
84 E & H DD, page 119.
85 E & H DD, pages 118–119.
86 Lord, page 210.
87 E & H DD, page 121–122.
88 E & H TT, page 278.
89 E & H DD, page 122.

CHAPTER 7

1 Beveridge and Hall, page 165.
2 See the article by Paul Lee and I, 'The
  Gigantic Question', in *Titanic Commutator*,
  Titanic Historical Society, 2007. It examines
  numerous sources as to the ship's name, from
  newspaper and journal reports, to our discovery of the Messrs Noah Hingley & Sons
  chain and anchor order book. Several new
  sources came to attention in a short space of
  time. The article by Simon Mills, '*Britannic*
  or *Gigantic*: *Titanic* Myth Busters', *Titanic
  Commutator*, *Titanic* Historical Society, 2007,
  was the first to publish the Harland & Wolff
  order book which gave the ship's name as
  Britannic. Jonathan Smith's '*Gigantic*: What's in
  a Name?' published the material from Messrs
  Noah Hingley & Sons for the first time and

was made available by the *Titanic* Research & Modelling Association online in 2007.

3 Voices, page 266.

4 John P. Eaton's article, 'What's in a name?', *Voyage*, *Titanic* International Society, 2006.

5 See my article, '*Olympic*'s Expansion Joints', in *Titanic Commutator*, *Titanic* Historical Society, 2007

6 *The Liners* pages 52–53.

7 *Shipbuilder*, page 153.

8 (Information about Ballin's ships.) *Shipbuilder 2*, pages 221–261, 271–283, 304; *The Liners*, pages 42 and 64; *Lost Liners*, page 103.

9 National Maritime Museum, Greenwich. 'Historic Photograph Record: *Britannic* (Br.)…1915'.

10 Last voyage, page 16; top photograph.

11 E & H TT, page 30.

12 *Shipbuilder 2*, page 173.

13 *Shipbuilder 2*, *Aquitania*, *Imperator* and *Vaterland* plans. Author's discussion with Michail Michailakis, Remco Hillen and Rolf Vonk.

14 Voices, page 266.

15 Power, page 106.

16 Last voyage, page 41, note 10, quoting *Engineering*, February 1914.

17 E & H FS, page 169.

18 Golden age, page 83.

19 Lynch, pages 22–23.

20 Description of the launching and press reports are taken from *The Times*, February 26th and 27th 1914; The *Daily Telegraph*, February 26th and 27th 1914 and others.

21 E & H DD, pages 58–59.

22 Hutchings, page 8.

23 E & H TT, page 22; Mills, pages 15 and 16; Golden age, pages 82–83; Butler, page 16.

24 *White Star*, page 110.

25 Many thanks to Gerry Livadas for sharing generously his research.

26 'HMHS *Britannic*: A Mystery of Numbers', *Titanic Commutator*, *Titanic* Historical Society, 2008.

27 Last voyage, page 10.

28 Last voyage, page 11.

29 *Titanic and her Sisters*, page 394.

30 *Atlantic Daily Bulletin*, Journal of the British *Titanic* Society, number 3, 1999, page 27.

31 Mills, page 30.

32 *Hospital Ships*, page 129. (information on the trains and various five areas)

33 National Archives Document BT 165 1569.

34 E & H FS, page 171.

35 Forgotten sister, paragraph 14, page 2–3.

36 National Archives Document BT 165 1569.

37 *Testament of Youth*, Vera Brittain, William Clowes & Son Ltd., London and Beccles, cheap war edition, fifteenth reprint, 1943, page 206.

38 National Archives Document BT 165 1569.

39 National Archives file MT 23/637

40 *Hospital Ships*, page 132. (Carrying numbers.)

41 Last voyage, page 8.

42 Imperial War Museum diary transcript, Ms Ada Garland (77/571).

43 *Testament of Youth*, Vera Brittain, 1943, fifteenth reprint, William Clowes & Sons Ltd, London and Beccles; page 210.

44 *Testament of Youth*, Vera Brittain, 1943, fifteenth reprint, William Clowes & Sons Ltd, London and Beccles; page 209.

45 *Testament of Youth*, Vera Brittain, 1943, fifteenth reprint, William Clowes & Sons Ltd, London and Beccles; page 216.

46 National Archives file MT 23/593

47 Imperial War Museum diary transcript, Mrs E. B. Moor, (98/9/1).

48 Imperial War Museum diary transcript, Miss W. Greenwood, (87/33/1).

49 E & H F S, page 174.

50 Jessop, page 169.

51 Jessop, page 170.

52 *Testament of Youth*, Vera Brittain, Virago Press, 1997, pages 297–298.

53 'Down to the *Britannic*', by Robert H. Gibbons, Vice President of the *Titanic* Historical Society, *Sea Classics*, 1975. Subsequent quotes and information from Sheila Macbeth is taken from here unless otherwise referenced.

54 (Both sentences.) Last voyage, page 14 (bottom).

55 Last voyage, pages 15 and 17.

56 Mills, page 41.

57 Jessop, page 172.

58 Jessop, page 172.

59 E & H F S, page 176.

60 *Ghost Liners*, page 42.

61 National Archives files ADM 53/42159; ADM 53/59512; ADM 53/44209

62 Last voyage, page 18.

63 E & H F S, pages 175–176.

64 Jessop, page 172.

65 Jessop, page 173; *Testament of Youth*, Vera Brittain, Virago Press, 1997; page 312.

66 Ms W. Greenwood, Imperial War Museum diary, 87/33/1.

67 'The *Britannic* Saga. Part Four: The Final Journey: A Personal Account…', *Titanic Commutator*, *Titanic* Historical Society, 1991. The officer who wrote the diary confirmed that he was in his stateroom when the explosion occurred, ruling out the possibility that he was the ship's fourth officer, Duncan Campbell McTavish, or the chief officer, Robert Hume. It makes reference to her captain, assistant commander, first officer, third officer, fourth officer and sixth officer, and of

the remaining possibilities – second or fifth officer – it is believed to be *Britannic*'s fifth officer, twenty-four-year-old Gordon Bell Fielding. It was kindly donated to the society, so that other researchers could see it, by his great-grandson Richard Kirk.

68 Ms W. Greenwood, Imperial War Museum diary, 87/33/1.

69 *Ghost Liners*, page 42.

70 Jessop, pages 172–174. Paragraph info.

71 Jessop, pages 175–176.

72 *Testament of Youth*, Vera Brittain, 1943, fifteenth reprint, William Clowes & Sons Ltd, London and Beccles; page 222.

73 Mills, page 42.

74 *Lost Liners*, page 132.

75 E & H F S, page 176.

76 Last Voyage, pages 19, 21.

77 E & H F S, page 177.

78 Last voyage, page 21.

79 *Ghost Liners*, page 42.

80 *Britannic Four Years On: Part 2*, by Simon Mills, *The Titanic Commutator*, Number 147, Volume 23, November 1999.

81 Last voyage, page 21.

82 Jessop, page 177.

83 Diary of Ms A. Garland, Imperial War Museum, 77/57/1.

84 *Ghost Liners*, page 42.

85 Jessop, page 177.

86 *Testament of Youth*, Vera Brittain, 1943, fifteenth reprint, William Clowes & Sons Ltd, London and Beccles; page 223.

87 Jessop, pages 178–179.

88 Mills, page 44.

89 Jessop, page 180.

90 Jessop, page 182.

91 *Sea Classics*, '*Britannic*', by Robert H. Gibbons, President of *Titanic* Historical Society, 1975.

92 *Testament of Youth*, Vera Brittain, Virago Press, 1997, pages 313–314.

93 Last voyage, pages 25–26.

94 E & H JJ, page 172; E & H DD, page 72.

95 *Testament of Youth*, Vera Brittain, 1943, fifteenth reprint, William Clowes & Sons Ltd, London and Beccles; page 222–223.

96 Last voyage, page 23.

97 Last voyage, page 33.

98 *Atlantic Daily Bulletin*, Journal of the British *Titanic* Society, number 4, 1999; page 23.

99 Jessop, page 183.

100 Last voyage, page 5.

101 Last voyage, page 17.

102 I would like to thank Michael Lowrey for the details from *U73*'s war diary and his continuing assistance, and Günter Bäbler for his translation of the original German text.

103 McGreal, pages 123–24.

104 I am grateful to Alan Geddes for transcribing the original newspaper article and sharing it publicly.

CHAPTER 8

1 (All Calypso information.) *Life and Death in a Coral Sea*, by Jacques Yves Cousteau with Philippe Diolé, Cassell and Company Ltd, 1972; pages 32–34; 50–51; 34–38.

2 'Expedition diary: Friday September 18th 1998'. The expedition diary and other materials were originally published online by the expedition at http://website.lineone. net/~britannic98 . The website no longer appears to be available, however my own printed copies were a great help; it may be possible for the dedicated researcher to access the old webpages via internet archives.

3 'Project Results Overview' 1999 expedition: 'http://www.ocean-discovery.org/Britannic_ results.htm'

4 Article entitled 'Death of the *Britannic*: An Autopsy' by Daniel Pendick, reporting on a 1998 paper on *Britannic*'s sinking by the American Society of Naval Architecture and Marine Engineering's Marine Forensics Panel. Accessed via: 'http://www.pbs.org/wnet/ saveseas/captain-side-britannic.html'

5 Article entitled 'Death of the *Britannic*: An Autopsy' by Daniel Pendick, reporting on a 1998 paper on *Britannic*'s sinking by the American Society of Naval Architecture and Marine Engineering's Marine Forensics Panel. Accessed via: 'http://www.pbs.org/wnet/ saveseas/captain-side-britannic.html'

6 Lost.

7 *Lost Liners*, page 136.

8 Lost.

9 Lost.

10 *Lost Liners*, page 12.

11 *Art of Titanic*, page 133.

12 *Ghost Liners*, pages 6, 44.

13 Lost (Whole paragraph.)

14 Lost.

15 *Ghost Liners*, pages 7, 44–45.

16 Lost.

17 Whopper, page 3 (of 3).

18 Whopper, page 1 (of 3).

19 Whopper, page 1 (top statement) (of 3).

20 Whopper, page 2 (of 3).

21 'Euphoric on the *Britannic*' appearing in 'Diver', 1999. accessed via 'http://www. divernet.com/wrecks/britt199.htm'

22 Unless otherwise indicated, all information about the 1999 expedition is taken from 'Global Underwater Explorers: *Britannic* 99' website: 'http://www.gue.com/research/

Britannic/index.shtml'.

23 Leigh Bishop's article, 'Unlocking the Final Secrets of *Titanic*'s Forgotten Sister', *Beyond the Blue*, 2003.

24 Carl Spencer's remarks are quoted from the answers to questions posed to him by *Britannic* researcher Michail Michailakis, with input from Remco Hillen and myself.

25 George Papatheodorou's article, 'Ghostly Images of HMHS *Britannic*', *Hydro International*, 2008.

26 Simon Mills' article, 'Making Waves: on the Subject of Retrieval or Raising *Britannic*', *Titanic Commutator, Titanic* Historical Society, 2003.

CHAPTER 9

1 E & H DD, pages 131–132.
2 E & H DD, page 132.
3 Marriott, page 141.
4 Lord, pages 232–233.
5 Lord, page 233.
6 E & H DD, page 133.
7 Marriott, page 143.
8 Lynch, page 202.
9 Discovery *Titanic*, page 91.
10 *Exploring the Titanic*, page 30.
11 Gardiner, page 259.
12 *Exploring the Titanic*, page 31.
13 Legacy, page 116.
14 Lord, page 237.
15 Marriott, page 144.
16 Marriott, page 144.
17 Butler, page 214.
18 Lynch, page 203.
19 Lord, page 239.
20 E & H JJ, page 191.
21 E & H JJ, page 192.
22 E & H TT, page 308.
23 E & H TT, page 310.
24 Legacy, page 121.
25 Legacy, page 126.
26 *Exploring the Titanic*, page 38.
27 *Exploring the Titanic*, pages 38–39.
28 *Exploring the Titanic*, pages 40–41.
29 Legacy, page 126.
30 E & H TT, page 309.
31 *Ghost Liners*, page 18.
32 E & H DD, page 146.
33 *Art of Titanic*, pages 124–125.
34 *Art of Titanic*, page 126–127.
35 *Art of Titanic*, pages 124–127.
36 *Art of Titanic*, page 112.
37 *Art of Titanic*, page 113.
38 Butler, page 214.
39 Discovery *Titanic*, page 231.
40 E & H DD, page 147.

41 E & H JJ, page 193.
42 Marriott, page 146.
43 E & H TT, page 310.
44 E & H JJ, page 194.
45 Marriott, page 147.
46 E & H JJ, page 196.
47 E & H JJ, page 197.
48 Lynch, page 208.
49 E & H TT, page 312.
50 E & H TT, page 313.
51 Lynch, page 209.
52 E & H JJ, page 197.
53 E & H JJ, page 198.
54 E & H JJ, page 199.
55 Marriott, page 149.
56 Riddle, page 315.
57 Wels, page 158.
58 Marsh, pages 3–8.
59 Heart of the Ocean.
60 Breaking New Ground.
61 Marsh, page 145.
62 E & H JJ, page 206.
63 Wels, page 132.
64 E & H JJ, page 208.
65 Wels, page 166.
66 Wels, page 169.
67 E & H JJ, page 218.
68 E & H JJ, page 224.
69 *Titanic* Live.
70 Encyclopedia Titanica: *Titanic* Research Articles: Biodeterioration of the RMS *Titanic*: Roy Cullimore: Summary [www.encyclopedia-titanica.org] Accessed Dec. 26 18:15:40 2000. by Roy Cullimore & Lori Johnston
71 Encyclopedia Titanica: *Titanic* Research Articles: Biodeterioration of the RMS *Titanic*: Roy Cullimore [www.encyclopedia-titanica.org] Accessed Dec. 26 18:14:18 2000. by Roy Cullimore & Lori Johnston
72 RMS *Titanic* Inc. published a series of Frequently Asked Questions (FAQs) dealing with various issues related to the shipwreck online in 2000.
73 Material relating to the expedition was published by RMS *Titanic* Inc. on its website in 2000. The addresses for specific pages on the company's website have changed, however the company still exists and maintains a website giving historical information about its previous expeditions.
74 Ghosts of the Abyss, pages 96, 100, 109 and 110.
75 Ghosts of the Abyss, page 53.
76 The selected quotes and summary are taken from Ken Marschall's report, 'James Cameron's *Titanic* Expedition 2001: What We Saw On and Inside the Wreck', published online at Parks Stephenson's website, Marconigraph.com in December 2001.

77 An article by Marc Davis, '*Titanic* Artefacts May Have been Plundered' appeared in *The Virginian-Pilot*, March 2003.

78 I am very appreciative of David Concannon's time and assistance. Much of the information about the expedition is drawn from his report to the Explorers Club on 26 March 2004, which gives a far more comprehensive outline of the different teams and objectives. The 'Explorers Club Flag No.132 was carried with dignity to the *Titanic* wreck site, where it served as a symbol of exploration that is older than the *Titanic* itself, and a testament to what the human spirit can achieve'.

79 Jeremy Weirich's summary was published on the National Oceanic and Atmospheric Administration's website shortly after the expedition ended, http://oceanexplorer.noaa.gov .

80 A useful summary was posted in the online NOAA Magazine at http://www.magazine.noaa.gov . The last issue was posted in August 2007 and the site has since been archived.

81 The signing was reported by the BBC News website, http://www.bbc.co.uk, on 6 November 2003.

82 These details are taken from RMS *Titanic* Inc.'s press release which explained the details of the reorganisation.

83 The expedition was documented day-by-day on the Discovery Channel's website, http://dsc.discovery.com, in June and July 2005.

84 Further information can be found at Deep Ocean Expeditions' website www.deepocean-expeditions.com .

85 Quoted from David Concannon's report to the Explorers Club on 17 November 2006.

86 The announcement was reported by press release on 27 July 2010.

87 The article '*Titanic* Explorers Delay Mission by a Day' was published online by CBC News on 22 August 2010.

88 McCarty and Foecke, pages 92 and 113.

89 McCarty and Foecke, page 114.

90 McCarty and Foecke, page 118.

91 McCarty and Foecke, page 136.

92 McCarty and Foecke, pages 144–47, 159, 164–66 and 170.

93 McCarty and Foecke, pages 171–72.

94 Thanks to J. Kent Layton for assisting me in finding, then supplying, the relevant articles in *Engineering*.

95 Simon Mills' 'More Questions Than Answers…', *Titanic Commutator*, Titanic Historical Society, 2006.

96 Parks Stephenson 'More Questions Than Answers, Part 2' *Titanic Commutator*, Titanic Historical Society, 2006.

97 Roy Mengot and Richard Woytowich, 'The Break-up of *Titanic*: A Progress Report from the Marine Forensics Panel' (SD-7) was presented during a meeting in New York between relevant naval architecture and engineering professionals in April 2009. It was subsequently published in *Marine Technology*, the journal of the Society of Naval Architects and Marine Engineers (SNAME), in January 2010.

98 JMS Newsletter, 'JMS Works with History Channel on New *Titanic* Documentary', 2008.

99 See also Gittins, who was the first researcher to reference Thearle's correspondence.

APPENDIX 2

1 *Merchant Fleets*, page 66 (whole paragraph).

2 *Merchant Fleets*, page 77.

3 E & H TT, page 92.

4 *Olympic*, page 61.

5 *Merchant Fleets*, page 77.

6 E & H TT, page 92.

7 Hutchings, page 7.

8 Hutchings, page 10.

9 E & H TT, page 93.

10 '*Olympic Titanic Britannic*' Fifth Avenue Films, 1994.

11 E & H F S, page 150.

12 E & H F S, page 213.

13 E & H F S, page 213.

14 I am indebted to Philippe Delaunoy for sharing generously his research.

15 *Olympic*, page 62.

16 (From [12]) *Merchant Fleets*, page 77.

17 Gardiner, page 71.

18 *Merchant Fleets*, page 78.

APPENDIX 8

1 Lord, page 169.

2 E & H, page 165.

3 E & H DD, page 40.

4 E & H, page 165.

5 Lord, page 170.

6 E & H DD, page 40.

7 Gardiner, page 177.

8 E & H, page 165.

9 E & H, page 165.

10 Lord, page 187.

11 Lord, pages 165–166.

12 Lord, page 176.

13 Lord, page 177.

14 Gardiner, pages 167–168.

15 Lord, page 178.

APPENDIX 9

1 Shipbuilders to the World, pages 165–68.

APPENDIX 10

1 *Famous Ships of the Clyde*, Jack Webster, the
Glasgow Royal Concert Hall, 1995; page 40.
2 *Famous Ships of the Clyde*, Jack Webster, the
Glasgow Royal Concert Hall, 1995; page 40.
3 *Famous Ships of the Clyde*, Jack Webster, the
Glasgow Royal Concert Hall, 1995; page 40.
4 (Safety features of *Aquitania*) *Aquitania*, page
10.
5 Golden age, page 78.
6 *Glory Days: Cunard*, David L Williams, Ian
Allan, 1998; pages 52 and 54.

APPENDIX 12

1 *Glory Days: Cunard*, David L. Williams, Ian
Allan, 1998; page 95.
2 *The Great Luxury Liners, 1927–1954*, William
H. Miller, Jnr., Dover Publications Inc., 1981;
page 9.
3 *White Star*, page 214, '*Majestic* (II)'.

APPENDIX 14

1 My thanks to Ian Edwards for having the
kindness to share his research on Rebecca
Munro.

BIBLIOGRAPHY

Sources listed below, as well as in the notes at the end of each chapter or appendix, provided such a wealth of information for this book, in addition to those people or institutions that are mentioned in the acknowledgements that follow.

BOOKS/ARTICLES (REFERENCE IN BRACKETS AT END OF EACH ENTRY)

Anderson, Roy, *White Star*, Stephenson & Sons Ltd., 1964. (*White Star*)

Archbold, Rick, & Ballard, Dr Robert D., *Lost Liners*, Madison Press, 1997. (*Lost Liners*)

Archbold, Rick, Ballard, Dr Robert D., & Marschall, Ken, *Ghost Liners: Exploring the World's Greatest Lost Ships* Madison Press, 1998. (*Ghost Liners*)

Archbold, Rick, Ken Marschall's *Art of Titanic*, Madison Press, 1997. (*Art of Titanic*)

Ballard, Dr Robert D., & Dunmore, Spencer, *Exploring the Lusitania* Madison Press, 1995. (*Lusitania*)

Ballard, Dr Robert D., *Exploring the Titanic* Madison Press, 1994. (*Exploring Titanic*)

Ballard, Dr Robert D., *The Discovery of the Titanic*, Madison Press, 1987. (*Discovery Titanic*)

Behe, George, *Archie Volume 3*, Lulu, 2010. (Archie)

Behe, George, *Titanic: Safety, Speed & Sacrifice*, Transportation Trails, 1997. (Behe)

Bemis, Albert Farwell, *A Journey to India*, Private Printing, 1923

Beveridge, Bruce, and Hall, Steve, *Olympic & Titanic: The Truth Behind the Conspiracy*, Six Star Publishing, 2004. (Beveridge and Hall)

Bonsall, Thomas E., *Titanic: The Story of the Great White Star Trio: the Olympic, the Titanic and the Britannic*, Gallery Books, 1987. (Bonsall)

Bullock, Shan F., *Thomas Andrews: Shipbuilder*, Maunsel & Company Ltd, 1912. (Bullock)

Butler, Daniel Allen, *Unsinkable: the Full Story of the RMS Titanic*, Stackpole Books, 1998. (Butler)

Cameron, James, Kirkland, Douglas, & Marsh, Ed W., *James Cameron's Titanic*, Boxtree, 1998. (Marsh)

Dekerbrech, Richard P., & Williams, David L., *Cunard White Star Liners of the 1930s*, Conway Marine Press Ltd, 1988. (1930S)

Eaton, John P. & Haas, Charles A., *Titanic: Triumph and Tragedy*, Patrick Stephens Ltd 1994. (E & H TT)

Eaton, John P., & Haas, Charles A., *Titanic: A Journey Through Time*, Patrick Stephens Ltd., 1999. (E & H JJ)

Eaton, John P., & Haas, Charles A., *Titanic: Destination Disaster*, Patrick Stephens Ltd, 1996. (E & H DD)

Eaton, John P., & Haas, Charles A., *Falling Star: Misadventures of White Star Line Ships*, Patrick Stephens Ltd, 1989. (E & H F S)

Flayhart, William H., & Shaum, John H., *Majesty at Sea: The Four Stackers*, Patrick Stephens, 1981. (*Four Stackers*)

Fleming, Rev. John, & Mills, Simon, *The Last Voyage of His Majesty's Hospital Ship Britannic*, Rev John Fleming M.A.C.F., Wordsmith Publications 1998. (Last Voyage)

Forsyth, Alastair, Hyslop, Donald, & Jemima, Sheila, *Titanic Voices – Memories from the Fateful Voyage*, Sutton Publishing Ltd, 1997. (Voices)

Fox, Robert, *Liners – the Golden Age*, Könemann, 1999. (Golden Age)

Gardiner, Robin, & Van der Vat, Dan, *The Riddle of the Titanic*, Orion, sixth impression, 1998. (Riddle)

Garzke, William H., & Woodward, John, *Titanic Ships: Titanic Disasters: An Analysis of Early White Star and Cunard Superliners*, The Society of Naval Architects and Marine Engineers, 2002. (Garzke and Woodward)

Gardiner, Robin, *Titanic: The Ship That Never Sank?* Ian Allan, 1998 (Gardiner)

Gittins, Dave, *Titanic: Monument & Warning*, Self-published electronically, 2005. (Gittins)

Gracie, Colonel Archibald, *Titanic – A Survivor's Story*, Sutton Publishing, 1998. (Gracie)

Green, Edwin and Moss, Michael, *A Business of National Importance: The Royal Mail Shipping Group, 1902–1937*, Methuen, 1982. (Green and Moss)

Griffiths, Denis, *Power of the Great Liners*, Patrick Stephens Ltd, 1990. (Power)

Haws, Duncan, *Merchant Fleets: White Star Line (Oceanic Steam Navigation Co)*, Travel Creatours Ltd (trading as TCL publications), 1990. (Merchant Fleets)

Hayes, Captain Bertram F., *Hull Down*, Cassell & Co., 1925. (Hull Down)

Hutchings, David F., RMS *Titanic: A Modern Legend*, Waterfront Publications, 1995. (Hutchings)

Jenkins, Alan C., *Eye Witness*, Blackie & Son Ltd, 1972. (Chapter 3: *Titanic* Disaster, an extract of the account by Lawrence Beesley.) (Witness)

Jessop, Violet, *Titanic Survivor: Memoirs of Violet Jessop Stewardess*, ed. Maxtone-Graham, John, Sheridan House Inc., 1997. (Jessop)

Lord, Walter, *A Night To Remember* (Illustrated Edition) Penguin, 1976. (Lord 1)

Lord, Walter, *The Night Lives On* Walter Lord, Penguin, 1986 (Lord)

Lynch, Don & Marschall, Ken, *Ghosts of the Abyss: A Journey into the Heart of the Titanic*, Da Capo Press/ Madison Press, 2003. (Ghosts of the Abyss)

Lynch, Don, & Marschall, Ken, *Titanic: An Illustrated History*, int. Ballard, Dr Robert D., Madison Press, 1998. (Lynch)

Marriott, Leo, McCluskie, Tom, & Sharpe, Michael, *Titanic and her Sisters Olympic* and *Britannic*, PRC Publishing Ltd 1998. (*Tianic and her Sisters*))

Marriott, Leo, *Titanic*, PRC Publishing, 1997. (Marriott)

Marschall, Ken, *Inside the Titanic*, Madison Press, 1997. (*Inside the Titanic*)

Maxtone-Graham, John, *Shipbuilder:Olympic* and *Titanic*: Ocean Liners of the Past, Amereon House, 1995. (*Shipbuilder*)

McCarty, Jennifer Hooper, and Foecke, Tim, *What Really Sank the Titanic*, Citadel Press, 2008. (McCarty and Foecke)

McCaughan, Michael, The Birth of the *Titanic*, the Blackstaff Press, 1998. (Birth)

McCauley, Robert, *The Liners: a voyage of discovery*, Boxtree, 1997. (*The Liners*)

McCluskie, Tom, *The Wall Chart of the Titanic*, PRC Publishing, 1998. (Wall Chart)

McGreal, Stephen, *The War on Hospital Ships: 1914–1918*, Pen & Sword, 2008. (McGreal)

Miller, Nina. D., Fall of *Titanic*'s Sistership Remains a Mystery; Maritime Reporter & Engineering News, January 1997. (Accessible through http://www.marinelink.com/jan97/mr01304.html) (Fall Of Sister)

Mills, Simon, *HMHS Britannic: The Last Titan* (Second Edition) Shipping Books Press, 1996. (Mills)

Mills, Simon, *RMS Olympic: Old Reliable*, Waterfront Publications, 1995. (*Olympic*)

Moss, Michael, and Hume, John R., *Shipbuilders to the World: 125 Years of Harland & Wolff, Belfast 1861–1986*, Blackstaff Press, 1986. (Shipbuilders to the World)

Oldham, Wilton J., *The Ismay Line*, The Journal of Commerce, 1961. (*Ismay Line*)

Plumridge, John H., *Hospital Ships and Ambulance Trains*, Seeley, Service & Co., 1975. (*Hospital Ships*)

Smith, Ken, *Mauretania: Pride of the Tyne*, Newcastle Libraries and Information Service in Association with Tyne and Wear Museums, 1997 (Mauretania)

Streater, L., & R.A, *Aquitania: Cunard's Greatest Dream*, the Maritime Publishing Company, 1997. (*Aquitania*)

Wade, Wyn Craig, *The Titanic: End of a Dream*, McClelland and Steward Ltd, 1979. (Wade)

Warren, Mark. D, *Distinguished Liners from 'The Shipbuilder'*, 1907 – 1914, Volume 2, ed., with a new introduction by Mark D. Warren, Blue Ribband Publications, Inc., 1997. (*Shipbuilder 2*)

Wels, Susan, *Titanic: Legacy of the World's Greatest Ocean Liner*, Tehabi Books, 1997. (Wels or Legacy)

NEWSPAPERS

Daily Sketch
Shields Gazette
Southampton Times
Southern Daily Echo
The Daily Graphic
The Daily Mail
The Daily Mirror
The New York Times
The Sunday Telegraph
The Telegraph
The Times

MAGAZINES/PERIODILCALS

Atlantic Daily Bulletin (British Titanic Society)
Diver; What a Whopper! February 1998. (Accessible at http://www.divernet.com/ wrecks/brit298.htm)
    (Whopper)
Engineering
Maritime Reporter & Engineering News (accessed via internet)
National Geographic
Sea Breezes
Sea Classics
The Titanic Commutator (Titanic Historical Society)

TELEVISION

Heart of the Ocean: the making of Titanic, Granada, 1997. (Heart Of The Ocean)
Secrets of the Deep: the Mystery of the Lusitania, Channel 4, 1999. (Mystery)
The Titanic*'s Lost Sister*, a Nova Production by varied directors for WGBH in association with
    Channel 4 television, 1996. (Lost)
Titanic *Live 1998*, Discovery Channel in association with NBC Dateline, Sardust Visual Inc. and
    RMS *Titanic* Inc. (*Titanic* Live 1998)
Titanic*: Breaking New Ground*, ©1998 Fox Broadcasting Company. Zaloom Mayfield Productions.
    (Breaking New Ground)

ACKNOWLEDGEMENTS

Some of the sources listed in the bibliography were those that first aroused my interest in the *Titanic* and her sister-ships. It may rightly be said that 'the shelves are groaning with books about the *Titanic*', but there are very few regarding her sister vessels.

In addition to the books, television broadcasts and other sources mentioned in the bibliography, many people and institutions have provided gratefully acknowledged information and advice.

Much of the information was collected not specifically for this book, but for general interest. The United Kingdom Hydrographic Office provided information from their vast wreck database of the wreck of the *Britannic*; the willing, enthusiastic and caring staff of the National Maritime Museum provided much information regarding photographs, as did the Imperial War Museum (thanks are due here to Archivist Anthony Richards); the Ulster Folk & Transport Museum was also very helpful. Thanks are due to the Commonwealth War Graves Commission, who do such a wonderful job preserving information, and whose information made such a contribution to the list of those casualties from *Britannic*, which I believe to be the most comprehensive yet published in book form.

I wish to thank the following for permission to reproduce and quote from archival documents: the copyright holder of the papers of Miss A. Garland; the copyright holder of the papers of Mrs E.B. Moor. Thanks to Mike Stammers and the Trustees of National Museums and Galleries on Merseyside for permission to quote from Merseyside Maritime Museum archival material, and Dr Alan Scarth. Despite every effort being made, it was not possible to contact the copyright holders of the papers of Nurse Greenwood, Lieutenant Colonel Anderson. Thanks also to William Garzke, and RMS *Titanic* Inc.

The helpful staff of the Merseyside Maritime Museum's Maritime Archives & Library gave me every assistance with my research there. The British Library's Newspaper Library at Colindale, London, proved very useful. Thanks are due to the helpful staff at the Sydney Jones Library's Special Collections and Archives, at Liverpool University, which look after the bulk of the Cunard Archives.

My thanks to Kevin Gurr and the team of the 1997 *Britannic* expedition; Nick Hope, John Chatterton, John Yurga, Geraint Ffoulkes-Jones and the 1998 expedition team; Jarrod Jablonski and the 1999 expedition team. Their efforts have ensured that our knowledge of the *Britannic* has grown considerably over the past few years.

I would like to thank the following for information, time or interesting historical discussion: Scott Andrews for pointing out several errors; George Behe, for *Olympic* log extracts, but particularly for sharing his analysis and giving an enjoyable discussion about the post-collision damage inspection aboard *Titanic*; Bruce Beveridge; Joseph Carvalho who supplied much appreciated information about *Olympic*; Richard Edkins; Ian Edwards; Nigel Hampson; Remco Hillen; Daniel Klistorner for his generosity in sharing his *Titanic* accommodation research (any errors are most certainly *mine* alone); Peter Kohler; Michail Michailakis; Lester Mitcham, who allowed me to cite his comprehensive research into the total number of *Titanic* survivors, and for drawing my attention to some inaccuracies which should really have caught my focus earlier; and Simon Mills. Further special thanks are due to the numerous individuals who I have had discussions with. Thanks to everyone who offered me advice and encouragement in getting my work published – the hardest (and often longest) task for any writer.

Major sources included the British inquiry report: 'Loss of the SS "*Titanic*." Court of Enquiry. Report, Evidence, & C. 1912.' (Reprinted 1998: ISBN number 1 873162 70 7.) My thanks to Brian Ticehurst of the British *Titanic* Society for the help he gave me in getting a reprint copy. Another good source was the American inquiry transcript: 'Subcommittee of the Committee on Commerce, United States Senate, Sixty-second Congress, Second Session, Pursuant to Senate Resolution 283, Directing the Committee on Commerce to Investigate the Causes Leading to the Wreck of the White Star Liner "*Titanic*." 1912.' (Both enquiries and their complete minutes are now online for those who wish to read them, thanks to an exhaustive effort by the *Titanic* Inquiry Project.) Lord Mersey's 1915 report on the *Lusitania*'s loss (REPORT) provided some detail on her fate (the report's text was published by 7C's Press in the mid-1970s for those who might want to obtain a copy.)

A great deal of information came from newspaper cuttings archaic and recent, for newspapers are a very treasured and useful but often underrated source; of particular usefulness were several of the 1912 editions of the *Daily Mirror*, *Daily Telegraph* and the *Daily Graphic*, as well as the *New York Times*. The *Daily Mail* printed several articles by Christopher Hudson several years ago, which provided some background information about a number of subjects, including *Titanic*'s officers, J. Bruce Ismay, Sir Cosmo Duff Gordon and Captain Smith. Several magazines proved useful, including *Diver* magazine for information on the wreck of *Britannic*; the *Atlantic Daily Bulletin*, of the British *Titanic* Society; and *The Titanic Commutator*, of the *Titanic* Historical Society. My thanks to those who kindly allowed me to quote from them, including the *National Geographic* magazine. For the appendix about prophecies and mysteries regarding *Titanic*'s fate, the book, *The Wreck of the Titan*, (first Published in the USA by M.F. Mansfield, 1898, as *Futility* [printed 1912 as *The Wreck of the Titan*]; republished in Great Britain by Pocket Books, 1998) was very useful for details and general information regarding the fictional ship of 1898 – *Titan* – and the original novel.

Many people suggested useful sources and provided information. I was able to locate the 1998 *Britannic* expedition's website (and other information through the website) through a request in the *Atlantic Daily Bulletin* (of the British *Titanic* Society); other information, as mentioned before, included that from *Diver* magazines. Mr D. and Mrs G. Chirnside and Miss Sharanjeet Mundey read the text and gave freely many observations, much advice and time. Several people offered enthusiasm and encouragement.

My thanks to those people who have always kept me informed of new television programs, articles, magazines and recently published books, etc. Many thanks are also offered to any people who may have been inadvertently omitted from these acknowledgements.

Last but not least, I would like to thank Campbell McCutcheon and everyone at Tempus Publishing, who believed in the project and made its publication possible.

It was such very helpful, very kind people and institutions, as mentioned above, that made this work possible. Before I finish, I would like to once again offer my apologies to anybody that I was unable to contact, or who feels they might have been inadvertently omitted; I will be more than glad to put this right. If any errors have occurred, which they surely have done considering the size of the work, the responsibility is mine alone.

October 2004

ACKNOWLEDGEMENTS TO THE
SECOND EDITION

It goes without saying that I continue to owe a debt of gratitude to the many kind people who did so much to help me as the first edition was being written. At the time, I had no previous titles to my name, and any scepticism could have been easily justified – for there are many people who intend to write a book but do not necessarily finish the task. There are many books that are written and never published; many of which are surely a great loss. Every person and organisation listed should therefore be highlighted again. First and foremost, I want to acknowledge the support of my parents – to whom this book is dedicated – and wider family and friends.

I have learned a great deal from correspondence and discussion with numerous individuals since the original book was published. In many cases, people have shared information which has been referenced specifically in the endnotes. At other times, information obtained for other projects or for my own general interest nonetheless proved useful in revising the first edition. There are many people who were generous in sharing their time, knowledge and expertise, as well as commenting on early drafts and making documented corrections. I have benefited from their suggestions, but any errors remaining are entirely my own responsibility.

I would like to thank: Steve Anderson; Scott Andrews; Taylor Andrews; Nigel Aspdin; Gunter Bäbler; Mark Bamford; George Behe; Bruce Beveridge; Leigh Bishop; Campbell McCutcheon;

Malcolm Cheape; Ed Coghlan; David Concannon; Philippe Delaunoy; John Eaton; Mark Evans; Trevor Ferris; Ioannis Georgiou; Charles Haas; Steve Hall; Sam Halpern; Jennifer Irwin; Jarrod Jablonski; Ed and Karen Kamuda; Daniel Klistorner; Arnold Kludas; J. Kent Layton; Mandy le Boutillier; Paul Lee; Ray Lepien; Gerry Livadas; Oliver Loerscher; Michael Lowrey; Richard Lundgren; Ken Marschall; John Maxtone-Graham; Roy Mengot; Michail Michailakis; Susie Millar; Simon Mills; Norman Morse; Una Reilly; David Rumsey; Brigitte Saar; Severin Schwendener; Bill Smith; Jonathan Smith; Tarn Stephanos; Parks Stephenson; Richard Stevenson; Nick Thearle; Hilary Thomas; Thorsten Totzke; Timothy Trower; Mark Warren; John White (White Star Memories); and Rich Woytowich.

I owe a special thanks to Gunter Bäbler; Ioannis Georgiou; Daniel Klistorner and J. Kent Layton for their considerable assistance in sharing generously their knowledge and images from their own collections, often at short notice. Eric Longo has shared his expertise, restoring images such as the rare shot of *Britannic*, despite many demands on his time. The talented Stuart Williamson painted the wonderful view of *Britannic* as she began to sink. For enquiries about purchasing prints of his existing paintings or commissioning new artwork, Stuart can be contacted online through his website: http://website.lineone.net/~stu_williamson.

A number of people and organisations have helped with both my ongoing research in general and some specific enquiries for the purpose of this project: Rob Cousins and his colleagues at the Department of Transport; Steve van Dulken, Lisa Kenny and the staff of the British Library; Christoph Haenggi and the *Museum für Musikautomaten* Seewen, Switzerland; Alison Heald and the staff of the curator's department at Hampton Court Palace; Jane Humphrey, Diane Matthews and the staff of Dudley Archives and Local History Service; the staff of the Guildhall Library; Melanie Oelgeschlager and the staff of the National Maritime Museum; Simon Offord, Anthony Richards and the staff of the Imperial War Museum; the staff of the National Archives (formerly the Public Records Office); the staff of the New York Public Library; the staff of the Public Records Office of Northern Ireland (PRONI), with thanks given to the Deputy Keeper of the Records at the Public Records Office of Northern Ireland and Harland & Wolff; Rebecca Parker and Misty Ann Tilson of RMS *Titanic* Inc.; Michelle Ashmore, George Wright, Michael McCaughan and the staff of the Ulster Folk and Transport Museum and National Museums Northern Ireland.

I also owe my sincere apologies to anyone who may have been inadvertently missed out, or those I have not been able to contact. Although every effort was made, it was not possible to contact the copyright holders of the papers of Walter Alexander Goodwin.

Finally, my thanks to everyone involved in the mammoth tasks of the original book's completion and the preparation of this new edition, including my commissioning editor Amy Rigg and her team, Emily Locke and Marc Williams, at the History Press.

May 2011

INDEX

Page numbers in **bold** typeface denote illustrations; and a **bold C** refers to the colour section.

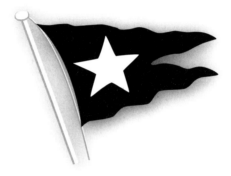